*A General Introduction
to Sociology*

A General Introduction to Sociology

A theoretical perspective

Guy Rocher

Translated from the French by
Peta Sheriff

The Macmillan Company of Canada
Limited/ Toronto

© Macmillan Company of Canada Limited 1972

This book was originally published
in French by Editions HMH Ltée
under the title *Introduction à la
sociologie générale.* Droits réservés 1968

ISBN 0-7705-0877-4
Library of Congress Catalogue
Card No. 74-187792

This book has been published with the help
of a grant from the Social Science Research
Council of Canada, using funds provided
by the Canada Council.

Text and cover design by Bob Frank

Printed in Canada for
The Macmillan Company of Canada
70 Bond Street, Toronto

Contents

Chapter 2: The Normative Foundations of Social Action

Part Two: Social Organization

Chapter 6: Classifications and Types of Social Organization

Part Three: Social Change and Historical Action

terminism in modern capitalism; A different interpretation: Lefebvre and Desroches; Conclusion.

three errors; Social conflicts and class conflicts; Class conflicts and revolution; Classes, class conflicts and ownership; The aim of Dahrendorf's model; The unequal distribution of authority; The dichotomy of authority; The dichotomy of authority and conflict of interests; Quasi-group and interest group; Latent and manifest interests; Pluralism and the superimposition of groups and conflicts; Two scales; The intensity of conflicts; The violence of conflicts; Radical change and sudden change; Dahrendorf's contribution; A theoretical step forward; Complementarity of approaches; A critical analysis of Marx; Some useful distinctions; A reservation: hypothetical propositions; A criticism: the duality of the opponents; A discussion: conflict of interests and social conflict; The concept of structural contradictions; The age of the elements of the social system; Society experienced in perspective; The broken rhythm of change; Some agents of contradiction; Contradictions and social complexity; Conclusion.

Chapter 12: The Agents of Social Change

Chapter 14: The Colonial System and Decolonization

Preface

This book is dedicated to the many groups of students who, over the past fifteen years, have taken my course in introductory sociology either at Laval University of Quebec or at the University of Montreal. Their comments, questions and suggestions have greatly assisted me in planning the content of the course and in teaching it. I am grateful to all of them for the contribution they have made to the book through their active and voluntary participation.

It is in the hope that I can continue to be useful to their colleagues of today and tomorrow — and also to others who are interested in sociology — that I have decided to write this book. With this purpose in mind, I have conceived of it as both an introduction to sociology and a work of reference. My approach is based partly on the content of my lectures, but some important changes have been made in the process of translating a spoken course into a written work. For example, I have added a large number of references to major sociological works, as well as to various articles published in the leading journals of sociology, anthropology and psychology. The reader who would like to go beyond an introduction to the discipline can use these references as a basic bibliography for each chapter. I should point out, however, that I have been necessarily selective in referring to other works, citing only those among the great number available which are essential to an understanding of the foundations of sociology.

It will be noticed that in writing this book I have drawn as much on French language as on English language sociology. I have often deplored the rigid linguistic barriers that exist in social science research. One of the advantages that Quebec offers the student, the teacher and the researcher is to place them at the crossroads of studies in both languages. We should therefore try to profit from this situation, for these two languages at present embody the main stream of sociological thought.

Before the reader begins Part One, some preliminary remarks should be made regarding my approach to this introductory text. As the title indicates, it is a *general* introduction to sociology. It therefore excludes two things in particular. First, it excludes specialized sociology — that is, analyses of particular sectors of social reality, such as the sociology of the family, of social classes, of political power, or of rural or urban areas. Second, there is no description or analysis in this book of a particular society; I did not wish to write an introduction to the sociology of Quebec, Canada, or North America.

In fact, I am firmly convinced that it is impossible to approach specialized sociology or the sociology of a particular area without first having a knowledge of the general foundations of sociological analysis. Although sociology is a young science, it has its own traditions and its own foundation of theoretical and methodological knowledge; a special language has been created for it, concepts have been defined, typologies have been elaborated, and models or theoretical schema have been constructed. It is with the aid of this theoretical and conceptual apparatus that sociology views social reality. Initiation to the discipline consists of progressively learning to view reality from the perspective that is particular to this field of study. For this, it is necessary to acquire some knowledge of the major works and the outstanding research in sociology; and, above all, to become familiar with the basic concepts and theories.

Since this book is concerned primarily with an introduction to the general and basic elements of sociology, it has a strong and well-developed theoretical emphasis. This will perhaps startle some readers who expect sociology to provide them with recipes or a direct confirmation of their own ideas, rather than a rigorous and systematic perspective for the study of social reality. But anyone who is willing to make the effort to understand the underlying theory will be better prepared to approach the specialized studies which are concerned with the social environment or with a particular sector of society, since he will have first familiarized himself with the more general framework of sociological analysis.

It is not my intention to create the impression that sociology has already become a unified science, supported by a collection of unanimously accepted theoretical works. In fact, I have devoted a large part of the book to discussion of the various points of view espoused by early and contemporary sociologists. I believe that all these different approaches contribute as much towards a knowledge of social life and contemporary sociology as do the facts and theories on which there is a sociological consensus.

For the same reason I have emphasized the traditions that link contemporary sociologists to their predecessors. Not having a general theory which unanimously unites its researchers, sociology today is an extension of the works of the first great thinkers who established its foundations. It is impossible to understand the sociology of the second half of the twentieth century without going back to Auguste Comte, Karl Marx, Herbert Spencer and the German historians of the eighteenth and nineteenth centuries. Therefore there should be no great surprise that their contributions have been accorded considerable importance in this book. This is not a history of sociology. But I have tried to show that contemporary sociology still integrates the thinking of its predecessors, and for the most part continues to focus on the problems they posed.

From this approach the reader will notice that sociologists elaborate their concepts and theories on the basis of historical societies with which they are familiar and in which they are involved; thus, the evolution of societies constantly stimulates them to pose new questions. Sociology is no more divorced from history than are the societies it studies. It does not exist beyond and exclusive of history, as it was long believed that philosophy existed. Rather, it is constructed within history, drawing on it and at the same time sharing its uncertainties.

One of the greatest problems facing sociology and the sociologist is the necessary involvement of the science in historical societies. Indeed, the sociologist is inspired by them at the same time as he seeks to stand at a distance from them, so that he can construct a generally applicable theory. We will be in a position to discuss this problem at the end of the book.

Beyond contingent historical influences and beyond theoretical divergences, sufficient unanimity has been attained among the main contemporary theorists as to make possible a fairly coherent introduction to sociology. On this subject, I can say that I have tried to take into account all the points of convergence of modern theories with the aim of deriving from these divergent viewpoints a general, unified and integrated perspective. Despite the differen-

ces of point of view which separate and often oppose these thinkers, the approach adopted — which is based on the concept of social action, on the search for a systematic framework of analysis,
and on the attempt to integrate within it an explanation of social
change — brings together the main contemporary theorists: Sorokin, Parsons, Homans, Gurvitch, Merton, Firth, Mannheim and
Touraine.

I hope, finally, that I have presented a true picture of contemporary sociological theory, of the problems that are posed, of the solutions that are suggested, and of the research that continues to be
undertaken. Granted, this has been no easy task. Sociology develops by following a variety of dynamic courses in a way that often
appears incoherent and even anarchic to those who are concerned
about rigour and method. But in this introductory work I have
specifically tried to direct the sociological approach back to the
area of its fundamental problems — that is, to concentrate attention on the essential elements of sociology — thereby avoiding the
distraction and the inhibition of imagination which is often experienced by those who are introduced to this science.

This type of problem is obviously that of a scientific discipline.
And such is sociology. The questions that sociology poses on the
basis of social reality are not necessarily the same as those which
are posed by men of action. The relevant questions in sociology
are concerned with knowledge and explanation; and it is on the
condition that sociology will remain faithful to what it is — a
scientific discipline — that its contribution to social policy will be
counted as valid.

In my opinion, three main problems dominate the theoretical
and empirical research in general sociology. These can be formulated in the following terms:
1. Why do human collectivities exist and how do they sustain
themselves? And, as a corollary, how is the individual attached to
these collectivities?
2. How is the social framework of human life organized and structured?
3. How is change, or the evolution of human societies, produced
and explained?

This introduction to sociology is written around these three
fundamental questions. Each of the three parts of the work attempts, in fact, to group together the replies of various sociologists
to each question. Transposed in terms of sociological problems,
the first question poses the problem of social action; the second,

that of social organization; and the third, that of historical action. This explains the division of the work into three parts.

None of the parts, however, is independent of the two others: they touch many of the same points and are interdependent. In this, it appears that sociology must always have the widest possible perspective, and must always try to take into account all the possible dimensions of social reality.

Part One
Social Action

Chapter 1
Social Action

The subject matter of sociology

Our first task is to place the procedure that we will be using clearly within the context of the whole field of study covered by sociology.

If one can claim that the sociologist studies man in his social environment or, even more generally, that he studies "society," it must be recognized that society is presented to the observer in different ways. A number of examples will illustrate this point. A civilization, such as Western or American civilization, is certainly a social environment, and it is hardly necessary to emphasize that each person who is part of a civilization is marked by it. A country, while it is part of a civilization, also possesses distinguishing characteristics that set it off from other countries; thus it is easy, sometimes at first glance, to differentiate an Italian from a Frenchman or from an American. Westerners may have some difficulty in appreciating the difference between a Chinese, a Japanese, a Korean or a Vietnamese, who, from their point of view, are all "Asiatics"; but this results only from their ignorance of the national traits which are specific to each of these Eastern countries, and which are evident even in the physical appearance of their peoples. Similarly, within a country, social classes, towns and cities, and industrial firms all represent unique social environments, which can be — and indeed have been — studied in their own separate contexts. Numerous monographs on American communities have shown both the similarities and the differences between the

New England town and the town of the Western plains or of the South. To narrow our focus even further, each family has its own traditions, habits, way of life and emotional climate. Every teacher agrees, too, that no class of children resembles another, and that different groups of children cannot be taught by the same methods. In the social sciences, an important branch of social psychology is concerned with group dynamics. This term refers to the way in which members of a small group who act in direct relationship with each other (the so-called face-to-face relationship) organize and structure themselves, establish links with each other and develop individually, thereby forming a real social microcosm. And finally, to give our last example, when two people meet on the street and stop to chat for a few minutes, signs, gestures and words are exchanged which constitute a social phenomenon as much in the content of this exchange as in its form. It could be said that this meeting between two people creates a social milieu, for if a third person arrives, within a few minutes the tone and atmosphere of the conversation can be radically transformed from seriousness to jesting.

Between the brief chance encounter of two people and a thousand-year-old civilization, the gulf is enormous. These are two completely different kinds of reality and, at least in appearance, they are in total contrast to each other. They are both social realities, however, because *they have in common the fact that they form an environment, a framework, a milieu, which results from a collective human activity and which conditions individual human activities.* If the sociologist is interested in understanding and explaining man in his social environment, he must include in his perspective the complete range of different social environments that man creates and in which he evolves.

The subject matter of sociology therefore is vast, since it covers at the same time immense aggregates, groups of varying sizes and small units of observation. The extent of this field of research explains, on the one hand, the great diversity of empirical and theoretical studies in sociology and, on the other hand, the difficulty of developing one coherent theory which is unanimously accepted by sociologists.

Microsociology and macrosociology

The French sociologist Georges Gurvitch has suggested a classificatory system which helps to create some order in this picture. He distinguishes three horizontal planes of description or, more precisely, "three kinds of social types" (these should not be confused with the vertical levels of his "sociology in depth"). The first is the macrosociological plane of total societies, which includes social groups that are sufficiently complete to satisfy all the needs of their members — such as a country, or Western civilization. These groups are considered as wholes or units. The second is the plane of partial groupings which form part of total societies, such as the family, lineal groupings, voluntary associations, social classes, and so forth. Finally, there is the microsociological plane of different types of social links (which Gurvitch also calls the "forms of sociability"). These are the various social relationships which are established between the members of a collectivity and the different ways in which these members are linked to and by the total society.[1]

This distinction between microsociology and macrosociology, borrowed from Gurvitch, can often be found among French language sociologists; it appears only rarely in American and English sociology. But many French sociologists use this terminology with a rather different meaning from the one which Gurvitch employs. Thus, microsociology often refers to the study of restricted units of observation — either groups which include only a small number of persons, such as a family, a clique or a gang, or actions or reactions which can be apprehended and analyzed directly only through the people concerned at the individual or interpersonal level. Such an approach, for example, would be used in studying the educational methods in operation in a society, or the attitudes and aspirations of a given sector of a population.

Whatever meaning might be given to these terms, it is important to see them only as certain points of reference which are intended to guide perception and analysis. In the study of reality, these three planes interpenetrate and link up: total societies are formed of particular groupings; total societies and particular groupings are formed on the basis of different types of social ties. Gurvitch emphasizes this point:

> It would not be possible to study with any precision a concrete grouping, whatever it might be, without on the one hand integrating it within a particular total society and on the other hand describing the specific constellation or microcosm of social ties which are charac-

---

1. Georges Gurvitch, *La vocation actuelle de la sociologie*, 3rd edition (Paris: Presses Universitaires de France, 1963), vol. 1, pp. 11-14.

teristic of it. One could thus formulate the following methodological observation: it is equally impossible to carry out a microsociological analysis without taking into account the differential typology of groupings and the typology of total societies, as to carry out a macrosociological analysis while neglecting the microsociological aspect. These three horizontal aspects of sociology are mutually interdependent, for they are inextricably linked in the reality of things.[2]

A dual approach

This discussion suggests that sociological analysis could commence as easily at the macrosociological as at the microsociological level. Each of the two approaches is valid. It could perhaps be claimed, however, that it is theoretically preferable to begin at the macrosociological plane. In fact, one of the fundamental rules of sociological analysis — we will have occasion to repeat it several times — requires that one seek to understand and explain all phenomena studied by referring back to the total context. Confronted with the social facts that he is attempting to interpret, the sociologist directs his investigation, not towards the structure of the individual personality, but rather towards the structure and organization of society. Microsociology is not a framework of research which is sufficient in itself; it is really a level of observation, from which analysis necessarily leads the sociologist towards total phenomena, in the same way as it leads the psychologist to the study of individual personalities. Thus, it is only after considering the society in its totality and its main constituent parts that one should embark on the study of microsociological facts.

The contrary is the case in terms of teaching or for the purpose of clarity of presentation. Macrosociological analysis uses or presupposes a battery of concepts which cannot be easily defined except in microsociological terms. This is particularly true within the perspective of the sociology of social action, which is the one that we have adopted. One cannot pursue the analysis of the total society, or of a particular total society, without constantly referring to ideas that have been acquired through the inventory of determinisms and freedoms which are provided by microsociological study. While it is true that a microsociological phenomenon must

2. *Ibid.*, p. 119.

lead to the macrosociological complex within which it is observed, it must be recognized equally that the study of the total society refers the sociologist constantly to the microsociological fact of which the total society is composed. This switching between the smallest and widest units of observation is the normal and necessary procedure of the sociologist; it is one of the most characteristic traits of the field of sociological study and at the same time constitutes one of its greatest difficulties. For the sociologist, there is no break in continuity between the microsociological and macrosociological planes, but rather interpenetration and complementarity of two levels of social reality and two levels of analysis.

At least at the beginning, microsociological analysis is relatively close to the concrete realities which comprise the daily experience of each person in his environment. Thus, these existential data can serve to support the initial steps of sociological reflection in such a way that the break with everyday perception is neither too abrupt nor too startling. The progression towards more abstract thought follows a normal route, for it advances from what is known best to what is known least, the process that occurs in all science and research.

Because the procedure which leads from the microsociological level to the macrosociological level provides a number of teaching advantages, this is the approach that we will adopt. We will follow an ascending route, starting with the smallest units of immediate observation which interest the sociologist and progressively encompassing the larger and more complex units of social organization.

Social Interaction

The discussion up to this point enables us to define the subject matter of sociology as *social action*, or human action in various social environments. This formula, which at first glance appears simple and lucid, conceals a number of difficulties. The social reality hidden within our definition must be disclosed and examined.

Following the procedure outlined earlier, we will try to define and analyze the reality of social action, first from the perspective of the smallest concrete unit of observation that we can find, so that we may proceed towards the study of larger social aggregates.

If a sociologist were asked to identify the smallest concrete unit of observation in his field of study, he could not properly reply that it is the individual or the unit-member of a collectivity. This cannot be stated too categorically: the departure point in sociology — unlike psychology — is not the individual person. For the sociologist, the smallest concrete unit of observation is the relationship between two people, their contacts with each other or, more precisely, their interaction.

In order to understand the meaning of these terms, let us use two concrete examples of interaction: first impressions in getting to know another person, and the relationship between two people who have known each other for some time.

First impressions

First of all, let us consider an encounter between two people who do not know each other. What happens? A very simple experiment carried out by the American social psychologist Solomon Asch throws some light on the subject.[3] Asch asked a group of students, whom we will call Group A, to draw up in their own words the description of a person to whom he attributed six qualities. He read this list slowly, leaving about ten seconds between each one:

> Intelligent
> Industrious
> Impulsive
> Critical
> Stubborn
> Envious

A second group, Group B, was asked to perform the same task, but this time Asch reversed the order of presentation of the qualities, so that "envious" came first and "intelligent" last. Analysis of the descriptions completed by the two groups showed that those of Group A were generally more favourable than those of Group B. Asch interprets this result on the basis of Gestalt psychology, the psychology of the unified whole: the subjects of Group A took in first the positive qualities (intelligent, industrious); a picture was formed which was favourable to the person described; the less positive qualities were then perceived within the framework which

---

3. Solomon Asch, *Social Psychology* (New York: Prentice-Hall, Inc., 1952), p. 212.

had already been constructed and were adapted to this framework. For example, a critical spirit and stubbornness can become positive qualities in an intelligent person who sticks to his ideas and defends them. The subjects of Group B, who heard the negative qualities enumerated first (envious, stubborn), formed an unfavourable first impression which subsequently influenced their perception of the positive qualities. Thus, the person was described as having "a certain intelligence despite the fact that he is envious and critical."

Structured perception

This experiment allows us to perceive, as if in a laboratory, the organization of first impressions in the relationship with another person. For each person, the image of the other is not made up on the basis of a mere accumulation of random observations or impressions, but is rather the product of a structuring of perceptions. The perception of another, like any perception, does not proceed in a disorganized fashion, but is an arrangement of various elements in order to construct a portrait — or in other words, to give these elements a "form" (gestalt). Psychologists have often studied the various physiological, emotional and intellectual factors that are likely to influence the organization of this form. This is not the place, however, to pursue the matter.

The original perceptual structure, which is built on the basis of first impressions, is obviously not definitive or unchangeable; it is only a preliminary mode of adaptation to the other person. If, after getting to know each other, two people come to see a great deal of each other or to live together, the process of adaptation will continue and the image of the other person will be restructured as new observations emerge to confirm, correct or weaken previous impressions. Furthermore, it is impossible for this adaptation to end, or for the structuring of the picture of the other person to terminate. It will continue as long as the two people know each other, taking into account changes in the situation or circumstances which may arise, the maturation of each, and the various experiences which they undergo either together or separately. Even after the death of one of them, his image continues to change in the eyes of the survivor, either because of new information that he obtains, or mainly because of the unconscious effects of memory. Some characteristics of the dead person are emphasized while others are minimized, generally to produce what psychologists have called "the best form" — or in other words, an embellish-ment of the true picture.

Structured interaction

Solomon Asch's experiment teaches us something else as well. In fact, Asch developed the experiment a little further. He repeated the same procedure with two groups of students, this time telling them that the description they were going to draw up on the basis of the qualities mentioned was that of a teaching assistant who would be in charge of their laboratory work. Following this, the same assistant directed the work of Group A and Group B. Through observation of the groups at work, it appeared that members of Group A, who had formed a positive image of the fu-ture assistant, were clearly more cooperative than those of Group B. Thus it can be said that *the structuring of action with another person is an extension of the structuring of knowledge of this other person*. In other words, *action with another person is no more the product of chance than is knowledge of another person: action is also directed by the form of organization or structure; it also seeks "the best form."*

The first meeting between two people is perhaps the most ele-mentary concrete social phenomenon. It is here that one can see the origin of an interpersonal relationship which is still embry-onic, the first moments of knowledge of the other person and ad-aptation to the other person, and the first moments of structuring and perception of action. At the same time, it is almost possible to see the division between psychological and social phenomena. On the one hand, each person knows the other with his whole person-ality — that is, with his senses, his emotions, his memory and his intellect. On the other hand, social experience, social background and culture provide the elements for forming first impressions and for constructing the image of the other person. Although it is ele-mentary, the first social phenomenon we have encountered is al-ready infinitely complex because of the psychological mechanisms involved in it, and because of the social components that it pre-supposes.

Mutual expectations

Let us now discuss the second example — the relationship be-tween two people who have known each other for some time. It is sufficient to arrest the adaptation process that takes place between them at a given moment. Through their considerable knowledge of each other, their mutual perception has become refined and at the same time they have developed *mutual expectations*. A expects that B will act in a certain way under certain circumstances, and the same holds for B.

Reality, however, is much more complex. An attempt can be made to delineate it partially, according to certain propositions, by adopting the point of view of a single person — that of Ego as related to Alter.

> Ego knows that Alter expects that Ego will act in a certain way.
> Ego knows that Alter knows that Ego expects Alter to act in a certain way.
> Ego knows that Alter knows that Ego knows that Alter expects Ego to act in a certain way.
> Ego believes that Alter expects that Ego will act in a certain way.
> Ego believes that Alter believes that Ego expects that Alter will act in a certain way.
> Ego believes that Alter believes that Ego believes that Alter expects that Ego will act in a certain way.
> Ego wants Alter to expect that Ego will act in a certain way.
> Ego wants Alter to wish that Ego expects that Alter will act in a certain way.
> Ego believes that Alter wishes that Ego expects that Alter will act in a certain way.
> Ego knows that Alter wishes that Ego expects that Alter will act in such a way.
> Ego would like Alter to expect that Ego act in a certain way.
> Ego would like Alter to believe that Ego expects Alter to act in a certain way.
> Ego would like Alter to know that Ego expects that Alter will act in a certain way.

Although the mere reading of these propositions is staggering, it must be recognized that they cover only a few of the many possible expectations. Then, too, the list must be doubled to include Alter's point of view with regard to Ego.

What must be seen, over and above the complexity of interpersonal relationships described by these propositions, is the basic structure, some elements of which the propositions attempt to delineate. It is a commonplace to say that two people who have known each other for a long time and who live together have learned to guess each other's thoughts; these people have a presentiment, and can often predict each other's reactions. A large part of this knowledge of each other, however, must be intuitive and can never be expressed verbally. Linked to this knowledge of the other person, a whole network of common habits and mutual expectations has formed and become organized, structured and crystallized. This by no means indicates that nothing changes; even in an interpersonal relationship which is based on living together for a long time, both people constantly adapt to what are often imperceptible changes in mutual relationships, to new situations, and to changing circumstances. The structure of interpersonal relationships is thus never definitive, rigid or final. Adaptation to the other person is always at the same time readaptation.

It is just because the interpersonal relationship requires this constant adaptation, in terms of both stability and change, that it is the source of mutual influence or, to use the term that is most commonly used in sociology, of *interaction.* Jean Piaget expresses this idea of mutual influence as follows:

> The relationship between the subject and the material object modifies the subject and that object both by the assimilation of the latter to the former and by the accommodation of the former to the latter. . . . But, if the interaction between the subject and the object changes them both in this way, it is obvious, *a fortiori*, that each interaction between individual subjects will change them both, one with regard to the other. Consequently, each social relationship in itself forms a whole which is productive of new characteristics and transforms the mental structure of the individual. From the interaction between two individuals to the whole which is formed by all relationships among individuals in the same society, there is thus continuity, and the whole that is so conceived appears consistent, not as a sum of individuals but as a system of interactions which modifies the latter even in their structure.[4]

4. Jean Piaget, *Etudes sociologiques* (Geneva: Librairie Droz, 1965), pp. 30-31.

Society: a multitude of interactions

From what has been said, and from the quotation from Jean Piaget, it follows that at the most elementary microsociological level, social action appears first of all as reciprocal influence between two people, or as interaction. This interaction is not guided by chance; it is structured and organized in what Piaget calls "a system of interactions." We will return later to the meaning of this last expression and we will see how exact it is.

It can also now be better understood why we said earlier that the departure point in sociology is not the individual person. In the eyes of the sociologist, what is called society is not, as Piaget says, "a sum of individuals" who are linked together by some contract or understanding; for the sociologist, *it is the multitude of interactions of human beings that forms the basis and elementary material of society, giving it at the same time both existence and life.*

Psychological and social phenomena

But the following objection immediately comes to mind. Isn't it true that modern psychology studies personality and its action within the context of interpersonal relationships and the social environment — or, more precisely, the different social environments to which a person belongs? In what way, then, are the relationships of interaction more social than psychological? Where is the line that divides what is sociological from what is psychological?

This objection is obviously important. It poses the problem of what, in the whole of human action, is the specific subject matter of sociology — what could be called, in philosophical language, its formal object.

First, of course, we must point out that social action is always psychological and social at the same time. As we indicated earlier, it draws on both psychological mechanisms and social components. From this point of view, social human action is a total, global reality which involves and influences the individual personality and which, at the same time, comprises the material of the social environment. At the microsociological and most elementary level, from which we started, the overlapping of psychological and social phenomena is even more apparent.

But if psychological and social phenomena are closely intertwined in the concrete reality of social action, it is all the more necessary to distinguish what is sociological from what is psychological or, more precisely, to specify the perspective from which sociology approaches and analyzes social action.

As a first distinction, we may suggest that the psychologist concentrates his attention on the total personality and that the environment, for him, is one of the variables which influences the structuring and dynamics of personality. The sociologist, for his part, studies the social environment or the totality of social relationships among people (and groups), taking into account those personality traits which can influence this environment. This simple reply contains some truth but does not resolve the problem we posed. Its solution can lie only in better delineation of the reality of social action in which the sociologist is interested.

Two Definitions of Social Action

For this purpose, two sociological definitions will serve as guides: one, formulated by Max Weber, defines social action in a subjective manner — that is, according to criteria which are within living subjects; the other, proposed by Emile Durkheim, can be called objective in contrast to the first, because it determines the social character of action on the basis of external constraints which are exerted on the subjects' action. Let us consider the two successively.

Max Weber's subjective definition

For Max Weber "... [Human] action is social insofar as, by virtue of the subjective meaning attached to it by the acting individual (or individuals), it takes account of the behaviour of others and is thereby oriented in its course."[5]

This short definition enables us to establish three criteria for determining the social character of action. First, people must take into account the behaviour of others and, equally, the presence or existence of others. Two young children who play beside each other, each occupied with a completely independent activity, have not yet attained a sufficiently advanced stage of sociability to share

5. Max Weber, *Theory of Social and Economic Organization* (New York: Oxford University Press, 1947). Quoted from the Free Press paperback edition (1964), p. 88.

the same games. The most that can be said is that the presence and the activity of the other encourages each to stay where he is and to continue his solitary game. This is a case of a very elementary interaction. One of the children may even go away without the other noticing. In this case, social action is non-existent. The distracted person who passes by you without seeing you because he is completely absorbed by his thoughts is perhaps having an internal conversation with an invisible questioner, but his action is not social in his immediate environment. It would be necessary to stop him, tap him on the shoulder, and bring him down to earth for him to become conscious of your presence and to take it into account. The numerous caricatures of the husband who eats his breakfast in front of his wife, hidden behind his newspaper, are well known; he is not having breakfast *with* her, even though they are physically very close. The newspaper screen symbolizes very well the absence of communication, or even refusal to communicate, with the other person.

In all these examples, the social character of action is either very limited or non-existent because one or both of the two subjects acts without taking into account the presence or behaviour of the other person.

The second criterion that Weber attributes to social action is meaning. This term must be understood in its most literal sense: the action of the subject must have the value of *a sign or a symbol* for others, as their action equally must have for him. In other words, taking others into account is not sufficient to make an action social; the subject must indicate by his action that he has understood the expectations of others, and that he intends to respond either positively or negatively to these expectations. When two people meet on the street and one of them puts out his hand, he clearly indicates by this sign (at least in Western civilization) that he expects that the other will, in turn, extend his hand, according to the accustomed form of greeting. If the second person does not take the hand that is extended to him, the first will quickly be able to understand, on the basis of other signs provided by the person's behaviour, whether his action can be interpreted as simple distraction or voluntary refusal. To attach a meaning to behaviour is to attribute to it a symbolic meaning which can be transmitted and understood through a code of indices or signs; more precisely, behaviour is inserted into a *system of communication*. We will later discuss at greater length the role of communication in social life. Here, it is sufficient to note that among animals, and even more among men, collective activity requires the transmission of messages to subjects who are in a position to collect, interpret and understand them. What makes human society superior to animal society, what gives it its power and richness, is that the system of communication is much more developed and more refined than in animal society, and that it can take many forms. If psychologists have been more interested to date than sociologists in the social activity of animals, it is because animals obey instincts and biological imperatives more directly. For man, the possibilities of communication have permitted the creation and accumulation of an immense reservoir of knowledge, traditions and customs, giving his social life a new dimension which no other animal species has been able to experience.

Of course, it must be recognized — and we will return to this too — that human communication is not always efficient. The meaning attributed to signs (the written or spoken word, a gesture, sign language) by those who interpret them is not necessarily the same as that which the sender of the message has given them. Misunderstanding is the extreme case of a gross error in the meaning of words or gestures. Without going as far as that, the imperfect interpretation of signs is a common thing in social life; it can even be said that an "objectively" perfect equation in the meaning that various people attribute to the same action in which they are involved is relatively rare. In reality, social action generally does not require such an exact equation. It is sufficient that the variation in meaning attributed by each subject, the "subjective" meaning that Weber mentions, should not be so great as to prevent all collective or common action.

Finally, according to the third criterion of Weber's definition, the behaviour of people involved in social action is necessarily influenced by their perception and interpretation of the action of others and of their own action. In other words, subjects must prove, through their behaviour, that they have understood the expectations of others and that they are either willing or unwilling to respond to them. This third criterion is in a sense the external complement of the two preceding criteria, the latter being internal to the subjects involved. In fact, it is through behaviour which is observable externally that it is possible to judge the two subjective conditions. Thus, Max Weber locates the essential characteristics of action that is really social within the subjects, in their perception and their understanding of the conduct of others. External behaviour, which is observable, serves as an index to this perception and understanding. The "subjective" character that we attribute to Weber's definition must be understood with this very precise meaning.

Emile Durkheim's objective definition

Emile Durkheim's definition of social action is very different from Weber's thinking and feeling. He writes:

> [Social action consists of] ways of acting that present the noteworthy property of existing outside the individual consciousness.
>
> These types of conduct or thought are not only external to the individual but are, moreover, endowed with coercive power, by virtue of which they impose themselves upon him independent of his individual will.[6]

From this definition, it is clear that Durkheim does not seek the characteristics of social action in the subjective state of individuals, as does Max Weber, but rather in the realities which are external to individuals and which exercise constraints on them. Durkheim uses two "objective" criteria to determine the social characteristics of human action: the externality of ways of acting, thinking and feeling, and the constraints to which individuals are subjected.

To understand the meaning that Durkheim attributes to these two criteria, one must go back to his theory of two consciousnesses. The collective consciousness is formed by all the ways of acting, thinking and feeling which comprise the common inheritance of a given society. These ways of acting, thinking and feeling have become established in the course of history, are transmitted from generation to generation, and are accepted and practised by the majority or the average of the members of this society. They are external to individuals in that they have preceded them, go beyond them, and outlive them. According to Durkheim's analogy, the collective consciousness is the psychological prototype of a specific society. It gives a society its distinctive and specific characteristics. It is this collective consciousness which sets off a Frenchman from a Belgian, or a Canadian from an American.

The individual consciousness comprises what could be called

---

6. Emile Durkheim, *The Rules of Sociological Method*, trans. Sarah Solovay and John H. Mueller (Chicago: University of Chicago Press, 1938), p. 2.

the private world of each person — his personality traits or temperament, his heredity, the personal experiences which make him a particular human being. The individual consciousness, for Durkheim, is the relative personal autonomy which each person employs in his use and adaptation of collective ways of acting, thinking and feeling.

In each person, the individual consciousness can be more or less strong or developed. But what interested Durkheim most, as we shall see later, is that from one society to another the collective consciousness does not impose itself on individuals with the same force or strength. Societies vary in the degree of constraint that the collective consciousness exerts on individuals, and in the degree of autonomy which is left to the individual consciousness. Whatever the degree of constraint, however, the collective consciousness is characterized by the fact that it is always necessarily constricting and coercive. In order to belong to a society, whichever one it might be, one must adapt to the collective ways of acting, thinking and feeling; one must accept and practise them.

Of course, members of a society do not generally feel the constraints of the collective consciousness. They have absorbed and assimilated it, mainly through the education that they have received. It has become theirs, and has become their own moral conscience. The external and constricting character of the collective consciousness, then, does not impinge on the members of a society; for the collective consciousness, while external to the individual, is at the same time part of him, and the constraints that it exerts are replaced, for each person, by habit and by his moral conscience. In this way, Durkheim re-establishes the continuity which he seemed at first to break, between the individual and society and between psychological and social phenomena.

Durkheim's definition helps to expand the notion of social action by making two important points. First, his definition clearly is not exclusively interactionist, as is Weber's. It encompasses in social action, personal or even intimate activities, thoughts and emotions, insofar as these activities, thoughts and feelings correspond to collective ways of acting, thinking and feeling. Interaction between individuals, whether or not they are physically present, now appears as only one part of the reality of social action. Individual action can be influenced by the social environment in the absence of effective interaction, but it is nonetheless social action.

Second, Durkheim's definition locates social action in its environment or milieu. In effect, it identifies a reality which is both external and internal to individuals, which goes beyond them and is assimilated by them; this reality is what Durkheim calls the collective consciousness. The following chapters will bring out still more clearly the importance of this concept.

Two Complementary Traditions

The comprehensive tradition

The two definitions discussed above should not be viewed as either opposite or contradictory. The difference in the viewpoints of these two authors stems mainly from the context and the intellectual tradition which influenced each of them. Max Weber, an historian, lawyer and economist as well as a sociologist, had to struggle against a very strong current of thought in Germany which viewed the natural sciences and the social sciences as extreme opposites. The natural order, it was said, is ruled by determinism; it is the world of inevitability. With conditions kept constant, the same phenomenon will be reproduced indefinitely. Moreover, a causal link can always be established between a physical or chemical event and preceding events or conditions. This stability and continuity enable the natural sciences to construct laws and explanatory theories. In contrast, human activity bears the hallmark of spontaneity, creativity and freedom. It escapes from the rigidity of determinism, and it cannot be enclosed by an explanatory law. History is the only real social science, provided that the sequence of events is seen in terms of their specificity.

Weber had to struggle against this tradition, both to obtain recognition for the scientific character of history, and to free sociology from the hold of history. Recognizing the distinction between the natural and social sciences, he tried by his ingenuity to develop a method that would be scientifically valid, but specific to the social sciences. In addition to demonstrating that it was possible to find a causal explanation for successive historical events, Weber concentrated on underlining the advantage of the social sciences over the natural sciences — of being able to understand "from the inside" the phenomena or facts studied. The historian, the sociologist, the psychologist and the economist can interpret phenomena by mentally taking the place of their subjects, by associating themselves with the subjects' feelings, or by adopting their representation of the facts. The physicist does not have to ask himself what the falling stone feels; but the historian must share the feelings of the conquered general and accompany him in his defeat.

This conception, which was inspired mainly by the philosopher and psychologist Karl Jaspers, made Weber the sociologist of the *Verstehen* — that is, of the *understanding* of social and historical reality from the inside, by penetrating to the heart of human action. It must not be thought, however, that Weber denies or neglects causal explanation. He believes that in the social sciences, understanding is the foundation of causal explanation. To be convinced of this, one only has to read his definition of sociology:

> Sociology (in the sense in which this highly ambiguous word is used here) is a science which attempts the interpretive understanding of social action in order thereby to arrive at a causal explanation of its course and effects.[7]

We can understand now why Max Weber sought the characteristic trait of social action in the perception that subjects have of the meaning of their action and the action of others. Here we can see the application of the comprehensive method to the analysis of the elementary fact of social action.

The positive tradition

Emile Durkheim, for his part, worked in the context of French positivism, where he was strongly influenced by Auguste Comte. Comte had dreamed of unifying human knowledge on the basis of the scientific method. Far from recognizing the dualism of the natural and social sciences, he proposed, on the contrary, to base the social sciences on the method that had succeeded so well in the natural sciences. If Comte is recognized as the father of sociology, it is because he wished (as we shall see in more detail in a later chapter) to oust all non-scientific consideration of political and social facts, and to encourage instead an objective, rigorous and methodological — that is, a truly scientific — analysis of society and its development.

Inspired by Auguste Comte, in *The Rules of the Sociological*

---

7. Weber, *Social and Economic Organization*, p. 88.

Method, Durkheim undertook the task of establishing a rigorous code of scientific sociology. The first rule that he suggests can be explained as follows:

> Social phenomena are things and ought to be treated as things . . . All that is given, all that is subject to observation, has thereby the character of a thing. To treat phenomena as things is to treat them as *data*, and these constitute the point of departure in science.[8]

This so-called social reductionism of Durkheim has been greatly criticized, though his intended meaning has not always been understood. Above all, Durkheim wished this rule to ensure the objectivity and empiricism which are essential for all scientific knowledge. The fact that social phenomena are considered as things, or as objects of observation, led Durkheim to seek and perceive in these phenomena the traits which are presented to the external observer. In accordance with this procedure, he defined social facts through the constraints which are imposed on individuals by ways of acting which are external to them.

In addition, Durkheim was concerned to distinguish sociology, not from history, but from psychology. In the positivist context, it was this latter discipline which could claim the exclusive scientific explanation of both social and individual human behaviour. He also wished to demonstrate that one must not confuse psychological and social phenomena, and still less reduce the latter to the former. This explains his distinction between the individual consciousness, a psychological reality, and the collective consciousness, a social reality. This distinction led him to contrast and separate psychological from social or sociological phenomena to a greater degree than would be accepted in the social sciences today.

In spite of the very clear differences which separate them, the Durkheimian and Weberian approaches to social action, stemming from these two traditions, are not contradictory or opposed to each other; rather, they are complementary. Generally, today it is recognized that sociology is both understanding and explanation, both subjective (in the sense indicated earlier) and objective. The sociologist who observes a phenomenon from the outside — whether it be a group, a strike or industrial work — is often led by the logic of the research process in which he is involved to borrow

---

8. Durkheim, *The Rules of Sociological Method*, p. 27.

the perspective of the different subjects or groups in question, and to adopt their point of view in order to arrive at an explanation which is either more complete or nearer to reality.

The definition of social action as the basic or elementary unit of society has immediately enabled us to appreciate this double perspective which is characteristic of sociology, and also of some other social sciences. *Social reality is neither exclusively internal to the subjects which experience it nor exclusively external to them: such reality is experienced by the individuals concerned on whom constraints and limitations are imposed simultaneously from the outside on the basis of their perspective on this reality.* The theoretical and methodological consequences of this conclusion are considerable; and we shall return to it at several points in this discussion.

The conditioning of orientation of action

But doesn't this conclusion lead us even further away from any solution to the problem raised earlier, of the distinction between psychological and social phenomena? On the contrary, it is in fact a solution to the problem. Our conclusion suggests, first of all, that Durkheim's distinction between the individual and the social consciousness is much too artificial and arbitrary, and that psychology and sociology thus have much more in common than Durkheim was prepared to recognize. In addition, if it is true that social phenomena are experienced psychologically by individuals, it is no less true that psychological activity consists, for the most part, of adaptation (or accommodation, to use Piaget's term) to social facts which remain external to individuals even when they have been assimilated. Such social facts may be comprised of other people, of groups, of collective ways of acting, thinking and feeling. It is in accordance with these social facts that *orientation of action* is organized and structured.

Orientation of action is subject, obviously, to the influence of psychological conditioning. Psychology and particularly psychoanalysis have taught us that human action obeys impulses which are largely unconscious. Action is to some extent guided by preceding experiences which may have occurred long ago and of which the individual is no longer conscious. Thus, the decision to act is made with reference to a reality which is only partially perceived or even distorted. In short, the individual always acts with his total personality — that is, with his temperament, his inherited characteristics, his neuro-physiological make-up, and with all the experiences that he has known and which have marked him since the time of his birth.

But there also exists a social conditioning of orientation of action. The interactions we described earlier, the collective ways of acting, thinking and feeling of which Durkheim speaks, are examples of this. The sociologist is interested in precisely this social conditioning of behaviour and seeks to describe, clarify and analyze it. Thus he is led to pursue his search, not among underlying personality traits, but in the underlying social facts. He approaches social action, not through its biological or psychological foundations, but through its truly *social* foundations.

This understood, we can assert that it is not the difference between psychology and sociology, but rather the continuity from one discipline to the other in the study of global reality, that carries with it perspectives which are different but always complementary. The respective tasks of the psychologist and the sociologist are in the same line of endeavour; they are mutually supporting and contribute to each other.

The following chapters, which will be concerned with the genuinely social foundations of action, will bring out more clearly the specific contributions of sociology.

Recent Theoretical and Empirical Contributions

Before we proceed with the analysis of the social foundation of human action, a final point must be covered. This is the contribution of modern theoretical and empirical research to the analysis of social action.

The definitions by Weber and Durkheim, which up to this point have specified the main characteristics of social action, have been fruitful and pedagogically useful. More recent research has not questioned their validity, but rather has served to confirm the intuitions of these first sociologists. It has also given us a further and deeper knowledge of social action. For the moment, it will suffice to outline three ways in which our knowledge has been advanced.

The psychological foundations
of social action

In the first place, the psychological foundations of social action have been explored much further than ever before, while at the same time the continuity of psychological and social phenomena have been theoretically demonstrated and explained in a way that can now be considered definitive. Later, when we discuss socialization, we will note the contribution of psychologists and sociologists to these developments. At this point, however, we will talk only about certain studies.

The first we will consider are the studies by George Mead, which have had great influence in the United States.[9] Most important, Mead showed how the individual personality is developed and structured by contact with others, through others, and by assimilation with others. The psychological personality, even in its origins, is a social phenomenon or at least a social product. It is not, however, a mere reflection of the surrounding environment, for it is always an individual adaptation and reconstruction of this environment.

For his part, Kurt Lewin[10] has developed an explanation of behaviour by his theory of what he calls "the social field." He summarizes the dynamics of action in the following equation: $B = f(PE)$, in which B represents behaviour, P represents the personality, and E the environment. Thus, behaviour is a function of both the personality and its environment. But, according to Lewin, P and E do not vary independently of each other. As Roger Girod points out:

> The structure of the environment, as it is perceived, depends on the wishes and needs of the individual, in other words on his attitudes, while the content of the environment puts the individual in a certain state of mind. This dynamic relationship of reciprocal influence creates the situation from which behaviour results.[11]

9. George Herbert Mead, *Mind, Self and Society* (Chicago: University of Chicago Press, 1934).

10. See in particular Kurt Lewin, *A Dynamic Theory of Personality* (New York: McGraw-Hill Book Company, Inc., 1935) and *Resolving Social Conflicts* (New York: Harper and Brothers, 1948).

11. Roger Girod, *Attitudes collectives et relations humaines* (Paris: Presses universitaires de France, 1953), p. 69.

Thus, the person is not outside the situation, but is part of it and within it; there is no clearly defined and rigid boundary between the individual consciousness and the environment. The permeability of the boundaries between the self and the outside varies according to the aspects of the person which are considered, the surrounding culture, and the atmosphere of the moment. Thus, one goes by imperceptible transitions from the individual to the collective level, and from the conscious to the objective act. The individual, objects, institutions, societies and events are all equally elements of the situation. These elements are dynamically interrelated, and the total of these relationships determines the structure of the socio-psychological field.[12]

Clearly the theories proposed by Mead and Lewin are a long way from the opposition between individual and collective consciousness that Durkheim suggested. Psychological activity is sustained by the social environment, while at the same time it impinges on it. The social milieu is both the individual's environment and part of his context.

The environment of social action

This discussion of Lewin's theory leads us immediately to the second contribution of a number of modern studies which have been concerned with the environment of social action. Weber's definition seemed to abstract the interaction between individuals from the surrounding environment. The social psychology of Kurt Lewin replaces this interaction in its total environment, which is undoubtedly social but is also biological and physical. The physical state of individuals, the objects that surround them or are manipulated by them, are part of the total context of social action and can sometimes influence it in a marked way. In an attempt to provide empirical proof of the theoretical studies by Mead and Lewin, various researchers have conducted laboratory studies on what has subsequently been called group dynamics, as well as on interpersonal relationships. All these studies have helped, among other things, to clarify the influence of the diverse elements of the environment.

One example will be sufficient. Various studies have been concerned with the conditions in which friendships are made and maintained among people who are required to work together in

---

12. *Ibid.*, pp. 70 and 71.

teams (work teams in a factory, flight teams) or to live together (in student residences, for example). One of these studies, by Priest and Sawyer, was concerned with interpersonal relationships among 320 people living in a student residence. The authors followed the development of these relationships over a period of four years. From their observations and from the careful statistical analysis to which these were subjected, it appeared that students have a clear tendency to make friends with companions in nearby rooms, and that this same physical proximity is an equally favourable factor in the permanence of friendships.[13] In the same vein, Festinger, Schachter and Back found that in a residence for married students, the physical location of apartments had an influence on the "popularity" which residents enjoyed; the most popular generally had an apartment which was close to a circulation point of the residence (such as a common staircase) or an apartment which was more immediately and easily accessible to the others.[14]

Such research demonstrates very clearly that social action is subject to the influence of various physical conditions. The influence of some of these conditions has been empirically verified at the microsociological level in different countries and in different contexts of interpersonal relationships.

Theoretical models of social action

Above all, it must not be thought that the studies that have just been described are only pure empiricism. In fact, they are directly linked to certain theories which they serve to confirm or to modify. The third contribution of most recent studies is an attempt to elaborate various theoretical models of social action on which a general sociological theory can later be built. It would be premature at this point to go into details on these theoretical models; too many essential elements are missing for this to be done. Let us only mention as a reminder that it is in this area that Talcott Parsons' general theory of action[15] is to be found, as well

13. Robert F. Priest and Jack Sawyer, "Proximity and Peership; Bases of Balance in Interpersonal Attraction," in *American Journal of Sociology* 72, no. 6 (May 1967): 633-49.
14. Leon Festinger, Stanley Schacter and Kurt W. Back, *Social Pressures in Informal Groups* (New York: Harper and Brothers, 1950), p. 54.
15. Talcott Parsons and Edward Shils, *Toward a General Theory of Action* (Cambridge, Mass.: Harvard University Press, 1951); Talcott Parsons, *The Social System* (New York: The Free Press of Glencoe, Inc., 1951).

as George Homans' theory of exchange.[16] There will be many occasions later to present particular aspects of these theories. It must be said here, however, that the descriptions of interaction and social action that have been given in this chapter have been inspired largely by these theories, although we have made no specific mention of them.

16. George C. Homans, *The Human Group* (New York: Harcourt, Brace and World, Inc., 1950); *Social Behaviour: Its Elementary Forms* (New York: Harcourt, Brace and World, Inc., 1961).

Chapter 2
The Normative Foundations of Social Action

In the preceding chapter, we tried to clarify the main aspects emphasized by the sociologist when he considers social reality from the point of view of social action. Guided by the definitions by Weber and Durkheim, and by more recent psychological and sociological research, we have progressed from the phenomenon of interaction to the idea of social action. Our analysis must now be taken further. In this chapter we will attempt to define the social foundations of orientation of action.

The Norms of Orientation of Action

Let us start, once again, with Durkheim's definition of social action. It will be remembered that, for Durkheim, the social nature of human action stems from the fact that such action follows collective ways of acting, thinking and feeling, which are external to individuals and which exert a constraining power on their conduct. We must now try to answer a new question: *in what way do these collective ways of acting, thinking and feeling exert constraints on behaviour*?

Once again, let us use a few concrete examples. When two people shake hands on meeting, both of them are following a normal pattern of action in Western civilization — in other words, they are obeying a certain rule of etiquette or politeness. In other civilizations, such as India or Pakistan, each would bring his hands together, bowing respectfully to the other; in Melanesia, they would rub noses. The Westerner who avoids making a noise when he eats and the Japanese who makes a great noise to indicate his pleasure are both obeying rules of politeness accepted in their own countries. The citizen who pays income tax, the driver who respects the speed limit, the Catholic who goes to Sunday Mass, the husband who is faithful to his wife, the person who sneezes into his handkerchief — all are obeying civic, religious, moral or health rules which have been derived from their environment and which they have been taught to respect.

Thus, without our being constantly aware of the fact, at almost every moment our behaviour is inspired by norms, which provide us with guides or patterns. Our hairstyles, our clothing, the language that we use, our culinary or aesthetic tastes, our way of expressing joy, sorrow or anger, and sometimes even our most intimate thoughts — these are all suggested, provided and taught by the environment in which we have grown up or in which we are developing. Very little of all this is the result of our individual initiative and belongs to us alone, even if we have made it ours through usage. These are, in effect, the ways of acting that we borrow to give our action the orientation that is most appropriate to the civilization, the environment or the groups in which we live.

The normative orientation of social action

From this it follows that "ways of acting, thinking and feeling" exert constraints because they are presented to us in the form of rules, norms or patterns which we must follow if we wish our behaviour to be acceptable to the society in which we live. The social constraints of which Durkheim spoke (regretting, himself, that he had to use the term) thus correspond to what the contemporary sociologist calls the normative orientation of action — that is, action which is oriented according to collective rules or norms. For all practical purposes, we can consider these two expressions — social constraints and the normative orientation of action — to be synonymous. But Durkheim's expression has the inconvenience of carrying a negative connotation, at least in everyday language, and also appears to personify society, for which suggestion Durkheim was often criticized. In contrast, the expression *the normative orientation of action* is more neutral and also nearer to the approach of contemporary sociology, which takes into account the point of view of the social subjects or actors rather more than Durkheim did.

If we return to the examples of social interaction given in the previous chapter, it is not difficult to discover the constraints that are exerted by the norms of behaviour — that is, the orientation of action of the subjects that are involved. If Ego can perceive the expectations of Alter and if he can fulfill them in a way that satisfies Alter, it is because Ego and Alter refer to *norms which are known and accepted by both of them.* If Ego can ascribe meaning to Alter's behaviour and act in such a way that Alter in turn can interpret the meaning of Ego's action, it is because Ego and Alter are guided by the same rules or the same code for reading the meaning of behaviour. Communication is possible because the words, gestures and signs used have the same meaning for both persons. The relationship between individuals — which we have made the elementary social unit — and the interaction which results are not possible unless norms of action are known and accepted by all the individuals concerned, and unless each person orients his action with others in the light of these rules. Interpersonal relationships presuppose a consensus, or a degree of unanimity, concerning at least a minimum of common norms which are accepted by each person as guiding the orientation of his behaviour. Otherwise, human relationships would become incoherent and dissolve into anarchy and chaos.

The normative structure of social action

In the previous chapter, when we described interaction between two people, we emphasized that such interaction is not guided by chance. As in the perception of another person, this interaction is guided by a *structure*; it adopts a "form" (gestalt) or a configuration. *But the principle of the structure of action must be sought in the collective norms which guide actors.* This is the case not only for interaction, but also for all social action. Human action — even the most private and personal action which involves the most secret thoughts and feelings — obeys common and collec-

tive external rules. When we think, we use the language, concepts
and ideas which have been provided by the society and the groups
among which we have grown up and continue to live. Our "inner
conversation" is always an exchange between two Selves — of
which one plays the role of an Alter, formed on the basis of many
Others. We satisfy our elementary physiological needs, our impulses, our feelings and our desires by obeying prefabricated norms
that familiarity and the education that we have received generally
prevent us from recognizing as such. To the innermost recesses of
his being, man is a product of the "tribes" to which he has belonged and continues to belong: civilization, country, nation, ethnic group, social class, religion, region, family, school and so forth.

At this point, we will not stop to ask ourselves where to place
the dividing line between what is personal to each person and
what is social: posed in this way, the problem cannot be solved. It
is a false problem, given that — as we stated earlier — there is continuity rather than opposition between individual and social phenomena. What is important is to emphasize that *it is through reference to a structure of rules or collective norms that all human
behaviour is meaningful and coherent, in the eyes both of the subject himself and of those with whom or among whom the subject
acts.* Transposed into the sociological perspective, this conclusion
takes the form of the following axiom: *human action is social because it is inserted into a structure of action which is provided by
the collective or common norms or rules by which it must be
guided.* This can be said to be the most fundamental axiom of sociological theory, or the elementary starting point of its perspective on social reality.

One of the most important consequences of this normative
structure of action is to make *foresight* possible. In effect, interaction demands that Ego foresee not only the expectations, but
also the behaviour of Alter, and that Ego make his own behaviour
sufficiently foreseeable in the eyes of Alter. To take an example
that has already been used, if I see a friend coming towards me
with his hand extended, I foresee that he wishes to shake my hand.
I can further suppose that he foresees, by his gesture, that he will
lead me in turn to hold out my hand. If I betray his foresight and
I leave him with his hand extended, immediately starting a conversation, I will have made his gesture ridiculous — as happens to
us all at times. Thus, all social action is based on a series of uninterrupted forecasts, which follow one after the other and which are
concerned with the behaviour of the actor himself, and with the

conduct of the person or persons with whom he is in touch. In some cases, foreseeing the expectations and responses of the other person or persons becomes an important aspect of an art. The lawyer who questions his client in court, or cross-examines a witness for the other side, has often worked long in advance in order to foresee the replies to his questions and thus be able to formulate such questions in the most appropriate way. The public relations expert tries to foresee in detail the favourable and unfavourable reaction of an eventual client. As a general rule, we are seldom conscious of this constant forecast of the actions and reactions of others to which we must devote ourselves in our daily conduct. This does not prevent us, however, from doing so constantly in every interpersonal relationship. And this foresight is made possible only because each person can take as given at least certain rules which serve to structure the orientation of the action of others as well as of his own action.

Cultural patterns

These rules and norms which serve as guides or standards in the orientation of action are generally designated by anthropologists and sociologists by the term *cultural patterns*. The pattern is by definition the model, the design or the example that one follows or copies, or by which one is guided. The dressmaker tailors a dress on a paper pattern; the Catholic is invited to walk in the steps of his patron (pattern) saint. Thus, pattern evokes the idea of what is exemplary. We will also use the term *norm*, however, particularly in this chapter, mainly to remind the reader of the link between cultural patterns and the normative orientation of action. Finally, we speak of a *cultural* pattern because the patterns are part of what anthropologists and sociologists call *culture*. This latter term will be used provisionally without being defined, for it covers many facets of reality which still remain to be explored.

The definition of social action

By clarifying the Durkheimian idea of social constraint, we have rediscovered the language and the perspective of contemporary sociology, and in particular those of a sociology of social action. The constraints of which Durkheim spoke are nothing other than the normative orientation of action which follows the patterns that are suggested by the culture of a given collectivity. This procedure now allows us to define social action better than we could in the preceding chapter. *Social action consists of all ways of acting, thinking and feeling, whose orientation is structured according to patterns which are collective — that is, which are shared by the members of some collectivity of individuals.*

The Social Role

Definition

The structure of action, which results from the constraints exerted by collective patterns of behaviour, will be further clarified through an analysis of what contemporary sociologists call the social role. The social role is, in effect, composed of norms which guide the action of subjects who occupy a particular position or function in a collectivity. In almost every collectivity, however small it might be, a differentiation of functions is produced, either between persons or between groups, in such a way that each one brings to the whole a specific and sometimes unique contribution. Even in the smallest groups, sociometric tests and studies have demonstrated this division of functions. One member acts as the leader, another exercises a less obvious but stronger influence, another provides information or puts forth new ideas, while another fulfills the function of critic. Even in the superficial observation of a small group, this phenomenon of differentiation can be discerned. Methodical studies have permitted a refinement and extension of the analysis.

To each of these functions there corresponds specific behaviour — ways of doing things which fulfill the expectations of others. Certain tasks must be carried out in one way and not in another. Consequently, in addition to the common norms which apply to all the members of the group, there are others which serve to guide different members of the group according to the functions that they perform. *The social role is made up of the patterns which are specific to a function or a position in a collectivity.*

Of course, there are as many ways of acting as the leader of a group as there are group leaders. Each group leader conforms to the norms of his role in his own terms; obviously, the normative orientation of behaviour does not cancel out individual personality. But beyond individual differences and adaptations, there exists a common fund of patterns of action on which each leader draws according to his personality. It is because his behaviour conforms to particular norms that he is recognized as acting as a group leader. Thus, the social role specifies patterns of behaviour which transcend individual differences and which serve to orient the action of subjects who occupy a given position.

The family as an example

The family serves as a classic example in the analysis of social roles. It is, in effect, a social microcosm, in which role differentiation appears very clearly as a function of the differentiation of positions and activities. Each member of the family follows patterns which define his action in a way that conforms to the position he occupies. The division of tasks between father and mother is not arbitrary; in a given society or in a specific social class within the society, the father is expected to carry out specific tasks while the mother is responsible for other duties. For example, important financial decisions may fall within paternal authority, while the mother makes the daily decisions required in the normal administration of the family budget. Punishment incurred as a result of serious misbehaviour on the part of a child is often reserved for the father, while the mother is responsible for daily discipline. The father will not do the laundry, except under abnormal circumstances, but he can be counted on for other domestic work. Similarly, roles are not the same for all children in a family. The eldest enjoys some rights, but also has certain responsibilities imposed on him, particularly if the family is a large one. The youngest benefits from privileges that his elders have not known or that they have enjoyed at a later age. Psychology has demonstrated that the rank occupied by an individual in his parental family can exert a deep and permanent influence on the structure of his personality. In addition, from the beginning the sex of a young child affects the definition of his role in the family. Certain behaviour will be accepted in a young girl that is not tolerated in a boy, and vice versa; each will perform different tasks and participate in different games. Thus, the child learns from an early age the role that conforms to his sex, and even the "temperament" that is ascribed to his sex.

Obviously, each parent and child plays his role in his own idiosyncratic way. Moreover, the behaviour of each member of the family varies from one civilization to another, from one society to another, or from one social class to another. The tasks, responsibilities and behaviour that are expected of the father and mother are not the same; the privileges and duties of each child vary and the roles which are attached to each sex are different. One of the many studies on the subject will illustrate these variations. Research workers have compared the roles of the father and mother in the American family with those in the German family. From their research, it is clear that in the German family the role of the father includes more direct disciplinary control over the children, as well as a greater expression of affection for them, than in the American family. In the American family, the father is expected to have more active relationships with his son and the mother with her daughter; this is not the case in the German family where the relationship between parents and their children is not as clearly drawn by differences of sex.[1] Thus, each role is defined by the behaviour that is expected uniformly of the father, mother and child in a given society, in spite of and beyond individual variations.

From this discussion, it is clear that social role and function must not be confused. The social role is neither the function that a person fulfills, nor his contribution to the life or functioning of a collectivity. It is the pattern of behaviour which, in a given society, is assumed to characterize the activities of individuals in carrying out a particular function.

Social and theatrical rôles

The idea of social role quite naturally suggests the theatre, and it can be further clarified by using this analogy. Max Weber and Talcott Parsons often speak of the social subject as the actor; in addition, Parsons gives great theoretical importance to the idea of social role.[2] Through the role that he fulfills, each person in a sense takes on the trappings of a social character and enters into the role expected, for example, of a father or mother in a family. The person adopts behaviour and attitudes for which society has at least suggested the outline of a script, in a way which is a little like a cinéma-vérité film. In a theatrical play, each actor is free to give a personal interpretation of his role — indeed, he is expected

---

1. E. C. Devereux, Jr., Urie Bronfenbrenner and George Suci, "Le comportement des parents aux Etats-Unis d'Amérique et dans la République fédérale allemande," *Revue internationale des sciences sociales* 14, no. 3 (1962).
2. See in particular Talcott Parsons in Talcott Parsons et al., eds., *Theories of Society* (New York: The Free Press of Glencoe, Inc., 1961), vol. 1, introduction, pp. 41-42.

to do so. But this freedom can be exerted only within certain limits which are defined by the role itself, by the author of the play, and by the whole theatrical environment — that is, by the interdependence between the different roles and their place and respective importance in the play. It is the same in social life, where a role imposes a certain outline of pre-established behaviour and fixes the limits of personal freedom and spontaneity in carrying out the prescribed tasks. The complementarity and interdependence of roles, which together form the collectivity, impose additional limits on the creativity of each person.

On stage, an actor may be called upon to play different parts within the same play or in different plays. Similarly, in complex social units, such as the total society, each person performs several roles: father of a family, civil servant at a particular level in a Ministry, member of several associations, town magistrate, the participant in a group of friends or card players. Each of these contexts obliges the individual to take on a "character," to adopt various forms of behaviour according to whether he finds himself within his family, at his office, in the company of other civil servants of the same rank or of a higher or lower rank, with his friends, or at the municipal council table. And he must avoid confusing roles; he should not behave with his secretary as he does with his wife or vice versa, or correct his subordinates in the same way as he corrects his children, or joke with his children in the same way as he allows himself to joke with his friends.

The multiple roles of each person serve to reinforce the picture of the social subject as an actor, who must successively take on different characters; fulfill the tasks of each one of them; respond to the expectations of others who are attached to each of these positions; and adopt, as guides to action, norms which differ from one role to another. Not everyone is able to pass from one role to another with equal agility; neither is it possible for everyone to maintain his personal identity successfully throughout this diversity of roles. But these are psychological difficulties which are linked to the demands of social life.

Finally, some social ceremonies naturally suggest the theatre, both by the arrangement of the main actors and the public, and by the pre-established script which each actor must follow according to the role that he fulfills. This similarity has been demonstrated very convincingly by the French sociologist Jean Duvignaud:

> A religious service at a mosque or synagogue, a family anniversary, a court hearing, an inauguration of an

official building, an installation of a sorcerer or a priest, a coronation — all these are ceremonies where men play a role according to rules established by a "script," which they are not in a position to modify since no one escapes from the social roles that he must assume. Certainly, social life cannot be reduced to these spontaneous theatricals, but the existence of such collective behaviour brings society and the theatre closer together, and suggests a continuity between social and dramatic ceremony.[3]

In closing, let us add that the concept of social role is often used in both theoretical sociology and empirical research. For example, it is a central concept in analyses of the family, working environments, small groups and the bureaucratic type of organization. In these different contexts, the term social role is generally employed by contemporary sociologists with the meaning that has just been given.

Sanctions

Up to this point, we have tried to show *how* constraints are exerted on the action of subjects or actors through collective patterns of behaviour and social roles. But we have not explained *why* cultural patterns exert such constraints — that is, what allows them to be imposed in such a way on all members of the same collectivity. Obviously, a complete reply to this question would be long and complex. At this point, it is sufficient to emphasize the two main factors which confer on cultural patterns their power of persuasion: these are the *sanctions* which are attached to such patterns and the process of *socialization*. Let us analyze these two constraining factors.

The classification of sanctions

Patterns of behaviour are not theoretical or abstract norms. Part of their strength of persuasion and dissuasion comes from the sanctions that accompany them. The term *sanction*, however, must not be understood only in the sense of punishment. A sanction can be

---

3. Jean Duvignaud, "Situation dramatique et situation sociale," *Cahiers internationaux de sociologie*, 36 (January–June 1964): 47.

positive as well as negative: it can be the reward or punishment, the approval or disapproval incurred through an action by the person who performs it. In each collectivity, *conformity to patterns of behaviour can bring forth certain rewards and non-submission can result in the imposition of certain punishments.* To illustrate concretely this function of sanctions, we will distinguish four main types of sanctions in negative terms — that is, by the punishment that is incurred through non-conformity.

1. *Physical sanctions* are those which involve the use of violence or physical force to correct the recalcitrant person, to bring him back in line, or to prevent him from continuing to harm others. The most extreme physical sanction of course is the death penalty, whether it is employed by the judiciary, by hired killers in the service of a gang leader, or on the occasion of a vendetta or a duel. All societies have officially resorted to the threat of the death penalty in one form or another, against what is considered a crime; this does not imply, however, that the same act is necessarily considered criminal from one society to another. It is only recently that the death penalty has been questioned in certain countries as much on a moral basis as for doubt of its effectiveness. Torture, imprisonment and parole are other uses of force as a sanction: according to the point of view, these can be defined as punishment, protection for society, correction or rehabilitation. Judicial sanctions are unique in the official use of force by the representatives of public power. But there also exist minimal physical sanctions which are commonly used: parents slap or spank a child, or more often threaten to spank him. Between adults, the slap is also a means of defence or sometimes of attack, which a woman can occasionally use more easily than a man. Kicking under the table someone who makes a faux-pas, keeping in a student after class or on a holiday — these also are physical sanctions.

2. *Economic sanctions* may be of a public or official nature, such as a fine or the cost of damages imposed by a court of law. But most are more indirect and subtle and sometimes are even hidden: for example, boycotting a disagreeable industrialist or businessman, or those whose political opinions one does not share; cancelling one's subscription to a publication, or better still, withdrawing an advertisement; stabilizing or lowering a salary, or dismissing an employee for trade union or political activity, for bad conduct or incompetence; cancelling the scholarship of a student who fails his exams. It must not be thought that this type of sanction is specific to a particular economic structure; it can be found

as easily in socialist as in capitalist countries, and in archaic societies which had no exchange system as well as in modern industrial
societies.

3. *Supernatural sanctions* can be either religious or magical.
Religious sanctions are concerned with the relationship between
man and God or the spirits, or with his destiny after death. They
can be found mainly in the following forms: anger and vengeance
or punishment by God and the spirits, loss of privileges, withdrawal of the possibility of survival or resurrection, damnation or
eternal death, or the promise of a new life in a degraded or inferior form. In any religion, one of the dominant aspects of sacrifice
is that it represents a restoring or expiatory offering which is
destined to erase faults and to pacify the wrath of the gods. Magical sanctions are of another kind. They do not necessarily call on
the spirits, but consist rather in the ritual manipulation of supernatural forces (that is, those forces which are above or below directly observable phenomena) which are invisible, but also real
and more powerful than natural forces. Thus, according to some
rites, it may be possible to cause the death of an enemy at a distance by sticking pins into his effigy. Similarly, it may be possible
to provoke someone's illness by throwing the seeds of a certain
plant into his field, according to a precise ritual. Magical sanctions
have undoubtedly lost a great deal of their strength in modern
scientific society. Traces of them are still found, however, among
those who are afraid to light three cigarettes with the same match,
to pass under a ladder, or to cross the path of a black cat. The
number thirteen is still a fateful omen: the large North American
hotels do not have either a thirteenth floor or a room with the
number thirteen, and many people would be upset to find themselves one of thirteen at a table.

4. *Strictly social sanctions* are very numerous and can take on a
variety of forms. Expulsion from a group, rejection and ostracism
are the strongest social sanctions. By more or less planned action,
someone who has behaved reprehensibly is isolated, and sometimes his family receives the same treatment. But there are other
less extreme ways of expressing blame or reproach: a recall to order, explicit or implied; a frown; silence or a disapproving look;
withdrawal of confidence or friendship, and so forth. Gossip is a
powerful and feared sanction, particularly in small communities;
it is based on the fear of what-will-be-said, with all that this can include of exaggeration or distortion of reality. Finally, if ridicule
does not always kill (in fact, far from it), it often wounds and
serves as a corrective; mockery, a laugh or a smile are sanctions

which at times can be more efficient than many others, particularly in the case of eccentric behaviour which oversteps established limits. In his excellent essay on *Laughter*, Henri Bergson has shown the social role of laughter in such cases.[4]

So far, we have considered only the negative aspect of sanctions — in other words, repressive, punitive or corrective sanctions. But a sanction can equally be positive and can serve to gratify, encourage and reward. In fact, the two aspects, positive and negative, are generally inseparable because they are two sides of the same coin; for the most part punitive sanctions consist of the retraction of gratification or of what is desired, whether it is freedom, material riches, prestige, a good reputation or the friendship of others. Each of the four types of sanctions that have just been described can thus be inverted and presented in a positive way, in terms of rewards and gratifications.

Social control

Whether they are positive or negative, sanctions all have a similar function: to ensure sufficient conformity to the norms of orientation of action to safeguard the necessary common denominator for the cohesiveness and functioning of the members of a given collectivity. Conversely, they have the function of discouraging all forms of non-conformity to the established norms of a collectivity.

This is why all sanctions, both positive and negative, which serve to ensure conformity of behaviour can be entered under the idea of social control. This expression was used for the first time in 1901 by the American sociologist Edward Ross,[5] but in a much wider sense than we have attached to it here; for by it he referred not only to the norms themselves, but also to any kind of social constraint that may be exerted on the individual. The term has been adopted by many writers, mainly in American sociology where it is commonly employed, but essentially without any unanimity concerning its meaning. We propose to use the term here in a more restricted way to designate *all the positive or negative sanctions to which a society resorts in order to ensure conformity of conduct to established patterns.*

---

4. Henri Bergson, *Laughter: An Essay on the Meaning of the Comic*, trans. Cloudesley Brereton and Fred Rothwell (London: Macmillan and Co., Limited, 1911), pp. 19-20.
5. E. A. Ross, *Social Control, A Survey of the Foundations of Order* (New York: The Macmillan Company, 1901).

Socialization

The second factor which makes patterns of behaviour efficient is the process of socialization of human subjects. By this, we mean the ways in which the members of a collectivity learn the patterns of their society, assimilate them, and make them the rules of their own personal life. Given the importance of the socialization process, later we will devote a complete chapter to it (Chapter 5). For the moment, it will be sufficient to cover the concept very briefly.

The concept of socialization

Cultural patterns possess the essential characteristic of not being inscribed from birth on the biological organism of the human being. They are not transmitted by heredity from one generation to the next. Each new generation must learn the patterns of the society in which it must live. But the works of Sigmund Freud and his disciples, and of Mead and Piaget, have demonstrated the importance of the process of socialization, through which social norms are internalized, assimilated and incorporated by the personality, becoming an integral part of it. During his education and throughout his life, man develops predispositions, tendencies and needs for which conformity to norms is the desired response. Most of the desires, expectations and needs of man are not formed in a free way, following a kind of biological or even psychological necessity; these desires, expectations and needs are selected and channelled as a function of the gratifications that are offered. They are formed and take root to the extent that they receive a satisfactory response. This must not be understood, however, in an exclusively hedonistic perspective. Unselfishness, giving of oneself, and even the purest spirit of sacrifice also grow in response to a need — that is, to the demand for a certain image of oneself and for a moral conscience.

From the process of socialization it follows that cultural patterns, while they are within society, are at the same time within the member-individuals of society. Although they are external to individuals, as Durkheim asserted, they are also internalized by each person. After this internalization of patterns of behaviour, the constraints that they impose are no longer felt by the subjects who submit to them. It seems as natural for the Westerner to eat with a knife, fork and spoon as it is for the Easterner to eat with his fingers or with chopsticks. What is natural is that both follow good manners which are practised in their respective environments, for the rules have only a relative and conventional character. In the same way, to the Westerner monogamy may appear to be the natural form of marriage; however, it must be conceded that for many Africans, polygamy appeared, and still appears, much more normal.

For sociology *as a scientific discipline,* a norm in itself is neither better nor more moral than another; it has no absolute value. A norm is good and moral when the members of a collectivity recognize it as such, when they have internalized it and conform to it according to their conscience. Here, we are concerned with the non-moralistic character of the sociological approach, or with the *relativism which is inherent to the scientific point of view,* and which separates sociology from philosophy and social morality.

At the same time we are concerned with the *relativity* of cultural patterns. Since they are not fixed by heredity but learned, the patterns vary in space and time; they vary from one civilization to another, from one society to another, from one social class to another, and from one university to another. Over time, the patterns change too; some fall into disuse, others remain and take on a new meaning. A particular way of doing things which was considered unquestionably right and unalterable a short time ago today is abandoned and even forgotten. Modern society, in which the generation gap is more evident than ever before, abundantly illustrates the rapid change of the norms of behaviour, even in matters in which such a rhythm of change would have appeared impossible or unthinkable a few years or even months ago.

The individual and society

The process of socialization once more underlines the fact that there is neither opposition nor discontinuity between the individual and society, or between individual and collective phenomena, but rather continuity and interpenetration. Following the socialization of individuals, there is — according to the expression used by Georges Gurvitch — a "reciprocity of perspectives" between the psychological and the sociological, or between the subjective and the social, aspects of behaviour. The same rules of conduct or the same norms are found within individual consciences and within institutions (such as law or religion), within the individual and within society. Georges Gurvitch writes:

Psychological reality is universal. Besides outdated philosophical prejudices, there doesn't exist the least reason to ascribe to individuals (Selfs) taken in isolation or in their relationships with each other (Others), the exclusive capacity for mental states, opinions and psychological actions which are denied to collectivities — to Communities, to Groups, to Social Classes, and to World Societies. The individual, the interpersonal and the collective mentalities are only three dimensions of the total psychological phenomenon. . . .[6]

This quotation from Gurvitch summarizes well the present position in sociology. It shows how the paradox is resolved that Durkheim seemed to presuppose between the individual and collective consciousness, and how the falsely assumed opposition between the individual and society is dissolved. It stresses the reciprocity, or better the interpenetration, of psychological and sociological phenomena, and of individual and collective phenomena. Common sense leads us too easily to perceive social reality either in terms of individualism and elementary psychology ("human nature is always the same," "in society, each person pursues his own interests"), or in terms of nominalist sociology ("the society," "they," "the people," "the mass"). It is important, therefore, to assert strongly the total perspective — which is both more realistic and more securely founded on theory — that sociology adopts in its definition of social action: that individualized patterns are also extra-individual patterns, that they are immanent to individuals and transcend them, that they are integral to each consciousness but also imposed from outside. The standardization of conduct is based on repressive and rewarding sanctions and is consequently the product of constraints; but as Talcott Parsons has shown, this idea of constraints — even for Durkheim — represents much less an external pressure exerted on individuals than a personal moral obligation which each person recognizes.[7] If one wishes to speak of social constraints, it must be said that *in every collectivity each member is at the same time the object of constraints exerted by others, the agent of constraints which are exerted on others, and subject to constraints that he imposes on himself.*

Of course, social control can be represented or exerted more particularly by certain institutions or agents — the law courts, the

---

6. Gurvitch, *La vocation actuelle*, vol. 1, p. 110.
7. Talcott Parsons, *The Structure of Social Action*, 2nd edition (Glencoe, Ill.: The Free Press, 1949), pp. 376-90.

police force, a foreman — but it is simultaneously diffused and generalized, each person exerting it on himself and on others, each person being both the agent and the object.

Thus, sanctions and the process of socialization are mutually reinforcing and give patterns of behaviour what we have earlier called their powers of persuasion and dissuasion. Sanctions are, in effect, part of the process of socialization: the agents of socialization employ them to support the internalization of norms. Moreover, as a result of this support by sanctions, the effects of socialization become widespread and enduring. Finally, through socialization, patterns, roles and sanctions become such an integral part of the personality of the individual that *correspondence between behaviour and norms is not only accepted, but also desired, wished and sought by the actors themselves.*

The Natural Social Order

Social determinism

The preceding discussion of the normative orientation of action, based on sanctions and the process of socialization, brings us to an important conclusion: *human action in society responds to a certain order because it obeys certain rules.*

The goal of all science is to seek amid the apparent chaos of things or events the order which reigns, the constants and repetitions which can be transcribed into laws and theories, the necessary sequences of events which contradict or assert determinism. Although this statement might displease or shock at first glance, it must be recognized that human action in society obeys a certain *determinism*; for it reveals to the observer certain constancies, or a standardization of individual behaviour, which is sufficient to permit foresight or prediction. It is the product of this determinism that we call order. It should be added that in the eyes of the sociologist, this order does not result from a superior will which is mysterious and superhuman, or from a contract or an explicit understanding which has been established among the members of a society. This order, because it is a basic requirement, is inherent to social life. In this sense it can be called a *natural order.*[8]

---

8. On this question of determinism of the natural social order and of human freedom, see in particular Jacques Leclercq, *Introduction à la sociologie*, revised edition (Louvain: Editions E. Nauwelaerts, 1959), especially chap. 7.

In effect, it is because such an order exists that life in society is possible. In all our actions, we rely on its existence; we act in response to this order and as part of it. When a professor arrives at a certain time in a certain room to give his class, he expects to find there the group of students registered for the course; the students who come to the same room at the same time expect the professor to give his lecture. And if the professor gives his lecture in one hour (at least, in the traditional lecture system), he relies on the students to adopt the behaviour that is the rule in such a situation — to remain seated and at least relatively attentive and silent. Lack of discipline in a lecture hall is a deviation from the rules and can result in negative sanctions. Thus, the professor who, acting on a whim or impulse, got up onto the table during his class and struck up obscene or drinking songs would be breaking the rules of the game and would risk losing his job or being committed for a mental breakdown, depending on the particular case. At the very least, he would be subjected to the sanction of ridicule.

It is easy to multiply the concrete examples of regulations, standardizations and repetitions which comprise the natural social order. It is known that an urban population is not distributed indiscriminately over the territory of a town; rather, what operates is a reordering of ethnic, linguistic and social groups according to level of income and education. Social ecology has studied the constants or laws of these groupings. If there is an accident or a fire in a street, we know that a mob of onlookers will gather, and we can predict individual and collective behaviour; consequently, we can foresee the presence of the police on the spot and their behaviour. The approach of a holiday period (for example, Christmas or New Year) brings a succession of events each year which it is possible to foresee: the special decoration of business offices, the rise in the level of sales of certain articles and of the volume of letters exchanged, family reunions which follow particular customs, the exchange of gifts, and so on.

The example of suicide

Undoubtedly the most striking research which has been conducted on this subject, and which as a result retains a certain classical aura, is Emile Durkheim's study of suicide.[9]

Also useful, though more complex and difficult, is the work by Georges Gurvitch, *Déterminismes sociaux et liberté humaine* (Paris: Presses universitaires de France, 1963).

9. Emile Durkheim, *Suicide*, trans. John A. Spaulding and George Simpson (London: Routledge and Kegan Paul, 1952).

Suicide is assuredly the most extreme way of escaping from one's obligations and retreating from society; and most societies consider it as eminently anti-social. Furthermore, suicide, as a general rule, has the characteristic of a private and intimate gesture. The person who plans to commit suicide speaks of it to no one and carries out the act in private (apart from suicides of the exhibitionist type), to such a degree that the exact and profound reasons which have motivated his decision often remain unknown. Nevertheless, Durkheim showed that suicide is, at the same time, an act which has all the characteristics of a social phenomenon. The suicide rate is relatively constant within each country, while it varies considerably from one country to another. It varies also from one group to another: fewer Catholics than Protestants commit suicide, and fewer Jews than Catholics. Fewer married people than single people commit suicide; married people with children are less likely to commit suicide than are those who have no children. Suicide is committed more frequently during periods of economic crisis, but also during periods of great prosperity. The number of suicides diminishes during wars and during periods of political and national crisis. Briefly, according to Durkheim, the suicide rate diminishes to the extent that people are integrated into social groups by strong and permanent ties. While the suicide takes his life for personal reasons that a psychologist or psychiatrist may be able to analyze, at the same time the constancy and variation in the volume of suicides suggests an order which requires another type of explanation. At least there may be an explanation which, without invalidating it, complements the psychological explanation of each suicide at another level of analysis.

Of course, the sociological explanation that Durkheim wished to give of suicide has been reviewed, discussed and refined since his time; Maurice Halbwach's study in particular should be mentioned.[10] But, in general, subsequent studies have confirmed Durkheim's thesis concerning the social nature of suicide.[11] Durkheim was able to put his finger on the social nature of an action which is apparently most intimate, by demonstrating the regularity of the suicide rate and thus showing that it is part of the social order. This social order, or this determinism of social action,

---

10. Maurice Halbwachs, *Les causes du suicide* (Paris: Librairie Félix Alcan, 1930).

11. This is particularly true of the following studies: Peter Sainsbury, *Suicide in London* (London: Chapman and Hall Ltd., 1955); Andrew F. Henry and James F. Short, *Suicide and Homicide* (Glencoe, Ill.: The Free Press, 1954); Albert Pierce, "The Economic Cycle and the Social Suicide Rate," *American Sociological Review* 32 (June 1967): 457-62.

should not be observed only as reality but should be established by sociology as a *postulate*. The sociologist, at the beginning, performs an act of faith concerning the existence of an order which underlies the incoherence and the apparent spontaneity of human events and actions. By using this postulate as a basis, he can disclose the factors and conditions which serve to explain these events and actions, can undertake the analysis of the interplay of variables and their interdependence, and can disclose the hidden structure of a society or a series of facts. We can thus conclude that without determinism society would be anarchic and chaotic, and that without the postulate of social determinism sociology as a science would not exist.

Determinism and Freedom

The preceding assertions obviously raise the question: does sociology not recognize the existence of human freedom; does it not take into account spontaneity, invention and innovation, which exist in social life and action?

In answering this question, we will establish four points.

The postulate of a natural social order: a starting point

We have suggested the *postulate* of determinism or social order as a *starting point*, not as a conclusion, and it can be viewed as a starting point in two ways. First, from the theoretical point of view, we have just said that sociology must pose the postulate of determinism in order to support its scientific view of social reality. Otherwise, the discipline would be reduced to merely a history of what is particular and unusual — a view that was held by a school of thought in Germany in the nineteenth century, as we mentioned in the preceding chapter. Sociology can go beyond a history of events, in order to develop a science of what is general and universal, only by suggesting this postulate of the natural social order as a basis of social reality. Let us add that this postulate of the natural social order in a way acts as a backdrop against which sociology can better detect free actions, spontaneity, invention and creativity. In fact, the search for, or the invention of, new norms of conduct always involves primarily and necessarily a break with those which are presently in operation and are commonly accepted. Social creation is a reaction and struggle against common attitudes and opinions, and against a given state of things; it is the opposition to what we call in everyday language the established order. The surest and firmest basis on which the sociologist can perceive and analyze spontaneity is that of conformity; free and creative action stands out from it and courts the risk of conflict with it.

The postulate of a natural social order can also be regarded as a starting point for the teaching of sociology. It is important to emphasize from the beginning that determinism can be clearly observed in life and in social action. In fact, it is much easier for us to admit without question the existence of human freedom than to recognize the existence of psychological and social limits to freedom. In modern industrial society in particular, we are more ready to believe in social change, in progress, in technical, scientific and cultural inventions than in the various conditions of change and progress. Thus, for someone who is beginning to study sociology, it is essential to start with a clear understanding of this determinist perspective and to learn, first of all, to recognize the different facets and bases of the social order. The student's understanding of movement, change, innovation and the creative drive will later be enriched, for he will know how to locate these phenomena in the context of inhibition, resistance and opposition which they always encounter and from which they emerge. From this stems our emphasis up to this point on the Durkheimian idea of the constraints imposed on the social subject by collective behaviour patterns.

Various degrees of social obligation

This said, it must now be added that, whether they are generalized or specific to a role, cultural patterns do not all impose themselves with equal strength and require the same degree of conformity. There are two reasons for this variation in obligation, and they concern patterns of behaviour. First, it is possible in each society to establish a scale of behaviour patterns ranging from the strictest to the least strict. Certain norms demand strict and general conformity — for example, the norm against killing or physically wounding another individual, which is accepted at least in our so-called developed societies; or the norm of respecting the property of others. Other patterns suggest behaviour that is highly recommended, but society accepts and tolerates deviations from it. This is the case, for example, with norms which apply to marital fidelity and extramarital sexual relationships. Let us note a particularly clear example: in our Western societies, adultery can be a sufficient reason for divorce, but it does not constitute a criminal act which is liable to fine or imprisonment. Homosexuality, however — even between consenting adults — is generally defined and sanctioned as a criminal act. Generally it can be said that Western societies have adopted a margin of tolerance which is greater for the patterns which regulate extramarital heterosexual relationships than for patterns which prohibit homosexuality. Finally, other patterns suggest conduct that is preferable, but it is openly recognized that members of a society are permitted to deviate from these patterns of behaviour. This is the case in fashion and with a number of rules of etiquette (for example, that a man should give up his seat to a lady on the subway). Obviously, among the three cases that have just been cited — mandatory patterns, patterns that are highly recommended, and preferred patterns — there exists a series of nuances; but it would not be useful to go into more detail at this point.

In the second place, it is expected in every society that a gap will exist between patterns of behaviour and behaviour in practice, because patterns are not all as easily applicable and thus do not exhibit the same degree of "realism." Some patterns are recognized as ideals, or reminders of what one should do, which are not easy to put into practice; only saints and heroes can be constantly and totally guided by them, and this gives their lives an exemplary value. Here, once again, a graduated scale of patterns of behaviour can be established, ranging from those which represent the highest ideal to those which are more "realistic," more easily carried out, and generally observed by the members of a collectivity.

Variation

The preceding comments on the variations in conformity demanded by patterns of behaviour should be completed by consideration of another feature of patterns. If patterns of behaviour do not require conformity in a formal and imperative way, it is generally because society offers a choice between two or more patterns. One of the patterns may be the one most generally observed in a particular society and, because of this, it has a preferred character; but recourse to other patterns is permitted or tolerated, according to the particular case. Up to this point, we have spoken of the normative orientation of action as being submission to collective patterns which have been accepted and internalized. Another dimension is added to social action by the fact that the normative orientation of action includes, equally and simultaneously, a certain decision on the part of the individual. Individuals, as well as collectivities, must choose between more or less divergent patterns. The margin of decision that is left to individuals or groups may be more or less great according to the society and the situation; it may also be more or less perceptible. We have already alluded on several occasions to the individual adaptations that are authorized by patterns and roles. It could be said that this is a socio-psychological necessity which is at the core of social action. In fact, the diversity of personalities which stems from heredity as well as from unique individual histories requires that society offer the possibility of variations in conformity, and that it authorize or tolerate choices among permitted patterns of behaviour. To return to an example used earlier, the social role of the father in a given society includes a choice, within limits, among various patterns of behaviour which are more or less equally recommended and practised. No society offers the father only one mandatory set of behaviour patterns.

The variation that is permitted by accepted patterns of behaviour will be further clarified in the following chapter, when we show that this variation is based on a diversity of values. Here we shall simply emphasize that we are concerned with an essential aspect of the freedom of social subjects. Freedom is not necessarily synonymous with invention and creation. It consists for a large part in choosing, within given limits, among various patterns of action that are suggested by a particular society.

Deviance

Finally, beyond variation we find what sociologists call *deviance*. The distinction between the two is not always easy to draw in reality. Variation involves choice between permitted models from which the members of a society benefit; deviance is the recourse to patterns of behaviour which are found on the margin of, or beyond, what is permitted. What makes the distinction between variation and deviance a difficult one is that deviant behaviour, while being rejected by a great majority of the members of a society, is still tolerated. The tramp is someone who is economically non-productive, who lives completely at the fringe of society, and who does not obey the most common social norms; society cannot recognize this way of life as "normal," but tolerates the fact that certain individuals who are sick, depraved or unusual will adopt this way of life.[12] Prostitution is a similar case. Whether or not it is officially recognized and even regulated, prostitution appears to be at best a necessary evil; and when it is not openly condemned, it is merely tolerated.[13]

But, contrary to what may be suggested by the examples we have chosen so far, deviance is not only anti-social or asocial; it is also the source of social change. Later we will see, for example, that the modernization of the developing countries often results from the action of deviant or marginal individuals or groups who have opted in favour of norms of action which are more favourable to economic expansion than those to which the majority of the members of the society adhere. Similarly, the revolutionary process demands, at the beginning, that individuals and groups choose ideas, attitudes and actions which are unacceptable to the society of which they are a part. Finally, the kind of person whom Max Weber has called a charismatic leader is recognized as a person of authority by those who follow him because of his gifts, virtues and special powers which set him apart and make him very definitely a marginal, if not a deviant, person.

We should note that, except in some unusual cases such as that of the charismatic leader, deviance implies mainly that an individual adheres to patterns which are not accepted by the total society, but which are condoned by a marginal group. The prostitute, the Parisian tramp, the American hobo and hippie conform to certain norms which are imposed on them, sometimes in a brutal fashion, by the milieu to which they belong. Thus, deviance is generally an inverted way of conforming; it is conformity to a way of living which is anti-conformist or anti-social.

Finally, let us underline one more point — namely, the "statistical" nature of the ideas that have just been developed. In speaking of conformity we refer to behaviour that is most generally accepted in a given collectivity; variation and deviance apply to the

---

12. On the tramp as a socio-psychological type, see particularly the study by Alexandre Vexliard, *Le clochard: étude de psychologie sociale* (Bruges: Desclée de Brouwer, 1957).
13. Prostitution has been the subject of a number of studies. One of the best is Harold Greenwald, *The Call Girl, A Social and Psychoanalytic Study* (New York: Ballantine Books, 1958).

behaviour of minority groups. Variant or deviant patterns may finally gain the support of the majority. In such a case variation and deviance would then change sides.

The System of Social Action

The elements of a system

The different facets of social action which have been considered up to this point allow us to clarify two important conclusions to this chapter. The first is that *social action shows all the characteristics of a real system which can be analyzed as such.* In fact, in it are found the four main constituent elements of a system.

1. *Units or parts.* These are not individual people, but are either the social acts undertaken by these people — that is, the acts that are oriented in a normative way; or the actors — that is, the individuals considered not as individuals, but in their relationships with others and with a collectivity, according to the position that they occupy within the collectivity and the role or roles that they play.

2. *Organizing and structuring factors of the units.* These are the patterns, roles and sanctions by which the units are linked to each other and arranged in such a way as to form a whole, which is the collectivity or common action.

3. *Interdependence.* The structuring of units is particularly underlined by their interdependence. Each actor fulfills his role according to the expectations of others, the other roles that are included in the collectivity, and the way in which others fulfill their roles. The social acts which are effected by the actors succeed each other according to the new expectations to which each gives rise, to the responses that it brings or suggests, and to the frustrations or gratifications which it arouses.

4. *Equilibrium.* Finally, from this organization and interdependence results a sort of equilibrium of exchange, of complementarity, and of interaction. It is an equilibrium which constantly fluctuates and changes, and which is subject to the forces of both interdependence and the spontaneity of the actors; that is to say, it is dynamic.

What has earlier been called the natural social order can now be expressed in more scientific language; in analytical terms, it is the *system of social action.* This expression is important. Later (in Chapters 8 and 9), we will see how important is this idea of social reality, conceived as a system, in contemporary sociology.

Two levels of analysis

The second conclusion is linked to the first and follows on from our analysis up to this point. We have shown that social action is defined by the normative orientation of action, and by the structure that such action forms by modelling itself on accepted and shared norms. But the two expressions that have been employed — the normative orientation of action and the normative structure of action — indicate that *social action, as it has been defined, refers to two levels of reality and analysis*:

1. The level of the behaviour of subjects, to which the preceding analysis refers particularly. This is the level of the action and interaction of individuals, to which the microsociological level of analysis corresponds in particular. It is at this level that one can speak of the normative orientation of action.

2. The level of the collectivity, the environment or the social unit, whatever it might be (civilization, nation, social class, family), which provides the common patterns that guide subjects in their orientation of action. It is this level of analysis which is really macrosociological, for it refers to social units as the source of the normative structure of action.

Thus, "the normative orientation of action" and "the normative structure of action" are not two synonymous expressions. They indicate rather the double perspective through which the same reality appears. In fact, the two expressions refer to social action; but *the first applies to behaviour while the second refers to social units.*

In this way, the distinction that has been made from the beginning between microsociology and macrosociology becomes clearer. These are two different approaches to the same "total social phenomenon," to borrow an expression from Marcel Mauss. But it is necessary to distinguish analytical levels in this total social phenomenon, if one wishes to appreciate its different dimensions and to grasp all of it. The sociologist must never lose sight of these dual levels of analysis and reality, with respect to both theoretical analysis and empirical research. And if, keeping in mind this dual approach, we were to recapitulate the procedure that has been followed up to now, it would be apparent that on the basis of the most limited and elementary level of social behaviour — that is, the interaction between two people — we have progressively broadened our view to that of the social unit. Collective patterns have provided the pivot, allowing us to move from the level of behaviour to that of collectivities, and similarly they have at times brought us back from the level of collectivities to that of behaviour.

This transition from the microsociological to the macrosociological level will be developed further in the next two chapters.

Chapter 3
The Symbolic and Ideal Foundations of Social Action

In the search for the normative foundations of social action, the analysis of patterns of behaviour and their sanctions, as well as of social roles, takes place at what might be called a first level of abstraction. An external observer can, in fact, deduce the existence of patterns of behaviour and roles on the basis of the observation of a concrete situation involving a certain number of individuals or groups. Observable constants, repetitions and similarities over a certain period of time enable one to conclude that patterns exist which guide these individuals or groups.

But the patterns and roles revealed by induction can be considered the expression, manifestation or *symbol* of what Georges Gurvitch calls a "deeper level" of the consciousness of individuals and social reality. This deeper level represents a second level of abstraction in that it is beyond norms and roles, and is generally reached by passing through norms, which are its symbolic expression. This deeper level, corresponding to the second level of abstraction, is called the realm of *values*.

We shall first define the concept of value and then try, on the basis of this definition, to discern the reality that it encompasses. We will then understand how values and patterns of behaviour are incorporated into social reality, and how they become active through the symbolic quality they assume. Finally, we will analyze the various functions of symbolism in relation to social action.

Values: Definition and Characteristics

A value is *a way of being or acting which a person or a collectivity recognizes as ideal and which renders desirable or worthy of respect the persons or the behaviour to which it is attributed*. With the help of this definition, we can isolate some of the characteristics of values.

First, values belong to the ideal world and not to the world of concrete objects or events. The latter can express or represent a value, they can suggest a value or be influenced by it; but it is with reference to a certain moral, aesthetic or intellectual order, of which these concrete objects or events bear the imprint, that they merit or receive respect. As ideals, values thus imply the quality of being or acting which is superior, to which man aspires and by which he is inspired. *A value is no less real, however, than the behaviour or the objects in which it is concretely represented or through which it is expressed*. The world of ideals is a reality for the people who adhere to it. It is as much a part of society as is property or a network of roads.

A value has a dual existence in reality: first, it is presented as an ideal to be adhered to or respected; second, it is manifested in things or behaviour which express the value in a concrete, or more precisely a symbolic, manner.

This is what Durkheim meant when he wrote: "Values have the same objective reality as things."[1]

Values and value judgements

In the article from which we have just quoted, Durkheim established the distinction between *reality judgements* and *value judgements*. The former "are limited to expressing given facts, or relationships between given facts"; thus, they are judgements which define reality or explain its existence. I make a reality judgement when I say that events have taken place in a certain way, or that they have been caused by a certain combination of factors. In contrast, value judgements are concerned with the quality of things,

---

1. Emile Durkheim, "Jugements de valeur et jugements de réalité," *Revue de métaphysique et de morale* 19 (1911): 438.

or the worth that is attributed to them. I make a value judgement if I say that events are fortuitous because they favour the progress of religion or atheism.

Durkheim's distinction leads us to another distinction, this time between *a value* and *a value judgement*. A value judgement is concerned with persons or behaviour judged in the light of certain values, or with the illumination of certain values; thus, it is a judgement which is inspired by values. Such a judgement presupposes that the subject adheres to an ideal to which he compares the things or events he observes. Values therefore precede value judgements. We judge as excellent the behaviour of a person who exhibits certain qualities which are highly esteemed, to which we ourselves aspire, or at least which we respect in others. These are qualities that we attribute to an ideal human type.

In practice, a value and a value judgement are easily confused. Indeed, we often adhere to values because of value judgements: values are learned and accepted through the intermediary of such judgements; and for a person, as for a collectivity, a value becomes clearer by means of the value judgements that are made about concrete reality. Clearly our definition is concerned with this link; for in the first part we speak of the value itself and in the second, of the judgements of things, persons and behaviour through which the value is expressed. We must emphasize this distinction in order to show how values belong to an ideal reality by which judgements are inspired.

Values and behaviour

But if values inspire judgements, they equally inspire behaviour. This is a second characteristic of values. Earlier, we presented patterns of behaviour and values as two superposed levels, with values underlying patterns. This method of representing reality has the obvious disadvantage of being mechanical and oversimplified. Nevertheless, it is an image which allows us to outline more easily the dynamic foundations of patterns in the orientation of action. We might say, in fact, that a lot of patterns are norms of conduct of a specific kind in that they serve as guides to the orientation of action in particular circumstances and at a particular time, place and position. Their range of influence is to some degree limited and restricted. This is the case, for example, with etiquette, protocol, rules for the conduct of ceremonies and rituals, and a great number of norms which guide the actions of our daily lives. Moreover, because of their specificity, these patterns appear to be quite unimportant when they are considered by themselves. Even the links between them are not readily apparent. Patterns considered in this way, at this one level, are difficult to understand and their meaning cannot easily be grasped.

This meaning is disclosed, however, when patterns of behaviour are perceived in relation to values. Then the constraints they exert, the adherence they require, and the ties that unite them are clarified; for the patterns take the form of specific applications, in concrete situations, of more general and universal judgements. The power and efficiency of patterns are understood more easily when we see that they are supported by a deeper level of judgements and feelings which we call values. This level serves as a support, both because it reaches down into the central core of the personality and because its sphere of influence is wider than that of patterns.

A concrete example will illustrate this point. The rules of etiquette or politeness have no sense in themselves and can even appear ridiculous in many ways. What gives them a real meaning is that they concretely express something that is much deeper — perhaps a respect for other people. A person is not an object like any other, but has a superior "value" and deserves some respect. Alternatively, perhaps rules of politeness express a respect for society, or for communal social life, which they protect and make possible. In one way or another, the rules of politeness can be explained by "something else." Probably a study would verify the hypothesis that rules of etiquette vary with the individual's conception of man and society, and with the type of value he assigns to them.

The constraining power of patterns of behaviour and roles is not based only on positive and negative sanctions. It is much more firmly supported by adherence to values, by what can be called *the orientation to values*, which is only one facet — though undoubtedly the most significant — of the normative orientation of action.

Although values and patterns of behaviour are very closely linked, it is not necessarily possible to move directly from values to patterns, nor is there perfect agreement between patterns and values. In the first place, different patterns of behaviour can express the same value equally well, or express it more or less well, and can all be acceptable in the same society. In addition, it sometimes happens that patterns of behaviour are cut off from the values that have inspired them, but continue to serve as rules of conduct. Or the link between certain patterns and one or more values may become less and less clear. Such patterns may then be followed with a routine conformity which is void of meaning, without necessarily losing their power of constraint.

In this sense, the image used earlier of the superposed levels of patterns and values has a heuristic value. But we can already see that reality is neither as simple nor as mechanical as this. The relationships between patterns and values are complex and cannot be circumscribed by one narrow formula.

The relativity of values

The third characteristic of values which is inherent in our definition is their relativity. To the sociologist, the only real values are always those of a particular society; these are the ideals that a collectivity constructs for itself and to which it adheres. Values are also specific to a given historical period, for they vary over time, as well as from one society to another. In the preceding chapter, we emphasized the relativity of patterns of behaviour. What was said for patterns is equally true of values, with the added condition that values take longer to change than patterns — or rather, their modification encounters greater resistance.

The emotional force of values

This greater resistance to change relates to a fourth characteristic of values which is not clearly brought out by our definition but which has enormous importance in sociology. Adherence to a value generally does not stem from an exclusively rational and logical step, but rather from a mixture of reasoning and spontaneous and direct intuition, in which emotion plays an important role. Adherence to values shares certain characteristics with conversion, in the religious sense of the word. It includes an impulse which springs up in each person and carries him vigorously towards recognition of an ideal in particular ways of being or acting. Values do not necessarily require an impassioned devotion, but at least an affective attachment. In other words, adherence is not in itself guided by emotion, but it is not generally exempt from strong feelings.

This affectivity surrounding a value makes it a powerful factor in the orientation of action of individuals and collectivities. Moreover, it at least partially explains the stability of values over time and the resistance usually encountered by a change in values within a society. Finally, it explains the fact that contradictory values can coexist easily. Emotions are often able to link values in a way that reason alone would have some difficulty in defending.

The hierarchy of values

Finally, the fifth characteristic of values is their *hierarchical nature*. In everyday language, we sometimes speak of a scale of values to indicate the hierarchical order according to which a person or a collectivity appreciates or respects the ideals to which he adheres. This expression corresponds to a reality that sociological research has been able to verify and measure. Among such research, the study by Florence Kluckhohn and Fred Strodtbeck is particularly detailed and carefully executed.[2] These authors started from the following postulates:

1. There is a limited number of common human problems for which all people at all times must find some solution.

2. The number of solutions to each problem is limited.

3. When the members of a society adopt one solution in preference to any other, this solution corresponds to a *dominant value* in this society.

4. The non-preferred solutions remain present within this society in the form of *variant or substitute values*.

Kluckhohn and Strodtbeck decided to consider five basic problems of human existence: (1) the character of innate human nature; (2) the relation of man to nature (and the supernatural); (3) the temporal focus of human life; (4) the modality of human activity; and (5) the modality of man's relationship to other men. To each of these problems, there is a limited number of solutions. Human nature can be defined as basically good, basically evil, or both good and evil; it can also be considered as mutable or immutable. The relation of man to nature can be one of subjugation, harmony or mastery. In terms of time, he can orient himself to the past, the present or the future. In his activity, man can opt in favour of the free expression of his wishes and needs (Being); or he can seek increasing control of himself through meditation, wisdom and det-

---

2. Florence R. Kluckhohn and Fred L. Strodtbeck, *Variations in Value Orientations* (Evanston, Ill.: Row, Peterson and Company, 1961).

achment (Being-in-Becoming); or he can seek active effectiveness or productivity (Doing). Finally, in his interpersonal relationships, man can attach greater importance to linear relationships, which link him to his ancestors and his descendants, or to collateral relationships, which he has with his equals; or he can prefer individualistic forms of human relationships.

Kluckhohn and Strodtbeck summarize the problems and their solutions in the following table:

TABLE 1

The Five Value Orientations and the Range of Variations
Postulated for Each

Orientation	Postulated Range of Variations			
	Evil	Neutral	Mixture of Good-and-Evil	Good
Human nature	mutable immutable	mutable	immutable	mutable immutable
Man-nature	Subjugation-to-Nature		Harmony-with-Nature	Mastery-over-Nature
Time	Past		Present	Future
Activity	Being		Being-in-Becoming	Doing
Relational	Lineality		Collaterality	Individualism

Source: Florence R. Kluckhohn and Fred L. Strodtbeck, *Variations in Value Orientations* (Evanston, Ill.: Row, Peterson and Company, 1961), p. 12.

Clearly the various responses to these five problems correspond very well to our definition of values. In fact, with respect to each problem, any of the possible responses can be considered to be the way of acting which is preferable to any other, and which corresponds best to a particular human ideal. Moreover, on closer examination it appears that these five basic problems correspond to the elements of a definition of man based on his main activities.

On the basis of this chart, Kluckhohn and Strodtbeck constructed a very elaborate questionnaire which sought to discover how the individual chooses, in varying circumstances, one concrete solution which corresponds to one or the other of the more general or more abstract solutions of the table. With the help of this questionnaire and other observations, the authors studied five different communities, all located in the southwestern United States — Spanish Americans, Navaho Indians, Zuni Indians, a Mormon village and a rural village of Texas.

The results of this study show that —

> 1. in each community, a choice is carried out in favour of one solution to each of the five problems of man;
> 2. the solution which is preferred or valued varies from one community to another;
> 3. substitute values, which are always present, permit different individual adaptations on the part of the same person;
> 4. the system of values of a society is not made up of only dominant values, but forms a whole in which dominant and substitute values are intermixed in a variable hierarchy.

Such constellations and the hierarchy of values that they reveal must be taken into account when one wishes to trace the profile of the total range of values of a given society. Anthropologists and sociologists have given the name *ethos* to the profile of values of a society (a term which designated mores, or norms, in Greek), or more often that of *world view* (*Weltanschauung* in German and *vision du monde* in French).

The complete hierarchical profile of values can become particularly important in the explanation, and even in the prediction, of social change, since substitute values can serve as indices of the evolution of a society. When the circumstances of a society change, the substitute values tend to become dominant. They also may be adopted by an active and influential minority, who will determine the course of the evolution. We can thus conclude that very few really new values ever appear in a society. A change in values is more often a transformation in the hierarchy of values than the creation of new ones.

Value Choices

Kluckhohn and Strodtbeck's study, which has enabled us to illustrate the hierarchical structure of values, also demonstrates an aspect of social action that was mentioned in the preceding chapter and that merits further attention now. Social action necessarily implies that subject-actors and collectivities must choose among various possible ways of acting. In the preceding chapter, we said that social actors and collectivities must choose among differing or

even contradictory patterns of behaviour — among one or sometimes several preferred patterns, and one or more substitute and
deviant patterns. It now appears that the choice among patterns of
behaviour presupposes a choice among values, and that the former
flows from the latter. The decision that actors and collectivities
make when confronted with various possible patterns is guided by
the values to which they adhere; but in any case, their choice concretely expresses a more or less conscious adherence to a certain order of values. In fact, the decisions that must be taken are not usually presented in the form of an option between one pattern which
would be appropriate and others which would not be appropriate.
Often, many patterns can be generally appropriate when everything is taken into account. It is the choice among values which
leads individuals and collectivities to decide that some patterns
conform better than others to their world view, to their ideal of
life and to the ideal that they have of man, his nature and his destiny.

Talcott Parsons' classification

Kluckhohn and Strodtbeck's chart presents several value choices
which serve to define the world view of individuals and collectivities. Talcott Parsons has developed another rather different
classification of these choices which is better known and more frequently used than that of Kluckhohn and Strodtbeck. His
classification will help us to advance a little further in our analysis
of this question.[3]

Parsons has presented his classification in the form of "pattern
variables." He observes that human actors constantly encounter a
series of "dilemmas": they are obliged to choose among various
orientations of action which are in opposition and clearly unreconcilable. Parsons states that, in any given situation, it is possible
to reduce the number of these dilemmas to five and that, in the
face of each of them, two contrasting orientations or options are
offered to the actor. Each of the five dilemmas is manifest in almost every social action — in other words, in every action where

---

3. This classification can be found in the volume by Parsons and Shils, *General
   Theory of Action*, and also in Talcott Parsons, R. F. Bales and Edward Shils,
   Working Papers in the Theory of Action (Glencoe, Ill.: The Free Press,
   1953). Parsons has elaborated his classification more fully in his article,
   "Pattern Variables Revisited: A response to Robert Dubin," *American Socio-
   logical Review* 25, no. 4 (August 1960): 467-83.

the actor is in a relationship with other actors or with objects or realities which have social significance.

The five dilemmas, to which a total of ten value choices correspond, are as follows:

1. The actor may choose to give free expression to his feelings and seek the immediate gratification of his impulses. This is the choice of *affectivity.* Alternatively, he may control his feelings, restrict or inhibit their expression, and minimize their importance. This is the choice of *neutrality.*

2. The actor may judge situations, things or other actors according to generally applicable criteria which are universal for all actors, situations and analogous objects. This is the option of *universalism.* If instead the actor puts aside general criteria of judgement and uses standards which apply only to the particular actors with whom he is in relationship or to a single unique situation, then he is choosing *particularism.*

3. The actor who relates to other people and respects them by taking into account what they are, independently of what they do, opts in favour of *quality.* If he judges them in the light of what they do and the results of their actions, he opts in favour of *performance.*

4. The actor may consider individuals as a whole and relate to them as total units; thus he opts for *diffuseness.* But if he considers only one aspect of them — one isolated portion of their being and qualities — he chooses *specificity.*

5. Finally, the actor may choose to act in accordance with his personal goals, which are linked to his personal interests. Here he opts for *self-orientation.* Alternatively, he may act in accordance with the goals and interests which he shares with other actors, and which are those of the collectivity to which he belongs. Then he opts in favour of *collectivity-orientation.* Let us note, however, that this is not a question of selfishness as opposed to altruism. The student who prepares for his exams acts in a self-centred way. If he agrees to share his lecture notes with others, he accommodates community behaviour in an action whose orientation necessarily remains completely self-centred — that is to say, he is still guided by the wish to succeed in his exams.

A few examples

The meaning of these different value choices can be better understood with the help of a few examples. The role of husband and father, which we have mentioned before, is guided by affectivity, by particularism (the husband does not judge his wife or his children according to the same general criteria that he uses to judge all women and all children), by quality (he does not love his child any the less if he does not succeed in his exams), by diffuseness (he is not interested in his child only as a student, patient or client, but as a total person), and by collectivity-orientation.

In contrast, the relationship between a businessman and his client is generally marked by affective neutrality, by universality (the businessman will fix his price and the conditions of sale according to universal criteria, unless he decides to "offer a special deal" in which case he may in fact be influenced by particularism), by performance (the client chooses his merchant according to the quality of his goods and according to his reputation, and the merchant does business with a client who he knows will pay), by specificity (the merchant acts with the client as a client and not as a total person), and finally by self-centredness (both the client and the merchant pursue their own personal interests).

These examples show that the same person will adopt one set of value choices in a given context and another set in another context. The same man must, as a merchant, make the opposite choices to those that he must make as a husband and father. The value choice is not identical for the same subject in every situation; on the contrary, it is linked to the context. More precisely, to choose in a given context in favour of one way of acting rather than another is to have already made a value choice. In fact, the contrast that we have just demonstrated between the behaviour of a father and that of a merchant is true only in a particular economic structure, where rationality and the valuation of profit and success dominate — that is, in a modern industrial economy. But in many non-industrialized countries, the economic mentality will be different, so that the behaviour of the businessman will be more particularist, less specific and less influenced by performance. In a later chapter, we will see that the change in value choices is one of the main problems of the developing countries.

Two levels of analysis

Our last remarks show that ultimately the problem of value choices can be analyzed only by carefully distinguishing between the level of the behaviour of actors and that of social units. Considering first the level of collectivities, it appears that there must be choices among different or contrasting values and patterns of behaviour. In fact, what this means is that one can observe, in a given collectivity and in a given context, that the majority of individuals will make one choice rather than another. As noted in the previous chapter, this is a statistical viewpoint: the structure of the profile, or the world view, of a collectivity stems from all the decisions that the majority of its members make in different contexts.

It is on this statistical basis that sociologists can carry out comparative studies in different societies. Kluckhohn and Strodtbeck used it in their study to compare particular cultures within American society. Seymour M. Lipset has used Parsons' classification to compare American society with other Anglo-Saxon societies.[4] Similarly, Parsons and Lipset have used this design to compare Latin America with the United States,[5] particularly with respect to economic attitudes. Gathering together different studies, Lipset has revealed that, on the whole, the Latin American entrepreneur is guided in his behaviour mainly by particularism, diffuseness and quality in contrast to the American entrepreneur, who tends to emphasize universalism, specificity and performance.

Proceeding to the level of the actors themselves, we note at once that their individual choices are already conditioned by what could be called collective choices — that is, by the orientations that are characteristic of their society and of the majority of its members. The American businessman who opts in favour of particularism, diffuseness and quality in his business dealings is deviant and, above all, risks failure. In contrast, as Lipset emphasizes, the minority of South American entrepreners who have opted in favour of universalism, performance and specificity are innovators in their context and have become active contributors to the economic development of their countries. In one case as in the other, deviance (or variation) is not easy for the individual subjects, but is more profitable for entrepreneurs and for the collectivity in the latter case than in the former.

Thus, the freedom that social actors enjoy in their value choices is itself conditioned by the general context. In a given society, the majority of actors opt in favour of the preferred orientation in

---

4. Seymour M. Lipset, *The First New Nation* (New York: Basic Books, Inc., 1963).
5. Parsons, *The Social System*, particularly pp. 198-200; Seymour M. Lipset, "Values, Education and Entrepreneurship" in Seymour M. Lipset and Aldo Solari, eds., *Elites in Latin America* (New York: Oxford University Press, 1957).

each sector of activity. They always have the freedom to make other choices. But it is only a limited number of actors who deliberately choose another orientation in a particular sector (such as economic activity) or in several sectors at the same time (economic, political and religious activity); and they do it to the extent that these orientations really appear more remunerative to them (in the broadest sense of the word) or more gratifying than the others, either for themselves or for the collectivity.

It follows that value choices are not the same for all actors and groups within the same collectivity, particularly when the collectivity is as complex as is modern industrial society. Not all divergences are necessarily desired and sought consciously and deliberately by individual actors. Some are, but others are the result of the multiple and diverse structures within which the actors function.

The Social Functions of Values

Our definition of values and the preceding comments enable us to summarize the functions that are fulfilled by values in social life and social action. These functions are mainly of three kinds.

The coherence of patterns

First, values contribute to the coherence of all the rules or patterns of behaviour in a given society. We said earlier that patterns are difficult to explain when considered by themselves, and that the ties that bind them together are not always apparent. It is in relation to the values which support and connect them that patterns of behaviour have a deeper relevance and meaning, and that the links which join them become clear at the level of both the actors and the collectivity. But the coherence of which we speak always remains relative. This is because, on the one hand, the values to which a collectivity adheres are not always very clear or precise; it has already been said that one of the characteristic traits of values is that they are often surrounded by an aura of confusion and ambiguity. On the other hand, the realm of values itself is not necessarily coherent; conflicting or contradictory values can coexist in a society. The emotive force attached to them often enables people to link together contradictory values that rational logic must certainly challenge.

The psychological unity of individuals

In the second place, values constitute an important element of the psychological unity of individuals. This is a case of a socio-psychological function that it is not possible to elaborate here. Let us say simply that the psychologist Gordon Allport has emphasized this point of the psychological unity of the personality, showing that it is achieved by individuals who succeed in attaining a level of maturity such that the whole of their personality is unified in a "philosophy of life," which is influenced by certain dominant values.[6] In a more general way, even when the personality has not achieved the unity described by Allport, values contribute towards the cohesion and integration of self-perception and the perception of the world, and towards some unity of motivation.

Social integration

Finally, the realm of values is an essential element in what Comte has called social consensus, what Durkheim refers to as social solidarity, and what today is more commonly called social integration. If we can say that patterns of behaviour are a common denominator in a collectivity, we can add that values are also a kind of common denominator. Values, like patterns of behaviour, must be shared by the members of a collectivity; adherence to common values is a condition of participation in the collectivity. Here again, however, the social integration which is achieved through values remains relative — first, because the members of a collectivity do not all share the common values with equal intensity; and second, because value choices divide collectivities, particularly complex collectivities. But the division and opposition between the holders of conflicting or different values is only, in reality, the reverse of the solidarity which is created between those who adhere to the same values. Solidarity through shared values can thus be both a source of social unity and — because it engenders such unity — a source of social conflict, or at least of social diversity.

Symbolism and Social Action

The preceding discussion of the relationship between patterns of behaviour and values, and the social functions of values has pre-

---

6. Gordon Allport, *Personality: A Psychological Interpretation* (New York: H. Holt and Co., 1937).

pared the way for us to approach the problem of symbolism in social action. In fact, we can say that as ideals, values constantly need to be asserted concretely by something else — that is, the adherence of an individual or a collectivity to certain values must be demonstrated through observable behaviour. Thus, patterns of behaviour become the symbolic expression of values; or, perhaps more precisely, external conformity of behaviour to patterns symbolizes internal adherence of the subject to a certain realm of values. Adherence to values in its turn symbolizes membership in a society or a given collectivity. Consequently, *the realm of patterns of behaviour and values takes on the appearance of a vast symbolic world* in which social actors, groups, collectivities and civilizations move. It is therefore not an exaggeration to say that *social action is constantly and entirely submerged in symbolism,* that it calls on symbolism in many ways, and that it is both motivated and fashioned by different types of symbols. It can even be said that human action is social because it is symbolic; symbolism is an essential component of social action and one of its main foundations. Clearly it is important to discuss symbolism at this point.

The definition of symbols

The simplest way to define a symbol is to say that it is something which takes the place of something else, or that it is something that replaces and evokes something else. A statue symbolically recalls a person, an event or an idea, and thus ensures their continuous presence or action. A word symbolically replaces a thing and enables one to evoke it without the necessity for the physical presence of the thing.

According to the examples that have just been given, it appears that a symbol requires three elements: (1) that which signifies, or the object that takes the place of another — that is, the symbol itself in the strict and concrete meaning of the term; (2) that which is signified, or the thing whose place is taken by the symbol; (3) the signification, or the relationship between that which signifies and that which is signified, a relationship which must be perceived and interpreted by the person or persons to whom the symbol is addressed. It sometimes happens that the thing that signifies has a natural relationship with what is signified — smoke indicates the presence of fire; moist ground indicates that it has rained. But these are really *signs* or elementary symbols rather than real symbols. Almost all social symbols have a conventional relationship only with that which they signify. This implies the need for a fourth element of symbolism — the existence of a *code* which defines the relationship between the things that signify and the thing that is signified. For symbols to be meaningful, this code must be known and learned by the subjects to whom they are addressed.

Symbolism and human development

It is precisely this capacity to understand and learn the relationship between that which is signified and that which signifies that is the fundamental difference between man and the other animal species. If this capacity exists at all among animals, it always remains very limited; what characterizes the human species is the extension of this symbolic aptitude. This extension has required certain physiological developments, notably of the brain, the cranial cavity and the face, but also the hand, as the French ethnologist André Leroi-Gourhan has shown.[7] In effect, he has maintained that the fabrication of tools and the elaboration of symbols "are linked neurologically . . . calling on the same basic equipment in the brain." The capacity to produce and use symbols has thus been the culmination of a slow evolution which has occurred over many hundreds of thousands of years. This evolution has divided the human species from neighbouring animal branches and has set it apart in the animal world. According to Ernst Cassirer,[8] man can be defined as a symbolic animal; for if man is rational, it is because of the extensive aptitude that he has acquired to represent things to himself in a symbolic way through words and concepts, and to manipulate reality symbolically. This ability to manipulate symbols has enabled man to increase infinitely more than the other animal species his capacity for invention, and finally his power over the rest of the world. Man exerts a hold on the world which is in no way proportionate to his physical strength. He owes this power to the use that he has been able to make of symbols.

---

7. André Leroi-Gourhan, *Le geste et la parole*, 2 vols. (Paris: Editions Albin Michel, 1964). This is an excellent and detailed study of the development of symbolism and communication in the human species.
8. Many of the writings of Ernst Cassirer have been translated from German into English; see in particular *The Philosophy of Symbolic Forms*, 3 vols. (New Haven: Yale University Press, 1953). For a summary of Cassirer's thought, see his two works *An Essay on Man* (New Haven: Yale University Press, 1944) and *Language and Myth* (New York: Harper and Brothers, 1946).

The symbolism which gives man his sway over the world is the result not only of biological evolution, but also of social evolution. Through social interaction, man has been able to develop his ability to manipulate symbols, while society has acted as the depository of accumulated symbols. Symbolism — which, like tools, originated in and through collective human action — has in its turn favoured a more organized, complex and dynamic social life. Symbolism and society have thus been closely associated in their evolution; it is not surprising that one cannot be considered without the other.

With respect to social action, symbols fulfill two essential functions which are concerned with the very foundations of the normative orientation of action. These are *communication* and *participation*. The first is the means by which symbolism serves to transmit messages between two subjects or between a plurality of subjects. The second is the means by which symbolism encourages or elicits the feeling of belonging to groups or collectivities, or serves to express forms of membership. It renders more concrete certain characteristics of the organization of groups or collectivities by being directed to those who participate, and sometimes also to others who have a relationship with these groups or collectivities. Of course, the two functions of symbols are not mutually exclusive. The symbolism of communication encourages participation and the symbolism of participation establishes various ways of communicating. In practice, nearly all symbols fulfill the two functions at the same time and in different forms, even though — as we shall see later — some symbols have the specific task of promoting the participation of the members of a collectivity, while others are essentially symbols of communication.

Symbolism: The Function of Communication

Thought and language

Let us analyze in greater detail the two social functions of symbolism — first, its function of communication. We have already said that interaction and social action are basically phenomena of communication. Every form of interaction and a very large proportion of social action require the sending and receiving of symbols by actors. For this purpose, subjects can use various symbols: spoken language uses a range of sounds to compose a great diversity of symbols which are words. Language can be written, and it gains much wider dispersal when the written word is printed. Language can also take other forms, such as the telegraphic code and semaphore. Communication can also be effected without the necessity for subjects to resort to language in the strict sense, by the use of a gesture, by the position of the body, or by a facial expression. This latter form of communication generally accompanies the spoken language; it can supplement language on occasion and often completes it. In fact, the gesture and facial expression that accompany a sentence may give it a very different meaning from that which it would have had without these supplementary messages.

These various forms of communication form a first level of symbolism. Concepts, which evoke reality, comprise a second level of symbolism in that they are images or mental representations which take the place of the things and beings to which they refer. And concepts, while particular to each person, for the most part are also essentially a social product — for example, all the concepts which express virtues, qualities, faults or myths, or those which refer to past history or to social, economic and political activities.

There is a close and constant link between concepts and language. Not only do concepts express themselves in words, but also words give rise to concepts or provide access to them. This fact has been illustrated in a particularly dramatic fashion by the case of Helen Keller, which has often been cited. She became blind and deaf at the age of eighteen months, and would have grown up and lived cut off from almost all contact with people and things if she had not benefited from the help of an ingenious and devoted nurse. The nurse forced Helen Keller to learn words. The method she found was to place Helen's hands on her mouth and throat and to repeat a word, until the girl had felt the movements of all the muscles and could repeat them. In her autobiography,[9] Helen Keller recounts that the words that she learned had absolutely no meaning for her at the beginning; she repeated them only for the pleasure that she derived from the movements she made with her mouth and throat. One day, at the age of nine, Helen was playing with water from a pump while the nurse beside her repeated the

---

9. Helen Keller, *The Story of My Life* (New York: Doubleday, Page and Company, 1903).

word *water*. She suddenly understood that the liquid which was running over her finger had a name, and that the words that she was learning corresponded to objects. As she says, she understood that "everything has a name." For her, this was a revelation; in fact, it was a realization of symbolism and its power. From this time on, her mental life became organized. She was able to communicate with her environment and she became a social being. Despite her handicap, Helen Keller even wrote several books and led an active life for the benefit of blind and dumb people; and her example has helped in the education of several other similar cases. Her story has also revealed the extent to which human thought depends on symbolism, particularly on the relationship between linguistic and conceptual symbols.

This idea has been developed even further. In a series of articles on the languages of the American Indians, Benjamin Lee Whorf[10] sought to prove that the representation of certain realities — such as time, space and movement — is not the same universally and that the variation stems from the structure of the language in which one learns to perceive and think of these realities. A language already includes a world view which is necessarily adopted by those who speak it. This hypothesis had been suggested in the nineteenth century by the German linguist von Humboldt; later it was taken up by the American anthropologist and linguist Edward Sapir and elaborated by Whorf.

We come to the conclusion, then, that language consists not only of the use of symbols to express concepts which themselves represent reality; linguistic symbols are also involved in the creation of concepts and ideas, in the same way that they can determine the very content of concepts, if one accepts the Sapir–Whorf hypothesis. We can now see the extent to which symbolism, thought and communication are interrelated, and mutually influence and condition each other.

The effectiveness and ambiguity of symbols

Precisely because human communication depends on the use of different forms and levels of symbolism, its effectiveness depends on many conditions: the equivalence between what signifies and

---

10. These articles, which were originally published by Whorf in technical journals, were edited after the death of the author in one volume entitled *Language, Thought and Reality* (Cambridge, Mass.: M.I.T. Press, 1962).

what is signified; the use of the most appropriate symbols on the part of the sender of the message; the complete transmission of the message, free from interference; and the exact interpretation of the message by the receiver. The enumeration of these few conditions already indicates the degree of error and distortion which can arise in human communication. The relationship between that which signifies and what is signified is not always unequivocal. This is because, although it evokes reality, by taking its place the symbol masks it; it does not reveal reality completely or exactly, but distorts and reconstructs it. The same symbol or the same words do not suggest the same facets of a thing for different people. And further misunderstandings may arise between individuals who belong to different groups, different social classes or different societies. The study of the failures of communication and their consequences has begun, particularly with regard to international relations, inter-ethnic relations, relationships between management and workers, and work relationships within bureaucratic organizations.[11] In fact, what is astonishing is not that there are so many errors in communication but that there are not more of them, and that despite the many conditions necessary for its functioning, human communication remains a relatively efficient process.

In ending this section, let us emphasize, without going into detail, that communication has become the object of many different studies over the past few years. This new interest can be explained by several factors:

> 1. It has been realized that communication can have tremendous importance for the efficiency of large modern working organizations.
> 2. Progress in the techniques of mass communication has given communication a new dimension by increasing its range of diffusion to an unprecedented extent.
> 3. The mathematics of communication have progressed rapidly and are destined to render an increasingly valuable service in various sectors.
> 4. Cybernetics, in which the process of communication is fundamental, today is recognized as almost a science, and its applications are multiplying.

---

11. See, for example, William V. Harvey, *Communication: Patterns and Incidents* (Homewood, Ill.: Richard D. Irwin, Inc., 1960).

Symbolism: The Function of Participation

Aside from communication, symbols influence social life in other ways. Primarily, they serve to make concrete, tangible and visible the abstract, mental or moral realities of a society. In this way, they contribute to the recollection and maintenance of feelings of belonging, and to the instigation or assurance of the appropriate participation of members according to the position and the role that each one occupies; they also contribute to the maintenance of the natural social order and the solidarity that it presupposes.

Earlier we analyzed the relationships between patterns of behaviour and values. These relationships are deeply symbolic in that patterns can be considered the symbolic form of values. Orientation to action which conforms to certain patterns also symbolically demonstrates the adherence of the subject to given values. Finally, adherence to values in itself symbolizes, both to the subject and to other actors, his participation in a particular society or collectivity.

This predominantly social function of symbolism, however, adopts numerous and diverse concrete forms, of which we will try to describe the main ones. These will be grouped under four headings: symbols which encourage solidarity, symbols which define the hierarchical organization of collectivities, symbols which link the present to the past, and symbols which represent supernatural forces and beings.

Symbols of solidarity

Collectivities are abstract entities which require symbols in order to remind their members of their existence, to distinguish such collectivities from others, and to ensure their existence for other people. This is the case with national or ethnic collectivities which are represented for us by various symbols — a flag, a coat of arms, a patriotic song, a distinctive colour, a statesman (such as the king, the chief of state, the president), a political institution (the British crown, the American constitution), an animal (the Soviet bear, the American eagle, the British lion, the Canadian beaver) or a typical personality (the English John Bull, the French Marianne, the French-Canadian Jean Baptiste, the Black American Jim Crow). Not only do these symbols help to represent collectivities concretely, but they can also serve to provoke or maintain the feeling of belonging and the solidarity of members. This is what is sought, and provoked, by a crowd singing the national anthem, by the chief of state's tour at an appropriate moment, by a caricature showing the typical personality facing the contemporary difficulties of the collectivity (during an international crisis or following a rise in taxes), by the hoisting of the flag, or by the oath of allegiance to the flag. The almost fetishist respect for the flag with which the young American grows up is well known, as is the extent to which he is taught to respect the etiquette surrounding the flag. One of the problems of a young nation is to create such symbolism, and above all to succeed in making it meaningful and vital for the whole of the population.

Collectivities that are not as big as a nation or an ethnic group also use symbolic forms of participation. This is the case with political parties in particular, which must maintain the solidarity of their followers and encourage new members. The strategy of political parties includes a great preoccupation with this symbolic aspect — finding the slogan which symbolizes the spirit and the program of the party, or constructing a symbolic image of their leaders which will be understood and well received. During the electoral period, the symbolism of political life proliferates and can become very varied. In the United States, in his study of Yankee City,[12] Warner particularly analyzed the symbolism that is attached to a politician, and how he uses it.

In general, voluntary associations, particularly those of an ideological nature, call on varied symbolism to arouse the solidarity of their members and to give evidence of their existence — flags, insignia, costumes, songs, slogans. Studies of gangs have shown how these groups often resort to the symbolism of participation when they are organized — initiation rites, insignia, decoration, jargon, activities and behaviour. All these groups adopt a symbolic context in order to assert, maintain and reinforce the solidarity of their membership.[13]

At the microsociological level, many family entertainments and

---

12. W. L. Warner, *The Living and The Dead: A Study of the Symbolic Life of Americans* (New Haven: Yale University Press, 1959). This is surely the most important and the richest empirical study of symbolic phenomena.

13. On this subject see, for example, F. M. Thrasher, *The Gang: A Study of 1313 Gangs in Chicago*, 2nd edition (Chicago: University of Chicago Press, 1936); and also William Foote Whyte, *Street Corner Society* (Chicago: University of Chicago Press, 1943).

ceremonies are characterized by the symbolism of participation. One attends a marriage or the funeral of a parent to show solidarity; to be absent would be to show a regrettable indifference to the family. The exchange of presents, greeting cards and visits on specific occasions are other symbolic manifestations of the family spirit.

The symbolic nature of alcoholic drink would in itself merit a complete study. Drinking together recalls the links that tie people together, the feelings that they share, and the events that they celebrate. Family celebrations and ceremonies include the offering of drinks — births, marriages, departures, arrivals, birthdays (and even death formerly). Friends who meet celebrate with a drink. In many religions, alcoholic drink symbolizes the communion of the believers.

Symbols of hierarchical organization

The internal, often complex, organization of collectivities is constantly represented by various symbols. Durkheim saw this and illustrated the fact in the case of primitive societies. Following him, many anthropologists have studied symbolism in archaic societies.

We will limit ourselves here to the symbolism which concerns the hierarchy of collectivities, contenting ourselves with familiar examples. In fact, all social hierarchies are accompanied by a very rich symbolism, as if it were particularly important that distinctions of rank and of power should be clearly advertised. Thus, many symbols express differences of class and prestige in society. Everything takes on the value of a symbol. The residential area, the type of housing, the car, the children's school, the associations or clubs to which one belongs, clothes, leisure time activities, the place where holidays are taken, language — all these serve as indicators, signs or symbols of the status that the individual occupies, the power that he exerts, and the prestige that he enjoys. Societies which are supposedly highly democratic or egalitarian do not escape this. Obviously, this does not mean that the social scale is only symbolic; it certainly has other bases. Moreover, the symbolism that surrounds the social scale does not only express it; symbolism reinforces it, increases its rigidity, and often contributes towards perfecting its fine points.

Since bureaucratic organization is hierarchical by its very nature, one would expect that this type of symbolism would proliferate within it. The public service can serve as a good example. The rank, power and jurisdiction of civil servants is expressed symbolically in various ways: the size of the office, whether or not there is an outside office, the size of this outside office, the type of furnishing, the carpet, the hangings, the private secretary or the status of the private secretary. This can continue up to the colour of the suit the civil servant wears (generally darker as one goes up the scale) and his choice of tie. All these accessories help to identify the status of each civil servant and — what is still more important — show the extent of his authority and the behaviour that should be adopted towards him. The surroundings in which a Minister or higher civil servant receives you does not only indicate the status of the individual, but also inspires you with the necessary respect for him.

To varying degrees, this symbolic apparatus is characteristic of all bureaucracies. One need only observe casually the organization and life of a university, a factory, an office, a religious community or a hospital to glean a rich collection of hierarchical symbols in a very short time.

In all these hierarchies, the clothing and accessories that may be worn merit a special study. As Leroi-Gourhan writes:

> The protective value of man's clothing is no more important than its form; it is on this basis and on the basis of the decorative accessories that accompany the clothing, that the first degree of social recognition is established. . . . Each individual, male or female, whether dressed in a suit with a waistcoat or a dress, carries a certain number of insignia which — by the colour of the tie, the style of the shoes, the decoration in the buttonhole, the quality of the cloth, the perfume that is used — enable one to locate him or her with great precision in the social structure. What is true of our society is just as true of Melanesia, of the Eskimos or of China.[14]

Clothing in itself serves to distinguish the sexes, age groups, manual from non-manual workers (blue-collar from white-collar workers), military from civil personnel, clergy from their flock; and to this must be added all the distinctions of rank that such clothing can indicate. Think of the problems of protocol that clothing poses on the occasion of a marriage, an official dinner, a public

---

14. Leroi-Gourhan, *Le geste*, vol. 2, p. 188.

ceremony or a society reception. In the religious world, clothing can simultaneously indicate membership and status; one says of a priest that he has been "defrocked" while still recognizing that "the habit does not make a monk!" The Cardinal "receives the hat" or is "clothed in scarlet"; the bishop receives a ring and the cleric the tonsure. Religious dress has always been the sign of the special character of the clergy, who are thereby "separated" because they "do not belong to the world." Thus, the simplification of religious dress today is intended to symbolize the coming together of the Church and the rest of the world.

Symbols of the past

As in the case of individuals, the past provides a collectivity with part of its identity. A society also is defined partly by its origins, its history, its evolution, and by certain remarkable events. Maurice Halbwachs has brilliantly defended this thesis on the subject of what he called the collective memory,[15] whose analogy with the individual memory is often striking.

The collective memory is not necessarily history as written by the historians, even though it is inspired by this history. Rather, it must simplify, summarize, prune, distort and legendize the past; for this purpose, it often resorts to symbolism. A few names of great personalities with a mythical halo are sufficient — a few dates, a few places full of memories, and certain events which have been more or less distorted. In illiterate societies, history and the collective memory are fused to a greater extent with mythical thought, where time is telescoped and where the plausibility of events is no problem. The collective memory has thus resolved the problem, by retaining a limited number of facts.

Though it simplifies and distorts reality, the collective memory is nonetheless a very powerful agent of social solidarity. The symbols that it uses are full of meaning. The memories that are evoked by these symbols are charged with a community emotion, and they are the source of psychological communion which is almost biological. They provide an explanation of the present situation, or at least a rationalization; they suggest lessons for the future. Thus these symbols contribute powerfully to the solidarity of collectivities, to the participation of their members, and to the orientation of individual and collective action.

---

15. Maurice Halbwachs, *La mémoire collective*, published after his death by Jeanne Alexandre (Paris: Presses universitaires de France, 1950).

Religious and magical symbols

Religious and magical symbolism is of a different order from the preceding kinds, for its goal is to link man to a supernatural order. But it can be claimed that religious symbolism is no less profoundly social. At the extreme, we can say that the majority of the relationships between man and the supernatural world are interpersonal relationships which have a great deal in common with social relationships. But without going that far, what is certain is that religious symbolism is sustained and strengthened by the social context, that it expresses social realities, and that it has social significance and consequences. Thus, religious symbolism serves to distinguish the faithful from the rest, the clergy from the faithful, the places that are sanctified or sacred from those that are not, pure objects from impure objects and so on. Such symbolism cuts through the very fabric of society to effect groupings, trace dividing lines, and set up hierarchies. In clothing, rites, sacraments and invisible signs, religion is rich in symbols which divide in order to regroup the parts in a better fashion.

In addition, religious life itself is almost universally a social activity in which mystical solidarity plays a central role. This solidarity is manifested and developed through a great diversity of symbols. Such is the case, for example, in the formation of human communities which are geographically and demographically identifiable (the parish, the diocese) and which are at the same time spiritually united. This is also the case with ceremonies which require the participation of those who attend in various symbolic ways (offertory, physical communion, bodily gestures, sign language, the carrying of insignia). Other ceremonies emphasize stages in religious life which are also stages in human life, and serve to mark or recall devotion — for example, initiation rites, the marriage ceremony and funeral rites.

Coming now to magic, we can quickly recognize that it is essentially symbolic. Magic consists of man's manipulation of supernatural, invisible and untouchable forces by the use of the appropriate symbols. Here the symbol itself is given an active power; it is both a symbol and a force. Indeed, the analogy between the symbol and the effect that it seeks to produce may be unambiguous, as in the examples that were given in the preceding chapter. A man can kill his enemy by sticking pins in a ritual fashion into his effigy; he can attack his enemy's health by throwing evil objects into his field.

In archaic societies, magic is an intimate part of social life. It accompanies work, war and all important undertakings. It is inscribed in human relationships and projects, and defends the collectivity as much as individuals. If magic has been considerably minimized in modern societies, it has not disappeared; but it no longer fulfills the important functions that used to be attributed to it.

Finally, let us add that the case of magical symbolism, and mainly of religious symbols, is instructive for us from another point of view. Religion and magic are richly endowed with various symbols because they refer to an invisible world which is not directly accessible, and they must thus follow a symbolic course to keep man in contact with this world. But, in many ways, society shows the same characteristics: it transcends each person and demands solidarity in vast communities which are complex and even difficult to perceive. Society forces relationships between groups and collectivities, and now between masses; it divides and subdivides into units and subunits which are constantly more refined. Society, as a moral entity with a complex organization, could no more exist and be perpetuated than could religion without symbolism's various forms of support — both the participation or identification that symbolism encourages, and the communication of which it is the instrument.

Conclusion

At the end of this analysis, we can now say that symbols serve to link social actors through the diverse means of communication that they put at the actors' disposal. They also serve to link patterns of behaviour to values, of which they are a more concrete and more immediately observable expression. Finally, symbols constantly recreate the participation and identification of individuals and groups with collectivities, and renew the solidarities which are necessary to social life. Through symbols, the ideal realm of values is translated into reality and becomes reality. If we were able at the beginning of this chapter to agree with Durkheim that values are part of society, as much as are property and the network of roads, it is because symbols make values more concrete and actualize them in the most literal sense of the word.

Beyond the normative foundations of social action have appeared the ideal foundations that we have identified in the realm of values, and the symbolic foundations which are essential to the actualization of these values. The normative orientation of social action is supported by this deeper level of orientation to values, through and by means of a great richness of symbolic forms. It is these ideal and symbolic foundations which give the normative orientation of action its real meaning and its internal coherence. For its part, the normative orientation of action confers life and reality on values which it actualizes in concrete and/or symbolic behaviour.

Thus, the structure of social action results from the interplay of a series of elements, which can be said to be ranged in tiers and which above all are interdependent. The interplay of these elements is infinitely complex and its subtlety goes far beyond our analysis in this chapter. All the same, this analysis now leads us to the macrosociological idea of culture, to which the next chapter will be devoted.

Chapter 4
Culture, Civilization and Ideology

Let us recapitulate the procedure that has been followed up to this point. It will be remembered that we have approached social reality starting from the smallest unit of observation in sociology — the relationship between two people — from which we have developed the idea of social action, based on the concept of interaction. Observing that social action has a structure, we have sought the foundations of this structure and have identified them as the patterns, roles and sanctions which give the behaviour of subject-actors its normative orientation. Our subsequent analysis of the normative orientation of action has sent us back to a deeper level of social action, that of values, which are given life and reality through a great variety of symbols and which are expressed in patterns of behaviour. On several occasions, we have underlined the fact that patterns, roles, sanctions, values and symbols, as foundations of social action, are both external to individuals and internalized by them. They are thus both "objective" and "subjective," and must be perceived through the reciprocal perspectives which link psychology and sociology.

The ideas we have presented in order to clarify and explain social action correspond to fragmentary and partial elements of social reality. These different elements are obviously linked and interlocking. We have tried, therefore, to show the links which unite roles and patterns, patterns and sanctions, patterns and values, and symbols, values and patterns, thereby avoiding an isolated analysis of each element. Anthropology and sociology have elaborated a concept — culture — which gathers together all these elements. Since it is a much more comprehensive concept than the preceding ones, in approaching it we will clearly move on to the macrosociological level of social reality.

The idea of culture is now a part of the everyday language of the human sciences. The meaning of the term *culture* has varied, however, and the definitions that have been given have sometimes been unfortunate in that they have not always helped to clarify its meaning and relevance. It is important, then, that we analyze this concept in some detail.

A Brief History of the Idea of Culture

Given that the meaning that the social sciences today attribute to the term *culture* is very different from that which everyday language gives it, it is useful to retrace its development and to see how it has acquired its present meaning.[1]

In universal history

The concept originated in Germany, where it was first used at the end of the eighteenth century in studies that can be called universal history. These studies sought to reconstruct a general history of humanity and societies since their beginning, painting this vast picture with broad strokes. But the historians of this school were less interested in political and military history than in the history of mores, institutions, ideas, arts and sciences. They were motivated by a remarkable curiosity for the diversity of societies and civilizations, and accumulated quantities of valuable data on all historical periods and all known societies. At the same time, however, they were convinced that the history of man is also the history of man's progress, and that the comparative study of societies and

---

1. In this section, we have been guided to a great extent by the study by A. L. Kroeber and C. Kluckhohn, *Culture: A Critical Review of Concepts and Definitions* (New York: Vintage Books, Random House, n.d.). This was originally published in 1952 in the *Papers of the Peabody Museum of American Archaeology and Ethnology*, Harvard University.

civilizations would reveal the outline of this development. In particular, they considered that comparative history should make it possible to discern periods of history and societies which have represented different stages in human progress. For this, it was necessary to determine the moments of history which were marked by the extension of knowledge, the advancement of the arts, the refinement of mores, or the improvement of social institutions; these could be considered indicative of a more advanced phase of progress.

The term *culture* was employed to describe this evolution of progress. In 1782, for example, one of the most famous of these historians, Johann Christophe Adelung (1732-1806), published an *Essay on the History of the Culture of the Human Species*; in this work he distinguished eight historical periods since the origins of man and identified them by comparing them with the ages in individual human life. Kroeber and Kluckhohn give many other examples of similar use of the term *culture* by German historians who were contemporaries of Adelung.[2]

It seems fairly certain that these historians borrowed the term from the French language where, however, it did not have this meaning. They spelled the term *Cultur*, and it was only at the end of the nineteenth century that it was written as *Kultur*. In the French language of the Middle Ages, the term indicated a religious cult. The word *couture* or *coture* was used to designate a field that had been ploughed and sowed; there was the verb *culturer* and also *couturer* to designate the act of cultivating the ground. The terms *coutiveure, cultiveure, cultivure, cultivoure, cultivoison* were all used in the sense of cultivation.[3] Apparently it was not until the seventeenth century that culture came to mean cultivating the ground; then, by extension of analogy, it was used in such expressions as literary culture or scientific culture.

It was only in the eighteenth century that writers started to use the term to designate in a general way the development of the mind.[4] At this time, culture came to mean *the intellectual progress of an individual* or the work necessary for this progress. Translated into German by Von Irwing, Adelung and their col-

---

2. *Ibid.*, pp. 30-42.
3. For these different terms, see Frédéric Godefroy, *Dictionnaire de l'ancienne langue française et de tous ses dialectes du IXe au XVe siècle*, also Edmund Huguet, *Dictionnaire de la langue française du seizième siècle*.
4. According to Emile Tonnelat, *Civilisation: le mot et l'idée*, quoted in Kroeber and Kluckhohn, *Culture: A Critical Review*, pp. 11 and 70-73.

leagues, the term took on a wider meaning, once again by analogy, and referred to *the intellectual and social progress of man in general and of collectivities and humanity.* Thus it had for the first time a collective connotation. But it continued to include the idea of progress, improvement and development.

It is important to emphasize, as do Kroeber and Kluckhohn, that the viewpoint of universal history was not the same as that of the philosophy of history, according to the conception developed particularly by Hegel. Hegel was to substitute the idea of mind (*Geist*) for that of culture, a substitution that symbolized all that set him apart from the universal historians. In contrast, these historians were empiricists and meticulous researchers, who were preoccupied with the idea of conducting a scientific study rather than a philosophical one; many of them eventually undertook genuine ethnographic studies. It is an interesting aspect of the sociological notion of culture that it comes from history and not from philosophy. Too often, the social sciences are attributed sources that are exclusively philosophical, and the important debt to history — above all, through the German tradition, as we emphasized earlier with reference to Max Weber (Chapter 1) — is neglected.

In anthropology and sociology

Moving from German to English, the idea of culture was to undergo another transformation. It is because of British anthropology — in particular, because of E. B. Tylor, whose book on *Primitive Culture* appeared in 1871 — that this transition was made. Guided primarily by the works of Gustav Klemm, who between 1843 and 1852 had published a monumental work in ten volumes on *The Universal History of the Culture of Humanity*, followed by two volumes on the *Science of Culture*, Tylor derived the elements that he needed to compose the idea of culture, which he used as a synonym for civilization. At the beginning of his work, Tylor gave a definition of culture which has since been quoted many times: "Culture or civilization, taken in its wide ethnographic sense, is that complex whole which includes knowledge, belief, art, morals, law, custom, and any other capabilities and habits acquired by man as a member of society." This definition, which is largely descriptive, is particularly original in that culture is no longer taken to imply progress or development; the term refers rather to a set of facts, which can be directly observed at a given moment in time and whose development can be followed — as it was by Tylor himself.

Thus the anthropological notion of culture was born. Though not used with this meaning by Herbert Spencer, it was taken up by the first British and American anthropologists — Sumner, Keller, Malinowski, Lowie, Wissler, Sapir, Boas and Benedict. In the United States, anthropology even came to be defined as the science of culture. While in Britain physical anthropology (the study of the development and growth of the human body) was distinguished from social anthropology, the Americans contrasted cultural anthropology with physical anthropology.

In sociology, the term *culture* was quickly adopted also by the first American sociologists — Albion Small, Park, Burgess and particularly Ogburn. It did not come into wide use as quickly as it did in anthropology, however, very likely because the great forerunners of sociology — Comte, Marx, Weber, Tönnies and Durkheim — did not use it. But now it is just as much a part of the vocabulary of sociology as it is of anthropology.

French-language sociology and anthropology incorporated this newly coined word much more slowly. Dictionaries, which always and necessarily lag behind the development of a language, provide proof. While English dictionaries all include a sociological or anthropological definition of culture, which is often very clear, the equivalent cannot be found even in the most recent French dictionaries. This is due in part to the fact that sociology in the French language has been marked by the very special vocabulary that Durkheim adopted. Another explanation can be found in the decline of French sociology between the two wars, when the idea of culture was being clarified and spread. It was only with the new generation of French sociologists that surged up after the Second World War that the term *culture* became popular in France, under the influence of American sociology. And perhaps we might risk a last interpretation. Since the term *culture* has been associated with a classical period of French thought, it still carries a humanist meaning. The French language would thus hesitate to recognize simultaneously a precise scientific meaning, for the logic of the language would thus be questioned.

This brief history has perhaps served to clarify the meaning that is now given to the term *culture* in sociology, and this meaning will become even clearer in the following pages. But this history of a term and an idea is also an outstanding case of the process of diffusion that has been studied by a number of anthropologists. Borrowed from the French, retranslated from German into English, the term added a new connotation each time, always by extension or by analogy, never losing its original meaning but taking on new meanings which were always further from it. From the ploughed and sowed field which it designated in Old French to the sociological meaning it has today, there is undoubtedly a great distance. Nevertheless, this distance is the result of an evolution which has occurred in a coherent way — that is, without a break and without discontinuity.

Culture and civilization

The development that has just been described inevitably led to a confrontation between the idea of culture and that of civilization. With the meaning that the German historians ultimately gave it, the word *culture* took on a meaning that was very close to that understood by the term *civilization*. Various distinctions were suggested, notably in Germany; but they can almost all be included within two main categories. In the first, culture is taken to mean all the collective means by which man or a society controls and manipulates the physical environment or the natural world. This would include mainly science and technology, and their applications. Civilization includes all the collective means by which man may exert control on himself in order to grow intellectually, morally and spiritually. Thus, the arts, philosophy, religion and law are part of civilization.

The second category of meaning is almost the exact inverse of the first. The concept of civilization is applied to means which serve utilitarian and material goals of collective human life; civilization has a rational character which requires the progress of physical and material conditions of work, production and technology. In contrast, culture includes the more disinterested and spiritual aspects of collective life which are the fruits of pure reflection and thought, of sensibility and idealism.

Since these two distinctions received almost equal support in Germany, it is difficult to assert that one was regarded more favourably than the other. In American sociology, however, those writers who have found it either necessary or useful to pursue this distinction have opted more frequently for the second alternative. Their choice probably can be attributed to the influence of German scholars — notably Ferdinand Tönnies, whose work will be analyzed later (in Chapter 6), and Alfred Weber. This is particularly true of Robert MacIver and Robert K. Merton,[5] both of whom have maintained a distinction between culture and civilization which is directly inspired by Alfred Weber, although couched in different terms.

In general, however, sociologists and anthropologists have not been preoccupied with pursuing this distinction. It appears artificial to them, tainted by an equivocal dualism and guided by a false opposition between mind and matter, sensibility and rationality, ideas and things. The great majority of sociologists and anthropologists avoid employing the term *civilization*, or instead use the word *culture* (which they prefer) to mean civilization; for they consider that the two are interchangeable. Thus, following Tylor's example, the French ethnologist Claude Lévi-Strauss talks of "primitive civilization."[6] As we saw earlier, while Tylor may have given the two terms slightly different meanings, he defined them as being identical.

Occasionally it happens, however, that two distinctions are found among some contemporary sociologists and anthropologists. First, the term *civilization* is used to designate a group of specific cultures which possess common origins or affinities. According to this meaning, we can speak of Western civilization, which includes the French, English, German, Italian and American cultures; or perhaps we can speak of American civilization, referring to the extension of the characteristic American way of life in the modern world. Thus, the idea of culture is associated with a given identifiable society, while the term *civilization* serves to designate wider groupings which are more inclusive in space and time.[7]

Second, civilization can also refer to societies which exhibit a more advanced stage of development, characterized by scientific and technical progress, urbanization, complexity of social organization and so forth. This goes back to the meaning given to the term some time ago (which still exists in everyday language) of civ-

5. Robert M. MacIver, *Society, Its Structure and Changes* (New York: R. Long and R. R. Smith, Inc., 1931); Robert K. Merton, "Civilization and Culture," *Sociology and Social Research* 21: 103-13. Quoted in Kroeber and Kluckhohn, *Culture: A Critical Review*, pp. 21-23.

6. Particularly in his book, *Du miel aux cendres* (Paris: Plon, 1966), p. 408.

7. For example, it is precisely this meaning that Durkheim and Mauss attribute to the concept of civilization, by which they mean "social phenomena which are not strictly attached to a specific social organism; they are spread out over areas which go beyond a national territory, or they develop over periods of time which go beyond the life of one society alone. They exist on the basis of a sort of supernatural life." In "Note sur la notion de Civilisation," *L'année sociologique* 12 (1909-1912): 47.

ilizing, or being civilized.[8] Thus, the term has an evolutionary connotation. But as we shall see later, the social sciences now use such words as industrialization, development and modernization to avoid the value judgements implicit in the term *civilization*.

The Definition of Culture

The brief history given in the preceding pages brings us now to a more specific definition of culture than we have attempted so far. Tylor's definition, which was cited earlier, is often quoted; for although it dates from 1871, it is astonishingly complete and precise. It has been criticized as being a little too descriptive, however, and in addition it does not specify all the characteristics that are now attributed to culture. Since Tylor's time, many other definitions of culture have been proposed; Kroeber and Kluckhohn have collected, classified and commented on them.[9] A considerable number of these definitions are far from being as useful as Tylor's; however, several have helped to delineate cultural reality a little more precisely.

Guided by Tylor's and other definitions, we can define culture as *an interconnected set of ways of thinking, feeling and acting which are more or less formalized and which, having been learned and shared by a plurality of individuals, serve both objectively and symbolically to unite these individuals in a particular and distinct collectivity.* An elaboration of this definition will enable us to specify the main characteristics that anthropologists and sociologists have agreed to attribute to culture.

The main characteristics of culture

First, it will be noticed that we have included Durkheim's useful formula in referring to ways of thinking, feeling and acting. This formula is more comprehensive and also more general than Tylor's definition; it is also more explicit than the standard "way of life" that is found in many other definitions. Our phrasing has the

---

8. Examples of this, as related by Arden R. King, can be found under the word "Civilization" in Julius Gould and William L. Kolb, eds., *A Dictionary of the Social Sciences* (New York: The Free Press of Glencoe, Inc., 1964), pp. 93-94.
9. Kroeber and Kluckhohn, *Culture: A Critical Review*, pp. 75-154.

advantage of emphasizing that patterns of behaviour, values and symbols which comprise culture include knowledge, ideas and thought, and expand to include all forms of expression of feelings as well as the rules which regulate actions and which are objectively observable. Culture thus includes all human activity, whether it is cognitive, affective, conative (concerned with acting in the strict sense) or even sensory-motor. Finally, this expression emphasizes that culture is action, and that it is first and above all lived by individuals. It is on the basis of the observation of this action that the existence of culture can be inferred and its outlines traced. In the same way, it is because the action of individuals conforms to a given culture that it can be called social action.

Second, these ways of thinking, feeling and acting may be more or less formalized. They are highly formalized in a code of laws, in ritual activities, ceremonies and protocol, in scientific knowledge, technology and theology. They are less formalized, to varying degrees, in the arts, in common law, and in certain rules of etiquette, notably those which govern the interpersonal relationships between individuals who have known each other and have been together for some time. When ways of thinking, feeling and acting are less formalized, interpretation and personal adaptation are permitted — and sometimes required — to a greater extent.

The third characteristic of culture which is included in our definition is absolutely central and essential. A culture is distinguished first and foremost by the fact that particular ways of thinking, feeling and acting are shared by a plurality of individuals. The number of individuals is not very important; a few people are sufficient to create the culture of a small group (a gang), while the culture of a total society is necessarily shared by a great number of individuals. The essential thing is that ways of living should be considered ideal or normal by a sufficient number of individuals that they can be recognized as rules of life which have acquired a *collective* and thus social character. Although it is individualized, culture in the anthropological and sociological sense is not individual in its nature. Rather, it is common to a plurality of individuals. We have already seen how the idea of culture, which at the beginning could be applied only to individuals, has come to have a new collective meaning. At the same time, it clearly does not apply only to a total society. Sociologists often talk of the culture of a social class, a region, an industry or a gang. And the expression *sub-culture* may be used to designate a partial unit within a total society (the sub-culture of youth), or to link one culture with another broader culture within which it exists.

A fourth characteristic of culture, to which a number of writers have given almost as much importance as the preceding one, concerns its mode of acquisition or transmission. Nothing cultural is inherited biologically or genetically, or is inscribed in the biological organism at birth. The acquisition of culture results from various forms of *learning* (where this latter term is understood in a wider meaning than the one that will be given to it in the following chapter). Cultural traits, then, are not shared by a plurality of individuals in the same way as are physical traits. It could be said that the latter are the result of *heredity*, while the former are an *inheritance* that each person must draw together and make his own. Many authors have defined culture as a social inheritance; others have said that it is all that an individual must learn in order to live in a particular society. A great number of definitions of culture, including Tylor's, while resorting to different formulae, have retained this characteristic; and some have even set it up as the main or dominant trait of culture.

Objective and symbolic aspects of culture

Cultural norms and values, which are learned and shared, contribute towards the formation of a certain number of persons into a particular collectivity which it is possible and even relatively easy to recognize and distinguish from other collectivities. Culture contributes towards the formation of this collectivity in two ways (and this is another essential trait of culture which often does not appear in the definition): objectively and symbolically. First, the ways of thinking, feeling and acting that individuals have in common establish links between them which each person feels to be very real. For each and every person, this common denominator is a reality that is as "objective" and as observable as other more tangible shared realities, such as a territory, public property, monuments, material goods and so forth. Culture is thus one of the factors that is found at the origin of what Durkheim called social solidarity, and what Auguste Comte called the consensus of society.

But more important, culture lays the foundation of this relative unity of a collectivity and gives it its distinctive character in a symbolic way. First of all, collective ways of thinking, feeling and acting are, for the most part, symbols of communication or at least symbols that make communication possible. The case of language is particularly clear; but players in a hockey team, for example, communicate with each other in a non-verbal way, through the sometimes unconscious knowledge they have of the meaning of the behaviour of other players. Thus, ways of acting themselves serve as symbols of communication in social action.

But primarily, collective ways of thinking, feeling and acting are laden with symbols of participation. As we said earlier, respect for patterns of behaviour generally symbolizes adherence to values, which in turn symbolize membership in a given collectivity. It follows that if the solidarity between the members of a collectivity is regarded as a reality, it is because it is sensed, perceived and expressed through a vast symbolic framework to which each of the members contributes. In other words, adherence to the culture is constantly reaffirmed by each and every member of the collectivity through the symbolic meaning of participation which is attached to their externally observable behaviour. Moreover, the symbolic meaning of conduct enables members of a collectivity, as well as those who are not members, to draw the intangible dividing line between members and non-members, between citizens and foreigners, and between the faithful and heathens. The Catholic who deliberately abstains from going to Sunday Mass symbolically demonstrates to himself, to other members of his religion, and to everybody else that he is in the process of separating himself, or that he is already separated, from the collectivity of the Church. Membership in a religious collectivity of a mystical nature obviously cannot be expressed except through symbols of this kind; but the same requirement is imposed, in a more or less obvious way, in every other collectivity, whether it is a nation, a political party, a trade union or even a family. To abstain from participating in meetings, from wearing insignia, or from signing a petition shows symbolically that one is separating oneself from a party, a trade union or an association. How do sociologists and ethnologists discern the groupings, collectivities, societies and their boundaries if not through the symbols of participation furnished by the contact of individuals? Thus, culture takes on the characteristic of a great symbolic unit, whose roots draw from socio-psychological realities a meaning and signs which are essential to collective human life.

The cultural system

Another and final characteristic of culture is that it forms what we have called an interconnected set — that is, a system. The different elements which form a given culture do not exist merely in juxtaposition to each other; when changes are effected in one sector of a culture, they entail changes in others. These links and relationships generally are not inevitable, in the sense that they do not result from a necessary logical and rational process. Rather, they are felt subjectively by the members of a society. Thus, the coherence of a society is above all a *subjective reality* — that is, a reality that is experienced subjectively by the members of a society. It is through and for the subjects that a culture takes on the character of a system. In fact, many different arrangements of the elements of a culture are possible. Kluckhohn and Strodtbeck's study of values proves that it is very difficult, at least in our present state of knowledge, to demonstrate objectively necessary links between certain values (for example, between the importance of the present and the importance of productivity). The only "necessary" links are those which the subjects themselves judge to be necessary, which appear to them as such and which they consequently accept.

This subjective nature of the cultural system distinguishes it from the system of social action. The latter is inferred by the observer, while the cultural system is directly demonstrated to the observer by the social actors themselves. In order to speak of the existence and structure of the cultural system, the sociologist therefore must first take note of the perception that the members of a collectivity have of it. If, therefore, we can speak of the system of *culture*, it is because we perceive and experience *a particular culture* as a system. As a rule, this aspect of the cultural system has not been sufficiently emphasized and analyzed by writers on the subject.

The Functions of Culture

The social function of culture

On the basis of preceding sections, it is now relatively easy to set down the socio-psychological functions of culture. First of all, sociologically, we have seen that the essential function of culture is to unite a plurality of individuals in a specific collectivity. Other factors also contribute to the same result — blood ties, geographical proximity, cohabitation of the same territory or the division of labour. But these factors, which could be called objective, are themselves transposed and reinterpreted within and through culture, thereby taking on a meaning and a relevance which go far beyond their original nature. For example, on the basis of biological blood ties, men have elaborated many varying family forms through culture. Thus, blood ties become family ties, and are subsequently widened and complicated by the prohibition against incest, by the rules which define permitted and prohibited marriages, and by the norms which regulate the relationships among individuals of the same family group and so forth. The same is true of the cohabitation of a territory, or the division of labour. Culture uses these conditions to forge the concept of nation, fatherland, property, social hierarchy, social prestige or social class. These are not merely ideas, however, but they become facts which culture helps to create and maintain.

Thus, culture appears as the mental, moral and symbolic world which is common to a plurality of individuals, because of which and through which these individuals can communicate with each other; can recognize ties, attachments and common interests, differences and contrasts; and finally can feel, individually and collectively, that they are members of a single unit, which transcends them and which is called a group, association, collectivity or society.

The psychological function of culture

If this is the case, it is because culture also performs, on the psychological level, the function of shaping individual personalities. In fact, a culture is a kind of mold in which the individual personalities are cast; this mold suggests and provides patterns of thinking, knowledge, ideas, preferred channels of expression for the feelings, means of satisfying or heightening physiological needs and so forth. *De gustibus non est disputandum* (there is no disputing about tastes) is valid not only among individuals but also among cultures. The child who is born and grows up in a particular culture (national, regional, class) will inevitably like certain food, eat it in a certain way, link certain feelings to certain colours, marry according to certain rites, adopt certain gestures or expressions, perceive foreigners from a particular perspective and so forth. If the same child were taken away at birth and subjected to another culture, he would like other foods, eat them in a different way, marry according to other rites, use different expressions, and perceive the same strangers in a different way.

If culture can be likened to a mold which shapes the personality, it must be added that this mold is not absolutely rigid. It is sufficiently flexible to permit individual adaptations; each person assimilates culture in an idiosyncratic way, and to a certain extent reconstructs it in his own fashion. In addition, culture offers choices — options between dominant and substitute values, or among preferred, variant or deviant patterns of behaviour — as we have seen in the preceding chapters. Culture can also authorize and sometimes even require a degree of innovation by social actors, though not all societies give their members the same latitude in this respect.

But this flexibility of the cultural mold always operates within certain limits. If the individual goes beyond these limits, he moves to the periphery of the society of which he is a member, or he leaves this society and joins another. Above all, this flexibility does not prevent culture from shaping the personality, through the choices that it authorizes and the variation that it offers, as well by the constraints that it imposes. Culture offers a choice between patterns of behaviour, values and symbolic meanings; but this choice is never limitless and certain preferred choices are always indicated.

Thus, we can say that culture *informs* the personality in the sense that it gives it a *form*, a configuration or a physiognomy that permits it to function within a given society. This aspect of culture will be further elaborated when we discuss socialization in the next chapter.

The double function of culture, sociological and psychological, can be understood and explained only within the context of another more general and fundamental function — that which permits and favours the adaptation of men and societies to the environment, and to all the realities with which they must live. This function can be better understood if culture is compared to instinct, with which it shares certain similarities and differences. Clearly, this is not the place to enter into a detailed discussion of instinct, a subject which preoccupies many biologists and psychologists; instinct is still a very obscure and mysterious reality. Some elements of it will be sufficient for our purposes.

Culture and Instinct

Definitions of instinct

The psychologist Henri Piéron defines instinct in the following way: "Instinct can serve to designate a category of more or less complex acts, which generally represent the participation of the whole organism, and which are carried out immediately, completely and usually without further development; they are relatively flexible within fairly narrow limits, are more or less influenced by the circumstances of the moment, but stem from a congenital mechanism which is by no means acquired through individual experience."[10] Ronald Fletcher gives a more elaborate definition which indicates its main characteristics:

> The term *instinct* as employed in the context of biology refers to those recurring sequences of animal experience and behaviour together with their underlying neuro-physical conditions which (a) appear to terminate in specific consequences; (b) are functionally beneficial to both the individual and the species; (c) are well adapted to the natural environmental circumstances of the species (though they are often "blind" and maladapted to unusual conditions); (d) are common to all the individual members of the species (though their particular manifestations may vary from individual to individual); (e) emerge with a definite order and regularity in the life of the individual in close relation to the process of growth and maturation; and (f) are not learnt on the basis of individual experience (though they may emerge in the context of learning, and though learning may take place in relation to them).[11]

The main point that emerges from these definitions, on which almost all specialists agree, is the congenital nature of instinct; or in other words, the fact that instinct is transmitted by heredity and inscribed in the organism at birth, at least in an embryonic fashion, and that it develops with the maturation of the organism. Thus, instinctive behaviour is necessarily behaviour that is not learned. It can sometimes be improved through learning or experience, but its essential nature is to be endogenous. That is, it results from internal mechanisms which are initiated by needs, motivation or perception. Thus, instinctive behaviour is the product, not of learning, but of maturation or chronological organic development.

---

10. Henri Piéron, *De l'actinie à l'homme*, vol. 2 (Paris: Presses universitaires de France, 1959), p. 90.
11. Ronald Fletcher, under the word "Instinct" in Gould and Kolb, eds., *A Dictionary of the Social Sciences*, pp. 336-37.

Instinct and intelligence

Both these definitions, and Piéron's in particular, are careful and carry many implications with them. According to a long intellectual tradition which goes back to antiquity, man has commonly been contrasted with animals, intelligence with instinct, reason with the unconscious. Biologists and psychologists are just beginning to free themselves from these dichotomies. But the studies carried out by naturalists of the last century bore many marks of such contrasts. They can be found, for example, in the work of J. H. Fabre, which inspired Henri Bergson in his volume on *Creative Evolution* (1904) to distinguish two divergent routes for the evolution of living beings — instinct, which was followed by arthropods and higher insects; and intelligence, which was pursued by the vertebrates and finally by man. Today it is thought that such a radical contrast does not correspond to the facts observed by researchers. On the one hand, instinctive behaviour is often accompanied by reflexes and tropisms. Reflexes are elements of behaviour, while tropisms are the total behaviour of the organism, both being automatic responses to the action of external stimuli (light, warmth and so forth). On the other hand, instinctive activity is complemented by acts that can be called intelligent, if one agrees with Gaston Viaud that "intelligence is always understanding and invention, both in animals and in Man. This means an understanding of the relationships among objects, facts, elements of thought and so forth, and then the invention or inspiration of possibilities of action."[12] In insects, and still more in higher mammals, biologists have observed behaviour that can be explained only by the fact that the animal has had to resort to a certain reasoning, that it has developed a certain perception of causality, which proves that it can imagine ahead of time the sequence of its acts and draw up a sort of plan of action. According to Ronald Fletcher:

> Among the lower species intelligence may be almost negligible; capable of only very minor adjustments in connection with the reactions involved in immediate activity; but among the higher species, intelligence be-

---

12. Gaston Viaud, *Les instincts* (Paris: Presses universitaires de France, 1959), pp. 150-51. This clearly and precisely written little book is based largely on the elaborate studies presented at the Round Table of the Singer-Polignac Foundation, held in June 1954. The papers were published under the title *L'Instinct dans le comportement des animaux et de l'homme* (Paris: Masson et Cie, 1956).

comes capable of grasping the relations between impulses, ends, and behavioural means. . . . Instinct and
intelligence are therefore not regarded as being separate
and distinct from each other but as mingling modes of
correlation, the one determined by heredity and the
other coming into play, within this given context, during the course of individual experience.[13]

Thus, animal behaviour is not necessarily instinctive behaviour
in its pure state. Gaston Viaud comes to the following conclusion:

The types of behaviour that the animal psychologists
have learned to define — tropisms, instincts, habits and
intelligent acts — are, in a way, abstractions rather like
chemical species: NaCl, $CaCl_2$ and so forth. This means
that they are not often encountered in a pure state in
nature. *These kinds of behaviour are above all the product of our analyses.* But it would be wrong to consider
them as arbitrary ideas, for they correspond to observable phenomena; they can also appear on their own.
Real behaviour, however, is more often made up of
combinations of them; instinctive behaviour integrates
tropisms, other behaviour incorporates habits or intelligent acts, and some behaviour may incorporate all the
types of behaviour at the same time.[14]

It is perhaps more appropriate, then, to speak of *instincts* rather
than *instinct* as Viaud does himself.

Instinct and the goals of action

Another essential aspect of instinct concerns the problem of the
goals of instinctive activity. By this, we mean that instincts "obviously aim at goals whose importance is major for the life of organisms; nourishment, reproduction, the search for a favourable habi-
tat, the arrangement or construction of a shelter."[15]

This question of the goals of instinct is hotly debated. Henri Piéron, for example, refuses to recognize such a characteristic in in-

---

13. Ronald Fletcher, *Instinct in Man, In the Light of Recent Work in Compara-
    tive Psychology* (New York: International Universities Press, Inc., 1957), p.
    294.
14. Viaud, *Les instincts*, p. 167. Emphasis in the original.
15. *Ibid.*, p. 2.

stinct, particularly bringing up the fact that it is easy to observe cases of instinct which are harmful or even fatal to the animal or the species. But even he is forced to recognize that "the harmful reactions are really rare, for since they entail the more or less complete disappearance of the species which demonstrates them systematically, one can only find examples of them when the conditions specific to the manifestation of harmful behaviour are not too frequently encountered."[16] Let us forget the term goals, then, since it carries too many anthropomorphic connotations which a mind as scientific as Henri Piéron's mistrusts — and for good reason. *On the whole*, however, instincts (accompanied by reflexes, tropisms, habits and intelligent acts) do enable the animal and the species to adapt themselves to an environment, to survive and proliferate within it, and to satisfy the various needs of the organism. Instinct guides and directs the action of the animal according to pre-established plans which are fairly rigid. It is through instinct that the animal responds to the surrounding reality, that it can protect or defend itself, that it can use this reality and even transform it to respond to its needs. In brief, it can be said that instinct is the animal's main mode of adaptation to his needs and his environment.

A comparison between instinct and culture

To return to culture, our discussion of instinct enables us to make a brief comparison between the two. First, instinctive behaviour is essentially congenital and unlearned, while culture is necessarily not inherited and learned. Second, instinct is endogenous — that is, it is inscribed in each organism and is not social in nature. While instinctive behaviour unquestionably is more or less the same for all the animals of the same family, this is because each individual organism is endowed with the same mechanisms. In contrast, culture is social in nature; it is a collective asset in which each individual has a part (albeit an unequal one) and which is simultaneously within and external to each individual. Here again, the contrast is total.

Third, while instinct is associated with reflexes, tropisms and intelligent acts, culture is supported by instincts; it is constructed on the basis of them, and complements and refines them. Viaud's comments on animal activity can also be applied to human activ-

---

16. Piéron, *De l'actinie à l'homme*, vol. 2, p. 90.

ity: cultural activity is not encountered in its pure state, but is always mingled with reflexes, habits, impulses and instinctive activities. In this, culture and instinct are alike.

Finally, and this is the particular point that we wanted to reach, *culture fulfills for man the same function of adaptation to himself and to the environment that instinct fulfills for the animal.* Through instinct the animal responds to and controls the surrounding reality. Through culture man enters into contact with himself, and with his physical and social environment; exerts a control on himself, his feelings, his needs and his impulses; and manipulates things and beings, making them serve his needs and his goals. Even among the higher vertebrates, instinct is accompanied by spontaneous and intelligent acts. For man, instinct has withdrawn and weakened in the face of the progress of intelligence, of symbolism, and consequently of culture.

Thus, it can be said that culture is like a prism through which man perceives reality. He uses it to adapt to this reality and to control it. Culture is therefore specific to man, because he alone has been able to develop sufficiently the symbolic system and to accumulate a reservoir of symbols at various levels of abstraction. In return, culture enables each individual to become part of the species of man, by allowing him to benefit from what has been accumulated before him — a legacy which cannot be transmitted to the biological organism.

Beyond the psychological and social functions, or perhaps more accurately *through* them, culture asserts its most basic function — to enable man to become human.

Culture and Ideology

The Marxist concept of ideology

Before we finish this chapter, a final ambiguity remains: one that can exist between culture and ideology. This ambiguity arises from the fact that we owe the general use of the concept of ideology in the social sciences to Karl Marx; for Marx gave the concept a very broad and equivocal meaning. First, he employs the term in such a wide sense that it overlaps virtually all of what we now call culture. In *German Ideology*, he speaks of "morals, religion, metaphysics and the rest of ideology"; specifically, the rest of ideology is law, politics, ideas, the representations and the consciousness that men have of things and of society, and finally language, which serves to penetrate all this spiritual or mental "production" of thought and behaviour.[17] Marx uses the same concept of ideology in the Foreword to *A Contribution to the Critique of Political Economy*, where he says that ideology includes "the legal, political, religious, artistic and philosophical forms"; and it seems, from the context, that he widens it to include science.[18] Briefly, ideology for Marx covers "all the products of a civilization," to use Georges Gurvitch's phrase.[19]

At the same time, the notion of ideology clearly had a pejorative connotation for Marx. As Gurvitch has remarked, this connotation existed before him; but Marx amplified and extended it. Norman Birnbaum explains this pejorative connotation as follows:

> The Marxist notion of ideology can be understood only in terms of the connected notions of alienation, reification and mystification. ... Ideology itself is only a part of this general process of alienation, by which the products of human activity escape from human control and rule over men, without being recognized as the incarnation of their life and work. Reification is the process through which one attributes to things an existence that is independent of their creators (illustrated by the fetish that is made of material goods). Attributing a real existence to the products of thought constitutes mystification. ... In the class society, the class that controls the means of production also controls the means of ideological production.[20]

In *German Ideology*, Marx states:

> The ideas of the ruling class are in every epoch the ruling ideas; i.e., the class which is the ruling *material* force of society is at the same time its ruling *intellectual* force. The class which has the means of material production at its disposal has control at the same time over

---

17. Karl Marx, *German Ideology*, R. Pascal, ed. (London: Lawrence and Wishart, 1938), Parts 1 and 3.
18. Karl Marx, *A Contribution to the Critique of Political Economy* (New York: New York and International Library Publishing Co., 1904).
19. Gurvitch, *La vocation actuelle*, vol. 2, p. 285.
20. Norman Birnbaum, "The Sociological Study of Ideology 1940-60: A Trend report and bibliography," *Current Sociology* 9, no. 2 (1962).

the means of mental production, so that thereby, generally speaking, the ideas of those who lack the means of mental production are subject to it. The ruling ideas are nothing more than the ideal expression of the dominant material relationships, the dominant material relationships grasped as ideas. . . .[21]

Thus, ideology is definitely the consciousness and the representation that the dominant class forms of reality, according to its position and interests. This perspective inevitably must be absorbed by all those "to whom the means of spiritual production are lacking" because they are alienated from the means of material production. Consequently, ideology can only be a "false consciousness" of reality, which is biased, basically corrupted, alienating and mystifying — an "erroneous view of human history" and an "opium of the people."

Expressed firmly by Marx, and as part of a work which was to have a very profound influence on modern thought, the concept of ideology was a great success — perhaps too successful. After identifying thirteen different meanings which have been attributed to the term ideology by Marx himself and by the Marxist tradition, Gurvitch concludes: "It cannot be disputed that Marxist sociology must make a selection among these thirteen meanings of the term ideology. Without this, the term risks losing its scientific value."[22]

The definition of ideology

We will not try to retrace the history of the concept of ideology since Marx's time. Such an undertaking would be far too complex for our purposes.[23] To summarize this history, briefly we can say that, at least outside the Marxist tradition, an attempt was made to give the concept a more limited meaning which would make ideology an element of culture instead of a synonym for it; and at the same time, to abstract the pejorative meaning which had long been attached to the term, and which continues to be associated with it in everyday language and in some scientific or philosophical works.

---

21. Marx, *German Ideology*, p. 39.
22. Gurvitch, *La vocation actuelle*, vol. 2, pp. 287-88.
23. The main elements of this history can be found in the very compact study by Birnbaum, "Sociological Study of Ideology."

On the basis of the most recent empirical and theoretical studies of ideology, notably that of Fernand Dumont,[24] it can be said that contemporary sociologists usually employ this term to designate *a system of ideas and judgements, which are explicit and generally organized; which serve to describe, explain, interpret or justify the situation of a group or collectivity; and which, largely on the basis of values, suggest a precise orientation to the historical action of this group or collectivity.* Defined in this way, ideology approaches what W. I. Thomas has called "the definition of the situation" — that is, the way that a collectivity or the members of a collectivity explain and interpret their present situation and give it meaning. But three elements in particular which are included in our definition of ideology must be added to the idea of the definition of the situation:

1. Ideology has a systematic, coherent and organized form because it is explicit and verbalized; it thus takes on the character of a doctrine, in the widest meaning of the term. This systematization requires that particular aspects of the situation be thrown into relief, and that a special emphasis be placed on certain links among the elements of the situation — links which have given ideology what Dumont calls its syncretism.[25]

2. Ideology refers a great deal to values, by which it is inspired, and which are reorganized in the scheme of thought that it formulates. Dumont says that ideology can be considered "the rationalization of a world view (or of a system of values)."[26]

3. Ideology has a conative function; it pushes or incites a collectivity to action, or at least directs this collectivity by providing goals and means.

Ideology in culture

With the more precise meaning we have just outlined, ideology is understood to be not all of culture, but only an element of it. In addition, it is no longer necessarily linked to the total society, as Marx wished in defining it as the product of a dominant social class. Ideology can refer to the guiding philosophy of a limited or

---

24. See in particular Fernand Dumont, "Notes sur l'analyse des idéologies," *Recherches sociographiques* 4, no. 2 (1963): 155-65; and Fernand Dumont, "Idéologie et savoir historique," *Cahiers internationaux de sociologie* 35 (July–December, 1963): 43-60.

25. Dumont, "Idéologie et savoir historique," p. 50.

26. Dumont, "Notes sur l'analyse des idéologies," p. 163.

partial group (political party, trade union, army, profession), as well as to that of a total society (nation, country, ethnic group).

But if ideology is only an element of culture, one is tempted to consider it as a particularly central element — "its real core," in Dumont's words.[27] More particularly, ideology is a sort of sociology of the first degree, or a natural sociology, for a given collectivity. In ideology, the collectivity constructs an image of itself and provides itself with an interpretation of what exists, at the same time clarifying its aspirations. Guided both by certain values and by certain elements of the situation, which it seeks to join together, and guiding in turn a collectivity's cultural patterns, sanctions and symbols, ideology surely occupies a privileged position within culture. From this stems the visibly growing interest among contemporary sociologists in the empirical study of ideologies. Ideologies give the sociologist direct access to a subjective perspective on the collectivity, which can serve as the starting point for his own analysis and enable him to pinpoint the main sources and agents of social change, as we will see in another chapter. Thus, one is far from the Marxist concept of ideology as a false consciousness of reality.

Our concept of ideology presupposes that it does not necessarily have a conservative or radical orientation. For Marx ideology, which is harboured by the dominant class, is conservative by definition. It is rather paradoxical that later the concept was often associated with radical or revolutionary thought. For us, ideology as it has been defined can be radical or conservative, extremist or moderate, totalitarian or liberal; and it can suggest either changes in or the maintenance of the status quo. Its content and the orientation that it suggests do not affect its nature, as it has been defined and explained.

What is more important is that ideology always seeks to encourage, maintain or safeguard unanimity — unanimity of representation, motivation and action. It does not always succeed; indeed, we can even say that it does not generally succeed. It is often a dividing principle, or the source of conflict within a collectivity and among collectivities. And it is here that ideology is distinguished most clearly from values and culture, and appears as an element of culture. Ideology carries within it a *will* towards unanimity, while culture and values require a consensus which is in a way natural and which can be said to go without saying. Thus, within culture,

---

27. *Ibid.*, p. 156.

ideology takes on a more rational, explicit and militant aura than do either patterns of behaviour or values. It forms a firm and solid core within the looser and less compact structure of culture.

This brief analysis of ideology has enabled us to discern another aspect of the cultural system and the influence that it exerts on orientation of action. If all culture is orientation of action, ideology is that sector of culture which suggests an orientation of action in the most explicit, the firmest and the least ambiguous way.

Chapter 5
Socialization, Conformity and Deviance

Culture and society are found within each person and each person is integrated into the social organization — we have emphasized several times this reciprocity of social and psychological perspectives which is fundamental in the analysis of the total social phenomenon. It remains for us to explain more clearly why and how the individual and socio-cultural phenomena interpenetrate. By the interaction of what mechanisms, and through the influence of what agents and milieux, does the individual personality internalize the culture of a given society? To what extent are these mechanisms and agents effective in encouraging conformity or standardization in the behaviour of one person and in that of the members of the same collectivity? In this chapter we will discuss these various problems.

Three Systems: Society, Culture and Personality

Through the influence of Pitirim Sorokin[1] and more especially Talcott Parsons,[2] sociologists have been accustomed to distin-

---

1. P. Sorokin, *Society, Culture, and Personality: Their Structure and Dynamics* (New York: Harper, 1947).
2. Parsons and Shils, *General Theory of Action*.

guishing three interrelated and complementary systems of action. The first is the social system, as it has been defined in Chapter 2, consisting of the structuring of the elements of social action in a set of interdependent parts which form a functional unit. The second is culture, which — as we said in Chapter 4 — similarly can be considered as a system. And finally, there is the personality — not to be confused with the individual person — which is formed by the organization of the various psychological components of the human being: temperament or character traits, impulses, needs, aptitudes, attitudes, interests, traces of former experiences and so forth, which together comprise a structured whole.

A fourth system could be added which is also related to the other three; this is the organic system, or the biochemical and physiological organization of the human body. But while there is sufficient knowledge of the relationships between organic and psychological phenomena, the relationships between the organic structure of man on the one hand, and culture and the social system on the other, have been studied very little. Since this biological aspect of social action is still imperfectly understood, for all practical purposes it can be omitted from our discussion.

Interpenetration of the three systems

The three systems — social, cultural and psychological — have in common the fact that they are all present and involved in all human social action. Moreover, all three are equally necessary for such action. In effect, social action is comprised of a network of interactions and roles which are based on mutual expectations; but, these expectations exist and have a meaning for each actor because of the patterns of behaviour and the values of the culture, as well as the symbolic expressions which surround and represent them. In addition, each person becomes involved in social action through a more or less important part of his personality. The individual acts and reacts according to what he is — in other words, according to the traits which make him a particular and unique person.

Thus, while it may be possible to distinguish these three systems analytically, in reality none of the three is autonomous, isolated or self-contained. Their boundaries touch one another; or more accurately, there are no boundaries between them, for each system needs the other two in order to exist and function. It is from the joining together of the three systems that all concrete social action is derived. The social system can exist as a normative system of interactions and roles only because culture provides shared values which guide behaviour and confer on it a communicable meaning. Culture exists only because it is created and re-created continuously within and through interaction and social action, of which it is both a condition and a consequence. Finally, the personality contributes to the two preceding systems the life element, or the essential spark to light the fire — it is the source of all the motivations which make each actor act and react in the social situation.

In fact, the three systems are not merely united; rather, they truly interact. Not only is each system related to the other two, but both in concrete action and also theoretically, it is enclosed within them and fashioned from elements provided by them.

The preceding chapters have enabled us to appreciate the complementarity of the social system and culture, as well as the analytical distinction that must be maintained between the two. The relationship between personality and the other two systems will now become clearer, through the analysis of what sociologists and social psychologists call the process of socialization. In fact, because of the knowledge of socialization that has been accumulated, it is possible to bridge the gap between the person and society, to link them together, to distinguish them from one another and to understand their complementarity.

The Process of Socialization

We define socialization as *the process through which the human individual learns and internalizes, throughout his life, the sociocultural elements of his environment, integrating them into the structure of his personality under the influence of meaningful social agents and personal experiences, and thus adapting himself to the social environment in which he must live.*

This definition includes a number of elements that will be developed and clarified in the following sections of this chapter. In particular, it suggests three fundamental aspects of socialization that should be emphasized immediately, for they will then serve as points of reference.

The acquisition of culture

First of all, socialization is the process of acquiring knowledge, patterns of behaviour, values and symbols — in brief, "ways of acting, thinking and feeling" — which are specific to groups, to society, and to the civilization in which an individual is required to live. This process starts at birth, continues throughout life, and ends only with death. Childhood is unquestionably the most intense period of socialization. It is not only the period when the human being has the most to learn (cleanliness, culinary tastes, etiquette, language, roles and so forth), but also the period when he is most pliable and most apt to learn, for he does it with a facility and a speed which he will never again experience. Modern society tends to prolong this period of intense socialization into adolescence, in contrast with non-industrial societies where the adolescent achieves the status of an adult at a much younger age. This is one of the consequences, in particular, of increasingly generalized access to secondary education for all the population.

Once this intense period of learning through childhood and youth has passed, the adult continues his socialization throughout the rest of his life. At certain stages, he will experience more intensive socialization than at others. Think, for example, of all the adaptations that are required by one's first job in modern industrial society — the acquisition of new technical knowledge; the understanding of an official and unofficial (or hidden) system of roles, interactions, communications and sanctions; and the training for methods and a new rhythm of work, for new living conditions, and sometimes also for a new standard of living. Every promotion and change of employment similarly gives rise to a new period of socialization. Marriage and the birth and marriage of the first child are stages which equally require new adaptations. The resettlement of an immigrant in an adopted country is probably the most difficult test of resocialization that one can experience at an adult age. Clearly the experience is not equally successful for everyone, at every age, under all circumstances. In fact, the acculturation of the immigrant, or his socialization in a new society and a new culture, is completed only over a period of two or even three generations. In our society, where old people have lost the status and functions that they used to enjoy, there is an emphasis on the art of knowing how to grow old to prevent the individual from suffering from the process and from making others suffer. Strictly speaking, this is a case of socialization to a new role, which society dictates to elderly people. One must also learn to die well; each society has its standards, essentially based on religion, which define how one should die. Finally, between these stages, each day brings with it the need to adapt to new situations, which impose on the individual the acquisition of new elements of the vast social code that legislates the life of each of us.

The integration of culture
into the personality

Second, our definition specifies that, as a result of socialization, the elements of society and culture become an integral part of the structure of the personality, to the point where they become the fabric or a part of the content of this structure. It is impossible to measure what proportion of culture and the social system is thus integrated into the personality; the extent varies, of course, from one person to another. But we can assert that, once they have been integrated into the personality, culture and the social system become a moral obligation or a rule of conscience, as well as a standard of "natural" or "normal" behaviour, thought or feeling.

It is because of this integration of socio-cultural elements into the personality that the weight of social control, or the imperatives and requirements of the social environment, is felt very little, at least consciously, by each social actor. The actor is not aware of bending at every moment under the pressure of an external authority, or of being the object of constraints imposed by institutions or other actors. The source of his conformity springs from his own conscience, undoubtedly as much to give himself the comfort of appearing neither unique nor out of place, as to merit respect in his own eyes and in those of invisible witnesses, whether they be God or the mother who died years ago.

Adaptation to the social environment

The third aspect of socialization that is raised by our definition is really the main result of it, from the sociological point of view: this is the *adaptation* of the person to his social environment. The socialized person is part of the milieu; he "belongs" to his family, to the group, to the firm, to the religion and the nation, in the sense that he is part of them and has his place among them. Thus, it is because he has a sufficient number of things in common with the other members of these collectivities that he is able to communicate with them, to share in their feelings, to share their aspirations, tastes, needs and activities — or briefly, to resemble them, not so much physically (which is also sometimes the case), but mentally and psychologically. To belong to a collectivity is to share with the other members a sufficient number of ideals or common traits to be able to recognize oneself within the in-group that is formed ("we of the university," "we Canadians," "we women").

By belonging, the individual can identify sufficiently with this in-group to draw from it, at least partly, his own psychological and social identity.

This adaptation involves the depths of the personality, for it is produced simultaneously at three levels — biological or psycho-motor, emotional and mental. *At the biological and psychomotor level*, the individual who has been socialized to a culture and a society has developed physiological needs, tastes and attitudes of the body, which have required a conditioning of his neuro-physiological organism and sensory-motor apparatus. The Italian, the Jew or the Frenchman are recognizable because certain gestures, facial expressions and mannerisms characterize them. The Mexican takes pleasure in eating certain foods which seem so strongly spiced to others that they literally burn the mouth and throat; the Englishman needs to start his day with a full breakfast and a cup of tea, while the Frenchman will be satisfied with a cup of coffee and a piece of bread. The body and its habits must thus experience a socialization process which is designed to adapt the individual to a given socio-cultural environment.

At the emotional level, not only can the expression of feelings be channelled by the patterns, limitations and sanctions of a culture; but they can also be smothered, restrained or denied by a culture or society. Ethnological studies have amply demonstrated that some societies more than others favour the development and expression of aggression, tenderness or love. Let us take a familiar example. In modern Western society, everyone strains his ingenuity and concentrates on making marriage a love affair, and the marriage of self-interest and the marriage of convenience tend to be deprecated in favour of what has been called romantic love. Nevertheless, in many societies over long historical periods, the marriage of young people was arranged by their parents and was essentially an economic affair that was treated as such. And this type of marriage was much more stable than the one based on romantic love. The value placed on romantic love is in fact a relatively recent cultural phenomenon in the history of humanity. Henri Bergson wrote:

> From time immemorial woman must have inspired man with an inclination distinct from desire, but in immediate contact as though welded to it, and pertaining both to feeling and to sensation. But romantic love has a definite date: it sprang up during the Middle Ages when some person or persons conceived the idea of ab-

sorbing love into a kind of supernatural feeling, into religious emotion as created by Christianity and launched by the new religion into the world. When critics reproach mysticism with expressing itself in the same terms as passionate love, they forget that it was love which began by plagiarizing mysticism, borrowing from it its fervour, its raptures, its ecstasies: in using the language of a passion it has transfigured, mysticism has only resumed possession of its own.[3]

Today love between young people is a feeling that is not only authorized, but also valued, encouraged and even exaggerated, presumably because it is believed that a marriage based on this feeling merits more confidence than a marriage of convenience. It has even come to be considered that a marriage that is no longer inspired by love should be dissolved, and that the man and the woman can or should look for a new love. In comparison with other civilizations and other periods, modern society thus favours among its members the birth, development and expression of the feeling of love. In our society, there are many definitions of love, ranging from pure eroticism to the most spiritual conception; but one cannot deny love, nor smother its development, among individuals who have been socialized in this type of society.

Finally, *at the level of thought*, socialization furnishes mental categories, representations, images, knowledge, prejudices and stereotypes — "ways of thinking" — without which intelligence, memory and the imagination cannot blossom, grow and produce. It is through incorporating elements of culture that intellectual faculties develop and are able to create new cultural elements.

Thus, the normal result of socialization — from the sociological point of view — is to produce sufficient conformity in ways of acting, thinking and feeling among each of the members of a collectivity that, on the one hand, each person will adapt and be integrated into this collectivity; and that, on the other hand, this collectivity will be self-sustaining and enduring. Must it be deduced from this that the result of socialization necessarily is conformity, or even conformism, in behaviour and attitudes and that any other result indicates a failure of socialization? Certainly not. We shall return to this problem at the end of the chapter; for, before being able to resolve it, we must study in greater depth the process

---

3. Henri Bergson, *The Two Sources of Morality and Religion* (London: Macmillan and Co., Limited, 1935), pp. 30-31.

of socialization. In other words, we must describe its main mechanisms, and analyze the role of the agents and milieux of socialization.

Mechanisms of Socialization

When the question is to explain the mechanisms which regulate the socialization of the individual, we turn naturally to the psychologists of various schools. At this point, however, it is not necessary to go through the whole process of the development and structuring of the personality. In sociology, it is sufficient to draw on psychological research that is specifically concerned with the formation of what can be called the social personality, or more precisely, the development of the aptitude for social action and the acquisition of the prerequisites for this — norms, values, symbols and so forth. Undoubtedly, this is a distinction which will not please all psychologists; they may say, and with good reason, that the personality is a whole, and does not lend itself to such surgery. But all the same, we are forced to maintain this analytical distinction, at least for the purposes of our presentation.

The problem of social motivation

The problem which must be resolved is posed in terms of motivation and can be formulated as follows: how is a human individual — particularly the child, but also the adult — led to orient his action according to the motives, aspirations and goals which are suggested to him by a culture, and which are dominant in a given collectivity in such a way that, seen from the outside, his behaviour appears subject to constraints and gives the impression of conformity or standardization? More briefly, it could be asked: how does the human individual develop the necessary motivation for normatively oriented action? If an individual, acting in conformity with the norms and values of a collectivity or culture, thus follows his own moral conscience and responds to a need which he considers "normal" or "natural," it is because he is positively motivated to act in this way. But it is known that such a motivation is not inherent in the biological nature of man, and that it is not a part of the essence of human nature, since different objects and various ways of acting can satisfy such motivation. The young puppy who laps milk for the first time seems to obey an internal impulse or instinct, for he can do it even before opening his eyes and seeing his mother; it is the order of *nature* that rules. But the Westerner who prefers to eat with a knife and fork, and who knows the difference between "right" and "wrong" ways of handling them, has inherited neither this preference nor this judgement with the biological need that he feels to eat and to drink; it is the order of *culture* that rules. How does the cultural order impose itself on man?

In a more general sense, this is the problem that was posed by Hobbes in *Leviathan*. In fact, Hobbes emphatically showed that it was necessary to explain why society exists and lasts without being "a war of all against all." In other words, Hobbes asked himself how it came about that all men do not resort to fraud and violence in pursuing their personal goals. How is it that they can maintain a relatively stable society, instead of constantly attacking or killing one another? How is it that men generally are internally motivated to follow social norms, to adhere to the values of their environment, and to identify with in-groups?

The reply, or at least part of it, obviously lies in the psychological mechanisms of human socialization. Without going into too much detail, and by greatly simplifying reality, it can be said that there are *two main mechanisms* of socialization: *learning*, and *the internalization of others*. These two mechanisms will be considered separately, but it must be remembered that in fact they are closely linked.

Learning

Learning consists of the acquisition of reflexes, habits, attitudes and so forth, which are inscribed in the organism and the personality of the individual and which guide his behaviour. The dog that the Russian psychologist Pavlov trained to salivate on hearing a bell or receiving an electric shock was subjected to a period of learning. In fact, Pavlov inculcated into the dog what he called a conditioned reflex. The dog salivated through a natural or spontaneous reflex when he saw or smelt his food; through training, Pavlov constructed an unnatural reflex in the neuro-physiological organism of the animal, which consisted of salivating on hearing a sound or on receiving an electric shock which announced or reminded him of food. The child who is trained in cleanliness, good manners and etiquette by his parents also has been subjected to a learning program through the repetition of the same gestures which are designed to develop in him conditioned reflexes and habits. The child learns a new game by watching others and imitating them; then he tries himself and corrects his errors. This is another form of learning. Similarly, the person who memorizes a text by repeating it several times and correcting his errors imposes a certain learning pattern on his memory, which will inscribe a series of successive sounds in his neuro-cerebral system. Finally, the child is punished for his thoughtlessness and rewarded for his generosity in the hope of developing within him habits of attention and kindness.

From the examples that have just been given, it can be seen that repetition, imitation, the application of rewards and punishments, and trial and error are the four main procedures through which learning operates. Whether in training animals or children, in teaching, education or socialization in general, the socializing agent and/or the person being socialized resort constantly to one or another of these learning processes.

Heredity or social environment

The studies on learning carried out by psychologists have involved them in a long and continuing discussion on the respective roles of *heredity* and *the external environment* in the learning process. The influence of the environment has been defended mainly by behavioural psychologists who, guided by the work of Pavlov, consider learning as mainly the development of the organism's responses to external stimuli. From this perspective, education and socialization would consist above all in the learning of appropriate responses to situations, events and external objects which acted as stimuli; this learning would be carried out mainly by repetition and the interplay of sanctions. Behavioural psychology has often been criticized for the fact that its definition of human conduct and education is too molecular or atomized; it has also been accused of neglecting the goal that is pursued by the human subject in his behaviour and actions, and of tending to treat the human subject as an automaton or a machine. In reply to these criticisms, psychologists (not necessarily behaviourists) have developed new theoretical schema. For example, Tolman has elaborated a theory of the cognitive map to describe the representation that the subject constructs mentally for himself of his environment, and of the objects of the environment which affect him and act on him as stimuli. Kurt Lewin has demonstrated that this cognitive map is structured according to a "field of force" — that is, around certain stimulus-objects of the physical and social milieu which take on a greater value than others for the satisfaction of the subject.

In opposition to environmental psychology, theories of instinct have emphasized heredity in the explanation of human conduct. Some psychologists, and notably William McDougall, have claimed that human action is basically the product of instincts which are inherent in the biological organism. An attempt has been made to compile a complete list of these instincts; they explain the needs of animals and man, as well as the feelings and behaviour which they motivate. Thus, McDougall attaches to each instinct an emotion which initiates human activity. The emotion of fear corresponds to the instinct of flight, the emotion of surprise to the instinct of curiosity, and the emotion of anger to the instinct of combat.

But instincts and needs are diffused in man: for example, various foods can satisfy the need to eat. Learning would therefore consist of channelling the progressive development of instincts and needs in man by suggesting specific objects which would be apt to satisfy them — one food rather than another, one way of eating rather than another. In this way, learning becomes a reconstruction of primary needs, instincts and their emotions, according to socially recognized and acceptable methods of gratification. While for the behaviourists the learning process begins with a tabula rasa and acts on a pliable organism in which the surrounding environment inculcates the appropriate responses and reactions through various means of conditioning, the instinct theorists have defined learning on the basis of a hereditary instinctive quality whose development must be guided.

The contrast between these two positions has been minimized today, if in fact it still exists. In particular, some agreement has been achieved on two major points. First, it was recognized that a theory of learning could not ignore either heredity or the influence of the external environment; on the contrary, *it must take into account these two elements and their constant interaction*. It is probably impossible to specify the importance which should be given to each element, and as a result one may be emphasized more than the other; but it is no longer possible to neglect either.

Second, whatever position is adopted concerning the respective roles of heredity and environment, it is recognized that a satisfactory explanation of learning must include the *meaning*, for the subject, of the different individuals who surround him and who are the active agents of learning, the relationships which he has with them, as well as his own behaviour towards them. Thus, it is not only the reward or punishment in itself that counts, but also the fact that the reward or punishment stems from a certain person, that it affects the relationship with this person in a particular way and entails a certain feeling towards him.

The internalization of others

To complete the first mechanism, the second mechanism of socialization, the *internalization of others*, now enters the picture. As early as 1902, the American sociologist Charles Cooley developed in detail the idea that the "self," or the feeling of being an entity or a person who can say "I," "me" and "mine," is largely social in its origins and content. By looking at himself in the mirror that others provide, a person constructs his Self, through the image of himself that he believes he is giving them, and through the judgements about himself that he attributes to them. To this concept of the Self reflected in the reactions of others, Cooley gave the name "the looking-glass self." The existential consciousness, or the consciousness of existing and being a Self, is thus the product of both the perception of one's self by others, which Cooley calls sympathy, and communication with others. But, for Cooley, the feeling of well-being and obligation results from the synthesis of the influences to which a person is subjected, as a result of his sympathetic sensitivity to the judgement of others.[4]

George H. Mead

In a study which is at the same time philosophical, psychological and sociological, George H. Mead[5] has continued the analysis of the social Self in great depth. On the basis of observations of the functions of language, play and the game (which is distinguished from simple play), he has demonstrated how the child develops mentally and socializes himself by playing the roles of others (pa-

4. Charles H. Cooley, *Human Nature and Social Order*, revised edition (New York: Charles Scribner's Sons, 1922), especially chaps. 5 and 10.
5. Mead, *Mind, Self and Society*.

rents, playmates, heroes) and by internalizing their attitudes. In this way, while he learns the rules of the game, he learns to think of himself as a member of the group and as different from others because of the role that he himself fulfills. Mead states that what happens in play and in the game is only an illustration of what happens in everyday life: the child's Self is developed through identifying with other people in the roles that they fulfill, and particularly through internalizing the "generalized other," or the organized and structured set of other roles on which he depends. The child also constructs his Self through the distinction that his own role enables him to make between his person and others. In addition, through the internalization of other roles, the child becomes familiar with the rules that regulate them, the attitudes that are related to them, and the principles that guide them; this is the basis of the progressive internalization of the socio-cultural elements of the environment. It is understandable why Mead's work, which has had a great influence in the United States, has been the foundation of the importance that American sociologists and social psychologists attach to social role in the socialization process.

In addition, through the function that he attributes to thought and intelligence in learning and action, Mead greatly contributed to freeing American psychology from the physiological limits within which strict behaviourism had enclosed it. In fact, according to Mead, thought is essentially social in character; it is social in its origins, because it necessarily develops through and in communication with others. It is also social in its content, because of the collective symbols that are used in constructing and communicating it.

Jean Piaget

It is here that Mead and Piaget come together. In fact, Piaget's works were mainly concerned with the development of thought and intelligence in the child, but Piaget has always considered this development as much a social as a psychological process. According to him, childhood is characterized, as much from the point of view of knowledge as from that of morals, by what he calls "egocentrism." This is how he explains and defines it:

> Just as at first the mind, before it can dissociate what belongs to objective laws from what is bound up with the sum of subjective conditions, confuses itself with

universe, so does the individual begin by understanding and feeling everything through the medium of himself before distinguishing what belongs to things and other people from what is the result of his own particular intellectual and affective perspective. At this stage, therefore, the individual cannot be conscious of his own thought, since consciousness of self implies a perpetual comparison of the self with other people. Thus, from the logical point of view egocentrism would seem to involve a sort of alogicality, such that sometimes affectivity gains the ascendant over objectivity and sometimes the relations arising from personal activity prove stronger than the relations that are independent of the self. And from the moral point of view, egocentrism involves a sort of anomy such that tenderness and disinterestedness can go hand in hand with a naive selfishness, and yet the child not feel spontaneously himself to be better in one case than the other. Just as the ideas which enter his mind appear from the first in the forming of beliefs and not of hypotheses requiring verification, so do the feelings that arise in the child's consciousness appear to him from the first as having value and not as having to be submitted to some ulterior evaluation. It is only through contact with the judgements and evaluations of others that this intellectual and affective anomy will gradually yield to the pressure of collective logical and moral laws.[6]

This contact with others, however, takes on two successive and very different forms, according to Piaget. Until the age of about seven, the relationship with adults, mainly parents, predominates. Because of the respect that adults inspire in him and the place that his parents occupy in his life, the child has a relationship with adults that is marked by coercion or constraint; the child thinks and acts as the adult wishes or prescribes. Thought and the moral conscience are still external to the child, who receives them in the same way as he accepts these adults — unconditionally. Following the childhood period of pure egocentrism comes a period when a child alternates between primitive egocentrism and the passive ac-

6. Jean Piaget, *The Moral Judgement of the Child*, trans. Marjorie Gabain (London: Kegan Paul, Trench, Trubner & Co. Ltd., 1932), pp. 407-8.

ceptance of the thought and judgement of others. During this phase "My pleasure is simply replaced by the pleasure of a sovereign authority."[7]

From the age of seven a second form of social relationship appears, based on cooperation. This is possible, not with adults, but with equals or companions of the same age. Cooperation allows discussion and criticism; based on the diversity and the complementarity of functions in collective play, it also enables the child to understand the diversity and complementarity of points of view. Thus cooperation has "a role which is both liberating and constructive . . . : [it] alone leads to autonomy"[8] of thought and of the moral conscience. Discussion engenders reflection, verification and criticism; it sharpens intelligence and judgement. Through cooperation and discussion, the ideas and categories which have been accepted up to then are progressively sifted, and those which endure take on a more personal character. From the moral point of view, the rules and principles which the child obeys submissively and passively become convictions or personal moral judgements; they have been submitted to the reflection and criticism which are required by cooperation. Thus, knowledge, norms and values of the environment, having been imposed from the outside, are gradually internalized and become the reason and the conscience of each person. Piaget, like Mead, clearly attaches great importance to the progress of language and to the symbolic function, which are the foundations of communication. Indeed, he suggests that in the socialized adult, even the most intimate and private language is social. The same is true of thought, because it is always addressed to another — real, imaginary or hypothetical.[9]

Sigmund Freud

While Piaget was concerned with describing the phases of the development of the intelligence, almost taking as given the social ties and feelings which accompany them, it is to Freud and his disciples that we owe the investigation and clarification of the emotional bases of human behaviour and social relationships. In addition, psychoanalysis contributed in a large measure to the expla-

---

7. *Ibid.*, p. 467.
8. *Ibid.*, p. 469.
9. Jean Piaget, *The Language and Thought of the Child*, trans. Marjorie Warden (London: Kegan Paul, Trench, Trubner & Co. Ltd., 1926), p. 246.

nation of the process of socialization. Here we can indicate only a few salient points of this contribution. We will consider four in particular.

First, Freud clarified *the relationship of the child with his parents* by showing its sexual roots, which he called libidinal. The various physical contacts between the young child and his mother, or whoever takes her place, give the child his first erotic pleasure, develop in him the feeling of love, and prepare him for the birth of sexual desire. It is the anguish of losing the object of this pleasure which creates in the child the need for emotional security which he invests in his parents. The search for affection and love thus surrounds all the phases of the child's early training, as much through the pleasures and the security that this love brings as through the deprivations and frustrations which accompany it, and the resulting antagonism and hostility. The dynamics of the human being's early learning are consequently inscribed within a context of intense emotional relationships which multiply tenfold both the relevance and the significance of the methods employed by the parents or their substitutes. It is during the oedipal phase, however, that the relationship between the child and his parents takes on its most intensely sexual character — an attachment to the parent of the opposite sex and an identification with the parent of the same sex. This identification constitutes the internalization of the other in its most extreme and powerful form; it consists of playing the role of the other in a very complete way in order to annihilate him and replace him in his role. This capacity of the child to identify is important for an understanding and explanation of the child's propensity to assume the roles and attitudes of others.

Through his analysis of the relationships between the child and his parents, particularly during the oedipal phase, Freud highlighted a second very important phenomenon — *the ambivalence of feelings*, or the human being's capacity to experience simultaneously contradictory feelings of love and hate towards the same people. The frustrations that parents must make their child undergo during his education are resented by the child all the more strongly because they come from loved ones; they only facilitate the development of contrary feelings of hostility. In the oedipal phase in particular, the identification with the parent of the same sex in the competition for the love of the parent of the opposite sex engenders the desire to kill the competing parent or to see him die. The murder of the father, at least in its symbolic form, is part of the normal development of the boy, and the same is true for the daughter with regard to her mother. On the social level, this ambivalence of feelings plays an important role in the relationship between generations, particularly between young people and adults. Later, it will be seen that writers have accorded this ambivalence an important place in the explanation of relationships between colonized peoples and their colonizers.

A third phenomenon which was fully analyzed by Freud is that of _transference_, or the capacity to attach to various people, roles and objects the feelings which were originally attached to another person, role or object. It is in the relationship between the psychoanalyst and his patient that transference occurs in the most intense and dramatic way. The psychoanalyst initially directs towards himself, for a temporary period, the feelings of love and hate that the patient entertains with regard to another person, in order to be able, later on, to break a former identification which has become pathological. This aptitude for transfer plays an important role in adult life and becomes necessary, in particular, at specific stages of adaptation and socialization — marriage, loss of a loved one, change of employment, emigration, growing old and so forth. In addition, studies of the social phenomenon of the scapegoat (in certain cases of anti-semitism, for example) have shown that feelings of hostility which cannot be directly expressed against the individuals or groups who have provoked these feelings are diverted through transference towards a more vulnerable group (such as a minority group). This group thus fulfills the function of a scapegoat, to which one can impute all the sins of Israel.[10]

Finally, the fourth contribution of psychoanalysis to the understanding of the socialization process stems from the Freudian analysis of the _Superego_. In the structure of the personality, the Superego is formed by the internalization of emotionally important figures, of the rules of life that they symbolize for the subject, and of the sanctions that these figures impose or with which they are associated. This is what psychoanalysts have called the series of censures which are applied to impulses and to their immediate and direct satisfaction. As Parsons[11] has emphasized, in his analysis of the Superego, Freud incorporates the Durkheimian idea of

10. This analysis of the scapegoat has been elaborated in Talcott Parsons, _Essays in Sociological Theory_ (Glencoe, Ill.: The Free Press, 1954), chap. 7.
11. Particularly in his analysis of the socialization process: Talcott Parsons et al., _Family, Socialization and Interaction Process_ (Glencoe, Ill.: The Free Press, 1955).

constraints, since these, like the Superego, represent the principle and the social source of moral obligation. The Superego is social control which has been internalized and assimilated in such a way that it enters into the dialectic established between the instinctive impulses, the objects that satisfy or frustrate them, and the constraints that the subject believes must be imposed.

This rapid excursion into the field of psychology enables us to gain a slightly better understanding of the interplay of the two main mechanisms in the process of socialization and the interaction between them. Learning, which is a much longer and more complex process for the child of man than for any other animal, is reinforced by the different forms of internalization of the other. These are both mental and emotional, and man is capable of them primarily as a result of his much greater emotional depth and, above all, his ability to manipulate reality symbolically.

The Agents of Socialization

Given the importance accorded to individuals and groups in the mechanisms which have just been discussed, our account must be completed by a brief study of the main agents in the socialization process. Obviously it is impossible to enumerate them all: we will content ourselves with mentioning those which have been the subject of the most important studies by sociologists and psychologists.

Three criteria of classification

Rather than make a mere enumeration according to some artificial order of importance, we shall try to classify the agents of socialization according to three criteria. First, a distinction can be made between socialization which operates within identifiable groups or institutionalized bodies, such as the family or the school, and socialization which is carried out in a more diffuse fashion because it is concerned with the whole of a collectivity and is aimed at a mass — as is the case, for example, of socialization through radio and television.

Second, the agents of socialization can be classified according to whether they have the explicit and recognized goal of educating and inculcating principles or dispensing knowledge; or, on the contrary, whether they carry out this function in an instrumental fashion, pursuing other activities or objectives as explicit goals.

Finally, the groups and institutions which carry out a socializing function can be distinguished according to whether they form heterogeneous age groups (members belonging to these groups or institutions are of different ages) or homogeneous age groups. S. N. Eisenstadt has used this last distinction to advantage in his important study of generations or age groups.[12] We should complete Eisenstadt's distinction, however, by adding that groups or institutions can also be characterized simultaneously by homogeneity and heterogeneity of age.

If only the last two criteria are used initially, the main agents of socialization can be presented in the following way:

TABLE 2

	Groups having socialization as an explicit goal	*Groups not having socialization as an explicit goal*
Heterogeneous age groups	Families Churches or sects	Business firms Trade unions
Homogeneous age groups	"Age-villages" Groups of old people	Groups of friends Youth movements Age groups
Both	Schools Educational movements Relatives	Political parties Social movements

The family and the school

From the table, it can be seen that a certain number of groups or institutions have the explicit and recognized goal of socializing some or all of their members. But these groups and institutions are structured differently in terms of age. Thus, the family and the school can be very clearly distinguished from one another. At school, the child lives among other children of his age with whom he shares his life and work, and the contacts between children of the same age are considered an element of education; at the same time, the child is submitted to the authority of adults who are in

---

12. S. N. Eisenstadt, *From Generation to Generation* (Glencoe, Ill.: The Free Press, 1956, paperback edition 1964), pp. 36 ff.

charge of teaching and discipline. In the family also, this distinction between adults and children is present; but the children are not always of (approximately) the same age, and this becomes an important element in socialization. Modern psychology has fully demonstrated the influence that the rank occupied in a family can exert on personality.

The same distinction holds in the case of relatives when they are ascribed the explicit function of education — which is seldom the case any longer in industrial society. In the extended family, for example, the children of several families (married brothers or sisters living together) are brought up together, generally under the joint authority of several people (in addition to the father and mother, the grandparents and/or the eldest brother and/or his wife). In these circumstances, there may be strata of children of the same age, similar to those at school.

Age groups

In sociology and anthropology, age groups are often accorded great importance. As we will show in Chapter 7, they form a basic element of the organization of traditional or non-urban societies; and in modern society, there is much talk of the youth culture and youth movements. From Table 2, it can be seen that age groups and youth movements can be of three different types. First, there are those which have socialization as an explicit goal and which include only individuals of the same age. In fact, few examples of this first type can be found. We could mention the Nyakyusa "age-villages" of Africa, which have been studied by G. and M. Wilson.[13] They are composed entirely of adolescents, and are considered quite exceptional in anthropological literature. The groups of elderly people which are multiplying in certain modern countries are perhaps another example of this type, since they have the fairly clear goal of encouraging the art of growing old.

The second type is composed of groups and movements which have socialization as an explicit goal, and in which adults have a responsibility in the education of young people. This second type is much more common, and can be found in a number of non-urban societies. L. Warner, for example, has studied this type among

---

13. G. Wilson, "An Introduction to Nyakyusa Society," *Bantu Studies* 10 (1936); and M. Wilson, *Good Company* (Oxford: International African Institute, 1951).

the Muengins of Africa, where the adolescents withdraw to a camp under the authority of adults and older boys.[14] Also, all youth movements of an educational nature — such as the scout movement, holiday camps, the young pioneers of socialist countries — are either directed or guided by adults or older people.

Finally, the third type is composed of age groups or associations which, in order to fulfill their functions or to carry out certain activities, must socialize their members. In this case, socialization appears as a means of accomplishing certain functions or activities and consequently is instrumental. Groups of friends and gangs, such as those studied by Thrasher[15] and Whyte,[16] have certain activities in view and pursue certain objectives; more or less "official" or explicit procedures of socialization provide for the initiation or acceptance of new members, but socialization is not asserted as a goal or as the manifest goal of the group. The same holds true for youth movements which are oriented towards student, social or political action, and which "educate" their members or their milieu as a function of the objectives of the movement. This is the case, for example, of student syndicalism. Most of the age groups of traditional societies fulfill political or economic functions first of all and through these carry out an indirect and inexplicit socializing function.

Business firms, trade unions, social movements

Like the third type of age groups (which are by definition homogeneous age groups), many other groups or institutions carry out a secondary socializing function which is generally based on the activities that they pursue. Thus, industrial or commercial firms resort to more or less organized methods for the integration of their new employees: periods of apprenticeship, training and sometimes education, which may be long or short according to the position and the firm. Trade unionism has developed social education or trade union education structures; cooperatives have study groups; social movements have study sessions, work camps and intensive sessions. Usually this socializing function is performed in relation to individuals of different ages. But in some cases, age is taken into

---

14. L. Warner, *A Black Civilization* (New York: Harper, 1937).
15. Thrasher, *The Gang*.
16. Whyte, *Street Corner Society*.

account: political parties and social movements, for example, have developed youth sections (Young Liberals, Young Conservatives, Young Republicans, Young Trade Unionists) within the framework of the party, so that age groups are seen to be clearly defined.

It is now possible to draw two main conclusions from this classification. First, groups and institutions which have socialization as an explicit goal generally manifest a total and diffuse attitude. They tend to want to socialize the total person and to exert an influence on his whole life, or at least on all aspects of his life. This is the case with the family, the school, churches and sects, and many educational movements. In contrast, when socialization is not the explicit goal of groups and institutions, these generally have a socializing function that is more limited or that touches only a segment of the personality. This is certainly true of business firms, trade unions and social movements, and political parties; it is perhaps less often true of homogeneous age groups, which frequently have broader goals.

Second, this classification makes it clear that socialization is not necessarily a transmission of culture by older to younger people. This transmission also occurs between individuals of the same age. In the groups and institutions which have socialization as an explicit goal, however, it is generally older people who have authority over the younger, or who are responsible for their education. We have had some difficulty in finding examples of homogeneous age groups which have the socialization of their members as an explicit goal. But in many homogeneous age groups which do not have socialization as an explicit goal, intense and efficient socialization is carried out among individuals of the same age, notably among young people (for example, in gangs, youth movements, and youth sections of trade unions).

Mass communication techniques

Finally, a special category must be set up for the socializing agents who direct their efforts, in a general way, to the whole of a collectivity or a mass. In modern society, this phenomenon is more powerful and more prevalent than ever before, because mass communication techniques have become an important socializing agent for adults as well as for young people. Since the invention of the printing press, it has become increasingly easy to address a whole collectivity, or a mass, through the circulation of various forms of printed material. More recently, the advent and progress of radio, films and television have made remarkable advances in mass communication. The expression itself — *mass communication* — is a new term which has been created to designate this special form of communication, whether simultaneous or not, with a great number of people.

Part of the socializing function which is carried out through mass communication techniques is undoubtedly direct; this is the case with educational and information broadcasts on radio and television, and of printed matter and films of a didactic kind. But most often, these new techniques socialize in an indirect way, particularly when they direct their efforts to the spectator or reader in order to amuse him, make him relax, and forget everything else.

We cannot go into a great deal of detail here. It will be sufficient to mention a few recent studies in various countries concerning the influence of television on young people.[17] Himmelweit, Oppenheim and Vince have come to the conclusion that young children learn and retain much more from dramatic broadcasts, which do not aim to instruct or inform, than from educational broadcasts.[18] Television exerts its influence particularly through values and idealized patterns which are presented with a powerful emotional impact. Himmelweit, Oppenheim and Vince also found that television sets up middle-class patterns of behaviour and values as ideals (kind of job, living conditions, kind of housing, behaviour traits), and that children who watch television are much more sensitive to these patterns and values than children who do not watch.[19] J. Komorowska notes: "The T.V. has supplied additional material in the class struggle fought by women, mothers and daughters to attain a new style of a life and to achieve a new ideal," with the result that it has "increased the levelling process in the social functions of boys and girls in the family."[20] In analyzing French magazines for young girls, Marie-José Chombart de Lauwe has noticed that the boys and girls who star in them

17. The most important are, for England, the study by H. Himmelweit, A. N. Oppenheim and P. Vince, *Television and the Child: An Empirical Study of the Effect of Television on the Young* (London: Oxford University Press, 1958); for the United States and Canada, the study by W. Schramm, J. Lyle and E. B. Parker, *Television in the Lives of Children* (Stanford: Stanford University Press, 1961); for Poland, the study by J. Komorowska, *La télévision dans la vie des enfants* (summarized and translated into French in a special number of the journal), *Enfance* 2-3 (April–September, 1964).
18. Himmelweit, Oppenheim and Vince, *Television and the Child*, p. 310.
19. *Ibid.*, chaps. 17-21.
20. Komorowska, pp. 145 and 153.

"are often on an equal footing, or even that the character of the boy is the weaker because he is younger." She continues:

> The young fragile girl who is the victim of circumstances or of nasty people, who was so often described in the preceding century, is absolutely exceptional. The soft, passive, submissive and obedient model is increasingly rare. The quality traditionally called "feminine" that can be found in these heroines is devotion, but it is also frequent in young boys. Members of both sexes are involved in the same adventures, track down the guilty and defend the victims.[21]

In a more general way, the same author emphasizes the disagreements or conflicts between the different models of the "ideal child" which are offered by movies, children's magazines, schools, advertisements and novelists, as well as the lack of continuity between the roles suggested to children at various stages of their development (for example, the little girl who identified with masculine heroes must learn to take on more "feminine" roles in adolescence).

These examples only serve to illustrate how mass communication techniques suggest and express patterns, values and ideals which can be imposed with so much more force and persuasion when they are presented in a dramatic or emotional context which contributes towards the inhibition of critical judgement.

The Milieux of Socialization

It is not sufficient merely to identify the main agents of socialization. In order for us to understand their influence fully, they must be located within the milieux to which they belong; or in other words, the milieux by which they are guided in their transmission of patterns, values and symbols must be known. It is useful here to distinguish between *membership milieux* and *reference milieux*.

Membership milieux are the various milieux into which the socializing agents and those who are socialized are integrated — ecologically, economically and sociologically. These are the milieux

---

21. M. J. Chombart de Lauwe, "La représentation de l'enfant dans la société urbaine française contemporaine," *Enfance* 1 (January–February 1962): p. 64.

of which they are a part, and to which they belong in the strict sense. The family is certainly the best example of a membership milieu in which intense socialization is carried out — the socialization of children by their parents, and sometimes also the socialization of parents by their children, particularly during periods of rapid social change or in the case of an immigrant family. But the family in turn is part of various membership milieux, through its ancestors, relatives, parents and also the children. Before we can understand the socialization that occurs within the family, we must know the membership milieux of that family. Let us enumerate a few of them.

Rural and urban milieux

First of all, the family may belong to a rural or an urban milieu. The family in the rural milieu generally offers the child fewer opportunities for intellectual development than does the family in the urban milieu. In a study conducted in Poland by S. Szuman, rural and urban children were presented with pictures of common objects and asked to identify them. Rural children tended not to differentiate clearly between one object and another, while city children did; and city children were more often able to identify objects by their exact names than were rural children. It is not surprising that studies in comparative psychology have consistently found that the intellectual quotient of rural children is, on the average, lower than that of urban children of the same age.[22] This is not to suggest that rural children are born with less intelligence than urban children; but their living environment is less favourable to the development of their intellectual ability.

Continuing with this comparison, in France G. Lanneau and P. Malrieu have shown that educational and teaching methods differ a great deal between rural and urban families. The education of children in the country is more uniform from one family to another than is the case in the city. The development of sociability is retarded in the rural child because of the delay in learning language skills, limitations imposed on collective play, deficiency in cultural contacts, and more frequent periods of solitude. The education of the rural child is characterized by alternating freedom

---

22. S. Szuman, "L'identification des objets représentés en image chez les enfants des villes et des campagnes âgés de 3 à 10 ans," *Enfance* 4 (September–October 1957): 425-42.

and constraints, depending on his age, and by the greater importance attached to duty. The city child succeeds in achieving his autonomy at an earlier stage and in a more complete way, but he is also subjected to a multiplicity of influences which are less homogeneous and less coherent than in the case of the country child.[23]

Racial, ethnic and cultural groups

In a complex society, the family belongs to a racial, ethnic or cultural group, or to a minority group, which may be more or less privileged. The influence of this factor on the psychology of the child and the way in which the young child and the adolescent learn to identify with norms, constraints and limits which regulate the conduct of the members of their group have been particularly highlighted in a series of American studies undertaken in the 1930's on the education of young Negroes.[24]

In an explicit or implicit way, by watching his parents, friends and whites and by progressively becoming conscious of the limits that are imposed on him, the young Negro learns that in the eyes of whites all Negroes are childish; they have primitive instincts that they cannot control; they are far from having the intelligence of the white man, and consequently can devote themselves only to the most menial work; and they are doomed to live in poverty. He learns from those around him that an immense unbridgeable gap separates him from the white man, that the white man has the

---

23. Gaston Lanneau and Philippe Malrieu, "Enquête sur l'éducation en milieu rural et en milieu urbain," *Enfance* 4 (September–October 1957): 465-82 and *Enfance* 1 (January–February 1958): 31-62.
24. Allison Davis and John Dollard, *Children of Bondage: The Personality Development of Negro Youth in the Rural South* (Washington, D.C.: American Council on Education, 1940); Charles S. Johnson, *Growing Up in the Black Belt: Negro Youth in the Rural South* (Washington, D.C.: American Council on Education, 1941); E. Franklin Frazier, *Negro Youth at the Crossways: Their Personality Development in the Middle States* (Washington, D.C.: American Council on Education, 1940). These studies were carried out with the support of the American Youth Commission of the American Council on Education between 1937 and 1940. If the lessons which were derived from these and many other studies carried out during the period 1930-1940 had been taken into account to a greater extent in the United States, the racial troubles which continue to rage through the country could have been avoided. These four authors have undertaken other studies on the American Negro which could be cited; let us mention in particular one which is concerned with the subject which interests us at the moment, by E. Franklin Frazier, *The Negro Family in Chicago* (Chicago: University of Chicago Press, 1932).

power and the right to scoff at him, and even to strike him or to put him into prison, and that he must at all costs avoid displeasing or annoying him. Through his family and his milieu, the Negro child understands that from every point of view, he lives in an inferior environment, and he learns the behaviour and attitudes which are suitable for individuals of this status.

Social class

In a similar way, differences exist among the educational methods that parents employ according to the social class to which they belong. In the United States, where a number of studies have been carried out on this subject, class differences have been observed between families of both the Negro and the white communities.[25] In particular, there are differences in the aspirations and expectations of parents of different social classes with regard to their children. In recent years, American sociologists and social psychologists have carried out numerous studies of achievement motivation; this is the motivation that impels an individual to set up increasingly difficult objectives for himself, to impose standards of competence, to want to succeed in what he has undertaken, and to wish to succeed in life in general.[26] Some of these studies have shown beyond any doubt that parents of different social classes in the United States do not encourage achievement motivation either to the same extent or in the same way. Middle-class children are more firmly encouraged to develop this type of motivation than are working-class children.[27] At the same time, the aspiration level of young people with regard to their education and their future profession is conditioned to a large extent by the social status of their family, the main values adopted by their particular social class, and the attitudes which stem from them.[28] For this reason,

25. Allison Davis and R. Havighurst show these differences, by class and by racial group, in a very striking fashion in their article, "Social Class and Color Differences in Child-Rearing," *American Sociological Review* 2, no. 6 (December 1946): 698-710. This article was reproduced in H. D. Stein and R. A. Cloward, eds., *Social Perspectives on Behavior* (Glencoe, Ill.: The Free Press, 1958), pp. 415-31.
26. The foundation of these studies is the book by D. C. McClelland et al., *The Achievement Motive* (New York: Appleton-Century-Crofts, Inc., 1953).
27. Bernard C. Rosen, "The Achievement Syndrome: A Psychocultural Dimension of Social Stratification," *American Sociological Review* 21 (April 1956): 203-11.
28. See, for example, the study by W. H. Sewell, A. O. Haller and M. A. Straus, "Social Status and Educational and Occupational Aspiration," *American Sociological Review* 22 (February 1957): 67-73; and more particularly that by

the socio-economic status of the parents is increasingly considered by researchers and educators as a reliable predictor of a child's success at school.

The French sociologist Maurice Halbwachs summarized the socializing influence of social class very well at the conclusion of his brilliant essay on the psychology of the peasant, bourgeois, working and middle classes:

> . . . No one is born a peasant, a large landowner, a farmer or a farm labourer in the sense that he is born with all the qualities ready-made that characterize the men following these different callings. Similarly, people are not born as bourgeois, entrepreneurs, lawyers, magistrates or industrial workers. The character of the clerical worker, the minor civil servant or small tradesman is not a spontaneous growth on the tree of humanity. And, on the other hand, social categories do exist. More often than not they are well defined: altogether distinct, if we consider such cases as the difference between peasants and town dwellers, or between manual workers and others; scarcely distinguishable when the comparison is between high-grade electrical workers and entrepreneurs, or low-grade clerical workers and manual workers. Each of these categories determines the conduct of its members and imposes definite motivations on them; it stamps each category with such a peculiar and distinctive mark, and so sharply, that men of different classes, even though they live in the same surroundings and are contemporaries, sometimes strike us as belonging to different species of humanity. Thus the motives and tendencies governing the majority of men seem entirely correlative to their social conditions.[29]

To the milieux that have just been enumerated, we should add that the family lives in a given region of a country, it may be part of a church or sect, it is attached to groups of friends, and it may

Herbert H. Hyman, "The Value Systems of Different Classes: A Social Psychological Contribution to the Analysis of Stratification" in Reinhard Bendix and Seymour M. Lipset, eds., *Class, Status and Power* (Glencoe, Ill.: The Free Press, 1953), pp. 426-42 and also reproduced in Stein and Cloward, *Social Perspectives on Behavior*, pp. 315-30.

29. Maurice Halbwachs, *The Psychology of Social Class*, trans. Claire Delevany (London: William Heinemann Ltd., 1958), pp. 119-120.

belong to associations or movements. Thus, it is from the outside that the family as a socializing agent takes images, values and patterns, which the parents transmit to their children, which the children introduce to each other, and which they sometimes also introduce to their parents.

Reference milieux

It is not enough to consider membership milieux alone, for *reference milieux* must also be taken into account. These are the milieux from which a socializing agent borrows patterns of behaviour and values which guide him in his socializing action, although he is not a member of these milieux. In the preceding section, we noted that Himmelweit, Oppenheim and Vince have emphasized that English television refers in particular to the norms and values of the middle class. In the United States, many writers have noticed that the school is guided largely by the norms and values of the middle class. A conflict results for the children of the working class, particularly for those of the most underprivileged slum environments, between adherence to the values of their membership class and acceptance of the values of the middle class which is adopted by the school as a reference milieu.

It is mainly the notion of the reference *group* that is used in sociology, particularly in American sociology. The first analysis of this notion was carried out by Robert K. Merton, and subsequently the term has been widely used. In terms of socialization, however, one can speak of reference milieux as well as reference groups.

Reference milieux are as important in the socialization process as membership milieux. For various reasons, in performing their function socializing agents often follow the norms, not of their membership group or milieu, but of other milieux with which they wish to identify. This is the case, for example, with parents who aim to raise the social status of their children. They educate them according to the norms of a higher social class, and this class thus serves as their reference milieu. The case of immigrant families also could be cited. In educating their children, these families are guided by the patterns of behaviour and the values of their adopted country, while they themselves continue to refer to the patterns and values of their country of origin.

The dual socializing function of milieux

It could be said that membership and reference milieux have a dual socializing function. First, it is these milieux that provide the norms, values and symbols which guide socializing agents; for it is through the adaptation to these milieux and also, to a certain extent, through action on these milieux that the socialization process is carried out. Second, it is in terms of the various milieux to which a person belongs or refers that he develops his *identity*, or the definition he presents to himself and to others of what he is as a person, both as an individual and socially. We can call this identity the social personality. It ensures a place for the person in society and a certain unity or coherence of his existence and behaviour. Identity is necessary both psychologically and socially: it contributes to psychological stability; it is an essential condition of the maturity of the personality; and it is a prerequisite to the harmonious social functioning of a person in his environment as well as to the cohesion of groups. Each person partly defines himself and acts through various social identities — national, ethnic, religious, professional, class, regional and so forth. Groups, collectivities and associations, however, are cohesive to the extent that they obtain for their members the feeling of belonging and identifying with an entity that really exists, which is distinct from others and clearly characteristic — in other words, these groups, collectivities and associations themselves have a collective identity.

Conformity, Variation
and Deviance

The concept of social adaptation

The two main mechanisms of socialization — learning and the internalization of others — and the influence of various socializing agents, the pressures of membership milieux, and the attraction of reference milieux clearly result in an *adaptation* of the individual to his total social environment. As has already been indicated, the adaptation of a person to his social environment means that this person has sufficiently internalized the patterns of behaviour, val-

ues and symbols of his environment and that these have been
sufficiently integrated into the structure of his personality that he
can communicate and live with the members of the collectivities
in which he participates; he can function with them and among
them in such a way that in effect he belongs to these collectivities.
Following from this, to permit adaptation to a social milieu, all
the individuals who form this milieu must have a common denominator. This is comprised of the norms, patterns of behaviour, values and symbols which are shared by all and which enable them to
participate in the same collective identities. Thus, the psychological idea of adaptation resembles the sociological idea of conformity, or the standardization and uniformity of behaviour.

But isn't this a very static and even dangerously conservative
conception of socialization and society? Is sociology finally
brought to the point of denying all spontaneity, all innovation
and thus all sources of social change? These questions have been
raised recently by several sociologists and psychologists, notably
Dennis Wrong, who has denounced what he has called "an oversocialized conception of man" in contemporary sociology,[30] and by
Paul-Henry Chombart de Lauwe who has compared French and
American studies on personality development.[31]

Adaptation, conformity and non-conformity

The most general answer to the problem as it has been posed
could be expressed in the following terms: *adaptation to the social
milieu which results from socialization can assume different forms
and different degrees of conformity as well as different forms of
non-conformity*. In other words, *social adaptation does not necessarily imply social conformity*.

In Chapters 2, 3 and 4 we emphasized the fact that society and
culture always offer a number of choices between dominant and
secondary values, and between preferred and accepted or tolerated
patterns of behaviour. Thus, adherence to norms and values implies a certain area of decision on the part of actors. Consequently,

---

30. Dennis H. Wrong, "The Oversocialized Conception of Man in Sociology,"
    American Sociological Review 26 (April 1961): 183-93.
31. Paul-Henry Chombart de Lauwe, "The Interaction of Person and Society,"
    American Sociological Review 31 (April 1966): 237-48. John A. Clausen's
    reply to some of Chombart de Lauwe's criticisms also should be consulted:
    "Research on Socialization and Personality Development in the United
    States and France: Remarks on the Paper by Professor Chombart de Lauwe,"
    American Sociological Review 31 (April 1966): 248-57.

in every society, one finds variant and deviant behaviour which is tolerated to varying degrees. Adaptation to a given environment presupposes the use of the margin of freedom or autonomy which this milieu provides.

It must be added, however, that this margin of freedom is not the same from one collectivity to another. In fact, it is obvious that while no collectivity can exist unless a certain common denominator is shared by its members, groups and societies do not all require the same adherence to established norms or conformity to an identical degree. Some societies or collectivities require stricter and more complete conformity than others, and variation and deviance are tolerated less. This requirement of conformity may be completely explicit, as in the case of certain parties, movements or associations, or under totalitarian regimes where individuals are required to adhere and submit fully to collective goals. Or it may be simply part of the normal order, as in the traditional society (which will be discussed later). One of the differences between the small town and the city is that the town imposes stricter conformity through its social and demographic structure; originality cannot pass unnoticed, and it is more likely to incur various sanctions than it would in the city. In this type of restrictive collectivity, all the mechanisms of socialization tend to encourage social conformity to a marked degree.

Other collectivities combine a greater or lesser degree of autonomy in individual or collective behaviour with the need to conform. For example, while the urban environment requires a degree of conformity, it allows greater freedom than does the rural environment in the choice of clothes, the rhythm of life, habits, attitudes and opinions. In some cases, individual autonomy is not only authorized but sought or demanded, or at least suggested and encouraged. The pattern of behaviour which regulates the education of young people in families and at school includes, as a norm, the accession of the adolescent to some personal autonomy, the progress of his spirit of initiative, resourcefulness and even criticism. The socialization of youth seeks a more or less constant equilibrium between conformity and personal autonomy.

In his lectures on moral education, Durkheim suggested that teachers should pursue the ideal of helping to prepare young people to build a new lay moral code:

> A society like ours cannot, therefore, content itself with a complacent possession of moral results that have been handed down to it. It must go on to new conquests; it is

> necessary that the teacher prepare the children who are
> in his trust for those necessary advances. He must be on
> his guard against transmitting the moral gospel of our
> elders as a sort of closed book. On the contrary, he must
> excite in them a desire to add a few lines of their own,
> and give them the tools to satisfy this legitimate ambi-
> tion.[32]

In this, Durkheim simply expressed the expectations of at least
some members of a complex and rapidly developing society with
regard to the school system; for the school has the function of socializing the adult of tomorrow to a society which does not yet exist,
but which we know will be or should be different from society
today.

From these considerations, an initial conclusion emerges: *in
every collectivity, socialization includes a greater or lesser degree
of adaptation to personal autonomy.*

Conformity in variation and deviance

It is important to note at this point that, for two reasons, *variation
and deviance must not be confused with non-conformity*. First,
adopting variant or deviant values or behaviour does not imply,
for all who do it, an equal break with the dominant values or preferred patterns. For example, children who grow up in city slums
are in immediate contact with the delinquent world; for them, to
enter into this world and to adopt its norms can be a normal consequence of the socialization to which their environment has subjected them. It is quite another question for someone who has
grown up in a rigorously strict and moral atmosphere; for, in order to become delinquent, he must break away completely from
his environment. In his case, delinquency is a much greater deviance than it is for the slum dweller, and it presupposes a much
more radical move away from the norms to which the individual
was originally socialized.

Second, variation and deviance are rarely individual; generally,
in a new environment of variation and deviance, a new conformity
can be found. Behaviour that is judged to be variant or deviant
from the point of view of one collectivity is simultaneously con-
formist from the perspective of another. Behaviour that is consid-

---

32. Emile Durkheim, *Moral Education*, trans. Everett K. Wilson and Herman
    Schnurer (New York: The Free Press of Glencoe, Inc., 1961), pp. 13-14.

ered anti-social is generally as profoundly social in its roots as any other: it is social in a different way, or more precisely, it is social with regard to other norms, groups or milieux. In order to live within a non-conformist group or collectivity (such as among American hobos or hippies), the individual must adhere to ways of acting and thinking, to patterns of behaviour and values which regulate these milieux. A great deal of conformity can be found within anti-conformity. In the same way, reforming or revolutionary movements necessarily provide mechanisms of socialization for their members, old members as well as new, which are destined to maintain the necessary unity of thought and action.

From these considerations, a second conclusion emerges: *within these milieux of non-conformity and anti-conformity one can find the same gradation of strict conformity, tolerance or recognition of the freedom to innovate as in any other milieu.*

Innovating adaptation

Proceeding to the psychological level, it must be recognized that the socialization mechanisms described earlier allow for various forms of social adaptation. In particular, phenomena of ambivalence and transference are probably fairly important in social reform movements. In fact, it is frequently from the most privileged milieux that these movements and their leaders are derived, and it is often in the well-to-do classes that a kind of Populism develops. For the well-to-do, ambivalence with regard to their milieu and its principles — which may originate with an ambivalence towards their own parents and a revolt against the father — has been the foundation for many social changes. In addition, the attachment to a charismatic revolutionary leader — the leader whose power is based on exceptional personal gifts, or those judged as such — can result from a transference of identification with a parental figure.

On this subject, Everett Hagen[33] has sought to explain the development of the personality of the reformer and the innovator on the basis of certain difficulties that the adolescent may encounter in identifying with a father figure. Such difficulties often arise when the father is too authoritarian or too weak, or when he has accepted a very low and disparaged social status. The son may experience distress, insecurity, hostility or psychological conflict

---

33. Everett C. Hagen, *On the Theory of Social Change* (Homewood, Ill.: The Dorsey Press Inc., 1962).

which can be resolved by the transfer of his identification to a cause, a nation, a class or a leader.

In such cases, adaptation to the milieu takes on the form of a desire to change this milieu, to contribute new elements, and to exert a dynamic influence on it. It is very difficult to explain completely the appearance of strong personalities who have an impact on their environment. But at least, we can assert that such facts do not — or at least should not — appear to sociologists to be accidents in a socialization process which is designed to produce conformists. The theory of socialization provides us with enough factors that such phenomena can be seen to be natural and even foreseeable when social conditions are propitious.

A third conclusion emerges from this discussion: *socialization can have, as a natural result, a social adaptation which is expressed as much by the wish to change the milieu or to innovate as to conform.*

Pathological adaptation

Finally, it must be added that it is often the same elements of the socialization process which engender behaviour that society would term pathological — crime, prostitution, delinquency, suicide and so forth. As has already been said, this behaviour can sometimes result from the "normal" socialization process, given that the individual is educated in a milieu in which behaviour that is deplored by the total society is tolerated or expected. But in many cases, pathological behaviour can result from the same frustrations, distress and insecurity which develop in other cases the desire for social reform or innovation. Behind anti-social behaviour, there is the same rejection of society that is found in the reformer, the prophet or the saint. It is very difficult to interpret the influence or interplay of factors which determine or encourage one life orientation rather than another. This is a mysterious area that the human sciences have yet to explore. Colloquial language expresses it very well when it is said of a certain child that he will be a villain or a saint.

Thus, we can put forward, as a fourth and final conclusion, that *the frontier that separates innovating or dynamic social adaptation from what can be considered pathological maladaptation is often not very great, for the same socio-psychological mechanisms may lie at the origin of both of them.*

Conclusion

The study of socialization has enabled us to go still further in our analysis of the social nature of human action, or what Durkheim called social constraint. As we have seen, this constraint is less external than internal to the conscience: it is the internalized social obligation which has become a moral obligation; it is the perception of the Self by others, incorporated into one's own perception of the Self; it is the presence within the Self of the personalities, patterns of behaviour, ideals and sanctions which have been transmitted over centuries and generations.

But at the same time, socialization has revealed other aspects of human activity which, in a way, help to make constraint less rigid. In fact, we have seen that socialization does not necessarily result in conformity. On the one hand, societies, groups and collectivities differ in the rigour with which they prescribe and impose conformity to values and patterns of behaviour, and in the freedom or personal autonomy that they tolerate, permit, encourage and sometimes impose. The strictest conformity is not necessarily a requirement of "society"; it is the case only for certain specific societies, collectivities or groups. And the same can be said of conformity within deviance; certain deviant groups impose a stricter conformity to their norms than others.

On the other hand, any socialization process has the object of adapting the individual to his environment. But social adaptation does not necessarily mean conformity. Adaptation to a milieu can also mean the wish to innovate within this milieu or to modify it. The socialization process can encourage dynamic and innovating agents, anti-social individuals, as well as conformists and passive subjects.

Finally, on concluding Part One, which has been devoted to social action, it is appropriate to add that the socio-psychological importance and relevance of conformity must not be underestimated. Even within conformity, man seeks values, pursues personal aspirations, and obeys his conscience. Conformity can sometimes be the easy solution; but frequently it is also obedience to duty, the imposition of an effort against internal and external resistance, the movement of the will, and the transcending of the Self. The fact that ubiquitous society, even when the individual is alone, affords the necessary support, encouragement or ambition, does not remove from individual acts the essential virtue that distinguishes them from acts that the individual would perform if he obeyed only his primitive impulses and instinctive needs. An obligation can at the same time appear to be an aspiration; the two are intermingled and mutually supporting.

In short, normative social action now more clearly appears to be the product of numerous tensions among conformity, freedom and innovation, between impulses and ideals, between requirements of the individual personality and those of the social environment, between social obligation and personal aspiration.

Part Two
Social Organization

Chapter 6
Classifications and Typologies of Social Organization

In this second part of the book we will take an important step. In the preceding chapters, social action has been analyzed exclusively within the framework of various cultural elements (patterns of behaviour, values, symbols and ideologies) which condition, organize and initiate it. If we confined ourselves to this single perspective, we could be justifiably criticized for reducing all social reality to culture, and reducing sociology to culturalism. A certain anthropological approach, particularly that of B. Malinowski, has this shortcoming. While the culturalist approach can be an excellent starting point in sociology (although it is not the only one), it must lead to a larger view of social reality.

Thus, the time has come to enlarge our view of social action, by locating it within a wider context than that of culture alone — in other words, within the context of total social organization. First, let us see what this means; then we can present what we will call the two sociological traditions of the study of social organization.

Culture, Structure and Social Organization

Previously we have emphasized the necessity of distinguishing, within social action, the level of the behaviour of actors from that of social units or collectivities. Since the study of social organization takes place at the macrosociological level of social units, a second distinction becomes necessary between the *cultural elements* of a collectivity and what we will here call the *structural elements*.

Cultural elements

In order to understand the meaning of these terms, let us start with a concrete example, that of the university. The action of different individuals who comprise and participate in a university is guided by a *cultural* world which is characteristic of all universities and at the same time is specific to each of them. In the first place, these actors have certain values in common; they respect knowledge in its different forms, value research, and hold intellectual work in high esteem. While these ideals are not pursued to the same extent by each professor, student and university, they are upheld in every university. To be convinced of this, one need only imagine the reaction that would be provoked if the president of any university publicly praised ignorance, obscurantism, laziness and intellectual passiveness.

Concrete patterns of behaviour correspond to these university values. Some are valid for all actors (such as silence in the library) and others are attached to the different roles within the university. We can cite, for example, the ethical code, more implicit than explicit, which regulates the behaviour of the university professor. This code indicates the time that he must devote to the preparation of his classes, to his students, and to research. It guides the quality and objectivity of his teaching and research, the share of various administrative tasks that he must take on, his relationships with the head of his department, the deans, the president and the administrative and secretarial personnel; it affects his diligence and even his way of dressing. We can easily multiply the examples of the symbolism which characterizes university life. It is the place where knowledge is transmitted; here, the spoken and written language obviously occupy a privileged position in all the communication processes attached to the educational function of the university. But there is also a symbolism which is specific to university life and through which the relationships between the actors are structured — symbols of role, position, prestige and authority; symbols of participation in celebrations, anniversaries, ceremonies, or artistic, sports and political activities.

Structural elements

These cultural elements are only one aspect of the total life of the university. A concrete analysis of a university would reveal many other *non-cultural* elements. Let us enumerate the main ones:

1. First, the various actors are occupied every day with a great number of *activities* or *tasks* — attendance at courses, participation in seminars or laboratory work, library research, reception of visitors, upkeep of the building, looking after the books, typing, committee meetings and so on. All these activities are organized with reference to the particular functions of the university (teaching and research), and each contributes to them in its own way.

2. Each of these individual and collective activities contributes towards the functions and objectives of the university through *the division of labour,* which determines role and status. The allocation of tasks among all the actors means that some teach, others study, others administer, others handle secretarial work, others maintain the buildings and furniture and so forth.

3. The performance of these various tasks entails the creation of a great number of *networks of social relationships*. It is not necessary for every professor to know all the students, but there are some that he must know. A dean does not need to know the carpenters, locksmiths, janitors and painters who work within the university, but the manager of the physical plant must know each of them.

4. These networks of social relationships and the division of labour are formalized in *organized frameworks* called faculties, departments, sections, institutes or administrative services. There are other similar groupings of individuals in trade unions, associations, clubs, parties, movements and sometimes secret societies.

5. In addition to the formal framework in which the various actors are grouped together and work, the networks of social relationships entail the formation of *less formal groups* which are relatively spontaneous — groups of friends, cliques, unorganized groups for discussion, research or the preparation of exams.

6. Social relationships develop within the framework of various *hierarchies* which are formed by the ranking of levels of authority, title and status, degree and so forth. Thus, there are distinctions among professors, between junior and senior students, and among the categories or classes which are concerned with the hiring and promotion of non-teaching personnel.

7. Social relationships within the university may be characterized by collaboration, but they may also include a certain element

of competition between actors or groups of actors (between faculties, departments or institutes). They may also be relationships of opposition, conflict or almost overt war, for these too are *forms of social relationship*.

8. The activities of various university actors and the networks of relationships which are organized stem in part from different *physical or material conditions*. Whether the university has 2,000 or 30,000 students, whether the campus is large or small, whether the buildings are concentrated in the same place or spread out over a vast area, whether the buildings are new or decaying, whether they are located in the centre of a large town or in the country — all are important factors. Similarly, the work and social relationships of actors are conditioned by the arrangement of facilities — amphitheatres, rooms for lectures or seminars, laboratories, libraries, professors' offices, secretarial offices, recreational and cultural centres, dining rooms and residences. The furnishing of these buildings also is significant, as is the quantity and quality of the material objects which are used by the actors in their various activities — books, documents, laboratory equipment, audiovisual aids and so forth.

9. The university has *financial requirements* and must count on particular sources of finance. These may be various — state grants, students' fees or endowments. The activities of the actors will be affected by the source and the extent of the financial resources of the university, by whether the university is poor or richly endowed, and by whether its development is encouraged or restrained.

10. The university is also located within time, which gives it its *age*. Its organization and activities can vary according to whether it is a new university, or one that is both rich in and burdened with tradition.

11. Finally, the *environment* within which it exists will condition the life of a university. This can vary according to whether the university is in an industrialized country or in a young developing nation, whether it is surrounded by other university institutions or is isolated, whether it exists within a totalitarian political regime or a democratic one.

Structure and culture

All these aspects of university life which specify, condition, determine or enclose the social action of actors cannot be included in what is identified as university culture. Generally, they can be assembled under the heading *the structural elements of social organization*. In contrast to the abundance of definitions of culture to be found in sociology and anthropology, it is very difficult to find a satisfactory definition of structural elements. Usually writers attempt to define the term by means of a fairly extensive list, as we have just done, and as the Canadian sociologist Fernand Dumont also does in the following passage:

> Sociology as well as anthropology constantly circle around the fundamental distinction between *structure* and *culture* without arriving at any precise definitions. On the one hand, from the perspective of structure, social reality is considered in its objective form, with emphasis on demographic and economic data, on certain aspects of social organization (those, for example, which are translated by roles and status), and on certain groupings which *appear* to impose themselves immediately on the perception (such as nations or classes). On the other hand, from the perspective of the various conceptions of culture, social reality is presented as a spiritual configuration or a "collective consciousness," as a mental world in which individuals participate and by which they are defined.[1]

It should be noted that these structural elements can be classified in two distinct sub-groups: the *morphological* elements, and the elements which are *strictly social*. Emile Durkheim and his disciples, particularly Marcel Mauss and Maurice Halbwachs, used the expression *social morphology* or *morphological substratum* to designate "the mass of individuals who form the society, the way in which they are arranged on the land, the nature and the configuration of things of all kinds which affect collective relationships."[2] Thus, the morphological elements of the university would be those which were enumerated earlier in points 8 and 9, and also in part of 11. The strictly social elements are all the forms of arrangement of social relationships in groupings, organizations, associations, hierarchies and networks of collaboration, competition, conflict and so forth.

---

1. Fernand Dumont, "Notes sur l'analyse des idéologies," p. 157. Emphasis in the original.
2. Note by Emile Durkheim in *L'année sociologique* 2 (1897-1898): 520.

The definition of social organization

All the elements that we have called structural are part of the collective life of the university and contribute towards its organization in close liaison with the cultural elements. The two constantly interact. Culture reflects the structural elements; it is guided by them in the creation of models, symbols and sanctions and in the identification of the normative content of roles. To a certain extent, the structural elements follow cultural representations, values, ideologies and symbols; at the same time they condition, resist or contradict the cultural pattern. Thus, if it is necessary for the purposes of analysis to know how to distinguish between cultural and structural elements, for the purposes of synthesis it is necessary also to be able to discern their interpenetrations and interactions — for it is from the synthesis of the cultural and structural elements that the *social organization* of a collectivity is derived. We can now define social organization as *the total arrangement of all the elements which serve to structure social action into a whole which has an image or a particular form which is different from its constituent parts and also different from other possible arrangements.*

It therefore can be said of the university (in general) that it has a social organization which distinguishes it from other types of arrangements of social action (a factory, a family, a court of justice). Similarly, a particular university (Harvard University, the University of London, the University of Toronto) has a social organization which characterizes it and gives it its own identity which is distinct from that of other universities.

The example that has been used is perhaps particularly suitable for illustrating the distinction between cultural and structural elements and their synthesis in a social organization. But the same analytical procedure and the same theoretical framework could be applied to any other collectivity — a factory, town, region, social class, profession, family, kinship system, or total society. Each is a social organization, in the sense defined above, in that within it are intertwined structural and cultural elements.

As we have expressed it here, social organization is *the most complete analytical context in which social action exists* for any collectivity of social actors. In effect, social organization results from the entire range of social action within a given collectivity and takes into account all the structural and cultural elements, all the variables and all the factors which determine, organize, guide and initiate the action of each of its members.

In this part of the book we will concentrate on the study of social organization. This amounts to saying that we have reached the macrosociological level of analysis. But in order to focus our analysis even more securely at this level, in particular we will examine the way in which sociology has approached the study of the *social organization of total societies.* Being the most complete concrete collectivities, total societies permit the most general sociological analysis. In addition, if we were to study the social organization of other more limited collectivities (a working environment, a family, a bureaucratic organization), we would have to cover a vast and extremely diversified area.

A Note on Semantics

Before we embark on this study, we should offer a comment on semantics. It is an amusing, sometimes distressing and always paradoxical fact that sociologists and anthropologists hardly ever use the same linguistic symbols; they have the sad reputation of not agreeing on terms. At the macrosociological level the vocabulary becomes most uncertain. Terms are used interchangeably, or they lack precise definition and confusion reigns.

As a result, we must resort to what the linguist R. Jakobson calls the metalinguistic function of language, which arises whenever "the sender and/or receiver find it necessary to verify that they are using the same code."[3] In other words, before we go any further, we will have to explain the terminology we are using.

Social types

Durkheim used the expression *social types* to designate what we call social organization, particularly in the case of total societies.[4] M. Steinmetz followed his example,[5] but the expression was not

---

3. Quoted by Henri Lefebvre, *Le langage et la société* (Paris: Gallimard, 1966), p. 100.
4. Specifically in Emile Durkheim, *The Division of Labour in Society*, trans. George Simpson (London: The Free Press of Glencoe and Collier-Macmillan Limited, 1964); and Durkheim, *The Rules of Sociological Method*.
5. M. Steinmetz, "Classification des types sociaux," *L'année sociologique* 3 (1898-1899): 43-147.

widely used. It is an ambiguous phrase, for it is too closely linked to the tradition of typologies (this will be discussed later).

Social structure

Many writers refer to social organization as social structure.[6] This expression is widely used in contemporary sociology and anthropology, but it is no less ambiguous than the preceding one. In a later chapter, we will see the extent to which the idea of structure is discussed, today more than ever before. For example, we have talked of structural elements, as distinguished from cultural elements, of a collectivity. Fernand Dumont distinguishes between structure and culture; and the American sociologist Seymour Lipset contrasts and compares structural conditions and cultural factors in his explanation of economic development.[7] Since we have already used the term *structure* in this context, and since in previous chapters we have emphasized the structured nature of social action, to give it a third meaning would simply risk confusion.

Social organization

The term *social organization* that we have adopted also has its drawbacks; for *organization* is now used in sociology with another precise meaning — to designate the formal bureaucratic arrangement of roles designed to pursue defined functions. Thus, it could be said that the university is a bureaucratic organization in the same sense that an industrial firm, a business office, the federal government, a hospital and the Army are bureaucratic organizations. In general, however, organization is used in this latter context and social organization in the context defined earlier, thus reducing the risk of confusion. One other drawback of the term is that it has had a rather troubled history in English anthropology.

In spite of these difficulties, there is some solid support for our use of the phrase. In *A Dictionary of the Social Sciences*, Robert Faris defines social organization as follows: "In social science us-

---

6. This is certainly the case with Raymond Firth in his article "Social Organization and Social Change," *Journal of the Royal Anthropological Institute* 84 (1954): 9, and in his book *Elements of Social Organization* (Boston: Beacon Press, 1963), pp. 28-40.

7. Lipset, "Values, Education and Entrepreneurship" in Lipset and Solari, eds., *Elites in Latin America*, chap. 1.

age, *social organization* denotes a relatively stable set of functioning interrelations among component parts (persons or groups)
which results in characteristics not present in the components and
produces an entity *sui generis.*"[8] This definition is sufficiently similar to ours to convince us that we are employing the expression
with a generally accepted meaning.

Social forms

Finally, we might have used the expression *social forms* to designate social organization. The German sociologist Georg Simmel
popularized this term, which he defined to mean "the forms that
affect the groups of men who are united in order to live beside
each other, for each other or with each other."[9]

But Simmel had the unfortunate idea of contrasting "the matter
of social life" with the forms of social life — a distinction from
which he could not later disentangle himself, and which became a
flaw in his sociological theory. Contemporary writers sometimes
use Simmel's phrase to designate social organization.[10] But in fact,
it is so rarely employed that for us to use it would be almost a form
of deviance!

A Dual Tradition in
the Study of the Social
Organization of Societies

Having resolved the semantic problem, we can directly begin our
discussion of the sociology of social organization.

When an attempt is made to understand the way in which sociology has approached the study of the social organization of total.
societies, two traditions can easily be discerned. The first will be
called *classificatory*, the second *analytical*.

---

8. Gould and Kolb, eds., *A Dictionary of the Social Sciences*, p. 661.
9. Georg Simmel, "Comment les formes sociales se maintiennent," *L'année sociologique* 1 (1896-1897): 72.
10. For example, E. Franklin Frazier, "The Impact of Colonialism on African
    Social Forms and Personality" in Calvin W. Stillman, ed., *Africa in the Mod-
    ern World* (Chicago: University of Chicago Press, 1955), pp. 70-96.

The two traditions

In the *classificatory tradition*, sociology seeks to identify the common as well as the different traits that can be observed in comparing concrete, historical societies. The aim of this approach is to arrive at a typology or system of classification which will enable us to reduce the multiplicity and variety of existing societies to a few large categories.

Sociology of the *analytical tradition* attempts to elaborate a conceptual and theoretical schema which would account for the organization of society, its functioning, the arrangement of its different parts, its internal coherence, its divisions and contradictions, its progress and decline. The proposed object of this approach is to construct a theoretical model which will enable us to analyze society, as a whole and in part, in order to understand and explain its organization and change.

Their common goal of universality

This dual tradition characterizes scientific work in almost every field. All scientific research consists of a mental reconstruction of reality, with the goal of discovering the order that underlies the apparent diversity and disparity of observed phenomena. The scholar comes to perceive this hidden order, first by reducing the great number of phenomena to a few classes, formed on the basis of certain criteria according to which the phenomena resemble or differ from each other. Such a classification not only allows him to reduce the totality of facts or phenomena to a manipulatable number of units, but also places each fact in the total context of which it is a part. Second, the researcher reconstructs the order underlying phenomena by elaborating an abstract model which is logically coherent, and which translates into general propositions the principles of organization and the movement of the observed phenomena.

Thus, classification and theoretical analysis both have *universality* as their goal, but they approach it in two different ways. The first seeks to construct a limited number of classes into which all the observed facts can be inserted; the second tries to construct a theoretical framework which accounts for all phenomena. This aim of universality is found in sociology, as in all the other sciences, and it underlies the two traditions.

It is important to emphasize that these two traditions — in sociology as in other sciences — are not independent of each other. Attempts to classify societies have helped to formulate the pertinent questions to which analytical theory must find an answer; in addition, advances made by the analytical tradition have led to the revision and refinement of former classifications, notably the criteria used in the elaboration of typologies. We will see that many writers are linked to one tradition or the other, depending on the part of their work that we are considering.

We will devote this chapter and the next to the study of the classifications of societies that have been suggested by some authors. Then, in Chapters 8 and 9, we will consider the analytical theories in sociology.

Two Problems in the Classification of Societies

To clarify the subsequent discussion, we should begin by pointing out that the classification of societies poses two major problems. The first is that of the criterion or criteria used to group and distinguish societies; the second is the evolutionary dimension in typologies.

The problems of criteria

What are the characteristics or elements of societies which are sufficiently dominant or fundamental that they can serve as principles of classification and give such classification validity and universal significance? This question has initiated many debates in sociology. Researchers have not agreed on the reply, and it is from this disagreement that the basic differences between sociologists or schools of sociology arise. Unfortunately it cannot be said that contemporary sociology has achieved unanimity on the subject, even if the problem is discussed less enthusiastically today than it was in the early days of the discipline. As a result, a number of classifications of societies can be found in sociology, each based on a different criterion.

While the typologies are numerous, however, they are not as dissimilar as one might expect. It is possible to select a few of the most representative and best-known classifications — as will be done here — in order to indicate the main trends in this area of sociology from its beginning to the present. And it will be seen that in spite of all differences, there is a certain amount of unanimity concerning the main types of societies.

The problem of evolution

The second problem is the evolutionary or historical factor which is part of any classification of societies. In fact, as soon as we compare societies in order to grasp their common and contrasting traits, we are obliged to separate them according to their degree of development, to organize them according to whether they are more or less advanced or developed, or according to the type of development that is characteristic of them. Thus, all comparative sociology ultimately postulates a judgement on the level of advancement of different societies, and arranges them according to a certain order of development. As Talcott Parsons notes, the culture and social organization of a central Australian tribe and those of the Soviet Union cannot be considered equal from every point of view. Independent of any value judgement of the human or moral quality of these two societies, one must conclude that the second is more "advanced" than the first, from various points of view.[11] Therefore, the criteria used to classify societies are at the same time used to judge their degree of "advancement." It can be better understood now why we said earlier that the basic differences among sociologists arise over this point.

Comparative sociology is inevitably evolutionary — it seeks to retrace the various successive steps of the development of societies from the most ancient or primitive stages up to the most advanced. Because of this, sociology is linked with anthropology, where research has been concerned mainly with less advanced societies. Sociology is also dependent on history for its knowledge of ancient societies and of the past of contemporary societies.

After enjoying great popularity and being widely adopted in the social sciences at the end of the nineteenth century and the beginning of the twentieth, evolutionism was later discredited. At the same time, interest in comparative sociology diminshed and was replaced by an emphasis on more analytical sociology. This accounts for the fact that most of the writers whose works will be studied in this chapter belong to earlier periods. Over the past few

---

11. Talcott Parsons, *Societies: Evolutionary and Comparative Perspectives* (Englewood Cliffs, N.J.: Prentice-Hall, Inc., 1966), p. 110.

years, however, there has been a renewed interest in evolutionism, particularly in anthropology and now in sociology. As we shall see later, this neo-evolutionism has adopted certain theses of the first evolutionists and modified them. At the same time interest in comparative sociology has revived, and further attempts have been made to elaborate typologies of total societies or certain parts of societies.

We will now present a few classifications of societies according to the criteria used by different writers in making comparisons and in determining their stage of social development. Two types of criteria employed by sociologists can be distinguished. Some criteria are external to the social organization itself, such as the state of knowledge or working techniques, or perhaps relate to only part of it, such as the power structure or the economy. Other criteria are concerned directly with the characteristics of the social organization itself — for example, its degree of simplicity or complexity.

For clarity of presentation, we will adopt this distinction in the following discussion.

Criteria External to the Social Organization and Partial Criteria

Auguste Comte: The State of Knowledge

Auguste Comte (1798–1857) is generally considered the father of sociology. He was the first to call it by this name (after first naming it *social physics*); but more important, he developed the first systematic theory of the subject. His two major works in this regard are *Cours de philosophie positive* (*Positive Philosophy*), which he published in six volumes between 1830 and 1842, and his famous *Discours sur l'esprit positif* (*A Discourse on the Positive Spirit*).

Three basic principles

Three basic principles underlie and explain Comte's sociology. First, according to Comte, it is no more possible to understand and explain a particular social phenomenon without placing it within the total social context to which it belongs, than it is possible in biology to explain an organ and its functions without considering them in relation to the total organism. This principle of *the primacy of the whole over the parts* applies to the analysis of what Comte calls "the spontaneous order of human societies," which is the subject matter of "static sociology." It also applies — and this is what interests us particularly at this point — to historical societies and to their development over time, which is the subject matter of "dynamic sociology." In fact, the society of a given period can be understood and explained only in relation to its history, or better still in relation to the history of the whole of humanity. Thus, Comte's sociology is necessarily comparative sociology whose general framework is universal history.

The second principle maintains that the *progress of knowledge* is the main guiding force of history. Man acts according to the knowledge that is available to him; his relationships with the world and with other men depend on what he knows of nature and society. One cannot quite say that ideas guide the world; rather, the dominant element of history is knowledge, or more precisely forms of knowledge. While we cannot speak of the determinism of knowledge in Comte's sociology, he does assert that there is a necessary coherence — necessary, because it is logical — between the state of knowledge and the social organization. Later we will see why and how this may be so.

Finally, the third principle is that *man is the same everywhere and in every period*, because of his biological make-up and particularly because of his cerebral system. Thus, one must expect that every society will develop in the same way and in the same direction, and that humanity as a whole will move towards the same goal of a more advanced society.

The law of the three states

Keeping these three principles in mind, we can begin to understand the classification of societies that Comte established. An historical law that he said he had discovered provides the clue: this is *the law of the three states,* according to which the progress of human knowledge is accomplished through three states or stages:

1. In *the theological state,* man explains things and events by attributing either to the things themselves, or to supernatural and invisible forces or beings, his own nature, will, feelings, passions and so forth. When man attributes life and action to things, his state of mind is called fetishist; this is the initial phase of the theological state. Then man confers certain traits of human nature (virtues, vices, motivations) on supernatural powers, giving rise to polytheism and monotheism successively.

2. In *the metaphysical state,* man calls on abstract entities or ideals to explain the nature of things and the cause of events. Because these abstract entities are treated as real agents or persons, Comte said, they replace the supernatural powers of the theological stage.

3. In *the positive state,* through observation and reasoning, man seeks to grasp the necessary relationships between things and events and to explain them through the formulation of laws. This state differs fundamentally from the two preceding ones — first, in that man becomes more modest and renounces knowledge of the intimate nature of things and of first and final causes; and second, in that knowledge becomes effective in assuring man's mastery and control of the universe. To Comte, the positive state is obviously the superior stage which ultimately must be achieved by the individual, by science, and by all humanity.

The verification of this law

The sequential emergence of the three states can be verified in two ways: first, in the individual development of each person; and second, in the history of science. "Now does not each of us," wrote Comte, "in contemplating his own history, recollect that he has been successively — as regards the most important ideas — a *theologian* in his childhood, a *metaphysician* in his youth, and a *natural philosopher* in manhood?"[12] But if each person can today accede to the positive state, that of the natural philosopher, it is because in our century knowledge has become increasingly positive as a result of the progress of science. Formerly the adult could be

---

12. Auguste Comte, *Cours de philosophie positive,* 3rd edition (Paris: J. B. Baillière et Fils, 1869), vol. 1, p. 11.

theologian or a metaphysician only according to the state of knowledge current in the period when he lived.

It is therefore mainly in the history of science that the successive development of the three states can be verified. The evolution of science shows us, in fact, that each discipline has achieved maturity by detaching itself progressively from theological and metaphysical considerations in order to become positive. Not all the sciences, however, have experienced this progress at the same rate and at the same time. The differences in their development can be explained by the fact that those sciences which are concerned with "the most general phenomena or the most simple, which are necessarily the most foreign to man"[13] have been able to achieve the positive state first. From this observation, Comte derives a hierarchy of sciences based on three criteria: the degree of complexity of the phenomena studied, the degree to which their subject matter is external to man, and the point in time when they achieve the positive state. Mathematics was the first science to detach itself from theological and metaphysical thought in order to become positive; there followed, successively, astronomy, physics, chemistry and biology.

The need for a new science: sociology

This hierarchy of sciences reveals that positive knowledge was first concerned with objects that were furthest away from man (numbers, stars) and then gradually approached man, through chemistry and particularly through biology. In order to complete the table of sciences, it remained to create a positive science of man, of human history and society — that is, a social physics or sociology. The absence of this science explains social anarchy; for although man now knows nature sufficiently to dominate and control it, he still represents society and history in a theological and metaphysical context. Positive reason must triumph over this last bastion of theology and metaphysics — the knowledge of man and society — for this is the only way to ensure that the progress of human history will be based no longer on fiction and imagination (both characteristic of the theological and metaphysical states), but on scientific knowledge of social laws, on prediction, and on efficient action. Through sociology, Comte suggested the application to social phenomena of the adage "know in order to predict;

---

13. *Ibid.*, vol. 1, p. 69.

predict in order to act" to ensure the mastery of man over nature.

For Auguste Comte, these are the theoretical and practical foundations of the new science of societies. Sociology, then, has a dual purpose: it will contribute to the progress of knowledge by completing the table of positive sciences, and it will facilitate the progress of society and all humanity to the positive state. To Comte, sociology is both knowledge and action; more precisely, it is action because it is knowledge. In fact, the organization and history of present society is still guided by the theological or metaphysical image men have of it. Since — in the absence of any positive or scientific knowledge of society and its history — men mold, organize and govern society according to this image, disorder, crises and a permanent state of social anarchy result. It is the responsibility of sociology to provide, through a more exact knowledge of the mechanisms of society and the meaning of history, the means by which man can take charge of his destiny.

This appears all the more certain to Comte because past history teaches us that a particular type of society is linked to each stage of knowledge. *The evolution of societies, like the evolution of individuals and knowledge, obeys the law of the three states*. Because this law summarizes the progress of knowledge, it is the great law of history. From this premise, Comte distinguishes three main types of society which correspond to the three states of knowledge.

The military society

When knowledge was predominantly theological, society was of the *military* type. In fact, there was a great affinity between the two, for both were fundamentally authoritarian and hierarchically unified. Moreover, from the time of earliest civilization and for centuries after, political leaders were invested with a sacred and even priestly character, which ensured for both them and the clergy absolute and total power. It is true that in the cases where the civil and religious authorities were distinct, they were often in conflict; but even so, they always supported each other.

Being by nature anti-scientific, military–religious society was necessarily agricultural and based on the ownership and exploitation of land. The family was the central unit and the main economic institution. Through it were transmitted not only the ownership of goods, but also political and priestly power.

A strongly controlled society was necessary when men first drew together in collective groups, in order to establish and maintain social order, to assist the transition from a nomadic way of life to the cultivation of the earth, to guarantee the security of individuals and communities, and to organize and structure community life. Military society responded to these needs and taught men to discipline themselves, so that eventually they were able to develop the rudiments of civilization.

The society of jurists

The society of jurists corresponded to the metaphysical state of knowledge. It was characterized by a clear distinction between spiritual and temporal power, and by the progressive independence of the latter. The weakening of religious authority led to an increase in the powers of civil authority. The concepts of State and Fatherland became predominant, and the unity that had been assured by religious authority disintegrated. Gradually two groups of men emerged who strongly contributed to the definition and extension of the functions and power of the State: these were ministers, to whom kings must delegate an increasing part of their authority; and diplomats, who established and manipulated relationships between States. Ministers and diplomats acquired the powers formerly held by generals, who subsequently were forced to acknowledge civil authority.

This type of society was unique in that it represented a "critical age." In the realm of knowledge, the metaphysical state is a transitory stage, a critical phase, which questions established religious prejudices, rejects them, and thus prepares for the positive state. The positive state cannot emerge without the existence of this critical phase.

The same holds true for social evolution. The society of jurists served to dissolve the sovereign authority and unity of the theocratic society; it was a period of disorganization, marked by crises and revolutions. But all this was necessary, for the positive society could not have immediately followed the military society, which was fundamentally religious, anti-scientific and authoritarian. In Western history, the critical period appeared in the fourteenth century and lasted five centuries, leading up to the French revolution, parliamentarianism and the emergence of modern nations.

Industrial society

The transition society of jurists laid the foundation for the third stage, which humanity has now entered — *the industrial society*. This corresponds to the positive state of knowledge. The positive sciences applied to the natural order are in the process of transforming working conditions with the appearance of industry. According to Comte, industry is "destined, with the inspiration of science, to develop the rational action of humanity on the external world."[14] In a way, industry is the spearhead of the positive mentality. Through industry and through the teaching of the positive sciences, the positive mentality will spread throughout society, stimulating a radical transformation of social organization and attitudes.

To Comte, then, industrial society is only in its initial stages. But the main features it will develop are already discernible:

1. The scientific mentality will dominate the industrial society. The progress of positive thought is inescapable; but it will occur at the expense of theological and metaphysical thought, which are destined to disappear. On this subject, Raymond Aron notes:

> Auguste Comte's guiding ideas of his youth were not his alone. From the climate of his time, he gained the conviction that theological thought belonged to the past, that God was dead (to use Nietzsche's formula) and that scientific thought would henceforth dominate the intelligence of modern men.[15]

2. Industry is the first concrete and social manifestation of the scientific spirit, but it will also be the heart or kernel of industrial society. Military society was based on the family unit, the society of jurists on the nation, but industrial society will be based on industry and industrial production.

3. The increase in industrial production will be effected by a concentration of the working masses around factories and in the towns. The fate of these working masses, who are today the proletariat, will improve with the growth of resources and education.

4. Social inequality is inherent in the structure of society: riches and power are necessarily in the hands of a small group of people. Thus, private property will not disappear, but will remain the motive force of the industrial economy. Power will be profoundly transformed. The feudal structure and the monarchy, vestiges of the military and theocratic society, are destined to disappear; the State of the jurists and parliamentarianism also will end shortly.

---

14. *Ibid.*, vol. 6, p. 270.
15. Raymond Aron, *Main Currents in Sociological Thought*, trans. Richard Howard and Helen Weaver (London: Penguin Books, 1965), p. 72.

Two new groups will accede to power: the industrialists and their engineers, who will organize and manage industry and the work world; and scholars, mainly sociologists (that is, social scientists), who will inherit political power and take responsibility for the organization of society.

5. The new industrial society will have to pass through crises and revolutions, but this will be a transitory phase. International and social peace will progress as industry develops, as the scientific or positive spirit spreads, and as the actions of scholars and sociologists make their impact on the organization and history of societies.

6. If, at the beginning, industrial society is experiencing a period of social troubles, it is because it suffers from an excess of specialization which gives rise to divisions and struggles between various interest groups (employers and employees, producers and consumers). Specialization will dwindle with technical progress and with improvements in the organization of work and society. But it is rather ignorance and the absence of social morals which are at the source of the present conflicts. Instructed in the positive sciences, the masses will understand and accept the requirements of social life and history. It is therefore the responsibility of the positive sciences, particularly sociology, to create a new moral code, based no longer on God or abstract ideas, but on respect for the social community and a better knowledge of the function of each person and each group for the well-being of the collectivity. Because of this new moral social code, industrial society will no longer have wars and revolution will erupt less frequently. At the end of his life, however, Comte came to the conclusion that the social moral code needed religious support; thus he initiated a new religion, without a God, which would be exclusively secular and based on the cult of humanity.

7. Finally, industrial society will result in the demise of large nations, which stemmed from the military period and were the product of the actions of diplomats and ministers. These great countries will split up into a multitude of small countries, each comprised of no more than a few million people. The new collectivities will be founded, not on the outdated concept of the nation, but on actual industrial production.

Comte's social thought

Clearly the development of industrial society that Comte believed he could discern at the beginning of the nineteenth century was basically different from that which was predicted by the socialists of his time — Saint-Simon, Proudhon, Marx and Engels. Comte did not believe that the disappearance of private property was a scientifically valid and demonstrable concept; nor did he admit that this disappearance could entail the formation of an egalitarian society. But Comte was by no means a liberal; he did not share the optimism of economists, who attributed providential and magical virtues to free competition.

In fact, Comte was already "the organization man." He wrote of the bureaucratization of industrial society; he foresaw the growing role of the technocrats of industry and politics; and more important, he took up the cause of a society based on the rationality of its planners and organizers. Comte's industrial society is definitely the Plan.

The influence of Comte's sociology

In contrast to the work of socialist sociologists, Comte's writings are not linked to an ideological and militant current of thought. Nonetheless, his influence is far from negligible. Comte was the first to present and systematize a scientific sociological framework. Perhaps his sociology was too strongly influenced by the model of the natural sciences and by philosophy, helping to make it a sociology of humanity rather than one of concrete societies; and perhaps he attributed excessive social functions to sociology. But he saw very clearly that the technical and scientific mentality would overflow from the natural sciences to the social sciences, and that industrial society would begin to make major demands on these social sciences.

Moreover, Comte was the first sociologist to analyze industrial society in depth. He did not consider it to be mainly a bourgeois or capitalist society, as did the socialist sociologists; rather, he sought to understand industrial society in itself and to outline its future. From this point of view, a long uninterrupted tradition links Comte to contemporary sociology.

As to Comte's view of the future development of industrial society, history has not always proved him right. He did not sufficiently appreciate the chances for the survival of national ideologies; he was not able to measure the role that the State was going to play; he exaggerated the historical and moral significance of education; and finally, industrial society has not brought the peace that he anticipated. He did, however, foresee the impact of the technical and scientific spirit on the mentality and social or-

ganization of industrial society; he was able to predict the secularization of industrial society; he understood the organizing tendencies inherent in this type of society; and he foresaw the role that
the technocrats occupy within it today. Finally, as will be seen in
the following pages, the contrast between military and industrial
society that Comte described has been echoed by many in sociology and is still found in various forms in contemporary writing.

Marx and Engels:
Relations of Production

Karl Marx (1818–1883) and Friedrich Engels (1820–1895) — it is
important to associate the two collaborators — were contemporaries of Auguste Comte. Like him, they were theoreticians
and reformers; like him, they suggested an interpretation of contemporary society and attempted to predict the next stages of its
history. But for the most part, the similarities end here. Their theories of society diverge considerably from Comte's.

Marx and Engels: sociologists?

The place given here to Marx and Engels in sociological thought
may be considered surprising. It is true that their contribution to
sociology is not explicitly recognized by the majority of sociologists. Too many prejudices and stereotypes — as much on the part
of Marxists as on that of non-Marxists — are still attached to
Marx's work and obscure its interpretation. For our part, we agree
with the judgement of the Belgian sociologist Henri Janne:

> Some people, even though they deny it — mainly those
> who proclaim that Marxism is a scientific method —
> practise Marxism as a faith. For them, Marx, Engels
> and Lenin are always right and in a way have foreseen
> everything. . . . But for others — and this includes the
> pretentious bureaucrats of "operational" sociology —
> Marxism is outdated. It belongs to the era of the great
> systems of social philosophy. This attitude is just as ex-
> cessive as the first. Marx's superiority over the other
> great systems of the nineteenth century resides in the
> fact that his dialectic prefigures, for the most part
> correctly, the functionalist approach in sociology.

Thus, he did not build a social philosophy, but rather the first macrosociological system which was worthy of the name.... A little sociology makes one despise Marxism; a lot brings one nearer to it.[16]

Georges Gurvitch is even more explicit:

Marx was the greatest and the least dogmatic of all the founders of sociology. And this in spite of all the philosophical or political dogmatisms that one wrongly believes can be derived from him.... Marx was first and foremost a sociologist, and it is sociology which unifies his work.... *Das Kapital* — which struggles against the prejudices of abstract economic man, against the "fetishism" of goods and capital, against the universal "economic laws" of which the classical economists spoke — can be understood as a scientific work only if it is considered as *economic sociology*, revealing that economic phenomena, economic activities and economic categories lose their meaning and their character when they are separated from the whole of society, from its structure, from the nature of its structure, from "the total social phenomenon", or from "the whole man." From this point of view, *to assert that Marx reduced all social life to economic life is basically false*, for he did exactly the opposite; he revealed that economic life is only an integral part of social life, and that our image of what goes on in economic life is falsified to the extent that we do not realize that society and the men who participate in it are hidden under capital, goods, value, price and the distribution of goods.... The interest of Marx's emphasis on total man, total society and total action does not reside in his humanist philosophy, *but in his search for a new dimension*, neglected by the philosophers and the economists — this is social reality, taken at all its vertical levels whose moving units are studied and classified by sociology.[17]

16. Henri Janne, "La technique et le système social" in Henri Janne et al., *Technique, développement économique et technocratie* (Brussels: Université libre de Bruxelles, 1963), pp. 75-76.
17. Georges Gurvitch, "La sociologie de Marx," *La vocation actuelle*, vol. 2, chap. 12, pp. 220, 222, 224 and 225. Emphasis in the original. It should be

Being more circumspect than Gurvitch, Henri Lefebvre writes: "For many reasons . . . *Marx is not a sociologist, but there is sociology in Marxism.*"[18] Lefebvre is sensitive to the fact that Marx's work goes beyond the specialized and thus necessarily narrow framework of various modern social sciences — political science, political economy, sociology, social psychology and anthropology. Marx approached social reality in a total way which was simultaneously historical, economic, political and sociological. Thus, Lefebvre refuses to identify Marx's work with any one of these fields. But this does not prevent him from recognizing, along with Gurvitch and Janne, that Marx and Engels made an important contribution to contemporary sociology.

Two texts from Marx

In order to analyze the sociological thought of Marx and Engels, we will start with two texts from Marx in which he briefly summarizes the bases of their sociology. The first, which is often cited, is taken from the Foreword that Marx wrote for his work called *A Contribution to the Critique of Political Economy*:

In the social production which men carry on they enter into definite relations that are indispensable and independent of their will: these relations of production correspond to a definite stage of development of their material forces of production. The sum total of these relations of production constitutes the economic structure of society — the real foundation on which rises a legal and political superstructure and to which correspond definite forms of social consciousness. The mode of production in material life determines the social, political and intellectual life processes in general. It is not the consciousness of men that determines their being, but, on the contrary, their social being that determines their consciousness. At a certain stage of their development, the material forces of production in society come into conflict with the existing relations of production, or — what is but a legal expression for the

noted that this chapter by Gurvitch remains undoubtedly the most complete analysis of Marx's sociology.

18. Henri Lefebvre, *The Sociology of Marx*, trans. Norbert Guterman (New York: Pantheon Books, 1968). Emphasis in the original.

same thing — with the property relations within which they have been at work before. From forms of development of the forces of production these relations turn into their fetters. Then begins an epoch of social revolution. With the change of the economic foundation the entire immense superstructure is more or less rapidly transformed. . . . In broad outlines, we can designate the Asiatic, the ancient, the feudal, and the modern bourgeois modes of production as so many epochs in the progress of the economic formation of society.[19]

In the second text, Marx takes up certain ideas from the first text and adds others. This quotation, taken from an article that Marx published in 1849 under the title *Wage-Labour and Capital*, is perhaps simpler and clearer:

In production, men stand in relation not only to nature but to each other. They only produce by working together in a certain way, and mutually exchanging their activities. In order to produce, they mutually enter into certain relations and conditions, and only within the limits of these social relations and conditions does their influence affect nature and production become possible.

These social relations between the producers, and the conditions under which they exchange their activities and take part in the collective act of production, will naturally vary according to the character of the means of production. With the invention of fire-arms the whole internal organization of the army was necessarily altered, the conditions changed under which individuals compose an army and work as an army, and the relation of different armies to one another was also changed.

The social relations within which individuals produce, *the social relations of production, thus change, transform themselves with the change and development of the material means of production, the forces of production. The relations of production in their totality constitute that which we call social rela-*

19. Karl Marx, *Selected Works*, ed. V. Adoratsky (London: Lawrence and Wishart Ltd., 1942), pp. 356-57.

tions, or society. Moreover, a society founded upon a definite stage of historic development is a society with a peculiar, distinctive character. *Ancient* society, *feudal* society, *bourgeois* society are totalities of conditions of production, each of which signifies a particular stage of development in the history of mankind.[20]

Forces of production and relations of production

From these extracts it is clear that Marx and Engels rejected the intellectualism of traditional philosophy and wished to find a more realistic and objective perspective on man, society and history. Man appears to them, first of all, as a "being with needs" — the elementary needs for food, clothing and shelter, and the more sophisticated need for comfort. The satisfaction of these needs involves man in a struggle with nature and with the forces of nature, obliging him to develop working techniques and to elaborate forms of organization for collective work. These material requirements of human existence, which the philosophers have always neglected, become the first and fundamental fact for Marx and Engels. It is in fact by and through this *praxis*, this material action on nature and on himself, that man develops his consciousness, his knowledge and his world view; it is on the basis of this praxis that all social and political organization is erected; and it is this praxis that clarifies the history of societies and humanity. From this stems the expression *historical materialism* which has been employed to designate the thought of Marx and Engels — an expression that they themselves did not use.

Thus, it could be said that the sociology of Marx and Engels is based entirely on the idea that the production of goods necessary to the satisfaction of needs is the main activity of man and the basis of all social life. The conditions under which this production takes place determine the organization of societies and influence their history.

The production of goods is first of all conditioned by what Marx and Engels called the forces of production, which include natural resources, the knowledge and techniques used in

---

20. Karl Marx, *Wage-Labour and Capital*, trans. Florence Baldwin (London: Communist Party of Great Britain, 1925), pp. 16-17. Emphasis in the translation.

production, and all forms of labour organization. In Raymond Aron's words, this is "the capacity of a given society to produce."[21] Productive capacity has developed over time; it has grown because of scientific and technological knowledge. But history shows us that a given stage in the development of forces of production corresponds with a specific type of "relations of production," which are all the relations established between men with a view to production. More precisely, the relations of production are essentially, for Marx and Engels, relations of ownership, or working relationships between owners and non-owners of the forces of production, betweens exploiters and exploited, or between the dominant and the dominated classes. They are not the product of either the will of individuals or a social contract; but they are "necessary" because they are basically determined by the material conditions of production.

The class struggle

The relations of production, which as a whole form the economic structure of a society, are by their very nature contradictory or conflicting relationships between groups with opposite interests. These conflicting relationships are crystallized and expressed through class relationships and conflicts — that is, through the class struggle, which is the inevitable consequence of property relationships. The dominant class organizes and maintains the legal and political framework which responds to its interests, and which, in a more general way, corresponds with its social consciousness (the way it perceives and thinks of society in accordance with the place that it occupies within it). The social and political organization of a society should therefore reflect its economic structure.

The progress of the forces of production, however, leads to a collision with or contradiction of the relations of production, which finally become shackles on the development of production. Thus a period of more or less rapid social change is reached, culminating in the transformation of the old society into a new one which is better adapted to the state of the forces of production. This transformation is carried out mainly through the organized struggle that the oppressed class — which is alienated from the means of production, from political power, and even from culture — under-

21. Aron, *Main Currents in Sociological Thought*, p. 119.

takes against the dominant class. The oppressed class gradually becomes conscious of the contradictions between the forces and the relations of production which contribute to its alienation, and it becomes involved in revolutionary action with a view to reversing the order established and maintained by the dominant class. It is this revolutionary process that Marx described at the beginning of the *Communist Manifesto*:

> The history of all hitherto existing society is the history of class struggles. Freeman and slave, patrician and plebeian, lord and serf, guild-master and journeyman, in a word, oppressor and oppressed stood in constant opposition to one another, carried on an uninterrupted, now hidden, now open fight, a fight that each time ended either in a revolutionary reconstitution of society at large, or in the common ruin of the contending classes.[22]

Classification of societies by Marx and Engels

It is from this historical perspective that Marx and Engels were led to describe more fully the historical development of different types of societies. It is now understood that both men sought to define these societies on the basis of the stage of development of the forces of production, and according to the consequent relations of production. Marx clearly indicates this in the quotation taken from *Wage-Labour and Capital*. In contrast to Auguste Comte, however, Marx and Engels elaborated their classification of societies very little; the past interested them less than the present and the future. While Comte mainly analyzed modern society as an industrial society, which he sought to interpret through its historical antecedents, Marx and Engels were concerned particularly with the capitalist and bourgeois nature of modern society. Their intention was to construct a systematic and — they hoped — irrefutable critique of capitalism.

Nevertheless, at many points in their writing, Marx and Engels outlined the historical development of various types of societies. Two examples can be found in the extracts quoted earlier. The most elaborate presentations, however, can be found in the first

---

22. This text is obviously a very brief condensation of the history of humanity. It should be remembered that Marx wished to give it a dramatic tone to suit the context of the *Manifesto*. Marx, *Selected Works*, pp. 204-5.

part of *German Ideology* and particularly in *A Contribution to the Critique of Political Economy* by Marx, and in Engels' *The Origin of the Family*. In fact, their classification of societies developed as they clarified their ideas and extended their studies. It will already have been noticed that Marx mentions four types of society in the first passage we quoted, and three in the second.[23]

By drawing on different parts of the works of Marx and Engels, we can identify six types in their classification of societies.

The tribal community

The tribal community is the oldest known form of society. In Marx's words, it is "an extension of the family" or of the first social unit, and results from bringing together several families through marriage or in some other way. The division of labour is very limited within the tribal community — hardly more elaborate than in the family — and it corresponds to archaic working techniques and low productivity. The goal of work is not production, strictly speaking, but rather the strict subsistence of the collectivity and its members.

Private ownership of the means of production counts for very little in this community; the type of property that dominates is communal. In other words, the territory or land belongs to the entire tribe, and each productive member considers himself a co-owner. Under these conditions, social organization is simple, based on the family and kinship ties, and social differentiation scarcely exists.

At the beginning, the tribal community is nomadic and pastoral, then later settles down and becomes agricultural. As the society becomes larger and trade develops, and as war and barter appear, it adopts the use of slaves in order to increase its productivity. Slavery was already latent in the family, according to Marx.

The tribal community is thus a form of primitive communism. Even slaves, who represent the first evidence of man's exploitation of his fellow man, are often considered communal property. At the same time, this society has no social classes.

The tribal community is a particularly important type of soci-

---

23. On the development of the thought of Marx and Engels concerning different types of societies, see E. J. Hobsbawm's introduction in Karl Marx, *Pre-Capitalist Economic Formation* (London: Lawrence and Wishart Ltd., 1964).

ety because it is the common trunk from which the three following types of societies have sprung.

The Asiatic society

The Asiatic society is the most direct continuation of the tribal community. In fact, there is no evidence in this society of private ownership of the means of production. All land is owned by a supreme power, and families or local groups are grantees of their domain. Thus, a communal form of property develops, each family sharing the ownership of land with the highest authority. The production surplus belongs either to the highest authority or to the local community, both of which use it in the common interest.

The political regime of such a society generally falls under the authority of a despot (this is the origin of the expression *oriental despotism*, which is also used to designate this type of society); but it may also take on a democratic character, with authority vested mainly in heads of families.

In this type of society, the town has very little importance. It is primarily a rural society; or it is formed from small local communities which are for the most part economically autonomous, depending on their ability to divide their energies and resources between industry and agriculture. Towns may develop in order to encourage external trade, or they may emerge if the leaders employ the production surplus to create work for the labour force.

The Asiatic society is generally a classless society; if classes do exist, they appear in their most primitive form. Furthermore, for various reasons that Marx hesitated to enumerate, the Asiatic society has shown itself the most stable and the least likely to change and develop.

The Asiatic society has existed and still exists in the East (where its name obviously originates), particularly in certain regions of India. It could be found also in the pre-Columbian societies of Mexico and Peru, and among the ancient Celts.[24]

---

24. Let us mention, in passing, that the society of the Asiatic type has caused and still causes lively debates among Marxists. Marx himself appears to have hesitated to recognize it; Engels omits it in *The Origin of the Family*; Lenin returns to it, but Stalin bans it formally. On this subject, other than Hobsbawm's introduction previously cited, the following studies may be consulted: Karl A. Wittfogel, *Oriental Despotism: A Comparative Study of Total Power* (Yale University Press and Oxford University Press, 1957); George Lichtheim, "Marx and the Asiatic Mode of Production," *St. Antony's Papers*, no. 14 (London: Chatto & Windus, 1963); F. Tokei, *Sur le mode de production asiatique* (Budapest: Akadémiai Kiado, 1966).

The ancient city

The ancient city is formed initially by the union of several tribes. The most highly developed classical examples of this are the ancient Greek and Roman cities. The axis of development and the centre of this society is no longer the country but the town. Power and wealth are concentrated in the town; the country becomes a territory that is dependent on it and develops according to its needs.

At first the social organization of the town is basically military, since war is the only means of appropriating and keeping it. From this it follows that the ownership of land is communal and national. Land belongs to the national community, to the State, and only the citizens who are members of this community can share the common property. Alongside communal property, private ownership of goods and real estate appears and grows; however, communal property (*ager publicus*) always remains important. It is only through his participation in the community that the citizen has the right to benefit from property and also to possess personal goods. At first, this right is granted only to patricians; then it is extended to plebeians, but never to slaves. The right to own slaves, like the right to possess other goods, is still communal. Slaves are a common labour force that is shared by the citizen-owners.

Thus, the division of property parallels the division of labour. The ancient city is a class society in which the main class relationships are established between citizens and slaves. But there are also other oppositions — between States which compete and engage in wars, between town and country (an opposition which is asserted for the first time in this type of society), between industry and commerce within the town, and finally among the peasants, who are the first rural proletariat.

The Germanic society

The Germanic society of the Middle Ages is a good example of another type of society, which has existed also in other regions at other times. It is a rural society. If a town exists, it is only the residence of the king and his court and has no economic basis.

The Germanic society is characterized by the fact that it is based on the dispersal and autonomy of small landed property. Each family unit lives independently on the farm which it owns and exploits for its needs. There is no concentration of owners, but rather a juxtaposition of working units and small properties.

It is an atomized and strongly individualistic society. If there is communal property, it exists only to supplement private property; it consists of land which is owned in common by the small landowners and which serves certain specific ends. Thus, in contrast to the ancient city where membership in the community is based on the right to own property, and to the Asiatic society where it permits participation in co-ownership, membership in the Germanic society is not related to property in any way. It is based, rather, on a common language, kinship ties, religion and so forth. It is a community in which ties are loose, and which exists mainly to ensure protection in case of war and to afford certain minor services to the small landowners.

The Quebec countryside of the eighteenth and nineteenth centuries corresponds quite well to this type of society. Its rural economy was based on farms which were cultivated individually by family units; the small landowners were relatively independent of each other and strongly individualistic; and in the oldest villages one still finds today the common — property owned collectively, which is used mainly for the grazing of cattle during the summer.

Feudal society

In the Western world, after the decline of the ancient city and the invasion of the Barbarians, *the feudal society* was able to develop from either a society of Germanic type, or a disorganized rural society which had been looted. Feudal society can be simultaneously rural and urban, but its origins are necessarily rural. The ownership of land is in the hands of large landowners who cultivate their property by bringing in serfs, on whom they levy dues or rent and to whom they assure protection in return.

Rural feudal society is a class society which is highly differentiated. There is a class of seigneurs and large landowners, and a class of serfs. The serfs can work and live only by the grace of their master and on his property. To this rural differentiation based on large landed property corresponds the trade guild hierarchy of the towns, to which all artisans must belong and which establishes and maintains the relationships between masters, journeymen and apprentices.

The division of labour is relatively limited. It appears mainly between the town and the country, and in the town it is structured by the trade guild organization. The division between industry and commerce appears only at a later stage of development in the feudal town. The feudal guild has already introduced capitalism. It serves to protect the artisans, whose capital, while modest, supports the work of journeymen and apprentices.

Bourgeois capitalist society

Bourgeois capitalist society is characterized by technical development and a more elaborate division of labour than exists in any other type of society, and by clearly identifiable class relationships. This society is marked mainly by the domination of a new class which emerges with the extension of commerce and industry — the bourgeois class of urban origins. Through the accumulation of considerable capital, this class opens up new commercial employment, creates manufacturing, and increases the productivity of labour. This increased economic activity can be carried out only through the concentration of workers, who are increasingly alienated from the means of production and from the goods produced. In this way, the working-class proletariat is formed.

Two stages of development can be distinguished in the capitalist society: the stage of commercial capitalism, during which the bourgeois class is formed and enriched by the extension of markets and by the discovery of new products and new sources of supplies; and the stage of manufacturing and industrial capitalism, which is centred on increasingly massive production. The working proletariat appears during this second phase, and becomes concentrated in the towns. The progressive urbanization of the countryside also takes place during this phase. According to the works of Lenin, a third phase of financial and colonial capitalism can be added. During his lifetime, Marx did not see this last stage evolve, at least in its modern form.

Marx declares that the internal logic of capitalism will lead it to its own destruction; for the opposition between the bourgeoisie and the proletariat can only become increasingly radical, eventually resulting in the overthrow and defeat of the bourgeoisie by the proletariat. Subsequently, through the dictatorship of the proletariat, a new type of society will be established, *the communist classless society*, based on the abolition of private property and a return to communal property. Only then will man no longer be subjected to the demands of production, for — in contrast to the pattern of the capitalist society — production will then be a function of the needs of each man and all men. It is through this liberation of man that what Marx called the pre-history of humanity will end and human history will really commence. This great humanist hope, which is at the heart of the work of Marx and Engels, is too often forgotten by the unconditional detractors of Marxism. But these last remarks have led us to the frontiers of sociology and prophecy.

Marx, Engels and Comte

Before we complete this brief presentation of some of the work of Marx and Engels, it will be useful to compare Marxist sociology with that of Comte. Like Marx and Engels, Comte was preoccupied by the state of contemporary industrial society; like theirs, his concern for social reform was both the source and the goal of his sociology. Thus, the two sociological approaches are clearly socially involved. For Comte, sociology itself provides a solution to social problems. Scientific knowledge of society will enable humanity to direct itself better by knowing itself better. The action to which Comte's sociology leads is the education of the masses to the new positive spirit; this was an action to which Comte personally devoted himself over a long period of his life, by giving weekly courses of the kind that are now called adult education. Marx's sociology, in contrast, leads to revolutionary action, through the organization of the proletarian masses with a view to overthrowing the bourgeois class.

The intellectualist or rationalist postulate of Comte and the materialist postulate of Marx and Engels can be discussed at great length. Let us only emphasize here that the "economic materialism" of Marx and Engels is really — as we shall emphasize in the third part of this book — less simple than Marxists, as well as non-Marxists, often give one to understand.

We should note another distinction which is more immediately pertinent to our subject. The evolution of societies as described by Comte is clearly uni-linear; his principle of the unity of the human race leads him to assert that all societies must uniformly pass through the three states described by his famous law. He recognizes that certain conditions of climate, natural resources and isolation, and also perhaps race, can influence the rhythm of this progression, but he believes that they cannot modify the course of it. Comte foresees that humanity is moving towards unity, as a result of the growing unanimity of the positive state.

Marx and Engels are much more sensitive to historical variations and to diverse routes of development. In particular, they believe that the tribal community was at the origin of various types
of society — Asiatic society, the ancient city and Germanic society.
Local conditions, combined with various physical, economic and
social factors, can thus multiply the courses of history. Besides, certain types of society more than others include dynamic elements
built into the structure of their organization. This is true of the
ancient city, Germanic society and feudal society, which carry
within them promises of development that would not be found in
Asiatic society, which is more stable and less conducive to change.
This more supple and more historical perspective of Marx and
Engels, leading to a multi-linear development, corresponds much
better to the modern neo-evolutionist point of view than does the
uni-linear evolutionary theory of Auguste Comte.

Ferdinand Tönnies:
The Psychological Foundations
of Social Relationships

Compared to the evolutionist or historical classifications suggested
by Comte, Marx and Engels, the typology of Ferdinand Tönnies
(1855–1936) is very different, as much because of the criterion employed as because of the classes or sociological categories of which
it is formed, and which constitute the core of Tönnies' sociology.
In a later chapter, we will examine the particular influence of
Tönnies' work on sociology.

The two wills

The starting point that Tönnies[25] adopts originates in individual
psychology. In this, Tönnies was influenced by a psychological

---

25. See Ferdinand Tönnies, *Community and Society*, trans. Charles P. Loomis
(East Lansing: The Michigan State University Press, 1957). This is preceded
by an introduction by John C. McKinney and Charles P. Loomis which directly concerns the subject of the present chapter (see particularly pp. 12-29).
In French, J. Leif has published a very good presentation of Tönnies' work:
La sociologie de Tönnies (Paris: Presses universitaires de France, 1946). The
study by V. Leemans, *Ferdinand Tönnies et la sociologie contemporaine en
Allemagne* (Paris: Alcan, 1933) also is excellent but presupposes a knowledge
of Tönnies' work.

school of the social sciences which was important in Germany at the end of the nineteenth century. The research of this school was concerned either with the psychology of peoples (Lazarus and Steinthal), or with the psychological foundations of law (R. Von Ihering, O. Gierke) or of political economy (A. Wagner). Tönnies undertook to analyze the psychological foundations of social relationships which comprise the fabric of any collectivity. For him, these social relationships are relationships between human wills. Here the term *will* has a rather imprecise meaning; it appears to designate all the mechanisms which motivate and direct the behaviour of men with regard to each other.

But human will in this sense is manifested in two very different and perhaps opposing ways: the *Wesenwille*, which has been translated into English as *natural will*; and *Kürwille*, or *rational will*. Natural will is "natural" in that it is directly linked to the biological organism from which it derives its force and impetus. It is the direct expression of the vital need of man, and also of his whole being which is made up of biological states, feelings and thoughts. Natural will does not exclude thought; rather, it integrates thought into all the motivations and mechanisms of human action. This is the main difference between natural will and rational will; the latter is dominated by thought, and is consequently artificial, for it is a will that man has had to construct for himself, by submitting a part of his action to the control of rationality and intelligence. According to Tönnies, then, natural will is a will that includes thought, while rational will is thought that envelops the will.

The forms of will

Natural will can take one of three forms, according to the different levels of activity to which it corresponds. At the level of vegetative activity, which is internal to the organism, the natural will is liking; at the level of animal activity, through which the organism relates to the external world, the natural will corresponds to habit; finally, at the level of mental activity, natural will takes on the form of memory, which Tönnies defines as the capacity to reproduce appropriate acts in order to obtain specific goals. Habit and memory are intimately linked; both are acquired by learning, and thus they are the basis of morality. The relationship which exists among the three forms of natural will confers on each person his specific moral character.

Similarly the rational will is manifested in three simple forms: deliberation, discrimination and conceptions. Let us summarize — if very briefly — Tönnies' thought, by quoting a passage by J. Leif: "Deliberation is the consideration of the intention or of the goal; discrimination is the search for reasons when the goal is chosen; and conceptions, finally, are the rational and general representations of objects or goals."[26] It should be added that, according to Tönnies, there also exist complex forms of the rational will; but we do not need to analyze them here.

The opposition of the two wills

The two wills, natural and rational, imprint different and even contrary orientations on human activity. Leif summarizes the contrast between the two wills in the following terms:

> The natural will and the rational will are opposed by their very nature. The one translates the impulses of the *heart*; the other is the expression of an activity of the *head*. The former stems from an organic and affective concrete field; the latter is purely intellectual and abstract.[27]

The opposition between the two wills is apparent in the different behaviour that they motivate. The natural will is at the origin of action inspired by passion, by love or hate, affection or loathing, courage or fear, good will or malice, and so forth. Any rational, calculated action, responding to personal interest, ambition or the search for power or money, is the expression of the rational will.

In each person, the two wills confront each other, and one must necessarily win over the other. It follows that the natural will is stronger in certain people, the rational will in others. This leads Tönnies to distinguish people according to the will that dominates them.

The opposition between the two wills is evident not only in individual activities and in individuals; it can also be found in groups and in social categories. Tönnies' individual psychology thus becomes social psychology. For example, he explains the contrast between the sexes in terms of the two wills: the woman is

---

26. Leif, *La sociologie de Tönnies*, p. 29.
27. *Ibid.*, p. 33.

guided to a greater extent by the natural will, since she is more sensitive, intuitive and sentimental than the man. The man is involved, more than the woman, in an active and often hard life, and must be guided more by the rational will. In the same way, poets, artists and geniuses are generally of a more "feminine" nature, for it is the natural will which prevails in them. In childhood and youth, the human being is guided mainly by the natural will, which is more primitive; in maturity and old age, the rational will progresses and increasingly dominates. Finally, education encourages the rational will to the extent that it awakens and sharpens the critical spirit, and develops rationality and freedom of thought. The educated classes of society are thus distinguished by the fact that the rational will dominates in them, while the non-educated classes obey the natural will to a greater degree.

Community and society relationships

If the two types of will can distinguish and contrast individual behaviour and categories or groups of people, it is understandable that they similarly distinguish and contrast two types of social relationships between men. In the relationships which unite men, action is guided by one or other form of will, as is all the rest of their conduct. It is in this way that Tönnies' formula — that social relationships are relationships between human wills — is explained. Social relationships obeying the natural will are those that Tönnies calls *community* relationships; those guided by the rational will are called *society* relationships. These two forms of social relationships are, in Tönnies' view, the *fundamental categories* of all social reality; in fact, all the forms of human social life can be attached to one or the other of these two categories. Of course, community and society relationships are never found in a perfect and isolated state in concrete collectivities; no group is based solely on one or the other. The community and the society nature of social relationships are thus categories of theoretical or pure sociology. Observation of concrete social reality, however, enables one to isolate analytically the two forms of social relationships and to determine in each case which is dominant. The grouping or the collectivity in which social relationships of a community nature form a type of social organization is the community (*Gemeinschaft*); those where society relationships dominate form the opposite type of social organization, the society (*Gesellschaft*).

The community

The community is comprised of individuals who are united by natural or spontaneous ties, as well as by common objectives which transcend the particular interests of each individual. A feeling of belonging to the same collectivity dominates the thought and actions of individuals, ensuring the cooperation of each member and the unity of the group. The community is thus an organic whole within which the life and interest of the members is identified with the life and interest of the whole.

This type of social organization can be found concretely in three main forms. *The blood community,* such as the family, kinship groups, the clan and so forth, is the most natural community. It is of a biological origin, and consequently it is also the most primitive. *The community of place,* which is formed through proximity, is found in the small village or in a rural environment. Finally, there is *the community of mind,* which is established on the basis of friendship, agreement and a certain unanimity of spirit and feelings. The community of mind is found mainly in small towns where individuals know each other, in the national community, and in religious groups.

Let us emphasize that these three types of community correspond, in Tönnies' mind, to the three forms of natural will: the first corresponds to liking, for it is the most biologically natural and primitive; the second corresponds to habit, because it is based on physical proximity or living together in the same limited territory; and the third corresponds to memory which is essential to all mental and spiritual communication between men.

The society

In *the society,* relationships between individuals are established on the basis of individual interests; thus, they are competitive, or at least characterized by indifference to the concerns of others. In contrast to the community, which is made up of warm and emotional relationships, the society is the social organization of cold relationships in which diversity of interests and a calculating approach dominate.

Commercial exchange is the most typical example of a society relationship. Each participant in this exchange seeks to obtain the highest possible profit; indeed, this is the rule of the game. Thus, the commercial, business and industrial world are forms of social organization of a society nature. The large town, which is the preferred location of commercial and industrial activity, is another form of society; the same holds for the political State which is superimposed on these towns, which protects or defends economic interests and must often obey them, and which represents the particular interests of a national community. Law, which stems from Roman law, is similarly an institution of the society type; for it is guided by a concept of man as a reasonable, rational and therefore responsible being. Furthermore, it is the expression of an essentially contractual notion of social relationships. Science is also a society world, for it tries to be a system of thought that is exclusively rational, critical, logical and universal. Finally, public opinion is a society activity. It is thought to be enlightened because it closely copies scientific thought, by which it is also guided; it is, in addition, based mainly on the State and on the interests that the State obeys.

From the community to society

In his final work *The Spirit of Modern Times*,[28] Tönnies applied his sociology of the community and society to the historical development of modern Western society. (For Tönnies, modern times necessarily includes the Middle Ages; the period that the historians call the modern period, which they date back to the end of the Middle Ages, can be explained only by including the Middle Ages, of which it is a part). The history of the Western world, from the Middle Ages to our times, outlines the change from a social organization of a community nature to one of a society type. The foundations of social organization in the Middle Ages were mainly the family unit, kinship ties and links formed by the neighbourhood, the village and the borough. Lords and serfs in effect shared the ownership of the land. The common law reflected the mores and customs of the community spirit. The political state was practically non-existent, and community of thought was expressed in religious unanimity.

The emergence and progress of individualism led to the evolution of the mediaeval community, and ultimately to its disin-

---

28. Ferdinand Tönnies, *Geist der Neuzeit* (Leipzig: Hans Buske, 1935). This volume has not been translated.

tegration and the birth of modern society. This individualism expressed itself first through the progressive commercialization of relationships between masters and subordinates: lords demanded increasingly high rents from their serfs; artisans organized themselves into guilds for self-protection from each other; princes taxed their subjects; the Church itself commercialized the relationships between the faithful, the clergy and God. Thus, relationships of opposition and domination replaced the former relationships of unity and cooperation. But domination could only engender emancipation movements, and these have existed since the end of the Middle Ages — movements for the emancipation of serfs and peasants; for the liberation of towns; for commercial, political and economic demands; for freedom of religious thought and equal rights for citizens. The freedom and equality that individuals demanded and obtained entailed, in turn, the appearance of a new type of contractual agreement between men, and thus the emergence of a new type of social organization based on it. This agreement recognized the divergence of individual interests and built it into a system; it was a substitute for the community agreement and the feeling of belonging. Thus, historical development from the Middle Ages to our times can be summarized as follows: social organization of a society nature — urban, industrial, capitalist, democratic and scientific — gradually replaced the former mediaeval social organization of the community — rural, artisan, cooperative, hierarchical and religious in nature.

In his later work, Tönnies develops an historical application of his sociological theory. The two basic categories of pure sociology — the community and the society — become two types of concrete and historical social organizations which can be compared, and whose sequence over time can be followed; undoubtedly, they can also be compared in different places during the same historical period.

The first attempt at a fundamental theory

The great influence of Tönnies' sociological work obviously is not due to the psychological foundations on which he believed sociology rested. This psychology no longer has any interest today except to serve as a background to his typology of social relationships and social organization. And his applications of psychology to groups of individuals are often oversimplifications, to say the least. In particular, the contrasts that he establishes between men and women presuppose masculine and feminine temperaments which are inscribed in the biological nature of men and women; but the most recent studies show that culture intervenes to a great extent in distributing psychological traits between the sexes.

Rather, the success of Tönnies' sociology results from the fact that it represents the first attempt to elaborate a model which stems from basic theory — a model whose applicability to concrete historical societies Tönnies hoped to demonstrate. *Gemeinschaft und Gesellschaft* mark the beginning of general sociological theory. From this point of view, Tönnies' work belongs as much to the analytical as to the comparative and classificatory tradition in the study of social organization.

Bipolar typologies

The classification of the forms of social organization on which Tönnies' sociology is founded inaugurated a long series of bipolar or dichotomic typologies, all of which are more or less directly inspired by that of Tönnies. We should recognize that Tönnies was not the first to suggest such a dichotomy; he was influenced specifically by the work of Henry Sumner Maine. In his study of ancient law and particularly of Roman law, Maine concluded that its development began with a law that established the *status* of individuals and progressed to a law which regulated the *contract* between individuals. In this juridical development, Maine saw the reflection of the development of a society marked by "the gradual dissolution of family dependency and the progress of individual obligation."[29] The law governing the status of individuals is linked directly to the dominance of the family; contractual law results from growing individualism. Here we can recognize certain ideas that Tönnies borrowed directly from Maine — notably, the idea of the progress of individualism in history and the attendant rise of contractual law.

Tönnies' work was original in that he constructed his two types of social organization as two "pure types" (to use the expression made popular by Max Weber) — that is, two abstract types so different from each other that they represent two extreme and totally opposite poles. Concrete reality rarely, if ever, attains such purity but is located at some point between the two extremes, generally

---

29. Henry Sumner Maine, *Ancient Law* (New York: Henry Holt and Company, 1885), p. 163. The first edition dates from 1861.

closer to one than to the other. It was left to Max Weber to system-atize this methodology, which Tönnies had only outlined but which he did use.

This method, which is called the pure type or the ideal type, has been used in sociology by several writers in dealing with various realities. Without claiming to be exhaustive, let us mention in particular Charles Cooley's distinction between *primary groups* — for example, the family: a limited group in which social relation-ships are personalized and intimate, and which exert a profound influence on the formation of the individual (it is mainly with this meaning that they are called primary) — and all the wider groups to which the individual belongs. Cooley did not call the latter groups *secondary* but many other sociologists who have subse-quently used the same distinction have not hesitated to do so.

Howard Becker has distinguished between sacred and secular societies; Karl Popper contrasts the open and closed society; Mac-Iver compares community relationships and associational relation-ships. Similarly (as we will discuss in more detail later), Spencer distinguishes between military and industrial society, Durkheim between mechanical and organic solidarity, and Redfield between folk and urban society. Moreover, all the scales used in social psychology and sociology to measure attitudes are essentially based on similar dichotomies — conservatism–progressivism, tol-erance–intolerance, segregation–integration, localism–cosmopoli-tanism, and so forth. Thus, Tönnies is the initiator of a method that, even if it was and is criticized, was nonetheless useful and widely adopted in sociology, anthropology and social psychology.

Tönnies' political influence

Tönnies influenced not only sociology, but also German political and national life. It is only too obvious that his sympathy was for relationships of a community type, which he regarded as a sort of natural moral code. His intention, in fact, was to prepare a moral as much as a sociological work. Also, it has been suggested that his work contributed to the proliferation of the German romantic and nationalist movements, including Nazism. But it must be recog-nized that Tönnies is not the only sociologist to have revealed his personal inclinations through his work. Many other sociologists have had difficulty in hiding their sympathy for the "superiority" of modern society over less advanced societies. Personal value judgements are always on the threshold of sociology's doorway to the world.

Criteria Internal to
Social Organization

Strictly speaking, the classifications presented in the first part of this chapter are all based on principles external to social organization. For Comte, social organization follows the progress of knowledge; for Marx, it is the superstructure of relations of production or forms of appropriation of the means of production; for Tönnies, the principle of social organization is located in individual psychology, relating to the type of will that inspires human action and social relationships.

We will now consider typologies that can be said to be more strictly sociological, in the sense that their authors have sought their principle or principles in the different characteristic ways in which the organization of societies is structured.

Herbert Spencer:
The Increasing Complexity
of Societies

The general law of evolution

All the philosophical writings of Herbert Spencer (1820–1903) were devoted to showing that the unity of human knowledge can be achieved on the basis of a single great scientific law which is universally applicable — the general law of evolution. Guided by works (particularly those of Lamarck and Darwin) which in the nineteenth century established the merits of evolutionist or transformist theories in biology, Spencer formulated a general law according to which evolution — not only in biology, but in all spheres — occurs through the transition from a primitive stage, characterized by the homogeneity or simplicity of the structure, towards increasingly advanced stages which are marked by a growing heterogeneity of the parts, and accompanied by new forms of integration of these parts. The more that a body includes different and heterogeneous parts in a more complex organization, the more one can say that it is advanced or developed. Provided that it is accompanied by the integration of the whole, the specialization of organs is in fact a progressive development for the body; for in this way the body's field of action is extended and its chances of survival multiplied in the struggle for life which prevails in every order of nature.

After applying his law of evolution to biology and psychology, eventually Spencer related the same law to the development of societies. In his view, society must be considered as a living being which obeys this law just as biological organisms do. To emphasize the link between biological and social evolution, Spencer calls society a supra-organic reality, whose evolution is comparable in many respects to that of organic beings. It is not surprising that Herbert Spencer's name became the symbol of evolutionist theory in the second half of the nineteenth century.

With this in mind, Spencer sought to define different types of societies corresponding to a similar number of stages in human and social evolution. His universal law of evolution applied to the history of societies would, he believed, enable him to identify these stages and show their chronological sequence.[30]

From simple to complex societies

With the support of the ethnographic studies available at the time, Spencer undertook to show that, according to the law of evolution, at the beginning human societies were simple, small collectivities, undifferentiated and homogeneous, and that they evolved by becoming ever more complex, differentiated and heterogeneous. The simplest societies are nomadic groups which have no political organization and live by hunting or fishing, for which they use very archaic technical methods, reducing the division of labour to its most primitive form. Societies become more complex or heterogeneous to the extent that they are composed of a hierarchy of numerous and different groups. Political authority is organized and differentiated, economic and social functions multiply, and production requires a division of labour that becomes increasingly elaborate.

The first typology

This criterion of the increasing complexity of social organization led Spencer to distinguish four types of societies, corresponding to four stages of social evolution, each of these types being divided into sub-types.

---

30. Herbert Spencer's main sociological work can be found in *The Principles of Sociology*, 3rd edition, 3 vols. (London: D. Appleton and Company, 1925).

1. Among *simple societies* Spencer distinguishes four sub-types: those which have no political authority; those which have an occasional leader; those which only have a vague and unstable authority; and, finally, those in which political authority has been organized in a permanent way. Within these sub-types, Spencer then distinguishes between nomadic, semi-nomadic and stable societies. All these sub-types of simple societies have one thing in common: there are no separate cohesive groups within the society group. Political authority, when it exists, is exerted directly on all the members of society without passing through intermediate authorities.

2. Within *compound societies* Spencer again distinguishes sub-types: those which have an occasional leader (there are none without authority); those with unstable authority and those with permanent authority. Within each of these Spencer again distinguishes those which are nomadic, semi-nomadic or stable. In these societies, particularly when political power is organized, intermediate levels can be observed, each of which is endowed with authority and is subject to the highest authority — for example, the heads of families or clans; military or religious leaders who have a specific jurisdiction and whose powers are subject to or coordinated by the highest authority. The existence of family groups, clans and moieties (clans which divide the tribe into two halves) gives these societies a more complex nature than simple societies.

3. In *doubly compound societies* the groups are doubled, authority is multiplied and new means of integration must be elaborated. All these societies are settled, and they have a power organization which may be either stable or unstable. It is in these collectivities that towns and transportation systems develop, that working techniques progress, and that positive law appears and is formalized.

4. *Triply compound societies* are the great civilizations from which empires and the great religions have arisen, and which have led to the advancement of science and the arts. The great modern nations and industrialized countries obviously fall into this final category.

The second typology

But Spencer does not stop there. In fact, he sees that it is possible and even necessary to elaborate a second classification of societies, which is parallel to the first and overlaps it to a certain extent. Here he distinguishes two types of society which are *clearly op-*

posed to each other, when they are considered in their extreme form. His second classification is thus, strictly speaking, *a dichotomic or bipolar typology*, like that of Tönnies. These two opposite types are the militant type and the industrial type.

The militant type of society

The militant type of society, which is the oldest, includes mainly the simple and compound societies. In effect, almost all these societies are in a constant state of war, either because they must conquer new territories or because they must protect themselves against real or potential aggressors. Thus, war is a dominant, necessary and permanent activity in the least developed societies; the military function wins over the productive function or, more accurately, the productive function is conditioned by and dependent on the military one.

It follows that social organization closely copies military organization. The society is regulated, administered and organized on the model of the army. It is a society that is highly centralized and rigidly hierarchical, in which political, religious and military power are fused or vaguely differentiated. Religion itself bears the mark of this military trait, both in its language and in its images of supernatural powers; religion also has an absolute and authoritarian nature which encourages and values complete and blind submission. Work, too, is often organized on a military basis, and in some of these societies, the authority of the leaders extends to the smallest details of daily life.

Briefly, the dominant characteristic of these societies is that men are subjected to what Spencer calls compulsory cooperation.

The industrial type of society

The industrial type of society, according to Spencer, is still in the process of formation; but on the basis of what we already know about it, we can discern its main characteristics — the autonomy and freedom of individuals. This tendency has been manifested historically in various sectors of social life — increasingly democratic political institutions, less interference from State authority in the private lives of individuals, increasing religious individualism, the progress of freedom in business and work, and so forth. The growth of individualism is explained by the fact that, to the extent that societies live in peace with each other, they turn increasingly to productive activities. The need for military organization in society is felt less; the army becomes one of the structures of society instead of being the central structure. The military function is thus subordinated to the productive function, in contrast to the relationship that prevailed in the militant type of society.

Consequently, the compulsory cooperation which is characteristic of the militant type of society is succeeded by the voluntary cooperation typical of industrial society. The contract, whose development Henry Maine traced in ancient law, is the main and the most perfect form of voluntary cooperation; in addition, it becomes the most general and universal link in fully developed industrial society.

Spencer's thought can be summarized as follows. In the militant type of society, a central, constraining authority establishes and maintains social links and the cooperation necessary to the society in order to facilitate permanent war. In industrial society, cooperation is effected spontaneously and freely, and is the result of the meeting of individual interests; the contractual relationship is thus the most typical and ultimately the most generalized social link.

Spencer, Comte, Tönnies and evolutionism

Spencer's sociology obviously takes us back to that of Comte: in both, industrial society is contrasted with military society, and Spencer employs much the same terminology as does Comte. But while their descriptions of military society are comparable on the whole, quite the opposite is true of their representations of industrial society. According to Comte, the new industrial society will be bureaucratic and planned, and subject to the authority of engineers and scholars. In contrast, Spencer sees industrial society developing towards an individualistic and free society in which political authority will be reduced to a minimum; order will be observed in accordance with an implicit agreement resulting from the convergence and complementarity of individual interests.

Perhaps Spencer understood better than Comte that the new industrial society would favour an increased autonomy of individuals; but he was wrong to see a principle of social organization in this individualism. What is certain is that Comte discerned more clearly than Spencer the bureaucratic tendencies inherent in industrial society, and the role that technocrats and experts play within it today.

Contrary to Tönnies, who was troubled by the progress of an individualism that he judged amoral or even immoral, Spencer — who was a fervent believer in economic liberalism, a confirmed anti-associationist, and a fierce opponent of socialism — found scientific justification for his ideas in history; he believed that he could demonstrate that individualism necessarily accompanied progress.

As a philosopher of evolutionism and economic and political liberalism, Spencer enjoyed quite a large audience in his time, particularly in the Anglo–Saxon countries. Early American sociology bears his stamp. But after evolutionism was rejected by British and American anthropologists, Spencer's writings were long considered to date from the pre-history of sociology. Later we will see that neo-evolutionism in anthropology and sociology is now bringing back theses which are curiously close to Spencer's.

Emile Durkheim: Types of Solidarity

Although Spencer's influence was strongest in the Anglo–Saxon environment, the French sociological school also owes him something. Emile Durkheim in fact quarrelled a great deal with Spencer; and because of this, he was led to "correct" and transform certain of Spencer's theories and, consequently, to borrow them. Durkheim's sociological writings, particularly his early works, therefore cannot be fully understood without reference to Spencer.

From the simple to the composite

On the question of the classification of societies, Durkheim recognized at once that "Spencer understood very well that the methodical classification of social types could have no other foundation" than to go from the simple to the composite.[31] And he himself states the principle of classification of social types in the following terms:

> We shall begin by classifying societies according to the degree of organization they present, taking as a basis

---

31. Durkheim, *The Rules of Sociological Method*, p. 81.

the perfectly simple society or the society of one segment. Within these types we shall distinguish different varieties according to whether a complete coalescence of the initial segments does or does not appear.[32]

Durkheim criticized Spencer, however, for not defining more clearly what he means by the "simplicity" of a society, and for identifying the simple society with "a certain crudity of organization." Durkheim provides his own definition: "A simple society is . . . a society which does not include others more simple than itself, and which not only at present contains but a single segment but also presents no trace of previous segmentation."[33] But it seems to us that in this definition Durkheim only expressed Spencer's own notion of simplicity more clearly than Spencer did himself.

Having defined the criterion for a classification of societies, Durkheim did not undertake the construction of such a classification. At the most, he rapidly enumerated a few social types, which are little different from those of Spencer and are presented in a less elaborate way than Spencer himself devised.

The two solidarities

It is on another point that Durkheim's contribution is original. It will be remembered that Spencer presented two classifications of societies and that he did not seem to recognize any link between them. Durkheim was to show that the two classifications are closely linked, or more precisely that the evolution of cooperation is closely associated with the increasing complexity of societies. According to Durkheim, Spencer correctly grasped the growing autonomy of the individual during social evolution; but he incorrectly analyzed its causes and consequences.

It is true that in primitive or archaic societies, the individual personality is largely absorbed by the society; or, in Durkheim's words, the "collective consciousness" almost completely overlaps the "individual consciousness." Primitive man thinks, feels and acts as the collectivity to which he belongs prescribes or commands; the external constraints that he experiences are too powerful to permit his individual consciousness to develop. This individual consciousness is asserted much more strongly in mod-

---

32. *Ibid.*, p. 86.
33. *Ibid.*, p. 82.

ern society. Man detaches himself from constraints that are too immediate and pressing, and he achieves a margin of personal autonomy over the collective consciousness.

If this is the case, however, it is not, as Spencer thought, because the very strong authority of a centralized military society has been gradually weakened, following gaps between wars. On the contrary, primitive society is no more centralized than industrial society — Durkheim even claims that it is not at all centralized. Primitive society is, in fact, formed by the juxtaposition of similar groups. A tribe is comprised of a certain number of families or clans which are all of the same kind and fulfill the same functions. Thus, the principle that is at the root of the social organization of such a collectivity is not the diversity of groups and individuals, but their *similarity*. The link that unites these individuals and groups is consequently a particular type of solidarity, the solidarity of similarity, which Durkheim calls *mechanical solidarity*. A strong collective consciousness necessarily corresponds to mechanical solidarity because such a society, in order to survive, cannot tolerate dissimilarities, originality or particularisms among individuals or groups.

It is the progress of the division of labour that brings about the transformation of a society based on mechanical solidarity. The principle of the division of labour itself is the diversity of individuals and groups — a principle which is directly contrary to that of the solidarity of similarity. The increasing sophistication of the division of labour thus dissolves and destroys mechanical solidarity; but it does not lead to purely spontaneous or voluntary cooperation, as Spencer believed. Rather it engenders a new type of solidarity, based on the complementarity of diversified parts. This merging of complementary interests is not, in itself, a principle of pure individualism, free from all constraints; but it is a social link of a new kind, or another principle of solidarity, having its own morale and leading to a new form of social organization. Because this solidarity is founded not on the resemblance of individuals and groups, but on their interdependence, Durkheim gives it the name of *organic solidarity*. Being based on diversity, this type of solidarity presupposes and indeed encourages a greater autonomy of individuals and a more extensive individual consciousness.

Types of law and types of solidarity

Solidarity and states of individual or collective consciousness are psychological or subjective realities which are not easy to delineate and measure concretely. How, then, are the two types of solidarity to be distinguished? According to Durkheim, law is the objective index that enables one to make this distinction. Corresponding to mechanical solidarity and to a strong state of the collective consciousness is a type of law that Durkheim calls repressive, whose function is to deal severely with everything that a society considers or defines as criminal. The fact that repressive law predominates expresses a strong repudiation of everything that menaces the unity and existence of the group. Corresponding to organic solidarity, which emerges from the increasing division of labour, is restitutive law. Its purpose is not to punish but to restore things that have been dislodged, to preserve the normal order of things. Contracts and the legislation protecting them are the most typical examples.

Thus, the emergence and development of restitutive law enable one to measure the degree of evolution of a society. Its presence in a society indicates that the division of labour is quite advanced, that the individual consciousness is winning over the collective consciousness, and that organic solidarity is replacing mechanical solidarity.

Two social types

Although he uses Spencer's typology, Durkheim identifies what he calls two social types — two types of society which are quite different from the militant and industrial societies of Spencer. The essential difference between the two typologies lies in *the principle of order or social organization* which is presupposed by the two writers. The society based on mechanical solidarity is a primitive society, like the militant society; the division of labour is elementary or weakly developed. The strong constraints that can be observed do not stem, however, from the coercion of a central military authority, as Spencer believed, but rather from *a strong collective consciousness* resulting from the resemblance of the constituent parts, and reflected in a law which is predominantly repressive or penal.

The society based on organic solidarity is, like industrial society, more advanced because the division of labour has progressed. But, to Durkheim, the diversification of the observable parts gives rise to new moral rules based on cooperation; such cooperation is not spontaneous, but rather is inscribed in the very fact of the interdependence of the parts. Restitutive law is its juridical formulation. Organic solidarity thus does not require the dissolution of political authority and the disappearance of all rules, as Spencer wished; it requires, on the contrary, that various authorities formulate *a wider and more complex set of regulations* than were needed in the society based on mechanical solidarity.

In this way, Durkheim comes to reconcile individualism, which Spencer had rightly perceived in industrial society, with the growing power of the State, which Spencer did not wish to recognize:

> The place of the individual becomes greater and the governmental power becomes *less absolute*. But there is no contradiction in the fact that the sphere of individual action grows at the same time as that of the State, or that the functions which are not made immediately dependent upon the central regulative system develop at the same time as it.[34]

The autonomy of individuals and social organization

One of Durkheim's most important sociological contributions was to show that the growing autonomy of individuals, which accompanies increasing division of labour, is linked to a type of social organization. Personal autonomy does not result from an absence of norms, patterns of behaviour and social control, as Spencer believed. In his study of suicide, Durkheim showed that this absence of norms, which he called anomie, on the contrary provokes pathological reactions — suicides, crime, delinquency and so forth. Social organization of industrial society is not spontaneous and cannot count on voluntary cooperation alone. Collaboration among members and among different and complementary groups requires a consensus on values and patterns of behaviour, and thus a degree of social control. Industrial society is no more based on the complete freedom of individuals than is any other type of society. What characterizes it is that the greater social differentiation enables members to choose between various norms and values, and thus individuals can exert their judgement to a greater extent. Division of labour encourages diversity between individuals as well as between groups; it requires dissimilarity rather than similarity, complementarity rather than identity. The growth of

---

34. Durkheim, *The Division of Labour*, p. 220.

personal autonomy therefore is not the consequence of a break-down of social organization. Rather, it results from the functional requirements of a certain type of total society.

Talcott Parsons: The Capacity for Adaptation

Parsons and neo-evolutionism

The lack of interest in evolutionism in the social sciences at the beginning of the twentieth century was accompanied by indifference towards comparative studies of societies. In recent years, however, there has been a return to evolutionary theories in sociology and anthropology through the birth of neo-evolutionism; and this in turn has sparked a new interest in comparative studies.

It may be surprising to some to find Talcott Parsons associated with neo-evolutionism. In fact, Parsons, whose general theory will later be the object of a detailed analysis (in Chapter 9) has earned himself, rightly or wrongly, the reputation of being a sociologist of social statics. It has been said that his theories disregard history, that they minimize the importance of social change and consider factors of change to be only marginal to the social system whose model he constructed. In fact, Parsons' work has followed a kind of cycle. It started with an analysis in depth of a few pioneers in sociology, particularly Durkheim and Weber. The interest these writers had in evolution and history obviously did not escape Parsons.[35] Later, however, Parsons devoted several years to the elaboration of a general theory, conscious that such theory was seriously inadequate for the purposes of sociology. It was only after he had constructed a theoretical and highly abstract model that Parsons believed he was able to return to comparative studies, with the aid of a more appropriate intellectual instrument than was available to the sociologists of the nineteenth century. This is what he has undertaken in his most recent publications.[36]

But, as Parsons aptly remarks, every comparative study of societies is necessarily evolutionist. At the beginning of this chapter, we

---

35. Parsons, *The Structure of Social Action*.
36. Parsons, *Societies: Evolutionary and Comparative Perspectives*.

mentioned his comment that one cannot compare the social organization of an isolated tribe of central Australia with that of a
great modern nation, such as the Soviet Union or the United
States, by treating them as equals in all respects. It must be recognized that one is more developed or advanced than the other, the
ambiguity of these terms notwithstanding. The comparative study
of societies thus requires that one make a value judgement on the
degree of development of the social organization.

The problem of the objective criterion

The danger that still awaits every researcher is that such a decision will express a value judgement rather than a reality judgement (to use Durkheim's expression); or in other words that the
sociologist will define development in terms of a moral judgement,
or a social or political philosophy. To avoid the influence of value
judgements, it is important, according to Parsons, to use a
criterion that is authentically "objective" for the classification and
arrangement of societies. This is not the place to discuss the considerable epistemological problem posed by this "objectivity" of a
principle of classification in the social sciences; the importance of
such "objectivity" has already been demonstrated in our discussion throughout this chapter.

Parsons resolves this problem by adopting a criterion which
conforms, as far as possible, to that which is used in biology. He
claims that there is no break in continuity between organic and
socio-cultural evolution; thus, a criterion whose validity has been
proved in biology provides a guarantee of objectivity for the social
sciences that can hardly be questioned. This is the criterion he selected: a society is "advanced" to the extent that its social organization manifests *a generalized adaptive capacity*. Every vital
process, whether it is that of a biological organism, an animal species or a society, is a process of adaptation to external and internal
realities, to stable situations, or to slow or rapid change. But here
adaptation does not only mean adjustment to given conditions; it
also includes the effort required to achieve a more satisfactory
state, a more productive one, or even one which corresponds better to latent aptitudes and available energies. Thus, adaptation is
not merely passive, but it is also a form of creativity and innovation. Consequently, a living being which is endowed with a
greater capacity for adaptation than another is better suited to
survival and progress.

Differentiation and integration

Starting with this principle, Parsons unequivocally rejoins the evolutionist theories of Spencer and Durkheim. He considers that, for societies, the generalized adaptive capacity is manifested mainly in the growing complexity of the social organization. The process of differentiation thus becomes a central criterion in the understanding of social evolution. Differentiation operates through the division of units which fulfill two or several functions into sub-units, each of which fulfills at least one of the functions of the original unit. For example, the peasant family was a unit of both residence and production; with the progress of the division of labour, the function of production was transferred from the family to the shop, factory or office. But it must be added that differentiation is not in itself an index of advancement; it becomes such an index only when the functions of the original unit are fulfilled in a "more adapted" way by the new sub-units than would have been the case with the first unit.

The process of differentiation also requires a rearrangement or a reintegration of the parts; the multiplication of sub-units must not lead to disorganization or anarchy, but to a new order between the units and sub-units. Finally — and this distinguishes social evolution from organic evolution — the process of differentiation and reintegration requires modifications in the realm of values. In a social organization whose complexity increases, the most appropriate system of values is that which includes the most general values — that is, values whose application to specific situations are relatively inexplicit, and whose relevance is universal. In a simple society, values can be more directly explicit for each situation or event; in a complex and differentiated society, values must be expressed in a more general fashion, and in such a way as to be applicable to a plurality of situations or events.

Such are the main lines of the theoretical framework of evolution and comparative sociology that Parsons suggests. He then applies it by distinguishing three main stages in the development of societies, each corresponding to a type of social organization.

Primitive societies

Primitive societies are the least differentiated societies. The low degree of differentiation appears at several levels of analysis. First of all, the kinship system is a central element of social organization in these societies, as the anthropologists have amply demonstrated. But the kinship system may be more or less differentiated. In certain Australian tribes, contrary to many other primitive societies, kinship groups or clans are not differentiated according to any particular function or hierarchy. Thus, we can correctly judge these Australian tribes to be less advanced than other primitive societies. When the kinship system comes to be differentiated, it usually serves as the ground for developing the political and administrative organization of the tribe; it is within and through the kinship system that political power is created and established. In addition, the family and the kinship system fulfill the economic functions of production, mutual help and commerce, thus performing the role of real economic structures.

In his study of the elementary forms of religious life, Durkheim showed the religious — or perhaps more precisely, the sacred — nature of primitive society. Parsons takes up and develops Durkheim's analysis, showing that in the primitive society religion serves to express the social organization symbolically, and thus to reinforce it. Primitive religion therefore has no universal character, since it is always very closely associated with a particular society. This sociological localism of primitive religions is expressed particularly in their beliefs and rites, which serve mainly to recall in mythological terms the origins and history of the tribe.

Religion and magic more often serve as a complement to the techniques used for hunting, fishing, cultivation and war. In a sense, they are part of the technology which is specific to each primitive society.

Finally, social, political and cultural frontiers between primitive societies are often vague. Tribes are not clearly distinguished from each other.

To be sure, these are general characteristics. With the help of concrete examples, Parsons himself shows that some societies are more primitive than others. Primitive societies are more advanced when, in particular, they have elaborated a political organization that is differentiated to some degree, and still more when this political organization begins to be separated from religious functions.

Intermediate societies

To Parsons, the main element which distinguishes primitive societies from *intermediate societies* is written language. The idea is not new; anthropologists have long used the expression *non-liter-ate societies* to designate primitive societies. But Parsons gives several explanations. Writing confers a new autonomy on culture — in other words, it permits culture to be relatively independent of the concrete and moving context of interactions. It thus ensures greater cultural stability, and also makes history possible. Moreover, written language gives culture a greater universality, thus encouraging its diffusion over time as well as space. Writing helps to stabilize some aspects of human relations, particularly through written contracts. Finally, while Parsons recognizes that writing may contribute to the inhibition of thought through the rigid respect with which classical texts are surrounded, he emphasizes the new possibilities of cultural innovation that writing introduces.

The intermediate societies, then, are necessarily those which are endowed with a written language. Parsons distinguishes two phases within this stage, or two sub-types of the intermediate society. His distinction rests on two main criteria: the use that is made of writing; and the type of religion adopted by the society. In the first sub-type, which Parsons calls the *archaic intermediate society*, writing is used exclusively for technical or useful goals — for example, accounting, administration, and magical or religious rites. In this society, religion is of the cosmic type; it no longer has the sociological quality that it possesses in primitive societies, but it remains a sort of supernaturalization of physical nature — the stars, animals, natural phenomena and so forth. This archaic stage of the intermediate society is represented by Ancient Egypt and by the Mesopotamian, Persian, Aztec, Mayan and Inca empires.

The more advanced sub-type, which Parsons calls *the historical intermediate society*, is distinguished from the preceding one in that it includes a higher social class which is thoroughly educated. Writing is no longer limited to only practical uses, but also serves. as an instrument for general or abstract reflection, and for the accumulation of a literary, philosophic and scientific tradition. In this society, religion is universal and systematic; it becomes supernatural, strictly speaking, in that it is differentiated and freed from any natural order, whether sociological or cosmic. The cases which Parsons cites to illustrate and explain this stage are the Chinese Empire after 200 B.C., India before the Musulman invasion, the Musulman Empire and the Roman Empire.

Over and above writing and religion, many other features differentiate the intermediate from the primitive society. Parsons emphasizes the existence of a political organization, which is well structured and which generally adopts the form of royalty in the archaic stage, later adopting more complex forms in the historical stage. A system of social stratification divides the societies rather rigidly into various ranks, orders, strata or classes, and in a much more complex manner than in primitive societies. Finally, all intermediate societies have social, political and cultural frontiers which are much better defined than is generally the case with primitive societies.

Modern societies

Modern societies are distinguished from the preceding ones by the existence of a legal system which has two essential traits: a universal character and an elaborate procedure, both of which are inspired by what Weber called formal rationality. Such a system is necessarily indicative of the pronounced autonomy of the normative apparatus of a society (rules of conduct, patterns of behaviour, values) with regard to the immediate and often changing requirements of political and economic interests, and also with regard to the influence of individual biological and psychological factors. Consequently, considered from the point of view of the norms of conduct which regulate the interaction of the members of a society, culture is relatively stable and resistant to rapid change.

Parsons recognizes that this criterion of the legal system, which he employs to distinguish modern from intermediate societies, is neither simple nor easy to apply. In addition, it is not very clear why Roman law does not fulfill the two conditions that he has posed. But it is difficult to explain and comprehend more clearly Parson's modern type of society, for that is about all he says about it for the moment. To date, his study has been concerned with the first two types of society, and he has reserved the analysis of the third for a future work.

"Seed-bed" societies

There is another aspect of Parsons' study which deserves to be mentioned. He paid particular attention to the special case of some societies which have served as "seed-beds." These societies have not themselves survived, but they have had a profound influence on other societies which have not followed them directly in the evolutionary sequence. This was the case for Israel and Ancient Greece, in particular. An important part of the culture of these two societies extended into other societies which were very different from the two original societies in their time.

Multi-linear evolutionism

It would not be useful to discuss Parsons in more detail at this point. This last part of our discussion, however, serves to illustrate that he refuses (as he has explicitly said) to accept a uni-linear evolutionary framework. He emphasizes that it is not necessary to presuppose one origin alone for human and social evolution, as did the classic evolutionists; and it is no more realistic to seek an evolutionary line which follows a well-defined path. Human social evolution has been multiple and varied. It has produced numerous cases of strong, commanding societies which have not been able to survive various crises or certain tests. Other societies have disappeared, such as those of Israel or Greece, but have exerted a profound influence. Many societies, particularly the primitive ones, have been stuck in an insulated niche and have not taken the steps necessary to progress to more advanced stages. Social evolution is no less complex than biological evolution.

In this, Parsons expresses very well the point of view of contemporary neo-evolutionism, which is the only acceptable position if one wishes to avoid falling back into the excessive simplifications of nineteenth-century evolutionism. From this perspective, the stages that one can attempt to delineate are no longer stages that must be experienced by every society in order to arrive at maturity, as Auguste Comte in particular imagined. These stages correspond rather to certain thresholds which are particularly important or significant, which certain societies have been able to cross and from which they have then been able to undertake new development.

The explanatory factor

If we wish to explain social evolution, with all its variations and variables, by a single causal factor, according to Parsons we are going back to the infancy of the social sciences. It must now be recognized that the interpretation of evolution requires an analytical theory which is capable of taking into account simultaneously a great diversity of factors and an equally great variety of conditions. The evolutionists of the nineteenth century lacked such a theory; and like Parsons, we can believe that sociology has made sufficient theoretical progress to justify the hope that an analytical and interpretive framework of social evolution can now be elaborated. Such optimism, however, is not yet shared by all contemporary sociologists.

Finally, let us emphasize that Parsons, while objecting to any form of social determinism, comes to the conclusion that the dominant element in evolution, when this is considered over a long period, is the progressive differentiation between culture and social organization, when the latter term is understood to have the strict meaning of all the interactions and structures of the society. This differentiation entails much greater cultural autonomy and stability. At the same time, culture has an increasing influence on history and on the evolution of more advanced societies. We can at least recognize that Parsons has given the idea of increased differentiation, which characterizes more advanced societies — an idea that had already been stated and developed by Spencer and Durkheim — a new meaning and a more elaborate theoretical foundation.

Conclusions

We have reviewed a few of the classifications of societies suggested by various sociologists, choosing the best known, those to which one refers most frequently and which have exerted the most influence. The conclusions which arise from these classifications should now be formulated. These conclusions first of all concern the similarities and dissimilarities of point of view among the writers whose works have been presented, and then touch on some of the methodological problems that are posed by this kind of sociology.

Four points of similarity

If we stop to consider the content of the classifications that have just been analyzed, we can easily distinguish similarities among the authors studied in this chapter. First, they all agree that some societies should be considered more "advanced" than others; and they all describe, at two extreme poles, an archaic, primitive or traditional society and an industrial, technological or modern society. This comparative and evolutionist framework has been present in sociology from its beginning and has served as a backdrop to a great number of empirical and theoretical studies. We will see, however, (in the next chapter and in Part Three) that this opposition between two types of society has been the subject of various discussions among sociologists. It has been questioned and certainly has not yet been unanimously accepted.

Second, many scholars, from Spencer and Durkheim to Parsons, are in agreement that society has evolved towards a growing complexity, a more differentiated structure, a multiplication and diversification of its parts, units or elements. It can even be said that there exists in sociology a continuous tradition which supports a certain theory of change through the processes of differentiation and reintegration.

Third, all the authors recognize that evolution has been accompanied by profound changes in culture, in values and value-scales, in mentalities and attitudes. It is this transformation that Auguste Comte wished to emphasize by focusing on the mental and psychological revolution which the positive state represents for mankind. Durkheim and Tönnies have in turn emphasized different aspects of the same revolution. Finally, Parsons extends the same idea, though in rather different terms from those of the preceding authors.

Fourth, it has been possible to observe a rather surprising consensus on an aspect which is perhaps fundamental to this transformation: the growing autonomy of the individual or individuality which accompanies evolution. This idea was present in Comte's work; it was at the centre of Spencer's thought, and Durkheim also expressed it in different terms. For Marx and Engels, modern capitalist society marks the last stage of the pre-history of humanity; from this, a new society will arise which will be at the service of man when finally he is no longer alienated. The English sociologist R. M. MacIver has expressed an evolutionary law stating that "the differentiation of community is relative to the growth of personality in social individuals."[37] For MacIver, the main index of the growth of personality is the individual's capacity for free expression and self-determination. Finally, let us mention that the American sociologist Robert Bellah has more recently suggested an evolutionary five-stage classification of religion, in which one of the criteria is the increasingly personal nature of the relationship between man and divinity.[38]

37. Robert M. MacIver, *Community: A Sociological Study*, 2nd edition (London: Macmillan and Co., Limited, 1920), p. 231.
38. Robert Bellah, "Religious Evolution," *American Sociological Review* 29, no. 3 (June 1964).

One main dissimilarity

There is one last point on which there is clearly no agreement, and that is the relationship between, on the one hand, the cultural sphere or the realm of ideas and values and, on the other hand, the technical, economic and material aspects of social life. Since the beginning of the nineteenth century, we have witnessed the confrontation of two theses — that of Comte on the predominant role of thought and the progress of knowledge, and that of Marx and Engels on the primary role of the material relations of production. It seems that this confrontation between two apparently contradictory theses must continue. To find it, it is not even necessary to seek opponents within the Marxist and "bourgeois" camps in sociology; examples can be found within American sociology itself. The sociologist William Ogburn has developed the theory of cultural lag. According to this theory, changes are generally produced first in the material conditions of the life of societies — physical environment, natural resources, techniques of production, working conditions and so forth. Non-material culture must then adapt itself to these changes, but adaptation is necessarily delayed to a varying degree. It is this delay that Ogburn calls cultural lag.[39]

We have seen that Parsons is strongly opposed to any theory which gives primacy to material facts in social evolution. It may be said that Ogburn's perspective is short term and Parsons' long term. But it is still true that their respective positions remain unreconcilable.

This — the causal explanation of change — is a problem to which we will return later. For the moment, we wish to limit ourselves to the descriptions of different types of societies that are found in the works of some sociologists, and to which contemporary sociology continues to refer. It is clear, however, that these classifications become meaningful to the extent that we can explain how and through which factors the change from one type of society to another is effected. This question will be treated in the third part of this book.

Three methodological problems

On the question of the methods of research and analysis which are applied to studies of this type, we have indicated, from the begin-

---

39. William F. Ogburn, *Social Change: With Respect to Culture and Original Nature* (New York: The Viking Press, Inc., 1922).

ning of this chapter, that two main problems are posed. The first is that of the objective and authentically scientific criterion for the classification of societies. We have seen that this problem was raised for all the writers that we have studied; and they, in turn, have been identified and classified according to the main criterion they used. They suggested various solutions to this problem; all of them, however, had the aim of choosing a scientifically valid criterion — even those scholars whose sociological research was coloured by moral implications.

The second problem is that of the necessarily historical or evolutionary nature of comparative and classificatory studies of societies. The main part of this chapter has clearly demonstrated this issue. Even Tönnies, whose basic categories of the community and society came closest to a pure sociology, used his categories to interpret the historical evolution of modern times.

There is a third methodological problem, however, which has appeared during the course of our presentation. Is it preferable to make use of a dichotomic typology, contrasting two extreme and pure types of societies, or to elaborate a more complex and continuous classification? Herbert Spencer first recognized this problem and resolved it by presenting two parallel classifications, one of which was complex and the other bipolar. Subsequently, Durkheim came to grips with the same problem; and although he saw, better than Spencer, the possible link between the two classifications, he finally concentrated his attention solely on the dichotomic typology.

The popularity of bipolar typologies

It should be recognized that dichotomic typologies have been more popular and have exerted a greater influence on sociological research than have continuous classifications. Spencer's complex classification is seldom mentioned, but his opposition between militant and industrial society is often referred to. Similarly, Durkheim's distinction between mechanical and organic solidarity has remained classic in sociology, while his classification of societies on the basis of nomadic tribes is forgotten. Tönnies' dichotomy of community-society is acknowledged by all sociologists, even those who ignore the psychological foundations of its historical applications. Finally, as we said, typologies of this kind have been popular and have multiplied in sociology.

Even when scholars have constructed a continuous classification, their classification masks a certain bipolar basis. In

Comte's law of the three states, the metaphysical state is described
as an intermediate and transitory period which serves to break
down the theological state and prepare for the positive state. The
two states that interested Comte particularly and which he analyzed in depth were the theological state and its opposite, the
positive state. Similarly, without making Parsons say something
that he did not say, we cannot help noticing that he used the term
intermediate society to designate the stage between the primitive
and the industrial societies. We believe that Parsons has too much
historical sense and his evolutionism is too purified of any linear
postulate for him to attribute to intermediate societies the same
characteristics that Comte gave them. But we can still find a
definite trace of the dichotomic typologies that he wished to reject.

Let us add that recent studies of socio-economic development
have drawn heavily on the tradition of dichotomic classifications.
Many writers have defined development as the splintering or the
breaking up of a traditional society and its transformation into a
modern society. For the past few years, the expression *modernization* has been used to designate this process, or to refer to
an aspect of this process.[40] Interest in the problems of development is a significant factor in the renewal of comparative studies
that we mentioned earlier, and in the progress of neo-evolutionism. Since Durkheim, most sociologists, with a few exceptions,
have no longer been interested in the sort of social botany created
by attempts to classify societies. They have preferred either studies
that are almost exclusively empirical or works of analytical theory.
Recent studies concerned with developing countries have shown
the need for a general classification of types of societies and the
stages of their evolution.

Finally, in American sociology and anthropology, the dichotomy to which we refer so often and which, in a way, includes all
the others is that which contrasts folk society with urban society
(or industrial or modern society). This dichotomy was made
popular particularly by the anthropologist Robert Redfield,[41] to
the point where his name has been attached to it and has become
a symbol of it. In the next chapter, we will return to Redfield's
work in further detail.

---

40. See chap. 12.
41. Robert Redfield, *Tepoztlan: A Mexican Village: A Study of Folk Life* (Chi-
    cago: University of Chicago Press, 1930); the author first formulated his di-
    chotomy in this study of a Mexican village. Also interesting is the article by
    the same author, "The Folk Society," *The American Journal of Sociology* 52
    (January 1947): 293-308.

Working through this long and rich tradition of bipolar typologies, we will devote the next chapter to establishing a parallel between traditional and technological society, by drawing on different descriptions that anthropologists and sociologists have furnished of these two types. This will enable us to illustrate the use that contemporary sociology makes of the classifications we have just studied.

Chapter 7
Traditional Society and Technological Society

As we explained in the preceding chapter, the main impetus of sociological research, and its principal support, is the desire to understand modern society better. Since the beginning of the nineteenth century, observers have rightly felt that the industrial revolution has transformed man's living conditions and his social organization. The discipline of sociology was developed in an attempt to describe and explain these changes, and to predict future events.

It was felt that in order to analyze the new society in its formative stages and to highlight its main characteristics, one should compare it with other types of society. Thus evolved comparative and evolutionary sociology. Similarly, it appeared that modern society should be contrasted with the most opposite, the furthest removed, and the most primitive society. The stronger the contrast between these two types of society, the more clearly would the dominant features of modern society stand out. On the basis of this approach, the dichotomic typologies emerged and flourished.

It is not difficult to retrace in contemporary sociology the background of the various classifications we studied in the preceding chapter. The dichotomic typologies in particular continue to exert a very strong influence. Almost all of them are expressed in the distinction or contrast established by contemporary sociology between *technological society* and *traditional society*.[1] Since this distinction between two extreme types of society forms a kind of backdrop for a large part of modern sociology, it should be discussed in some detail. This will be the subject matter of the present chapter.

The two types of society will be compared from three points of view: their economic structure, their social organization and their ideology.

Traditional Society

The Economic Structure of Traditional Society

A simple economy

The economic structure of traditional society is *simple*; for in order to satisfy their needs, members of this society use *directly* the goods provided by nature, adapting them only slightly. To provide for their needs, they employ one or the other of the following techniques: cultivation of the land, breeding of cattle, hunting, fishing or the gathering of fruits, herbs and roots. As a rule, the members of a traditional society simultaneously or successively engage in two or more of these activities. For example, fishing or

---

1. We have used these expressions in preference to others. The term *traditional society* is often used in sociology, and more or less corresponds to *folk society*. The expression *technological society* is perhaps less widely used. Robert Redfield, from whom we have borrowed liberally, contrasts folk society with urban society. As will be seen later on, we believe that its urban nature is only one aspect of technological society and, consequently, that this latter term is more exact because it is broader. It is mainly in *The Primitive World and its Transformations* (Ithaca, N.Y.: Cornell University Press, 1953) that Redfield presents his penetrating analysis of traditional society; also useful is his article "The Folk Society." Other writers contrast industrial society with traditional society. We are of the opinion (and will later explain why) that industrial society is a sub-type of technological society. Finally, American writers have recently used such expressions as *communal society* in contrast to *associational society* to designate what we are calling traditional society and technological society. An example will be found in Ely Chinoy, *Sociological Perspective*, 2nd edition (New York: Random House, 1968), pp. 81-86.

hunting may be combined with agriculture; or the breeding of animals and agriculture may be practised as the seasons alternate. Often, though, one of these activities is dominant, while others complement it. Consequently, ethnologists usually classify traditional societies according to their main activity. They speak of agricultural peoples, hunters, fishermen, pastoral peoples·and gatherers.[2] In fact, social organization may differ according to the dominant activity of a particular society. The adoption of agriculture is particularly important, in that it effects the change from a nomadic to a sedentary society.

For housing and tools, the traditional society employs materials provided by the natural environment — wood, stone, clay, leaves, animal bones and so forth. For clothing, which can be more or less rudimentary, the people use the fur or skin of animals, wool, tree bark and various plants (flax or hemp). Often it is in clothing that raw materials undergo the greatest transformation, through the curing of skins, weaving, the dying of fibres and so forth.

A second factor gives the traditional economy its simple nature and this is the *archaic technology* employed in various production activities. The technology of this society is called archaic because it is characterized by the three following features: (1) the use of natural energy, such as animal power, or the force of wind and water; (2) the use of tools, which are a direct extension of the limbs of the human body (the hammer or the mallet give the arms and the fist a greater driving force); (3) the use of simple weapons such as axes, arrows, javelins.

Finally, the traditional economy is simple because it is based on a very elementary division of labour which generally consists of the distribution of tasks between the sexes and among age groups. Some tasks are ascribed to men and others to women; children and old people are assigned activities which are simpler or less tiring than others. Because it is rudimentary, the division of labour is often rigid. Men never undertake the work of women, and vice versa. It should be added, however, that specializations of a professional nature also may exist in traditional society. This is true, for example, of the sorcerer or the shaman, but it is also true of various craftsmen who specialize in the production of certain tools and artifacts.

---

2. For example, André Varagnac, *De la préhistoire au monde moderne: Essai d'une Anthropodynamique* (Paris: Plon, 1954), p. 35.

A subsistence economy

Archaic technology and an elementary division of labour result in low productivity. From this emerges a *subsistence economy*, which is characteristic of traditional society. In this type of economy, society produces the goods that it needs immediately for its survival and defence. No surplus is accumulated except over a short period (a few days or months, or at most a year). Thus, the problem of providing food is almost a daily one; it dominates the activity of every individual, as well as his thoughts and conversation. The subsistence economy is constantly threatened by the prospect of drought and famine. If game and fish are in short supply, or if the harvest is spoiled, it is disastrous for the entire human community. Therefore, in societies where circumstances are particularly precarious, the main quality required of the leader and his primary concern is the safeguarding of the survival of his people.[3]

Under these conditions, the traditional society can export only in exceptional circumstances. In any event, the available means of transport are very slow, and as a result the society's area of contact is limited. Exchanges — when they exist — can be carried out only with immediately neighbouring societies and concern only a very limited number of articles. Even within the traditional society, commercial exchanges are almost non-existent or very limited. Usually money does not exist; if it does, it is seldom used. Barter is the main form of exchange, often conducted ceremoniously or by ritual (on the occasion of a celebration, games, or a funeral), rather than for purely commercial ends.

A limited society

A subsistence economy has important demographic implications. First, it explains why the traditional society is always limited in number and why the population density is very low. Given the natural resources available for survival and an archaic technology, this type of society must be able to exploit a rather extensive territory in relation to the size of its population. Furthermore, the demographic growth of this type of society cannot be rapid; otherwise, the equilibrium between the population and the natural re-

---

3. Striking examples can be found among the Indian tribes of Brazil, described by Claude Lévi-Strauss in *Tristes Tropiques* (Paris: Plon, 1955). Translated as *World on the Wane*.

sources will soon break down. In fact, because of unfavourable hygienic conditions and rudimentary medical knowledge, life expectancy is very short and the rate of infant mortality is high. Occasionally, too, migrations and wars help to check population growth. Thus, through various means, a traditional society is led to respect a given demographic maximum or ceiling, which it cannot exceed without endangering its very existence.

The Social Organization of Traditional Society

The kinship system

The organization of traditional society rests on two main axes: the kinship system, and age groups. The kinship system is based on the recognition of blood and marriage ties which unite a group of people. These ties give rise to a complex network of relationships among individuals of different ages, based on rights, duties and obligations which are explicitly defined and regulated by norms and rules of conduct that sometimes may be very strict. Through his membership in a kinship group, each individual finds himself obliged to adopt certain attitudes towards various people, to show more respect for certain persons than for others, and to help some more than others.

The functions of the kinship system

In traditional society, the kinship system fulfills very important functions. First, it is this system which confers on each member his social personality: the individual is integrated into traditional society according to the place that he occupies in the kinship system. The name by which he is known and called is often only a description of this position ("Hector's Pierre"). Many missionaries and ethnologists, in order to be admitted to a traditional society, have had to be adopted by a family which gave them a name, status, and above all the confidence of the people. In a traditional society, not to belong to any kinship group is to be a foreigner, and this is often equivalent to being an enemy, or at least a potential one.

In addition, the kinship system forms a vast network of interdependence and mutual help, because of the numerous obligations that it creates between its members. In case of need, one can always count on the help of members of the kinship system. In a subsistence economy, this help is most valuable for those who benefit from it, although it can be costly and burdensome for those who must contribute to it. In a later chapter, we will see the problems that can result in traditional countries in the process of development.

Above all, it can be said that, in almost every traditional society, the kinship system forms the basic framework of social organization. All the collective life of the community is organized around the kinship system and reflects its form. Thus, many traditional societies are divided into clans or moieties, which are nothing more than groups of kinship systems; all the members of a clan or moiety consider themselves related in one way or another. In these societies, most of the religious, recreational, economic and military activities are organized according to the lines dividing clans or moieties. Political power also very often arises from the power of heads of families or leaders of clans. Indeed, sometimes the division of kinship groups is reflected concretely in the physical arrangement of a village and in the location of dwellings in such a way as to ensure that the members of the same clan or moiety live close to one another.[4]

Thus, in traditional society, the kinship system is an essential means of social differentiation: it provides for distinctions and groupings within the society. But it is also an important factor in social integration. Inspired by *The Gift* by Marcel Mauss, Lévi-Strauss has shown that in traditional societies, marriage is basically a form of exchange of women, and this creates a complex network of ties among kinship groups, clans and moieties. These groups are consequently linked together by a series of various obligations, debts, responsibilities and affective relationships which ensure the solidarity of the total society and prevent it from becoming fragmented into more limited groups.[5]

The complexity of the forms of kinship systems

It should not be supposed that because social organization is based on the kinship system, it is simple. Contrary to the economic structure, the social organization of traditional societies is often

---

4. For example, the case of the Bororo village in Brazil, *ibid.*, pp. 187 ff.
5. Claude Lévi-Strauss, *The Elementary Structures of Kinship*, trans. James Harle Bell, John Richard von Sturmer and Rodney Needham (London: Eyre and Spottiswoode, 1969).

quite complex, for kinship systems themselves take on a complex form. The American anthropologist George Murdock has been able to show that there exist at least twenty main forms of kinship systems, with variations.[6] In practice, when the anthropologist first makes contact with a new society, he must often devote a great deal of time to unravelling the skein of kinship links, which each member of the society appears to understand very easily. It is as if these traditional societies specialized in the art of inventing and refining the forms of kinship systems, since these constitute the nucleus of their social organization.

Age groups and categories

The second axis of the social organization of traditional societies is age groups and categories which horizontally overlap kinship groups. In traditional society, rights and obligations are attached to different stages of human life; and as proof of their importance, in most cases various symbols are created to express these rights and duties. In addition, the transition of an individual from one age to another is often marked by group ceremonies and celebrations. Van Gennep has called these ceremonies *rites de passage*.[7]

In France

An extract from André Varagnac's book *De la préhistoire au monde moderne* (*From Prehistory to Modern Times*) summarizes well the history and importance of age categories in traditional societies. Describing prehistoric social life before the Iron Age, Varagnac writes:

> Clearly, families were organized in communal groupings. The community or the tribe (which could include several hamlets) was in turn noticeably structured according to a type of organization that ethnographers call age categories. *All* the members of the community were arranged in a particular group according to age. Children, young people, fathers and mothers, and old people formed distinct groups, characterized by special rights and duties and by particular roles and behaviour. All the inhabitants were obliged to be members

---

6. George P. Murdock, *Social Structure* (New York: Macmillan Co., 1949).
7. Arnold Van Gennep, *Les rites de passage* (Paris: Nourry, 1909).

of these successive groups. Ethnographers have noticed this form of division and social organization among the oldest known peoples, a form which at this stage showed no evidence of social caste or class divisions. But studies by sociologists and folklorists in all the countries of Europe have demonstrated the survival up to the present day of this very ancient social organization, even though nearly four thousand years have passed since the Iron Age and since the division of societies into castes and socio-economic classes.[8]

Varagnac himself is among those who have studied this survival of age categories in contemporary society. In another work, he gives a very good example of age groups and categories among French peasants.[9] Guided by the folklore of the different regions of France in distinguishing the symbols attached to stages of human life, Varagnac distinguishes eight age categories.

1. *The first age* (from conception until the end of the nursing period). Since the foetus and the nursing infant are frail and defenceless, they need protection, mainly because they are "subject to attacks from wicked spirits and from witches. . . . From birth, the nursing infants have to be guarded night and day by an adult who is often armed." The infant, who still belongs to the Other World whence he comes, is a sign of sanctification and blessing for the home that receives him.

2. *Childhood.* The end of the nursing period, which generally comes when the child is two or three years old, marks the transition to childhood. The child continues to be considered as a "messenger from the Other World," but he can now call down blessings not only on his own home, but also on others that he visits, as illustrated by the celebrations and ceremonies mentioned by Varagnac.

3. *Young people.* Young girls and boys are still invested with certain magico-religious functions, and this gives them a special place in certain celebrations and ceremonies. But their social role is asserted more and more strongly. For young girls, it is a period of temporary autonomy before they finally become submissive to a man in marriage; thus, they are the object of courtship. Young boys have more civic responsibilities; they "must prepare for the

---

8. Varagnac, *De la préhistoire au monde moderne*, pp. 162-163.
9. André Varagnac, *Civilisation traditionnelle et genres de vie* (Paris: Albin Michel, 1948), pp. 113-245.

formation of new households, control the peace of households, and generally supervise the customs which define the respective duties and rights of the age categories. . . . They form the essential part of the military force of the community. . . . Finally, it seems that in various regions they have been specifically charged with looking after the upkeep of the public roads. . . ."

4. *Young marrieds.* Marriage is a real *rite de passage*, which profoundly changes the status of the newlyweds. During the first year of marriage, they fall into a special category between youth and maturity. The folklore about them is rich and varied. Varagnac summarizes it as follows: "A certain number of customs relative to recently married people stem from elementary sexual symbolism; others relate to the birth of a child; others impose dues on the recently married; others require gifts for them; others subject them to jokes, and still others transform them into temporary leaders of youth. . . ."

5. *Fathers and mothers.* "The birth of the child separates the newly married from the group of young people." They enter a new category which is more diffuse but still clearly distinguished by the authority and the numerous and heavy responsibilities carried by its members. "Being in charge of work and daily subsistence, fathers and mothers are also the workmen responsible for the accumulation of reserves and riches. . . . To conserve living capital — the people and animals of the household — and perishable reserves is a daily and nightly struggle against a world of invisible dangers. . . ."

6. *Widows and widowers.* Widows and widowers are expected to carry alone, and courageously, the responsibilities of the former household. French peasantry does not favourably regard a remarriage with a younger person. The widow or widower who remarries risks being the victim of a charivari conducted by young people, who see themselves deprived of a possible spouse.

7. *Old people.* The marriage of the last child marks the transition to this age category. A varied folklore accompanies this marriage, and its symbols express the retirement of the old parents. This is the period of physical decline, and retirement from work and sexual life.

8. *The deceased.* To Varagnac, these form a real age category; for they continue to live among the living, at least for a certain period. They make various demands on the living; they have certain rights; and, on occasion, they can punish or reward according to whether or not they are helped.

In Quebec

Varagnac claims that age categories were not the same for all French peasants, and that variations from this general picture could be observed from one region to another. On this question, the American anthropologist Horace Miner provides us with a useful point of comparison. In his monograph on the rural village of St-Denis de Kamouraska in Quebec, where he stayed in 1936 and 1937, Miner[10] identified six age categories.

1. *Young children*, from their birth to their entry into school. This is a period of relative independence, combined with the training undertaken by parents and older brothers and sisters. It is a non-productive period, dominated by play among children and sometimes with adults.

2. *Children of school age*, from the age of six to ten or fifteen. This is the beginning of serious living. The child must go to school, and at home he must start performing small services, which vary according to his or her sex. This period is marked by two religious *rites de passage* which are particularly important: the "petite communion," or first communion, when the child is about seven; and the "grande communion," or declaration of faith, which marks the beginning of adolescence about the age of twelve.

3. *Adolescents.* The end of formal school studies marks the definite transition from childhood to adolescence. For the adolescent, the realm of social relationships is enlarged; he participates in social evenings, and he has a group of friends that he sees on various occasions. In addition, he participates actively in work on the farm and in the house. Varagnac did not find in France the same separation between adolescents and young people which Miner found in Quebec.

4. *Young people.* The transition to this age category is gradual, evidenced by changes in styles of clothing, the right to smoke for the boy, the beginning of dating, and above all growing responsibilities in preparation for the future.

5. *Fathers and mothers.* In St-Denis, there does not seem to be a special category for the newly marrieds, such as that described by Varagnac for the French peasantry. Much more than among the French peasantry, here marriage marks the direct entry into matu-

---

10. Horace Miner, *St-Denis, A French Canadian Parish* (Chicago: University of Chicago Press, 1939).

rity. After the important *rite de passage* of marriage, Miner observed a progressive transformation in the couple. The woman adopts longer and more somber clothes and no longer curls her hair; the period of courtship is finished. The man starts to wear a moustache. But mainly — and in this they are like the French peasants — the two take on increasingly heavy responsibilities.

6. *Old people*. The marriage of the last child does not appear to have the importance in St-Denis that it had among the French peasantry. Perhaps when the couple give up their land and goods to the son who will succeed them, they start their retirement. During this period, they are mainly occupied with preparing for death and ensuring their eternal salvation.

While Miner does not specifically consider the deceased as an age category, he still gives a number of indications that they remain present in the spirit of the living, who have certain debts towards them and who fulfill certain obligations.

The unified nature of social organization

A remarkable feature of age categories, which has been amply emphasized by Varagnac and Miner, is that magic, religion and secular activities are intermingled and confused. In the *rites de passage* and in the rights and duties attributed to different categories, a fusion of the supernatural and the temporal can usually be observed. This brings us to note that, in a general way, the social organization of traditional societies is closely linked to magic or religion. One achieves a certain status, or changes status, by participating in magical or religious rites. Power at all levels — the family, the kinship system, the total society — is both religious and political. If there is a distinction between political power and religious power, the two always remain closely associated and interdependent. And the rhythm of daily life from year to year is marked by a great number of celebrations which are both religious and social. These celebrations are often directed towards a category or group of the social organization; they can impose on parents or on another age category heavy responsibilities for the preparation and enactment of ritual ceremonies (dances, song, games, exchanges).

This fusion of the sacred and the secular gives the social organization of traditional society *a certain wholeness or a unified nature* which has led many anthropologists to treat it as a strongly integrated whole. But this is not always the case. Traditional man obeys norms and patterns of behaviour which are imposed on him in the name of both that which is held sacred and society; for the same action, he incurs sanctions immediately and in the Other World. Political power demands the support of supernatural spirits, as well as the support of tradition and law. Legal acts (treaties, marriages, promises) similarly have a magical character. Thus, both here and in the next world, the entire future is almost always involved in the social behaviour of the members of traditional society.

Social control

It should be added that, in traditional society, social control is exerted in a direct and immediate way, because the social universe is limited and everyone knows everyone else. In the village, the deviant is more quickly located than in the large town and undergoes almost immediate punishment. In a limited and self-examining community, the control of each person by the group is exerted almost constantly. And among the control mechanisms of traditional society, a special place must be accorded to gossip. This phenomenon has been studied by many anthropologists. Gossip breaks the monotony and routine of daily life, taking the place of the press or spoken news. It brings an element of novelty and gaiety to a social life which often lacks these elements — all the more so because imagination is inevitably mixed up with it. It is these characteristics that make gossip a powerful factor of social control.

Thus, it can be said that each member of a traditional society belongs to it totally and unconditionally. According to Parsons' terminology, the individual is linked to the society in a diffuse rather than a specific way. Because of this, the organization appears particularly stable and well-knit.

The Mentality of Traditional Society

Empiricism

One of the strongest prejudices which retarded the progress of modern anthropology was the belief that there existed a primitive mentality which was basically different from that of civilized man. Lévy-Bruhl was undoubtedly the most typical representative of this theory; it was he who formulated it most clearly and in its most extreme form, even though at the end of his life he doubted his own hypotheses.[11]

Lévy-Bruhl contrasted the "logical mentality" of Western civilization with the "pre-logical mentality" of primitive man, showing that the latter operated on the basis of certain *principles* which were fundamentally different from those of rational logic. Because of this, primitive man could not establish the same relations between objects as we can; and consequently, he could only construct different classifications from ours. From this, Lévy-Bruhl concluded that the two mentalities were totally unreconcilable.

Today this theory has been completely abandoned — not because differences between the two mentalities are no longer recognized, but because differences have been sought in other areas.

First of all, it must be recognized that a vast reservoir of knowledge exists in traditional societies, even the most "primitive" ones, which is scientifically valid. A great many facts bear witness to this. In the most archaic societies, men have a profound knowledge of nature, of the properties of plants, of the movements of the stars, of the habits of animals and so forth. But this knowledge is essentially *empirical*; it lacks the framework and the theoretical basis that comprise modern science. Such knowledge forms a unit of partial and juxtaposed information which, while it is all true and consequently useful and practical, does not thereby form a science. For example, one might be able to foretell the weather according to a flight of birds, the provisions that certain animals make, or the rheumatic pains one feels, and seldom be wrong. But all this knowledge does not form a science of meteorology which is theoretically based. The meteorological forecasts may more often be proved wrong than those of Indians or peasants — it doesn't matter; for it is still true that the knowledge of the meteorologists is scientific and that of Indians and peasants is empirical.

The nature of traditional empiricism

Lévi-Strauss, who has analyzed traditional mentality in depth, explains it by using an enlightening comparison between the handyman and the engineer. The handyman possesses empirical, practical and efficient knowledge or knacks. He knows how to

---

11. Lucien Lévy-Bruhl, *Primitive Mentality*, trans. Lilian A. Clare (New York: Macmillan Co., 1923). It was in *Les carnets* (Paris: Presses universitaires de France, 1949), published after his death, that Lévy-Bruhl questioned his own ideas.

make use of materials and tools; he manages with the minimum of resources; he can carry out a great number of jobs in his house without needing complicated theoretical knowledge. The engineer, while he is sometimes less well equipped than the handyman for the normal upkeep of his house, possesses theoretical and experimental knowledge which is more developed, and which enables him to conceive and supervise large work projects. The handyman's knowledge is no less scientifically valid than that of the engineer, but it is not of the same kind, not at the same level. The handyman's knowledge is at the empirical level; that of the engineer is scientific and experimental.[12]

Empirical knowledge is the result of patient and attentive observation of life; it is constructed by accumulating detailed and fragmentary information. Its basis is neither logical deduction nor laboratory experiment, but rather a long *tradition of accuracy*. It is supported by the fact that the flight of birds has never been wrong about the forthcoming weather. Strictly speaking, this type of knowledge is traditional, in the sense that the tradition transmitted since time immemorial vouches for it. Here we are able to grasp the deepest and most real meaning of the expression *traditional* society.

Conservatism

From this perspective, it can be understood that change and innovation are not warmly welcomed and may even appear threatening. They question and threaten to break up the very basis of the intellectual order and the mental and practical relationship with life. It is therefore thought to be safer to continue to trust in useful knowledge, which has been proved over time, than to accept new ideas, particularly when these are foreign to the normal intellectual process. The *conservatism* which characterizes traditional mentality is thus basically a protection against everything that menaces tradition as the basis of the intellectual order and the foundation of successful adaptation to the environment.

Mythical thought

In order to understand such conservatism better, we shall return to the example of the handyman. There is an important difference

---

12. Claude Lévi-Strauss, *The Savage Mind* (London: Weidenfeld and Nicolson, 1966).

between the mentality of the handyman and that of primitive man. The former realizes that a theoretical science exists that he does not know, or knows only a little, but that he respects. The latter ignores such theory, if indeed he knows it exists; he is not interested in it or he distrusts it, as can be seen from several instances reported by Lévi-Strauss. In traditional society, *mythology* takes the place of theoretical science. It is myth which links together disparate and incoherent fragments of knowledge, and which gives these fragments meaning and coherence. In traditional society, mythology at the same time takes the place of natural science, history and the social sciences. It *recounts* more than it explains why things are as they are; it tells of the origins and development of things, and names ancient sources of its stories. In this way, it contributes to the foundation of tradition within an order that is both human and superhuman, where the sacred world and daily practical events are linked.

Relationships between the sacred and the secular

The important role of mythical thought in the state of knowledge also explains another characteristic of traditional mentality — *the fusion of the sacred and the secular.* Mircea Eliade[13] has clearly illustrated how, in traditional mentality, things and events refer back to "something else," to an invisible order which exists and develops parallel to the visible order, and of which the latter is a part. From that perspective, what is visible is only a part of the total cosmos, and a no less real part escapes our view. This invisible order is sacred; it completes the visible order and gives it its real meaning. Events and things are not self-explanatory but their truth must be revealed with reference to the sacred world, for it is there that their original model and source is located. This concept gives rise to the great variety in traditional society of symbols for the manifestation of the gods to man.

The same is true of collective life, which also follows an invisible model. The divisions of society, the arrangement of houses, the rhythm and cycle of nature and of human life, all reflect the sacred order. For example, celebrations — which are generally numerous in traditional society and which occur at specific times in the annual cycle — are designed to permit the community to par-

---

13. Mircea Eliade, *Le sacré et le profane* (Paris: Gallimard, Collection "Idées," 1965).

ticipate in the progress of invisible events which are repeated from year to year. The members' perception and explanation of traditional society (their natural sociology) are thus necessarily integrated into a vast cosmological system in which the natural and social orders belong to a higher order, which simultaneously serves as a model for them. Thus, what we earlier called the unified nature of the social organization of traditional society can now be better understood, for mythical thought is both its origin and its support.

Confined within restricted geographical limits, traditional thought nonetheless opens out, through the intermediary of mythology, onto the entire universe. But it is a universe that is perceived by the members of most traditional societies as having themselves at its centre. Mircea Eliade observes that in many religions a tree, a mountain, a temple, a sanctuary or a town are said to be the centre and the pillar of the world.[14] And many anthropologists have noted that the name of a people or of a tribe simultaneously means *man* or *humanity*. As a result, a foreigner is generally perceived as another human species or an inferior man, if not an enemy. From this arise the rites of adoption mentioned earlier, by which a stranger may be admitted to the community.

Magical thought

In this context of mythical and sacred thought, *magic*, which is constantly present in the life of traditional society, becomes comprehensible. Magic consists essentially of the manipulation by man of invisible forces or forms of energy which were bestowed on things at the beginning of time or which are simply part of their nature. In contrast to religion, magic is necessarily effective, provided that one knows and practises the rites correctly. Thus, like technology or empirical knowledge, it has a practical applied goal. As Malinowski has clearly shown,[15] however, magic does not replace technology and does not ignore empirical science; rather, it completes and extends them. The Trobriander Islanders, described by Malinowski, do not use magic when they fish in the lagoons, where fish are abundant and where there is no danger; but they use it for open sea fishing, which is more uncertain and dangerous. Magic is to action what myth is to thought; the two effect the synthesis of the sacred and the secular, or the integration of the visible and the invisible worlds.

14. *Ibid.*, pp. 31-44.
15. B. Malinowski, *Magic, Science and Religion* (Glencoe, Ill.: The Free Press, 1948), p. 14.

Technological Society

The Economic Structure of Technological Society

The natural environment and the technical environment

Georges Friedmann has distinguished between the *natural environment* and the *technical environment*.[16] In the natural environment man lives in direct and immediate contact with nature, he adopts its rhythms and adapts himself to its requirements and constraints. Thus we can say that in traditional society, as it has just been described, he lives absolutely in a natural environment.

In contrast, the technical environment interjects between man and nature a network of machines, complex techniques, knowledge, and manufactured, transformed and adapted objects. Man is no longer dependent on nature; instead, he tends to subject it to his needs, desires and ambitions. He exploits nature in the literal sense of the term; he dominates it and uses it for his own ends. As Friedmann emphasizes, the technical environment is a new environment, for it has appeared recently in the history of humanity. It stems from the industrial revolution — that is, from the transition from the tool to the machine and from manual work to mechanized work — but it also arises from the discovery of new materials and unexploited energy. The technical milieu really characterizes modern society; it is both its cause and its product.

The technical environment and the production economy

Following the extension of the technical environment, the economic structure of technological society has become infinitely more complex than that of traditional society. The technological economy is an *economy of production*, characterized by very high labour productivity complementing the use of machines, electricity, electronics and nuclear energy. In contrast to the subsistence economy, the production economy cannot be stable without de-

16. Georges Friedmann, *Sept études sur l'homme et la technique* (Paris: Gonthier, 1966), pp. 7-69 and 203-6.

clining; its natural state is dynamic. Thus, by its very nature, the technological economy is necessarily vast and international, and is based on an extended network of exchanges which are supported by an abundant use of money and credit. While fear of drought dominates traditional society, overproduction constantly threatens the technological economy. The only solution is the expansion of the internal and external market, and finally a reduction in man's working hours. Developed to its extreme, the production economy ends, paradoxically, by becoming the leisure civilization.

Three other factors of high productivity

Technology alone is not sufficient to explain the growth in productivity. There are three other contributing factors. First, there is the enormous investment of capital. The industrial revolution was possible only because enormous fortunes were available for the creation of the first factories, machines, modern industry, and means of transport and communication. The technological society thus requires a complex financial structure, based as much on credit as on money itself.

Second, the technological economy was made possible only through an increasingly complex division of labour. In his analysis in *The Wealth of Nations*, Adam Smith showed, through his classic example of the manufacture of pins, that productivity increased when the assembly line replaced the production of a complete pin by each worker.[17] More than any other society, the technological society has pushed the division of labour to the extreme point of the fragmentation of tasks, which Georges Friedmann has called the anatomy of work. But it is not only in the factory that this fragmentation has taken place; the whole society is characterized by the specialization of functions and by professionalization.

Third, technological society has effected a considerable movement of the labour force from the sector of production that is called primary, towards the secondary and tertiary sectors. The primary sector is based on the exploitation of natural resources — that is, agriculture, fishing, hunting, mining and the breeding of stock. The secondary sector includes all activities which transform raw material into finished products, and thus covers all forms of industrial activity. The tertiary sector includes all business activi-

17. Adam Smith, *The Wealth of Nations* (London: J. M. Dent and Sons Ltd., 1933), p. 5.

ties, transportation, communications, professional and public services, the professions and, in a general way, non-manual employment. As the economists Colin Clark and Jean Fourastié[18] have
shown (see Figure 1), from the beginning of the industrial period
there has been a movement of the labour force from the formerly
dominant primary sector towards the secondary sector, and then
increasingly towards the tertiary sector. In the more industrialized
countries, a levelling off can be observed, and even the beginning
of a decline in the secondary sector in favour of the tertiary sector.
Already we can foresee that the majority of the population will
soon be located in this latter sector, as a result of the rising educational standards of the population and the progress of automation.

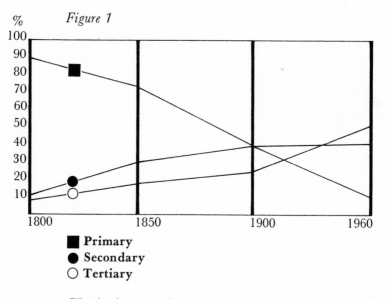

■ **Primary**
● **Secondary**
○ **Tertiary**

*The development of the primary, secondary and tertiary
sectors of production in the main industrialized countries
from 1800 to the present*

---

18. Colin Clark, *The Conditions of Economic Progress*, 3rd edition (London:
Macmillan, 1957); Jean Fourastié, *Le grand espoir du XXe Siècle* (Paris:
Presses universitaires de France, édition définitive, 1958).

The break between the producer
and the consumer

The evolution of the division of labour and the structure of employment has had an important result which is characteristic of technological society — the break between the producer and the consumer. In traditional society, the family consumes what it produces; it is simultaneously the unit of production and the unit of consumption. In technological society, the family is generally no more than a unit of consumption. The worker labours for a market that he often does not know himself; the work place is separated from the home and production is radically separated from rest, leisure and consumption.

The constant increase in consumption demands

One last characteristic of the industrial economy should be emphasized, and this is that the sustained expansion of such an economy essentially depends on a constant increase in consumption. As Halbwachs and following him Chombart de Lauwe[19] have clearly shown, human needs are neither fixed nor firmly established; they increase or decrease in relation to the economic cycle. "The phases of (economic) expansion provoke the appearance of new needs, which then seek to consolidate themselves."[20] During a period of economic prosperity, certain needs become more sophisticated; this is true for the demand for food, clothing and housing. New demands are created — in Western civilization the demand for televisions and cars has become almost as elementary as the need for food. New kinds of needs appear — intellectual, aesthetic and spiritual. The level of need is thus not an abstract or general fact; it is a changing cultural and psychological reality, or at least it can be. In industrial society, it is this change in the level of needs which is the mainspring of what the economists call the elasticity of demand, an essential factor in industrial expansion. Advertising and all forms of promotion of products tend to increase demand

---

19. Maurice Halbwachs, *L'évolution des besoins dans les classes ouvrières* (Paris: Alcan, 1933); Paul-Henry Chombart de Lauwe, *La vie quotidienne des familles ouvrières* (Paris: Centre national de la recherche scientifique, 1956). In Quebec, a similar study has been conducted by Marc A. Tremblay and Gérald Fortin, *Les comportements économiques de la famille salariée du Québec* (Québec: Les Presses de l'Université Laval, 1964).
20. Chombart de Lauwe, *Familles ouvrières*, p. 11.

by constantly raising the level of the needs of consumers. It is the inverse situation to that which prevails in traditional society, where the level of needs is low and more or less stable.

The Social Organization of Technological Society

A complex social organization

While it is fairly easy to pin down the main bases of the social organization of traditional society, such as the kinship system and age groups, it is much more difficult to do this for technological society. The latter includes a much greater number of elements or structures than does traditional society. In addition to the kinship system, which continues to fulfill certain specific functions, and age categories, which continue to exist (this is evident particularly in the importance that the so-called youth culture has taken on in recent years), technological society includes the professions, social classes, voluntary associations, political parties, churches, trade unions and other interest groups. Thus it can be said that the dominant trait of the social organization of technological society is its *complexity*, to the point that, in spite of all the studies carried out, it is still very difficult to compile a coherent and integrated description of it. In sociology, technological society is quite frequently called complex society, in contrast to traditional society, which is relatively simple (or so it appears to us).

Many sociologists have shown that each individual must assume *multiple roles* in technological society. One man is simultaneously the father of a family, an employee of a certain office or factory, and a member of a club, a political party, a trade union, a church and various associations. The risks of role conflict are consequently much greater here than in traditional society. Such a complex society imposes on its members a great number of relationships which Parsons has called specific, in which the individual is involved with only a part of his total being. The society must also develop rules which Parsons calls universalist, for individuality would be equivalent to anarchy. These are various ways of expressing the complexity of technological society: the fragmentation of the personality corresponds, at the level of individuals and their behaviour, to the diversity of the structures of society.

A society based on production

If we had to bring together in one formula the essential character-istics of the organization of technological society, we would say that it is *based mainly on production, its conditions and con-sequences.* In a technological society, man must be a producer not only in industry, but also in the intellectual, artistic, political and even religious realms (there is a constant demand for new ideas, new values, a new philosophy and scientific discoveries). Man must continuously produce a great deal, because he consumes enormous amounts of material goods, ideas, images, works of art and all kinds of idols. It follows that technological society is characterized in particular by the predominant part played by the work world, and by the attendant economic organization and structure. Work is forever present in the daily life of traditional so-ciety also, given that subsistence is a daily struggle. But one does not find *a work world* which is organized, structured and domi-nant, as it is in technological society. In addition, as we empha-sized earlier, in traditional society there is only a rudimentary and simple economic structure.

Thus, it is not surprising that Marx attributed a central position in his definition of man to productive work and praxis, and that he gave the economy a predominant role in human his-tory. Applied to industrial society, which he saw developing in his lifetime, his analysis was valid.

Now, let us look a little more closely at how this predominance of production and the work world is manifested concretely in so-cial organization.

The predominance of achieved status

Let us start with the following fact. In traditional society, the two foundations of social organization confer on individuals a status whose bases are purely biological — blood ties and age. Ralph Linton[21] writes that in this type of society, the individual enjoys an ascribed status — that is, a social status which he receives at birth, or at some other stage of his life, without having had to win it or necessarily deserve it (for example, the status of son, brother-in-law, young person or old). In contrast, in industrial society, it is

---

21. Ralph Linton, *The Study of Man* (New York: Appleton-Century-Crofts, Inc., 1936), chap. 8.

achieved status which dominates, or the social status which a person obtains through what he does or which results from his own activity; thus, it is a status that he can attempt to improve if he wishes, and if he is capable of it. Ascribed status is contrasted with achieved status in rather the same way as Being is contrasted with Doing. When one wishes to know someone in traditional society, one asks "Whose son is he?" In technological society, one asks "What does he do?" or perhaps "What does her husband do?" Thus, it is mainly through the work world that achieved status and the social personality that it confers are acquired. One fact that demonstrates this very well is that survey questionnaires almost inevitably include one or two questions on the occupation of the respondent. This information is much more useful than his name or his family background, for it enables us to locate him quite precisely in society, according to his level of education, his income, his life habits, and sometimes even his place of residence.

A professionalized society

Because it is a productive society, the technological society is, from the sociological point of view, a *professionalized* society. On the one hand, the work world is highly diversified; it is broken up into a multitude of occupations that result from an unending division of tasks. And this enormous network of varying occupations encloses the whole society like netting. It is ubiquitous — it is found whatever one does or wherever one goes. On the other hand, because of this constant presence of the occupational structure, each person must define his social identity (and that of others) in relation to this network of occupations. And it is through and within this network that he acquires a precise and recognizable status. In this context, to be unemployed entails not only a loss of income, but also a loss of status and prestige. Also, many housebound women and students say that they suffer from deprivation of a recognized status in this society based on the division of labour and production.

While the occupations of technological society are numerous and diversified, they are nevertheless distributed according to *a hierarchical order*. It is remarkable that, without any preconceived plan, the members of technological society all have in mind the same representation of this hierarchical distribution of occupations. A number of sociologists have verified this fact by carrying out empirical studies of the scale of occupational prestige.[22] Similar studies, carried out in several industrialized countries, have even shown that with some minor variations the same scale of prestige can be discovered in the United States, Great Britain, France, the Soviet Union, Japan and Canada.[23] This quasi-unanimity is all the more striking because it is generally very difficult to explain satisfactorily why and according to what criteria one occupation is considered to be more prestigious than another.

A bureaucratic society

The work world of technological society manifests another specific characteristic which is very important: it is highly *bureaucratic*. Max Weber has analyzed Western bureaucracy, and bureaucracy in general, in the greatest depth; to him in particular we owe the image of the main features of a bureaucracy in its pure state.[24] Let us summarize them briefly:

---

22. The study that was most instrumental in revealing this fact is without doubt the one carried out by the National Opinion Research Center of the United States, under the direction of C. C. North and Paul L. Hatt, "Jobs and Occupations: A Popular Evaluation," *Opinion News* 9 (September 1, 1947): 3-13. In this study, a national sample of individuals was asked to attribute a rank to ninety occupations; the high correlation between the replies was very striking. The method developed by North and Hatt served as the starting point for a great number of similar studies in several countries.

23. Alex Inkeles and Peter H. Rossi, "National Comparisons of Occupational Prestige," *American Journal of Sociology* 61 (January 1956): 329-39. In this article, the authors compare the scales of prestige in six countries — Germany, Great Britain, Japan, New Zealand, the Soviet Union and the United States. Recently, the analysis has been extended to include a greater number of countries as well as developing countries: R. W. Hodge, D. J. Treiman and Peter H. Rossi, "A Comparative Study of Occupational Prestige" in Bendix and Lipset, eds., *Class, Status and Power*, 2nd edition (1966), pp. 309-21. In addition, it has been possible to demonstrate, at least for the United States, the stability of the occupational prestige scale by repeating in 1963 the NORC study of 1947: R. W. Hodge, Paul M. Seigel and Peter H. Rossi, "Occupational Prestige in the United States, 1925-1963," *American Journal of Sociology* 70 (November 1964): 286-302. For Canada, two studies using different techniques have highlighted the similarity between the American and Canadian scales of prestige and also the similarity, with some minor differences, between English and French Canada: Peter C. Pineo and John Porter, "Occupational Prestige in Canada," *Canadian Review of Sociology and Anthropology* 4 (February 1967): 24-40; Bernard R. Blishen, "A Socio-Economic Index for Occupations in Canada," *Canadian Review of Sociology and Anthropology* 4 (February 1967): 41-53.

24. Max Weber, *From Max Weber: Essays in Sociology*, trans. H. H. Gerth and C. Wright Mills (New York: Oxford University Press, 1946), pp. 196-244.

1. A bureaucracy is essentially a rational organization of the work of a great number of individuals who all contribute to the production of the same good or service.

2. A bureaucracy is always a hierarchical juxtaposition of areas of responsibility, so that each person is responsible for his work to an immediate superior, who himself is responsible to another superior and so on up to the highest level.*

3. Detailed rules specify the tasks of each person, the way in which he must carry them out, the area of his responsibilities, his immediate superior and so on.

4. The bureaucrat receives a fixed salary which is established according to norms which take into account his previous education, his years of service, his experience and his competence.

5. Entry into the bureaucracy and promotion from one level to the other are permitted according to objective, defined criteria which enable one to judge the competence of the candidate to occupy the post.

6. The bureaucrat is not the owner of his position or his work tools.

Again, we note that these traits are those of a bureaucracy in a pure state. In practice, bureaucracies can deviate to a greater or lesser extent, even to the point of becoming irrational and inefficient; this is the main source of criticism by modern observers.[25]

Bureaucracy did not first appear in the last century; it has always existed. It was well developed in Ancient Egypt, where even the prophet became an official. This is shown by the biblical story of the Israeli, Joseph, who was sold by his brothers as a slave and who, after interpreting the Pharoah's dream, became the prime minister and was put in charge of applying the economic policy that arose from his interpretation of this dream. In modern society, the multiplication of occupations and the development of large firms have made bureaucracy more necessary than ever. The State, commercial or industrial firms, banks, the educational system, hospitals, churches, trade unions and even social movements

---

25. See in particular William H. Whyte, Jr., *The Organization Man* (New York: Simon and Schuster, 1956). The terms *bureaucracy* and *bureaucrat* clearly have a pejorative connotation in general everyday language.

are all organizations of the bureaucratic type. Thus, bureaucracy is not reserved for the public sector alone, but is found just as much in private enterprise. Formerly independent professions — medicine, law and business — are becoming increasingly bureaucratic.

An urban society

A work world that is professionalized and bureaucratic presupposes a population that is highly concentrated; thus, technological society is necessarily an *urban* society. The large city is perhaps the most obvious symbol and the most striking aspect of technological society. A modern town is the most perfect illustration of the technical environment of which Georges Friedmann speaks. In addition, it has been the object of a great number of studies to which we can only refer the reader.[26]

The pre-eminence of the economic structure

The predominance of the work world is necessarily accompanied by *the pre-eminence of the economic structure within the social organization.* One cannot exist without the other. The position that is occupied by the economic structure in technological society appears at many points. Thus, while political power was separated from religious power, it was only to move closer to economic power. Politicians cannot dissociate themselves from the holders of economic power — financiers, industrialists, and labour leaders. Labour leaders in particular have become a sort of power behind

---

26. The interested reader can consult, in particular, Max Weber, *The City*, trans. Don Martindale and Gertrud Neuwirth (Glencoe, Ill.: The Free Press, 1958); R. E. Park, E. W. Burgess and R. D. McKenzie, *The City* (Chicago: University of Chicago Press, 1925); Georges Friedmann, ed., *Villes et campagnes* (Paris: Armand Colin, 1953); Paul-Henry Chombart de Lauwe, *Paris et l'agglomération parisienne* (Paris: Presses universitaires de France, 1952) and by the same author, *Des hommes et des villes* (Paris: Payot, 1965); Michel Quoist, *La ville et l'homme* (Paris: Editions ouvrières, 1952); Louis Wirth, "Urbanism as a Way of Life," *American Journal of Sociology* 44 (July 1938): 1-24; Pierre George, *La ville* (Paris: Presses universitaires de France, 1952). In Canada, two studies have been concerned with the suburbs of Toronto: John R. Seeley, R. Alexander Sim and E. W. Loosley, *Crestwood Heights* (New York: Basic Books, Inc., 1956); and S. D. Clark, *The Suburban Society* (Toronto: University of Toronto Press, 1966). The metropolitan region of Montreal has been studied in depth by Norbert Lacoste, *Les caractéristiques sociales de la population du Grand Montréal* (Montreal: Université de Montréal, 1958).

the throne, exerting their influence in a variety of ways. For example, the many lobbies that surround the United States Government are well known, and other governments are not exempt from similar pressures.[27]

Money becomes a precise and essential measure that is used in a thousand and one ways. The whole work organization in our present technological society would crumble without money. The time devoted to work, the competence of the worker, his experience, his years of service, former services rendered — all these are estimated in terms of their monetary value, which becomes the main standard. A good man is worth so much, each year of experience is worth so much, a consultation is worth this or that price according to whether it requires an hour or a day's work, because time is money.

Money is also a measure of prestige, authority, and duties and responsibilities attached to a position. It is not the quality of the individuals involved, but rather the position that commands the salary. In the university, it is thought that the president's salary should be higher than that of the dean, and that of the dean higher than that of the professors (or at least most of the professors). The same is true for the secretary to the president in comparison with the dean's secretary. Thus, money serves as a symbol of the hierarchical levels within a bureaucracy and within the whole society.

A class society

Social classes are another socio-economic reality of great importance in technological society. As Marx amply demonstrated, their roots lie in relationships of production, and in differential access to the means of production. Social classes are manifest in the economic structure, in the work world, and in the entire social organization. It is not surprising, then, that in technological societies they have crystallized, becoming real and recognized and a central element of modern history. Social classes are the direct consequence of a society of production and work. They result from the diverse economic situations of the owners of the means of production (capitalists, the bourgeoisie, the large landowners, industrialists) and various groups of workers (rural workers, industrial workers, artisans, white-collar workers and technicians). The

---

27. In Canada, links between the holders of economic and political power have been emphasized by John Porter, *The Vertical Mosaic: An Analysis of Social Class and Power in Canada* (Toronto: University of Toronto Press, 1965).

economic interests of administrators and capitalists on the one hand and workers on the other, while they are sometimes complementary, are also very often divergent or even opposite. But divergent interests of different groups of workers can also be observed — for example, of rural and urban workers, of white-collar workers and blue-collar workers, of artisans and industrial workers — so that class struggles can oppose workers to each other, as well as industrialists to workers.

The concentration of a number of workers in large firms and in towns has led to a collective awareness of the interests that are common to all the members of the same category, or of the same economic group. Thus, it is only in the industrial and urban milieu that social classes can form, in the strict sense of the term, and that a real consciousness of class and class struggles can develop.

Voluntary associations and social movements

The awareness of common interests is not unique to social classes. It has also led to the formation of *a great number of voluntary associations and social movements of all kinds*, from political parties to secret societies for cooperation or conspiracy, and including trade unions, national associations, recreational clubs, professional associations, religious or philanthropic societies, reformist or revolutionary societies and so forth. Each of these associations can become a pressure group on the holders of power (politicians, religious leaders, administrators) in order to promote or defend specific interests.

The multiplicity of elites

Another distinctive characteristic of technological society is that *a multiplicity of elites* corresponds to this multiplicity of associations. By elites we mean the individuals or groups who represent or who are said to represent some community (an ethnic group, social class or group of workers, for example). While the system of elites in traditional society is relatively simple and generally stable, in technological society it is extremely mobile and complex. Elites can often succeed each other rapidly; they collide with, crowd and oppose each other. While traditional society is also marked by internal divisions and struggles, it appears that conflict is a permanent element of the fragmented and diversified organization of technological society.

In the context of this brief analysis, it can now be better understood why technological society is sometimes called complex society. It is certainly complex from many points of view, so that it is
difficult to disentangle the main bases of its organization. Perhaps
also it can now be realized why sociology has arisen in such a society, which has felt the need to know and understand itself better.

The Mentality of
Technological Society

In comparison with traditional mentality, the mentality of technological society is profoundly *demystified*, even though many traces
of magical and mythical thought can be discerned in it. And this
demystification can be observed on the two levels of knowledge
and mental attitudes, and the moral order.

The demystification of knowledge:
rationality

First, at the level of knowledge, it has often been said that science
has demystified the world — that is, science has replaced many explanations of a mystical kind with rational or scientific explanations. These are undoubtedly less poetic and blunter, but they aim
to be more "objectively" true because they are based on experiment and scientific knowledge. It is this state of mind and the
practical attitudes which stem from it that Max Weber called *rationality*, as contrasted with traditionalism. Rationality is based
on the conviction that phenomena find their explanation within
and not outside themselves, whether this be in myth or in tradition. A truth is accepted and recognized not because it is a traditional or revealed truth, but because it is logically or experimentally demonstrable — that is, it can be explained in an objective
manner. At the level of practical action, rationality entails the constant search for the most objectively efficient means with the aim
of reaching goals that are defined as achievable. Ends and means
are no longer freely accepted; they are always subject to revision
and question.

It is obviously this practical mental attitude of rationality
which was at the root of the industrial revolution and of scientific
and technical progress. Within the social organization, this same
rational attitude is manifested concretely in bureaucracy; for bu-

reaucracy at least has the intention of being an application of rational thought to the efficient organization of the work of a group of people.

Faith in science and progress

Rationality can thus be reduced to *faith in science*, which is the main basis and the most characteristic trait of technological mentality. It is faith in the science which explores the secrets of nature, demystifies the origins of the world and of the human species, explains the mechanisms of economic and social organization, and even reveals the mysteries of thought and of the human soul. Thus, it is faith in a science which is general and comprehensive, whose capacity for explanation extends to all fields, and which knows no limits. In addition, science is accepted and recognized as being constantly changing and in a state of continuous progress. Faith in science thus necessarily leads to *faith in progress* and in infinite progress.

It is obviously on the scientific level that this faith in progress is most firmly established. What amazes technological man is not that a vaccine against poliomyelitis has been discovered, but rather that it is taking so long to discover the causes of cancer. To him, no scientific problem can remain for very long without a solution. And the same is true of technical problems, economic and social problems, and obstacles to the individual and collective well-being of men. Change and innovation are no longer threatening, but instead are regarded as the essential road to progress and the improvement of human life.

In contrast to traditional mentality, the technological mentality *values change because it values progress*. The two go together: the conviction that it is always possible to improve things means not only that one accepts and expects change, but also that one desires and seeks it. The scientist, the administrator and the politician are judged in relation to their contribution to progress within their field. The productive society and the value attributed to progress join together in order to reinforce each other: the productive society, which is constantly expanding, is supported by constant innovation and requires a mentality that is favourable to change.

The value accorded to education

It is natural that *the value accorded to education* should be linked with rationality and faith in science — the former is the route to and the condition of the two latter. In fact, it is in technological society that the educational system has developed and been extended the farthest; and it is in this society that education is most separate from the institution of the family. In many countries, there has long been opposition to the legal imposition of compulsory schooling on each child up to a certain age, because this appears to be an attack on the rights of the family. Today this law exists in all the industrialized countries and in many developing countries, because it is thought that education is a right, even a duty, for each person. The child's right to education takes priority over the family's right over the child; this is an important change which illustrates a profound transformation of attitude with regard to science.

It is easy, however, to discern a certain *ambivalence* with regard to education in technological society. While it is considered essential and useful, its excesses are feared. The excessively educated man who advocates abstract ideas and lacks a sense of reality is not trusted. The word *intellectual* is often used in a pejorative way. And popular folklore recognizes certain caricatures of the intellectual. He is said to be a pipe dreamer, absent-minded and idealistic; in the United States, he is often described as an egghead, a term which suggests that his head has absorbed so much knowledge that it has finally taken the shape of an egg. In fact, in a society haunted by production, pure and disinterested research and art always need to prove that one day or another, they can be useful; without this proof, they have no place in society. And there is constant conflict — sometimes latent and sometimes open — between theoreticians and practitioners, between researchers and administrators, and between thinkers and men of action.

The mixing of ideas

The progress of education and science has another important consequence, however: technological society is a milieu for *the mixing of ideas*, and one in which questioning is constant. In order to evolve fully, rationality requires a large margin of freedom of thought. In a totalitarian country, it is the university people, professors and students that are the most distrusted, for it is among them first of all that the taste for freedom has the chance to grow. This climate of freedom and discussion presupposes a mentality which accepts change and innovation, and which can tolerate the conflict of values; for this cannot fail to arise and be perpetuated in such an atmosphere. These conflicts between different or contradictory values correspond, at the level of culture and ideas, to the conflicts between elites and associations which we mentioned earlier in connection with social organization. The greater the development and extension of education in technological society, the more numerous are its new sources of social criticism, of aspirations to the freedom of thought and expression, and consequently, of conflict of values. Thus, it is a type of society which requires from its members extensive adaptability to novelty and the capacity to defend themselves against the resultant psychological insecurity. From this point of view, technological society is clearly less reassuring for its members than is traditional society.

Moral demystification: secularization

This brings us to the level of *the moral order*. The demystification of the world through rationality and science has entailed a radical transformation of the foundations of moral life. This transformation has been called *secularization*. In fact, in a society of technological mentality, motivations of metasocial inspiration — that is, motivations which are guided by moral imperatives based on mythological or theological considerations — can be seen to weaken in favour of a more exclusively social moral code. Individually and collectively, men are less strongly impelled than they are in traditional society by motives and sanctions of a supernatural nature — the desire for eternal salvation, fear of the spirits or recourse to providence. Man, temporal life, and individual and collective well-being are valued for themselves to a greater extent, independently of a reference to "something else," to a superhuman sacred order.

The separation of the sacred and the secular

This does not necessarily mean that religion disappears from technological society. It cannot be denied that it continues to exist; and in some cases, there is even a resurgence of religious activity. But secularization is characterized by two distinctive features. First, there is a clear and radical differentiation, in the mind and in institutions, between the sacred and the secular. Religious life no longer has a collective and societal character, as it does in traditional society; the social organization is no longer completely involved in religious activities and cycles. Following the example of political power, which is radically separated from religious power, technological society has a lay character: the work world and the secular world are clearly separate from the world of prayer and relationships with the supernatural order. This distinction is manifested in institutions, which lose their religious or confessional connotation (the State, schools, voluntary associations and so forth become neutral) and in the daily life of individuals, where religion takes on a more individualistic and, in a way, a more internalized character.

Religious and moral pluralism

Second, the secularization of technological society also takes the form of *a moral and religious pluralism*. The religious and moral unanimity that generally characterizes traditional societies disappears. At the level of religion, as at the moral level, the critical spirit and freedom of thought entail a great diversity of personal choices, a splitting up of religious allegiances, and a multiplicity of different moral attitudes which are sometimes contradictory. This means that the culture of technological society does not show the same unity and cohesion as that of traditional society. One finds different creeds and behaviour that is guided by different values and moral codes, and this leads to the formation of sub-cultures. At the level of mentality, cultural pluralism is a reflection of the complexity which characterizes the social organization of technological society.

The feeling of superiority

Finally, there is a last aspect of the technological mentality which should be emphasized — even though it is of a completely different kind — and this is its enormous feeling of superiority over traditional society. While within traditional society it is believed that all humanity is assimilated in the tribe, in technological society there is the conviction that this community of men monopolizes light, science and truth. In fact, it is generally from the large city, which is the brain and nervous system of technological society, that new ideas emerge and spread out — ideas such as reform movements and new fashions. Technological and urban culture is all-encompassing for surrounding traditional societies; it is very rare that the inverse can be observed. But besides that, the city-dweller tends to treat the country-dweller with unkindness and distrust, for he considers him to be backward. On this subject, a varied urban folklore can be found which caricatures the slow and loutish peasant, with clay on his shoes and a poultry basket under his arm. In all technological societies, to treat someone as a peasant is to insult him.

But here again, a certain ambivalence can be seen. In the city-dweller, pity is mixed with a certain envy for the man who lives close to nature and who is the lord and master of his farm. In the heart of urban man, imprisoned in his technical environment, there remains a romantic nostalgia for the natural life, which he idealizes all the more because he finally knows it only through his cottage or the campsite where he pitches his modern tent.

Ideal Types and Sub-types

Two ideal types

The two types of society which have been described are in fact mental constructs which Max Weber called ideal types. By ideal he meant, not an exemplary or superior type, but a pure type, perhaps one to which no concrete society corresponds on every point. Ideal types are obviously constructed on the basis of empirical observation of real societies, but the elements are drawn and put together with the intention of pushing each one of the traits and the whole picture to the extreme, in order to present a pure image or concept.

Thus, these two types of society are not designed to describe real societies. Instead, they are intellectual instruments or, in Margaret Mead's words, conceptual models. These conceptual models have enabled us to contrast modern society with the most extremely different type of society, which we have called traditional society, in such a way as to highlight the characteristics of each.

The debate between Lewis and Redfield

It is important to mention at this point that the distinction between traditional and technological society (or urban or industrial society, depending on the author) has been the object of various attacks from some sociologists and anthropologists, and it has sparked lively debates. The most violent attack to date was launched by the anthropologist Oscar Lewis who, twenty years after Redfield, restudied the same Mexican village, Tepoztlan.[28] Lewis presented a description of social life in this village that was very different from Redfield's, mainly emphasizing the sources of tension and conflict that Redfield had neglected. He came to the conclusion that Redfield had been led to distort reality because of the model of traditional society through which he had perceived it. Lewis criticized this model particularly for offering a picture of social reality that was too integrated and too stable, and that was imbued with a Rousseauistic romanticism about primitive societies. This criticism is certainly not unfounded and puts one on guard against the weakness of a bipolar typology, at least in the way that this has often been employed.

But Redfield replied, also with good reason, that his analysis of Tepoztlan was not necessarily invalidated by Lewis' findings; for the same social reality can be perceived from several complementary and not necessarily opposing points of view. In this way, different analytical models permit one to reveal different aspects of the same reality. Redfield insists that he did not suggest his model of traditional society to the exclusion of any other, and that he grants it no absolute value. But he defends his method as being *one*, among others, which is likely to reveal certain aspects of reality.

At this point, we are approaching an extremely important methodological principle in sociology: the same social reality can reveal several facets and can be seen from several perspectives (we will show in another chapter that it includes several structures). One perspective is not necessarily truer than another and does not exclude others. Confronted with the complexity of social reality, it must be recognized that no method has the monopoly of truth and validity. The diversity of perspectives is generally useful to permit complementary views from which a perception of the whole can ultimately be derived; but we can never know, finally, whether reality includes other aspects which have been overlooked.[29]

Let us note that, in addition to a question of method, it is really a conception of sociology which opposes Lewis to Redfield. Lewis

---

28. Redfield, *Tepoztlan, A Mexican Village*; Oscar Lewis, *Life in a Mexican Village: Tepoztlan Restudied* (Urbana, Ill.: University of Illinois Press, 1951).

29. On the subject of this debate, other interesting articles are Horace Miner, "The Folk-Urban Continuum," *American Sociological Review* 17 (October 1952):529-37, which comes to the defence of Robert Redfield's dichotomic classification; and Joseph Gusfield, "Tradition and Modernity: Misplaced Polarities in the Study of Social Change," *American Journal of Sociology* 72 (January 1967): 351-62, which takes up Lewis's attack.

is an upholder of sociology (and anthropology) based on the study of conflict, while Redfield works within the functionalist tradition. This is a question to which we will return in the following chapters.

Two conditions for the validity of this typology

In spite of the criticisms directed towards it, the bipolar typology remains the main framework for comparative sociology. But this is true on the condition that two essential facts are not forgotten. First, it should be remembered that the two types of society can co-exist within the same concrete total society. In fact, we can assert that, if societies exist which are uniquely traditional, there are none which are solely technological. In any modern society, even the most industrialized, whether this be Canada, the United States, Great Britain, France, the Soviet Union or Japan, forms of traditional society — in the country and, in North America, among the Indian tribes — exist at the boundaries of technological civilization.

Second, it should be noted that many variations of traditional society exist. The mass of anthropological and ethnological studies bear eloquent witness to this. Technological society also appears to be becoming increasingly diversified. And for both these types, a steadily increasing variety of transitory forms can be observed.

It is clearly impossible to go into the details of these distinctions at this point. But in order to complete the picture that has been presented in the preceding pages, we will introduce and discuss the main sub-types of traditional and technological society.

Archaic and Peasant Societies

Following Robert Redfield's suggestion,[30] two sub-types of traditional society can be distinguished — archaic society and peasant society. These can be differentiated from each other in two ways.

---

30. Robert Redfield, *Peasant Society and Culture* (Chicago: University of Chicago Press, 1956). This study has also been published by the same publisher, under the same title, with another of Redfield's studies entitled *The Little Community*.

Forms of subsistence and technology

First, peasant society is necessarily comprised of agricultural and pastoral people, while archaic society generally depends on hunting and fishing for its subsistence. And since peasant society is closely linked to the land, it is much more sedentary than the other. In order to cultivate the land, peasants resort to the domestication of animals (ox, buffalo, horse); in archaic societies, the animal is rarely associated with man's work. Peasant society also develops more extensive and sophisticated equipment than does archaic society. Finally, in peasant society, a law exists regulating land ownership. Land may belong to a large landowner in a feudal or manorial system, or to the collectivity in the zadruga, or to a group of families or individual families. In archaic society, when ownership of land exists, it is much looser and is never regulated by a detailed legal code.

Thus, in terms of human and social development, peasant society can be considered to be more advanced than archaic society. It is the product of the first important technical revolution — the agricultural revolution — which has gradually made man sedentary through the ownership of land.

Relationships with the town

The second difference between peasant and archaic society is that the former is generally located within the orbit of urban centres and within the framework of a great civilization, while archaic society is isolated, closed in on itself, with its own government and laws, and without any relationships with similar neighbouring societies. Members of peasant society are acquainted with the town, or at least are aware of its existence. They may even have frequent contacts with the urban milieu: the town is the market where they dispose of surplus agricultural production; it is the place that attracts young people who leave the country; it may be the residence of the large landowner or the peasants' creditor; and the town is also the principal seat of government. Thus, peasant society is subject to the influence of the town (to different degrees, depending on the case) and its fashions, ideas, inventions, laws, government, wars and economic cycles.

If it is taken out of isolation and abruptly exposed to urban and technological society, archaic society risks disintegration, or at least it will experience a violent shock and serious disturbances. Peasant society, in contrast, has long coexisted with the town. It has developed defence mechanisms and protection devices, and over a long period has learned to integrate what urban society offers in its own way and at its own pace.

Anthropological and sociological studies of peasant society

When Redfield describes what he calls folk society, it is clear that he is thinking mainly, and perhaps exclusively, of archaic society. This is obvious particularly in his article in the *American Journal of Sociology* which we cited earlier. Redfield recounts how anthropology, after concentrating its attention exclusively on archaic societies, progressively "discovered" peasant society through studies carried out in Latin America, in Africa, and in the Orient.[31] When he undertook his study of the Mexican village of Tepoztlan, Redfield came to the conclusion that peasant society is "intermediate between the tribe and modern society"[32] — an idea that he later developed and systematized.[33] Today it is mainly anthropologists and some geographers[34] who study the rural milieux. Sociologists have devoted themselves much more to an analysis of technological and urban society, perhaps to the neglect of rural areas. There does exist a certain tradition of rural sociology, however, which should be renewed and extended.[35]

The Pre-industrial City

Until the beginning of the nineteenth century, the great majority of men lived in traditional societies, either peasant or archaic, and

---

31. *Ibid.*, pp. 5-22.
32. Redfield, *Tepoztlan, A Mexican Village*, p. 217.
33. In addition to those studies by Redfield that we have mentioned previously, there is his interesting introduction on this subject in Horace Miner's book *St. Denis.*
34. Mainly those who belong to the tradition called human geography, which was initiated in France by Vidal de La Blache and Max Sorre. Of special interest is Max Sorre, *Rencontres de la géographie et de la sociologie* (Paris: Librairie Marcel Rivière, 1957). In this tradition also the studies by Pierre Deffontaines might be consulted, notably *Le rang, type de peuplement rural du Canada français* (Quebec: Presses de l'Université Laval, 1953) and *L'homme et l'hiver au Canada* (Quebec: Presses de l'Université Laval, 1957).
35. The interested reader can consult various issues of the American journal *Rural Sociology.*

this was true of all continents. A more or less important minority, depending on the civilization and the period, lived in cities. These obviously do not date from the industrial period: they have a history of at least 5,000, and probably of 7,000 to 8,000 years.[36] Until the eighteenth century, however, the city was quite different from its modern form in that it was a *pre-industrial city*. While peasant society can be considered a social type between archaic and modern society, the pre-industrial city also can be considered as *another type of society between traditional and technological society*. As such, it forms a special category which is worth examining.

Pre-industrial cities have often been studied by archaeologists and historians.[37] On the basis of these studies, Gideon Sjoberg constructed the pure type (which he calls the constructed type) of the pre-industrial city.[38] Let us summarize its main traits.

Social organization

The pre-industrial city is much less extensive than the modern city; it may contain more than 100,000 individuals, but usually it has no more than 5,000 to 10,000 inhabitants. The social organization is a rigid hierarchy of classes and/or castes. At the top, there is a small class or dominant caste which is rich and powerful; sometimes there is a middle class; then there is a large lower class; below that, a still less privileged group of outcasts, and sometimes slaves. Social mobility is practically non-existent. A man lives and dies in the same class or caste into which he was born.

In various ways the social hierarchy is reflected in social life. In the ecology of the city, classes or castes are distributed in easily identifiable districts. Dress, manners, language, and the standard and style of living are generally very different from one class to another. Only the dominant class has access to education, and it is in its hands that a good part of the riches and all political, economic and religious power are concentrated. The authority and power of this class is based on tradition and on certain absolute principles (such as divine right or hereditary human superiority).

---

36. Kingsley Davis, "The Origin and Growth of Urbanization in the World," *American Journal of Sociology* 60 (March 1955): 430.
37. For example, Henri Pirenne, *Les villes et les institutions urbaines*, 2 vols. (Paris: Alcan, 1939).
38. Gideon Sjoberg, *The Preindustrial City* (New York: The Free Press of Glencoe, Inc., 1960).

The economic structure

From the economic point of view, the pre-industrial city is a centre for artisans and for commerce. Artisans and merchants are generally grouped into guilds which have their own legal functions (control of competition and of the quality of merchandise) and educational functions (the training of apprentices). Very often, occupations are grouped on certain streets, which are named after the appropriate trade. But business suffers from a lack of standardization of prices, of money, and of weights and measures, and sometimes also from the low quality of products.

Social and political integration

From the political point of view, power is generally authoritarian and non-democratic. The monarch is often surrounded by a court of lords and is assisted by bureaucrats who are recruited on a particularistic rather than universalistic basis. Birth counts a great deal, but bureaucratic positions can also be bought.

Finally, religion is a powerful factor of control and integration. It is closely linked with political power, and there is generally only one religion, which is collective and almost obligatory. Religious celebrations and ceremonies are the main occasions that unite the disparate groups of this society. Foreigners who do not participate in the accepted religion of the society are set apart and are often included among the outcasts.

The pre-industrial city,
traditional society and technological society

Clearly the pre-industrial city includes certain characteristics of traditional society — its religious unanimity and its conception of power and authority. It differs, however, in the degree of concentration of the population, the way of life, and the extent to which the groups that form the society are separated. But the pre-industrial city is already a technical environment, and thus anticipates the modern city; and the modern city finds the pre-industrial city an environment conducive to its development. In fact, it is in the pre-industrial cities that the seeds of the industrial revolution grew and flourished.

The pre-industrial city differs from the modern city mainly in its artisan economy, its very low standard of living for the great majority of the population, its class system which is so rigid that it is really more of a caste system, and its religious and cultural unity. Now it can be understood why we have preferred to contrast traditional society with technological rather than urban society; for urban society is divided into two sub-types, the pre-industrial city and the modern city, which are very different.

Industrial Society and Post-industrial Society

We pointed out earlier that a number of writers contrast traditional society with industrial society. If we have preferred to talk of technological society, it is because a growing number of sociologists have recently begun to suggest that, at least in the most advanced countries, industrial society is in the process of developing into another type of society. The features of this new society are still not very clear, and there is a great deal of hesitation to give it a name. Some speak of the post-industrial society (which is at least prudent!), others of mass society, still others of the consumer or affluent society; and more recently, there have been references to the post-modern society. Thus, we come to the point of recognizing that industrial society and post-industrial society are two sub-types of technological society, which differ increasingly from each other.

Industrial society took shape in the Western world at the end of the eighteenth and the beginning of the nineteenth century. It resulted from the technical, scientific and intellectual revolution which took place during this period and from the impact that this revolution had on work, mores, ideas, socio-economic organization and political structure. It is towards this type of society that a good number of so-called developing countries are now evolving, as we will show in a later chapter. Technological society, as we described it earlier, corresponds very well to the industrial society sub-type, at least as it has existed in its most advanced form in the Western world of the first half of the twentieth century.

With the second half of the twentieth century, Western society has begun to experience such profound changes that we seem to be witnessing the emergence of a new sub-type of technological society. Just as industrial society appeared to the philosophers of the early nineteenth century to be in a period of gestation, so post-industrial society, as it can be described today, is in an embryonic state. Consequently, the new post-industrial society still has a great deal in common with industrial society, and our earlier description of technological society applies to it as well. Some traits, however, that are distinctive and characteristic of this new society are already apparent. It is worth briefly indicating a few of them.

The predominance of the tertiary sector

First, post-industrial society is witnessing the very rapid growth of the tertiary sector of production and employment, to the point where it is foreseeable that this sector will soon include the majority of the labour force. The typical worker of post-industrial society will not be the labourer, the manual worker or the blue-collar worker, but rather the technician, the engineer, the administrator and the white-collar worker. This is the product of technical progress. Many workers are replaced by increasingly automated machines, which are the product of the development of electronics and cybernetics. Automation requires, in turn, a new staff of technicians and additional employees in offices, business, transportation, the services and so forth. The working class, which was the nucleus of the industrial society of the nineteenth century, has itself been deeply transformed, following technological changes which have entailed a rapid development of the means and relations of production. A new working class has already appeared, more complex than that of the nineteenth century, in which former artisans and modern technicians work together, where the levels of specialization are multiplied, and where trade union and political attitudes are greatly diversified.[39]

The leisure civilization

Constant technical progress in production entails two more important consequences. First, there is a reduction in the hours of work. Of course, the beginning of the industrial revolution was marked by shameful exploitation of the labour force, which resulted from harsh competition between capitalist entrepreneurs and from the lure of gain that motivated them. It was not rare to

---

39. See in particular Serge Mallet, *La nouvelle classe ouvrière* (Paris: Editions du Seuil, 1963); Alain Touraine, *L'évolution du travail ouvrier aux usines Renault* (Paris: Centre national de la recherche scientifique, 1955); Jacques Dofny et al., *Les ouvriers et le progrès technique* (Paris: Colin, 1966).

find a work week of seventy to eighty hours, for women and children as well as for men. Workers averaged very low salaries and worked in extremely unhygienic conditions. This was still the situation at the end of the nineteenth century.[40] Today the normal work week is half that of the earlier period, and now it is claimed that we have already entered the leisure civilization. The worker benefits from longer leisure hours; but such leisure can itself become a problem if it is not used constructively, to raise the cultural level of the whole collectivity and each one of its members.[41] The commercial organization of leisure has taken on extraordinary proportions to the point where it has become an important sector of economic activity. One need only think, for example, of the considerable sums invested in various sports (private or professional) and in sports competitions, in the cinema, amusement halls of all kinds, tourism and so forth. The consumer society consists, to a great extent, of the consumption of leisure.

The importance of education

The second consequence of recent technical progress is the unprecedented expansion of the system of education and the importance accorded to it. Just a short time ago, the majority of the population could not benefit from primary education, and secondary education remained the privilege of a small minority of young people. Today, in the most industrialized societies, the great majority of young people attend secondary educational institutions. There is also talk of permanent or adult education as the necessary corollary both of a leisure civilization and of a constantly progressive technology. Soon, for the first time in the history of humanity, we will see societies in which almost all the population has completed at least a part of their secondary education. It is too

---

40. This situation has been described particularly for England by Charles Booth in his many studies reported in *Life and Labour of the People of London*, 17 vols. (London: Macmillan and Co., Limited, 1902–); and by B. S. Rowntree, *Poverty: A Study of Town Life* (London: Macmillan and Co., Limited, 1901). For France, the following could be consulted: G. Duveau, *La vie ouvrière en France sous le second Empire* (Paris: Gallimard, 1946); Paul Louis, *La condition ouvrière en France depuis cent ans* (Paris: Presses universitaires de France, 1950); Maurice Halbwachs, *La classe ouvrière et les niveaux de vie* (Paris: Alcan, 1913). For Canada, there is a very interesting work entitled *Report of the Royal Commission on the Relations of Labor and Capital in Canada*, 1889.
41. See in particular Joffre Dumazedier, *Vers une civilisation du loisir?* (Paris: Editions du Seuil, 1962); J. Dumazedier and Aline Ripert, *Le loisir et la ville* (Paris: Editions du Seuil, 1966).

soon to predict the type of society that will result from this, but it is certain that this advancement of education is a powerful factor of social and cultural change which will have a tremendous impact on the new post-industrial society.

Mass communication media

Among technology's improvements, those which most strongly affect contemporary social life and particularly modern mentality are the techniques of mass communication. Movies, radio and television have been added to printed matter, which itself has made such great progress that perhaps paperbacks should be counted among the mass media.[42] If we speak of a new mass society, it is partly because modern techniques of communication are aimed at an enormous audience which is constantly bombarded with new ideas, images and feelings, and which is encouraged through advertising or by other means to have constantly changing aspirations and needs. Various studies which have analyzed the influence exerted by these media have been mentioned in connection with socialization (Chapter 5). But this is a vast area which is relatively unexplored. In any case, it can be said that the mixing of ideas which is characteristic of technological society has undoubtedly been accentuated by modern techniques of communication, which force debates on the listener and even induce him to take an active part in them. In addition, mass communication breaks down barriers between the mentality of regions and countries; and with the imminent widespread use of satellites, communication will have an unprecedented world dimension. The interdependence of regional and national cultures, within and through mass culture, becomes a fact that is as important and vital as the interdependence of national economies.

The lonely crowd and political structures

It is perhaps mainly at the political level that the consequences of mass society have been, and still are, most fully analyzed and debated. Many researchers have emphasized that, in mass society, there is a weakening of the former local and intermediate structures which, in industrial as well as in traditional society, ensured the social integration of individuals — trade organizations, profes-

---

42. For example, see Robert Escarpit, *La révolution du livre* (Paris: UNESCO, 1965).

sions, voluntary associations and social classes. Political action will henceforth be based on vast organizations or mass movements in which individuals can no longer participate except in an anonymous, impersonal and very isolated way. A new form of alienation, that of the lonely crowd, is beginning to typify this society. In such a highly fragmented society, the bases of democratic government will be seriously compromised, because the social structure does not lend itself to the multiple representation of different interests and points of view. Thus, there is the risk of political power falling solely into the hands of political professionals, technocrats and a few specialists in the manipulation of public opinion. In addition, protest movements are often inspired by an extremism which is no less anti-democratic. Mass society thus offers an environment conducive to the emergence of new forms of dictatorship and totalitarianism.[43]

Social movements and participation

While this analysis is true in part, its pessimism has been mitigated by recent research on social and political movements, protest demonstrations, and various forms of political extremism.[44] These studies have emphasized that new forms of social and political participation are being elaborated through these movements; and groups, strata or social classes find new identities and a collective consciousness by which they seek to integrate or re-integrate themselves into the total society that, up to this point, has neglected or ignored them. In fact, mass society has awakened feelings of unity and solidarity in groups which were previously unorganized and

43. This point of view has been presented mainly by William Kornhauser, *The Politics of Mass Society* (Glencoe, Ill.: The Free Press, 1959); Philip Selznick, *The Organizational Weapon* (New York: McGraw-Hill Book Company, Inc., 1952); Erich Fromm, *Escape From Freedom* (New York: Rinehart, 1945); David Riesman, *The Lonely Crowd* (New Haven: Yale University Press, 1951).

44. In particular, Joseph Gusfield, "Mass Society and Extremist Politics," *American Sociological Review* 27 (February 1962): 19-30; Seymour Lipset, *Agrarian Socialism* (Berkeley: University of California Press, 1950), in which the author studied the Canadian socialist movement in Saskatchewan: also, Seymour M. Lipset, "Social Stratification and Right Wing Extremism," *British Journal of Sociology* 10 (December 1959): 1-32; Maurice Pinard, "Mass Society and Political Movements: A new Formulation," *American Journal of Sociology* 73 (May 1968): 682-90. A generally positive appraisal of mass society can be found in the detailed article by Edward Shils, "Mass Society and Its Culture," *Daedalus* 89 (Spring 1960): 288-314.

passive, such as the American Negroes, the poor or those on social welfare. Perhaps, finally, the fact that protest movements break the rules of the game of democracy is less attributable to the mass society itself than to the affluent society, in which gaps in status and in standards of living become more obvious and increasingly less tolerated and tolerable. In addition, it is among the social classes which have suffered from great frustration and alienation and have the least education that totalitarian attitudes have the strongest hold;[45] it is these social classes that are mainly involved in protest movements.

Agitation and protest

Mass society probably is destined to experience a tumultuous existence marked by many disturbances. Through the mixture of ideas that it encourages, through the aspirations that it awakens and nurtures within individuals and collectivities, through the new needs that it engenders and through the implicit frustrations, mass society will in all likelihood be characterized less by the standardization and cultural levelling that has often been attributed to it than by permanent social agitation, and by more or less violent protest movements. This might be one of the most remarkable features of this new society. What is known about it at the moment gives considerable weight to such a forecast.

---

45. Seymour M. Lipset, "Democracy and the Working-Class Authoritarianism," *American Sociological Review* 24 (August 1959): 482-501.

Chapter 8
Social Organization: Function, Structure and System

The two preceding chapters have been devoted to what we have called the classificatory tradition in the study of social organization. First, we reviewed briefly the typologies of societies suggested by various writers (Chapter 6), and then we considered in more detail the dichotomy of traditional society and technological society (Chapter 7) which, with its sub-types, is widely referred to in contemporary sociology (this will become apparent later, in our discussion of social evolution).

In this chapter and the following one, we will deal with the second tradition in the study of social organization — the analytical tradition. In fact, we used this tradition to a great extent in the first part of the book. In defining and analyzing social action, we have often emphasized the *structured* nature of action and of the norms which regulate it. We have stressed the fact that social action manifests itself as a *system* of interdependent elements, and we have indicated some of the *functional* relationships between the elements comprising the culture, which also is conceived as a system.

The time has now come to define these ideas — system, structure, function — which have been used up to this point without detailed discussion. The definition of these three concepts in fact serves as the main thread for the analytical tradition in sociology.

The Analytical Tradition

The difficulty of the subject

It should be said immediately that the analytical tradition in sociology is more difficult than the classificatory tradition, because it is more abstract. By analytical tradition, we mean *all the research which is carried out with the explicit goal of constructing a scientific and explanatory theory of social organization, its functioning and its changes.* The formulation of a theory is obviously located at a higher level of abstraction than the refinement of a classification. The latter is *conceptual* in nature — that is, it consists of the construction of classes or types which are broad enough to cover a great number of concrete cases. Auguste Comte's concepts of theological and positive society, and the notions of traditional and technological society, are such conceptual instruments, employed in order to represent concrete historical societies in a simplified or purified way. In contrast, the search for a theory is *hypothetical and deductive* in nature; or to express this differently, the guiding motif is to discern the often-hidden relationships which exist between phenomena and to link them to each other in order to form a whole or a unit that is logically explicable. The goal is to establish laws or principles which account for interdependent relationships between phenomena, and to combine the different propositions in the most general possible model. Thus, the theory is constructed, on the one hand, by the methical observation of concrete reality, which constitutes the empirical basis of scientific knowledge; and on the other hand, with the help of deductive reasoning, which suggests the relationships and links constituting the logical framework of the theory. The verification of theory is effected by testing the hypotheses which have been suggested by this procedure by means of further empirical research.

As we emphasized in Chapter 6, the elaboration of theories and the construction of classifications go together. In sociology, most of the writers whose classifications we have studied — Marx, Comte, Spencer, Durkheim and Parsons — also suggested theories to which their typologies were linked. For example, Comte based his classification of the theological, metaphysical and positive societies on the law of the three states. Parsons arrived at a typology of societies only after working for a long time on the elaboration of a general theory. The analytical and classificatory traditions are therefore not independent of each other.

But contrary to our approach to the study of the classificatory tradition, it will not be necessary to go back to the nineteenth century in order to discuss the analytical tradition. In fact, it can be asserted that theory-building has been profoundly and rapidly transformed since the beginning of the twentieth century. And the social sciences are probably the field of knowledge in which theoretical development has been most strongly affected by this change. This explains why contemporary theoretical research will now be our main focus.

Another point must be made here. Sociology has witnessed the development of a number of theories which apply to a particular sector of social organization — small group theories, social class theories, theories of bureaucratic organization and so forth. These are called limited theories, or theories of the middle range, as Merton has described them. Similarly, there is not only one general theory of society, but several — that is, theories dealing with the total society. Our discussion in this chapter of the analytical tradition is valid for both middle range and general theories; but we will be concerned mainly with the total society, and we will follow the approach adopted in the two preceding chapters, through which we considered social organization in the most general and comprehensive way possible.

Models of Society

The need for models

In order to understand the need that has been felt in sociology to elaborate a theory of social organization, one must start with a very elementary statement: philosophers, thinkers and researchers of every period who have asked themselves questions about human life in society have always had to resort to analogies or images in order to represent society. In fact, social organization is a complex, multiple and fleeting reality that the human mind has some difficulty in comprehending, both as a whole and in its modifications. In order to represent it and discuss it, and to be able to analyze its parts or compare concrete societies with one another, it has been necessary to resort to comparisons with more familiar and better known objects or beings — or at least those that are considered to be better known — which have served as models of society.

This approach is necessary because it is the normal and accepted way of perceiving things which are rather complicated. For example, I can represent the universe to myself as balls on a billiard table or as a sphere, or I can perhaps picture electricity as a current of water or as a river. Thus, I proceed on the basis of a more familiar and simpler reality, which serves as a supportive analogy in comprehending phenomena which are more complicated and thus more difficult to perceive and analyze as a whole. This is an intellectual procedure that we often use, sometimes without even realizing it, when we have to represent realities or phenomena which are unfamiliar to us. For example, I conceive of unknown cities in terms of those I know. But this approach, which consists of moving from what is best known to what is least known, is also part of scientific procedure, for the latter also uses analogy. The researcher very often uses it either to raise himself to a higher level of abstraction or generality, or to make the transition from known phenomena to phenomena that are as yet unexplored. Given that science has the goal of understanding and explaining, frequently it merely refines common modes of thought, by imposing on them a more rigorous and logical method. Thus, it is not surprising that in sociology, as in other fields of enquiry, various models are used to represent society.[1]

The evolution of models

It generally happens that with the development of a science, the nature of the models used is modified. The models employed at the beginning are often rough images or comparisons which are still very close to common sense; then, through subsequent empirical and theoretical research, they are refined and give rise to new models which are more abstract, general or logical. This development is easily observable in many sciences. In fact, the main dividing line between traditional and modern science was drawn when the latter detached itself from early models, which were still too concrete and too directly guided by common sense, in order to

1. A slightly different presentation of models of society will be found in Alex Inkeles, *What is Sociology: An Introduction to the Discipline and Profession* (Englewood Cliffs, N.J.: Prentice-Hall, Inc., 1964), chap. 3.

elaborate abstract and theoretical models; and this development was possible mainly through the use of mathematics. The transition from classical physics to modern physics is perhaps the best example, as Arthur March explains:

> The early physicists dealt with a world that was immediately accessible to the senses. From the beginning of this century, research has been oriented towards a world that forms the invisible substructure of the macrocosm and which is formed by particles of matter. . . .
>
> The development of quantum physics took the direction of increasing abstractness, which makes an understanding of the theory extremely difficult. For one thing, it turned out to be impossible to encompass the events of the microworld in visualizable pictures. This in turn was a consequence of the fact that the concepts used in speaking of the familiar everyday world are not suitable for a description of elementary particles. Modern physics was forced to undergo a radical revision of its mode of thought and to adopt concepts that are not pictorially interpretable but are capable of exact description only through the use of mathematical symbols.
>
> Today's physics has become non-pictorial and consequently largely incomprehensible to the outsider. The reason is not that its proponents have failed to exert themselves sufficiently to find an intelligible representation; its strangeness is inherent in the nature of the things it deals with, and this precludes the possibility of graphic description.[2]

Material Models

Sociology is obviously far from undergoing as radical a transformation as physics has experienced. Nevertheless, a development in the same direction can be observed. Here we will use Rosenblueth and Wiener's terminology to explain the progressive transition

---

2. An English adaptation of Arthur March's work, originally published in German, can be found in Arthur March and Ira M. Freeman, *The New World of Physics* (New York: Random House, 1962).

from *material models* to *formal models*: "A material model is the representation of a complex system by a system which is assumed to be simpler and which is also assumed to have some properties similar to those selected for study in the original complex system."[3] If the material model enables one to go from the simple to the complex, it is because it suggests a concrete and even tangible reality which supports the elaboration of more abstract thought.

Mechanical models

In sociology, the material models that are used can be classified under two main types: *mechanical models* and *organic models*. Mechanical models of varying complexity have served to represent different aspects of society. The Egyptian pyramid was useful to depict the social hierarchy, particularly in ancient societies of the authoritarian or feudal type. Today this image is still employed, although in a different sense, when we speak of the age pyramid in demography. The scale is a useful image to represent a hierarchy or stratification; we still speak of the scale of social prestige, the scale of power, and the scale of values. The balance has long been the symbol of the law, and consequently of justice in society. The chariot, which used to carry military and political leaders, has come to represent the State itself, which has to be directed and controlled and which also serves to guide its troops in battle. The progress of mechanics has resulted in more complex models, particularly that of the clock, which makes it possible to represent simultaneously the complexity of all of society, its harmony, the complementarity of its functions, and the arrangement of its parts.

This conception of society as a mechanism like the clock was all the more attractive to scientists of the Renaissance and Classical periods because the "new science," mainly mechanical physics,

---

3. Arturo Rosenblueth and Norbert Wiener, "The Role of Models in Science," *Philosophy of Science* 12 (October 1945): 316-21. On the development of models and their use in contemporary science, particularly in sociology, the following articles also may be consulted: Karl W. Deutsch, "Mechanism, Organism, and Society: Some Models in Natural and Social Science," *Philosophy of Science* 18 (July 1951): 230-52; Herman Meyer, "On the Heuristic Value of Scientific Models," *Philosophy of Science* 18 (April 1951): 111-23; Paul Meadows, "Models, Systems and Science," *American Sociological Review* 22 (February 1957): 32-38; Roger Nett, "System Building in Sociology: A Methodological Analysis," *Social Forces* 31 (October 1952). Several articles which are also concerned with this question will be found in Llewellyn Gross, ed., *Symposium on Sociological Theory* (New York: Harper and Row, 1959).

had facilitated the discovery of laws which really explained the world and which raised the hope of an efficient control over the forces of nature. In the same way, for Machiavelli, Hobbes, Montesquieu, Adam Smith and even Kant, it was a case of discovering the hidden laws of politics, economic life and history, in order to control the machinery of power. Machiavelli's work is particularly significant from this point of view, for it illustrates well the radical change in perspective which occurred at the time. Contrary to all the other philosophers, Machiavelli does not offer the Prince moral advice; his are scientific conclusions concerning the art of seizing and maintaining power. And these conclusions were scientific to Machiavelli because they were derived from an objective, rather than a moral, analysis of a number of historical cases which showed similarities and dissimilarities. Thus, the original Machiavellianism was based essentially on the scientific approach.

The mechanical model was attractive, too — mainly during the Renaissance period — because it was based on the simple principle that any phenomenon is necessarily the effect of a cause; thus, when the real cause is identified, the phenomenon can be understood and explained. This principle of causality in its most elementary form contrasted with the principle of finality, which had long prevailed and which claimed to explain phenomena by assigning a goal (or final cause) to them instead of seeking real causes.

Organic models

It is the *organic model*, however — the model which uses the living organism, generally the human body, in order to represent society — which has been most popular and has had the longest history. Many examples can be given, starting with the philosophers of Ancient Greece and continuing to the present. Aristotle compared society with the human body, in which the most worthy members are in command of the inferior members; in particular, this concept enabled him to justify the existence of the social hierarchy and to take up the defence of slavery. When Saint Paul wanted to explain to Christians the mystical solidarity which united them to each other and to Christ, he used the example of the living organism, pointing to the interdependence between the members and the organs; this is his famous analogy of the mystical body of Christ. In the tradition called universal history (mentioned in Chapter 4 in connection with the concept of culture), several German historians based the stages of civilization on the successive phases in the life of the human organism; this is evident, for example, in the work of Johann Adelung. This tradition has continued into the twentieth century. The contemporary philosopher of history Oswald Spengler describes the historical cycle of civilizations according to the cycle of human life: civilizations are born, mature, grow old and die.[4]

Similarly, in sociology the organic model has often been used, to the extent that we can speak of a school of social organicism. Generally Herbert Spencer is considered to be the father of this school, for it is he who compared society to the living organism in the most explicit and rigorous way. Emile Durkheim also employed the organic model; for example, he characterized industrial society by a type of solidarity which he called organic (see Chapter 6). As in the living organism, this solidarity was established on the basis of the division of labour among the members of the society, and of the complementarity of the functions fulfilled by each of them.

The organic model was frequently employed in a mechanical way — that is, by following the principle of simple causality. Nevertheless, it mainly served to illustrate the interdependence, complementarity and solidarity of the members of society. Thus it accentuated the relationships existing between members and between different elements of society. Later in this chapter, we will discuss the important methodological consequence that was to follow from this.

But every material model, whether mechanical or organic, must be employed with caution. Because it is only a simple comparison between two realities which always remain separate and dissimilar, the material model runs the risk of concealing the reality studied, while giving the illusion of clarifying it. The analogy is rarely perfect. It can create and maintain an incomplete view of reality which is biased or even false; it can hide important aspects of it; and because it focuses attention on some aspects of reality, it can camouflage others which are equally or more important. It is true that these dangers are always present in the use of any model; but they are more obvious in the use of material models.

---

4. Oswald Spengler, *The Decline of the West*, trans. Charles Francis Atkinson, 2 vols. (London: George Allen & Unwin, 1926-1929).

Formal Models

When it can, science seeks to detach itself from material models in order to use *formal models*. Rosenblueth and Wiener define this technique as follows: "A formal model is a symbolic assertion in logical terms of an idealized relatively simple situation sharing the structural properties of the original factual system."[5] In contrast to the material model, the formal model is not an analogy, for it does not employ a comparison with a reality of another kind or another order. Strictly speaking, it is a mental reconstruction of reality assisted by various symbols. It is really an *abstraction*, because it is constructed by extracting certain properties from the reality studied which, once represented by signs or concepts, can give this reality a logical interpretation and explanation.

Mathematical models

Undoubtedly the purest and most perfect formal model is the mathematical model. Verbal non-mathematical language always carries within it analogous, allegorical and figurative tendencies; it is easily charged with emotional overtones. Mathematical language, which is purified and stripped of these tendencies, is basically non-figurative. This explains why mathematics should become the scientific language *par excellence*, and why all sciences seek to use it as much as possible.

Of all the social sciences, to date economics has been the most successful in integrating mathematical language and constructing valid formal models. Its object of study easily lends itself to this; for goods produced, consumed or in circulation, and money, are two types of quantitative data. Demography, being by its very nature a science of quantifiable data, since it analyzes the characteristics and movements of populations, also can construct mathematical models, although it does so less than economics. The other social sciences (psychology, anthropology, sociology and political science) as yet have been able to make only a limited use of mathematical models. We should mention some notable attempts in sociology, however, mainly relating to the structure and dynamics of small groups and to networks of communication; and those in so-

---

5. Rosenblueth and Wiener, "Role of Models," p. 317.

cial psychology which relate to the measurement of attitudes.[6] With the exception of these tentative experiments, sociology uses mathematics relatively little, and its future in this connection is still not clear. But in our opinion, sociology probably will become increasingly mathematical in the next decades.

Non-mathematical models

One should avoid confusing formal and mathematical models. A model can be formal without being mathematical. In fact, non-mathematical models can attain a high level of abstraction and logic. This is the case, for example, wih theoretical models elaborated over the last few years in linguistics which, through very general rules, aim to explain aspects of the phonology or syntax of languages. And in biology, there is Cannon's homeostatic model, for example, which is designed to explain the equilibrium that every living organism achieves or constantly seeks.

Formal models in sociology

Like the other sciences, sociology seeks formal models — mathematical, and perhaps mainly non-mathematical — which are more abstract and more rigorously scientific than the material models used in the past. To date, this search has not been as fruitful as in other fields, such as economics and linguistics. But precisely because this is a pressing concern in contemporary sociology, and because the future of sociology as a science will depend largely on the success or lack of success of this theoretical research, it is important to know the present situation.

The Postulate of a Social System

The construction of a formal model is possible only on the basis of an essential *basic postulate*, which is that *the reality studied manifests the properties of a system*. In very general terms, this

6. Herbert A. Simon, *Models of Man, Social and Rational: Mathematical Essays on Rational Human Behavior in a Social Setting* (New York: John Wiley and Sons, Inc., 1957); James S. Coleman, *Introduction to Mathematical Sociology* (Glencoe, Ill.: The Free Press, 1964).

postulate means that the following properties are attributed to the reality studied:

  1. It is formed of elements which share mutually inter-dependent relationships.
  2. The whole formed by all of the elements cannot be reduced to the sum of these elements.
  3. The interdependent relationships between the elements, and the whole that results from them, are regulated by rules which can be expressed in logical terms.

This postulate was suggested by those who used material models of society. But either it was posed only in implicit terms, or the methodological consequences which were later seen to derive from it were not recognized. It is characteristic of the formal model to be based explicitly on this postulate of the systemic properties of reality; and it is because the consequences that this postulate implies have been derived from it that modern science has been so radically transformed.

Pareto's contribution

Probably the first to express unequivocally the need for formal models in sociology and the postulate of the social system was the Italian economist and sociologist Vilfredo Pareto. He explains his conception of sociological theory in a very important passage:

> Little or nothing can be inferred directly from the mere description, and in that sense the apothegm that "history never repeats itself" is very true. Concrete phenomena have to be broken up into ideal phenomena that are simpler, that we may so arrive at something more nearly constant than the complex and ever-shifting thing we have before us in the concrete. . . . In a quest for sociological uniformities, too many facts, details too minute, may be a hindrance rather than a help; for if one dwells on all the petty circumstances that figure in a situation, one easily loses one's way, like a person travelling in thick underbrush; one is prevented from assigning proper indices to the various elements, mistaking what is secondary for what is principal, what is very variable for what is quasi-constant, and so one ends by writing a piece of literature that is

devoid of the slightest scientific value.... If, accordingly, one would remould the social sciences on the model of the natural sciences, one must proceed in them as in the natural sciences, reducing highly complicated concrete phenomena to simpler theoretical phenomena, being exclusively guided all the while by the intent to discover experimental uniformities, and judging the efficacy of what one has done only by the experimental verifications that may be made of it.[7]

In this quotation, Pareto clearly indicates the need that exists in sociology to construct theoretical abstract models which are experimentally verifiable, and he specifies certain requirements of this procedure. Like Auguste Comte, Durkheim and Weber, Pareto wished to give the social sciences the same scientific character as the natural sciences; to this end, he saw no other solution than to introduce the same methodological rigour into the former as had been instrumental in the progress of the latter. This presupposes that one proceeds, in sociology as in the other sciences, towards a simplification of reality or, more precisely, towards a transposition of concrete and particular phenomena into abstract and general terms. But the first theoretical transposition of this kind that should be effected is to consider all concrete society as presenting the properties of a system:

But however many, however few, the elements that we choose to consider, we assume at any rate that they constitute a system which we may call the "social system"; and the nature and properties of that system we propose to investigate. The system changes both in form and in character in course of time. When, therefore, we speak of the "social system" we mean that system taken both at a specified moment and in the successive transformations which it undergoes within a specified period of time. So when one speaks of the solar system, one means that system taken both at a specified moment and in the successive moments which go to make up a greater or lesser period of time.[8]

---

7. Vilfredo Pareto, *The Mind and Society*, ed. Arthur Livingstone (London: Jonathan Cape, 1935), vol. 4, pp. 1735-39.
8. *Ibid.*, p. 1435.

Here, Pareto states very clearly the postulate of the systemic properties of society, adding immediately that it is a system which must be defined as dynamic and not static.

From the economic system to the social system

In order to understand better Pareto's contribution, we should note that he was mainly an economist; the majority of his work is in economic theory. But he was not satisfied that political economy should study only logical or rational behaviour isolated from its socio-psychological context. He himself explained that he undertook the study of sociology in order to complete his studies in political economy and to enlarge the relevance of his economic and political analyses. On the basis of the economic system, Pareto went on to study the social system, because in a sense the latter is an extension of the former. For Pareto, the social system is a modification of the economic system, serving to introduce into economics what has been left aside — namely, feelings: their manifestations, their rationalizations and the non-logical actions which result from them, and to which Pareto gave prime importance in social life. Thus, the analysis of the social system was intended, in his mind, to explain rationally the non-rationality of society.

To Pareto, society appeared to be a mixture of logical and non-logical actions, feelings and rationality. Economics studies logical and rational behaviour; but these are constantly affected by feelings and non-logical conduct. Thus, Pareto assigned to sociology, as its main goal, rational explanation — on the one hand, of the relations between feelings, rationalizations and non-logical actions; and, on the other hand, of the interdependent relationships between non-logical and logical conduct. Lawrence Henderson has emphasized the fact that scientists construct a theoretical system and use the systemic analysis of reality whenever reality does not lend itself to a simple causal explanation, but manifests a complex tangle of interdependent variations. For Pareto, the systemic analysis of society was precisely like "an application of the logical method that has been found useful in all physical sciences and elsewhere when complex situations involving many variables in a state of mutual dependence are described."[9] The sociologist's problem when faced with the complexity of social facts resembles that of the biologist confronting the complexity of the digestive

---

9. Lawrence J. Henderson, *Pareto's General Sociology: A Physiologist's Interpretation* (Cambridge, Mass.: Harvard University Press, 1935), p. 17.

apparatus; in both cases, it is useful to represent reality in a simplified and rather stylized way, in the form of a system.

We must recognize, however, that Pareto's suggestion that social reality be considered as a system passed almost unnoticed at the time. Perhaps only Lawrence Henderson — probably because he was a physiologist and not a sociologist — understood this suggestion in depth. In addition, Pareto himself scarcely did more than formulate his proposition, for he did not elaborate it further, nor did he really apply it.

In fact, before a theoretical model of the social system could be constructed (as it has been possible to do recently), it was necessary as a preliminary step to clarify two essential methodological concepts — function and structure. Since the beginning of the twentieth century, theoretical effort in sociology and anthropology has been devoted mainly to this. In order to follow this current of thought, we will now turn to a summary of the debates that these two concepts have initiated.

Function and Functionalism

We cannot explain the concept of function in sociology and anthropology without immediately talking of functionalism. This is due to the fact that functional analysis has been the source of considerable controversy, mainly in American sociology and anthropology.[10] The supporters and opponents of functional analysis have often thought it useful to distinguish themselves as functionalists and non-functionalists; so that now, by tradition, there exists a sort of functionalist school. Today it is recognized that there are many types of functionalism; one writer believes that he can enumerate about a dozen.[11]

It is important, then, to impose some order on the different meanings attributed to the terms *function* and *functionalism*; for they have varied connotations, a fact which has contributed more than a little to the debates that they have engendered.

---

10. A collection of some of these discussions can be found in a volume which brings together the main American articles published in various journals: N. J. Demerath and Richard A. Peterson, *System, Change and Conflict: A Reader on Contemporary Sociological Theory and the Debate Over Functionalism* (New York: The Free Press of Glencoe, Inc., 1967).
11. Melford E. Spiro, "A Typology of Functional Analysis," *Explorations 1* (1953).

The Concept of Function

Two simple meanings

The term *function* has at least four different meanings in sociology. First, it is used in the sense of status, position, profession or employment. It is in this sense that we talk of fulfilling one or several functions within a firm, ministry or bureaucracy; similarly, we speak of promotion from one function to another.

According to a second meaning, which is close to the first, function means all the tasks, duties and responsibilities incumbent on the person who occupies a position, fills a job, or practises a profession. For example, one might wonder whether a specific responsibility belongs to the dean's functions in a university or to a particular official in a ministry. It is said that someone is neglecting his functions when he does not accomplish all the tasks that are attached to the position he occupies.

These first two meanings of the term *function* do not pose any problem. They are part of everyday language and have the same meaning in sociology, where they are employed notably in analyses of the professions, the work world and organizations.

The mathematical meaning

Function may be used with a third meaning that can be called *mathematical*. In this case, we speak of function in the sense of *a relationship that exists between two or several elements, such that any change introduced into one provokes a modification in the other or others and entails an adaptation on their part.* Here, the link between the elements, their mutual relationships and thus their interdependence are emphasized. In simple mathematical language, it can be said that x is a function of y when the value of x depends on the value of y; thus, x and y are in a functional relationship with respect to each other. In sociology, it can be seen that a change in working techniques entails changes in the organization of the firm, in the conditions of work, in the standard of living of the workers, in their family life, in law and so forth. We could then say that the organization of the firm, working conditions, the standard of living of the workers are functionally dependent on working techniques.

An example: Durkheim's study of suicide

Durkheim's study *Suicide* is an example of this type of functional analysis. In fact, Durkheim showed that the suicide rate is linked to marital status (bachelors are more likely to commit suicide than are married persons), to whether or not one has children (childless couples are more likely to commit suicide than are those with children), to religion (Protestants are more inclined to commit suicide than are Catholics, and the latter more than Jews) and so forth.

Thus, the tendency to commit suicide is not equally distributed within a given population, for it rises or falls *as a function* of certain social characteristics of individuals. In drawing up a list of the different social characteristics which are favourable to suicidal tendencies, Durkheim finally derives a general conclusion which gives his analysis its originality: "Suicide varies inversely with the degree of integration of the social groups of which the individual forms a part."[12] Durkheim's formulation of this sort of sociological "law" of suicide amply demonstrates that it is a functional relationship between two phenomena: the suicide rate is functionally dependent on the degree of social integration.

Other examples

In a general way, a great number of empirical studies in sociology stem from this type of functional analysis. For example, it might be concluded: that a student's I.Q. and school achievement depend on the socio-economic status of the family; that political attitudes vary according to the individual's socio-economic status and his aspirations to upward social mobility; that a couple's fertility is a function of their social origins, their level of education and their aspirations to professional mobility.

The goal of this type of functional analysis

All these propositions, including Durkheim's, seek to establish or even measure the link which exists between *a dependent variable* and one or more *independent variables*. The dependent variable is the element or phenomenon which varies as a function of another or several others, and with regard to which it is thus found

---

12. Durkheim, *Suicide*, p. 209.

to be in a situation of dependence. Thus, the dependent variable is the variable to be explained, while the independent variable is the explanatory variable. In the examples given above, suicide, I.Q. and school achievements, political attitudes, and the fertility of a couple are the dependent variables; social integration, socio-economic status, aspirations to social mobility and so forth are the independent or explanatory variables.

The goal of this type of functional analysis is obviously to discern the most *weighty* independent variable — that is, the one which exerts the strongest influence on the dependent variable. Clearly not all the independent variables have the same influence on a given phenomenon. Some of the weaker variables can be considered to be favourable *conditions*. In Durkheim's study, for example, the fact that a population is Protestant rather than Catholic represents a condition that is more conducive to suicide than is the inverse. On the other hand, a variable becomes a *factor* when its action on the dependent variable is more immediate, more direct and stronger. For example, the socio-economic status of the family can be considered a factor in the school achievements of children. In fact, it is only a minority of children from the less privileged socio-economic backgrounds who reach a high level of education; therefore, the socio-economic status of the family is generally considered the best predictor of progress in school.

The use of functional analysis in sociology

It can be understood why this type of functional analysis is widely used in empirical sociological research. It is the closest to causal analysis, but remains sufficiently different from it. When confronted with the complexity of their subject matter, sociologists always hesitate to recognize the link of cause and effect between two or several phenomena; rather, each phenomenon appears to be the product of a bundle of variables, or of interaction among several variables. Functional analysis enables one to avoid the over-assertive language of causal analysis, by drawing out the cumulative action or the interaction of several variables. At the same time, functional analysis is similar to causal analysis in that it enables one to weigh each of the variables, and sometimes to discern the variables or group of variables which exert sufficient influence to be considered a factor and almost a cause.

Various mathematical and statistical techniques, such as factor analysis, have been elaborated in order to establish this weighting and to discern the weighty variables or factors. In reading through sociological journals, one can appreciate the use that is made of these quantitative techniques in analyzing appropriate subject matter.

In this case, can one speak of functionalism? We do not think so. *Functional analysis* is a technique practised in any empirical research, in sociology as in the other sciences. Understood in this way, functional analysis belongs to scientific methodology; it is one of the procedures that can be used by the researcher who is anxious to derive by induction certain laws or constants.

The biological meaning

It is really the fourth meaning attributed to the term *function* which is the foundation of functionalism or functionalisms in sociology and anthropology. Here, function means *the contribution that an element brings to the organization or action of the whole of which it is a part.* So defined, the concept of function takes us back to the organic model. In fact, biology was first developed by analyzing the several functions of the organs of the animal or human body — the liver, the kidneys or the heart — or the digestive or respiratory functions. The biological study of functions can focus either on a particular organ, such as the liver, or on the activity of a group of organs which comprise, for example, the digestive function. Similarly, in sociology one can study the function of the family — that is, its contribution to the organization, maintenance and activity of society. Or one can analyze the function of socialization — in other words, the action of various groups who contribute to the socialization of new members of society. This analogy with the living organism guided all Herbert Spencer's sociology, for he sought to find the equivalent in society of the main biological functions of production, consumption, transportation and communication.

Function and need

To speak of the contribution of an element is to draw on another idea — that of the *needs* of the organism. In fact, the function of an organ or an element within the whole can be understood only when we know the need or needs to which this organ or element responds. This link between function and social need was well illustrated by Durkheim. For while Durkheim carried out a *func-*

tional analysis of suicide, as has been seen earlier, his analysis of the division of labour is clearly *functionalist*. At the time that he undertook his study, he wondered, first of all, what function was fulfilled by the division of labour in society. And with the explicit guidance of the organic model, he writes:

> The word *function* is used in two quite different senses. Sometimes it suggests a system of vital movements without reference to their consequences; at other times it expresses the relation existing between these movements and corresponding needs of the organism. Thus, we speak of the function of digestion, respiration and so forth; but we also say that digestion has as its function the incorporation into the organism of liquid or solid substances designed to replenish its losses, that respiration has for its function the introduction of necessary gases into the tissues of an animal for the sustainment of life. It is in the second sense that we shall use the term. To ask what the function of the division of labour is, is to seek the need which it supplies.[13]

At the end of his analysis, Durkheim concludes that the division of labour responds to the need for social solidarity in a society which is developing and becoming more complex (see Chapter 6). And he insists that he is speaking of function because this idea corresponds more closely to the spirit of the scientific method than the strongly teleological ideas of ends or goals. To speak of an end or a goal, he says, would be to "presuppose that the division of labour exists in *the light of results* which we are going to determine. . . . What is important for our purposes is to establish its existence and the elements of its existence; not to enquire whether there has been a prior presentiment of it, nor even if it has been sensibly felt afterwards."[14]

The Three Functionalisms

Contrary to the impression that is sometimes conveyed, functionalism, of which Durkheim is one of the first representatives, is not

---

13. Durkheim, *The Division of Labour*, p. 49.
14. *Ibid.*, pp. 49-50. Emphasis in the original.

a simple concept. While it would be possible to refine the analysis further, we will content ourselves with distinguishing *three types of functionalism*: absolute functionalism, relative functionalism and structural functionalism. Let us look at each of these in turn.[15]

Absolute functionalism: Malinowski

Undoubtedly, the most typical representative of absolute functionalism is the English anthropologist of Polish descent Bronislaw Malinowski. Indeed, he is often considered to be the father of anthropological and sociological functionalism. Malinowski had the great merit of being the first anthropologist to study the mores of archaic peoples in the field while his predecessors — Tylor, Spencer and Durkheim — knew them only through the writings of explorers or missionaries. Thus he deserves the honour of being the initiator of the anthropological method of field research. Malinowski used this method because he was strongly opposed to evolutionary anthropology, which he considered unscientific and whose errors and sterility he denounced. He took particular exception to the fact that the theoreticians of evolutionism selected cultural traits, types of institutions and customs in different societies, detached them from their context, and then used them at their convenience to illustrate what they claimed to be human and social evolution.

Sharing the life of the archaic peoples that he studied, Malinowski was quickly convinced that each society is characterized and distinguished from the others by an original and particular culture. And what makes each culture original is the specific arrangement of its parts, the place that each element occupies, and the way in which all the elements are linked together. In addition, each culture forms a coherent, unified and integrated whole that one must seek to understand and explain as a totality. To isolate a cultural trait or an institution from its context, as the evolutionists did, is necessarily erroneous; for each cultural trait takes on its meaning only according to the place it occupies within the whole, and through its links with other cultural elements. "The atomizing or isolating treatment of cultural traits is regarded as sterile, because the significance of culture consists in the relation between

15. We have borrowed this terminology from Raymond Boudon, "Remarques sur la notion de fonction," *Revue Française de sociologie* 8 (1967): 198-206.

its elements, and the existence of accidental or fortuitous culture complexes is not admitted."[16] Unity of culture, which is the basis of social integration, thus figures as a fundamental principle in Malinowski's functionalism.

The method suggested by Malinowski

From this perspective, which represented at the time a revolt against evolutionism, how must the anthropologist proceed? Confronted with each material object, cultural trait and institution, he must ask himself why this particular element exists, and what contribution it offers which makes it essential and gives it its place within the cultural whole. To answer this question, he seeks out the needs of the individuals and the society to which the element responds. Just as cultural systems do not exist by chance, so there are no useless or accidental elements. Every cultural element exists because it responds to a need. Therefore, anthropological analysis will seek to identify its function or functions. In the article "Culture," which was cited earlier and which has often been called the manifesto of functionalism, Malinowski shows at length how all the material objects used in a society respond to physiological, technical, economic, social or cultural needs. This is the case not only with material objects, but also with everything that constitutes culture — customs, laws, art, education, magic and religion. This finally leads Malinowski to suggest the following principle: "The functional view of culture insists therefore on the principle that in every type of civilization, every custom, material object, idea and belief fulfills some vital function, has a task to accomplish, and represents an indispensable part of an organic whole."[17]

Four positive aspects of Malinowski's functionalism

Before we consider the criticisms that have been offered against this type of functionalism, it is useful to notice the positive con-

---

16. B. Malinowski, "Culture," *Encyclopaedia of the Social Sciences* (New York: Macmillan Co., 1931), vol. 4, p. 625.

17. B. Malinowski, "Anthropology," *Encyclopaedia Britannica*, quoted by Robert K. Merton, "Manifest and Latent Functions: Towards a Codification of Functional Analysis in Sociology," *Social Theory and Social Structure* (Glencoe, Ill.: The Free Press, 1949).

tribution that it made in its time. We shall comment on four particular points to its credit.

To begin with, Malinowski's functionalism represents the first attempt to establish a rigorous scientific method for the observation and analysis of archaic societies. At a time when Durkheim, despite his stated desire for scientific rigour, still held to the procedures valued by the evolutionists, Malinowski taught that it is necessary, first of all, to *observe* living reality in the field and perceive it as it is. And he suggested an intellectual approach which went beyond the mere observation of facts, by making it possible to group these facts together and to seek to *explain* them in a logical way.

Second, the approach Malinowski suggested was truly sociological in that it emphasized the placement of each cultural element within a total context — that of a given culture — and invited observation and explanation with reference to this context. Malinowski was anxious that each cultural element should be perceived as a genuinely social phenomenon, even if it could be explained in terms of the physiological or psychological needs of individuals.

Third, better than anyone, Malinowski knew how to present society and culture in a realistic and convincing way, as organized and integrated wholes, forming a totality comprised of the arrangement of diverse and multiple parts. It is obvious that he perceived society as a sort of coherent and orderly system.

Finally, in order to make his functionalist approach more precise, Malinowski developed a concept of culture which was more than a mere enumeration of its contents. He was able to grasp the profound meaning of culture by presenting it as ". . . essentially an instrumental reality which has come into existence to satisfy the needs of man in a manner far surpassing any direct adaptation to the environment."[18]

Relative functionalism: Merton

The second type of functionalism, which we have called *relative*, in part was constructed in opposition to Malinowski's functionalism, which was considered too absolute. The appearance of Robert Merton's study "Functional Analysis in Sociology" can be considered a significant point in this development.[19] It is not func-

---

18. Malinowski, "Culture," p. 645.
19. Merton, *Social Theory and Social Structure*.

tionalism itself, however, that Merton attacks. On the contrary, he believes that "the functional orientation is neither new nor confined to the social sciences"; he even states that functional analysis "appeared relatively late on the sociological scene, if one may judge by its earlier and extended use in a great variety of other disciplines." Thus, Merton announces himself publicly as a supporter of functionalism, but of a revived and more flexible functionalism, which is concerned less with the study of the contribution of cultural or social elements than with their *observable consequences*. This distinction is not unimportant; for by focusing analysis on the observable consequences of cultural elements, rather than on their contribution, Merton hopes to give an operational and empirically usable dimension to the concept of function. This was lacking in Malinowski's functionalism, which was sometimes too vague. It is only in this way that functionalism can fulfill its assigned role, identified by Merton as follows: "The central orientation of functionalism — expressed in *the practice of interpreting data by establishing their consequences for larger structures in which they are implicated* — has been found in virtually all the sciences of man — biology and physiology, psychology, economics and law, anthropology and sociology."[20]

Merton's critique of Malinowski

It is generally considered that Merton wrote the most pertinent and decisive critique of Malinowski's absolute functionalism. He showed that this functionalism was based on three highly debatable postulates:

> 1. *The postulate of the functional unity of society*, which states that cultural elements and social activities are "functional for the entire social or cultural system." Merton admits that "all human societies must have *some* degree of integration," but he shows empirically that one cannot claim, as Malinowski implies, that all societies have "this *high* degree of integration in which *every* culturally standardized activity or belief is functional for the society as a whole and uniformly functional for the people living in it." This postulate was perhaps acceptable in the case of certain small archaic societies which were highly integrated, but it proves to

20. *Ibid.*, pp. 46-47. Emphasis added.

be completely false in the case of complex, differentiated and literate societies.

2. *The postulate of universal functionalism,* according
to which every social or cultural element fulfills a function;

3. *The postulate of indispensability,* according to
which each cultural or social element is indispensable.

Merton shows that it is harmful to maintain that *every* cultural
element necessarily fulfills a function and is consequently indispensable. Using several examples, he illustrates the sometimes
glaring errors of interpretation that these two latter postulates
have led researchers to commit. To attempt, at all costs, to find a
function for each cultural element can sometimes lead one to fantastic or far-fetched explanations.

New operational concepts suggested by Merton

The discussion of Malinowski's three postulates ultimately leads
Merton to develop four new functional concepts which are designed to make these postulates more relative and flexible but,
above all, to make functionalism an operational concept. First, he
suggests the idea of *functional alternatives (functional equivalents
or substitutes).* To suggest that a cultural or social element is indispensable merely because it exists is to forget that the same social, psychological or physical need can be filled by various and
sometimes interchangeable cultural elements. As a replacement
for the postulate of indispensability, Merton proposes "a major
theorem of functional analysis: *just as the same item may have
multiple functions, so may the same function be diversely fulfilled
by alternative elements.*" Thus, several functional equivalents or
substitutes can correspond to the same cultural element; or a cultural element can itself be the substitute for another which would
be more efficient. Merton illustrates this by recalling:

> ... there is not seldom a readiness among some func-
> tionalists to conclude that magic or certain religious
> rites and beliefs are functional, because of their effect
> upon the state of mind or self-confidence of the be-
> liever. Yet it may well be in some instances that these
> magical practices obscure and take the place of acces-
> sible secular and more adaptive practices.

This last statement leads Merton to introduce a second idea, similarly designed to make functionalism less rigid, and this is the concept of *dysfunction*. While "functions are those observed consequences which make for the adaptation or adjustment of a given system," *dysfunctions* are those "which lessen the adaptation or the adjustment of the system." To return to the example cited earlier of magical or religious ceremonies and beliefs, in some cases it is apparent that these rites and beliefs are poor substitutes for other possible activities whose effect would be more certain. This is true, for example, with regard to the religious respect that continues to be attached to cows and monkeys in India, although it entails serious economic inconveniences. Annoying or disastrous consequences for individuals and for society can result from some magical or religious beliefs or practices; and under these circumstances, Merton suggests speaking of dysfunction, rather than function. Many authors have emphasized the danger that such a distinction presents, however: it can too easily serve to camouflage implicit value judgements on the part of the observer.

Finally, Merton suggests a distinction between the functions that he calls *manifest* and those that he calls *latent*: "the first referring to those objective consequences for a specified unit (person, subgroup, social or cultural system) which contribute to its adjustment or adaptation and were so intended; the second referring to unintended and unrecognized consequences of the same order." Merton adds that one can also speak of manifest and latent dysfunctions. In other words, this distinction is equivalent in functional analysis to separating *the point of view of individuals within the situation* — that is, those who belong to a given society and can explain the manifest functions of their activities — from *the point of view of the observer* who discovers functions (or dysfunctions) which are neither perceived nor sought by the members of the society.

While there are many slight differences in meaning, Merton's relative functionalism is fairly representative of that which is found among most modern sociologists who quote or practise functionalism. This is why we have thought it useful to summarize his study, for it remains a major document in the functionalist file. It is very often cited by both supporters and opponents of functionalism.

Structural functionalism

The third type of functionalism, which has been called *structural functionalism*, is different from the two former types in that it is not concerned with the analysis of cultural or social elements. *The starting point here is the society,* which is perceived both abstractly and totally. The question is, what essential functions must be fulfilled in order that a society may exist, and maintain and perpetuate itself? In other words, what are the *functional prerequisites or imperatives* in a given society? We can cite two examples of this type of functional analysis. In a joint article, five American sociologists establish a list of nine functional prerequisites.[21] In order to exist and maintain itself, every society must include:

1. Provision for adequate relationship to the environment, and for sexual recruitment
2. Role differentiation and role assignment
3. Communication
4. Shared cognitive orientations
5. A shared articulated set of goals
6. The normative regulation of means
7. The regulation of affective expression
8. Socialization
9. The effective control of disruptive forms of behaviour

In a later work, one of the authors, Marion Levy, added a tenth prerequisite: satisfactory institutionalization.[22]

Talcott Parsons adopted a viewpoint that is even more general. According to him, every society — or more abstractly, every social system — must respond to four functional problems: the pursuit of goals or "goal attainment"; normative or latent stability or "pattern-maintenance and tension management"; "adaptation" to the surrounding physical and social environment; "integration" of members into the social system.

In Chapter 9, we will explain in great detail Parsons' four functional imperatives and the place that they occupy in his general theory.

Conclusion

In order to assist in the understanding of the meaning of function and functionalism in sociology, we have thought it useful first to

21. D. F. Aberle et al., "The Functional Prerequisites of a Society," *Ethics* 9 (January 1950): 100-11.
22. Marion J. Levy, *The Structure of Society* (Princeton: Princeton University Press, 1952).

establish a distinction between functional analysis, which is widely employed in research, and functionalism in the strict sense; then we have distinguished three types of functionalism. We believe that a great many of the debates among sociologists could have been avoided, or would have been more useful, if these distinctions had been taken into account. In any case, the student of sociology will benefit from keeping these distinctions in mind. They will help him to appreciate the merit of different theoretical or empirical studies which refer to functionalism, and to maintain a sense of direction in the maze of different interpretations that have been given of functional analysis and functionalism.

Without going into the many discussions which functional analysis and types of functionalism have provoked — discussions which are too long to be reported here — we can draw an important conclusion. Functionalism and functional analysis have contributed very largely to stressing the study of society as a whole, and emphasizing the need always to relate every phenomenon studied to this totality and to its natural context. Functionalism in particular encourages the recognition of the interrelationships which exist between elements of culture and society, and simultaneously emphasizes the relationships between each element and the socio-cultural whole. From Malinowski and Durkheim to Parsons, and including all the others, the same global purpose, which characterizes sociology in both its empirical research and its theoretical developments, is asserted.

It is not surprising that functionalism should have encouraged the elaboration of the systemic model in sociology. As Alvin Gouldner states:

> The intellectual foundation of functional theory in sociology is the concept of a "system." Functionalism is nothing if it is not the analysis of social patterns as parts of larger systems of behaviour and belief. Ultimately, therefore, an understanding of functionalism in sociology requires an understanding of the resources of the concept of "system."[23]

Functional analysis, understood in the mathematical sense defined earlier, and the various functionalisms that we have just analyzed, must have the postulate of a social system as a starting

---

23. Alvin W. Gouldner, "Reciprocity and Autonomy in Functional Theory" in Gross, ed., *Symposium on Sociological Theory*, p. 241.

point, as Gouldner clearly emphasizes. Explicitly or implicitly, functional analysis and functionalism presuppose that society or the social phenomenon studied manifests the properties of a system that have already been specified. It is in this that the *global purpose* of functional analysis and of all functionalism resides. In other words, the aim is to study each social phenomenon by taking into account its widest possible context and by relating it to this context.

This same global purpose will be found in the concept of structure and structuralism to which we now turn.

Structure and Structuralism

The present vogue of structuralism

During the past thirty years, the concept of structure has experienced a new popularity, not only in sociology, but in all the social sciences. It is used in very different ways, however, and as a result is sometimes the source of heated controversy. Furthermore, it is very difficult to sort out the more or less subtle differences of meaning that have been suggested. The American anthropologist Kroeber has concluded:

> "Structure" appears to be just a yielding to a word that has a perfectly good meaning but suddenly becomes fashionably attractive for a decade or so — like "streamlining" — and during its vogue tends to be applied indiscriminately because of the pleasurable connotations of its sounds . . . everything that is not wholly amorphous has a structure. So what "structure" adds to the meaning of our phrase seems to be nothing, except to provoke a degree of pleasant puzzlement.[24]

To this defeatist and oversimplified attitude, Roger Bastide replied that if the term "constantly invades new fields of study, it is because it corresponds to a need; it is useful and, while it can lead to confusion, it can also enrich the fields of study that employ it."[25]

---

24. Quoted by Claude Lévi-Strauss, *Structural Anthropology*, trans. Claire Jacobson and Brooke Grundfest Schoepf (New York: Basic Books, 1963), p. 278.
25. Roger Bastide, ed., *Sens et usages du terme structure dans les sciences humaines et sociales* (La Haye: Mouton and Company, n.d.), introduction, p. 14.

It is clearly impossible to discuss the question exhaustively at this point. But we shall attempt to give a view of the issue which is general and, we hope, as "structured" as possible! Of course, we will emphasize those aspects which are of greatest interest to sociology.

Two main sources

At the risk of oversimplification, it can be said that the concept of social structure stems from two main sources: the first, which is older, is the organic model; the second, which is more recent, is linguistics or, perhaps more accurately, phonology. We will see that in the end *two very different concepts of structure* correspond to these two sources.

The Organicist Source

Spencer's organicism

We have previously mentioned several times the organic model in sociology, and we have pointed out that it was Herbert Spencer who used it most extensively. In *The Principles of Sociology*, of which the first volume was published in 1876, Spencer constructs a detailed parallel between the organization and evolution of living organisms and those of societies. He concludes that "society can be considered as an organism"[26] and refers to society as a social organism. The comparison between biological and social organisms enables him to establish a number of similarities between the two. He observes in particular that their evolution has come about, in both cases, through an increasing diversification and specialization of organs or parts and that, as a result, a multiplication of social structures and social functions has emerged that is comparable to that of biological structures and functions. He observes, further, that these two organisms are endowed with three systems of organs: the system of nutrition, the system of distribution and the system of control. The evolution of these systems has occurred

---

26. Spencer, *The Principles of Sociology*, vol. 1, p. 462. It is in this volume that Spencer developed his organicist thesis (pp. 447-597). On this thesis, see in particular the article devoted to it by Georges Gurvitch, "Une source oubliée des concepts de 'structure sociale,' 'fonction sociale' et 'institution,' Herbert Spencer," *Cahiers internationaux de sociologie* 23 (1957).

in both cases through an increasing interdependence of the constituent parts, and through a more integrated and more defined organization of each system and its reciprocal parts.

But Spencer is careful to note that there are also differences between the two organisms. He emphasizes, in particular, that the
political organ has no parallel in the living organism. This
provides him with an argument in support of his unyielding opposition to the State and to all government enterprise, and confirms
his extreme liberal philosophy. Finally, Spencer concludes that all
these analogies between the living and social organism are "but as
a scaffolding to help in building up a coherent body of sociological inductions. Let us take away the scaffolding: the inductions
will stand by themselves."[27]

It must be recognized that Spencer derived his perception of social reality, as a set of relationships between interdependent parts
which form an integrated whole, from his organicist analogy or his
model of the living organism, which he used to the full.

Spencer's concept of social structure

But what did Spencer mean by "social structure"? As the biologist
Etienne Wolff has said:

> The idea can occur to a group of biologists to organize
> a round table discussion on "structures" in biology. It
> would never occur to them to organize such a round
> table on *the meaning of the word structure*. In other
> words, the term is perfectly clear and indisputable.
> Within our field of study, it retains its etymological or
> commonplace meaning that one finds defined (as) ...
> "The way in which a building is constructed." One
> also finds: the way in which the parts of a whole are ar-
> ranged; the structure of the body. . . . The fact is there:
> structure is a simple concept which corresponds to a
> given fact and not simply to an idea. The concept of
> structure corresponds very closely to that of organiza-
> tion.[28]

Like the complacent biologists, Spencer poses no problems concerning the meaning of the words *structure* or *function*. For him,

---

27. Spencer, *The Principles of Sociology*, pp. 592-93.
28. Etienne Wolff, "Le sens et l'emploi du mot 'structure' en biologie" in Bastide, ed., *Le terme structure*, p. 23.

too, structure is a given fact; for him, ultimately the concept corresponds closely to that of organization. Any arrangement of cells, organs or parts is a structure, and he uses the term with this elementary and simple meaning.

Radcliffe-Brown

Spencer exerted a considerable and long-lasting influence on British social anthropology. A. R. Radcliffe-Brown, following Spencer's example, again took up the organicist analogy and the concept of social structure and function; but he sought to give them a more precise meaning than did Spencer. He writes:

> Social structure is an arrangement of persons in institutionally controlled or defined relationships, such as the relationship of king and subject, or that of husband and wife.... [He goes on to make a distinction between social structure and social organization, defining the latter as] an arrangement of activities.... The structure of a modern army consists, in the first place, of an arrangement into groups — regiments, divisions, army corps, etc. and in the second place an arrangement into ranks — generals, colonels, majors, corporals, etc. The organization of the army consists of the arrangement of the activities of its personnel whether in time of peace or in time of war. Within an organization, each person may be said to have a role. Thus we may say that when we are dealing with a structural system we are concerned with a system of social *positions* while in an organization we deal with a system of *roles*.[29]

It should be recognized that Radcliffe-Brown's distinctions are not always very clear. In addition, he sometimes seems to contradict himself. He insists, for example, that structure is not the concrete organism itself, but rather the "set of relationships" between the constituent units. Social structure, then, is the set of relationships between individuals or actors *when these relationships are described according to what standardizes them* — in other words, according to the institutionalized patterns of behaviour

---

29. A. R. Radcliffe-Brown, *Structure and Function in Primitive Society* (London: Cohen and West Ltd., 1952), p. 11.

which serve as norms for the conduct of individuals. But at the same time he distinguishes between, on the one hand, the structure that has a concrete existence in reality, which is directly observable and is constantly moving and changing within society, as within the organism; and, on the other hand, the structural form described by the observer, which underlies the concrete structure and which is much more stable and permanent.

Because of contradictions of this kind, Radcliffe-Brown's work has been the target of various criticisms, which are more or less deserved, formulated by authors who have not always understood him. In fact, it seems that these contradictions or ambiguities stem from Radcliffe-Brown's intuition concerning two distinctions that he did not manage to express very clearly. First, there is the distinction between the aspects of reality which lend themselves to structural analysis — that. is, aspects that Gurvitch has called astructural or non-structurable, which constantly change or are modified by spontaneity or creativity. Second, there is the much more important distinction (which we will encounter again in our discussion of Lévi-Strauss) between the structure experienced more or less consciously by the members of a society and the theoretical structure or model which is constructed by the researcher in an attempt to account for and explain reality.

Radcliffe-Brown's successors

Radcliffe-Brown's successors in British sociology and anthropology contributed nothing new to the idea of structure. Thus, for S. F. Nadel: "We arrive at the structure of a society through abstracting from the concrete population and its behaviour the pattern or network (or 'system') of relationships obtaining between actors in their capacity of playing roles relative to one another."[30] And in his sociological introduction, which is extremely good in other respects, T. B. Bottomore follows Morris Ginsberg in asserting: "Of the different conceptions we have discussed, the most useful seems to me that which regards social structure as the complex of major institutions and groups in society."[31] Unfortunately, such a definition of social structure is neither illuminating nor useful.

But Radcliffe-Brown's influence led British anthropology into

---

30. S. F. Nadel, *The Theory of Social Structure* (Glencoe, Ill.: The Free Press, 1957), p. 12.
31. T. B. Bottomore, *Sociology: A Guide to Problems and Literature* (London: Allen and Unwin Ltd., 1962), p. 111.

extremely valuable empirical research, mainly because of the structuralist approach by which he was guided. British anthropologists have made notable and important contributions to the empirical studies of kinship structure and of the political and legal structures of the African peoples.

The Linguistic Source

Ferdinand de Saussure

Structuralism's second source of inspiration is linguistics. The French linguist Ferdinand de Saussure can be found at the origins of this influence. In his *Course in General Linguistics*, which his former students published after his death in 1916, he was the first scholar to claim that language is a system and should be studied as such.

> Language is a system that has its own arrangement....[32] Language is a system whose parts can and must all be considered in their synchronic solidarity;[33] ... to consider a term as simply the union of a certain sound with a certain concept is grossly misleading. To define it in this way would isolate the term from its system; it would mean assuming that one can start from the terms and construct the system by adding them together when, on the contrary, it is from the interdependent whole that one must start and, through analysis, obtain its elements.[34]

As the linguist Roman Jakobson recognized in 1927:

> F. de Saussure's thesis defining language as a system of relative values is almost generally accepted in contemporary linguistics. However, all the practical conclusions of this thesis have not been consistently derived.[35]

---

32. Ferdinand de Saussure, *Course in General Linguistics*, trans. Wade Baskin (London: Peter Owen Limited, 1960), p. 22.
33. *Ibid.*, p. 87.
34. *Ibid.*, p. 113.
35. Roman Jakobson, "Proposition au premier congrès international de linguistes," reproduced in *Selected Writings* (La Haye: Mouton et Co., 1962), vol. 1, p. 4.

The Prague school

It was left to Roman Jakobson, N. Trubetzkoi and their colleagues of the so-called Prague school to develop structural linguistics. And it is now recognized that it is because linguistics has analyzed language as *a systemic whole* that it has made considerable progress. Indeed, it has the reputation of being the most advanced social science and the one to which one can turn for guidance.

Linguistics first accomplished its most remarkable progress in phonology — that is, in the study of phonemes, which are the voiced aspect of language. As early as 1933, Trubetzkoi could state: "Contemporary phonology is not limited to declaring that phonemes are always members of a system; it demonstrates concrete phonological systems and their structure."[36] More recently, by use of the same methods, identical progress has been achieved in semantics — the study of language as a symbolic system which is independent of the subjects who speak it.

From linguistics to anthropology: Lévi-Strauss

More than anyone, the French anthropologist Claude Lévi-Strauss was guided by the systemic approach in linguistics, and he attempted to transpose it to the analysis of social reality. He is considered the main representative of what he himself has called structural anthropology, a phrase used for the title of one of his books.[37]

This transposition from linguistics to the other social sciences is justified, according to Lévi-Strauss, for two reasons. First, man's vocal apparatus enables him to articulate a very wide range of sounds. But no language uses all possible sounds. Some sounds are selected and others omitted, and specific relationships between sounds are established. The same is true of society and culture. The biological and psychological apparatus acts as a very rich reservoir of diverse predispositions and opens up a wide range of various possible attitudes. Some of these possibilities are universally recognized; but at the same time, each socio-cultural unit chooses a certain number of them and eliminates others in order to form a particular coherent arrangement. Thus, the work of sociologists

---

36. N. Trubetzkoi, "La phonologie actuelle," *Psychologie du langage* (Paris: n.p., 1933). Quoted by Claude Lévi-Strauss, "L'analyse structurale en linguistique et en anthropologie," *Word* I (1945): 35.
37. Lévi-Strauss, *Structural Anthropology*.

and anthropologists consists of understanding and explaining the structure of the elements which have been retained among all those which are possible, just as linguists search for the system of sounds and signs which comprise a language.

Second, social life is based essentially on a vast symbolic apparatus, and language is only one of the systems of symbols that man employs in his exchange and communication with others. All the other means of symbolic representation and exchange in social life should lend themselves to the same analytical methods as language.[38] In his own experience, Lévi-Strauss achieved this transposition in his study of kinship, which he interpreted (guided by Marcel Mauss's *The Gift*) as a symbolic system of exchange or circulation of women, giving rise to a vast set of marriage relations which formed the main basis of the organization of non-industrial societies. This system shows a structure which is equivalent to the structure of language, and lends itself to the mathematical formulation of all the rules of marriage and, consequently, of all types of kinship.[39]

Lévi-Strauss's concept of social structure

The originality of his theory and the source of much subsequent discussion is the meaning that Lévi-Strauss attributed to the concept of structure. For him, the structure of social reality is not a concrete fact which is directly observable; it is rather, in his words, "latent," hidden within reality, and it must be discovered. But, he insists, there is no opposition here between the concrete and the abstract:

> Contrary to formalism, structuralism refuses to contrast the concrete and the abstract and to accord a preferential value to the latter. *Form* is defined in contrast to matter which is separate from it; but *structure* has no distinct content. Structure is itself the content which is apprehended within a logical organization, conceived in its turn as part of reality.[40]

Lévi-Strauss is solidly opposed to Spencer's and Radcliffe-Brown's conception of social structure, which he considers too realistic and

---

38. See in particular Lévi-Strauss, "L'analyse structurale."
39. Lévi-Strauss, *The Elementary Structures of Kinship.*
40. Claude Lévi-Strauss, "La structure et la forme," *Cahiers de l'Institut de science économique appliquée,* Série M, no. 7. (March 1960): 3.

too concrete. For him, social structure is neither the arrangement of social relationships, nor a set of groups; these are the directly observable facts that can be described, in their own terms, by those who participate in and experience them. Structure as defined by Lévi-Strauss is, strictly speaking, a theoretical *model* which the researcher constructs and which, in the extreme, should be able to be reduced to a mathematical formula. The function of structure is not to describe, as Spencer and Radcliffe-Brown claimed. Rather, it is *to make the observed facts intelligible* at a level other than that which is available to the participant himself — in other words, at the level of theoretical intelligibility, which is different from the level of common-sense knowledge.

Thus, the gap between reality and structure can be found elsewhere than in the opposition between the concrete and the abstract. Guided by the linguist Trubetzkoi, for whom "structural linguistics goes from the study of *conscious* linguistic phenomena to that of their *unconscious* infrastructure," Lévi-Strauss considers that ". . . phonemic systems are built by the mind at the level of unconscious thought."[41] The same is true of social structures. The structure that the observer describes is present, but "latent" in reality, in the sense of an order which is concealed behind events that are consciously experienced. Those who experience the events (whether a language that they speak or a kinship system to which they belong) are not aware of the underlying structure. It is the role of structural analysis to discover this hidden structure, to derive it from concrete reality and to express it in the form of a general rule, a scientific law or an explanatory model of reality. Thus, as defined by Lévi-Strauss, structuralism is "an attempt to order what is arbitrary in order to discover an immanent necessity within the illusion of liberty." Here, once again, we find the preoccupation that has already been encountered among other authors, notably Pareto, of elaborating theoretical models in the social sciences which make it possible to understand and interpret the social reality *experienced* by the members of a collectivity and mentally *reconstructed* by the researcher.

Lévi-Strauss and Pareto

By now, it is fairly clear that Lévi-Strauss's structure corresponds to what Pareto called a system. Lévi-Strauss guided by structural lin-

---

41. Lévi-Strauss, *Structural Anthropology*, pp. 33-34.

guistics, and Pareto by pure economics both suggest the elaboration of highly theoretical models as a goal for researchers in the social sciences. The two terms used, *structure* and *system*, should not mislead us; for these two authors have the same conception of the scientific task to be accomplished. The procedure they advocate consists of progressing from *observation* of what is incoherent, disjointed and arbitrary, to *explanation* through a logical, articulated and intelligible model. In fact, it can be said that by formulating the rules which regulate kinship structure, Lévi-Strauss conceived of a social system of which Pareto would have approved.

Lévi-Strauss and Radcliffe-Brown

There is a deeper and more rigid opposition between Radcliffe-Brown and Lévi-Strauss. But this opposition is didactically fruitful for us. In fact, these two authors can be considered as *the representatives of two different conceptions of the concept of structure* which are in general use; in their turn, these two concepts of structure correspond to *two types of scientific analytical models*.

Structure: a conceptual model

Radcliffe-Brown's social structure corresponds to what we will call a *conceptual model*, whose function is *descriptive*. To say that a university has a structure is to represent it as a set of positions, roles and stratified groups which are linked together according to functional relationships in a constantly readjusted equilibrium. Some parts of the structure can be described by the participants themselves, according to the position that they occupy within it and the consequent perspective that they have on the whole — the president, a dean, a full professor or a lecturer, a student, a laboratory technician, a stenographer, an official in charge of the maintenance services, a donor, a former student or the parent of a student. Each of these actors devotes a more or less important part of his life to participating, and thus sees this structure from a particular viewpoint. The sociologist is guided by these different perspectives, which he consolidates, integrates and merges, and also by his own observations of the conduct of various participants, of the communications network, and of particular groupings. On the basis of these, he will seek to construct a total coherent image of a specific university or of universities in general. This image will be based on a series of elements experienced by different participants at their own level in a conscious, though partial and localized, way. The sociologist's image of the university also may include structural properties of which none of the participants is aware; for them the revelation of such properties may be a surprise, and they may even deny them.

This image that the sociologist derives from his direct observation of the university is a conceptual model in that it permits him to describe reality in a way that is simultaneously total, coherent and articulated; and, in a sense, it is external, for it does not correspond to the partial image of each participant. It corresponds in other respects to reality as it is experienced, for it is directly extracted from this reality; but this correspondence is not perfect, because it is a reconstruction. Let us say, then, that it is *an abstraction of the first degree,* or that the structure described by the conceptual model is immediately and directly observable in reality as it is experienced, but that such reality is then reformulated.

Structure: a theoretical model

In contrast, structure as defined by Lévi-Strauss is a *theoretical model* whose function is *interpretative and explanatory,* rather than representative and descriptive. The conceptual model can be considered as a way of *perceiving* reality, and the theoretical model as a way of *understanding* reality. The members of a society can have at least a partial knowledge of its structure, in terms of a conceptual model; but structure as a theoretical model escapes them, for it presupposes a procedure other than direct observation. It presupposes a *translation* of observed facts at another level or at a second degree of abstraction.

The mechanical model and the statistical model

Lévi-Strauss has distinguished between two types of models which resemble ours: the mechanical model, which corresponds to our conceptual model; and the statistical model, which would be our theoretical model. He gives an example of each. The anthropologist or sociologist who observes the selection of spouses in the marriages of a given population derives a set of marriage rules which are observed by this population and which determine preferred, permitted and prohibited choices. These rules form a descriptive model that tells us which norms are obeyed by the members of a society in the choice of their spouses. It is well known, however, that in practice norms are not always rigorously observed. Marriages take place which are not in accordance with the rules. *The descriptive model does not allow us to predict the probability of marriages in which the choice of the spouse will break the rules.* This is Lévi-Strauss's mechanical model: it specifies general norms or rules, but does not permit the prediction of all individual conduct in practice.

If, at the same time, the anthropologist or sociologist keeps a register of all marriages over a fairly long period and makes a statistical count of all the effective choices of spouses, and if he subjects this account to mathematical treatment and finally derives a simplified formula which accounts for all the observed cases, he is then in the position to predict the margin of probability that marriage in practice will take place in accordance with the established rules. This statistical model is not located at the descriptive level; it presupposes *a translation of the facts to an interpretive level which permits prediction.*

We must be careful here, however. Both Lévi-Strauss's terminology and his example are confusing. A model is not theoretical just because it uses statistics. As Gilles Granger has emphasized, the mechanical model also may employ statistics.[42] Instead, the important point made by this example is the transition from the descriptive to the interpretive level; for it is in this transition that the difference lies between the conceptual and the theoretical model.

A Dual Theoretical Purpose

The two concepts of structure that have been described and the two types of models to which they correspond bring us to an important conclusion. In fact, it can be said that these two types of models express the two main purposes which have presided, and still preside, over all theoretical research in sociology and anthropology. *The conceptual model responds in particular to the global purpose, while the theoretical model responds to the purpose of logical-experimental abstraction.*

---

42. Gilles Granger, "Evénements et structures dans les Sciences de l'homme," *Cahiers de l'Institut de science économique appliquée,* Série M, no. 6, pp. 177-78.

The global purpose

By global purpose, we mean the attempt to perceive society (or a given society) as a set of interdependent parts which form a whole having a certain internal coherence, and to analyze each phenomenon in relation to this whole or in relation to other phenomena which are produced within this whole. This purpose has already been noticed in functional analysis and functionalism. It can similarly be found within structural analysis, particularly in the conceptual model. In addition, it is this global purpose which most modern definitions of structure express. For example, in his philosophical dictionary, André Lalande says of the term *structure*: "It is employed in opposition to a simple combination of elements to designate a whole which is formed by interdependent phenomena, such that each one depends on the others and can only be what it is within and through its relation with the others."[43] The same purpose is expressed in Piaget's definition of structure: "We say that structure exists (in its most general form) when the elements are united in a whole which shows certain properties as a whole and when the properties of the elements depend, entirely or partially, on the characteristics of this whole."[44] Finally, we may quote Gurvitch's definition, not of structure in general, but of social structure: "Every social structure is a precarious balance (which must be constantly re-established through renewed efforts) between a multiplicity of hierarchies within a total social phenomenon of the macrosociological kind; the structure represents only one sector or aspect of this total social phenomenon."[45]

All these definitions of structure and social structure have one thing in common: they remind the sociologist that within the slice of reality he has selected for study, facts and events are not isolated from each other. Such facts will become meaningful and consequently intelligible to the extent that he searches for the links which unite them to each other and to the whole, as well as for the properties which result for them and for the whole from the interdependent relationships that exist between them.

---

43. André Lalande, *Vocabulaire technique et critique de la philosophie* (Paris: Presses universitaires de France, 1960), pp. 1031-32.
44. Jean Piaget, *Introduction à l'épistémologie génétique* (Paris: Presses universitaires de France, n.d.), vol. 2, p. 34.
45. Georges Gurvitch, "Le concept de structure sociale," *Cahiers internationaux de sociologie* 19 (July–December 1955): 43.

The purpose of logical-experimental abstraction

The second purpose, which we have identified as logical-experimental abstraction, has been expressed by Lévi-Strauss. He gives the idea of structure the meaning of a theoretical and highly abstract model which is located beyond the consciousness of the subject-actor, and which is discovered by the researcher both through the observation of reality and through logical deduction. Perhaps it can be claimed that in the social sciences it is Lévi-Strauss who has specified most rigorously the requirements of an authentically scientific approach. As he properly reminds us, we cannot be satisfied with describing reality as it is presented to us; above all, scientific knowledge must explain phenomena. And this explanation must be such that it permits confident prediction of the phenomena, changes or conduct that will be observed under given conditions. In fact, in the light of the validity of the predictions that it permits, the merits of a scientific theory can be judged. But this is precisely what Lévi-Strauss requires from structural analysis, as he understands it. He writes:

> We can say that a structure consists of a model meeting with several requirements.
>
> First, the structure exhibits the characteristics of a system. It is made up of several elements, none, of which can undergo a change without effecting changes in all the other elements.
>
> Second, for any given model there should be a possibility of ordering a series of transformations resulting in a group of models of the same type.
>
> Third, the above properties make it possible to predict how the model will react if one or more of its elements are submitted to certain modifications.
>
> Finally, the model should be constituted so as to make immediately intelligible all the observed facts.[46]

In this passage, Lévi-Strauss unequivocally expresses, first, the global purpose of structural analysis: all structural analysis has the goal of describing and/or explaining the interdependence of the elements of a system. But, second, he adds two fundamental requirements — that the structural model should account for all observed facts, and that it should permit prediction. It is these two requirements which imply that structural analysis as presented by Lévi-Strauss is not at the same level as that proposed by Radcliffe-

46. Lévi-Strauss, *Structural Anthropology*, pp. 279-80.

Brown, Piaget and Gurvitch. It is located at a level which is much more clearly theoretical and more rigorously scientific.[47]

It should be noted, however, that in practice it is difficult to find sociological examples of structural analysis which fully satisfy the requirements suggested by Lévi-Strauss. When one speaks — as one often does in sociology — of *structural-functional analysis*, one is referring to the use of some comprehensive conceptual model which is either guided by functionalism or directed towards the goals of functional analysis. Structural analysis of the kind suggested by Lévi-Strauss remains, in sociology, an objective yet to be attained.

Systemic Analysis and the Social Dialectic

Among all the sociologists and anthropologists whose work has been mentioned, we have found the same preoccupation, or the same objective, of contributing to their field of study a rigorous and coherent theoretical apparatus. And for this, they all suggest studying social reality as a totality, or as an organic and ordered whole, whose principles or laws of arrangement must be sought. Whether they take the functionalist or structuralist route, these researchers are completely in agreement concerning the need for a *systemic analysis* of social reality — that is, for an analysis which stems from the postulate that social reality manifests the essential properties of a system. And they agree, too, that it is necessary to elaborate the conceptual and theoretical models required for the explanation of social phenomena as part of a social system.

The main criticism against systemic analysis

Various writers and scholars have criticized both structuralist and functionalist systemic analysis. The method has been, and still is, charged with being excessively static and neglectful of the influence of time; with not taking into account social change and

---

47. This chapter was completed when Raymond Boudon's illuminating and recently published study came to our attention: *A quoi sert la notion de "structure"? Essai sur la signification de la notion de structure dans les sciences humaines* (Paris: Gallimard, 1968). In a slightly different but related way, Boudon also distinguishes two different conceptions of the idea of structure.

the contradictions and conflicts which are inherent in social life — briefly, it has been charged with ignoring the social dialectic. It is true that a good number of sociologists and anthropologists have used systemic analysis in such a way as to lay themselves open to criticism. In their studies, many researchers have overemphasized the "harmonious" interdependent relationships and complementarities that they perceive between various elements of society. But as a number of writers have stressed, the fault stems, not from systemic analysis itself, but rather from the restricted use that has been made of it.

Here we must emphasize two important points. The first is concerned with the relationships between systemic analysis and time; the second, with the relationships between systemic analysis and the social dialectic.

Systemic analysis and time

It is possible to analyze a social system *at a given moment of time.* This is what is done in empirical research, for example, when interpretation is made of the responses of a group of subjects given at about the same time, to a series of questions concerning their present attitudes. But in a great number of cases, systemic analysis must be carried out *over a certain period of time* during which a given collectivity is observed, so that the researcher may discern the existing functions, functional relationships, structural wholes and so forth. For example, all monographic studies are necessarily of this type. Moreover, social time is an essential aspect of the analysis of a community — that is, time as perceived, measured and appreciated by the members of this community, which is different from chronological or historical time. In addition, a number of systemic analyses are concerned with change itself. For example, most of the mathematical models constructed in microsociology and social psychology seek to explain and predict *changes in attitudes* which can be observed between two or several moments in time.[48] Thus, systemic analysis, in itself, is not located "outside time."

Systemic analysis, change and conflicts

The second point is even more important. Can the contradictions and conflicts of social life be incorporated into systemic models? In

---

48. See in particular Coleman, *Introduction to Mathematical Sociology.*

our opinion, there is no reason to doubt that this is possible. As Jean Pouillon aptly says:

> Structuralism has been defined by its effort to apprehend as a whole, not totalities which are closed and well-defined, but rather wholes whose boundaries are questionable. To use Sartre's language, structuralism is global by its very nature, and what it seeks to make into a whole are not necessarily symmetrical or recurrent phenomena, but also oppositions and unbalanced phenomena, not in order to erase them but in order to understand the link that maintains them.[49]

On the same theme, many writers have used their ingenuity to show the dynamic nature of structural–functional analysis and to illustrate how the study of change can be integrated into a systemic model. Let us mention a few examples. Guided by Ernest Nadel's epistemology, Francesca Cancian indicates four ways in which change can be studied in a functional system, and she gives two examples. The first, taken from anthropology, is Leach's study of change in the political system of Burma; the second, taken from sociology, is Parsons and Smelser's analysis of the differentiation between ownership and control that has come about in the American economy.[50] Pierre van den Berghe shows both the convergence of and the complementarity between functionalism and dialectics; far from being in opposition to each other, the two methods have much in common and each has limitations that a synthesis of the two would make it possible to overcome.[51] Finally, Harold Fallding, in specifying the postulates of functional analysis, includes readiness to change as one of the requirements for the adaptation of a system, and mainly of a social system.[52]

Synchronic and diachronic analysis

For both structuralism and functionalism, not only the possibility is recognized, but also the necessity that systemic analysis should

---

49. Jean Pouillon, "Présentation: un essai de définition," *Les temps modernes*, no. 242 (November 1966): 783. This article serves as the introduction to a special issue devoted to "the problems of structuralism."
50. Francesca Cancian, "Functional Analysis of Change," *American Sociological Review* 25 (December 1960): 818-27.
51. Pierre van den Berghe, "Dialectic and Functionalism: Toward a Theoretical Synthesis," *American Sociological Review* 28 (October 1963): 695-705.
52. Harold Fallding, "Functional Analysis in Sociology," *American Sociological Review* 28 (February 1963): 5-13.

integrate conflicts, contradictions and social change into its conceptual and theoretical models. But a final source of confusion remains. It is often said that sociological research should give priority to the study of change, instead of devoting so much time and energy to the elaboration of structural-functional models, even if these include the analysis of social change. To reason in this way is to fail to recognize the elementary steps of every science and to repeat the error of the social evolutionists of the nineteenth century. The example of linguistics can be very useful in this respect. It was Ferdinand de Saussure who was the first to distinguish between what he called the *synchronic* and the *diachronic* in linguistics.

> Certainly all sciences would profit by indicating more precisely the coordinates along which their subject matter is aligned . . . . (1) *The axis of simultaneities*, which stands for the relations of co-existing things and from which the intervention of time is excluded; and (2) *the axis of successions*, on which only one thing can be considered at a time but upon which are located all the things on the first axis together with their changes. For a science concerned with values the distinction is a practical necessity and sometimes an absolute one. In these fields scholars cannot organize their research rigorously without considering both coordinates and making a distinction between the system of values per se and the same values as they relate to time.[53]

From this arose the distinction, established by de Saussure, between synchronic linguistics, which studies the "logical and psychological relations that bind together co-existing terms and form a system in the collective mind of speakers," and diachronic linguistics, which is concerned with "relations that bind together successive terms not perceived by the collective mind but substituted for each other without forming a system."[54]

From the systemic to the diachronic

It is generally recognized that linguistics owes its really remarkable scientific progress over the past thirty years to this distinction

---

53. Ferdinand de Saussure, *Course in General Linguistics*, pp. 79-80.
54. *Ibid.*, pp. 99-100.

between the synchronic and the diachronic, and to the structural method that this distinction facilitated. As Nicolas Ruwet writes:

> The linguists have this great merit of having been the first to understand *where it was necessary to start* if one wished to undertake an objective study of man. They were the first to stop putting the cart before the horse, and to recognize that before drawing up the history of a specific object and before asking themselves questions concerning its origins, evolution and decline, it was first of all necessary to circumscribe, define and describe this object. The immanent study, as Hjelmslev says, must precede and is the condition of every transcendent study of any object whatsoever.... To undertake the immanent study of a given object first of all means that one postulates the existence of a specific structure within the object.... In other words, analysis can only set itself the initial task of seeking the underlying system of the process which is manifest to experience.[55]

In different terms, Lévi-Strauss expresses the same requirement, for he was largely guided by the example of linguistics:

> I often say to my students that there would not have been a Darwin if there had not first been a Linné; it would not have been possible to pose the problem of the evolution of species if one had not started by defining what one meant by species and by constructing a typology. But we are far from having a taxonomy of societies, and perhaps we will never have one which will be even comparable to the pre-Linné taxonomies.[56]

Finally, Maurice Godelier has amply demonstrated that for Marx himself — who is often cited in support of a sociology of change as opposed to a systemic sociology — "the study of structures has priority over the study of their genesis and evolution." Speaking more specifically of Marx's economic analysis, Godelier writes:

55. Nicolas Ruwet, "Linguistique et sciences de l'homme," *Esprit* (November 1963): 566-67.
56. Claude Lévi-Strauss, "Réponses à quelques questions," *Esprit* (November 1963): 638.

Thus, Marx does not operate in the Hegelian way, by "deducing" one category on the basis of another. He specifies the functions of an element within a structure or of a structure within a system, and explains the order of these functions. . . . With Marx, there is a complete disclaimer of all historicism, or of any priority of the historical study of a system over its structural study; this anticipates, by more than half a century, the crises in linguistics and in sociology which have led de Saussure and Lowie to reject the evolutionist approach of the nineteenth century.[57]

All the evidence presented here leads to one conclusion: that there is no opposition between the analysis of social change and systemic analysis. On the contrary, the latter is the condition of the former.

Conclusion

What we have called *systemic analysis* in sociology can be understood in the light of the foregoing discussion. Systemic analysis is any research, theoretical or empirical, which, on the basis of the postulate that social reality manifests the characteristics of a system, interprets and explains social phenomena through the interdependent links which unite them and form a whole.

To seek the functions of an element or of a social phenomenon, to consider the functional relationships which link it to other realities or phenomena, to reconstitute the structure of an object, and to establish its structural relationships with other units — these are various forms of systemic analysis. Functional and structural research is thus, in a way, the application of the systemic postulate; at least, such research is the logical and necessary consequence of this postulate.

Clearly the concepts of system, function and structure are *intellectual instruments for the analysis of reality*. They stem from the methodology of scientific research. Contrary to other ideas, such as the concepts of actors, groups or milieux, these concepts do not cor-

---

57. Maurice Godelier, "Système, structure et contradiction dans 'Le Capital,'" *Les temps modernes*, no. 246 (November 1966): 843.

respond to concrete phenomena. Instead, they suggest a way of perceiving and explaining reality; it is in this sense that they are really analytical.

The analytical tradition raises more difficult and complex problems in sociology than does the classificatory tradition. As we have demonstrated, even the validity of systemic analysis is still questioned by some sociologists; and among those who are in agreement on its usefulness, various interpretations of such analysis are suggested.

Nevertheless, from the diversity and complexity of the various functionalist and structuralist approaches, we have been able to establish certain common denominators which at least demonstrate the same aim and the pursuit of the same goal — to give sociology a conceptual and theoretical apparatus which is increasingly rigorous. More specifically, Talcott Parsons considers that among most sociologists there is agreement on the following points:

> 1. The relevance of the classical rules of scientific method
> 2. The significance of analytical theory within this method
> 3. The necessity of analytical abstraction for theory
> 4. The utility of the concept of system
> 5. And, finally, the "action frame of reference" (which we presented in Part One)[58]

This list simultaneously takes into account the scope and the limits of the agreement that is presently found in sociological theory, and pinpoints the present state of the analytical tradition in sociology.

---

58. Talcott Parsons, "An Outline of the Social System," in Parsons et al., eds., *Theories of Society*, vol. 1, p. 33.

Chapter 9
The Social System

In the preceding chapter, we followed main lines of development of the analytical tradition in sociology in order to discover its dominant aims and points of consensus. We will now move from purpose to practice and see how the social organization can be analytically represented in a formal, conceptual and abstract model.

Talcott Parsons' theoretical contribution

For this, we shall refer mainly to the work of the American sociologist Talcott Parsons; for Parsons, who is one of the main theoreticians of contemporary sociology, is undoubtedly the one who has gone the furthest in elaborating a general theory in sociology. Over the past forty years, he has devoted a great number of writings to this task. These will guide us in our presentation.

It should be added, however, that it is not easy to interpret and summarize Parsons' work. This is due in part to the very abstract nature of his thought and to his style of writing. But it is also due to the fact that his work is still in progress, for Parsons' ideas constantly develop in many — sometimes surprising — directions.

In order to simplify the presentation and for greater clarity, we will limit ourselves to the systemic model suggested by Parsons in his latest writings.[1]

---

1. In particular, we will use the sections prepared by Parsons himself in Parsons et al., *Theories of Society*, as well as Chapter 2 of the small volume by

The System of Action and Its Sub-systems

The idea of action

The starting point of Parsonian analysis is *action* — that is to say, all human behaviour, whether individual or collective, conscious or unconscious. The terms *action* and *human behaviour* must be understood here in their broadest sense, including not only externally observable behaviour but also thoughts, feelings, aspirations and desires.

Human action is always located simultaneously in four contexts:

1. The biological context, which is that of the neuro-physiological organism with its wants and needs
2. The psychological context, which is that of the personality, studied through psychology
3. The social context, which is that of interactions between the actors and groups, mainly studied through sociology
4. The cultural context, which is that of norms, patterns of behaviour, values, ideologies and knowledge, studied particularly through anthropology

Concrete action is always total. This means that it takes place simultaneously within the four contexts and always results from the interaction of forces or influences stemming from each of them. It is only on the analytical or theoretical level that it is possible to establish distinctions among these four contexts. Each of the social sciences must therefore examine the context or the sector in which it specializes with reference to what Parsons calls *the frame of reference of action*; for this frame of reference is more general, and it is the only context which is theoretically and empirically valid. Thus, the frame of reference of action is the common ground on which all the social sciences meet.

Parsons, *Societies: Evolutionary and Comparative Perspectives*. Among his earlier works, let us particularly mention Parsons, *The Social System*; Parsons and Shils, *General Theory of Action*; Parsons, Bales and Shils, *Theory of Action*; and Parsons, *Essays in Sociological Theory*. Finally, the Cornell University symposium on Parsons' work should be mentioned: Max Black, ed., *The Social Theories of Talcott Parsons* (Englewood Cliffs, N.J.: Prentice-Hall, Inc., 1961).

The concept of system

Another common denominator links the social sciences, and this is the concept of system. For Parsons, this is a "concept . . . vital to science. . . . The concept of system is essentially nothing but an application of the criterion of logical integration of generalized propositions."[2] Systemic analysis or *systematization* thus consists of the transposition of empirical data into general or theoretical propositions, which have the property of being logically linked and interdependent.

This stage of development in scientific knowledge has already been reached in biology and also in psychology; it is now necessary for anthropology and sociology to attain it. This is to say that the four contexts of action are, or should be, considered from the analytical point of view as four systems: the biological system, the psychological system, the social system and the cultural system.

The four sub-systems of action

Each of these systems possesses its own internal logic and consequent boundaries which distinguish it from the others. This makes it possible to isolate it theoretically and analyze it in itself. But each system is, at the same time, an open system with respect to the others. The four systems are related in an interdependent and complementary fashion, so that the analysis of each must at least take into consideration the existence of the three others which form its environment. From this perspective of interdependence, the four systems can thus be considered as *four sub-systems of a more general system which is the system of action.*

As can be seen, from the very beginning Parsons places the social system and sociology within their most general possible context — that of human action and all of the social sciences. And it can be said that in his work Parsons has been faithful to this perspective; he is certainly one of the rare sociologists to have sought an overall view of human and social behaviour and of the social sciences. His first major work was specifically concerned with the structure of social action[3] (long before structuralism became fashionable). He has also devoted an important part of his work to the

---

2. Parsons et al., *Theories of Society*, vol. 1, p. 32.
3. Parsons, *The Structure of Social Action*.

analysis of personality,[4] as well as to economic and political analysis.[5] We should emphasize, therefore, that Parsons is a sociologist for whom sociology always remains *one of the social sciences*, whose subject matter is analytically separated within a set of data which manifest many other different, though complementary, dimensions.

The Ranking of the Sub-systems of Action

Another aspect which links the four systems is *the cybernetically controlled rank order* in which they find themselves. This is an element which has only recently appeared in Parsons' thought, but which has assumed increasing importance.

Cybernetics

In this regard, Parsons has been guided by cybernetics, which, as we know, has a great number of applications. Cybernetics emerged from the comparative study of automatic electronic machines, mainly computers, and of the human nervous system. The properties which are common to the two mechanisms have given rise to a certain theory of action, and to techniques of organizing and controlling this action. It has not been decided whether cybernetics is really a science, or more properly a technology. Louis Couffignal has defined it as "the art of making action efficient."[6] The action in this case is man's action, or that of the machine that replaces him.

With the aim of greater efficiency of action, cybernetics always takes into account two elements in particular: communication or

---

4. In addition to a great number of articles, in particular Talcott Parsons, *Social Structure and Personality* (New York: The Free Press of Glencoe, Inc., 1964); and Parsons et al., *Family, Socialization and Interaction Process*.

5. Parsons' economic analysis will be found in Talcott Parsons and Neil J. Smelser, *Economy and Society* (London: Routledge and Kegan Paul, Ltd., 1956). His political analyses can be found especially in Talcott Parsons, *Politics and Social Structure* (New York and London: The Free Press of Glencoe and Collier-Macmillan Limited, 1969).

6. L. Couffignal, *La cybernétique* (Paris: Presses universitaires de France, Collection "Que sais-je?," 1966), p. 23.

the transmission of information, and the various mechanisms which command, guide or control action. The meaning of communication is generally understood. The control of the efficiency of action is defined by Couffignal as follows: "Control consists of comparing the results obtained with the forecasts made previously. In the case of failure, it has the effect of putting the corrective operations into motion."[7]

The cybernetic ranking of the four sub-systems

In the case of human behaviour, each of the four sub-systems of action can be considered to include mechanisms which guide or control action. Physiological needs, psychological motivations, norms regulating the interaction of social actors, and cultural values are all mechanisms which serve to guide or control action, or in other words, to give it an orientation (to use the term adopted in earlier chapters). But what gives these control mechanisms their cybernetic character is that they are not located at the same level. The four sub-systems are arranged hierarchically from the point of view of the control that they exercise on action. The biological system is lowest on the scale; then comes the personality system, followed by the social system and the cultural system.

In cybernetic ranking, a system which is located towards the top of the scale is richer in *information*; when it is lower down the scale, it is richer in *energy*. Since the cultural system is essentially made up of symbolic elements (knowledge, values, ideologies), it guides and controls action exclusively through the information that it dispenses; thus it is located at the top of the hierarchy. In contrast, the biological system guides and controls action through the energy that it develops and releases; thus, it is located at the bottom of the scale.

Precisely because of this difference, a system that is higher up on the scale exerts a control over the lower systems through the information that it diffuses and procures for them. Thus, the personality is a control system for the biological organism; the social system is a control system for the personality; culture is a control system for the social system. It follows that through the personality, the social system also exerts control over the biological organism

---

7. *Ibid.*, p. 118.

and, through the social system, culture exerts a control over the personality and the biological organism. The higher a system on the scale, the more control it exerts over the other systems of action.

Consequently, when we referred earlier to the interdependence of the four sub-systems of the general system of action, we did not mean that this is a horizontal interdependence. Nor is it an interdependence which implies confusion or mixing. The cybernetic ranking shows that it is rather *a structure of interdependence based on the successive ranking of the control mechanisms of action.*

For Parsons, the cybernetic order also has the merit of avoiding reductionism, which has been the source of many errors in the social sciences. In effect, it avoids reducing the explanation of all human and social action to one single control mechanism, as would be the case if one wished to explain all human conduct on the basis of some physiological or psychological need. To explain fully total human action, one must refer to the four sub-systems; the cybernetic control order is there to provide us with a constructive reminder of this.

Social System and Cultural System

The distinction between the social system and culture

By now, it will have been noticed that the two systems at the bottom of the cybernetic scale of control are situated at the level of the individual; the two other systems concern the collectivity. It is these latter two systems (social system and culture), then, which are of particular interest to us.

Similarly, it will have been noticed that the Parsonian concept of the social system does not include all social reality. Social reality is analytically separated into two distinct systems: the social system and the cultural system. The cultural system includes values, knowledge and ideologies, or more generally, *the total symbolic apparatus* that guides all social action. The social system is concerned with "the conditions involved in the interaction of actual human individuals who constitute concrete collectivities with determinate membership."[8] In every concrete collectivity, whatever the size, whether a small group or a total society, these two systems necessarily interpenetrate. A social system cannot exist without a cultural system to furnish the essential symbolic elements; a cultural system without a social system is a dead civilization, such as those of Ancient Egypt and the Roman Empire.

Institutionalization

The key concept which simultaneously establishes the overlapping of the two systems and the distinction between them is that of institutionalization. This consists of the translation of the cultural elements (values, ideas and symbols), which by their very nature have a general character, into norms of roles and groups which exert direct and immediate control on the social action and interaction of the members of a collectivity. For example, the general value of justice is institutionalized in the role of the judge, in the judicial system and in the body of laws. Thus, institutionalization in a sense makes cultural elements concrete, and is a kind of transposition of them into applicable and applied forms.

Social organization, in terms of the meaning given to it in Chapter 6, thus appears analytically to be the complex compound of a social system and a cultural system which are closely connected. In what we have called social organization, the two systems exist in such a way that they overlap and are inseparable from each other, although it is theoretically possible to separate them, as Parsons does.

In the following pages, it is from this single perspective of social system that we will consider social organization, thus adhering to Parsons' analysis. And in order to give the most complete idea possible of the social system, we will consider in succession structural components, functional imperatives and finally the process of change.

---

8. Parsons et al., *Theories of Society*, vol. 1, p. 34.

The Structure of the Social System

The Parsonian idea of structure

In the preceding chapter, we spoke of Parsons as a representative of structural functionalism and we briefly enumerated the four functional imperatives of his theory. We will now return to them in more detail.

If Parsons is often identified with structural functionalism, it is because he has effectively elaborated his analysis of the social system and social organization in terms of structure and function. But he has given a rather special meaning to these concepts. Let us start with his idea of structure.

Parsons first defines structure in a general way by stating that it consists of institutionalized patterns of normative culture.[9] It immediately appears that the structure of the social system is closely linked to the cultural system; it could even be said that the idea of structure is the pivot between the two systems. Structure is in fact *the result of the process of institutionalization*; in other words, it is composed of the cultural elements transcribed into patterns of social action.

Because it consists of institutionalized models, structure is relatively stable. Parsons places tremendous importance on this point. In fact, structure includes "those elements of the patterning of the system which may be regarded as independent of the lower-amplitude and shorter time-range fluctuations in the relation of the system to its external situation."[10] It will be noticed immediately that Parsons does not say that these are elements which do not change; rather, they are *elements of the system which are sufficiently stable to be considered as constants for the purposes of analysis*. Concretely, in reality the elements of the system which are defined as structural change. They may change quickly, as will be seen later; but as a general rule, except during periods of rapid and profound social upheaval, they change slowly. It is permissible, therefore, at the beginning of analysis to regard them as constants. The structural elements provide a series of stable elements which can serve as the springboard for the analysis of the system.

---

9. *Ibid.*, p. 36.
10. *Ibid.*

The structural components
of the social system

What, more precisely, are the elements of the social system which are sufficiently stable over time to be considered as the structural components of the system? Parsons distinguishes the following four groups of structural components of the social system:

> 1. *Roles*, which define the forms of membership and participation of individuals in different collectivities of the system (the roles of father, professor, mayor and so forth)
> 2. *Collectivities*, formed around certain values, ideas and ideologies which they institutionalize by specifying the concrete forms of application for the social actors who are members of each collectivity (such as the family, university, factory or political party)
> 3. *Norms*, which, for Parsons, correspond more or less to what we earlier called patterns of behaviour
> 4. *Values*, which specify the desirable orientation for the entire system — that is, what the system seeks to be, do or become

This enumeration of the structural components enables us to comprehend better Parsons' definition of structure as "the institutionalized patterns of normative culture." The structural components in fact form four channels through which culture passes in order to be transcribed and materialize in the concrete life of a society and its members. By passing through these channels, culture becomes specific to a particular society, its groups and its members. This is precisely the process of institutionalization.

Concrete structural totalities

The process of institutionalization is similarly carried out through the formation of "concrete structural totalities" to which the name *social institutions* has often been given. These are, for example, the family and the kinship system, the economic structure, the political system and the judiciary. In each concrete structure of this kind, we will always find the four basic structural elements: roles, collectivities, norms and values. But to employ the term *structure* to designate these institutions is to give it a concrete meaning and abandon the analytical meaning given earlier.

The cybernetic ranking
of structural components

Finally, according to Parsons, another characteristic of structural components should be added: in them can be found the same cybernetic ranking as exists for the four sub-systems of action. In the order that they have been presented, the first structural components (roles, collectivities) are at the bottom of the scale of control; the last (norms, values) are at the top of the scale. Values and norms are in effect richer in information; in addition, they border on the two social and cultural systems. It can even be said that these two components belong simultaneously to both culture and the social system; it is the perspective from which they are considered which relates them to one or the other. In terms of their content and symbolic expression, they belong to the context of the cultural system. But on the basis of the guidance that they give to social action and the normative control that they exert on such action, they can be perceived as belonging to the social system.

In contrast, the first two components (roles and collectivities) are much richer in energy; they act more directly and immediately on individuals and groups than do norms and values. More precisely, roles and collectivities serve to "collectively organize the population" of a society[11] by establishing concrete frameworks and practical methods of interaction.

The Functional Analysis
of the Social System

The Parsonian concept of function

If the structural components provide a basis of constant elements for the analysis of the system, the concept of function contributes a more dynamic and changing perspective. In fact, Parsons defines the function of the social system as "those features in terms of which systematically ordered modes of adjustment operate in the changing relations between a given set of patterns of institu-

---

11. Parsons, *Societies: Evolutionary and Comparative Perspectives*, p. 18.

tionally established structures in the system and a given set of properties of the relevant environing systems."[12]

As we have seen, the social system is an open system; thus it constantly relates to its environment. This can include the physical milieu — geographical and climatic conditions, for example. But when Parsons speaks of the environment of the social system, it should be understood that he is referring to the three other subsystems of the general system of action — in other words, to the biological organism, personality and culture. Each of these sub-systems has its own development; and more important, each influences the others and creates continuing problems of adjustment or adaptation for the structure of the social system. Since the structure of the social system has been defined as being theoretically constant at the start, these are functional forms of adjustment which entail changes in the structure and modification of the various structural components.

The four functional imperatives

According to Parsons, four fundamental problems of adjustment can be identified which every social system must face. It is these four problems of adjustment that Parsons calls the functional imperatives of the social system; they are imperatives in the sense that every social system must constantly regulate these problems in order to exist and maintain itself. Consequently, within the social system, four functions can be distinguished, each of which is designed to respond to one of these problems. These four functions are the following:

1. The function of *pattern maintenance*. This consists of ensuring that the values of society are known by its members and that the latter are motivated to accept these values and their requirements. As Parsons emphasizes, pattern maintenance does not imply a static condition; change itself requires pattern maintenance, if only in the form of a certain "order within change." Parsons notes, however, that this first function is the least dynamic of the four, for it generally has the effect of maintaining and protecting the normative order. He even compares it with the concept of inertia in mechanics. The three other functions are much more dynamic and constantly give rise to problems of pattern maintenance.

---

12. Parsons et al., *Theories of Society*, vol. 1, pp. 36-37.

2. The function of *integration*. This consists of ensuring the necessary coordination between the units or parts of the system, particularly with regard to their contribution to the organization and functioning of the whole.

3. The function of *goal-attainment*. As its name suggests, this concerns the definition and achievement of objectives for the entire system and/or for its various constituent units.

4. The function of *adaptation*. This is concerned particularly with all the means that the system and its members must employ in the pursuit of goals.

The cybernetic ranking of functions

The four functions also possess the property of being hierarchically ranked according to the gradation of cybernetic control. The first two (pattern maintenance and integration) are located at the top of the scale of control since they are more immediately guided by the cultural system; the latter two (goal-attainment and adaptation), because they are in more direct contact with the concrete realities of social organization, are located at the bottom of the scale of control.

Thus, a parallel is established between the ranking of functions and that of structural components as described earlier:

> The structural component of values corresponds to the function of pattern maintenance.
> The structural component of norms corresponds to the function of integration.
> The structural component of collectivities corresponds to the function of goal-attainment.
> The structural component of roles corresponds to the function of adaptation.

Functions and concrete structural totalities

The parallel can be pushed even further so that each function more or less corresponds to a concrete structural totality. There is, in other words, a particular structural totality which in the social system has priority in fulfilling each of the basic functions. Thus:

> The structures of socialization (family, education) respond to the function of pattern maintenance.

> Law and the judiciary respond to the function of integration.
> The political structure responds to the function of goal-attainment.
> The economic structure responds to the function of adaptation.

There is no exclusive and exact correspondence, however, between structural totalities and functions. A concrete structural totality alone can never fully respond to a functional imperative; the latter is of too general a nature for the correspondence to be perfect, and it is not located at the same analytical level. The correspondence in question is therefore a question more of emphasis than of perfect agreement. For example, the definition of goals and goal-attainment are obviously not the exclusive prerogative of the political structure; but these are responsibilities that are attributed to political power or that it particularly attributes to itself. The same is true for each of the other structures with regard to each of the basic functions within the system.

Functional imperatives within the general system of action

It remains to clarify one final point which Parsons considers extremely important. The four functional imperatives that we have just presented do not belong to the social system alone; they are found also within the general system of action where they serve to distinguish the four sub-systems:

> The cultural sub-system corresponds to the function of pattern maintenance within the general system of action.
> The social sub-system corresponds to the function of integration.
> The personality sub-system corresponds to the function of goal-attainment.
> The sub-system of the biological organism corresponds to the function of adaptation.

Table 3 summarizes the main traits of the complex analytical model elaborated by Parsons in order to account for the general system of action and the social sub-system. Note the parallelism of the rank order of cybernetic control and the way in which the social sub-system is integrated into the general system of action.

TABLE 3 The General System of Action and the Social Sub-system

Functions of the general system of action	Sub-systems of the general system of action	The rank order of control of action
Pattern maintenance	Culture	Rich in information
Integration	Social system	− ← ← +
Goal-attainment	Personality	+ → → −
Adaptation	Biological organism	Rich in energy

SOCIAL SUB-SYSTEM

Functions of the social sub-system	Structural elements	Structural totalities	Rank order of control of social action
Pattern maintenance	Roles	Socialization	Rich in information
Integration	Norms	Law	− ← ← +
Goal-attainment	Collectivities	Political structure	+ → → −
Adaptation	Values	Economic structure	Rich in energy

Source: Adapted from Talcott Parsons, *Societies: Evolutionary and Comparative Perspectives* (Englewood Cliffs, N.J.: Prentice-Hall, Inc., 1966), pp. 28-29.

Social Evolution

The social system whose functions and structural elements have just been briefly described is not static. The transformations that it experiences can be analyzed from two perspectives: from the evolutionary perspective; and from the perspective of social change, strictly speaking.

Functional and structural differentiation

From the evolutionary perspective, the main phenomenon that is observed is the increasingly accentuated functional and structural differentiation that occurs as a society becomes more "advanced". In this specific sense, more advanced societies become complex societies.

In contrast to complex society, traditional society is characterized by the fact that the four functional sub-systems are less easily distinguished and, above all, that the same structural totality simultaneously fulfills more than one function. For example, the religious collectivity may be at the same time both a political collectivity and an economic one. This was the case in the Middle Ages, when the Catholic Church represented a political power that was actively involved in the struggles between nations and empires; it was also an economic collectivity through its large and valuable holdings. The Church thus simultaneously fulfilled the functions of integration, goal-attainment and adaptation, and at the same time contributed very largely to pattern-maintenance. Or we can cite the example of the union of political power and the judiciary in the hands of the same authorities. Thus, in traditional society, the tribal chief, the lord or the prince dispensed justice either himself or through the intermediation of his subordinates.

It is only in the more advanced societies that an increasingly clear differentiation exists among the four functions and among the structural totalities which correspond to them. For example, there will be a growing differentiation between the religious collectivity on the one hand and the political, economic and judicial collectivities on the other. Here we return, in a more analytical way, to a phenomenon that was described in Chapter 8 when we compared traditional and technological society.

Two processes of differentiation

Parsons emphasizes that this phenomenon of differentiation operates through two different processes: segmentation and specification. *Segmentation* consists of the appearance and proliferation of new sub-collectivities which divide among them the function formerly held by a single collectivity. The institution of the school, for example, was formed by the redistribution of the socializing function, which formerly belonged solely to the family. The labourer's trade union emerged as it assumed some of the economic functions formerly fulfilled by the corporation and the employer.

As a correlation to segmentation, a *specification* of the normative culture is produced. In effect, each sub-collectivity effects a redefinition of certain cultural elements in such a way that these become specific to it. For example, there is a redefinition of values and norms for new roles which arise in new sub-collectivities, and for new goals that are assigned. The complex society is distinguished from traditional society by a less homogeneous culture; the culture of complex societies becomes diversified as a result of the multiplication of concrete structures of collectivities and sub-collectivities.

The processes of structural segmentation and cultural specification obviously pose problems of integration. New forms of coordination are required each time that new structures are created — coordination between a new role and former roles, between a new collectivity and long-established collectivities. In the development of complex societies, the constantly dynamic nature of the function of integration takes on great importance. It is on the success of the integrative function that a so-called harmonious development largely depends.

Social Change

The evolutionary perspective focuses analysis on transformations operating over long periods of time which generally go beyond the life of one generation. When one adopts *the perspective of change*, which is the one most often preferred in sociology, the analysis is concerned with shorter periods; thus it cannot follow the same course.

The concept of equilibrium

For Parsons, the essential starting point is provided by the concept of *equilibrium*. This, he says, is "a fundamental reference point for analyzing the processes by which a system either comes to terms with the exigencies imposed by a *changing* environment, without essential change in its own structure, or fails to come to terms and undergoes other processes such as structural change, dissolution as a boundary-maintaining system (analogous to biological death for the organism), or the consolidation of some impairment leading to the establishment of secondary structures of a 'pathological' character."[13] Parsons has become the target of many attacks because of this appeal to the concept of equilibrium in the analysis of social change. He has been criticized — perhaps a little too easily — for constructing a sociology of the status quo. In fact, it should be recognized that the concept of equilibrium is, for Parsons, a purely methodological procedure which he believes that sociology should use as do many other sciences. Equilibrium corresponds to what in statistics is called a *null hypothesis*, designed to perceive better and to measure change. It is hypothesized that structure or structural elements are constant or stable at a given point in time. This structural stability theoretically constitutes a point of equilibrium between the social system and its environment, as well as within the social system. Faced with a disturbance, the natural tendency of every system is to maintain its equilibrium or to re-establish it. In the social system, it is the function of pattern maintenance, in particular, which tends to maintain equilibrium. The values internalized during socialization operate as a counterbalance to the requirements of change.

Two types of change

In practice, however, the equilibrium is often disturbed, and this entails a change in the system. Parsons distinguishes between two cases which represent two types of social change.

In the first case, the equilibrium is disturbed and gives way to a new equilibrium without the system itself being changed. The system, as a unit or whole, remains the same; and the new equilibrium is effected through modifications in certain parts and certain sub-systems of the system, without entailing important transformations of the total system. In this case, Parsons speaks of *a*

---

13. *Ibid.*, p. 37.

change in equilibrium, which is a normal phenomenon, common and even continuous in the life of every system, particularly of the social system.

But if the forces of change are too powerful and if the pressure exerted on the system from without and within is too strong, the disturbance of the equilibrium entails changes within the structure of the system. These accumulate to produce new states which are more and more different from the previous situation. This can be considered a different type of change from the preceding one. It is not only a change in equilibrium, but also *a structural change* which affects the nature of the entire system.

The difference between the two types of change

There are three essential differences between the two types of change. First, structural change results from an accumulation of strains which are increasingly strong within the social system. These strains are the consequence of an increasing lack of adaptation between two or among several units or sub-systems. The tension becomes such that the former relationships between these structural units or sub-systems appear increasingly untenable and unacceptable. Structural change thus seems to be the only form of adaptation which is likely to minimize or reduce the increasing strain. In contrast, change in equilibrium constantly reduces the strain resulting from adjustments, in such a way that these adjustments occur almost imperceptibly.

The second difference is based on the extent of the transformations. Changes in equilibrium affect only some units of the system; they are really methods of adaptation for the system, allowing it to maintain and perpetuate itself. Structural changes, on the other hand, affect the very nature of the system itself, its general orientation or its form of organization, or all of these at the same time. The difference between the two types of change can be illustrated in the following way. A colonial regime succeeds in maintaining itself through successive adaptations to new situations and problems — in other words, through a series of changes in equilibrium which do not modify either its nature or its general orientation. But when a colonial regime breaks down to give way to one or several independent nations, profound changes in structure are produced which transform the former social system into a new, different type of system. It should be added, however, that other, less spectacular structural changes also can take place, which are more gradual but also more profound — for example, the democratization of a society, or a decline in the birth rate.

Finally, a structural change can take place only through the intervention of the highest level in the cybernetic control hierarchy. Whatever the source of the impact to which the social system is subjected — whether it be the diffusion of new techniques or new ideas, or a disturbance in the physical environment — structural change always presupposes a transformation in the cultural realm of values and in the function of pattern maintenance. In other words, it is necessary that at least some of the members of society accept and internalize the new values which are likely to become institutionalized in the new structures. Given the extent of the control which it exerts on other sub-systems, the function of pattern maintenance is particularly important in the analysis of structural change. It can be either a force of inertia or resistance to change, or an active force in the transformation of structures, depending on its orientation.

Resistance to change

As a result of the function of pattern maintenance, it follows that even in the case of strong internal stress, the resistance to change in a social system can be such that it blocks any structural transformation. The system can then attempt to reject the sources of disturbance or to neutralize them. It is in this case that *a parallel protest sub-system* can be seen to develop, either within or outside the system; this will seek to obtain, through force or violence, the structural changes that have been refused. Such are revolutionary or anarchist movements, extremist groups, guerillas and so forth. Or perhaps the parallel sub-system will adopt behaviour that society considers pathological, such as juvenile delinquency, or the behaviour associated with the Hell's Angels, criminal gangs, the political underworld or a non-conformist sub-collectivity.

Systemic Analysis and Social Dynamics

It can be seen that Parsons has seriously sought to integrate change and evolution into his theoretical model of social organization. He can be, and has been, criticized for some of his earlier formulations of the social system, in which he treats change as an accident in the normal life of the system.[14] But in more recent presentations of his model, he has been able to introduce social change as an integral part of the social system.

In doing this, however, Parsons has not deviated from the theoretical attitude that we encountered among other writers in the preceding chapter — the view that the analysis of change can have a scientific value only within the context of a systemic analysis providing stable reference points. He explains very clearly his attitude on this subject:

> In our theoretical scheme, dynamic analysis must be referred to morphological premises, or else be subject to complete loss of orientation. The statement that everything empirical is subject to change may be metaphysically correct; but this is often translated into the scientifically untenable doctrine condemning as invalid a heuristic assumption that any reference point is structurally given, on the grounds that such an assumption would commit the investigator to deny the fluidity of ultimate reality. . . . The scientifically specific component of this scientific organization depends on the ability to establish reference-points structurally stable enough to justify the *simplification* of dynamic problems prerequisite to logically manageable analysis. Empirically, these reference-points are relative and may be expected to change as the science develops. The categorical assertion that any assumptions about structure are scientifically inadmissible because in the last analysis everything is in flux, denies the legitimacy of science. In any science, and in sociology in particular, the concept of change is meaningful only in terms of a definable *something*, i.e., something which can be described in structural terms.[15]

Obviously, it is possible to discuss the Parsonian model and its integration of dynamic phenomena in various ways. But to Parsons' credit, we must recognize that on the basis of his model of the social system, he has known better than most sociologists how to distinguish three types of social change which are too often confused: long-term evolution, change in equilibrium, and structural

14. This was particularly the case in Parsons, *The Social System*.
15. Parsons et al., *Theories of Society*, vol. 1, p. 70. Emphasis in the original.

change. Many debates on the subject of social change would perhaps have been more fruitful if the participants had distinguished more clearly between the different types of change at issue.

The Theory of Systems

Parsons' systemic model, which has been summarized very briefly, is without a doubt one of the sociological contributions in which theoretical and logical analysis of social organization have been pushed the furthest.[16] This is why we have thought it useful to present it here, to illustrate the methods of contemporary theoretical research which aim at elaborating analytical and formal models in sociology of the type discussed in the preceding chapter.

Sociology and systems theory

Parsons' work (and also that of Homans) locates sociology in the steadily developing current of theoretical research which is generally called *systems theory*. This is an attempt to reflect on the general properties of systems, as this concept is understood within a scientific framework. Profiting from recent progress in cybernetics, in information and communication theory, in mathematics, and in operational research, an effort is made to clarify and develop the theoretical implications of systemic analysis, both for scientific knowledge in general and within particular areas of research.

Up to now, it is mainly in some physical sciences, in biology, in psychology, and in various applied sectors of technology that systems theory has contributed a rich harvest of perspectives, ideas and new intuitions. Some authors are of the opinion that the analysis of the socio-cultural system also would benefit from a redefinition and reorientation in terms of systems theory research and results.

The sociologist Walter Buckley is one of these.[17] Starting with

16. Among other theoretical contributions, that of George C. Homans deserves more than the single mention that we can make here. In particular, see Homans, *The Human Group*. This chapter was already written when another recently published analysis came to our attention: Henri Janne, *Le système social: essai de théorie générale* (Brussels: Institut de sociologie de l'Université Libre de Bruxelles, 1968).
17. Walter Buckley, *Sociology and Modern Systems Theory* (Englewood Cliffs, N.J.: Prentice-Hall, Inc., 1967).

the systemic analyses of Parsons[18] and Homans, he has tried to demonstrate the need to reformulate, in a broader and more rigorous way, the concept of system as used in sociology.

From the simple to the complex system

The main conclusion of Buckley's work is that there is both *continuity and discontinuity* in systemic analysis. There is continuity in the sense that the same form of analysis, based on identical postulates and pursuing similar goals, is found and applied at all levels of reality, from the organic cell to the socio-cultural universe. It is a little as if Auguste Comte's great dreams were coming true: the unity of scientific knowledge operates from the base of a single aim and a single methodology for all fields of scientific study. But this continuity in scientific knowledge is accompanied by a discontinuity — *the same systemic model is not applicable at all levels of reality.* The transfer from one level to another may require the abandoning of a simple system for a complex systemic model.

This change from the simple to the complex system is necessary particularly in the analysis of socio-cultural reality. But according to Buckley, sociology has not yet been able to make the transition properly. Sociological theory was right to employ the systemic model. Its fault, up to now, has been to content itself with a concept of system which is still too close to the mechanical and organic models. In particular, Buckley criticizes Parsons' systemic model as being too strongly influenced by the concepts of equilibrium in mechanics and homeostasis in biology. These ideas are valid in the analysis of simple systems, as in mechanics, or of closed systems, as in biology. They become dangerously limiting and restrictive, however, when they are transposed directly into the analysis of a complex system which is vibrant and open, as is the socio-cultural system; and they are even less appropriate when applied to the general system of action. The analysis of these systems must integrate into its models phenomena that are not found at other levels of reality, particularly communication in various forms, the use and roles of symbols in action and interaction, and perhaps above all the purposeful nature of individual and collective human action. Buckley suggests that we should be guided,

---

18. It is regrettable that Buckley took into account only the early formulations of the Parsonian model, particularly that of *The Social System*.

more than in the past, by cybernetics and by information and exchange theory, so that we may construct one or several models of
the complex system which are capable of accounting for *all* the
facts of socio-cultural reality.

Here, once again, we find the main methodological and theoretical problem which was emphasized in our preceding chapter —
that of passing from the material model to the formal model. Parsons' systemic analysis certainly makes an important contribution
in this direction. And we have seen that Parsons, in the final formulations of his model, has particularly sought to profit from
cybernetics and information theory. But Buckley's criticism has
the great merit of putting us on our guard against certain strongly
organicist sources in the Parsonian scheme. It is still too soon,
however, to judge what general systems theory will, in fact, be able
to contribute to theoretical research in sociology.

To elaborate a purely formal model of the social system which is
capable of interpreting and explaining all the static and dynamic
elements of reality, and which can create verifiable predictions —
such is the task undertaken by Parsons, Homans, Buckley and
other researchers. And this search must be continued.

Part Three
Social Change and Historical Action

Chapter 10
Problems of Historical Sociology

Society is history. It is forever involved in a historical movement, in a transformation of itself, its members, its environment and other societies to which it is related. It constantly arouses, experiences or receives forces, either external or internal, which modify its nature, its orientation and its goals. Whether abruptly, slowly or imperceptibly, every society experiences daily changes which are more or less harmonious with its past and which follow a more or less explicit design or plan.

Society, then, is not merely the social action of a plurality of individuals; nor can it be reduced to some form of social organization. It is also the movement and change of a collectivity over time. Thus, having analyzed the foundations of social action in the first part of this book, and the forms of social organization in the second part, we will now approach the study of society from an historical perspective.

The Tradition and Weakness of Historical Sociology

When we consider the approach adopted to date by sociology in studying society from an historical perspective, we are struck by a curious paradox. On the one hand, change is one of the most obvious characteristics of society, and from the beginning sociology has been eager to explain and interpret such change. But, on the other hand, sociology is relatively backward in the analysis of social history. This is one of the areas where sociologists agree the least, and where they have barely managed to reach a consensus among themselves. In fact, the various sociological schools find their basis and origins in their diverse interpretations of social change and its nature, importance and orientation.

The first sociologists

There is much evidence to indicate that in sociology there has been a long tradition of interest in the historical aspects of society. From the beginning of sociology to the present, every sociologist has recognized that change is an integral part of social reality, and that it is a factor of prime importance. But it is particularly among the early sociologists, those of the nineteenth century and the beginning of the twentieth, that this interest in society in the process of development is most striking. For example, Auguste Comte suggested dividing sociology into two main parts: static sociology and dynamic sociology. Static sociology would study what he called *order*, or the means by which the members of a collectivity arrive at a consensus through which the society can exist, maintain itself, and function; this corresponds fairly closely to what we have called the foundations of social action and organization (see Part Two). *Dynamic* sociology would study *progress*, or the transformation of societies throughout the history of mankind. It is here that we can locate Comte's law of the three states, and the historical analysis that he derived from it (of which an outline was given in Chapter 6). To Comte, dynamic sociology was much more important than static sociology; in fact, he gave it a central place in his work.

That the sociology of Marx and Engels was a sociology of change is too obvious to require long explanation. Their intention was to explain the origin and evolution of capitalist society, to analyze its crystallization in the modern period, and to show how the struggle that it provokes and aggravates between the two opposing classes — those who own and control the means of production, and the totally alienated proletarian class — would inevitably entail the breakdown of this capitalist society and its replacement by a proletarian dictatorship, preparatory to the emergence of a new type of society — the classless, communist society. Sometimes, indeed, the works of Marx and Engels are quoted to support the suggestion that sociology should study society exclusively, or at least mainly, from the perspective of the change that is produced within it. As we mentioned in Chapter 9, however, it is not certain that this is a fair interpretation of their writings.

We might add that the sociological writings of Herbert Spencer (his law of universal evolution), Durkheim (notably his analysis of the division of labour), Simmel (his study of conflict), Pareto (his analysis of the circulation of elites) and Weber (his large historical pictures) have all been concerned with the history of society, and have sought to grasp some aspect of it. When we studied the works of some of these writers (such as Spencer and Durkheim) in earlier chapters, we tried to show this. Later we will discuss Weber's theses and indicate, at least, the influence of Simmel and Pareto.

Briefly, then, we can say that the early sociologists brought to social reality not the eye of a photographer, who grasps only a fixed moment outside time, but rather that of a film-maker who records on his film the movement of beings and the course of events.

Three influences

Sociology owes this original orientation largely to three main influences which were exerted on it at the beginning.

First, early sociology was strongly marked by *the philosophy of history*, which was itself inspired by a philosophy of man. Scholars and philosophers of the eighteenth and nineteenth centuries generally considered that man in their time was in the process of freeing himself from an oppressive and still menacing past. They wished to read in human history the efforts made to win this freedom; they sought to establish the stages of this progress, and to discern the various moments in the continuous transformations of societies. Thus, in their hands, sociology became an instrument designed to measure simultaneously the path travelled on this road to liberation and the route that remained to be traversed.

Second, *the transformist theories in biology* furnished an apparently useful model for the study of human and social evolution. Perhaps the influence of the works of Lamarck and Darwin on the social sciences at the end of the nineteenth and the beginning of the twentieth centuries is not sufficiently appreciated today. This influence was so profound, however, that without it one cannot explain the popularity enjoyed by anthropology and sociology at the beginning of the century, particularly in Anglo-Saxon countries.

And it would not be difficult to show that the echoes of Darwinian transformism still have repercussions on contemporary sociology and anthropology.

Finally, one is often tempted to neglect the influence that *the science of history* exerted on sociology. It could easily be claimed that sociology was first defined as a sort of social history or as a scientific method within history. In Germany, sociology emerged in reaction against a history that was too exclusively based on events and which wished to consider only that which was unique and original in human and social phenomena. Thus, history ultimately was denied its status as a science and was reduced to the mere recounting of the course of events. In contrast to this anti-scientific notion of history, Max Weber conceived of sociology as the comparative and explanatory science of history.

The functionalist pause

It is often said that after the impetus provided by the early sociologists for an historical sociology, functionalism broke with this tradition and diverted sociology from the science of history and from history as an object of study. There is a lot of truth in this statement.

In fact, as we saw earlier, functionalism was formed in opposition to evolutionism, as it was practised at the end of the nineteenth century. The functionalists emphasized the lack of scientific validity in the methods and conclusions of the great Spencerian evolutionist theories. They proposed a more rigorous method for the analysis of society, perceiving society as an integrated unit or system. But in suggesting a new orientation for sociological analysis, many functionalists considered the organization and functioning of society only at a given moment in its development. As a result, functionalism came to be identified with a sort of refusal of history and social change.

It should be added that it was mainly anthropologists who defined and practised functionalism. The archaic societies they studied generally had no known history, and this was an important factor in the a-historical approach adopted in functionalism. In the analysis of societies that possessed a history, however, this indifference to history obviously was an important limitation that ran counter to the original intentions of functionalism.

We can suggest, then, that the historical tradition in sociology experienced a pause during the two or three decades when functionalism dominated sociology and anthropology. The history of society was no longer the primary concern of either theoretical or empirical research. Instead, attention now concentrated too intensely on the description and analysis of the structures and the functioning of social organization.

The study of social change by a few functionalists

Contrary to the impression that is sometimes given, it should not be thought that functionalism inhibited all interest in the study of social change. During this period, several researchers provided us with some excellent analyses concerned either with certain actors in social change or with forms of social change. And often these researchers were confirmed functionalists; indeed, Kingsley Davis could assert that "... some of the best analyses of social change have come from people labeled as functionalists."[1]

For example, we should not minimize the importance of studies such as Kroeber's on the changes contributed by the diffusion of inventions, techniques and knowledge,[2] or Barnett's thorough analysis of various examples of innovation in archaic and advanced societies.[3] Even in sociology, Robert Merton (whose contribution to functionalism was mentioned in Chapter 8) has analyzed the role of various socio-cultural factors in the evolution of scientific and technological knowledge.[4] Later, we will have the opportunity to examine his studies. Let us mention also Neil Smelser, a colleague of Parsons, and his important theoretical and empirical analysis of the processes in the transformation of indus-

---

1. Kingsley Davis, "The Myth of Functional Analysis as a Special Method in Sociology and Anthropology," *American Sociological Review* 24 (December 1959): 766-67.
2. A. L. Kroeber, *Configurations of Culture Growth* (Berkeley: University of California Press, 1944). Following Kroeber's studies, research on diffusion phenomena have aroused much interest and inspired a number of anthropological studies. Belonging to this context is the famous Kon-Tiki expedition, which was designed to illustrate how a case of cultural diffusion could have occurred.
3. H. G. Barnett, *Innovation: The Basis of Cultural Change* (New York: McGraw-Hill Book Company, Inc., 1953). Barnett mainly sought to specify the socio-cultural conditions that favour innovation; he concluded by showing that innovation is really a very widespread phenomenon in society, and that each social actor is an innovator, often unconsciously.
4. Robert K. Merton, "Science, Technology, and Society in Seventeenth Century England" and "Puritanism, Pietism, and Science," *Social Theory and Social Structure*.

trial organization and work following the progressive introduction of machines in the English textile firms in the eighteenth and nineteenth centuries.[5]

The list could be extended even further. But these examples will be sufficient to demonstrate that the tradition of historical studies in sociology has not been broken, even if it paused and was temporarily put aside over the period dominated by functionalism.

The present revival in studies of change

Over the past dozen years, a renewed interest in the study of social change can be observed in sociology. To appreciate this, one need only consult a list of recently published studies or a summary of the articles that have appeared in the main sociological journals. The number of studies devoted to various aspects of social change is growing continuously. Several factors have contributed to this reorientation in sociology. Let us mention the main ones.

The rise of the Third World

First of all, the rise of the new nations, their efforts to break away from a long and lethargic history of underdevelopment, and the economic, political, social and cultural changes which took place in these countries aroused the interest of a number of sociologists. Important events occurred which shook the old established order and shattered the images and attitudes which had been accepted up to then. The Third World took shape — complex, diversified and at the same time revealing specific traits and characteristics. One of the traits common to all the developing countries was that they were deeply transformed, and at a rapid and even punishing pace.

The rulers and businessmen of the colonial countries followed these events with anxiety. Powerful economic and political interests were endangered, and attempts were made to protect them in the hope that at least the essential structure might be saved. In some cases even, the scientific curiosity of researchers was encouraged for purposes that were not purely disinterested. In fact, such

---

5. Neil J. Smelser, *Social Change in the Industrial Revolution: An Application of Theory to the Lancashire Cotton Industry, 1770-1840* (London: Routledge and Kegan Paul, Ltd., 1959).

a policy had been practised for several years; France and England, for example, had long financed research and scientific institutes in their colonies. The results of this research enabled them to administer the colonies in what seemed to be the best interests of the colonized and colonial countries. Following the move towards decolonization, financial aid for social research could be seen to increase, mainly with the massive participation of the United States, in such a way that political and financial aims became more obvious than in the past.

Crises in the developed societies

At about this time, most of the developed societies themselves were in the grip of profound structural crises. New types of militancy and extremism appeared: the peaceful and remote hobos of former times were replaced by the hippy or yippy movement, which was inspired by a proselytism in favour of a world of peace and love; at the same time, other right- and left-wing groups increasingly called on violence either to restore order or to establish a new order; in addition, students revolted in the name of a universal protest against industrial, bureaucratic and capitalist society, saying that they were seeking a just and purified society. All these phenomena indicated profound value conflicts, a revision of dominant ideologies, and certain structural changes in the process of being produced or in preparation.

In the Preface, we have already mentioned that sociology lives according to the rhythm of its era. Thus, it was only natural that the attention of a number of sociologists should be focused on these new phenomena in an attempt to analyze their origins, scope and development.

The influence of Marx's sociological work

Another extremely important factor should be added, and this is the more open and positive reception which has recently been accorded to Marx's work in sociology. Twenty-five years ago, very few sociologists would have conceded Marx's contribution to the history of sociological thought. Marx was regarded as a philosopher, a reformer, a prophet — anything but a sociologist. Today an increasing number of sociologists recognize Marx as one of the main forerunners of their field of study.

Non-Marxist as well as Marxist sociologists have contributed to the recognition and acceptance of Marxist sociology. Among the sociologists of a Marxist persuasion, Henri Lefebvre[6] and Lucien Goldman[7] can be counted among those whose theoretical and empirical work, carried out within the perspective of Marxist thought, has exerted the greatest influence. Those non-Marxist sociologists who turned to Marx were generally researchers who were interested in the analysis of social change, and did not feel at ease within the functionalist framework. This was the case notably with C. Wright Mills[8] who, through his non-conformist views, incurred the anger of American sociologists; and we should also add the name of Ralf Dahrendorf, whose works will be analyzed in the next chapter. Among the non-Marxist sociologists, a special place should be given to Georges Gurvitch, who was the first to demonstrate in a thorough and illuminating way Marx's sociological contribution.[9]

Undoubtedly the more positive reception given to Marx's work had its source in the renewed interest in the history of society. But at the same time, for a great number of sociologists a better knowledge of the sociology of Marx awakened a new taste for the theoretical and empirical problems which the development of societies, the class struggle, the revolutionary movement and structural changes pose for sociological knowledge.

In this way, intellectual influences and historical events interacted to create among contemporary sociologists a renewed and increased interest for the study of processes of change — their factors, their agents and their obstacles.

The sociologists' discomfort in the face of change

Although one can trace in sociology, as we have done, a long tradition of interest in the history of societies, sociologists feel that they

---

6. Henri Lefebvre's work is extensive. We will refer the reader only to his very interesting discussion in Lefebvre, *The Sociology of Marx*, as well as his articles in the Marxist journal of sociology, *L'homme et la société*.
7. Lucien Goldman, *Sociologie du roman* (Paris: Gallimard, Collection "Idées," 1965), as well as his articles in *L'homme et la société* can be consulted.
8. The essence of C. Wright Mills' thought on the orientation of sociology can be found in C. Wright Mills, *The Sociological Imagination* (New York: Oxford University Press, 1959).
9. See in particular the chapter previously cited: Gurvitch, "La sociologie de Marx," *La vocation actuelle*.

lack an explanation and interpretation of social change. They complain of the absence of conceptual and theoretical apparatus, research techniques and measuring instruments which are appropriate for the observation and interpretation of structural changes. Some blame this gap on the prolonged influence of functionalism; some even go so far as to suggest that in functionalism they can see the reflection in the social sciences of a middle-class attitude which is more interested in the status quo than in change. Others maintain that, on the contrary, it is the absence of a theoretical framework for systemic analysis which to date has delayed the progress of dynamic sociology.

Whatever reasons can be given (and these can be debated for a very long time) one fact remains only too obvious: the sociology of societies, viewed from the perspective of their history, suffers from a number of weaknesses of which three are outstanding.

Three weaknesses of contemporary historical sociology

First, *sociology still does not have available a general theory which would include within the same total framework the analysis of social organization and the analysis of social history or change.* The equivalent of Freud's contribution to psychology is lacking in sociology. Freud elaborated a theory or a model of the personality, conceived simultaneously as a system and as history, in which the structure of the personality was formed through the unique history of each individual. In sociology, Marx and Engels perhaps came closest to offering as comprehensive a model through their simultaneously functionalist and historical view of social reality. But their sociology was weakened by the philosophical, militant and polemical frame of thought which was its context; by the rigid orthodoxy of too many interpreters; and also, it should be recognized, by factors which value political and social history more than scientific history. This point illustrates again that sociology is itself a sociological phenomenon, and that it is subject to social conditioning and determinism.

In the absence of a general theory which would integrate the variable of time within its analytical framework, *the study of social change remains a sector or particular field* within the whole area of focus in sociology. One is forced to act as if the history of society were a phenomenon in itself, and an aspect that can be detached from the rest of total social reality. While sociologists hesitate to recognize explicitly the distinction that Auguste Comte made between static and dynamic sociology, it can always be found. Contemporary sociologists generally refuse to use this terminology. But in every sociological text or manual, the authors find themselves obliged to devote a section or a chapter to the special study of social change, as we have had to do ourselves.

The third weakness of the sociology of change is still more serious. *We can ask ourselves whether there really exists a sociological theory of change.* If such a theory existed, it should permit the *prediction* of future events. In fact, the verification of predictions is the only test of the validity of any theory of change. But sociologists are obliged to recognize that it is hardly possible for them to make predictions which are scientifically based. How can one maintain, then, that in sociology there exists a valid theory of change? This is a considerable problem to which we will return later.

Evolution and Social Change

Before approaching (in the following chapters) the basic problems that are posed by the history of societies, it is essential to make certain distinctions and to clarify certain definitions. The rest of this chapter will be devoted to this.

Social evolution

First, a distinction must be made between social evolution and social change. It will be generally agreed that *social evolution* consists of all the transformations that a society experiences over a long period — that is, a period which goes beyond the life of a single generation or even several generations. It is related to what could be called the trends of centuries, which cannot be observed on a reduced scale but which can be perceived from a very long-term perspective. At this level of analysis, small changes are blurred; there remains only the cumulative effect of a great many changes which form a line or path that delineates the direction or movement of a general trend. Social evolution therefore is observable only from a great distance, and the details of the landscape are merged in a single image or movement.

Social change

Social change consists of observable and verifiable transformations over shorter periods of time. During his life or even during a brief period of his life, a single observer can follow their development and know the outcome, or what can be provisionally considered the outcome. In addition, social change generally is geographically and sociologically localized; it can usually be observed within a geographical area or within a more limited socio-cultural framework than is possible with social evolution.

The importance of this distinction

This distinction between social evolution and social change is important. The early sociologists were particularly interested in social evolution. For Comte, Marx, Spencer and Durkheim, sociology primarily attempted to describe and explain the century-long changes of human societies or even of humanity. By contrast, in contemporary sociology it is the phenomena of social change that scholars are particularly eager to study, although neo-evolutionism has made some progress, as we noted earlier. The tradition of interest in the historical aspect of society, to which we have called attention in the preceding pages, has not been preserved without modification. Dynamic sociology, as we refer to it today, does not have exactly the same meaning that Auguste Comte gave it. He saw the possibility of painting large pictures of human history; today sociologists lean more modestly towards less sweeping changes.

Functionalism was opposed to the sociology of evolution, not to a sociology of change. This distinction has not always been taken into account either in criticizing or in practising functionalism. If he rejected the excessively vast perspective of evolutionism, it did not necessarily follow that the sociologist would then be confined to an exclusively static perception of social reality. It can be said that by rejecting history as well as evolutionism, some functionalists have thrown out the baby with the bath water.

The Concept of Social Change

A second distinction has already been provided by Talcott Parsons: it is the one that he suggests between change in equilibrium and structural change. We have previously summarized the general meaning of this distinction (in Chapter 9), which is part of the framework of the Parsonian system. It can now serve to clarify the meaning that is generally given in sociology to the expression *social change*.

It should be said that sociologists are rather miserly with their definitions of social change. They speak of it as if one should automatically know what it is, and as if everyone has the same conception of it. But this is not necessarily the case.

What social change is not

We can start by enumerating what social change is not, in the manner followed by Richard LaPiere, for example.[10] First, social change must be separated from single events. Thus, an election is an event, as is a strike, a meeting or a fire. The event may be part of social change, and may accompany it or provoke it; but this is not always and necessarily the case. An election, a strike or a fire does not in itself create social change.

Similarly, a change in personnel is not social change. There is a constant change of personnel in society: a new generation occupies the place of the one that is leaving, or a new board is elected to replace the former one. In these, the result or the sign of change may be seen. But again, this is by no means always true.

There is also a constant and vast quantity of exchange in the normal and daily order of social life — exchange of goods, presents, information, rights, responsibilities, insults and so forth. Many of these exchanges are part of what Parsons calls changes in equilibrium in the whole social organization; but they do not necessarily affect its structure. Most of these exchanges belong more properly to the normal functioning of the social organization.

Generally it can be considered that the changes that are required by the very functioning of the social organization are not usually of such a kind as to modify its structure. From Parsons' perspective, it could be said that they contribute to the continuous re-establishment of the equilibrium of the system. It is with this meaning that Parsons talks of them as changes in equilibrium, as distinguished from structural changes.

Finally, a change that affects only one or a few persons cannot be considered social change. Thus, the socialization of an individual causes deep changes within him, but these individual modifications may run counter to all social change, to the extent

---

10. Richard T. LaPiere, *Social Change* (New York: McGraw-Hill Book Company, Inc., 1965).

that they encourage conformity of conduct to established models. That one or a few persons change their opinion or attitude can be considered a social change only if this change is part of a larger collective context.

What social change is

The analysis of what social change is not can now help us to state more specifically what it is.

First, social change is necessarily a *collective phenomenon*. It must implicate a collectivity or a good sector of a collectivity; it must affect the conditions or life styles, or perhaps the intellectual atmosphere, of more than merely a few individuals. This is too obvious a requirement to need any further emphasis.

Second, social change must be *structural change*. One must be able to observe a modification of the social organization as a whole or of some of its components. It is essential, in fact, in speaking of social change, to be able to indicate the structural or cultural elements of the social organization which have been modified, and to describe these modifications with some precision. Thus, a strike can have the result of an adjustment in wages in relation to the standard of living or to some other point of comparison. In this case, the change is a change in equilibrium, not in structure. But if one can describe, for example, certain changes in the organization of the firm, in the delegation of authority, in the channels of communication and so forth, that have resulted directly from the strike, and if one can even predict the impact that these transformations will have on other similar firms, one can then assert that there has been social change.

Third, the idea of structural change presupposes that it can be identified *within time*. In other words, it must be possible to describe all the transformations or their sequences between two or more points in time (between the points T_1, T_2, ... T_n). In fact, social change cannot be appreciated and measured except in relation to a reference point in the past. On the basis of this reference point, it can be said that there has been change, and what has changed and the extent to which change has occurred can be specified.

Fourth, in order to be true structural change, all social change must show a degree of *permanence*. The transformations observed must not be merely superficial or ephemeral. They must at least appear to be more than transient.

Finally, the four preceding characteristics can be summarized by the statement that social change *affects the course of the history of a society*. In other words, the history of a society would have been different if social change had not taken place. In practice, it is obviously very difficult to prove this. Hypothetical history, as a working instrument, is extremely delicate to manipulate: it is not easy to reconstitute what would have been the historical development if such a change had or had not taken place. But it is a method that the social sciences should probably use more. In addition, simulation (the use of which is spreading) consists of projecting several courses of hypothetical history into the future, in an attempt to measure the influence of diverse variables.

The definition of social change

The preceding analysis has provided us with the necessary elements for the construction of a fairly simple and clear definition of social change. Social change is *every observable transformation over time which affects, in a way that is not provisional or ephemeral, the structure or the functioning of the social organization of a given collectivity, and which modifies the course of its history*.

Social Change, Historical Action and Social Process

This definition of social change enables us to go even further. Now we must distinguish among historical action, social change and social process. Too often these terms are used interchangeably in sociology.

Historical action

In particular, it is essential not to confuse historical action and social change. Historical action is to social change what social action is to social organization: historical action and social action describe the activity of social actors; social change and social organization are the observable product of this action.

Thus, we will define *historical action* as *all the activities of the members of a society which by their nature or by design provoke, intensify, restrain or prevent changes in the social organization as a whole or in some of its parts*. It is rare for all the members of a society or collectivity to be involved in historical action; more often, particular individuals, groups or movements at a given moment influence the orientation of a society, affect its destiny, and actively contribute to its history. Thus, historical action refers more precisely to the influence of these active elements or agents of change.

Let us note that the action of agents of change may be concerned with either the content or the rhythm of change. Some agents provide ideas or innovations, or initiate new values; others contribute to the propagation of ideas and values and, through this, to the intensification of the pace of change.

But agents of change may also play a negative role by actively opposing innovation and its acceptance, or by delaying its application. The active rejection of change is as much a part of the historical action of a collectivity as is innovation or the struggle against the status quo.

It can be said, then, that historical action is social change seen from the perspective of those who contribute to it in a positive or negative manner. Or again, it is that part of social action (as defined in Part One) which is based on innovation, in order either to extend it or to oppose it. In this sense, historical action appears as the truest sociological aspect of social change; in fact, it is located within the perspective of social action which we have made (in Part One) the basis of the sociological approach. Historical action is clearly only one aspect of social action.

Social change

In terms of *social change* itself, the definition given earlier now appears in its full meaning: *it is the structural change which results from the historical action of certain actors or certain groups within a given collectivity*. Historical action and social change are intimately linked but can be distinguished analytically. In particular, social change can be studied without consideration of the action of the actors who provoked it; indeed, social change has often been analyzed in this way. But it is important to know precisely what is being studied and what is being deliberately excluded.

The social process

Finally, there is a term which is often used by sociologists — that of *process* or *proceeding*. This refers to *the succession and chain of events, phenomena and actions which, as a whole, form the se-*

quence of change. The process accounts for how things happen, the order in which they occur, and their arrangement or pattern. The process does not explain change; it *recounts* its unfolding over time.

Factors, Conditions and Agents of Change

The important distinctions made in the preceding pages permit us to clarify three ideas which are often employed in the analysis of change: these are the factor, the condition and the agent of change. The first two are used in the analysis of social change as we have just defined the term. The idea of agent refers directly to historical action as defined above.

The factors of change

To speak of a *factor* of change is to suggest a strong determinant of social change. A factor is an element of a given situation which, by the very fact of its existence or through the action that it initiates, entails or produces a change. Thus, the introduction of new production techniques in a factory may entail modifications in the methods of work, in the organization of teams, in the levels of authority and so forth, in the same way that the establishment of a factory in a rural environment may lead to a transformation of the employment market, instigate population mobility, and bring changes in the mores, culture and social organization of the rural community. In both cases, it can be said that these are factors of change.

The conditions of change

The *conditions* of change are the elements of the situation which encourage or discourage, activate or halt, impel or impede the influence of a factor or several factors of change. Taking the same examples again, the attitude of the factory union faced with change, the perception that it has and that it propagates among the workers will be conditions, either favourable or unfavourable, of the change brought about by the introduction of new techniques. In the rural community, the type of agriculture, the degree of family prosperity, the general attitude towards change all may be favourable or unfavourable conditions of change which emerge subsequent to the establishment of a new industry.

Conditions and factors of change are therefore complementary. The conditions of change are the elements of a situation which encourage or discourage the action of factors; they permit the factors to exert their influence or, on the contrary, stifle the action of such factors. Moreover, the conditions may affect the rhythm of change, accelerating or impeding the action of factors. They may also influence the direction of change by bending it in one direction or another. Thus, following certain conditions which are inherent to a given situation, a new idea or technique may be modified during the course of its diffusion, and may not produce the anticipated change. Finally, the conditions of change may affect the extent of change. For example, a change may not encounter favourable conditions within a certain sector of society or in a particular region, and as a result either will not penetrate or will be accepted only after a delay.

The agents of change

As we noted earlier, the agents of change are the individuals, groups or associations who introduce change, support it, favour it, or oppose it. Thus, in some respects their social action takes on the character of historical action. Their action is motivated by goals, interests, values and ideologies which have an impact on the development of society.

Prophecy and Prediction

The analysis of social change and historical action requires a final clarification: is it possible to distinguish between prophecy and prediction? This distinction is obviously a very delicate one to establish, but it is nevertheless important to attempt to grasp it. In fact, given the great weakness of predictive sociology emphasized at the beginning of this chapter, it is only too easy to confuse the two and to prophesy under the guise of prediction.

Prophecy among the early sociologists

In fact, most of the great theoreticians of the development of social change have turned, in the end, to prophesying. Almost all of them have announced to their contemporaries better times for the future, and a more human, just, harmonious, free and peaceful society. Optimism was astonishingly widespread among the early sociologists.

This can be explained by the fact that most of the great theories of evolution or history were cumulative: in one way or another, they recognized a certain *progress* of humanity, and an improvement in individual and collective human life. This was clearly the case with Auguste Comte who saw in the positive state a superior stage of thought and social organization. Spencer read into social evolution an ascending road towards industrial, liberal and individualistic society. Marx and Engels announced the unavoidable breakdown of capitalism to make way for the more desirable classless society.

Those who, instead of reading history as a straight and continuous evolution, saw a cyclical movement[11] show a more moderate optimism. This is true of Sorokin, for example, who identified three stages of civilization ("good," "bad" and transitory) which followed each other in a cyclical fashion in a sort of eternal recommencement.[12] Oswald Spengler probably remains the outstanding prophet of doom. He describes the history of civilizations as that of a human life — birth, maturity, decline, and death — and thereby demonstrates the present decline of Western civilization and anticipates its eventual end.[13]

Five distinctive characteristics

But what is prophecy, and how can it be distinguished from prediction? It appears to us that there are five dominant distinctive traits of prophecy.

First, all prophecy starts with *a critical view of present society*

---

11. A simple and clear presentation of the various rectilinear, undulated, cyclical and declining theories of historical evolution and social change can be found in Wilbert Moore, *Social Change* (Englewood Cliffs, N.J.: Prentice-Hall, Inc., 1963), pp. 33-44.
12. P. Sorokin, *Social and Cultural Dynamics* (Boston: Porter Sargent, 1957).
13. Spengler, *The Decline of the West.*

and its origins. Ambiguities, contradictions, injustices and social inequalities are described, denounced and judged. And it is on the basis of this criticism that a new society is proposed and foreseen. But Herbert Marcuse, whose critique of what he calls advanced industrial society is well known, himself asserts: "The critical theory of society possesses no concepts which are capable of crossing the distance between the present and the future; it makes no promises; it has not succeeded; it has remained negative."[14] But all those who have criticized society have not had Marcuse's prudence; they have crossed the line which separates criticism from prophecy.

What facilitates this transition is that the second — and most important — source of inspiration for prophecy rests in what can be called *a meta-scientific kind of thought.* Prophecy follows a procedure which is guided, not by the canons of scientific research, but by reflection based on the adherence to new ideas, values and beliefs. The values to which the prophet adheres may be religious; and in this case, his reflection and predictions stem from divine or supernatural revelations, as was the case for the biblical prophets or the author of the Koran or, more recently, for Joseph Smith, the founder of the Mormon church. But modern prophecy is not generally religious; instead it results from philosophical or moral reflection on the essential nature and destiny of man and society.

Scientific prediction, in contrast, is neither critical nor guided by values. Based on the observation of the past and the present, it seeks to discern the possible routes of the future, according to whether various factors, conditions and agents will exert a greater or lesser influence. Thus, prediction is based essentially on an analysis of the weight of different variables and the consequences which may follow from them. It should be recognized, however, that in practice the dividing line between meta-scientific reflection and scientific research is, in the social sciences, subtle, debatable and often difficult to grasp. Prophecy and prediction can easily be confused. The following traits will assist still further in distinguishing one from the other.

Third, prophecy has a voluntaristic nature: *it wishes to inspire direction and seeks to influence the course of history.* While announcing the future, the prophet wishes to guide the forces which will make it what it ought to be. Prediction, in itself, does not have such aims. It does not suggest following one route rather

14. Herbert Marcuse, *One Dimensional Man* (London: Routledge and Kegan Paul, Ltd., 1964).

than another; it displays the range of the possible and the probable, taking into account the different operating variables.

Fourth, prophecy is generally marked by a certain *assurance*. It announces with certainty the inevitable direction of history. The prophet foretells the future with all the more conviction when he suggests, at the same time, that it should be so. Thus, a mixture of determinism and voluntarism can often be observed in almost all forms of prophecy. Prediction, on the contrary, is essentially relative and probable; it is based, for all practical purposes, on a probability calculation concerned with the possible influence of various elements of the present and future situation.

Finally, prophecy can generally be classified as *optimistic* or *pessimistic* according to the nature of the future that is foreseen. This is not the case with prediction. Prediction in a sense aims to describe the future as historians will write it — in other words, by weighing only the operative factors. A prediction can be said to be encouraging or depressing; this is not the same as saying that a prophecy is optimistic or pessimistic.

The complementarity of prophecy and prediction

One cautionary note should be added. In making these distinctions, our aim is not to say that either prediction or prophecy is "better" than the other. Both are necessary. Prophecy is a moral position; it is involvement in history. And history cannot be written without the value judgements of those who experience and create it. Prophecy is generally guided by an elevated view of man and his destiny; thus it can be considered the most noble of man's research on history as he wishes to live it.

But the value judgements and options that historical action imposes require scientific prediction. The value judgements will be that much clearer if the prediction has been seriously and thoroughly carried out. Prediction attempts to indicate, in an objective way, the different avenues which are open, and the requirements and conditions involved in each. It thus offers the most solid basis to inspire an authentic view of historical action.

Prediction without prophecy is empty and in vain, merely a game of the mind. Prophecy without prediction risks being illusory and utopic. This interdependence of the two attaches even more importance to the need to distinguish them. As it is easier to confuse them in sociology than in any other science, scientific prediction will make no more progress in the future than it has done in the past if people persist in believing that prophecy takes its place.

The Questions That Are Posed

Six major questions

The preceding distinctions have enabled us to clear the ground sufficiently that we can now describe how contemporary sociology approaches the problem of social change. This can be summarized by supposing that the sociologist, faced with change, asks himself six main questions.

1. He first asks *what is changing*? It is rather exceptional for an entire society to be involved in a radical change. Thus, it is important to locate the sectors where change is operating: to ask, for example, if it is in the structural elements or in the culture; and within culture, if it is occurring in patterns of behaviour, values or ideologies. One is too often tempted to wish to pass quickly to the explanation of change itself, without first circumscribing and locating it within the whole of a given society.

2. Then the sociologist asks *how is the change operating*? What course is it following? Is it continuous and regular? Or, instead, is it sporadic, broken and discontinuous? Does it encounter strong resistance? Where is this resistance located? What form does it take?

3. Third, the *rhythm* of change is important to notice. Is there a slow, progressive evolution, or are there abrupt and rapid changes?

4. Once the facts are known, the sociologist can then turn to their interpretation. It is here that the analysis of the *factors* that he seeks to identify to explain change, as well as the *conditions* which are favourable or unfavourable to change, are located.

5. Similarly, he asks what are the active *agents* which bring change, which symbolize it, which are its motivators or promoters? And what are the agents of opposition or resistance to change?

6. Finally, the whole of this analysis leads the sociologist to ask if he can *foresee* the future course of events, the different routes that society is likely to take within a given future, either immediate or long-term.

The procedure of the following chapters

It should be recognized that these six questions have not been equally explored in sociology. Perhaps not surprisingly, the explanation of change has excited researchers far more than its description. It is true that science, in the final analysis, owes itself, if possible, a causal interpretation of phenomena. But if sociology has not yet been able to throw more light on the causes of change, it is perhaps because there has been too great a concern with the study of explanatory factors and because the description of the facts themselves, of which change is comprised, has been neglected. It is in this way that we can explain the discussions and theories which have resulted from the search for the main or dominant factor capable of enlightening the entire course of history.

Given the importance of these discussions, as well as the richness of the underlying studies and research, it would be very difficult to proceed in a different way from that adopted by sociology. Thus, we will follow the development of sociological thought by asking ourselves the questions in the same order as we cited them above. In the next chapter, we will analyze the interplay of certain factors and conditions of change; in Chapter 12, we will study the role of the main agents of change. In Chapters 13 and 14, we will thoroughly examine and clarify the action of the factors and agents in a concrete case — in development. This will necessitate a more precise description of what changes, how the change operates, and according to what rhythm. Finally, we will conclude with the analysis of a process of social change — the revolutionary process.

Chapter 11
Factors and Conditions of Social Change

In studying factors and conditions of social change, there is one basic problem: is it possible to discern the factor, or factors, and their conditions which exert a preponderant influence on the history of human societies? In other words, is there a *dominant factor*, or factors, in the explanation of social change? In this, the aim is obvious — to come as close as possible to a causal interpretation of the history of societies.

The dominant factors

This question has been answered in many different ways. At first, it was thought that various dominant factors in history could be identified — for example, the physical environment, technological development, race, the structure of economic production, the state of knowledge, religious beliefs. Each of these factors has been supported by one or several scholars; some have even formed the basis of a school of thought.

The debate finally crystallized around a central question. In human history, should more importance be attached to things than to ideas, to material conditions than to spiritual conditions, to structural factors than to cultural factors? We have encountered this debate several times already. It was apparent at the beginning of the nineteenth century in the opposition between an intellectualist (Auguste Comte) or idealist (Hegel) conception of history and a materialistic one (Karl Marx).

Relativism in contemporary sociology

In contemporary sociology, a more relative perspective has been adopted, and it has a dual basis. First, even those who continue to emphasize a particular factor recognize that social change is always the product of *a plurality of factors* which act and interact simultaneously. In the cluster thus formed, the factors do not all have equal weight, some exerting a greater influence than others. Today, the relative weighting of factors is attempted by taking into account their mutual influence.

Second, many sociologists consider that it is not possible, at least in the present state of knowledge, to adopt a general model which describes the weighting of factors in absolute and universal terms. Rather, the weighting of factors is a problem for empirical research, and it must be resolved in the analysis of each concrete historical case. Weighting varies, then, according to the specific situation; it cannot be established finally and according to a universally applicable scale. From this perspective, if we can still speak of a dominant factor, it is only with respect to a particular context in a particular combination of circumstances within a given period.

Taking into account the form and direction of the debate on the factors and conditions of social change, in this chapter we will examine a few of the main explanatory factors which have held the attention of sociologists. At the same time, in the light of various studies, we will consistently emphasize the possible interdependence among these factors and the influence that various conditions can exert on them.

It is impossible to detail here all aspects of the debate. We will leave aside the discussions which have been concerned with the historical influence of certain factors — such as the physical environment, climate, and race — so that we may concentrate on the analysis of those which have been the object of the most important studies in sociology. These are mainly the demographic factor, technology, the economic infrastructure, values, ideologies and conflict. This approach will enable us to study the influence of *structural* or material factors (demography, technology, the economic infrastructure), as well as that of *cultural* factors (values, ideologies), and will lead us at last to the analysis of a factor of a particular type — conflict.

The Demographic Factor

Demographic density and the division of labour

Undoubtedly Durkheim went the furthest in analyzing the demographic factor in social change. We have seen that, for him, the progress of the division of labour entailed a radical transformation of societies; it was following an increasingly complex division of labour that the transition was effected from traditional society, based on mechanical solidarity, to industrial society, based on organic solidarity. But Durkheim then asked: to what causes should this progress of the division of labour be attributed?

For him, the answer to this question seemed to lie in the demographic characteristics of societies. When a society's population is small and scattered over a wide territory, it can survive without developing a complex division of labour. Being thinly dispersed over a large area, families and groups of families do not endanger each other's economic opportunities, but all have available to them the same resources (agriculture, hunting, fishing) and the same techniques for exploiting them. When the population increases in number and density, the survival of the group is possible only on the condition that a division of tasks is effected, and that subsequently specialization and complementarity of functions are developed. From this observation, Durkheim derives the following general proposition: "The division of labor varies in direct ratio with the volume and density of societies, and, if it progresses in a continuous manner in the course of social development, it is because societies become regularly denser and generally more voluminous."[1]

Demographic density and moral density

Durkheim pursued further his analysis of the consequences of demographic growth. Demographic density is not merely the cause of the division of labour; its relevance is much wider. In fact, *demographic density gives rise to what Durkheim called moral density*. When individuals live closer together, their relationships multiply, diversify and intensify; from this results a "general stim-

---

1. Durkheim, *The Division of Labour*, p. 262.

ulation," greater creativity and a raising of the level of civilization of the society. This led Durkheim to conclude:

> In determining the principal cause of the progress of the division of labor, we have at the same time determined the essential factor of what is called civilization. . . . From the time that the number of individuals among whom social relations are established begins to increase, they can maintain themselves only by greater specialization, harder work, and intensification of their faculties. From this general stimulation, there inevitably results a much higher degree of culture. From this point of view, civilization appears, not as an end which moves people by its attraction for them, not as a good foreseen and desired in advance, of which they seek to assure themselves the largest possible part, but as the effect of a cause, as the necessary resultant of a given state. . . . The more numerous they [the individuals] are and the more they act upon one another, the more they react with force and rapidity; consequently, the more intense social life becomes. But it is this intensification which constitutes civilization.[2]

In this quotation from Durkheim, *social interaction,* or the reciprocal influence of individuals in human relations with which we started at the very beginning of this book (Chapter 1), is found to be the main factor in civilization. Moral density, which motivates the development of societies and is the source of civilization, is really the product of both a multiplicity of interactions and the intensification of the reciprocal influence of individuals.

It should be added that Durkheim clearly distinguished between factors and conditions of social change. He criticized Spencer for perceiving population growth as merely an "adjunct condition" in the progress of the division of labour. So he wrote:

> We say, not that the growth and condensation of societies *permit*, but that they *necessitate* a greater division of labor. It is not an instrument by which the latter is realized; it is its determining cause.[3]

And he adds that moral density is the "essential factor in what is called civilization."

---

2. *Ibid.*, pp. 337 and 339.
3. *Ibid.*, p. 262. Emphasis in the original.

The law of gravity of the social world

Thus Durkheim arrives at a dual causal relationship. First, the growth in demographic density simultaneously engenders the development of the division of labour and moral density. Second, the division of labour and moral density are in turn the main factors in the progress of civilization — that is, of economic, social and cultural growth. This dual causal relationship appears so fundamental to Durkheim in the explanation of social history that, in an analogy with Newton's law of universal gravity in physics, he calls it the law of gravity of the social world.

What should we think of this law? How should it be interpreted? If, for the purposes of the discussion, we consider economic development alone, which is easier to identify than social and cultural development, unfortunately we can quickly find examples which disprove Durkheim's law. We have only to think of some regions of Asia, where the demographic density is one of the highest in the world, but where far less economic development has been experienced than in regions of lower density. We can also find examples where demographic decrease has led to greater economic development.

After analyzing a number of similar cases, Henri Janne concludes that "demographic growth and decline may be followed by either favourable or unfavourable periods at the economic level, for other factors interfere."[4] In other words, the causal relationship that Durkheim established is too simple. Other factors or conditions should be added to the factor of demographic density.

The interdependence of demographic, economic and cultural factors

For his part, Henri Janne emphasizes the role of two other factors or conditions which should be taken into account in order to appreciate the influence of the demographic factor:

> *The potential resources of the environment* and *the capacity for technical improvements* should be sufficient to respond to the needs resulting from population growth. When this is not the case, there is no technical progress but regression. A form of mysticism makes

---

4. Janne, "La technique" in Janne et al., *Technique, développement économique et technocratie*, pp. 38-39.

misery acceptable by placing spiritual values far beyond material values. The mystique is then the functional substitute of technical progress (for example, India up to the Second World War).[5]

Thus, demographic growth is a factor favourable to economic and social development only in conjunction with *an economic factor* (the presence of certain potential resources) and *a cultural factor* (the capacity to develop the necessary techniques). The thesis of a plurality of factors is substituted for the monist thesis that Durkheim suggested.

An empirical illustration

Georges Balandier provides us with an excellent illustration of this pluralist thesis. In comparing the adaptation to the colonial regime of two African peoples, the Fangs of Gabon and the Bakongo of the Congo, he concludes that the demographic factor is of prime importance:

> One notices that the Woleu-Ntem and the most dynamic Congo "countries" are the *only* regions supporting a relative concentration of population, and this leads one to take into account a series of *quantitative* characteristics. The social units considered as villages are numerically less reduced than in the other zones; they are less dispersed and distant from each other; they have retained — even in the Fang country, as is evident around Oyem — mutual links by which they are integrated into a social territory which is not confined to their own boundaries. These two human units have maintained a population volume which is not only favourable to a much greater vitality of the societies of which they are a part, but which also enable certain solutions requiring from the village groupings a minimum of importance and of relationships with the exterior. The capacity for reorganization and initiative is linked to these quantitative aspects at the level of the social territory within which the villages exist. Further proof of this theory can be found in the most depopulated areas of the Fang country, where there is

5. *Ibid.*, pp. 32-33. Emphasis added.

an increasing number of very small villages and where isolation is greater.[6]

This conclusion provides a strong confirmation of Durkheim's thesis on the dynamic role of demographic and moral density. Even if Balandier does not use Durkheim's terminology, it can almost be read between the lines.

Balandier adds, however, that economic aspects should be added to the demographic factor: "The demographic and economic characteristics of the groupings are closely linked; together they help to create (or not to create) conditions that are conducive to stimuli of social and cultural reorganization."[7] Finally, Balandier adds a third factor which he calls "the adaptability of groupings to the local economy"; and he emphasizes the importance that should be attached to the interrelationships among these three factors:

> One should stress the attention that should be given to the interrelationships among the quantitative characteristics of the villages, the potential of the *local* economy, and the adaptability of groupings to the latter. The third of these terms is the most imprecise, but its importance is equal to that of the other two. In Woleu-Ntem, as long as there was no adaptation of the groupings (with regard to the distribution of agricultural work between the sexes, the extension of the cultivation of cocoa, and its increased value), progress was slow in the improvement of demographic conditions, in the increase in the size of villages and in the expansion of the social territory. The comparison of these three terms for a whole series of specific societies of large ethnic units would permit the classification and ranking of them in terms of their capacity for arrangement and development.[8]

Briefly, for Balandier as for Henri Janne, the three factors — *demographic* (volume and density of the population), *economic* (potential of the local economy) and *cultural* (the capacity for adaptation to economic realities through norms and values appro-

---

6. Georges Balandier, *Sociologie actuelle de l'Afrique noire*, 2nd edition (Paris: Presses universitaires de France, 1963), p. 490.
7. *Ibid.*, p. 491.
8. *Ibid.*, p. 492.

priate to the culture) — are closely associated, and together they could even form the basis of a dynamic classificatory framework for the developing countries. This is a very important point to remember concerning the interdependence of factors in social change.

Certainly Durkheim's perception was accurate when he emphasized the dynamic importance of population growth. But this factor alone does not explain social and economic development. Too many examples demonstrate that when faced with population growth, many societies have used solutions other than the division of labour and technical progress — for example, the conquest of new territory; the emigration of part of the population; the mystical passivity stressed by Henri Janne; or simply the limitation of the population by different means, such as late marriage (as in Ireland),[9] infanticide, the religious virginity of women, human sacrifices, wars and so forth. Demographic density thus gives rise to moral density (as described by Durkheim) and economic and social development to the extent that it is joined together with other factors or with certain conditions of an economic, cultural, and perhaps also political and psychological kind.

Psychological repercussions of demographic density

Returning to Durkheim, we find that he goes further still. In his words, "With societies, individuals are transformed in accordance with the changes produced in the number of social units and their relations."[10] For him, then, population growth has psychological repercussions on the individual character, as well as economic and social consequences.

The American sociologist David Riesman has taken up Durkheim's thesis. In his well-known work, *The Lonely Crowd*, he presents the theme of his research as follows: ". . . I tentatively seek to link certain social and characterological developments, as cause and effect, with certain population shifts in Western society since the Middle Ages."[11]

---

9. C. M. Arensberg and S. T. Kimball, *Family and Community in Ireland* (Cambridge, Mass.: Harvard University Press, 1940).
10. Durkheim, *The Division of Labour*, p. 345.
11. Riesman, *The Lonely Crowd*, p. 7.

The demographic evolution of the West

David Riesman begins by recalling that the growth of Western population has followed a curve in the form of an S, in which three phases can be distinguished. The base of the S represents a phase of demographic stability, during which the number of deaths is almost equal to the number of births. This phase is said to include a "high growth potential," because the birth rate is high; but this does not produce an increase in the population because it is balanced by an equally high death rate. If the death rate diminishes, a demographic explosion is produced. The curve then rises very quickly and the second phase is entered — that of "transitional population growth." Rapid population growth is said to be transitional because the birth rate will soon decrease in proportion to the decrease in the death rate. In the third phase, a new demographic equilibrium will be established, this time based on a low birth rate.

Figure 2

Riesman's three demographic phases, with the corresponding types of society and social character

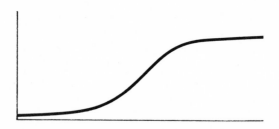

Demographic factor:	High growth potential	Transitional growth	Incipient decline of population
Type of society:	Subsistence society	Industrial society	Consumer society
Social character:	Tradition-directed	Inner-directed	Other-directed
Main sanction:	Shame	Guilt	Anxiety

Tradition-directed

Riesman maintains that a particular type of society and social character corresponds to each of these three demographic phases, as is illustrated in our diagram. A subsistence society, which is relatively stable and whose culture is strongly traditional, corresponds to the phase of high growth potential. Its members develop a conformity based on the tendency to accept and to follow tradition and the traditional order; this is the social character that Riesman calls tradition-directed. The main sanction corresponding to this type of character and behaviour is the fear of shame.

Inner-directed

The transitional growth phase started in the West with the Renaissance, when traditional society started to break down and give way to a new type of society characterized by invention, innovation and rapid change in all areas. This is the period of the growth of secondary industries — manufacturing and the transformation industries. The dominant social character among the members of this society is "inner-directed": the conduct of the individual is governed by general principles and goals which have been inculcated very early and which are supposed to guide him during his whole life. The main sanction for the inner-directed type is the feeling of guilt. The purest type of inner-directed individual can be found in the Protestant middle class.

Other-directed

In the third demographic phase, society enters a period of mass consumption in which the tertiary sector of employment and industry — services, communication, professions and administration — increasingly dominates. Riesman calls the social character corresponding to this type of society other-directed: the attitude of individuals is guided and determined by the different milieux to which they belong, whose approval they seek and with which they constantly strive to identify themselves. The main sanction for the other-directed individual is diffused anxiety, perhaps mainly the anxiety of disapproval. It is in the contemporary American middle class that this type of social character can mainly be found.

Discussion of Riesman's thesis

Riesman's thesis has been the object of some criticism. He has been criticized mainly with the preferential role that he accords the demographic factor. It is obvious that Riesman could just as easily have established his classification of the three types of society and social character on a wider basis than a mere population curve. He recognizes this himself:

> The use of demographic data in the first chapter of *The Lonely Crowd* has always seemed to me debatable.... It now appears to me much more clearly that the demographic cycle served our purposes badly, and that a study of the evolution of techniques or of mass communication would have been much more appropriate.[12]

But in correcting himself, Riesman calls on other factors which, he says, would have been much more appropriate. Is this really the case? One wonders whether Riesman did not remain rather too imprisoned by the idea that a single dominant factor should be explanatory; he seems only to regret not having used the best one. Instead, isn't it rather an interrelationship of factors or dynamic elements (to use Balandier's expression) that he should have used?

The following section will enable us to reply to this question. In fact, we will analyze the influence of one of the two factors that Riesman regrets not having used — the technical factor.

The Technical Factor

The technological revolution

Is the technical evolution proposed by Riesman a more valid explanatory factor in social change than the demographic factor? Certainly it is an explanatory factor which is often used. It has become customary to attribute to what is called the technological revolution the main upheavals that modern society has experienced over the past two centuries. In fact, how can one not be impressed by the profound and rapid changes that have taken place

---

12. David Riesman, *La foule solitaire: anatomie de la société moderne* (Paris: Arthaud, 1964), p. 15, note 1.

since the advent of the machine and electricity? Industrialization, urbanization, the rise in productivity and the acceleration of transportation and communications are only the most obvious manifestations. In reality, the whole of human and social life has been subjected to the influence of the technological revolution — family life, religious life, literature, the arts, political attitudes have all changed profoundly and radically and in a very short time.

The technological revolution still continues today. It transforms the rural world, breaks up old traditional cultures, and opens the road to economic, social and political development for countries and continents. The means of mass communication have invaded our individual lives and homes. And soon a powerful system of satellites will encircle the planet in an immense telecommunications network which will not only enable us to be in immediate contact with all points of the globe, but will also put at our disposal an infinite reservoir of varied information.

The technological revolution is far from complete; it inevitably pursues its course. We continue to experience its effects, and it is very difficult to predict precisely into what science-fiction world it will lead us.

When in Chapter 7 we wished to contrast the pre-industrial, traditional society with the type of society which would be furthest away and most different from it, we had to call it the technological society. In this, we were guided by Georges Friedmann, who distinguished between two types of environment — the natural environment and the technical environment. The technological revolution has really provoked the transition from one type of society to another, completely different, type; and in calling this new society technological we are able to specify precisely what is characteristic of it.

Technology and social types

Various writers have used the state of technology as a criterion for the construction of a classification of historical societies. The best known of these classifications is undoubtedly Lewis Mumford's.[13] He was guided by an English economist of the beginning of the century, Patrick Geddes,[14] who demonstrated that the modern in-

13. Lewis Mumford, *Technics and Civilization* (London: George Routledge and Sons Ltd., 1934).
14. Patrick Geddes, *Cities in Evolution* (London: 1915).

dustrial revolution developed according to two clearly distinct phases: the phase that he called paleotechnic, which was that of the coal and iron revolution of the eighteenth century; and the ne- · otechnic phase, which was that of electricity at the end of the nineteenth century. Adopting Geddes' idea and terminology, Mumford thoroughly studied and elaborated the distinction between the technological phases. He further showed the consequent implications for civilization; and finally he added a third phase, preceding and preparatory to the two others, which he called the eotechnic phase.

More recently, Henri Janne has adopted and amplified Mumford's model by adding two more preceding phases to the three already distinguished by Mumford and Geddes, and by developing the economic, social, political and ideological aspects characteristic of each.[15] It is Janne's formulation that we will follow at this point, reducing it to its main outlines.

The technological complexes

Each of the phases of technical development form what Mumford calls a technological complex, by which he means that to each period of the history of technology there corresponds a type of society and, more broadly, a real civilization. He explains this as follows:

> While each of these phases roughly represents a period of human history, it is characterized even more significantly by the fact that it forms a technological complex. Each phase, that is, has its origins in certain definite regions and tends to employ certain special resources and raw materials. Each phase has its specific means of utilizing and generating energy, and its special forms of production. Finally, each phase brings into existence particular types of workers, trains them in particular ways, develops certain aptitudes and discourages others, and draws upon and further develops certain aspects of the social heritage.[16]

We shall now outline the five phases or technological complexes described by Janne and Mumford.

1. *The lithotechnic era* is characterized by archaic tools and ob-

---

15. Janne, "La technique" in Janne et al., *Technique, développement économique et technocratie.* Janne takes up this analysis, almost without modification, in the recently published volume, *Le système social.*
16. Mumford, *Technics and Civilization*, pp. 109-110.

jects made out of elementary materials — wood, bone, skins and flint. The economy is necessarily local, exchange is limited, and productivity is very low. In fact, it is a subsistence economy. The dominant social structures are the family and the clan; the political organization is slightly developed and is in the hands of the elders. Thought is very predominantly magical. In this limited society, social constraints are strong, and from this results a great community homogeneity. Briefly, this is traditional society of the archaic type whose environment is the natural milieu in its purest state.

2. In *the anthropotechnic era*, the main technical innovations are the use of metals for tools and the use of slavery on a vast scale. The slave, the "domestic," is both the main labour force and an object which is part of the collection of tools. This dual technological development (the use of metals and slavery) has important repercussions. It facilitates a much more productive agriculture, resulting from new agricultural instruments and a cheap and plentiful labour-force. Commerce is initiated and extended by the rise in agricultural productivity and by the improvement in the means of transport that results from the development of the wagon and the boat. Towns spring up along the river banks and on the seashore. The political administration is organized and expands, initially establishing city states and ultimately founding the first great empires. Rational thought makes its appearance, mainly in a philosophical form, but the mentality of the people remains strongly magical and religious. The whole of the society is still predominantly rural, but the urban milieu plays an increasingly important political and economic role.

3. *The eotechnic era* started in the West in the tenth century and continued until the end of the eighteenth century. It was during this phase that the way was slowly prepared for the industrial revolution. This phase is marked by three technological developments: (1) the technical use of water and wind, particularly through the mill and the sail boat; (2) the use of animals (horse, ox, camel, elephant) for labour, replacing slavery; and (3) the invention of printing and the clock, both destined to exert a great influence on social life. The economy remains predominantly agrarian, but large-scale commercial capitalism appears and develops, constantly extending the frontiers of its markets and the exploration of the known world. In the towns, the progress of the artisan industry leads to the formation of trade guilds and the first labour unions, together with the appearance of the first forms of an urban proletariat. The political regime is of the feudal type,

based on absolute monarchical power. In the realm of knowledge, the reign of theology has been succeeded by that of philosophy; but one also sees the early progress of scientific knowledge and the emergence of the new spirit which results. Throughout most of this period, the mentality, however, remains profoundly religious; ecclesiastical power is strong and active and the monastical movement plays an important role, as much from the economic as from the cultural point of view. But the reaction has already started: the Renaissance and the Encyclopaedia prepare for the coming of the technical milieu.

4. *The paleotechnic era* is that of the industrial revolution, extending from the end of the eighteenth century to the beginning of the twentieth. Technically, it is characterized by the association of coal and iron. The new source of energy, which is linked to coal, is steam; it revolutionizes the means of transportation (the steam boat and the locomotive) and gives birth to industrial machinery. Iron replaces wood in tools and in transportation. Industrial and competitive capitalism replace commercial capitalism, the latter having paved the way for the former. Workers and the proletarian masses become concentrated in the urban centres; trade-unionism emerges and sets the class struggle in motion. The economic structure is marked increasingly by the predominance of the secondary sector of production. Political power passes from the hands of the former aristocracy to those of the bourgeoisie, thus nurturing parliamentary democracy. Scientific knowledge flourishes, mainly in chemistry and mechanics. The great social ideologies — liberalism, socialism, communism and social catholicism — appear and spread.

5. *The neotechnic era* is the one we have entered since the beginning of the twentieth century. New sources of energy have appeared — electricity, petroleum, gas and atomic energy — resulting in the proliferation, diversification and automation of the machine. Chemistry has revolutionized basic materials through the creation of new synthetic products — light alloys, fertilizers, fabrics, concrete, plastics and so forth. Industrial capitalism gives rise to financial capitalism; large monopolies are successors to competitive capitalism. State intervention takes over from liberal laissez-faire; trade unions extend beyond the working class and enter the tertiary sector, which is in a period of rapid growth; unions tend towards mass syndicalism. Two types of political structure dominate: mixed Western democracy, liberal and interventionist, of the welfare state type; and popular one-party democracy of a totalitarian kind. A positive climate for socialization and partici-

pation spreads in the political, economic and social structures. A certain weakening of ideologies can be sensed; the production society is transformed into the consumer society.

Definition of the technical factor

The description of these successive phases of civilization really contributes nothing particularly new; it reminds us of the different types of society which we described earlier in Chapters 6 and 7. The main interest in the classification lies in its basic criterion of the state of technology, which is used to separate the main stages in human history and to construct a certain typology of societies. But there again, it will undoubtedly have been noticed that this typology and the way in which the types are described is reminiscent of Marx's typology which, in fact, guided Mumford and Janne. The technological factor adopted by these two writers recalls some of Marx's formulae — for example, "the wind mill will give you the society with an overlord; the steam mill, the society with industrial capitalism" (*The Poverty of Philosophy*). In addition, the way in which Mumford and Janne talk of the technical factor strongly resembles what Marx means by the relations of production. Mumford writes: "It was Marx's great contribution as a sociological economist to see and partly to demonstrate that *each period of invention and production* had its own specific value for civilization, or, as he would have put it, its own historical mission."[17]

The comparison between technology and the relations of production enables one to comprehend better what should be understood by the so-called technical factor. To speak of the technical factor in history is really to resort to a simplified formula to designate simultaneously *the invention and/or use of tools, machines, energy and material, and the working conditions as well as the relations of groups of production which result from them.* Thus, the expression *the technical factor* should be understood, not in a restricted sense, but in a wider fashion as *the total form of production.*

The historical role of the technical factor

It will now be easier to appreciate the role of the technical factor

---

17. *Ibid.*, p. 110. Emphasis added.

in social history when defined in this way. It is certainly an important variable, whose influence has been felt profoundly and will perhaps be felt increasingly in the evolution of societies. This is amply demonstrated by the fact that one can successfully use it, as Mumford and Janne have done, as an independent variable to distinguish the great periods of human civilization. Modes of work linked to the state of technology are today considered — and justly so — as a particularly rich and valid explanatory factor by an increasing number of scholars. It is relevant to recognize the importance of the contribution of Marx and Engels to this discovery.

Nevertheless, the historical importance of the technical factor should be interpreted within its total framework. As Mumford notes: "The machine cannot be divorced from its larger social pattern; for it is this pattern that gives it meaning and purpose."[18] In fact, technology is not an historical factor which acts alone and of necessity. Its influence depends, to an important extent, on the attitude of a population towards it and on the way in which a population integrates technology and production into its projects and designs, and into its definition of what it is and what it wishes to be.

Thus, it can be maintained that the technical factor has not exerted an equally important role in all historical periods and civilizations. If it can be considered an important variable at the moment, it is because it occupies a predominant position both in the culture of contemporary society and in the daily life of all its members. Modern society is a society of production, in which the work world has taken on an importance that it appears never to have had in any other civilization. The aristocratic elite, in all the civilizations that it dominated, considered work an unworthy activity devolving on subordinate groups of men. The value accorded economically productive work has resulted, in the West, from the transfer of power which took place between the aristocracy and the bourgeoisie. Within the culture of the bourgeois class, technology and its practical consequences were integrated into a world view based on the productive activity of the individual and the collectivity.

The technical factor and other factors

While the technical factor can be considered an important variable in history, it is not a dominant factor; technical determinism

---

18. *Ibid.*

has no more validity than demographic determinism. Such is the conclusion of most contemporary sociologists. For example, following a detailed analysis of the role of technical progress in social evolution, Fred Cottrell concludes:

> Throughout this discussion we have asserted that values, organization, technology, and the inorganic world are together involved in producing and maintaining the patterns that govern energy flow. . . . Neither technological determinism nor "energetic determinism" has been demonstrated. But neither has the transcendental view of values or culture. If man makes himself, he does so in a world that includes other organisms and things that interact with man's purposes as they are reflected in his choices and resultant behavior.[19]

Again, when undertaking the analysis that we summarized earlier of the different types of civilization corresponding to the evolution of technology, Henri Janne starts with the following statement:

> We will take the technical factor as an independent "variable" and consider all the other aspects of history "in function" of it. Given technical changes, how do they react on the geography, demography, economy, ideology, religion and political power of a total society?
>
> This exercise does not imply that the technical factor should be considered the "primary factor" (technical monism). The evolution of Western humanity could be as easily explained by taking other significant factors as variables — politics or religion, for example. In reality, all these factors constantly interact with each other. It is their *correlations* which constitute the explanation of history.[20]

Finally, let us quote a particularly illuminating extract from Lewis Mumford:

> To understand the dominating role played by technics in modern civilization, one must explore in detail the preliminary period of ideological and social

---

19. Fred Cottrell, "Technological Progress and Evolutionary Theory," in Herbert R. Barringer, George I. Blanksten and Raymond W. Mack, eds., *Social Change in Developing Areas* (Cambridge, Mass.: Schenkman Publishing Company, 1965), p. 314.
20. Janne, *Le système social*, p. 314.

preparation. Not merely must one explain the existence of the new mechanical instruments: one must explain the culture that was ready to use them and profit
from them so extensively. For note this: mechanization
and regimentation are not new phenomena in history:
what is new is the fact that these functions have been
projected and embodied in organized forms which
dominate every aspect of our existence. Other civilizations reached a high degree of technical efficiency without, apparently, being profoundly influenced by the
methods and aims of technics. . . . Technics and civilization as a whole are the result of human choices and
aptitudes and strivings, deliberate as well as unconscious, often irrational when apparently they are most
objective and scientific. . . . It (technics) does not form
an independent system like the universe: it exists as an
element in human culture. . . . The world of technics is
not isolated and self contained: it reacts to forces and
impulses that come from apparently remote parts of
the environment.[21]

Technology and culture

As Mumford strongly emphasizes in the passage quoted above,
technology is not external to culture; on the contrary, it is part of
culture, as is religion, ideology or morality.

Technology is an element of culture in several ways. The
progress of technology is closely linked to the progress of science.
But the sociology of science has amply demonstrated that scientific
and technological progress is dependent on values, on a world
view, and even on the religious orientations of a collectivity. Thus,
in his classic study of the relationships between Protestantism and
capitalism (which will be discussed later), Max Weber showed
that the Puritans had a more receptive, positive and active attitude towards science than did the Catholics.

[To them] the knowledge of God and His designs can
be attained only through a knowledge of His works.
The favourite science of all Puritan, Baptist, or Pietist
Christianity was thus physics, and next to it all those

---

21. Mumford, *Technics and Civilization*, pp. 4 and 6.

other natural sciences which used a similar method, especially mathematics. It was hoped from the empirical knowledge of the divine laws of nature to ascend to a grasp of the essence of the world, which on account of the fragmentary nature of the divine revelations, a Calvinistic idea, could never be attained by the method of metaphysical speculation. The empiricism of the seventeenth century was the means for asceticism to seek God in nature. It seemed to lead to God, philosophical speculation away from Him.[22]

Taking up Weber's analysis, Robert K. Merton demonstrated that it was confirmed by a great number of facts. In particular, Merton established that in the seventeenth, eighteenth and nineteenth centuries, the Puritans contributed in a quite exceptional way to scientific progress in England, Germany and the United States; similarly, they were in the vanguard of the movement to introduce more science into educational programs. If this was the case, it was because, according to Merton: ". . . the religious ethic which stemmed from Calvin promoted a state of mind and a value-orientation which invited the pursuit of natural science."[23]

The Puritan ethic and the culture of the middle class reinforced each other and finally came to exert a dominant influence on the mentality of modern technological society. It can be asserted that, without this pairing of a religious morality and the culture of a dominant class which occurred in the seventeenth and eighteenth centuries, Western society would be very different from what it is today.

Conclusion

From this analysis it seems that the historical influence of the state and progress of technology is not a simple phenomenon. As we have said, the technical factor is an important variable. But this is true above all in the contemporary world. In addition, the real influence of technology cannot be appreciated without taking into account its cultural context. Technology is not located only at the

---

22. Max Weber, *The Protestant Ethic and the Spirit of Capitalism*, trans. Talcott Parsons (New York: Charles Scribner's Sons, 1958), pp. 168 and 249, n. 145.
23. Merton, "Puritanism, Pietism, and Science," *Social Theory and Social Structure*, p. 606.

level of the infrastructure, to use Marx's terminology; it simultaneously stems from the world of things and from the realm of thought, attitudes and values.

The Economic Infrastructure

The ambiguity of Marx and Engels

The relationship between the technical factor and culture raises the larger and more difficult problem of the relationships between structural elements and culture (these terms having the meaning that has already been given them in the preceding chapters, and particularly at the beginning of Chapter 6). This problem was posed mainly by Marx and Engels with regard to the dynamic role of productive forces (as defined in Chapter 6) in social change and in the history of societies. It should be recognized, however, that the position of Marx and Engels remains rather ambiguous on this point, and it is understandable that it has given rise, and still gives rise, to different interpretations. On the one hand, one can read passages from both writers in which the determinist meaning can hardly be doubted. Here are a few of them.

Economic determinism

> Social relations are intimately connected with the forces of production. In acquiring new forces of production, men change their mode of production, their way of earning their living; they change all their social relations. The hand mill will give you a society with the feudal lord, the steam mill a society with the industrial capitalist. The same men who establish social relations in conformity with their material power of production, also produce principles, laws, and categories, in conformity with their social relations. (Marx, *The Philosophy of Poverty*, 1847).

> Assume a particular state of development in the productive forces of man and you will get a particular form of commerce and consumption. Assume a particular stage of development in production, commerce and consumption and you will have a corresponding social order, a corresponding organization of the family and

the ranks and classes, in a word a corresponding civil society. Presuppose a particular civil society and you will get particular political conditions which are only the official expression of civil society. (Marx, Letter to Paul Annenkov, December 28, 1846.)

These relations of production correspond to a definite stage of development of their material forces of production. The sum total of these relations of production constitutes the economic structure of society — the real foundation, on which rises a legal and political superstructure and to which correspond definite forms of social consciousness. (Marx, Preface to *A Contribution to the Critique of Political Economy*, 1859.)

Another passage from Engels

In 1890 Engels wrote a curious letter in which he said:

Marx and I are ourselves partly to blame for the fact that younger writers sometimes lay more stress on the economic side than is due to it. We had to emphasize this main principle in opposition to our adversaries, who denied it, and we had not always the time, the place or the opportunity to allow the other elements involved in the interaction to come into their rights. But when it was a case of presenting a section of history, that is, of a practical application, the thing was different and there no error was possible. . . . There is an action and reaction of all the factors, and within this the economic movement ends by necessarily clearing a path through the infinite throng of risks. (Engels, Letter to Joseph Bloch, September 21, 1890.)

In reality, this letter does not basically modify the central thesis: Engels simply recognizes that there can be an interaction between the economic and other factors; but he firmly asserts that through the multiplicity of factors "the economic movement ends by necessarily clearing a path for itself." Thus, it remains true that the productive forces will, in the last resort, be the predominant dynamic factor; it is in the technical and economic infrastructure that the source of social organization and consciousness will be located.

What is the economic infrastructure?

In the preceding section, we posed the problem of the relations between the technical factor and culture; it is clear that the same problem is posed here. The technical and economic infrastructure is not independent of the cultural world. The productive forces are not a purely material basis of social organization and change; they have their roots in acquired scientific and technical knowledge and in the socio-psychological attitudes essential to the discovery, use and propagation of this knowledge. In his discussion of Marx's sociology, Raymond Aron raises this problem as follows:

> The ambiguity of Marx's sociology may also be revealed by an analysis and discussion of its essential concepts. Let us take, for example, the two terms *infrastructure* and *superstructure*. What are the elements of social reality which belong to the infrastructure? What are the ones that pertain to the superstructure? In general, it seems that infrastructure should refer to the economy, particularly the forces of production. But what are these so-called forces of production? All the technical apparatus of a civilization is inseparable from scientific knowledge; and the latter, in turn, seems to belong to the realm of ideas, of knowledge, and these last elements should derive from the superstructure, at least to the extent that scientific knowledge is, in many societies, inseparable from the way of thinking, from philosophy and ideology.[24]

It is clear, however, that Marx also posed this problem for himself. And he resolved it in a way that is very characteristic of him and which corresponds to the main lines of his thinking:

> The production of ideas, of conceptions, of consciousness is at first interwoven with the material activity and the material intercourse of men, the language of real life. Conceiving, thinking, the mental intercourse of men appear at this stage as the direct efflux of their material behaviour. The same applies to mental production as expressed in the language of the politics, laws, morality, religion, metaphysics of people. Men are the producers of their conceptions, ideas, etc. – real active men as they are conditioned by a definite development

---

24. Aron, *Main Currents in Sociological Thought*, vol. 1, p. 158.

of their productive forces, and of the intercourse corresponding to these, up to its furthest forms. (*The German Ideology*).

The concept of productive forces

In other words, Marx resolves the problem by referring thought, knowledge and science back to the economic infrastructure. But at the same time, he poses a new problem which appears insoluble; in the process of being extended, the idea of productive forces disintegrates. It is the total man who is involved in the activity of production at the same time that he is wholly determined by his work and his production; it is the whole of the social organization which is at the service of economic production — which in turn is modeled, guided and activated by the latter. Knowledge, thought and even the consciousness of man are involved in the material activity of production in two senses: they are at the service of production, and they are its product. What then becomes of the idea of productive forces, which is extended to all the activity and thought of man and of the collectivity?

Gurvitch saw this problem very clearly. Referring to the passage from Marx that has just been quoted, and to other similar texts, he wrote:

> From a certain angle, production or the "productive forces" are understood in the sociology of Marx, or at least of the young Marx, in such a broad fashion that they include all of social reality in all its manifestations. . . . In other words, the more that the productive forces are considered not as *isolated factors* but as the *total social cause*, the more this concept is extended to the maximal point, by being identified with all the levels of social reality.[25]

An expanded definition of productive forces

Understood in these terms, the concept of productive forces can almost be said to mean the generalized capacity for economic production of a given society. Thus, it is a case, not of a particular

---

25. Gurvitch, *La vocation actuelle*, vol. 2, pp. 259 and 261. Emphasis in the original.

factor, but of a collective aptitude which results from the combination or correlation of several factors. The elements which enter into the composition of this aptitude, the factors and conditions which form it, must be discovered and rearranged in each particular case; or at least, their arrangement is not necessarily the same in a universal and absolute way. It is for the researcher in each empirical study to discern the factors and conditions favourable or unfavourable to the productive capacity of a given society, or of the segment of a society or historical period that he is studying.

It could be maintained, and not without reason, as it has been by Gurvitch, that this interpretation of the productive forces corresponds better to Marx's and Engels' intentions than does the narrow and rigidly determinist meaning that was read into it. It was against this determinist meaning that Engels defended himself in his letter of 1890 to Joseph Bloch (see p. 371). The contribution of Marxist sociology would not thus be diminished. On the contrary, Marxist sociology has already made a substantial contribution by emphasizing the impact of the economic structure on social organization and history. A broader definition of productive capacity, which would be less strictly monist and causal, would enable one to make the link with the pluralist and correlationist conception of social change that is found in the modern social sciences.

It is in this direction that Henri Janne's criticism of Marxist sociology points, though his sympathies for Marxist thought cannot be questioned.

> What has been overlooked in Marx's work is all the parts conditioned by philosophical presuppositions. This includes his predictions, his over-organized historical considerations for the periods preceding the nineteenth century, and finally, his technico-economic monism, often called "economic." Of course, it is well known that Engels in a famous letter (of September 21, 1890) was indignant about this accusation, and pointed out that Marxist theory admits the action of the superstructure on the infrastructure, or "reciprocal action." This is understood; but it remains true that the fundamental action would be due to the infrastructure and that the economic factor is accorded predominance. In the final analysis, the error stems from reasoning elaborated in terms of classical causality. *Marx's dialectic*

would have led him to completely accurate results if it had been based on the principle of correlation among the factors.[26]

From simple to complex causality

Here Janne has probably touched on the crux of the problem, which is the transition that has taken place over a century in scientific thinking from classical, simple, direct, immediate causality to complex, multiple causality, resulting from the action and interaction of a plurality of factors. In the analysis of societies and concrete situations that the sociologist must pursue, it is no longer possible to resort to a simple and uniform model of causality. In other words, as Engels himself wrote in the letter to Joseph Bloch: "The application of the theory to any period of history would be easier than the solution of a simple equation of the first degree." The productive activity of a society and the productive capacity from which it results are extremely complex phenomena, and they are beyond the bounds of an analysis which uses only a simplified or rigid theoretical framework. Productive capacity does not depend exclusively on either structural elements (natural resources, technology, the working organization) or cultural elements (values, ideologies); it is the product of a joint action, an interaction and a correlation of factors located at one or another level of reality. All contemporary research points in this direction. Here we find once again Georges Balandier's idea, which was stated in the preceding section: social change is always the result of an interrelationship of structural and cultural factors.

Let us add the evidence of another researcher. In summarizing studies concerned with two societies which have experienced rapid economic development — the northern United States and English Canada — and two societies which have experienced slower development — the southern United States and French Canada — Seymour Lipset comes to the following conclusion:

> These comparisons between the United States North and South, and English and French Canada, show that structure and values are clearly interrelated. Structure such as a plantation system combined with a racially based hierarchy is functionally tied to a given set of

---

26. Janne, *Le système social*, p. 76. Emphasis added.

"aristocratic" values, and antipathetic to an emphasis on achievement, universalism and hard work. But any value system derived from given sets of historical experience institutionalized in religious systems, family structures, class relations, and education will affect the pace and even direction and content of social and economic change.[27]

An example of a rigid determinist interpretation: Bukharin

The preceding considerations bring us finally to make a very important point. Obviously Marx and Engels emphasized very strongly the role of economic structures in social organization and in history. In addition, it is on the basis of their work that we have posed the problem of the role of the economic infrastructure in social history. But too often, passages from Marx and Engels are used out of context and without regard to the objectives and intentions evidenced throughout their work. Thus there exists the risk of arriving at a rigid economic determinism.

This is the case, for example, of the Marxist sociology of Nikolai Bukharin: the social and ideological superstructures are placed in direct relationship with the technical and economic conditions of production, and appear merely to reflect them. Bukharin undoubtedly recognizes that "the superstructures are by no means a 'passive' element of the social process." But their action is always exerted as a function of "the preliminary state of economic relations." As Bukharin maintains:

> The *starting point* of any process should not be lost from view. Where is this starting point to be found? In the conflict between the evolution of productive forces and property relations. *This* is the basis of the process and the initial point in any social reorganization.[28]

Economic determinism in modern capitalism

It is permissible, however, to support another interpretation of Marx's and Engels' thought. Their work must be read above all as

27. Lipset, "Values, Education, and Entrepreneurship," in Lipset and Solari, eds., *Elites in Latin America*, p. 12.
28. Nikolai Bukharin, *Historical Materialism, A System of Sociology* (London: George Allen and Unwin, 1926). This manual was published in the

a criticism of modern capitalism, which is the extreme outcome of the regime of private property and the ultimate form of individual and collective alienation. Capitalist society, in effect, pushes to its extreme limits the enslavement of man by man and by matter. It assembles within it and condenses all the social and ideological contradictions which result from the private ownership of the *means* of production. More than any other form of society, it is directed by the forces and relations of production, because it is subjected totally to a dominant class that directly exploits a proletarian working mass. In addition, it is in capitalism that the fetishism of money and goods ultimately is most strongly asserted.

Economic determinism is thus a particularly dominant element in modern capitalism; it is even its fundamental vice. *The breakdown and the end of capitalism and the coming of communist society will be accompanied by the freeing of man from economic determinism*; and this will transpire when the labouring masses take their historical destiny in hand.

A different interpretation: Lefebvre and Desroches

This explanation of economic materialism can be found in the work of a particularly authoritative interpreter of Marxist thought, the sociologist Henri Lefebvre. His own writing expresses it best:

> Marx is still in many quarters looked upon as an economist. He is believed to have championed a certain "economic determinism," according to which the level of development of the productive forces mechanically or automatically determines the other relations and forms that constitute social life, property relations, institutions, ideas. For allegedly holding such a view he is sometimes criticized, sometimes approved. But (it should hardly be necessary to point out yet another time) this interpretation overlooks the subtitle *Das Kapital: A Critique of Political Economy*. After all, wasn't it capitalism that founded itself on economic reality: commodities, money, surplus value, profit? By contrast with capitalism, in which the mediation of money

U.S.S.R. in 1921 and was then translated into several languages. In the text cited, the emphasis is in the original.

changes relations between persons into the quantitative relations that obtain between abstract things, medieval society was founded on direct relations among human beings, relations between masters and serfs — no doubt relations of bondage, but perfectly clear ones. Once society has been transformed, human relations will again become clear and direct, only without servility. : . . To be sure, every society had and still has an economic "foundation" or "base." This base determines social relations, however, only to the extent that it limits the activities of groups and individuals; it imposes shackles on them; it arrests their potentialities by limiting them.[29]

The same interpretation of Marxist thought can be found in the work of Henri Desroches:

The formal declarations (of Marx) are that *matter takes precedence over the mind* — that if men make their own history, it is with determined premises and conditions, and that finally, "among all of them, it is the economic conditions which are finally determinant."

But this declaration is not of the abstract, reflective type, which would be universally valid over time. It is of the historical, philosophic kind, valid essentially for a period that is completely defined — ours — which is the period of necessity and which is still not the period of liberty.

Humanity thus effectively finds itself in the period when matter commands, since — and this is the fundamental fact that should not be ignored — the will of millions of men to exist is still more or less restricted to the will to find the means to live and to live materially, consequently to produce and in order to produce to alienate their liberty necessarily by linking their existence to the means of production. This is the elementary and brutal affirmation of Marxist materialism.

But there is another affirmation of the same materi-

---

29. Lefebvre, *The Sociology of Marx*. Emphasis in the original. Let us add that Lefebvre has expressed this idea many times in other writings, notably in Henri Lefebvre, *Dialectical Materialism*, trans. John Sturrock (London: Jonathan Cape, 1968).

alism, which is that this period when matter commands is precisely the inhuman period. It is this affirmation which is the basis of any of this materialism's humanism.[30]

Conclusion

We have thought it useful to quote these two long passages from Lefebvre and Desroches because they throw an unaccustomed light on the Marxist analysis of the economic factor in history. Without seeking to minimize the relevance of the economic variable in the study of social change, it can be said that Marx and Engels have demonstrated the very specific importance of the economic infrastructure in the history of contemporary, capitalist society without, to their minds, maintaining that this is exactly the same in the history of every society.

This important conclusion highlights the *historical nature* of the Marxist thesis on the influence of the economic factor in history. In fact, the importance of the economic factor no longer seems the result of some mysterious, historical and absolute determinism which acts as a deus ex machina. Rather, it is characteristic of an historical period of a type of society — modern capitalist society — in which the infrastructure exerts a stronger and more marked alienating function on the human collectivity than it does in other historical periods. If this is true, it is due to a particular correlation of conditions and factors which have come together in the history of modern Western society.

Thus relieved of the dogmatism and prophecy which is too often ascribed to it, Marxist sociological analysis of contemporary society becomes, for the sociologist, particularly rich in suggestions and hypotheses.

Cultural Values

In the preceding pages, we have referred on several occasions to the realm of cultural values as one of the factors in social change (or resistance to change). As in the case of the preceding factors, cultural values do not act in isolation or autonomously; the axiom

---

30. C. H. Desroches, *Signification du marxisme* (Paris: Les éditions ouvrières, 1949), pp. 36-37. Emphasis in the original.

that ideas lead the world has no scientific basis. Auguste Comte's broad picture of the types of society corresponding to the three states of knowledge (theological, metaphysical, positive) does not stand up to confrontation with history and socio-economic reality. This does not mean that knowledge, and perhaps still more attitudes with regard to knowledge, exert no influence on social change. Quite the contrary. But this influence is always linked to other factors that Auguste Comte too readily left aside. Here again, the classical causality that inspired Comte must give way to a more complex and pluralist causality.

Ideas, values and motivations

If ideas exert a partial influence on social change, how does this influence make itself felt? In what way does its effect operate? We can answer this question very simply by saying that ideas have a social impact to the extent that they activate and guide the *motivation* of social actors. As has often been said, society is above all the social action of a plurality of actors; it is the product of this social action. And social action is oriented and motivated by goals, knowledge, aims and projects that are formulated and entertained by actors and groups of actors, and which impel or encourage them to act in a given direction and to reject other possible routes or choices. Thus, ideas exert an influence on social change to the extent that they become *values* which are capable of arousing a fairly strong *motivation*; or again to the extent that they are integrated into an *ideological system,* which is suggested as an explanation and plan for the whole of a collectivity. It is mainly from the perspective of values and ideology, then, that contemporary sociology approaches the role of ideas in social change. First we will analyze the role of values in social change; the role of ideologies will be discussed in the following section.

Max Weber's thesis

The influence of religious values on the development and evolution of capitalism will serve as an illustration. This question has aroused a great number of discussions and has led to many studies of the relationships between structural and cultural factors. It is not possible to summarize all these studies at this point, for they are too many and varied to be recounted in a few pages. We will refer primarily to Max Weber's thesis (which remains the main thesis on the question) concerning the influence that religious values, and notably the Protestant ethic of Calvinist inspiration, exerted on the progress of Western capitalism.[31]

The spirit of capitalism

To Max Weber, capitalism is first of all a spirit or mentality, which does not consist merely of the pursuit of gain, or riches, or comfort; the desire for acquisition has existed and continues to exist outside capitalist structures. The spirit of capitalism can instead be defined as *a type of specific economic behaviour, characterized by the search for constantly increasing profits through the rational, calculated and methodical use of the means of production (resources, capital, techniques, work organization) as well as of market or exchange conditions.*

In this sense, the spirit of capitalism is neither new nor recent. It existed previously in different periods of history, in China, in Egypt, in Ancient Greece and Rome, and in Europe of the Middle Ages. But it is in the modern Western world that it has emerged in its most advanced and extensive form; it can even be said that modern Western capitalism constitutes a distinct and particular type of capitalism, which is characterized specifically by the systematic organization of the work of a free labour force (in other words, not composed of slaves or serfs), by the most developed use of science and technology, by the extension of its markets, and by a perfected accounting system. Briefly, what forms the historical specificity of this type of capitalism is the extreme *rationality* of behaviour and of the social, political, economic and legal structures.

Capitalism and rationality

The genesis of this type of capitalism cannot be explained without an analysis of *the sources of this rationality* which forms the kernel of what Weber calls the spirit of capitalism. If it is true that certain structural factors have favoured the progress of modern Western capitalism — the accumulation of capital, demographic conditions, the discovery of new continents and so forth — it was still necessary for men to be motivated to use these various elements rationally with a view to developing the capitalist type of

---

31. Weber, *The Protestant Ethic*. This was first published in *Archiv für Sozialwissenschaft und Sozialpolitik* 20 and 21 (1904-1905). Weber published it again in 1920 in the series of studies on the sociology of religion which his death prevented him from completing: *Gesammelte Aufsätze zur Religionssoziologie*, 3 vols. (Tübingen: J.C.B. Mohr, 1920-1921).

production. It was necessary that men should be animated by a spirit, by a world view, and by values favourable to rational, economic behaviour and practices. In other historical periods, the religious and magical world view which predominated and which guided behaviour had put a check on either economic objectives of the capitalist type or on rationality in organization and economic actions.

Calvinist morality and the capitalist spirit

In the seventeenth and eighteenth centuries, a religion appeared in the West which, on the contrary and for the first time, would involve the believer in the systematic and ordered pursuit of indefinite profit. This religion was Calvinist Protestantism. It would be false to say — and, besides, this would not correspond to Weber's thinking — that Calvinism gave birth to capitalism; the latter had existed elsewhere and already existed in Europe before Protestantism. But Calvinism was the spiritual force, the cultural factor, which explains why the capitalist spirit experienced a unique and curiously powerful impetus in the West.

Weber does not attribute this effect to all Protestantism. In particular, he shows that Lutheranism was not able to exert the same influence as Calvinism. In the current of religious thought following the Reformation, it was mainly the latter which, more than any other, was to play an active and dynamic role in modern economic development and in the history of Western capitalism. And if this was the case, it was not because the very content of Calvinist theology was more favourable to capitalism than was the theology of Luther or the Catholics. Instead — and this is Weber's fundamental point — it was that *the Calvinist doctrine, both through its own logic and through the psychological reaction that it stimulated, engendered an individual and economic morality that was favourable to behaviour of the capitalist type*. It was this particular Protestant ethic, stemming from the theological conceptions of Calvin and his disciples, that Weber claims contributed the spiritual foundations which gave modern Western capitalism its impetus and its originality.

Predestination, according to Calvin

The Calvinist idea of predestination is the main source of this ethic. Much more than Luther, Calvin pushed to the extreme the idea that man is saved or damned by an unfathomable and mysterious decree of God. Salvation is a pure act of grace that no man can earn, for no one is really worthy of it. In fact, salvation is not primarily arranged for man's happiness, but solely for God's glory; this is true of all creation, which — being God's work — is destined to manifest and express his glory. Puritanism is thoroughly imbued with the idea of the smallness and insignificance of man before God. The saint is really, in the strictest meaning of the term, God's *elect*. He does not earn his salvation, nor does he merit it; he receives it as an act of grace for the glory of God. Thus, no one can be certain of belonging to the invisible church of the Saints, particularly after Christ's warning that salvation is reserved only for an elected few.

The consequences of the doctrine of predestination

As Weber emphasizes, the spiritual solitude and the uncertainty of personal salvation into which this doctrine plunged the believer was difficult for the mass of believers to bear. The acceptance of the *decretum horrible* (the terrible divine decree of predestination) required the purest love of God and the most total faith to an heroic degree. It was natural, then, that Calvin's disciples should derive a theological and moral teaching from this doctrine that was more acceptable, if not more reassuring. It is therefore through an apparent paradox that Calvin's doctrine, based on grace and the glory of God, more than any other religion was to involve the believer in temporal and economic activity.

In fact, the Calvinist's secular activity, while operating within and on the world, was guided by an essentially religious vision of the world; at the moral level, asceticism was the answer to the theological doctrine of predestination. If the faithful person could not know whether he was elected or damned, he could at least be assured that God could not choose his elect among the sinners. Therefore, every form of human weakness should be excluded from the believer's life. In addition, not being able to count either on the sacraments to atone for his faults or on the accumulation of good works to save himself, the believer should lead a pure and saintly life, fully devoted to the glory of the Kingdom of God. The believer's attitude must thus be marked by dignity and self-control, by severity and seriousness. He who practised this asceticism during his whole life, even if he could not win his salvation, could at least gain a certain conviction of this salvation.

Moral asceticism

Moral asceticism included several important obligations. The first was *work*: laziness, idleness and leisure were the greatest sins, for they constituted a refusal to participate in the building of the Kingdom of God. The idea of a vocation became central to Calvinist thought. Each believer had to carry out his part in the Kingdom of God by seriously and efficiently fulfilling the function to which he had been called for the greater glory of God. To the Calvinist, work did not appear as a necessary evil, nor as punishment for a fault; it was man's positive and necessary contribution to the manifestation of God's glory. Consequently, it was not enough simply to work; the work had to be carried out well and, above all, to serve useful goals or be really *productive*. Work also had to be *continuous*. It was necessary to inculcate into the child very early the meaning of work and a vocation, and to teach him that man must work all his life, without resting or stopping.

Second, the believer should lead *an austere life*. Everything pleasing to the senses should be banished from his existence; this included not only every form of material comfort, but equally the arts, music, poetry and literature. If, through his work, the believer accumulated wealth, this was not to serve his ease and pleasure, nor to buy his salvation in any way whatsoever. The faithful person should avoid luxury and extravagance, but also avarice; he should neither spend nor hoard. Rather, he should use his wealth for new productive activities. Since man is only the steward of the goods of this world, he should, according to the parable in the Scriptures, make them multiply to the full extent of his capacities and efforts.

Third, *science*, and mainly experimental science, was a form of knowledge of the works of God. Every believer should have at least a minimum of education in order to be able to read the Word of God. If he could, he should also educate himself in the natural sciences, which through God's works would reveal His greatness and wisdom. He could, and even should, profit from the natural sciences in his work, in order to make this more efficient and useful.

The influence of ascetic morality

This ascetic morality was to have important practical consequences. The Puritan moralists mistrusted the pernicious effects of money, but their precepts involved the faithful in a life of work and economy which enriched them constantly. The rejection of any form of magical thought, the emphasis on self-control, and the respect for scientific and experimental knowledge predisposed believers to the rational organization of their lives, their work and all their undertakings. Basically opposed to a feudal life of laziness and extravagance, Calvinism was identified instead with the mentality of the entrepreneur and the commercial bourgeoisie. Consequently, wherever Calvinism took root, an intense economic activity of the capitalist type could be observed.

Before Max Weber, historians had already noticed this coincidence in Holland, in England, and above all in New England. Weber wished to explain its origins; at the same time he showed that religion is not *in itself* an obstacle to economic rationality, as has sometimes been maintained, but that it has been an important factor in the development of Western capitalism.

Two objections

As one might easily guess, Weber's thesis has had wide repercussions. Formulated at the beginning of the twentieth century, it has continually been commented on and discussed since that time. It would be impossible to summarize all the studies which have been concerned with this part of Weber's work.[32] Let us emphasize those that are related to this chapter.

It is generally recognized that Weber demonstrated the role of an important cultural factor — religious morality — in economic history. It is futile to object to Weber's thesis, as has been done,[33] on the grounds that the Puritan doctrine was opposed to the accu-

---

32. A fairly complete bibliography of articles and works in which Weber's thesis has been discussed, or which follow on from this thesis, would easily cover several pages. We will mention only a few titles here, in addition to those already mentioned in this section: Henri Sée, "Dans quelle mesure Puritains et Juifs ont-ils contribué au progrès du capitalisme moderne?" *Revue historique* 155 (1927), and by the same author, *Les origines du capitalisme moderne* (Paris: 1926); Maurice Halbwachs, "Les origines puritaines du capitalisme moderne," *Revue d'histoire et de philosophie religieuse* (March-April 1925); H. Hauser, *Les débuts du capitalisme moderne* (Paris: 1927); Amintore Fanfani, *Catholicism, Protestantism and Capitalism* (New York: Sheed and Ward, 1935); H. M. Robertson, *Aspects of the Rise of Economic Individualism: A Criticism of Max Weber and his School* (London: Cambridge University Press, 1933); Talcott Parsons, "Capitalism in Recent German Literature," *Journal of Political Economy* 36 (December 1928): 641-61 and 37 (February 1929): 31-51.
33. For example, Kurt Samuelsson, *Religion and Economic Action* (New York: Basic Books, Inc., 1961), p. 79.

mulation of wealth and to the faithful being completely involved in economic activity. Weber recognized this. It was not the Puritan doctrine to which he directly attributed a dynamic role; this doctrine, in itself, could *in fact* deter the faithful person from economic activity. It was the moral conclusions derived from it which were the important element; it was the Calvinist ethic, and not Calvinist theology, that was the active cultural factor.

Other writers have tried to show that the Catholic doctrine could favour the same practical behaviour as Calvinism.[34] To this, one can first of all reply that in Catholicism, the link between religious thought, morality and economic activity is less direct, and above all less central and less fundamental than in Calvinism; second, one can say that, in fact, Catholicism has not exerted as remarkable an influence as Calvinism on the economic motivations of the faithful. The active role of Protestants, notably Calvinists, in the history of industrialization and economic development in the West has been noticed by a number of observers and historians; the same cannot be said of Catholics.

The Calvinist ethic — a dominant factor?

But the central point in the discussion of Max Weber's thesis is this: can the Calvinist ethic be considered the *dominant factor*, or the main one, in the explanation of the evolution of Western capitalism? There has often been the temptation to contrast Weber's thesis with Marx's, as if Weber had proved or had wished to prove that cultural factors are more important than structural factors in economic change. It is certainly true that Weber's research follows in the wake of Marx's work. But it was from a new and different perspective that Weber wished to pursue the analysis of capitalism that Marx and Engels had undertaken. Weber did not seek to retrace the origins of capitalist institutions; instead, he wished to throw new light on the spirit of modern Western capitalism and on the values and mentality that characterize it, by showing the historical link which joins these values to a morality of religious origin.

Perhaps one could say more precisely that Weber demonstrated that capitalism would not have been able to develop as fully and broadly as it has done in the West if it had not received the support and impetus of a particularly favourable religious morality.

---

34. In particular, J. Broderick, s.j., *The Economic Morals of the Jesuits* (London: 1934).

In other sociological studies of religions, Weber showed that religious morality was generally unfavourable to the blossoming of the capitalist spirit; this was true in the case of Judaism, Hinduism, Buddhism, Confucianism and Taoism.[35] Ascetic Protestantism represents an exception, and this is what makes it a particularly important historical factor.

Three fundamental problems

In this sense, it can be said that Weber wished to demonstrate that religion, which Marx had considered an ideological reflection of the economic structure, could be a dynamic factor in economic change. But more specifically, what importance did Weber accord to this religious factor? In fact, this question poses three fundamental problems: (1) the link or *the interaction among the different factors*, and particularly among the cultural and structural factors, in the explanation of social and economic change; (2) *the continuity of the influence of the religious factor in modern Western history*; and (3) the *weighting* that it is possible to accord to different factors in change. Let us briefly analyze these three problems.

The interaction of factors

If one were reading Weber's brief thesis on Calvinism and capitalism alone, one would be tempted to believe that he had neglected all the other factors likely to explain the evolution of capitalism — the accumulation of capital; the formation of the middle class; urban development; geographical, technical and scientific discoveries and so forth. In the Preface that he wrote in 1930 for the English translation of the *Protestant Ethic and the Spirit of Capitalism*, R. H. Tawney wished to put readers on their guard against the dangerously unilateral view that he believed he could discern in Weber's thesis;[36] he corrected himself later, recognizing that his criticism and his reservations rested on erroneous premises.[37] In

---

35. Max Weber's main works in religious sociology have been translated into English: *The Religion of China: Confucianism and Taoism*, trans. H. H. Gerth (Glencoe, Ill.: The Free Press, 1950); *Ancient Judaism*, trans. H. H. Gerth and Don Martindale (Glencoe, Ill.: The Free Press, 1952); *The Religion of India: The Sociology of Hinduism and Buddhism*, trans. H. H. Gerth and Don Martindale (New York: The Free Press of Glencoe, Inc., 1958).

36. Weber, *The Protestant Ethic*.

37. R. H. Tawney in Max Weber, *Religion and the Rise of Capitalism* (New York: Harcourt, Brace and Company, 1937), preface.

another part of his work,[38] Weber unequivocally asserts the following points:

1. Religion is not the only factor which determines the economic ethic. This is influenced equally by economic, political and geographical conditions and imperatives.

2. Religion itself is not independent of the influence of economic, political and cultural factors.

3. In particular, it can be observed that all the great religions have been influenced by the life style of certain specific social categories, or certain social groups. Thus, Confucianism and Hinduism were long tied to a wealthy and educated class that was far removed from the people; Islam was spread by a class of warriors and knights; Christianity was influenced by the Ancient City, and was an urban religion, formulated by and for the citizens (and not the slaves).

4. The various influences which are exerted on the religious ethic and religious thought must not lead one to overlook another important fact: religious thought, and the morality that stems from it, are simultaneously responses to real *religious needs* which are endowed with a certain autonomy with respect to other spheres of human activity. This permits one to assert that the direction that a religion gives to life and behaviour is not merely an ideological reflection of material life conditions; it has other functions responding to the logic or structure of religious life itself which the purely Marxist analysis neglects or denies. Weber specifically used religious life as the means by which to trace the link between Calvinism and the spirit of capitalism, but at the same time he recognized the interplay of other influences on the evolution of both capitalism and ascetic Protestantism.

It is clear that Weber did not wish to suggest an explanation of modern Western capitalism on the basis of the religious factor alone. His historical knowledge was too broad and his scientific spirit too rigorous for him to be unaware of the multiplicity and complexity of the factors in play, of their mutual interaction and the joint or multiple influence that they have exerted on Western history. Weber would certainly not have repudiated Tawney's formula: "There was action and reaction, and while Puritanism helped to mold the social order, it was, in its turn, molded by it."[39]

---

38. Weber, "The Social Psychology of the World Religions," *Essays in Sociology*, pp. 264-301.
39. R. H. Tawney in Weber, *The Protestant Ethic*, preface, pp. 10-11.

In any case, it can be asserted that subsequent historical studies have amply demonstrated the merits of this position. To quote only one example, in a recent article Herman Israel demonstrated that if Puritanism effectively accelerated the emergence of industrial society in England in the seventeenth century, this action was part of "... the complex interaction of *interdependent* factors such as religion, the economy, and government with some consequent syntheses (resulting from the action of these factors and from their interaction)."[40]

The continuity of the influence of the religious factor

The second problem is the continuity of the influence of the religious factor in modern capitalism. If it is admitted that Calvinist morality exerted an influence on the development of capitalism in the eighteenth and nineteenth centuries, should it thus be concluded that this influence was maintained equally and continuously up to the present? This is equivalent to wondering whether the influence of the religious factor remains *constant* in history.

First, let us clearly establish that numerous studies have shown, without a doubt, that ascetic Protestantism was an active factor in the industrialization and economic development of the modern Western world. We can cite a brief example. It is admitted that scientific progress, and still more the acceptance and recognition of science and the scientific mentality, were essential to industrialization. But many studies have shown the predominant influence that ascetic Protestantism exerted on the scientific movement, not only through the educational institutions which grew from it, but still more through the favourable attitude it developed towards scientific studies and research and through the number of men of science that it supplied. Here let us mention particularly the studies of Robert Merton,[41] James B. Conant,[42] George

---

40. Herman Israel, "Some Religious Factors in the Emergence of Industrial Society in England," *American Sociological Review* 31 (October 1966): 590. Emphasis in the original.
41. Merton, "Puritanism, Pietism and Science," *Social Theory and Social Structure*.
42. James B. Conant, "The Advancement of Learning during the Puritan Commonwealth," *Proceedings of the Massachusetts Historical Society* 66 (1942): 3-31; also by the same author, *On Understanding Science* (New Haven: Yale University Press, 1947).

Rosen,[43] Paul Kocher[44] and Perry Miller.[45]

In a more general way, Protestantism (and not only ascetic Protestantism) is attributed a more favourable role in industrial development than is Catholicism. Taking electricity consumption per capita as the best universal index of the level of industrialization and economic activity of a country, and adjusting this index to allow for differences in natural resources, David McClelland showed that in 1950 the countries with a Protestant majority were, with a few exceptions, more advanced economically and technically than were the countries with a Catholic majority.[46] Knapp and Goodrich established that in the United States, Protestant institutions of higher learning educated many more men of science than did Catholic colleges or universities.[47] Bernard Rosen observed that American Catholics are more fatalistic, less optimistic and less disposed to foresee and plan the future than are Protestants;[48] H. W. Wendt discovered approximately the same differences in Germany.[49]

The gradual disappearance of religious differences

Other American studies have shown that if the economic attitudes of Catholics and Protestants were fairly different previously, they are much less so today. Both Catholics and Protestants participate in the culture and ethos of industrial American society. In a complex society like that of the United States, we can no longer expect to find completely homogeneous Catholic and Protestant religious communities which are insulated and clearly differentiated; instead, we observe sub-cultures within these two large religious

43. George Rosen, "Left-wing Puritanism and Science," *Bulletin of the Institute of the History of Science* 15 (1944): 375-80.
44. Paul H. Kocher, *Science and Religion in Elizabethan England* (San Marino, Calif.: The Huntingdon Library, 1953).
45. Perry Miller, *The New England Mind: From Colony to Province* (Cambridge, Mass.: Harvard University Press, 1954).
46. David C. McClelland, *The Achieving Society* (New York: The Free Press of Glencoe, Inc., 1961), pp. 50-53.
47. R. H. Knapp and H. B. Goodrich, *Origins of American Scientists* (Chicago: University of Chicago Press, 1952).
48. Bernard C. Rosen, "Race, Ethnicity, and the Achievement Syndrome," *American Sociological Review* 24, no. 1 (February 1959): 47-60.
49. Quoted by McClelland, *The Achieving Society*, pp. 360-61.

groups.[50] Miller and Swanson have observed that among the members of the middle class, the economic attitudes of American Catholics and Protestants are not differentiated; differences are apparent, however, among members of the lower class.[51] This observation supports the conclusions of several other researchers, particularly those of Bernard Rosen, who has noted that the ethnic group and social class to which the individual belongs are more important factors than religion in shaping attitudes towards life.[52] Thus we can conclude that the entrepreneurial spirit, which was initially closer to Protestantism and Calvinism than to Catholicism, is now part of American culture; recent immigrants who belong to various ethnic groups and the underprivileged classes share this spirit the least.

From all these studies, it is clear that Max Weber's perception was accurate when he suggested that ascetic Protestantism had played an active role in the evolution of capitalism and modern industrial society. But the influence of ascetic Protestantism has not remained constant; it has gradually weakened. As modern society becomes more complex, the influence of the religious factor on economic motivation and behaviour is less direct and immediate. It gradually gives way to such factors as class, ethnic group, regional location.

Here we return to an important point made earlier in this chapter: an historical factor does not act in an absolute fashion. Its influence depends on a particular context, on specific circumstances, and on the interplay of certain conditions. This rule may be called *the principle of the historical relativity of factors of social change.*

The weighting of factors

The third problem is more complicated. Once the simultaneous action and interaction of several factors is recognized, is it possible to weight these factors? Can we measure the degree of influence exerted on social change by each factor?

50. See in particular the survey by John Kosa and Leo D. Rachiele, "The Spirit of Capitalism, Traditionalism, and Religiousness: A Reexamination of Weber's Concepts," *The Sociological Quarterly* 4 (1963): 243-63.
51. D. R. Miller and G. E. Swanson, *The Changing American Parent* (New York: John Wiley and Sons, Inc., 1958).
52. Rosen, "Race and Ethnicity," pp. 55-60.

This is a methodological problem which the sociologist encounters very frequently in his studies, and to which he would like to be able to give a scientifically valid response. Let us notice that it is already a satisfying scientific achievement to have identified the main factors in social change. But we would like to go further and measure the weighting of each factor in history.

Some statistical techniques now exist which enable us to measure, with a fair amount of precision, the relative weight of several factors. But these techniques are still applicable only to relatively restricted problems, and in conditions where it is possible to reconstruct the equivalent of a laboratory experiment. But at the macrosociological level — where Max Weber's thesis is located — sociology does not possess satisfactory measuring instruments. It would be very daring to claim that, in the present state of knowledge, one could provide a scientific answer to the following questions: what was the exact weighting of Calvinism in the development of Western capitalism? What was the influence of the religious factor, as compared with other factors, in the history of capitalism?

Historical evolution at this macrosociological level is so complex that no one has yet succeeded in measuring with certainty the respective weight of each of the relevant factors. Historical and sociological science lead to approximations, if not to questions. This is why value judgements, personal choices and prophecy ultimately are substituted for strictly scientific analyses.

Conclusion

Although Weber's thesis, and the studies which it has inspired, stop short at this threshold and do not provide all the answers, they have provided some important lessons:

> 1. Values — in this case religious and moral values — can be factors of social and economic change.
> 2. The cultural factor (values in Weber's thesis), like the structural factor, cannot be considered to act exclusively; it acts jointly and in combination with other factors.
> 3. The studies subsequent to Weber's work, notably those carried out in the United States, confirm the principle of empirical relativism in the analysis of historical factors, and they provide a strong defence

against dogmatism — that is, against the idea of an absolute historical factor which exerts a constant and equal influence throughout history.

4. The questions which remain unanswered indicate the present limits of scientific knowledge insofar as it has not yet been possible to weight historical factors at the macrosociological level.

The study of human history requires at least as much intellectual humility as does the study of the evolution of the biological species. While biological evolution cannot be explained within the confines of magical or prefabricated formulae, this is even more true of the former. Social history results from particular *contingencies*, of which all the variables must be reconstructed. It is the product of the interaction of *a complex cluster of factors*, in which the relative weight of each is not always easy to measure precisely.

Ideologies

A long tradition

A long and solid tradition accords ideology a dynamic role in history. Many passages from Auguste Comte's work show that he saw in the positive state the product of an ideological revolution. The industrial society that he foresaw would result from the triumph of what could be called the ideology of technico-scientific organization. It was a new world view that would transform man's mentality as much as his living conditions. Similarly, the revolutionary class consciousness which, according to Marx and Engels, must initiate the class struggle and lead to the overthrow of capitalism could be clarified and motivated only by a new ideology which expressed the contradictions of society and the alienation of the proletariat. When Alexis de Tocqueville analyzed American democracy at the beginning of the nineteenth century, he considered it simultaneously as an egalitarian ideology, a style of life, and a governmental structure.

More recently, ideology has been the object of various specific studies. These studies have mainly examined the role that ideologies have played, and continue to play, in the young nations and in the developing countries. Other studies also have been concerned

with certain ideological phenomena in highly industrialized societies. We will try to summarize the main conclusions drawn from
this research.

Definition of ideology

Let us begin by recalling the definition of ideology stated in
Chapter 4: it is *a system of ideas and judgements, which are explicit and generally organized and which serve to describe, explain, interpret or justify the situation of a group or collectivity
and which, largely on the basis of values, suggest a precise orientation to the historical action of this group or collectivity.* Thus,
within culture, ideology appears as a particularly coherent and organized unit of perceptions and concepts. It is in this sense that it
can be described as a system, as the French-Canadian sociologist
Léon Dion has clearly demonstrated.[53]

Furthermore, the purpose of this system of thought is to explain
the social situation and to suggest the direction of historical action. In this way, from the viewpoint of sociologists, ideology is a
strategic phenomenon, enabling him to understand social reality
and its history *from the inside*. In fact, ideology is located at the
level of *society and history as they are experienced* — that is, at
the level of society as it is thought and felt, and of history as it is
desired, by the actors or a particular group of actors. By its very
nature, ideology is thus *an instrument of historical action*: it is
elaborated and diffused by actors who seek to influence the historical course of their society.

There are, however, other characteristics inherent to ideology
which help to make it a powerful dynamic factor. It is worth taking the time to consider them.

The rationality of ideology

First, since it takes the form of "a system of ideas and judgements," ideology is presented as *rational,* and sometimes even as
scientific. It is intended primarily to provide an explanation of a
reality which is often complicated and diffuse, if not confused.
This explanation generally is both logical and coherent, even if it

---

53. Léon Dion, "Opinion publique et systèmes idéologiques," *Ecrits du Canada
Français* 12 (1952): 9-171.

is also in most cases relatively simple. At least, it is *intellectually satisfying*, and it can be so both for the intelligentsia who develop it and for those who absorb only its framework or its elementary principles.

Enlightening or reassuring ideology

Second, this system of ideas and judgements enables those who experience a given situation to define it better, to comprehend its meaning, and to give it justification. Ideology says why and by whom one is exploited, why one's country is underdeveloped, why the white man can think himself superior, why the country is going to rack and ruin, why it is necessary to change the government. Thus, ideology may be *enlightening* or *reassuring*, depending on the particular case, or it may be both at the same time.

Ideology at the service of interests

Third, although it is a system of ideas and judgements, ideology is not abstract; it refers to *immediate individual and collective interests*. Whether it is addressed to someone who wishes to protect and maintain his position or to someone who wishes to improve it, ideology is always directed to the interested party. It refers to factual situations, which it justifies or questions according to the interests that it expresses and represents.

The appeal to powerful psychological states

Fourth, because it touches interests, ideology is linked to *powerful psychological states*, which are often diffused or latent. These psychological states are mainly of two kinds. They may be anxiety states, generally provoked by change or upsets, or by the mere possibility of changes and the insecurity or uncertainty that they entail. Anxiety may be weak, and may manifest itself in the form of uneasiness or a vague disquiet; or it may be acute, and take the form of a strong fear, distress or even panic. Anxiety states generally create ideologies of a conservative or reactionary type.

Psychological states may also be characterized by *aggression*, resulting from a long period of individual and collective frustration. Ordinarily, aggression entails a mixture of hostile attitudes to an adversary or scapegoat and new utopic or dream-like aspirations. Aggressive states are more likely to produce ideologies of a reformist or revolutionary type.

The common action of a community

Fifth, ideology seeks to satisfy these powerful psychological states by suggesting a *common action* which will bring a degree of security to the anxious, or open the door to the expression of anger and the attainment of aspirations among the aggressive. Thus, ideology appeals to a community; it encourages individuals to group within a unit with which they can be identified and which will bring them a feeling of power and strength. The community may be a social class, a political party, a nation, a social movement, and so forth.

The ideological community is often simplified and sometimes almost personalized in order to enable individuals to identify with it and what it represents, and to permit a transfer to it of their anxiety or aggression.

Values and ideology

Sixth, the ideological community generally serves to symbolize and crystallize the *values* to which ideology appeals and by which it is supported. These values may belong to a more or less distant past; they may pertain to the present, or they may be new.

Let us emphasize that ideology is one of the main areas where new values are created. Often diffuse or latent, these new values finally find their formulation in an ideological model which clarifies them. Moreover, what are called new values are really old or contemporary values which ideology redefines in a new context, or gives a meaning that was formerly implicit, or presents in a different light through the arrangement of these values in a new system of ideas and judgements.

It is this reference to values which mainly distinguishes ideology from science, with which it often seeks to be identified. Ideology simultaneously includes factual judgements and value judgements; it judges reality while describing it, and it explains it while judging it.

The voluntaristic nature of ideology

Finally, ideology is voluntaristic. It appeals to a will to act by suggesting goals to be attained, by indicating the means to attain them and by elaborating a more or less specific procedure. Its judgements lead to concrete solutions which aim to be realistic or realizable, and on such an active level as to permit their application in the near or distant future. Specifically, ideology attempts to bend the course of history in the direction that it desires. Whether this is under cover of determinism ("follow the direction of history") or whether its voluntaristic nature is openly suggested, ideology always seeks the same goal — to motivate the historical action of a collectivity.

Ideology: a socio-psychological phenomenon

The main characteristics of ideology that have just been enumerated show clearly that, strictly speaking, it is *a socio-psychological phenomenon*. First, it is linked to sociology in several respects: through the collective situation that it explains, justifies and judges; through the values by which it is supported; through the symbolism by which it is surrounded; through the adherence to the community that it encourages and through the common action that it suggests. For this reason, ideology has already been presented (in Chapter 4) as part of culture; it was even said to be a hard kernel of culture, precisely because of its systematic, rigorous, explicit and voluntaristic nature. In addition, ideologies have given rise to a number of sociological studies, mainly through the influence of Marx and Mannheim,[54] most of them from the perspective of the sociology of knowledge. Similarly, in political science, ideology has been the subject of a great number of studies.[55]

---

54. Karl Mannheim, *Ideology and Utopia*, trans. Louis Wirth and Edward Shils (New York: Harcourt, Brace and World, Inc., 1936). In particular the reader can consult the critical bibliography by Norman Birnbaum, "The Sociological Study of Ideology" (1940-1960), *Current Sociology* (London: Oxford University Press, 1961).

55. An example of this will be found in the analysis by Jean Meynaud and Alain Lancelot, *Les attitudes politiques* (Paris: Presses universitaires de France, Collection "Que sais-je?," 1964); see also Jean Meynaud, *Destin des idéologies* (Lausanne: 1961). An excellent bibliography will be found in David E. Apter, ed., *Ideology and Discontent* (Glencoe, Ill.: The Free Press, 1964).

But ideology is also linked to psychology. It is strengthened by the anxiety or aggression which is latent among the members of a collectivity; it encourages the transfer of these feelings to a community, through the identification of individuals with the group or collectivity that this community represents. Some authors have attempted to carry out a psychoanalysis of ideologies,[56] but little is known on this subject.

This fusion of the sociological and psychological levels in ideology clearly gives it an exceptional strength of action. Around it are concentrated obscure but powerful and sometimes explosive psychological energies, which are at the service of precisely defined collectivities, clearly identified objectives, and methodically elaborated schemes of action. The needs and aspirations of individuals join with the anxieties and ambitions of collectivities, in a union where individual psychological states and collective attitudes are cumulative and thus mutually reinforcing.

False consciousness and true consciousness

It is clear at this point that there is a great divergence between the Marxist analysis of ideology and the analysis of ideologies in contemporary sociology. In the Marxist model, ideology and its social functions are defined exclusively from the perspective of the dominant class; ideology is that class's perception of the situation according to its position and its interests. When adopted by other social classes, ideology is an opium for them, because it alienates their consciousness and stifles their revolutionary energies. Perceived in this way, ideology is a false consciousness of reality, because it is a distorted perception which is destined to maintain a status quo that is favourable to the dominant class.

Marx contrasts class consciousness with ideology. The former is an awakening of real class interests and of the political and revolutionary action necessary to overthrow the dominant class. Through class consciousness, the contradictions of the objective situation are clearly perceived, judged and fought.

This radical opposition between ideology and class consciousness neglects an essential point — that class consciousness also occurs through ideology. True consciousness, in contrast to

---

56. In particular, Charles Hanly, "A Psychoanalysis of Nationalist Sentiment" in *Nationalism in Canada*, ed. Peter Russell (Toronto: McGraw-Hill Company of Canada Limited, 1966), pp. 303-19.

false consciousness, does not emerge naturally and spontaneously from a state of unconsciousness. Usually, it results from a systematic explanation of the situation by the definers of a new ideology. This new ideology presents a view of the situation that is different from the one which prevailed before; in relation to the dominant ideology, the new system is a counter-ideology.

It is understandable, then, why in contemporary sociology it is believed that ideology can produce true consciousness as well as false consciousness. In itself, ideology is neither alienating nor enlightening; all depends on its context. But, because it contributes to true consciousness, ideology is a factor in social change, and it is mainly from this perspective that it has been studied in recent years.

Ideology and true consciousness

When we say that ideology can develop true consciousness among the members of a collectivity, or at least among some of them, we mean that, in describing and explaining a situation, in making the values explicit, in presenting a system of ideas and judgements, ideology brings to the conscious level feelings and thoughts which used to be unconscious or semi-conscious because they were confused, stifled, inhibited and unspoken. To these ideas and feelings, ideology gives words and formulae through which they can be expressed and recognized. What was felt only subjectively suddenly takes on an objective quality. Thus, ideology *reveals* to the members of a group or society what they already thought and felt obscurely, as if subconsciously. In an explicit way, it often presents itself as a "coming to consciousness."

Ideology also contributes to true consciousness through the objectives that it suggests and the means of action that it proposes. It paints a possible future; it specifies the meaning of unexpressed aspirations; it arouses and strengthens hopes, desires and ambitions. Ideology focuses on the future, and brings forward new hopes which were formerly repressed.

In addition, ideology generally simplifies. It selects certain elements of the situation, links them together through "obvious" or easily comprehensible reasoning, and constructs an apparently clear explanatory system. This is why ideology is often expressed in shock-language ("Blacks are lazy," "Jews are robbers"). This capacity for simplification makes ideology a powerful instrument for the process of "coming to consciousness."

The action of ideologies

Through the true consciousness that it develops, *ideology frees energies and at the same time channels them*. Some writers have hypothesized that with the decline of religious faith in the modern world, ideologies have gathered energies diffused in the supernatural, mystical and magical world, in order to use them in the temporal and social order. This hypothesis is interesting and well founded. In any case, it is certain that the modern world has witnessed the multiplication and increasing attraction of ideologies. And these ideologies — as many concrete examples show — have had the effect of raising the level of the aspirations of individuals and collectivites; awakening ambitions and hopes; supporting large collective undertakings; and in some cases, radically transforming the course of history.

Other writers have wondered whether we are not witnessing the end of ideology. In a book with precisely this title, Daniel Bell wrote in 1960: "In the last decade, we have witnessed an exhaustion of the nineteenth-century ideologies, particularly Marxism, as intellectual systems that could claim *truth* for their views of the world."[57] But it seems clear that we are witnessing, not the decline of ideologies, but their extension throughout the world. There is a great ideological resurgence in the West, and perhaps even more in Africa and Asia.

In advanced industrial society, which is characterized by the raising of the level of education and simultaneously by the complexity of social organization and power structures, it would be very astonishing to witness the decline of ideologies. Rather, it seems that they will continue to find the socio-psychological conditions favourable to their multiplication, diffusion and function.

Classification of ideologies

In order to explain fully the influence of ideologies, and to understand better the context in which they develop true rather than false consciousness, it is necessary to use a typology of ideologies. Up to now, we have spoken of ideology as a relatively simple phe-

---

57. Daniel Bell, *The End of Ideology* (Glencoe, Ill.: The Free Press, 1960), p. 16. On the subject of this debate, the reader can consult Raymond Aron, "Fin de l'âge idéologique?," *Sociologica*, Frankfurt am Main (1955): 219-33; and Meynaud, *Destin des idéologies*.

nomenon. In fact, it is a very complex phenomenon, according to its different concrete forms.

It is possible to classify ideologies according to at least four criteria: the group towards which the ideology is directed; the relationships between ideology and power; the means of action that it suggests; and its content.

1. *a*. Ideology may be directed towards one or several *particular groups* within a total society — a social class, a profession and so forth. Thus, trade union ideology is designed for workers and employees; there also exists an ideology of the liberal professions.

> *b*. Ideology may express the aspirations of a *total society*, as is notably the case with nationalism.
>
> *c*. Ideology may be addressed to an *international or super-national collectivity*. Marxist communism, particularly in its early days, was directed towards the international working class ("Workers of the world, unite!").

2. Ideology is always (or almost always) based on power, and consequently takes on a political aspect. Thus, one can distinguish between:

> *a*. the ideology which expresses the viewpoint of a *group in power* — for example, the ideology of a dominant class or of a technocracy;
>
> *b*. the ideology of a *group which aims at succeeding to power* — for example, that of a minority political party, or of the opposition;
>
> *c*. the ideology of a *group which seeks to influence power*, without coming to power — such as the ideology of pressure groups.

3. In terms of its means of action, ideology may be:

> *a. reformist*, if it suggests a progressive plan for the transformation of a given situation;
>
> *b. revolutionary*, if it suggests using violent and illegal means, such as agitation and subversion.

4. Finally, in its content, ideology may be:

> *a. reactionary*, if it suggests solutions which constitute a return to the past;
>
> *b. conservative*, if it values the status quo;
>
> *c. progressive* or *liberal*, if it suggests the abandonment

of certain traditions in favour of changes judged to be essential;

d. radical, if it desires a complete or almost complete break with the existing situation.

Also a distinction is made between:

1. *leftist* ideology, generally of Marxist, socialist or socialist-directed origins, or sometimes even of democratic ones; and

2. *rightist* ideology, of more traditional origins, which is more conservative or reactionary.

These last two expressions (*left* and *right*), which are often ambiguous in themselves, lead to even more subtle distinctions, such as the extreme left, left-of-centre, centre, right-of-centre and the extreme right.

We should note the richness of current vocabulary in ideology, the confusion which often accompanies it or which it perhaps serves to express, and the different meanings that all these expressions can take on, according to the context.

Ideology, then, is anything but a simple reality. A complete analysis of the phenomenon should be able to take into account all the distinctions of concrete reality. This is obviously not possible here; we will be giving only a few indications.

The conservative ideology of a particular group

The ideology of a particular group which has power and has easy access to political power generally will be conservative and sometimes reactionary. It will be located somewhere between the centre and the right; if it accepts or supports changes, it will always be through moderately reformist means.

This type of ideology is particularly well illustrated by the studies that American sociologists have made of the ideology of American businessmen.[58] Businessmen need to find a justification for their privileged status, their authority and power; in addition, they are subject to all sorts of tensions, constraints and pressures. Their ideology thus justifies and reassures them through its con-

---

58. Reinhard Bendix, *Work and Authority in Industry: Ideologies of Management in the Course of Industrialization* (New York: Harper and Row, 1956); F. X. Sutton et al., *The American Business Creed* (Cambridge, Mass.: Harvard University Press, 1956).

servatism and moderation and through the devalued perception that it provides of those under their command.

In addition, businessmen compete with those with whom they have common interests. Their ideology emphasizes what unites them over and above what opposes them.

Finally, they have ambiguous relationships with political power. They are close to it and, while fearing its intervention, seek its favours. This ambiguity is reflected in their ideology, which is a mixture of conservatism and liberalism.

In relation to social change, an ideology of this kind is adaptive. It does not provoke change but favours a progressive adaptation to change when it has occurred or has become inevitable. This is very clearly shown in Reinhard Bendix's historical study.

The reactionary or radical ideology of a particular group

A particular group which attacks power or which seeks to influence it can develop an ideology which is either reactionary and rightist, or progressive or radical and leftist. In fact, a rightist ideology often has more in common with a leftist ideology than with a central ideology. The ideology of the centre is a conservative and adaptive ideology; the ideologies of the right and left suggest changes for a situation considered unsatisfactory.

Thus, reactionary and radical ideologies may exist together simultaneously — for example, in the working class. Here they express its ambiguous situation and divided aspirations.[59] The same phenomenon can be observed in the ideologies of populist peasant movements and in the violent revolts which they provoke, and which are generally quickly suppressed.[60] Often, it is only after a period of such ambiguities that a radical ideology will finally take root among an underprivileged group, as is presently the case, for example, with the Black Power ideology among the Negroes of the United States.[61]

---

59. Certain analytical elements of an ideology of the working class will be found in the interesting study by Ely Chinoy, *Automobile Workers and the American Dream* (Garden City, New York: Doubleday and Company Inc., 1955); also in the older study by W. L. Warner and J. O. Low, *The Social System of the Modern Factory* (New Haven: Yale University Press, 1941).

60. See, for example, Roland Mousnier, *Fureurs paysannes, Les paysans dans les révoltes au XVIIe siècle (France, Russie, Chine)* (Paris: Calmann-Levy, 1967).

61. On this subject, see in particular Floyd B. Barbour, ed., *The Black Power Revolt. A Collection of Essays* (Boston: Porter Sargent, 1968).

Thus, the ideology of an underprivileged group which is far from power may be a factor in change, but in various and even opposite directions. It should not be believed that the ideology that is elaborated in these groups is always and necessarily radical; in fact, various ideologies can usually be found within them, covering a very wide spectrum from the extreme right to the extreme left.

The national ideology of a total society

An ethnic or national collectivity and a total society need a certain ideology to define what they are, and what is specific to them and characteristic of them. For every national or ethnic collectivity, and perhaps still more for the one which is seeking and questioning its identity and destiny, the national or nationalist ideology clearly establishes the territory that belongs to it, specifying its frontiers and sometimes giving it a new name; it demarcates the shape of the national group, identifying those who are of the community and those who are excluded from it; it defines its rights, aspirations and destiny; it names its enemies or adversaries; it reads its future in its past and its present.

Thus, nationalism serves to clarify what is called *national identity*, an expression which at the sociological level implies the definition of a collective entity, and at the psychological level suggests an encouragement to individuals to identify themselves with this community and to find within it a part of their personal identity. These socio-psychological functions of ideology are particularly essential to the young emerging and developing nations.[62]

The complexity of national ideology

National ideology is a complex phenomenon. It is directed at a total society (or one that aims to be) composed of many diversified groups and sub-groups. It is particularly important in this case, therefore, to know which group or groups define, support and propagate it. In the next chapter, we will study in more detail the elites and groups which define and diffuse national ideology. At this point let us simply note an important consequence: national ideology is not in itself conservative, reactionary or radical. Its orientation depends on the groups which express it.

---

62. An excellent example will be found in Bernard Lewis, *The Emergence of Modern Turkey* (London: Oxford University Press, 1961).

Also, national ideology can be profoundly changed in a short period of time. This evolution is directly related to the groups or elites which confront or succeed each other, and which claim to be or wish to be the spokesmen of the complete collectivity. Marcel Rioux has described such a development in the case of the nationalist ideology in Quebec.[63] He notes three successive national ideologies:

> 1. "the ideology of conservation," which was conservative and reactionary, and which dominated French Canada from the second half of the nineteenth century until the Second World War;
> 2. "the ideology of protest and recovery," which exerted a growing influence from 1940 to 1960; contrary to the preceding one, it "is resolutely centered on the present, and asks that the Quebec culture be brought up to date and spread throughout Canada";
> 3. finally, "the ideology of development and participation," which has appeared recently; "more radical" than the ideology of protest, it defines not French Canada, but rather an independent, socialist and secular Quebec.

This evolution of ideologies is both a reflection and a factor in social change. On the one hand, it is the index of structural changes; but, on the other hand, each of these ideologies has exerted and continues to exert an influence on the historical action of the national collectivity in Quebec.

Unanimity, division and opposition

From the various active forms that ideology adopts, as briefly outlined above, it is possible to derive some more general ideological influences. In fact, it can be stated that ideology initiates change, or opposes it, because *it creates unanimity at the same time that it entails division and opposition*. It is in the nature of ideology to unite and to separate simultaneously.

On the one hand, ideology creates *unanimity*. It encourages identification and participation in some community; it invokes common interests or a common cause; it suggests collective action.

---

63. Marcel Rioux, "Sur l'évolution des idéologies au Québec," *Revue de l'Institut de sociologie* 1 (1968): 95-124.

Sometimes ideology camouflages actual divisions or specifically asks that they be forgotten, at least temporarily. This is the case, in particular, of ideologies which are directed towards total societies — nationalism, patriotism, federalism and internationalism. But whether directed towards a particular group or a total society, the goal of ideology is always the same: the persons concerned discover themselves within the system of ideas that it suggests, and solidarity or unanimity arise from this fusion of interests and minds. In this sense, ideology provokes reactions and attitudes of the community rather than the society type, according to Tönnies' distinction.

On the other hand, however, ideology engenders *differentiations* and *social divisions*. To the extent that ideology unites some individuals, it distinguishes and separates them from others. It segregates those who belong to the community from those who cannot belong. It highlights the distinctive characteristics which are common to a collectivity (cultural and national traits, class interests, regional characteristics) and which permit it to be identified through confrontation with other collectivities. It is here that ideology will be particularly selective in its perception of reality: in its choice of the elements that comprise its system, all that serves to particularize a collectivity is highlighted and valued.

In some cases, the differentiation becomes *opposition*. Thus unanimity is created through the refusal or rejection of others or through conflict with others. For this purpose, others are described in the ideology as being dangerous, menacing and sometimes even perverse; their intentions are doubted, their good will is challenged, their motives and actions are reinterpreted, and their conspiracies denounced. Others are not only different; they become an adversary against which ideology encourages a struggle.

Ideologies and their context

If ideology is the powerful factor in change that we have claimed it to be, at the same time it cannot act by itself. It requires expression and manipulation through the agents of change, notably elites, pressure groups, parties and social movements (we will discuss this in greater detail in the following chapter).

Moreover, ideology in itself cannot be considered a unique factor in change. The analysis of ideologies always refers to their context. An ideology expresses the particular aspirations, fears or ambitions of a collectivity, and the struggles of a group or groups in a specific historical period.

Meynaud and Lancelot have emphasized that ideologies can acquire "a sort of autonomous life, or a kind of relative autonomy, which leads to placing some of them against the current of social evolution; some are seen to be in advance of the time while others no longer correspond to the requirements of the period." But it still remains true, according to the same authors, that "ideology expresses a perspective on the world; it is a rationalized and abstract system which stems, at least partially, from the social struggle while still helping to mold it."[64] The great point of interest of Bendix's study on the ideology of businessmen and entrepreneurs is that he showed how this ideology has evolved in its content and role, following changes in technology, the evolution of values, political changes and so forth. He writes: "Ideologies are formulated through the constant play of interactions between present contingencies and past heritage."[65] And Marcel Rioux notes: "In a complex society, the ideological conflict mainly translates the conflict of sub-groups who struggle to get their theory of society accepted by the majority and, finally, to direct this society."[66]

Thus, ideology belongs to a particular combination of factors. It is linked to structural forms, values and symbols. This is clearly demonstrated by the fact that some ideologies are born and die without exerting any influence, while others are engraved deeply in history. The factors and conditions which are favourable and unfavourable to the efficient action of ideologies are undoubtedly numerous and mysterious; they still remain to be studied.

Conflicts and Contradictions

When we referred in Chapter 7 to the debate which opposed Lewis and Redfield, we said that it was a question of a confrontation between two conceptions of sociology (and anthropology). One, supported by Redfield, emphasizes the integrated nature of social units and the processes which work together for the integration of

---

64. Meynaud and Lancelot, *Les attitudes politiques*, pp. 101 and 102.
65. Bendix, *Work and Authority*, p. 443.
66. Rioux, "Des idéologies au Quebec," p. 110.

the parts and the whole — the institutionalization of models, values and roles, socialization and social control. The other, upheld by Lewis, stresses the numerous conflicts which constantly disturb society and instigate structural changes within it that may be quite violent and abrupt.

Later we will discuss this opposition and consider to what other phenomenon it corresponds. But we must touch on it here as we approach our analysis of conflicts and contradictions as a factor in social change. Indeed, the study of this factor of change has provided the basis for a sociological school of conflict which claims, or is said, to be in opposition to the sociology of integration.

The sociology of conflict: Ralf Dahrendorf

It is obviously not difficult to trace the origins of the sociology of conflict to Marx and Engels. We have seen earlier, in this chapter and in Chapter 6, the historical role that Marx and Engels attributed to the class struggle, and to the revolutions which resulted from the necessary opposition between the owners of the means of production and the working masses. Since the time of Marx and Engels, however, the definition of social classes, and the roles of conflicts, class struggles and revolutions have been the subject of many analyses and discussions. In addition, the industrial society that Marx and Engels knew has itself evolved, and not necessarily in the way they foresaw.

Since Marx and Engels, then, the sociology of social classes and social conflicts has made important progress. For the purposes of our discussion, we will refer to the work of one of the main contemporary sociologists to have studied these problems. This is the German sociologist Ralf Dahrendorf.[67] He is often considered one of the main representatives of the sociology of conflicts (in addition to the American sociologist L. A. Coser[68]), although he was influenced more strongly by the work of Georg Simmel[69] than by Marxist sociology.

---

67. We will refer here to Ralf Dahrendorf, *Class and Class Conflict in Industrial Society* (Stanford: Stanford University Press, 1959).
68. L. A. Coser, *The Functions of Social Conflict* (Glencoe, Ill.: The Free Press, 1958) and by the same author, "Social Conflict and Social Change," *British Journal of Sociology* 8 (September 1957): 197-207.
69. See in particular Georg Simmel, *Conflict and the Web of Group-Affiliations*, trans. Kurt H. Wolff and Reinhard Bendix (Glencoe, Ill.: The Free Press, 1955).

Dahrendorf's aim is to construct a theoretical model with a dual goal: to explain the *formation* of conflict groups, and to account for the *action* by which they entail structural changes (in Parsons' meaning of the term) in the social system. According to Dahrendorf, this is the dual goal that every theory of social classes, and in a more general way, every sociology of conflict pursues.

For this purpose, Dahrendorf undertakes a long critical analysis of Marx's thought and of those who have been guided by Marx or have criticized him — notably Schumpeter, Renner, Geiger, Burnham, Lipset, Bendix and Parsons.

Marx's four fundamental contributions

According to Dahrendorf, in Marx's work we can find four basic contributions to the sociology of conflicts. First, Marx highlighted *the permanence of conflicts in every society*. Conflict, Dahrendorf remarks, always accompanies life; everything that lives experiences constant states of conflict. Society, which is a reality animated by living beings, is not exempt from this rule; conflict is inherent to its nature and functioning. Marx remains the main sociologist to have attributed to this fact the importance that it merits.

Second, Marx understood that *social conflicts, being conflicts of interest, necessarily set two groups, and only two groups, in opposition*. In society, every conflict of interests is reduced to an opposition between those who are interested in maintaining and perpetuating a situation from which they profit, and those who are interested, or believe they are interested, in changing the situation. Whatever might be the immediate object of a social conflict, the position of the opponents is always defined in relation to the status quo. And in relation to the status quo, the only possible choice, in the final analysis, is between maintaining it and changing it. Of course, there can be more or less radical positions among those who desire change, and more or less rigid positions among those who are opposed to it. But this does not negate the fact that conflict can always be analyzed in terms of two large units of persons and groups whose interests are irrevocably opposed.

Third, Marx understood perfectly that *conflict is the main motivating force of history*. Conflict necessarily brings change in either the long or the short run. It is in and through the opposition between various interest groups that social structures are transformed. As will be seen later, Marx was not able to analyze correctly the means by which conflict engenders change. But at least he established the principle of the explanation of change through conflict.

Finally, by his analysis of change through class conflict, Marx opened the door to the search for *structural factors in social change*. In fact, two main classes of factors of change can be distinguished:

> 1. *exogenous* forces, which intervene from outside the social system; this is the case, for example, with the influences of the physical environment and climate, and also with the diffusion of techniques and knowledge that have been studied by anthropologists;
> 2. *endogenous* forces of change are engendered by the social system itself; they arise from its own functioning and structure.

It is a characteristic of the social system that its functioning creates forces which change it. Marx understood this very well. It is this fact which lends particular interest — at least methodologically — to his analysis of the class struggle which results, according to Marx, from the structural contradictions within society and, more particularly, within capitalist society.

Marx's three errors

Dahrendorf considers that Marx committed certain analytical errors from which the sociology of conflicts has had to, and still must, disentangle itself. He criticizes Marxist analysis mainly for three fundamental errors.

Social conflicts and class conflicts

First, *Marx reduced all social conflicts, or at least the historically important social conflicts, to class conflicts*. This, according to Dahrendorf, is an extreme simplification. The class (as will be seen later) is only one of the interest groups which opposes the members of a society, and the class struggle is only one of the conflicts of interest which divide the society. All the other conflicts which agitate society cannot necessarily be reduced to the class struggle, as Marx supposed, even though this may happen under some circumstances. Marx generalized erroneously on the basis of a particular type of conflict — the class struggle — and a particular situation, in which all the social conflicts are reduced to class conflicts. The state of capitalist society at the beginning of the nineteenth century appeared to support him. Today, it is no longer possible to perpetuate this error.

Class conflicts and revolution

Second, *Marx believed that class conflict led inevitably to revolution.* This seemed to him the only possible outcome of the class struggle. But it can be empirically demonstrated that the class struggle can experience other outcomes than revolution. Again, the total overthrow of a regime by a violent revolution is only one particular case and, it can be added, an exceptional one in the history of class conflict. What is much more often observed is a dominant class which borrows new ideas and itself effects changes which are sufficient to nullify the potential revolutionary factors.

Here Dahrendorf offers an important criticism of Marx. He points out that Marx propounds a clearly *static analysis of the class struggle.* According to Marx, everything which precedes a revolution only contributes to the construction of a *system* of class opposition which, once it has attained its extreme point of perfection, explodes and destroys itself, giving way to a new system which, in turn, progressively builds itself up. Thus, in Marxist analysis, the revolution is the only really dynamic moment in history. But this interpretation of history, which is valid in some special cases, neglects all other forms of evolution without revolution. More precisely, it hides all the structural changes which can result from the very existence of the class struggle. This does not necessarily lead to the perfection of a system of class opposition; more often, it produces constant changes in the system itself, and these changes enable the system to perpetuate itself as it evolves. This is precisely why real revolutions are rare in history, and why the dominant classes are seldom overthrown.

Classes, class conflicts and ownership

Finally, *Dahrendorf's third criticism of Marx is that he located the origin of social classes and class conflicts in the ownership of the means of production.* This error lies at the foundation of Marx's utopic prophecy that a classless society would emerge following the disappearance of the principle of ownership. Undoubtedly, in the early nineteenth century capitalist society that Marx knew, ownership and control of the means of production appeared necessarily linked. The later evolution of capitalism, however, showed that they could be dissociated. In the large firm which is characteristic of modern capitalism, ownership is often shared among thousands of shareholders who exert no control; control effectively belongs to the technocrats and bureaucrats, who have no right of ownership in the firm. It is thus the control of the means of production, rather than its ownership, that is the essential and dominant factor in class conflict.

The aim of Dahrendorf's model

According to Dahrendorf, this statement entails important changes in perspective. In particular, it is necessary to find another source of social and class conflicts than the ownership of the means of production alone. Similarly, the concept of social class should be redefined; for it is not, as Marx believed, a reality which is primarily and essentially economic, since it is more closely linked to power than to ownership. Finally, it is necessary to re-analyze the historical role of class conflicts from this new perspective.

This is the task that Dahrendorf undertakes in elaborating his theoretical model of conflict and change. His critical analysis of Marxist sociology enabled him both to pose the problems of a sociology of conflict, and to indicate the routes for a solution to these problems.

Guided by Marx's teaching, Dahrendorf emphasizes the need to seek *the structural sources* of conflict. For example, it would not be sufficient to explain social conflicts in exclusively psychological terms, as if they resulted only from personal feelings, or from the mood or emotions of the members of society. It is in the structure of social organization and in its mode of functioning that the permanent source which stimulates and strengthens conflicts should be sought.

The unequal distribution of authority

According to Dahrendorf, the main structural source of social conflict is not the unequal distribution of the ownership of the means of production, as Marx believed; rather, it is *the unequal distribution of authority* among individuals and groups. In defining authority, Dahrendorf is guided by Max Weber: authority is the "probability that a command with a given specific content will be obeyed by a given group of persons." In these terms, authority is distinguished from power, which Weber defines as being "the probability that one actor within a social relationship will be in a position to carry out his own will despite resistance, regardless of the basis on which this probability rests." Power is attached to the individual; it can depend on an individual's physical force, his talent, his charisma, as well as on the position that he occupies. By contrast, authority is attached strictly to the position occupied, or to the role fulfilled in a social organization. If the structural source of conflicts is being sought, it is in authority and not in power that it may be found. Thus Dahrendorf is concerned with authority, and not with power.

Authority exists in every human collectivity; it is a necessary part of the very fabric of social organization. Obviously it can take different forms and be asserted in various ways. But it is constantly present, if only to coordinate the activities of actors. Social organization is theoretically and practically unthinkable without authority, and without a distribution of authority.

Thus, in every collectivity, there are always individuals or groups who exert a greater or lesser authority, and individuals and groups who are subject to this authority. Consequently, there are always relationships based on the opposition of domination–subjection among individuals and groups. Some individuals and groups dominate; others are subordinate.

The dichotomy of authority

Like wealth, authority is unequally distributed. But between wealth and authority, there is an important distinction. In the unequal distribution of goods, some have more than others; but even those who have the least still have something. In contrast, Dahrendorf maintains that authority is so distributed that some share it while others are totally deprived of it. This is what he calls *the dichotomy of authority*, and it is the essential feature of his explanation.

It is not always easy to observe this dichotomy concretely. In any case, it cannot generally be observed in a total society; we will see why later. Instead, a particular collectivity (for example, a church, a firm or an association) should be taken as the unit of observation if the dichotomy is to be discerned. In other words, the dichotomy of authority can be observed easily only within a limited collectivity whose activities are coordinated on an unvarying basis.

The dichotomy of authority and conflict of interests

The dichotomy of authority has a very important consequence: a conflict of interests necessarily results between those who wield authority and those who obey. Those who occupy positions of command have certain interests in common which cannot be shared by those who are subject to authority; conversely, those in a position of subjection share certain interests from the very fact of their common situation.

At the extreme, the divergent interests of those who command and those who obey are contrary interests. Thus, conflict of interests is always *an opposition of interests*. As we saw earlier, Marx correctly perceived that the main interest that those who command have in common is the maintenance of the status quo. The main interest shared by those who are subject to authority is the change or reversal of the status quo. The interests of both are unreconcilable by their very nature.

Consequently, conflict of interests always sets in opposition two sets of individuals or groups, and only two — those who are interested in maintaining the status quo, and those who are interested in changing it. As stated earlier, whatever might be the positions of the opposing parties in a conflict, they must always be able to be reduced analytically to this duality. *The dichotomy of authority logically entails the duality of opponents.*

In addition, as authority is an essential element in social organization, it can be deduced that conflict is always present in society. *The permanence of conflict in social life is thus explained by the structural origin of conflict.* Authority and the division of authority are inherent necessities in the structure and functioning of the social system; but at the same time, they constantly spark conflicts which affect and modify the system.

Quasi-group and interest group

It is important to distinguish between two types of opposing groups. For example, individuals occupying different positions of command in the same association do not necessarily form a group in the sociological meaning of the term. They may have certain interests in common, linked to their common situation, without forming a group as a result. To designate this unit, Dahrendorf employs the term *quasi-group*. Quasi-groups are really social categories rather than groups — for example, consumers, businessmen, students. In contrast, by *interest group* he means a group of individuals who possess a certain degree of organization, an explicit program of action, and fairly precise goals. This is the case, for example, with a trade union, a political party and a social movement.

According to Dahrendorf, it is the interest group and not the quasi-group which is the true active agent in the conflict of interests. The interest group in effect serves to crystallize the reasons for conflict, to make them explicit, and to polarize the actions of individuals and sub-groups.

Latent and manifest interests

For this to be true, however, one further condition must exist. What Dahrendorf calls *latent interests* must become *manifest interests*. Latent interests guide the behaviour of actors, without being consciously recognized by them; manifest interests are conscious motives which guide the action of actors. Obviously, latent interests provoke a conflict of interests; but being neither conscious nor explicit, they can only give rise to the formation of quasi-groups, which consequently are unlikely to defend common interests in an organized and premeditated way. In contrast, manifest interests are much more powerful factors of conflict; around them form active interest groups (political parties, trade unions, social movements), capable of specifying objectives, elaborating a policy of action and practising a strategy. Here is recognized, in different language and in another analytical context, what Marx called class consciousness and politicized consciousness, which he saw as an essential element in the class struggle.

It should be noticed, however, that Dahrendorf's notion of interest group does not correspond to Marx's notion of social class. As has already been said, Dahrendorf adopts as the analytical unit of departure the framework of a restricted and partial organization (a church, a firm and so on). It is with reference to this framework that he analyzes the dichotomy of authority and its consequences. In this context, it cannot be said that the interest groups defined by Dahrendorf are social classes, even if their behaviour and action resemble those that Marx attributed to social classes.

Pluralism and the superimposition of groups and conflicts

If we now consider a total society, we cannot observe within it a dichotomy of authority as clearly as we can in a partial organization. The reason for this is that individuals or groups exerting authority within a particular organization may lack authority in other sectors of society. The social actors and groups may belong to a dominant group or quasi-group in one context and to a subject group or quasi-group in another. This is what Dahrendorf calls a situation of *pluralism* of opposition and conflicts. It is impossible for a confrontation to result from this which will challenge the total society itself.

In practice, however, the pluralism of opposition and conflicts is much more limited than we have suggested. The same individuals, the same groups, exerting authority in one sector or organization generally enjoy authority in other sectors or organizations. Then what Dahrendorf calls a *superimposition* of interest groups is produced. Within the whole of the total society, to a very large extent one finds approximately the same cleavage as in partial organizations. It is thus that the notion of interest group encounters that of social class, and that the notion of conflict of interests rejoins that of the class struggle. Social class is the product of the superimposition of multiple groups and quasi-groups of interest which divide partial organizations; the class struggle results from the superimposition of multiple conflicts of interests in various sectors of society.

The degree of superimposition of interest groups and conflict groups is a subject for empirical enquiry in each concrete case. *A priori* one cannot suppose that there is always superimposition of conflicts; this is precisely the error that Marx committed in his analysis of the class struggle. For this danger to be avoided, the class struggle should be approached in a more empirical way, on the basis of numerous, more limited conflicts of interest which strengthen it and polarize it to various degrees. The analysis of social classes and the class struggle thus cannot have the total society as a starting point but rather restricted collectivities which comprise this society.

Two scales

For Dahrendorf as for Marx, conflict is the main structural factor in the history of societies. Inscribed in the very nature of the social organization, it constantly stimulates change, evolution and even revolution. Marx stopped at the single case of revolutions — that is, abrupt and radical change leading to the complete replacement of the individuals and groups who exert authority and control. But real revolutions are rare in history. Rather, history is written in terms of progressive structural changes; and it does not entail, either necessarily or abruptly, the displacement of dominant individuals and groups. Such changes need to be explained as much as do revolutions. A theoretical model of the sociology of conflict must be able to account for both.

For this purpose, Dahrendorf suggests *analyzing social conflicts according to two scales*: an intensity scale and a scale of violence. The intensity of a conflict refers to the sum of energy engaged in the conflict, to the passions and emotions that it arouses, and to the importance attached to victory or defeat. The violence of a conflict, in contrast, arises from the means employed and from the weapons which are used to express hostility and fight the opponent. A verbal struggle may be more or less violent according to the terms that are used by the parties concerned; violence increases if the opponents come to blows and if, finally, they use weapons.

The two scales are independent of each other. They are not affected by the same factors, even though some factors may influence the two scales equally. Dahrendorf puts forward several propositions describing variations in intensity and violence of conflicts on the two scales.

The intensity of conflicts

The intensity of conflicts decreases:

> 1. to the extent that the interest groups can organize themselves — for example, in totalitarian countries where the quasi-groups of opposition cannot be transformed into interest groups, the intensity of conflict is much greater than in countries where hostility can be expressed through organizations;
> 2. to the extent that conflicts, within different limited associations of society, remain dissociated from each other — that is, are not superimposed on each other;
> 3. to the extent that interest groups in the different limited associations of society are not superimposed on each other;
> 4. to the extent that the distribution of authority does not coincide with the distribution of other economic

and social advantages — that is, to the extent that wealth, prestige and culture are accessible to those who do not exert authority as well as to those who occupy positions of authority or control;

5. finally, to the extent that the structure of social classes is fairly open, permitting social mobility.

The violence of conflicts

The violence of conflicts diminishes:

1. to the extent that the interest groups can organize themselves;

2. to the extent that total deprivation of economic and social advantages for those who exert no authority evolves towards relative deprivation — that is, that those who are deprived of authority start to benefit from at least some economic and social advantages;

3. to the extent that conflicts are "effectively regularized"; this presupposes that the parties recognize what divides them, that each accepts the seriousness of the other party (not treating it, for example, as a necessary evil, or as if it were blind or foolishly idealistic), and that they observe some common rules in their mutual relationships.

Radical change and sudden change

Finally, Dahrendorf adds two other general propositions:

1. A change in structure is more radical as the intensity of the conflict increases.

2. A change in structure is more abrupt as the violence of conflict increases.

If we interpret Dahrendorf correctly, the violence of a conflict does not in itself entail a radical change in structure. The extent of change resulting from a conflict depends much more on the intensity of the conflict than on its violence.

Dahrendorf's contribution

Dahrendorf's contribution to the analysis of conflict leading to social change is important for contemporary sociology. He introduces positive elements into a dynamic or diachronic sociology;

but more than this, even the weaknesses of his propositions are highly instructive. Let us first consider the positive aspects of Dahrendorf's contribution, then we shall offer a few criticisms of his work.

A theoretical step forward

First, let us say that Dahrendorf, more than any other scholar, has contributed to the construction of a sociology of conflict on considered theoretical foundations. Some sociologists have mentioned the importance of conflict in social reality; some have empirically highlighted the role of conflicts — Oscar Lewis, for example, in his monograph on Tepoztlan. But Dahrendorf has gone further: he has sought to elaborate a logical and empirically verifiable theoretical model, designed to explain both the origins of social conflicts and their historical influence. In doing this, Dahrendorf has made a unique contribution which merits serious consideration.

Complementarity of approaches

It was not Dahrendorf's intention to advance his theory of conflict in opposition to any other. He recognizes, as we did at the beginning of this section, the existence of two approaches — that of the integrated social system, and that of the system in conflict. But contrary to other sociologists, he does not suggest abandoning one for the other. Instead, he insists several times that the two approaches are true and complementary — *society is simultaneously an integrated system and a system in conflict* — and that these two aspects of social reality can have a common source. Thus, authority as analyzed by Dahrendorf is a factor in social integration at the same time as it is a factor in conflict. *It is because it is a factor in integration that authority is simultaneously a factor in conflict.* Thus, conflict theory cannot be accepted to the exclusion of a theory of integration, and vice versa.

This way of approaching social reality is, in our opinion, particularly fortunate. In fact, we believe that the contrast that is sometimes drawn between the sociology of conflicts and the sociology of the social system is futile and can only delay the progress of sociological analysis. For various reasons — theoretical, empirical or practical — one aspect of social reality can be considered rather than another. But to feel obliged to deny the reality of any other aspect and the validity of any other approach is to impose useless limitations on one's own research. If, with Dahrendorf, one be-

lieves that conflict and social structure are closely linked, sociological research and theory can progress only to the extent that the
two aspects are analyzed within the same theoretical model.

A critical analysis of Marx

Third, it should be recognized that Dahrendorf has put forward a
vigorous criticism of Marx's sociology of conflict. He has been able
both to be guided by Marx's work and to dissociate himself from it
on important points. In particular, the distinction that he establishes between ownership and control of the means of production
is valid and useful; his criticism that Marx analyzed the class
struggle from too static a viewpoint has some foundation; his comment that Marx accorded an exaggerated role to revolutions in social change is well based. On the whole, Dahrendorf's study
provides an interesting discussion of that part of Marx's sociology
concerned with the class struggle.

Some useful distinctions

Finally, Dahrendorf suggests a number of distinctions which are
useful for the analysis of conflicts. For example, he distinguishes
between latent and manifest interests, quasi-groups and interest
groups, the intensity and the violence of conflict, and the radical-
ness and the abruptness of change. These distinctions are all the
more useful in that Dahrendorf has tried to define his concepts in
such a way that they are fairly easy to define in operational terms
for the purposes of empirical research. The sociology of conflicts,
like sociology in general, has suffered from an absence of precise
and operational concepts. It is fortunate that Dahrendorf sought
to define carefully the concepts that are already currently employed, as well as the new ones that he introduced.

A reservation: hypothetical propositions

Our consideration of Dahrendorf's contribution should be followed by the mention of certain criticisms or reservations. First,
his general propositions concerning the factors which affect the intensity and violence of conflicts require empirical verification; the
same is true of the propositions which link the extent of change to
the intensity of conflict and the abruptness of change to the violence of conflict. For the moment, these are hypotheses to be

verified, as Dahrendorf himself recognizes; and therefore they should be considered as such.

In the case of some of his other propositions, it is doubtful whether they are really supported by facts. As will be seen in a later chapter (Chapter 15), the evolution from total deprivation of economic and social advantages towards relative deprivation appears to be a factor that will favour the revolutionary process rather than nullify it. Consequently, there is doubt that a diminution in the intensity of conflicts results.

A criticism: the duality of the opponents

Another point should be met not only with reservations, but with criticism. Is it correct that the dichotomy of authority necessarily leads to the duality of opponents, as Dahrendorf suggests? This is a fairly central point in his model (as in Marx's sociology), but we wonder if it is well based in fact. Dahrendorf believes he can demonstrate it by maintaining that individuals and groups in authority are always interested in the maintenance of the status quo, which is advantageous for them, while individuals and groups in positions of subjection are interested in any change in the status quo. We can observe situations, however, where the individuals or groups in authority suggest and initiate changes which are refused by their subordinates. As will be seen in the next chapter, there are leaders who are ahead of their troops. Instead of fighting for the maintenance of the status quo, some individuals in authority seek to modify it, and not necessarily to their benefit or to the benefit of their authority. It seems that such phenomena cannot be explained by Dahrendorf's model.

The relationship of domination–subjection appears to us to be much more complex and dialectical than Dahrendorf supposes. He has described these relationships in terms that are too exclusively static. There exists the opportunity to enrich and expand Dahrendorf's model on this point, not discarding his concept of the duality of opponents, but giving it a greater flexibility.

A discussion: conflict of interests and social conflict

A third element in Dahrendorf's model requires discussion. He is right in criticizing Marx for considering only one case of social conflict, the class struggle; he suggests extending the analysis in order to include all conflicts of interest. But we can turn the same criticism against Dahrendorf, suggesting that he has reduced all social conflicts to conflicts of authority. His analysis of the dichotomy of authority as the structural source of conflict is, in our opinion, completely valid. But the danger, then, lies in interpreting all conflict in terms of authority conflict. It is not certain that Dahrendorf could resist this temptation.

In the preceding pages, we have noted that many sociologists have been tempted (and perhaps still are) to explain all social change on the basis of a simple and dominant factor. It appears there is little resistance to the same temptation in the study of social conflict; one would like to attribute the same source to all conflict and perhaps thus reduce it to the same type. There would be every advantage, however, in retracing the multiplicity of possible sources of conflict in social organization, instead of trying to identify a unique source.

The concept of structural contradictions

On this subject, we believe it useful to return to the idea of *structural contradictions* suggested by Marx — without accepting, however, that it is the product of the relations of production alone. Every social organization, and particularly that of complex societies, in effect includes various structural contradictions which are the constant source of frictions and conflicts. For example, the social structures of every society manifest its history. Like geological strata which are superimposed on each other and tell the Earth's history, the ancient institutions of society underlie more recent ones.

This is particularly apparent in law and in judicial institutions. New laws and more recent procedures and interpretations are added to earlier ones but do not replace them. The same is true in governmental administration, in the educational system, in religious institutions, and in bureaucratic organizations: more or less ancient practices and structures are found to exist beside those that are recently instituted. In the work world, young professions are added to traditional occupations; in industry, modern technicians work alongside craftsmen.[70]

---

70. Alain Touraine gives a very good example of this in *L'évolution du travail ouvrier aux usines Renault.*

The age of the elements of the social system

In brief, in the social system, each element has an age. It could even be said that there are "generations" of institutions, customs and social practices; for some have appeared together during the same period. Established at different periods and in different contexts, the institutions and customs which have survived (and many have disappeared) to comprise the present social system cannot be perfectly adjusted to each other. The old and the new cannot live together without being in some degree of contradiction with each other and without frictions, tensions and conflicts developing.

A simple example will illustrate the point. The appearance of new clinical professions arising from the social sciences — psychologists, psychiatrists, social workers, social aides and social animators — has led to a whole series of frictions and conflicts with the professions and groups which traditionally were in charge of individual and collective social problems — members of the clergy, doctors, lawyers, politicians, philanthropists and so forth. The new professions have similarly experienced various conflicts with the established institutions which refuse to recognize and integrate them — for example, churches, hospitals, universities and courts.

The same contradictions and conflicts can be observed in the cultural system. Values, patterns of behaviour and symbols also have an age. Or perhaps the meaning that is given to them varies over time. Words, patterns of behaviour and values survive by taking on different meanings which are sometimes quite opposite.

Taken together, the contradictions and conflicts between institutions, customs and cultural elements of different ages resemble the contradictions and conflicts between the human generations. In his analysis of generations and relationships between generations, Eisenstadt has clearly demonstrated that each generation has its own perception of society, of things, and of life, according to the context in which it has matured, the experiences that it has known, and the traumas through which it has passed. A generation that has grown up during war and suffering does not react in the same way as one that has known only peace and prosperity. In rapidly developing complex societies, generational conflicts are thus inevitable.[71]

---

71. Eisenstadt, *From Generation to Generation.*

Society experienced in perspective

The same analysis could be extended to all the sub-groups that form a society. Each sub-group (profession, social stratum, geographical region) sees society and experiences it *in perspective* — that is, according to its particular perspective of the society, depending on the place that it occupies, the functions that it fulfills, and the advantages from which it benefits. According to the seat that I occupy in a room, I will have a particular perspective on this room and on what is happening, and my perspective will be different from that of the other individuals who are present. It can be said that, by analogy, it is the same in society for the various groups and sub-groups which comprise it. Each of them has its own perspective on society according to the place that it occupies; its social perspective thus cannot be reduced to that of the others. This is an important structural source of contradiction and conflict.

The broken rhythm of change

Every social change, in its turn, leads to new conflicts. It is unrealistic to believe that change resolves conflicts; it simply creates new ones. In effect, no society changes entirely and all at once. Some parts of a society, some sectors and regions change before others or more rapidly than others. A minority first initiates change and welcomes innovation. Then the transformation follows certain channels and networks; it encounters pockets of resistance, and firm or modified refusals. In passing from one sector to another, or from one environment to another, a new idea experiences various changes and adaptations; a new value is diluted or reinforced according to the groups which receive it.

A small or large collectivity always experiences a *broken rhythm* of change. Each part of society evolves at a particular rate and along its own route. The progression of change thus necessarily engenders frictions which serve to encourage change, which influence its rhythm and its orientation. Every change operates in this way, in and through a succession of conflicts. And these conflicts are themselves factors in new changes; a new value or ideology, through the conflicts that it stimulates, is modified by the changes that it introduces.

Some agents of contradiction

Finally, it can be added that some groups, by their very nature, are more active agents of contradictions and conflicts than are others. This is the role, for example, of some elites. Thus, it is generally among the intelligentsia (a rather vague term which designates all those who are interested in strictly intellectual activity, as producers or consumers) that innovators are recruited. In effect, the intelligentsia possess the necessary resources for being more inventive, creative and critical than other social categories and groups; their perspective is also more effectively international, without their having to travel to develop this perspective, and thus they can provide a propitious environment for the diffusion of innovation. Some sectors of the intelligentsia exist in perpetual contradiction with their society, where they constantly initiate new conflicts.

Contradictions and social complexity

The preceding examples have served to illustrate the fact that the structure of a society always includes many and various contradictions, and that these contradictions are inherent to the social organization. Some contradictions will have no dynamic influence on society, at least during a given period; they coexist peacefully without provoking friction or conflict. In this case, the functions of integration and the reduction of tensions, which are always active in society, have been sufficiently strong to absorb these contradictions, render them tolerable, or conceal them. But this is not always so. Other contradictions resist the functions of integration; they arouse irrepressible tensions and lead directly to conflicts.

It is probable that the more complex a society and the more rapidly it evolves, the more contradictions it includes that the system cannot integrate. It is also likely that the more educated the population of a society, the more sensitive it is to structural contradictions and to the tensions that these provoke. This explains why post-industrial society, as described in Chapter 7, seems inevitably marked by a permanent state of protest and social agitation.

Conclusion

It has become clear, by the end of this analysis, that conflicts and contradictions are a factor in social change, but of a different order from the other factors previously discussed in this chapter.

The other factors of change (demographic, technical and cultural) exist, in a sense, beyond the action of social actors; they are imperatives which dominate collectivities and social action. Conflicts originate directly in social action, and are part of it. It has been seen that they even belong to the fabric and structure of the social organization. They are aroused by the normal functioning of every social system.

It can still be said that the other factors in change are also very often sources of conflict. Moreover, by provoking conflict they generally exert a dynamic influence on the social organization. Demographic conditions and technological changes initiate contradictions in the structure of society and then lead to tensions and conflicts.

Conflict, like the other factors, does not provide a unique explanation of social change. But it is one of the necessary routes along which society travels in its endless process of adaptation to new situations by which it can survive its own evolution.

Chapter 12
The Agents of
Social Change

Above and beyond the great historical factors analyzed in the preceding chapter, *it is men who make the history of societies*; it is their actions and decisions which determine the destiny of collectivities.

Karl Marx wished to remind the idealistic philosophers of precisely this point: social history results from the praxis of men who have needs that they can satisfy only through work and production. Similarly, Max Weber emphasized that the Protestant or ascetic ethic is expressed through the reaction of believers to the intolerable harshness of the doctrine of predestination. Thus, both scholars refer us back to man, his needs, his responses and his actions.

Following this guide, we distinguished earlier between social change and historical action. In the preceding chapter, we reviewed a number of explanations of social change on the basis of various factors and conditions of change. Now we can undertake the study of historical action — that is, the action of various agents who influence the course of their society's history.

In this chapter, then, we will study history from the perspective of its actual agents. In particular, we will analyze the respective roles of elite groups, social movements and pressure groups. We will also consider the relationships between elites or leaders and the movements or groups which support them. And finally, we will examine recent studies in social psychology concerning some of the psychological traits of innovating agents.

Elites

The idea of the elite is now used widely in contemporary sociology. But as a result of a rather interesting development, the term has acquired quite a different meaning from that which is attributed to it in everyday speech.

Pareto's definition

It was Vilfredo Pareto who made the term and the concept of the elite acceptable in sociology.[1] According to him, the elite is composed of all those who manifest exceptional qualities or who demonstrate outstanding aptitudes in their field or in some activity. Stated differently, those who, either through their own efforts or through their natural talents, are more successful than the average man are part of the elite. And Pareto gives the particular example of the famous chess player who merited fame and prestige.

As can be seen immediately, Pareto defines the elite in a way that is still very close to the everyday meaning; for he gives it a *qualitative value*. For him, the elite is composed of the "superior" members of a society, or those to whom exceptional qualities bring power or prestige.

The circulation of elites

Pareto's theory of the circulation of elites should be understood in the light of this meaning. According to this theory, membership in the elite is not necessarily hereditary, since children do not have all the exceptional qualities of their parents. Thus there is a continuous replacement of former elites by new ones drawn from the inferior strata of society. This constant circulation of elites helps to maintain the equilibrium of the social system in that it ensures the upward mobility of the best minds. At the same time it contributes to social change, for the circulation of elites entails the circulation of ideas.

Pareto's image of society could be called *elitist but not aristocratic.* His idea of the circulation of elites obviously questions the hereditary power of the nobles. Pareto also believes that power

---

1. Pareto, *The Mind and Society*, particularly vol. 2, pp. 1420-32.

and authority devolve only on individuals who are qualitatively and objectively superior. Thus, to him, the circulation of elites is at the same time both an observable *fact* and the necessary *condition* for the normal functioning and progress of a society.

The concepts of the elite and the circulation of elites as defined by Pareto were taken up and applied by Marie Kolabinska. In a study that was, for the period (1912), well documented, she attempted to show that the notion of the circulation of elites accounted very well for the social mobility observable in France.[2]

Mosca's definition

We are indebted to another Italian sociologist, Gaetano Mosca, for his thorough study of the concept of the elite.[3] For Mosca, the elite is composed of *the minority of individuals who have power in society*. This minority can be compared to a real social class, the directing or dominating class; for what gives it its strength and enables it to maintain itself in power is its organization and structure. In effect, different ties exist which link together the members of a dominant elite — ties of kinship, interests, culture and so forth. These ties provide the elite with a certain unity of thought and group cohesiveness that is characteristic of a class. Already endowed with powerful economic means, through its unity the elite is assured of wielding political power and cultural influence over the unorganized majority. This explains the historical role of the elite.

But the elite is not totally homogeneous; rather, it is *stratified*. Almost always, there is a directing nucleus composed of a limited number of individuals or families who enjoy greater power than the others. This directing nucleus fulfills a leadership role within the elite; it is, so to speak, a super-elite. This leadership gives the elite even greater strength and efficiency.

Mosca finally comes to the conclusion that a complete explanation of history can be constructed, based on an analysis of directing elites. In effect, history appears to him to be motivated essentially by the interests and ideas of an elite in power.

---

2. Marie Kolabinska, *La circulation des élites en France* (Lausanne: Librairie F. Rouge et Cie, 1912).
3. Gaetano Mosca *The Ruling Class*, trans. H. D. Kahn (New York: McGraw-Hill Book Company, Inc., 1939).

C. Wright Mills: the elite and social class

The American sociologist C. Wright Mills follows in Mosca's tradition but he dissociates himself from it on certain important points. In particular, Mills saw clearly that the elite is a much more complex and diversified reality than Mosca supposed. Also, to speak of it as a class is misleading and an extreme simplification of reality. In fact, Mosca confused two distinct phenomena — social classes and elites. The proof that they are distinct and separate lies in the fact that it is possible to identify elites within classes, such as the elite of the working class or that of the peasant class. It then becomes ambiguous to speak of an elite class.[4]

The power elite

Mills was guided by Mosca in undertaking the empirical study of what he called the power elite,[5] particularly in the United States. While they do not form a class in the sense suggested by Mosca, *the elites are associated to form a power unit which dominates society*. The ties which link the elites have different bases. They may arise from a community of interests among certain large groups or among large institutions. For example, there is always a community interest in the maintenance of the status quo among the dominant elites. The government and large capitalist corporations have certain financial interests in common; this explains, for example, the political and military protection that all colonial countries have accorded to capitalist firms investing in the colonies or in developing countries. Similarly, we can cite the example of common interests which tend to ally the military faction and the capitalist corporations which profit from war, with a view to influencing the decision of politicians concerning international policies.

In addition, there is a community among elites of a more psychological or personal kind — a similarity of ideas and attitudes based on common social origins, a similar education, ties of

---

4. An excellent presentation and discussion of this problem of the confusion between elite and social class can be found in T. B. Bottomore, *Elites and Society* (London: C. A. Watts and Company Ltd., 1964).
5. C. Wright Mills, *The Power Elite* (New York: Oxford University Press, 1956) and by the same author, *The New Men of Power: America's Labor Leaders* (New York: Harcourt Brace, 1948).

friendship, kinship or marriage, and the exchange of courtesies. These personal ties support and reinforce the community of interests among the elites.

In order to verify the cogency of this analysis, Mills suggested carrying out systematic studies of American elites — their composition, social origins of their members, means of access to these elites, and relationships among the different elites. Although they sometimes lack sufficient methodological rigour, Mills' studies have been illuminating and generally valid.

Mills' contribution

Mills' contribution was *important in three ways*: he was able to dissociate the idea of elite from that of social class; he traced the route for a sociology of power; and he opened up a new field in empirical research — the study of elites. He is generally considered one of the main pioneers of the sociology of power, as well as of the sociology of elites.

Mills also inspired a number of subsequent studies on elites and the distribution of power among elites. In particular, we should mention the study by the Canadian sociologist John Porter, who revealed both the distinguishing and the common features of the political, economic, technocratic, religious and trade-union elites in Canada.[6]

Studies of this kind, which follow the tradition of Pareto and Mosca, contribute to the analysis of social change in that they highlight the role of individuals and groups which, through the positions that they occupy and the power at their disposal, can influence the history of their society. The decisions made by these actors or groups may have immediate or long-term repercussions. Knowing the composition of elites and the way in which their members are recruited is an important element in explaining — and eventually predicting — the orientation of the thought and action of elites and, consequently, the direction they give to the history of their society.

It can be claimed, then, that such studies are concerned directly with *historical action*, for they focus on the contribution of particularly strategic agents in change, or resistance to change, in a given society.

---

6. Porter, *The Vertical Mosaic.*

The elite, authority and power

We should note an important ambiguity in the concept of the elite as it is used in these studies. Although it has been clearly dissociated from social class, this is not the case with regard to authority and power. Mills, Porter and Mosca all envision elites as being composed exclusively of individuals or groups who occupy positions of authority and power. Pareto distinguishes between the governmental elite and the non-governmental elite, but what he calls the non-governmental elite is no less a power elite than the other. While it has no political authority, it does exert power in other areas, notably in the economic sector.

Individuals and groups in power do form an important nucleus of elites. But to define elites solely in terms of their authority and power is to neglect those who also can be considered elites *according to the influence that they exert*, even though they do not hold a position of authority or possess recognized power. The distinction between authority and influence is frequently made in studies of small groups; in sociometry, for example, it is the basis for differentiating the apparent leader from the one who truly enjoys prestige within a group. The same distinction is valid in the analysis of elites. As well as power elites, there are elites of influence whose impact has perhaps been neglected in previous studies.

The definition of elite

An exhaustive definition of elites must at least take into account this distinction and include the two types of elites. We have attempted to do both in the following definition: *the elite includes the individuals and groups who, according to the power that they hold or the influence that they exert, contribute to the historical action of a collectivity either through the decisions that they make or through the ideas, feelings or emotions that they express or symbolize.*

This definition corresponds fairly closely to the current concept of the elite in sociology. It is different from Pareto's definition mainly in that it is not qualitative or normative. In everyday language, we are accustomed to speaking of elites, as well as ideologies (and pressure groups, which we will discuss later) in a qualitative way. We are for or against elites, or a certain image of elites, and we speak with respect or contempt, depending on the case —

that is, we make value judgements about them. In sociology, while the same terms are used, the elite is defined in a way that aims to be more objective or neutral. Becoming accustomed to using this terminology in a way that is free from all value judgements can, however, present a problem for the beginning student.

Typology of Elites

In sociological language, we generally speak of elites rather than the elite, suggesting that in fact there exists a plurality of elites, whatever might be the observable ties among them. We can therefore expect to find various classifications of elites. We will present one of them here; later we will encounter others.

Since we have defined elites on the basis of their authority and influence, we will adopt the classificatory criterion of *the basis of their authority or influence*. This is an idea that Max Weber used in making his famous distinction, which is often quoted, among three types of authority — traditional authority, legal authority and charismatic authority. But we have expanded his criterion to include the idea of influence, as well as authority, in analyzing elites.

By this criterion, we can distinguish six types of elite.

Traditional elites

Traditional elites enjoy an authority or influence which stems from ideas, beliefs or social structures whose roots go back to the distant past and which are reinforced by a long tradition. Thus, every aristocratic elite is a traditional elite: noble titles have more prestige if they can claim a long history. Similarly, a traditional tribal chief has authority because he is known to be the direct descendant of some ancestor or mythological God.

Usually, religious elites also are to some degree traditional. Their authority or influence is based on respect for certain truths which were revealed to men at some time in the past, or on a very long tradition which has taken on a value of its own.

Later we will examine the importance of traditional elites in the developing countries.

Technocratic elites

Technocratic elites exist within a legal or bureaucratic structure. Their authority is based on two facts: first, they have been named or elected according to established laws which are recognized and accepted; and second, they are attributed a certain competence, measured according to known criteria. Competence may be established through examinations, by a jury, by amount and type of education, or by acquired experience (length of service) and so forth. In some cases, competence may also be judged by popular vote.

Specifically, the technocratic elite is composed of the higher category of administrators found in the government, governmental agencies, and industrial or financial corporations — that is, higher civil servants or executives.

Technocratic elites have, in Max Weber's words, legal authority. They are elites of authority rather than influence; they occupy positions of command in bureaucratic hierarchies.

Property elites

Property elites are invested with authority or power according to the goods or capital they possess. These goods and capital give them power over the labour force they employ and support; but it is their potential for asserting power over other elites, traditional or technocratic, that gives them social power.

Property or economic elites are the large landowners, great industrialists and financiers whose decisions can influence political and often social life as much as the economy, and who are in a position either to slow down or to provoke political, economic or social change.

Charismatic elites

The elites that we call charismatic — to use Weber's term — are those to whom one attributes a certain charisma, certain qualities carried to an extraordinary degree (beyond the ordinary), or certain magical or almost magical virtues. The authority and influence that charismatic elites enjoy are thus attached to precise individuals, and not to positions or goods. It is what a person has done or what he is believed to be able to do that gives him charisma. Therefore, it is more appropriate to speak of charismatic leaders than of charismatic elites. But there are examples of charismatic elites, such as some social categories or classes of religious origin, or particular social or political movements. It can also happen that a leader's charismatic power is extended to those who surround him, or to the whole of his team.

Ideological elites

Ideological elites are those which develop and crystallize around ideologies. These are the individuals and groups who participate in the definition of an ideology, who diffuse it, or who are its spokesmen or appointed representatives.

Like charismatic elites, ideological elites are not necessarily part of the power elite, in Mills' sense. They may be influential, but they lack official authority. This is the case, for example, of counter-elites — that is to say, opposition or protest elites which contradict the power elite. These influential charismatic or ideological elites often forecast future structural changes and provoke a redirection of historical action.

The theory of the power elite and the studies by Mills and others can be criticized for neglecting the role of counter-elites, particularly ideological counter-elites, in historical action. The power elite generally seeks to oppose change, or sometimes to adapt to it. It is guided by what we called, in the preceding chapter, an adaptive ideology. If it suggests changes itself, they are usually moderate, often designed to thwart the action of those who suggest more profound ones. In contrast, the greatest amount of innovation is found among the charismatic and ideological elites which, because they are not in power and do not hold positions of authority, are free to play at prophesying. Dreams, utopian hopes and sometimes inefficient forms of extremism are the main weaknesses of the action of these counter-elites, and these faults can minimize their historical influence.

Symbolic elites

Symbolic elites are generally neglected in classifications of elites; however, they perform important functions.

Most elites have a symbolic character. The individuals who form them in effect take on a symbolic value for those who watch, follow or fight with them. Political leaders symbolize a cause, values and ideas; they are seen as the living symbols of the status quo, the Establishment, order, new ideas and so forth. Charismatic and ideological leaders in particular are likely to have this symbolic character.

But there are some elites whose function is more purely and explicitly symbolic. These are the individuals or groups who present themselves or are presented as the prototypes of certain ways of living, acting and thinking, or who represent certain qualities and values. Let us give a few examples. Popular artists correspond particularly well to this idea of the symbolic elite. Popular singers become heroes among adolescents because, to them, they symbolize youth, love, fantasy, novelty, non-conformism and so on. The influence of these singers among young people can be considerable; many young people can carry on a sustained dialogue most easily with them. Through television, transistor radios and magazines, the communication established between these idols and their young public contributes to the creation and maintenance of the cultural world of adolescents, which is relatively marginal but all the same real and present.

Professional sportsmen also form a symbolic elite by embodying certain human qualities. One need only read newspaper accounts of their lives, training and exploits to see that they are presented as the prototypes of courage, audacity, tenacity, skill, intelligence and so on; they also illustrate the virtues of an ethic that is called the sporting mentality.

We will give one final example. Newspaper articles (perhaps mainly in North America) on the wives of politicians, and the interviews with them that one finds in magazines and the women's pages, present them as a symbolic elite. Ways of living are emphasized, as are certain qualities or virtues which are considered particularly feminine. They are described as supporters of their husbands, guardians of the home, initiators or benefactors of various artistic or philanthropic undertakings, courageous in adversity, and modest and simple when they enjoy success.

Elites and Historical Action

In the light of the typology that we have just elaborated, we can now specify the various ways in which elites can participate in historical action — that is, the ways in which they can contribute to social change. In particular, there are three forms of action for elites.

Decision-making

First, some elites contribute to historical action through the weight that they carry *in the whole decision-making process within a society*. It is perhaps in this context that their influence is most directly apparent; and it is this aspect primarily that has been demonstrated in analyses of the power elite. In effect, social change or resistance to change can be considered to be the result of all the decisions taken by various particularly influential actors, or by those who occupy strategic positions. This is a very important, and perhaps the primary, aspect of historical action. In the life of institutions and societies, it is still true that major decisions are made by a limited number of individuals who thereby initiate long- or short-term historical action.

Andrew Hacker has illustrated this fact very well.[7] He says that, in the United States, the owners and executives of large corporations (which form the property elite and part of the technocratic elite) complain of the numerous constraints or limitations in decision-making which are imposed on them by the government, various government agencies, trade unions and so forth. Which decisions are still their responsibility? Hacker enumerates the main ones. They have some control in deciding the price of goods produced; they have a lot of freedom in determining the dividends to be distributed to shareholders; despite collective bargaining, they maintain a good portion of control over salaries, particularly for higher categories of personnel and for those that they wish to favour for one reason or another; they decide on the positions to be created and the number of such positions, the geographical mobility of their employees, and the technical changes in production procedures; they are free to locate their firms where they want, and to establish their own investment policy; and finally, they are free to use or not to use their power in furthering certain causes (freedom of speech, the defence of civil rights, educational democracy and so forth).

The decisions made by the owners and executives of large corporations, their actions and sometimes their inaction, can result in vast movements of population, modify the living conditions of thousands of individuals, influence the standard of living

---

7. Andrew Hacker, "Power to Do What?" in Irving L. Horowitz, ed., *The New Sociology* (New York: Oxford University Press, 1964).

of millions of people, and sometimes change the course of history. All this is not necessarily social change; but it is through and by such decisions that structural changes are initiated, designed and carried out.

This picture should be completed by emphasizing that, in a corporation, decision-making involves many individuals other than the higher executives. In effect, to a greater or lesser extent they take into account the opinions, information, and studies provided by subordinate personnel. But at the level of these subordinate personnel, a great number of decisions have had to be made which were already preparing for, and even influencing, the decisions of higher executives.

The definition of situations

Elites initiate a second form of historical action through the part that they play in collective definitions of situations — that is, in the true or false consciousness that a collectivity has of itself, of what it is and what it wishes to be.

This form of action is distinguished from decision-making in that it takes place mainly at the cultural and socio-psychological levels, while decision-making primarily affects institutions and living conditions. The definition of situations consists, in effect, of the effort which is made to describe and explain things as they are, to give them a meaning, and sometimes to criticize them and predict their preferable future orientation. The definition of situations thus appeals to mental images, to feelings, aspirations, motivations and so forth. Its aim is to create or maintain *states of consciousness*.

In fact, though, this form of elite action is not totally independent of the first. Decision-making necessarily entails some definition of situations. Those who, according to the positions that they occupy, must make decisions directly or indirectly affecting human collectivities, must also define situations; or more often, they borrow those that others have already elaborated; or perhaps they take into account definitions which already exist and which are accepted by the collectivity. Thus, decision-making is more or less in agreement with a certain definition of situations. In this way, power elites contribute to the elaboration of definitions of situations, or more often to the reinforcement of recognized definitions.

There is a case which deserves special attention — that of elites which attempt to elaborate or propagate new ideologies. This occurs generally among charismatic or ideological elites, sometimes among symbolic elites, but rarely among technocratic elites.

What distinguishes this form of action from the others is that its effects are often less immediately apparent. Those who make decisions or participate in decision-making usually are not slow to notice at least some effects of their decisions. But to elaborate a new ideology or counter-ideology, to propagate and spread it abroad, is to work for a more distant future which is often very remote.

Moreover, those who participate in decision-making are often assured of exerting some influence. This is not the case with those whose action is more long term. Despite the confidence that they may have in the cogency of their point of view, they have no assurance that their definition of the situation will be accepted and will finally prevail.

If their definition is eventually recognized, these elites exert an influence on the history of their society which is sometimes more profound and certainly more long term than that of any other elite. They have really contributed to historical action in the strongest meaning of the term.

Exemplary action

Finally, elites make their influence felt on the course of history in another way, through the exemplary value that they represent. As living symbols of ways of thinking, living and acting, they attract certain categories of individuals, or groups, or an entire collectivity. Thus they instigate a movement towards imitation, or perhaps more precisely towards identification.

This identification with elites may have many sources and result from various motivations. Personal ambition may be an important motivation in identifying with some elites. Those who aspire to climb the social ladder and to accede to wealth and important positions must assimilate the ideology of one of the power elites; they must identify with its interests, and sometimes they may even copy styles of behaving and living down to the last detail. In effect, it is very difficult to accede to a power elite without making the commitment to full identification with it. Members of the power elite thus serve as living models, whose force of attraction exerts pressure on those who aspire to power or to association with it.

In other cases, the exemplary value of elites is based on the general attraction of the values they suggest or symbolize. These may be values which are already present and widespread within society, or new values in the process of elaboration. This exemplary value may be of a higher or lower ideal order, sometimes extending to the highest degree of heroism, as in the case of the prophets or the saints.

Conclusion

As we have seen, elites form units of particularly active agents in the functioning of society and mainly in initiating change. Their contribution to historical action can take on different forms; we have reviewed the three main ones — decision-making, definition of situations, and example.

In Chapter 7 we noted that the multiplication of elites is a phenomenon which is characteristic of modern industrial societies, and which is part of the greater complexity of these societies. New elites appear and are the spokesmen of various sectors of society — the labour elite, peasant elite, student elite and so forth. In expressing different points of view, interests and values, these more numerous elites provoke an increase in the number and intensity of conflicts over values, interests and ideologies. This is one of the reasons for believing that modern society is not close to what Daniel Bell called the end of ideology (Chapter 11).

We can even suggest that factors and agents in change meet and reinforce each other mutually. The multiplication of elites entails the plurality of ideologies and values and, as a result, the proliferation of conflicts. And diverse conflicts provoke the appearance of new elites, which create new or as yet unexpressed ideologies, values or aspirations.

It is often said that, in the modern world, an acceleration of history has taken place, meaning by this that events occur much more quickly than formerly. Rapid transportation and communication have obviously been very important factors in this acceleration. But it is also clear that the multiplication of elites and the confrontations which result among them constitute another more strictly sociological factor in this acceleration of history. It could be said that *because of the proliferation of elites, modern society harbours more opportunity for the ferment of historical action and social change.*

Social Movements and Pressure Groups

It is no more possible to study elites without reference to the context of the social movements and pressure groups which support them or on which they are based, than to study ideologies and values without reference to elites and social movements. Ideologies and values do not exist on their own; they are expressed, propagated and symbolized by elites. These elites in turn represent or seek to represent social movements and pressure groups.

In addition, elites should not be confused with social movements. They are two completely distinct agents of historical action. In fact, complex relationships exist between elites and social movements, and these relationships are themselves part of the process of social change. They are an element of it and sometimes an important, and certainly not a negligible, factor. Later we will discuss this in more detail.

Social Movements

Definition of social movement

Let us say, first of all, that by a social movement we mean *a clearly structured and identifiable organization which has the explicit goal of grouping members with a view to the defence or promotion of certain precise objectives, generally with a social connotation.* The main characteristic of a social movement is that it is essentially demanding. It seeks recognition and acceptance of its ideas, interests and values. Thus, a social movement is neither an academic discussion group, nor a religious order. It necessarily occurs in the public view. It attempts to gain supporters and to retain the attention of the public, or some sector of the public, and the power elites.

The goals pursued by social movements are infinitely varied — the reversal of the established order, the prohibition of alcohol, the recognition of the legal and political equality of women, the abolition of capital punishment, nuclear disarmament and so on. The means of propagating the movement also vary, from publicity alone to moral pressure and even physical violence. But whatever the goals suggested and the means employed, social movements always exhibit the same basic proselytism.

It is around this act of making demands that the organization of each social movement is structured. The organization is designed to serve the pursuit of goals and the use of means; it is secondary to, and conditioned by, the movement itself. This is the perspective from which it must be studied.

Touraine's Three Principles of Social Movements

Alain Touraine, one of the sociologists to have recently studied social movements in depth, suggests a theoretical model which is designed to analyze their action as well as their structure.[8] In order to exist as an organization with demands, every social movement must *resolve certain problems of self-definition*; it must, in Touraine's terms, bring together certain principles of existence. The response to these problems — that is, the way in which it resolves the principles of existence — gives a social movement its specific nature and directs its action.

According to Touraine, there are three principles that must coexist in any social movement.

The principle of identity

A social movement must first give itself an *identity* by saying *whom it represents*, in whose name it speaks, and what interests it protects or defends. The problem to be resolved here is the socially identifiable and significant definition of the group that is making demands.

A social movement may assume an identity by claiming to be the spokesman of a particular group — for example, the working class, students, women, war veterans, or peasants. Or it can claim to be the spokesman of the interests of a total society, as is true, notably, of a patriotic, national or nationalist movement. In this case, a movement is identified with a quasi-total group — that is,

---

8. Alain Touraine, *Sociologie de l'action* (Paris: Editions du Seuil, 1965) and by the same author, *La conscience ouvrière* (Paris: Editions du Seuil, 1966).

one that comprises almost all of the society. An example would be a consumer movement.

In order to understand the nature and action of a social movement, it is necessary to ask questions such as these: Whom does the movement say it represents or wishes to represent? In the name of which group or groups does it speak or claim to speak? What interests does it defend or promote?

The principle of opposition

A social movement exists because certain ideas are not recognized, or because particular interests are neglected. Thus, it always struggles against resistance, obstruction or inertia. It seeks to break down opposition, apathy or indifference; and it necessarily has its opponents.

The principle of opposition is the second existential principle of social movements. Without opposition, a social movement no longer exists, or more precisely, it no longer exists as a social movement. Its nature is changed. It may become a party in power or an established institution. But it is no longer a social movement, for it has lost its essential characteristic quality — its proselytism.

In the analysis of social movements, then, it is equally essential to identify the opponents which the movement attacks as it is to recognize those whose interests it aims to defend. In addition, the group whose interests the movement represents and the group of opponents often complement each other in various ways.

As it develops, a social movement may change its adversary. A labour movement will attack the State, rather than employers; a religious movement will criticize another Church, rather than the world. The change in adversary sometimes indicates an important modification in the orientation of a social movement. In some cases, it may be the first sign of a transformation in its principle of identity, indicating that the movement is in the process of changing its public, In other circumstances, this event may be merely a tactical and provisional change. But in the analysis of social movements, a change in adversary should never be overlooked. Its relevance must be appreciated in each concrete case.

The principle of totality

A social movement acts in the name of certain higher values, grand ideals or some particular philosophy or theology. Its action is inspired by thought which aims to be the highest possible. Even when it represents or defends the interests of a particular group, a social movement claims to do so in the name of universal realities and values which are, or should be, recognized by all men and by the entire collectivity. Thus, the reasons cited by a social movement to motivate its action may be the national interest, the common good, human freedom, collective well-being, the rights of man, the health of all, God's desired order, history and so forth.

This is what Touraine calls *the principle of totality*. A social movement cannot make demands without doing so in the name of some basic truth which is recognized by all the members of a collectivity.

Like the two preceding principles, the principle of totality is important in explaining the nature and orientation of a social movement. Moreover, a change in orientation is generally accompanied by a change in the principle of totality. Thus, a patriotic movement of religious inspiration which becomes secular ceases to speak of God's desired order and instead substitutes the trend of history. And, at the same time, it often becomes more radical and even revolutionary.

Actionalism and social movements

In fact, Touraine's analysis of social movements has a still more general goal. He proposes an analytical method of historical action, which he calls *actionalist analysis*. This aims to explain *how values are created*, the logic on which they are based, and by what means they appear, are expressed and provoke the action of collectivities. Touraine emphasizes that he is not setting up his actionalism in opposition to functional and structural analysis; while these start with existing values, taking them as given, actionalism proposes going back to their origin and source.

In this actionalist analysis, Touraine gives social movements a privileged position. To him they appear to be the strategic place where new values are created and made explicit. Because of this, they become particularly central to the analysis of historical action and social change. It is mainly in and through social movements that innovating actors, as well as their opponents, organize their action and seek to influence the history of their society.

Let us look a little more closely at what this means.

The multiplication of social movements

To start with a factual observation, we can find a multiplication of social movements in modern societies as compared with traditional societies. This multiplication of social movements is correlated with the multiplication of elites that we mentioned earlier. It is also linked, as both cause and effect, to the acceleration of history.

In archaic societies, social movements are almost non-existent. They appear in peasant societies and have often been at the source of peasant uprisings and revolts, but here they are generally rather short term. Above all, they are not an integral part of the social organization of peasant societies to the extent that they are in the urban milieux of modern society.

In modern society, its rulers and public opinion are constantly solicited by a great number of social movements which seek to promote widely diverse causes and interests. The first act of a totalitarian regime is to liquidate the social movements which could or do protest against it. But they constantly threaten to revive secretly and overthrow the regime.

The number and diversity of social movements in modern society already indicate their importance. If only for this reason, they deserve the attention of the sociologist interested in social change.

Three Functions of Social Movements

Their importance becomes even more evident when one considers *the three functions of social movements*: mediation, clarification of the collective consciousness, and pressure. Let us examine these three functions in turn.

Mediation

Social movements are the active mediating agents between individuals, on the one hand, and structures and social realities on the other. This mediation operates in various ways. We shall emphasize two of them.

First, social movements serve to make the society and social structures known to their members, and often also to others. They explain certain social realities, in order to defend them, criticize them, or suggest changes. In this way, they fulfill a role as *socializing agents*, serving to convey social reality to the greatest possible number of actors.

Social movements are also a powerful medium of participation. Depending on their size and degree of differentiation, urban and industrial societies require more complex forms of participation in collective life than does traditional society. This fact was strongly emphasized by Emile Durkheim in his famous Preface to the second edition of his book *The Division of Labour in Society*. Durkheim showed the importance of intermediary groupings which serve to integrate individuals into complex societies; according to him, this integration was a necessary correlate of organic solidarity. More recently, Daniel Lerner has shown that in the transition from traditional to modern societies, the members of a society must acquire new aptitudes that enable them to adapt themselves to more complex forms of participation.

In the mass society, the social movement has become one of the main intermediary groups through which actors can protect their interests or assert their ideas, and thus participate to varying degrees in historical action.

Clarification of the collective consciousness

A social movement, by its nature, develops and maintains a clear and aggressive collective consciousness in a society or a particular sector of society. Since Marx's analysis of class consciousness, the importance of a politicized collective consciousness in social change has been recognized. But collective consciousness is an ambiguous term. It is all too easy to assume that it includes many phenomena and to accept it as the ultimate source of historical action.

Keeping this caution in mind, we must recognize the utility of the idea, for it can help us to perceive a reality that is often difficult to describe — *the collective state of true consciousness*. This occurs in a collectivity which discovers its interests, or what it believes to be its interests, and comprehends the action or changes that the situation requires.

It is obviously this second function of social movements which is most directly linked to historical action. Some degree of collective consciousness is an essential element of all historical action. But it is part of the very nature of social movements — because of their organization and proselytism, and also because of their three basic characteristics (Touraine's three principles) — to seek constantly to clarify the consciousness of a collectivity from their own point of view. In this way, they help to maintain or provoke a state of permanent alertness in the collective consciousness. It is particularly because of the influence that social movements exert on the state of consciousness of collectivities that Touraine accords them a privileged role in history.

Pressure

Third, social movements have an influence on the historical development of societies through the pressure that they are able to exert on individuals in authority and on the power elites. This pressure can be exerted in various ways — through publicity or propaganda campaigns, public opinion, threats, lobbying and so forth.

Pressure on the authorities is only one of the various forms of action adopted by social movements. But it is so widespread and common that it is often considered the main function of social movements. Consequently, a special phrase has been created to designate this characteristic, and social movements are then referred to as *pressure groups*.

Because of the popularity and frequent use of this expression, and because many studies focus on pressure groups, it is worth exploring this particular form of social movements a little further.

Pressure Groups

First, we must emphasize that *social movement* and *pressure group* are not synonymous terms, even though they are often used interchangeably. Confusion often arises because both phrases refer to the same reality — social movements frequently act like pressure groups, and most pressure groups are social movements.

What, then, should be understood by the term *pressure group*?

Definition of pressure groups

Pressure groups have been studied more thoroughly in political science than in sociology. In this discussion, we will refer particularly to the works of Jean Meynaud, who has written several books on this phenomenon.[9]

Meynaud clearly defines pressure groups as follows: Interest groups are transformed into pressure organisms only when those responsible for them influence government apparatus in order to make their aspirations and demands triumph. A manufacturers' trade union behaves as an interest group if it sets up and supervises the distribution of clients among its members by its own means; it becomes a pressure group if it tries to obtain a statement from those in authority regulating the entry of new elements into its area. On the whole, the category of "pressure groups" includes part of the activity of interest groups: more precisely, it consists of analyzing a specific aspect of these groups.[10]

This definition explains why social movements can, at the same time, be pressure groups: to speak of pressure groups is to emphasize a specific aspect of social movements and interest groups. We might suggest that the study of pressure groups highlights one of the main functions of social movements: *the pressure they can exert on government authorities.*

Classification of pressure groups

Meynaud divides pressure groups into two large classes according to the nature of the goals pursued.

Professional organizations include pressure-groups which have "the essential objective of obtaining material advantages for their adherents, or protecting existing situations, thus tending to improve the well-being of the persons represented." For the most part, these pressure groups are formed on the basis of occupation or profession. Within this category we find labour unions, employers' associations, professional associations, production cooperatives and so forth. But despite the name that Meynaud gives this class, other groups may be included, such as consumer and tenant associations, chambers of commerce, and all societies that pursue similar goals.

Groups with an ideological vocation "find their raison d'être in the disinterested defence of spiritual or moral positions, in the

---

9. Jean Meynaud, *Les groupes de pression* (Paris: Presses universitaires de France, Collection "Que sais-je?," 1965), and by the same author, *Les groupes de pression en France* (Paris: Librairie Armand Colin, 1958) and *Nouvelles études sur les groupes de pression en France* (Paris: Librairie Armand Colin, 1962).

10. Meynaud, *Les groupes de pression*, p. 10.

promotion of causes, or the affirmation of theses." In this category can be found religious and anti-religious groups, patriotic and internationalist groups, moralists, freedom fighters, philanthropists, naturalists and so forth. All causes find defenders — the protection of birds, elephants or animal life; the rights of man or those of women; or the battle against air and water pollution.

These two large classes include almost all pressure groups. But Meynaud emphasizes that these classes are not mutually exclusive. Professional organizations can also promote ideas and values, and thus give themselves an ideological vocation.

Conditions of effectiveness

More important for our purposes are the conditions for the effectiveness of pressure groups that Meynaud enumerates. He suggests four main ones.

1. *The number of members.* The likelihood that a pressure group can exert some influence on those in authority depends to some extent on the number of members it can claim. But this estimate is often difficult to make; for the members of a movement are not all equally active, and they are not involved to the same extent in the causes that the movement defends. In addition, politicians may take into account the potential adherents of a movement, rather than the number of its effective members.

2. *Financial capacity.* A pressure group lives, at least partly, on the contributions of its members. As these contributions are generally rather small, the number of members becomes an important element. Thus the financial position of a movement should be an indication of the number of its members. A movement whose financial bases are solid is in a better position to exert pressure on the State.

3. *Organization.* In general, it appears that a highly structured movement is a more powerful pressure group than one which is not as well organized. Meynaud emphasizes two organizational factors which, to him, seem particularly important: the quality of the leaders, and "the extent of the network of relationships that they succeed in establishing within parliamentary circles, ministerial offices, and organizations of the for-

mation of public opinion." Let us note in addition that, for other reasons, weakly organized movements also can capture the attention of those in authority.

4. *Social status.* Pressure groups, like individuals and some other groups, have a social status. They have a high or low reputation and various degrees of prestige in the opinion of the public. For reasons which are often difficult to discern, some pressure groups do not succeed in gaining public respect, while others enjoy a reputation which is hardly merited. Social status is often a primary factor in the influence of pressure groups on members of the government.

Means of action

Finally, let us quote the main forms of pressure group action on government authorities. Meynaud lists five.

1. *Persuasive efforts* can take the form of the submission of memoranda, documents, petitions and so forth to various members of the government. In this case, the pressure group hopes to win support through the (at least apparent) objectivity and the quality of information that it presents to the government.

2. *Threats* to the government obviously can take various forms — threats of boycott, strike, blackmail and sometimes physical violence.

3. *Money* also can serve to win political favour, either through subscriptions to political parties or through the corruption of members of government and civil servants.

4. *Sabotage of governmental action* can take the form of a refusal to cooperate with those in authority or to pay income tax, a boycott of certain governmental projects, and so forth.

5. Finally, *direct action* consists of the use of force and violence through strikes, mass demonstrations and the disruption of services.

The action of pressure groups

Despite all that can be said about the possible action of pressure groups and the methods at their disposal, there is no agreement concerning their real power. Meynaud emphasizes this on several occasions:

> In them, some see a powerful instrument for the anni-
> hilation of democracy; they go so far as to demand a
> strict regulation of their activities. Others consider
> such attitudes excessive, and regard them as an attempt
> to influence opinion. This is a controversy which seems
> far from solution, given the lack of factual data on the
> role of groups.[11]

It should be recognized, however, that in his various studies Meynaud accumulated a very impressive file on the role and activities of pressure groups. In a concrete way, he demonstrated their influence on politicians and higher civil servants; he illustrated the existence of numerous lobbies in France, England and the United States; he highlighted the means they use to convince, and sometimes to force, those in authority to satisfy their interests.

It is clearly no longer possible to deny the efficient action of pressure groups and their influence on the history of societies. This is a well-established fact, both scientifically and practically. But sometimes it is tempting to give them an importance which is not supported by the facts.

Failure of pressure groups

A recent study serves to guard against an exaggerated interpretation of the real influence of pressure groups. Léon Dion[12] has traced the succession of events when, in 1963, the Quebec government brought before the House a proposed law for the creation of a Ministry of Education. He analyzed the interplay of pressures exerted at the time by those who were opposed to the law and those who supported it.

Dion reviews the various pressure groups who expressed their opinions, the way in which they did so, and the direction of their opinions. He carefully aligns the opposing forces and gives a precise account of the interventions that were favourable or unfavourable to the law. The confrontation was an important one, and the groups opposed to the law as well as those who favoured it accorded great importance to the outcome of the debate.

---

11. *Ibid.*, pp. 5-6.
12. Léon Dion, *Le bill 60 et la société québécoise.*

At the end of this detailed analysis, Dion shows that all this feverish and noisy activity on the part of the pressure groups had practically no influence on the government's decision. Instead, the decision took the form of an agreement between two equal powers — the State and the Catholic Church. Behind the façade of the agitation of pressure groups, it was the discussions between the representatives of the Catholic episcopate and the government which formed the crux of the debate and determined the final outcome.

At the extreme, it could be suggested that the episcopate was the most powerful pressure group to influence the government. This is not Dion's feeling, for such a claim gives too wide a meaning to the idea of pressure group. In this debate, the Catholic Church represented a power similar to the State, and both were subjected to the assault of pressure groups. At the most, it could be said that the activity of the pressure groups made the two powers cooperate and understand each other; but equally it could be claimed that this would have happened in any case. In fact, once the agreement was concluded and announced, the pressure groups were silent.

This example is not cited in order to minimize the power of pressure groups. Rather, it helps to illustrate the fact that the real influence of pressure groups must not be estimated only on the basis of the noise they make. In order to measure their influence precisely, it is necessary to return, as Dion has done, to the decision-making process, and to be able to analyze its effective components.

Relationships Between Elites, Movements and Groups

Interactional relationships

Elites, movements and groups, whose influence we have analyzed separately, are in fact intimately associated. Elites create, activate and symbolize social movements and pressure groups. Social movements and groups, for their part, support or oppose their leaders, restrain or advance them, or sometimes change them. The historical action of elites, movements and groups is thus partly conditioned by the reciprocal relationships maintained among them.

The interaction between elites and their movements also becomes an important element in historical action. It often happens that the historical action of an elite is influenced by its relationships with its movement, in the same way that the action of a movement can be determined by its relationships with its elite.

Relationships between elites and their movements are complex and change constantly. Let us try at least to indicate the outlines.

The gap between leaders and members

First, we must state that there is never perfect agreement between the leaders and the members of a movement. If, for example, the leaders and then a certain number of members are questioned, frequently a clear difference can be observed in the respective viewpoints expressed by the two groups. The leaders usually have a more precise knowledge of the objectives pursued by the movement than do its members. They are in a better position to explain the structures and the functioning of the movement. They will know more about its history and previous development. They can more precisely identify its opponents, adversaries and so on. In brief, it can be asserted that the leaders of a movement generally have a clearer, more precise and detailed knowledge of it than do its members.

Similar differences can be observed among the members of a movement. Comparing the active members and the mere sympathizers, one can draw a series of concentric circles which move progressively farther from the centre. The most active members who are closest to the centre ordinarily have a better knowledge of their movement than do the sympathizers located at its periphery.

These differences between the leaders and the members, and among the members themselves, have important dynamic consequences for the life of a movement. These can be described with the help of two extreme situations.

Leaders ahead of their movement

In the first case, the leaders can be said to be ahead of their group — that is, *they hold more extreme positions than do the members, but in the same direction*. If the movement is reactionary, the leaders are more conservative than the members; if the movement is revolutionary, the leaders are more radical than the members.

In such a situation — which is very common — the leaders must devote an important part of their energies to the education of members. Their efforts to convert are directed towards those indifferent to the movement or to its opponents, as well as towards its members, but by different ways and means. In the case of non-members, the leaders will seek to awaken them, make them conscious, trouble and convert them. In the case of members, the leaders can presuppose that they already share certain basic convictions; therefore, they will concentrate on feeding the necessary information to members, helping them to develop and advance.

At the same time, the leaders must take care not to cut themselves off from their group. If they assume positions that are too far advanced, either publicly or officially, they risk rejection by their members. This can have the reverse effect of leading the members to support and defend attitudes which they first judged to be extreme. But, on the whole, leaders who find themselves in this situation are restrained in their activity, and the changes that they want to bring about require an enormous amount of time and energy. This is true particularly if the opponents of the group are able to play on the gap between the leadership and the members and thereby persuade the members to reject their present leaders and install more moderate ones.

An elite overtaken by its members

The situation is completely different when the leaders of a movement find themselves overtaken by a number of their members who adopt more extreme attitudes than their own. The leading elite must then confront *an opposition within its own movement*, and must struggle on two fronts — against its adversaries, and against its internal opposition.

Usually the internal opposition itself is directed by an opposition elite or counter-elite. Thus the members find themselves divided between two directing teams, both of which seek to gain their support. The distinction between the two teams sometimes can be reduced to mere nuances — a different strategy, or a question of emphasis. But when there is opposition on fundamental questions, the movement runs the risk of a crisis and of seriously weakening its influence. The leaders must then decide between pursuing the defence of their point of view or safeguarding the efficiency of the movement.

When the debate is concerned with fundamental questions and

when it becomes violent within a movement, the leaders face the possibility of dissension and the loss of some of the members. They can try to avoid such an eventuality by trying to arrive at a compromise with the opposition elite. But sometimes they prefer to lose a part of the group, in order to protect what they consider to be the integrity or authenticity of the movement.

The members who support an opposition elite risk having to resolve a dilemma of loyalty — loyalty to the movement as it is, or loyalty to an elite which represents another conception of what the movement can be or do. Sometimes their position can become as uncomfortable as that of the leaders in power.

Elite, movement and milieu

The relationships between the elites and a movement are still more complex if they are considered within the context of the milieu that the movement represents, or in which it works. A movement is always in danger of cutting itself off from its milieu, of isolating itself and functioning in a vacuum. In effect, because of its efforts to convert, a movement is never in perfect agreement with its milieu: it seeks to spread ideas within it, to protect interests and so forth. *Thus, between a movement and its milieu, there is generally an element of more or less acute tension.*

The social origins of the leaders of the movement will sometimes be an important factor in this tension. Leaders who are not from the milieu may benefit from being strangers, because of the prestige that they bring, because they cannot be suspected of defending personal interests, or perhaps because they do not arouse envy or jealousy. But their situation is always delicate within the movement and the milieu. The time may come when they must repress their origins, or ultimately they may resign in order to prevent damage to the action of the movement within the milieu.

In contrast, the leaders who can claim to be from the milieu often remain suspect for a long time in their own milieu. They are suspected of having personal ambitions and interests to protect, and of exploiting the position of their brothers for their own benefit. In the extreme, they are often accused of not really being from the milieu, and they are criticized either for accepting compromises or for promoting ideas which are too advanced and imported from outside the group.

Conclusion

The few examples that have just been given illustrate the complexity of relationships between elites, social movements and milieux. It is through this confused bundle of relationships and interactions that the historical action of elites and movements clears the way to exerting some influence on the course of history. Understandably, it is not easy to assess or measure the contribution of each. Here, perhaps more than on any other subject, it seems evident that a model of simple causality can be of no use in sociology.

Motivation and Need for Achievement

To complete our analysis of the agents of historical action, we will now explore in another direction. In the preceding pages, the action of agents involved in the process of change has been considered exclusively at the sociological level. In effect, we have considered elites as a social category of actors, and this has led us to locate them within the context of social movements, pressure groups and the total social milieu.

But elites and leaders are individuals with psychological traits and reactions. They act in response to needs, impulses and motivations which are not all located at an equal level of consciousness. In the analysis of the agents of social change, particularly leaders and elites, these psychological factors are far from negligible. On the contrary, they are likely to influence significantly the social and historical action of actors who perform a strategic role in the process of change in a society.

One of the psychological factors which can affect historical action has been studied particularly in social psychology; this is what has been called *motivation and the need for achievement*. A number of important studies have recently been devoted to this personality trait. Their conclusions are very pertinent in the analysis of social change, and we will try to summarize them.

Success as a value

Sociological and psychological studies of success follow clearly in the wake of Max Weber's studies. Weber showed that the en-

trepreneurial spirit was an essential element of the original mentality of capitalism; and he attempted to show that one of the
sources of this entrepreneurial spirit was the Puritans' need for
human success in order to prove to themselves that they could be
among the elect, predestined by God to salvation.

Several American sociologists, guided by Weber, have attempted to identify the social function of this need for achievement. Extending Weber's idea, they have shown that personal success is not
valued equally from one society to another and from one period to
another. This led Kluckhohn and Strodtbeck, and Talcott Parsons, to make achievement one of the value options in the theoretical models that they constructed (see Chapter 3). American sociologists have almost unanimously considered achievement as a characteristic value of the mentality of industrial society. Consequently, the industrialization process is difficult in a society in
which personal success is not strongly valued.

The value of achievement has also been associated with social
mobility, particularly in the United States system of social
stratification. It has been observed that the individuals and groups
who accord little value to achievement have less chance of rising
on the scale of stratification. To measure this phenomenon more
precisely, various research techniques have been developed,[13] such
as Fred Strodtbeck's V-scale.[14]

More recently, David McClelland has transposed the notion of
achievement from the level of values to the socio-psychological
level of motivation and need. He has studied what he has called
achievement motivation or achievement motive and the need for
achievement.[15]

Value and motivation

A value is presented as an ideal, a goal or an objective. Thus it is,
in some respects, external to individuals — mainly in its collective
aspect — in that it is a stimulus which can or must affect the motivation of individuals. Richard LaPiere has defined value as "the

---

13. On this subject, see particularly Joseph A. Kahl's article, "Some Measure-
    ments of Achievement Orientation," *American Journal of Sociology* 70 (May
    1966): 669-81.
14. Fred L. Strodtbeck, "Family Interaction, Values and Achievement" in David
    C. McClelland et al., *Talent and Society* (New York: D. Van Nostrand, 1958).
15. McClelland et al., *The Achievement Motive*; McClelland, *The Achieving So-
    ciety*. A number of articles on achievement motivation have been published;
    most are partially summarized in *The Achieving Society*. But we should

obverse of motives. . . . (It is) the object, quality, or condition that satisfies motivation."[16] On the other hand, motivation is the product of all the needs, impulses and desires, conscious or unconscious, which provoke a person to act.

This distinction is particularly apparent in the various methods employed to study values and motivation. Sociologists generally look for values at the conscious level; the individuals interviewed must be able to express them in an explicit way, to verbalize them, or at least to recognize them when asked to make precise choices. Psychologists, for their part, are sensitive to the unconscious mechanisms of motivation and they have been very skilful in discovering indices which reveal the unconscious needs and desires that are hidden behind adherence to values and the reasons for it.

Measuring techniques for the need for achievement

A psychologist by training, McClelland wished to isolate and measure what he called the need for achievement (which he symbolizes by *n Achievement* or *N Act*) in the motivation of social actors. For this purpose, he used as a research instrument a projection test inspired by Henry Murray's Thematic Aperception Test. Subjects are presented with ambiguous pictures and are asked to tell a story about them. The postulate of the projective test is that subjects project their unconscious needs and motivations into the imaginary story, and that these can be discerned by means of an appropriate code. McClelland's test is constructed to detect the reactions and emotions of subjects in competitive situations where behaviour and accomplishment are evaluated according to criteria of excellence. The imaginary story, written by the subject, reveals the need he feels to succeed in what he undertakes, the standard of excellence that he imposes on himself, and the confidence with which he undertakes and accomplishes tasks of varying difficulty.

Clearly McClelland considers the achievement motive to be *a*

---

mention particularly the article by Bernard C. Rosen, "The Achievement Syndrome." This article is of theoretical and methodological interest because the author has used two research instruments — one to measure achievement as a value, and the other to measure achievement motivation as defined by McClelland.

16. Richard T. LaPiere, *A Theory of Social Control* (New York: McGraw-Hill Book Company, Inc., 1954), p. 133.

personality trait. The test is designed to measure neither achievement as a value, nor the need for achievement when faced with specific tasks, but rather *the generalized attitude of an individual in every competitive situation requiring a standard of excellence.*

McClelland extended the application of his technique by developing a second instrument. He postulated that literary works, mainly tales, fables and short stories, show the same characteristic as a projective test, because their authors have unconsciously expressed their need for achievement. He drew up a code for measuring this need, in folklore as well as in written works. McClelland was able to use this second instrument to measure the achievement motive during past historical periods.

In the literate countries, he applied his test particularly to the analysis of tales that young children read or should read in their educational texts. He did this for the following reason: when the educational texts of a country present young children with examples of a strong need for achievement, it can be expected that, in subsequent years, there will be a general rise in the need for achievement in the population; and this rise in the need for achievement should, in turn, have a visible effect on the history of this country.

Through these two tests, McClelland was able to determine a *rate* of achievement motive among individuals and collectivities, and subsequently to locate these individuals and collectivities on a *scale* of need for achievement, ranging from those who manifest the highest need to those who show the weakest need.

Need for achievement and economic development

On the basis of numerous surveys in various countries and at various historical periods, McClelland formulates the following conclusions:

1. The need for achievement varies from one individual to another; but collectivities are also differentiated in the same way. Countries, religious groups, ethnic groups, social classes and historical periods have varying degrees of achievement motive.

2. The analysis of the economic development of a number of industrialized countries between 1925 and 1950 shows that those in which, in 1925, one could identify a strong achievement motive (through the study of educational texts) have experienced *more rapid expansion and economic development than the others.*

3. The study of forty-five archaic societies shows that those where the achievement motive is strongest have shown *a more intense economic activity*.

4. Analyses of particular historical periods reveal that *a high achievement motive immediately precedes a period of economic development, that the achievement motive diminishes at the time when economic development is at its highest level, and that a decrease in the achievement motive entails an economic regression*. This evolution has been observed in the following cases: Greece between 900 and 100 B.C., Spain from 1200 to the middle of the eighteenth century, England from 1400 to 1830, the United States from 1800 to 1950 and the Inca empire of Peru from 800 B.C. to A.D. 700.

5. If the achievement motive acts as a factor in economic development, the explanation is that it is *a basic element in the economic entrepreneurial spirit*, and more precisely in the mentality of the entrepreneur, in socialist or communist structures as well as in capitalist structures.

Social conditions favourable to the need for achievement

Faced with these statements, the obvious question is — what produces a strong achievement motive among certain individuals and not among others, within certain collectivities and not in others? To this question McClelland replies that, although the achievement motive is a psychological need or a personality trait, this does not mean that it is a purely psychological phenomenon. Its origin cannot be hereditary since it varies so rapidly from one generation to another. Instead, certain social conditions explain its different degrees of manifestation among individuals.

What are the environmental conditions which influence the degree of achievement motive? McClelland identifies a few of them.

The, first factor is *family education*. Children do not necessarily have the same need for achievement as do their parents. On the contrary, parents who themselves have a strong need for achievement, and who have succeeded, have a tendency to encourage a weaker need for achievement in their children. The education most favourable to the need for achievement is that which develops personal autonomy, self-control, specific ambitions and self-confidence sufficiently early in the child. It supposes, on the part of both parents, an equilibrium between the freedom that they accord to the child and the controls that they establish, between the affection that they demonstrate and the tasks and standards that they suggest. McClelland seems to believe that the degree of achievement motive is fixed once and for all during childhood and is not changed later.

Second, the *social class* of the parents influences the need for achievement. According to studies carried out to date, the need for achievement is highest in the middle class.

Third, it is among those individuals and groups who have the *strongest aspirations to social mobility* that the achievement motive is most marked. But two conditions seem to be necessary: that the individuals and groups have strong ambitions to improve their situation, and that they have the opportunity to hope for a real change. *Too distant an objective and too great a challenge are unfavourable to the achievement motive.* Here McClelland sees a confirmation of Toynbee's thesis, that challenges must be neither too weak nor too strong for a collectivity to deploy the energy and initiative necessary for its development. This observation is valid for both individuals and collectivities, as Atkinson demonstrated when he constructed, on an experimental basis, conditions within which a challenge provokes the desire and the ambition to succeed.[17] This model would explain the vicious circle in which particularly underprivileged groups — social classes, ethnic minorities, developing or colonized countries — are trapped.

Formal education does not seem to emphasize the need for achievement when individuals are elsewhere surrounded by a culture and groups where the achievement motive is weak. In this case, school experience is too partial and limited to exert a significant influence.

Ideology and need for achievement

McClelland adds a fourth factor (to family education, social class and aspirations to mobility) which is favourable to raising the level of the need for achievement — *the ideological climate.* A number of observations seem to demonstrate that a clear rise in

---

17. J. W. Atkinson, "Motivational Determinants of Risk-taking Behavior," *Psychological Review* 64 (1957): 359-72; J. W. Atkinson and G. H. Litwin, "Achievement motive and test anxiety conceived as motive to approach success and motive to avoid failure," *Journal of Abnormal and Social Psychology* 60 (1960): 52-63.

the need for achievement accompanies what McClelland calls a movement towards ideological conversion, whatever the ideology to which one is converted — a new religion, a religious revival, nationalism, socialism, communism and so forth. It seems that an active ideological climate which instigates the redefinition of a collectivity and its goals entails, at the same time and at least among some of the population, a great achievement motive.

This phenomenon has been observed in various circumstances. It was reported in the case of the Mexican revolution.[18] McClelland believes that the same phenomenon took place following the Soviet revolution.[19] He also mentions a significant rise in the need for achievement in the newly independent young nations.[20] In addition, he has analyzed the educational texts in what he calls the three Chinas — Republican China from 1920 to 1929, Nationalist China from 1950 to 1959, and Communist China at the same period. He notices a weak level of need for achievement in the first period, a higher level in the second, and the highest level in the third.[21]

Frustrating situations and the need for achievement

Pursuing McClelland's analysis, another psychologist, Everett Hagen,[22] has attempted to analyze the psychological mechanisms which, in situations of collective frustration (in the case, for example, of social classes, underprivileged ethnic minorities or colonized countries), can provoke revolt and the desire to innovate among certain individuals. Hagen locates the source of these mechanisms in the relationships between father and son. The image of the father who is crushed and abused is, for the son, a source of disappointment, disillusionment and revolt against the father. If, through transfer, this revolt against the father becomes a revolt against the oppressive group, the desire for a new personal and so-

---

18. On this subject, see Lipset, "Values, Education, and Entrepreneurship", in Lipset and Solari, eds., *Elites in Latin America*, pp. 36-39.
19. McClelland, *The Achieving Society*, pp. 412-13.
20. David C. McClelland, "Motivational Patterns in Southeast Asia with Special Reference to the Chinese Case," *Journal of Social Issues* 19 (1963): 10.
21. *Ibid.*, pp. 12-13.
22. Hagen, *Theory of Social Change*; and by the same author, "How Economic Growth Begins; A General Theory Applied to Japan," *Public Opinion Quarterly* 22 (1958): 373-90.

cial identity may emerge. And this search for a new identity will favour a rise in the need for achievement.

In this case, the need for achievement will be very strong. As McClelland noted earlier, the individuals who emerge from a group with a weak achievement motive manifest a particularly strong need for achievement. According to Hagen, it is this strong need for achievement which impels the innovating agents who try to break the vicious circle in which underprivileged collectivities are confined. These innovating agents will contribute to the elaboration and diffusion of a liberating or developmental ideology. Thus they are likely to create the *ideological climate* which is favourable to the need for achievement and to revolutionary or other collective action.

Other-directedness and social change

Let us report two more of McClelland's observations which are of particular interest at this point, for they add new elements to what we have just seen and thereby broaden the picture.

First, McClelland notes that a second psychological factor is added to the achievement motive in the explanation of economic development. Using David Riesman's terminology (which is already familiar to us — see Chapter 11), he calls this factor other-directedness. By this, McClelland means that in the economically advanced countries human relationships are observed to manifest a greater flexibility; they are less rigidly pre-established and defined than in the less advanced societies. This presupposes, on the part of the social actors, greater attention and sensitivity to others, particularly equals, and more adaptability and facility in recognizing, accepting and welcoming new norms of conduct. Mass communications play a particularly important role in the development of this sensibility and adaptability.

This observation agrees with the one that Daniel Lerner made earlier.[23] He noted the progress of what he called empathy in human relationships in the course of the modernization of societies. Empathy is the capacity to put oneself in the place of another, to understand quickly what he is and the role that he fulfills, and then to adapt oneself to very different people who are also differ-

---

23. Daniel Lerner, *The Passing of Traditional Society: Modernizing the Middle East* (New York: The Free Press of Glencoe, Inc., 1958), pp. 52-54.

ent from oneself. Modern society, which is vast and complex, requires that the social actor have numerous and brief relationships with various people, who are virtually strangers, in various roles. This psychological mobility is essential to the functioning of both individuals and the social organization in such a society.

Going back a bit further, we can suggest that on the basis of very different starting points, McClelland and Lerner confirm Durkheim's thesis on the solidarity of *complementarity*, which he called organic solidarity and which is characteristic of industrial society.

Psychological needs and the evolution of political structures

Second, McClelland identifies two other psychological needs which may be more or less pronounced among individuals and collectivities. These are the need for affiliation, and the need for power. The need for affiliation is characterized by the desire for " . . . establishing, maintaining or restoring a positive affective relationship with another person. This relationship is most adequately described by the word friendship."[24] This is a different and totally independent need from the other-directed attitude described above. The need for affiliation corresponds to a need to be loved, respected, accepted and forgiven. McClelland defines the need for power as a concern "with the control of the means of influencing a person."[25] It is the need to be able to command and punish, to have subordinates, and to impose one's will on them.

The complementary analysis of these two needs leads McClelland to conclude:

> A combination of low *n* (need for) Affiliation and a high *n* (need for) Power is very closely associated with the tendency of a nation to resort to totalitarian methods in governing its people. Every one of the more notorious police state regimes in our sample of countries (with one possible exception) was above the mean in *n* Power and below the mean in *n* Affiliation.[26]

This last observation reveals the possible existence of links be-

24. McClelland, *The Achieving Society*, p. 160.
25. *Ibid.*, p. 167.
26. *Ibid.*, p. 168.

tween psychological needs and the evolution of political structures. This is a vast research area which has not yet been explored.
To what profound psychological impulses are men responding
when they set themselves up as promoters of totalitarian or democratic political structures? What psychological needs lead them to
wish to restrict the freedom of others or to share their own?

These questions, and many others, come to mind when we examine the studies which have begun to discover the as yet un-
suspected aspects of the socio-psychological foundations of historical action.

Conclusion

These psychological studies by McClelland, Hagen and others illustrate particularly well, in the case of agents of historical action,
the reciprocity of psychological and social perspectives which we
have referred to since the beginning of this book. These studies
have led to the discovery of certain psychological foundations for
the elaboration of ideologies, and to the exploration of the impact
that ideologies can have on the psychological states of members of
a society. In the preceding chapter, we emphasized the socio-
psychological nature of ideologies. Studies on the need for achievement provide us with a striking example.

In addition, these studies reveal *certain psychological motives
for historical action*. They throw light on the impulses and motivations to which certain agents of change, and certain particularly
active and innovating elites, respond. This contribution by social
psychology perfectly complements the analysis of the factors and
agents of social change.

Conclusion

Throughout our analysis of the factors, conditions and agents of
social change, we have emphasized the fact that social change cannot be explained by a single cause or by a dominant factor. We
have tried to show both the *diversity* and the *interdependence* of
factors, conditions and agents of change. Finally, we have emphasized the reciprocity of psychological and sociological perspectives.

In conclusion, however, it is important to specify the exact
meaning of this multiplicity and interdependence. It is not a ques-

tion of erecting a system of causes (rightly condemned by C. Wright Mills as "a pluralist confusion of causes").[27] Rather, we have emphasized the fact that there is not, *in an absolute and general sense*, a hierarchy of causes of social change which would be universally applicable. But this does not mean that *in each concrete situation* there is no hierarchy of causes — that is to say, one or several dominant factors and one or more outstanding influential agents. On the contrary, it is almost an axiom of sociological research that one must presuppose the existence of such a hierarchy. It is on such an axiom that the theory of the interdependence and interaction of factors and agents is based. What Mills called the pluralist confusion of causes is the failure to recognize this axiom.

The hierarchy and interdependence of the causes of change — which we earlier called their interrelationships, in Georges Balandier's terminology — is clearly a problem which must be resolved in each empirical study. The sociologist must be firmly convinced that, in each concrete situation, dominant explanatory factors exist; but he must be equally convinced that in the absolute there does not exist a general model of causality which is always and uniformly applicable.

---

27. C. Wright Mills, *The Sociological Imagination*, p. 85.

Chapter 13
Industrialization, Development and Modernization

Our analysis in the last two chapters of the factors and conditions of social change and the agents of historical action is very general. We have reviewed studies, theories and hypotheses which attempt to measure the influence that can be attributed to certain factors and agents in social dynamics. We should keep in mind, however, that *all these studies have the same goal — to understand the evolution or history of modern industrial society*. As we have stressed on several occasions, it is through the effort to interpret and explain contemporary Western society that the discipline of sociology has been developed and refined.

The sociology of archaic peoples

Considered from this perspective, until very recently archaic or primitive societies have interested most sociologists only as *points of comparison*. By reference to these societies, it has been possible to identify the peculiar characteristics of Western society, which sociologists have placed at the forefront of human and social evolution. Taken to extremes, this perspective could lead one to the conclusion that the archaic peoples, who stopped at some point on the road to development and remained stationary for thousands of years, were destined never to evolve beyond that point. Perhaps they were victims of either unfavourable physical conditions or an inevitable innate inferiority. As we have seen, Lévy-Bruhl was con-

vinced that the intelligence of primitive men was stunted and restrained by a pre-logical mentality which was fundamentally different from that of civilized man.

Today this point of view has been completely modified. On the
one hand, as we mentioned earlier, there is no proof that the archaic peoples have been stationary over hundreds and thousands
of years; on the other hand, peoples who have been regarded as
primitive have recently become involved in industrialization and
urbanization, and have experienced rapid and profound changes
in their social environment. Particularly since the end of the Second World War, some of these peoples have started to agitate, to
throw off the yoke of colonizing civilizations, and to claim their
right to self-determination and economic and social progress. New
nations have been formed, encompassing tribes which formerly
were enemies. Education has touched at least part of these
populations, and there has been a mass migration towards urban
centres.

Three stages in the Western perception of archaic societies

The perception that the West has had of these "uncivilized" peoples has evolved in three stages, well expressed by the terms used
to designate these peoples. In the sixteenth and seventeenth centuries, the so-called savages were the object of both curiosity and
enthusiasm. Eye-witness accounts of their strange customs were
avidly heard and read. At the same time, some wished to West-
ernize them and convert them to true religion, in the hope that
they would become useful citizens of the Empire. There are in evidence long extracts from the letters of Louis XIV and Colbert to
the governors, administrators and clergy of New France, enjoining
them to "Gallicize the savages," according to the phrase then in
use, in order to make honest citizens of them.

Towards the middle of the eighteenth century, it became obvious that the civilizing and missionary undertakings had failed, especially in America, or had accomplished their objectives in a me-
diocre way. And in the nineteenth century, the evolutionist theories confirmed what people already suspected — that the small
savage tribes retained traces of, or were throwbacks to, former
stages of human and social evolution. These peoples, who had remained at the periphery of the forward march of civilization, were
then no longer called savages but were given the name *primitives*.
Reinforced by certain interpretations of the Bible, this notion of

primitiveness had the additional advantage of soothing the conscience of the Christian conquerors, who exploited the weakness of these peoples by seizing their territory and enslaving them.

In the twentieth century, the "undeveloped" peoples are no longer regarded as human documents, but have become a problem for the Western conscience. They represent the problem of hunger and, more explicitly, the problem of the gap between the rich and the poor or less developed countries. A new vocabulary has appeared. Now we speak of underdeveloped countries, developing countries, economic development, new nations and the Third World.

The influence of this development on the social sciences

It is in the nature of the social sciences to feel the impact of such an important and sudden change in perspective, while at the same time they help to a certain extent to bring it about. Thus, the way in which problems are posed in the social sciences has been changed. The developing countries are not so much a witness to the past as a project for the future. It is from this perspective that they now interest sociologists, and for this reason that upheavals in these countries hold their attention. The changes taking place have revealed new theoretical and practical problems for our sciences. They have enlarged the scope of our vision and opened new horizons for research.

The social sciences of the nineteenth and early twentieth centuries accustomed us to regarding industrialization as an innovatory process over a fairly long period, which passes through certain stages and operates at a constantly accelerating rhythm. Today, in contrast, we see some young nations passing very quickly from archaic styles of life to industrial society, from the bush to the factory and town. In addition, industrialization was considered to be an inescapable fact whose advance had only to be followed. Now, in the developing countries, it appears to be a consciously sought objective and a design to be achieved. Thus, industrialization is revealed in its ideological aspect. Finally, certain stereotypes of both traditional and industrial society which were exaggerated by the social sciences were forced to break down. In particular, it appears to be more difficult to establish an opposition between the two types of society than was once believed.

This said, it should not be concluded that studies of the developing countries mark a complete break with the earlier studies that we mentioned in Chapter 12. On the contrary, strong ties exist, and there is even some continuity between them. Studies of the developing countries could not have been conducted and refined without reference to the accumulated studies on industrialization in the West. Indeed, the modernization of the underdeveloped countries simply places in a new perspective the analysis of the whole problem of socio-economic change which until recently could be considered only in limited terms. In any case, the study of the developing countries has effected a return in sociology to the dynamic approach which early sociologists adopted almost instinctively, and which unfortunately later disappeared.

The procedure to follow

From this it can be understood why, in a text such as this, we attach importance to the phenomenon of the modernization of underdeveloped countries. Sociological studies of this phenomenon — and to an even greater extent, economic, political and anthropological studies — multiply each year. But above all, this new research area has, for us today, become *the equivalent of what the industrial revolution in the West was for the nineteenth-century scholars.* Thus, following our discussion of the industrial revolution in the preceding chapters, it seems quite natural to continue our study of social change by analyzing the developing countries.

First we shall define the concept of development. As will be seen, this idea must be understood in a wider sense than that which is usually attached to it. Then we will detail a model of change for the so-called developing countries, and subsequently discuss the concept of traditional society in the new framework of these changes.

To complete this model, in the next chapter we will focus our attention on the colonial situation and the process of decolonization, for this is the framework in which the development of most archaic and backward societies takes place.

Definitions and Distinctions

The richness and ambiguity of terminology

From the beginning, let us state that the terminology used to designate the processes taking place in the developing countries is not yet firmly established. We speak of industrialization and urbanization,[1] of economic growth,[2] of economic[3] and political development.[4] More recently, the term *modernization* has been adopted;[5] more graphic expressions also are used, such as the Third World[6] (analogous to the Third Estate in France in the eighteenth century) or, in Marxist language, the proletarian nations.[7]

This richness and ambiguity of terminology perhaps indicates the difficulty encountered in delimiting a new reality which is complex, mobile, extremely varied and in constant turmoil. Each of these terms undoubtedly has a different connotation, although in fact most writers use them indiscriminately. Here we shall use only those which are current among sociologists, political scientists and anthropologists — industrialization, economic growth or development, development and modernization. First, we shall try to grasp the exact meaning of each term.

What, in fact, is development or modernization? How can the phenomenon be defined, or at least its essential characteristics described, on the basis of the extremely varied concrete forms which it can assume?

Five Stages of
Economic Growth

To reply to this question, let us start with what W. W. Rostow has called the five stages of economic growth,[8] briefly summarizing the main points.

---

1. Daryll Forde, ed., *Aspects sociaux de l'industrialisation et de l'urbanisation en Afrique au sud du Sahara* (Paris: UNESCO, 1956).
2. W. W. Rostow, *The Process of Economic Growth* (New York: Oxford University Press, 1953) and by the same author, *The Stages of Economic Growth* (London: Cambridge University Press, 1960).
3. Albert O. Hirschman, *The Strategy of Economic Development* (New Haven: Yale University Press, 1958).
4. A. F. K. Organski, *The Stages of Political Development* (New York: Alfred A. Knopf, 1965).
5. David E. Apter, *The Politics of Modernization* (Chicago: University of Chicago Press, 1965).
6. Georges Balandier, ed., *Le "Tiers Monde"* (Paris: Presses universitaires de France, 1956); Peter Worsley, *The Third World* (Chicago: University of Chicago Press, 1964).
7. Pierre Moussa, *Les nations prolétaires* (Paris: Presses universitaires de France, 1959).
8. Rostow, *The Stages of Economic Growth*.

Traditional society

Traditional society is characterized by a science and technology which are still pre-Newtonian, and consequently by a ceiling on productivity. The production of traditional society is not necessarily static. It can increase, but only to a limited extent according to the ceiling imposed by the archaic state of scientific and technical knowledge.

Being mainly agricultural, traditional society is organized around the family and the clan. It permits only limited social mobility, and the attitude of the population is stamped with a certain long-term fatalism — that is, the general situation is accepted as it is. This does not, however, preclude the desire for limited individual improvement.

Pre-conditions for take-off

In order for the development process to take place within traditional society, *certain conditions and factors which are indispensable to take-off must appear.* In some sectors of the population, the idea spreads that economic progress is necessary in order to reach particular goals, such as general well-being, national pride or personal profit. Education contributes to the development of new needs and aspirations, at least among some of the population. Entrepreneurs mobilize savings for private or public firms. Banks and other financial institutions appear. Investment grows. Some industrial firms are established, and commerce is extended within and outside the country. A central political power forms, generally on the basis of coalitions which favour a new nationalist feeling.

This period is really a transitory stage between traditional society and take-off. Often, these changes are restricted to a limited sector of the population and the economy within a society which remains traditional and whose general productivity remains low.

Take-off

Take-off is the critical period and the decisive point which marks the difference between traditional society and developed society. Take-off presupposes that the forces favourable to economic expansion which were established during the preceding phase do not remain isolated within traditional society, but fan out to reach all of society, becoming its dominant agents and directing its evolution. By this time, of necessity, resistance to change — which traditional society holds to and perpetuates mainly in its mentality, attitudes and social structures — has been destroyed or at least largely eliminated.

Then, as a result of the increasing investment rate, of which a large proportion comes from foreign capital, industrial firms and services multiply. Agricultural productivity also must increase in order to free the workers who are needed in the new industrial labour force. Towns expand and new urban centres are created. The geographical and social mobility of the population becomes intense.

Great Britain went through this take-off period at the end of the eighteenth century; France and the United States in the first half of the nineteenth century; Germany and Japan in the second half of the nineteenth century; Russia and Canada at the end of the nineteenth and at the beginning of the twentieth. India and China have now in turn entered this take-off stage.

Maturity

Maturity is characterized mainly by the diversification of industrial production. In the preceding phase, industry could still develop only in some sectors of production, particularly in the basic sectors. But the sustained movement of investments soon permits the opening up of new sectors, the exploration of new natural resources, the discovery of new, more economical and efficient techniques. Rostow has estimated that economic maturity is attained about forty years after the end of the take-off period.

High mass consumption

The phase of *high mass consumption* is marked by a general rise in the standard of living of the whole population, an increase in the number of white-collar and skilled workers in the labour force, and the growth in investment devoted to social security, health and welfare. The European countries and Japan are now in this phase; the Soviet Union has just entered it; the United States is probably in the process of going beyond, into a sixth stage that Rostow has not yet been able to outline.

The place of the developing countries

Rostow's vast picture reveals that the developing countries are those which are located in the second and third stages that we have just described. Indeed, most are in the second phase, in which the necessary conditions for take-off are established. Thus, these countries are going through a transitory stage; the conditions favourable to their economic growth remain limited, and many obstacles must still be overcome.

This observation is equally valid for many newly independent countries, as well as for countries in a colonial situation. A number of the new nations — and even the not-so-new nations, such as South Africa — are tragically underdeveloped in economic terms. Political independence and economic growth do not necessarily go together.

A Few Definitions

This leads us to distinguish among some of the terms mentioned earlier — industrialization, economic development, development and modernization.

Industrialization and economic development

In the strictest sense, *industrialization is the search for constantly increasing work productivity through technical innovation and through the rational organization of the labour force.* In this precise sense, industrialization is essentially the arrangement of the working environment, which is only one aspect of economic development (or economic growth).

Economic development consists of the use of various economic factors with a view to raising the national income and the general standard of living of the population of a country or region, and benefiting its general well-being. Economic development, as Rostow's model demonstrates, presupposes capital investment, the establishment of banking systems and financial institutions, the creation of transportation and communication systems, various public services, a fiscal system and social security measures. Thus, strictly speaking, economic development is the goal set by economic policy.

Development or modernization

Finally, what we here call development or modernization[9] has a more general and a wider meaning which includes both industrialization and economic development. It is *all the actions undertaken to direct a society towards the realization of an ordered set of collective and individual living conditions which, on the basis of certain values, are judged desirable.*

Comments on these definitions

These definitions are important and should be commented on. First, it will be noted that the idea of modernization or total development necessarily entails normative judgements and a scale of values. The economist can consider the wish to raise the standard of living a fact; for the sociologist, this wish is functionally related to a scale of values. Not all human societies value equally the raising of the standard of living and give it the same importance. Thus, educational content can be conditioned by the requirements of industrialization and economic development; but it is also governed by certain human qualities and an image of the ideal man which express a scale of values. A political regime is not only a power organization; it is also the expression of the meaning given to freedom and of the importance given to it in itself, and in relation to other objectives. The same is true of economic structures and growth. They are not only objective realities, but also the result of certain value choices. They presuppose that a value is accorded to certain behaviour, types of men, life styles and so forth.

Let us emphasize that from the perspective of values, each society is a sub-system whose total system is the international society. Each society draws its guiding values from a larger system; and each can measure its development by referring to "more modern" societies or perhaps to societies considered as "more valid" models.

Second, our definition refers to "an ordered set of . . . living con-

---

9. It will be noticed that the two terms *development* and *modernization* are used interchangeably, although some authors have tried to give each a specific meaning. But the distinctions that have been made ultimately can be reduced to nuances that need not concern us here. The reader who is interested in these discussions can consult Apter, *The Politics of Modernization*, chap. 2; and also J. P. Nettl and R. Robertson, "Industrialization, development or modernization," *The British Journal of Sociology* 17 (September 1966): 274-91.

ditions." In effect, development seems to be the search for an equilibrium which is never attained, or perhaps for the resolution of constantly renewed tensions between different sectors of social and human life. For example, it is said that in modern society man's moral progress is not equal to his technical progress; or perhaps that mass culture lags behind the techniques of mass communication. Such expressions of opinion reveal not only a scale of values, but also the need for a sort of ideal harmony that a perfect society should be able to attain, according to a particular normative definition of man.

Third, our definition of development (as well as the definitions of economic development and industrialization) applies to the so-called developed or industrialized countries as well as to the developing countries. In the light of these definitions, there is no such thing as a developed country, in the sense of one that has attained a final stage of development. *The development process is found in all societies which have at least some degree of industrialization.*

The importance of the economic factor

The order in which we have presented the definitions of industrialization, economic development and modernization is not accidental. In contemporary society, modernization is very largely conditioned or determined by economic development, and this in turn results from the industrialization process which follows technological progress. In the two preceding chapters, we have stressed *the historical relativity of the hierarchy of factors.* But, in the case of the modernization process of backward societies, we are not falling into a strict and rigid technological and economic determinism if we grant economic development *a predominant place.* Undeniably it is this that acts as the main driving power and the essential condition of total development. In effect, in the modernization process, industrialization acts as the instrumental, if not the main, objective around which motives and energies are organized. In the name of industrialization, political and legal constraints and controls are formulated; in response to its needs, populations are displaced and life styles and social organization are altered. Too long ignored and then strongly emphasized by Marx and Engels (perhaps a little too much), the predominance of the economic and technical fact in social change is forcefully asserted in the analysis of modernization.

A Model of Development

Following our general definition of the terminology, we can now return to the analysis of a particular case of development — that of the so-called developing countries. These are societies which can be said to be in a period of rapid and sometimes profound transition, in which the type of society that we have called traditional breaks down and is transformed or adapted under the impact of industrialization and subsequent socio-cultural implications.

In the following pages, we will develop a model of this transition. First, however, let us emphasize that it is a general model, or a sort of ideal type, which cannot take into account the diversity of concrete situations revealed by empirical observation. Some societies may be better prepared than others to become industrialized, because of the natural resources at their disposal, because of their geographical situation, or perhaps because of their former development, certain cultural traits or the availability of the labour force. Therefore, the rhythm of modernization will not be the same from one society to another. The areas of resistance will vary; the obstacles to overcome will be different; the phenomena of disorganization will not be manifested in the same way or in the same sectors. Nevertheless, it remains true that beyond the diversity of individual cases, some traits of modernization are sufficiently common to most situations that a general picture or theoretical model can be derived.[10]

Our model will take into account the changes which operate in three sectors of developing societies: economic changes, changes in the social structure, and changes in culture and attitudes.

---

10. It would be unnecessarily weighty for the reader if we indicated all the bibliographical sources on which this model is based. We will mention only a few. The reader who is interested can consult, in particular, the excellent chapter by Wilbert E. Moore, "Industrialization and Social Change" in Bert F. Hoselitz and Wilbert E. Moore, eds., *Industrialization and Society* (UNESCO, Mouton, 1963); Forde, ed., *L'industrialisation en Afrique*; Lerner, *The Passing of Traditional Society*; Melville J. Herskovits, *The Human Factor in Changing Africa* (New York: Alfred A. Knopf, 1962); Georges Balandier, *Sociologie des Brazzavilles noires* (Paris: Cahiers de la Fondation nationale des Sciences politiques, no. 67, 1955).

Economic Changes

Basically, development presupposes that a subsistence economy — that is, an economy with low productivity which is designed to ensure local and short-term consumption responding to the basic necessities of life — be transformed into an economy of industrial production. In this sense, development first consists of a process of industrialization.

Capital investment

Industrialization requires a transfer of capital: capital invested in landed property and everything connected with it (herds, houses, servants) or in other non-productive activities (ceremonial, ritual, religious, magical) must be progressively freed and reinvested in the technical equipment necessary for industrial production, transportation and communications, as well as in commerce and service industries.

Shortage of capital is obviously the major obstacle to industrialization in many developing countries. Industrialization requires considerable investment, but it is often not possible to accumulate the required capital because of the general poverty of the population. When sufficient capital exists, it is often monopolized by a small number of people (the large landowners for example) who refuse to transfer it, either because of their attitude or the social prestige conferred by landed property, or because of the considerable financial risks involved in new undertakings. The same reasons prevent those with savings from investing in new undertakings. The small saver, in particular, does not change easily from a hoarder to a shareholder. For these various reasons, development and the acceleration of development in most cases require the contribution of foreign capital, and this opens the door to various forms of colonialism — economic, political, social and cultural.

The transfer and recruitment of the labour force

Industrialization also requires a transfer of the labour force. In the non-industrialized countries, more than eighty per cent of the labour force is involved in agriculture, other primary activities and crafts. An important proportion of this labour force must now be directed towards the secondary transformation occupations and also, to a lesser extent, towards the tertiary occupations (commerce, services, communications and professions). Let us emphasize that, in order to free the labour force without lowering the production necessary for food supplies, capital must also be invested in agricultural equipment so that the productivity of farms and livestock can be increased.

The recruitment of the industrial labour force forms the second main obstacle to the industrialization of developing countries. The problem is not that the labour force is unavailable; it is generally abundant and even overabundant, for the subsistence economy is almost always characterized by underemployment of the agricultural labour force, which will be attracted towards industry by the hope of profit. But this labour force is not prepared for the available specialized posts; it lacks education and technical preparation. Thus, economic development is often characterized by unemployment and the endemic underemployment of an illiterate and unskilled labour force, as well as by the scarcity of specialized labour.

Commerce, consumption and income

With industrial work, the use of money and credit spreads among the population, encouraging the appearance of new needs. Internal commerce is activated, extended and diversified in a more or less constant relationship with the growth of consumption and the rise of per capita income. In the developing countries, the relationships among commerce, consumption and income are very complex. For example, an excessive proportion of the labour force is often involved in commerce and the service industries (this is only one aspect of the underemployment of a population which is not qualified for industrial work). And consumption, particularly of certain prestige or luxury items, overtakes income, necessitating the establishment of a network of loans which drains savings and limits productive investment. The labour surplus also can lead to a lowering of salaries, entailing a depression in consumption and a decrease in the incentive to work.

The parallel traditional economy

The traditional economy continues to exist parallel to industrialization, but it is affected by it. Some forms of employment disappear following the introduction of new products; other traditional activities are commercialized as new markets — for food products, for example — emerge. Money modifies trade relationships within the traditional economy, as well as between it and the industrial economy.

The responsibilities of political power

Industrialization entails an extension of the obligations of those with political power. In particular, they must ensure the general and professional education of young people, and also the education of adults, unless they are able to count on help from other sources, such as the Church. In addition, the government must create transportation (railways, roads, aviation, ships), communication (telephone, telegraph, radio and television), welfare (clinics, hospitals) and social security services; or at least it must contribute to the building of part of these services. It also may wish to take on some industrial investment, or even all of it in a socialist state. For these purposes, those with political power must establish or extend a fiscal system, ensuring the necessary revenue to cope with these expenses. Thus, an important part of the revenue of individuals and of an already weak national revenue must be devoted to essential social investments.

Social Changes

Urbanization

Industrialization is necessarily accompanied by urbanization — that is, it entails a migration of the labour force, mainly young people, and families towards the towns. These towns may have been in existence before industrialization;[11] but now they begin to grow, spread and change in appearance. New towns grow up around mines and industries, and along communication routes.

In some cases, the developing countries experience an excessive influx of population into the towns. Either more workers come to establish themselves than are required for the available jobs; or more likely, too great a proportion of those who come are not sufficiently qualified for the urban labour market. If part of the new

---

11. Thus, contrary to what is often believed about Africa, the town existed before the arrival of the Europeans, and before the beginning of industrialization. Herskovits, *Changing Africa*, pp. 259-63.

urban population suffers from unemployment or under-employ-
ment, there is a proliferation of slum areas or shanty towns, generally in the centre of the town. The term *over-urbanization* is used
in this sense, to designate a rhythm of urban growth which does
not correspond to the rhythm of economic development.[12]

Geographical mobility: its motivations

There may be several motives for the migration of the rural
population to the towns, and they are often quite obscure. In his
study of Brazzaville, Balandier mentions both positive motives
(which attract people to the town) and negative ones (which make
them leave the country). Among the positive motives, he cites the
economic attractions of the town, where the rural people hope to
grow rich; the desire to improve their social status, not only by becoming richer, but also by adopting the life styles and acquiring
the symbols associated with the urban milieu; the need to help
their relatives financially; and the obligation to accompany a
parent or parents. The main negative motives are the desire to escape from the limitations and constraints of traditional society;
the breakdown in the traditional economy following industrialization, which eliminates the need for some craftsmen or de-
prives families of their means of subsistence; and the over-
population of the country, or its poverty.[13]

Urbanization also provokes other forms of geographical mobility. Not all of the new urban population settles permanently in
the city. A significant proportion may be transient. Some workers
will stay long enough to accumulate the savings they need to buy
land or herds, and then return to traditional life; others are only
occasional workers who come to work in the city with the goal of
amassing just the necessary money for specific or temporary needs.
For many reasons, urbanization entails a strong stream of geographical mobility between the country and the town.

Family, relatives and local loyalties

In traditional society, the dominant type of family is generally the
extended family, composed of several nuclear families (for ex-

---

12. Moore, "Industrialization and Social Change" in Hoselitz and Moore, eds.,
    Industrialization and Society, p. 335.
13. Georges Balandier, *Sociologie des Brazzaville noires*, pp. 40-43; Herskovits,
    Changing Africa, pp. 267-71.

ample, several married brothers living together with their families and their aging parents), or the polygamous family. Economic development and urbanization tend to disorganize this type of family, so that it breaks up and gives way to the nuclear family (father, mother and their unmarried children) which becomes neolocal (that is, which adopts its own residence). Certain factors contribute to this transformation; migration obliges the nuclear family to become more individualistic; social mobility on the new scale of prestige or stratification associated with the town and industrial work strains the ties between brother and sister; education causes a split within the extended family and leads to its disintegration; and the process is further accelerated by differences in the degree of assimilation of new values, attitudes and behaviour linked to industrialization, the town or the prestige of foreigners.

The same factors also impose a strain on family ties, tribal loyalties and attachments between individuals coming from the same region. Kinship relationships may continue to occupy a very important place in family life; but Moore emphasizes that they " . . . become permissive rather than obligatory; and the number of situations in which they are at all relevant decrease."[14] Tribal allegiances and regional attachments slowly blur in the most highly evolved sectors of the population. But despite everything, they retain a very strong hold on a large part of the population, as has been noticed in Africa, for example.

The status of women

Following the modification of the structure and functions of the family and also contributing towards the acceleration of this transformation, the status of women undergoes certain changes. Industry and the urban milieu offer women the possibility of employment outside the home; the social climate of the town favours their emancipation before and within marriage; within the family, which is the unit of consumption, they dispose of a portion of the budget, or at least the part devoted to current consumption; they benefit from greater freedom in the care and education of their children.

---

14. Moore, "Industrialization and Social Change" in Hoselitz and Moore, eds., *Industrialization and Society*, p. 339.

The status of young and old people

The transformation of the family also leads to the emancipation of young people, who tend to become financially independent, who are better educated than their parents or who, transplanted very early into the urban milieu if not actually born there, adapt to it more completely than do their parents. As a result, the authority of the parents, and particularly the father, is diminished and their role as socializing agents is greatly reduced in relation to what it was in traditional society.

Older people experience a serious loss of status. They no longer benefit from the prestige and authority with which they were honoured in traditional society. Indeed, they are identified with a past which is deprecated to some extent, and they are forced to live in a world to which they can no longer adapt. Thus, the generation conflict (opposing three generations) can become acute, both within the family and throughout the entire society.

Voluntary associations

Since the family and the individual have lost part of the support and security guaranteed by the organization of traditional society, in some developing countries — notably Africa — there is a proliferation of all kinds of voluntary associations. Their official or primary purpose may vary considerably; it may be religious, recreational, political, professional or economic. But in many cases, their real function is to organize mutual aid and cooperation with a view to ensuring security for their members in case of sickness, accident, unemployment, death or pregnancy. In this way, for example, it is possible to explain the great number of associations which bring together women or mothers. Some of these associations have been directly inspired by Europeans — old boys associations or religious associations. Some have been organized locally on the model of European associations — trade unions, professional associations and political cells. Some are local adaptations of European institutions — national churches, local religious sects, recreational or social clubs, and savings banks. And finally, some are clearly of local inspiration — mothers or women's clubs, secret societies, associations of tribes or clans.[15]

---

15. On this subject, detailed documents will be found in the studies by N. Xydias, P. Clément and E. Hellmann cited by Forde, *L'industrialisation en Afrique.*

Stratification and social classes

The urban environment and the new work structures in emerging industrial society encourage further splits within the population. To the distinctions arising from traditional society and based on the tribe, clan, relatives and region of origin are progressively added distinctions of class or pseudo-class, social strata, professional prestige or bureaucratic status. The industrial work environment engenders distinctions which initially are very general between white-collar workers and labourers, and are then refined as the workers become more specialized. This leads to the emergence of classes linked to income, level of education, and the authority exerted over other workers. Complex forms of social stratification are elaborated, incorporating elements of both traditional society and industrial society. New forms of status are created with the appearance of professions and employments hitherto unknown; the old and new scales of prestige and power become mixed, linked together, opposed, superimposed and entangled. The idea of social class was generally non-existent in traditional societies, although they did have their own hierarchy of authority and powers. It emerges and is extended in the developing countries, resulting from the economic changes that occur and from certain associations which appear, particularly trade-unionism and some political parties.

Political organization

Earlier we emphasized the wider obligations which fall to the State in the process of industrialization. Political power can no longer be restricted to a limited region and shared between small jurisdictions, as is generally the case in traditional society and in a subsistence economy. Groupings or coalitions must be effected in order to establish a central government which will extend its authority over a sufficiently vast territory to be able to organize public service utilities such as education, health, welfare, transportation and communication. In many cases, new nations have had to be created fairly artificially, by-passing tribal or regional divisions, in order to install quickly a government administration and the required public services.

New and traditional elites

Parallel to the former elites (tribal and family leaders, priests, sorcerers), new elites appear and grow, further encouraging structural change. These elites are identified with urban life, industrialization and the values of technological society. They emerge from voluntary associations (trade unions, political parties); from government or industry (administrators, technocrats, politicians); and from the advancing educational system (university personnel, scholars, teachers). Between the new and the old elites, the relationships are complex, often tense and sometimes hostile. The new elites extend and symbolize a style of life, ideologies and values which may seem to threaten the traditional elites. But the old and new elites sometimes may become temporary allies in a common cause — for example, in the fight against foreign administration and control.

Changes in Culture and Attitudes

Economic ideology

Industrialization, and the social changes that accompany it, cannot be effected without the intervention of a new world view which arises out of profound changes in spirit and mentality. Such changes are more difficult to discern, and still more difficult to measure, than are economic and social changes. There is a serious lack of detailed studies on the subject. It can be said, however, that a large proportion of the cultural and psychological changes associated with development are connected with economic ideology. The ideology implicit in the subsistence economy must give way to one which is propitious to industrial productivity. This latter ideology can be reduced to a few essential traits.

1. The physical environment may no longer be regarded as a power to which one submits or with which one lives harmoniously, but as a force that man can dominate and subject to his direction and control. The physical environment can be controlled on the condition that it is demystified — that is, as long as it is not attributed an arbitrary will (whether internal or external) but is recognized to have a determinism that man can exploit provided that he knows its laws.

2. The production of goods and the standard of living are not definitively stable, but can rise through scientific and technical innovation. The productivity of both work and capital can be in-

creased, if the rationale applied to the physical environment is extended to all working and economic relationships.

This ideology can exist in both a socialist context and a capitalist society; it is the cultural foundation of the entire economy of industrial production. In the developing countries, it may be more or less rapidly assimilated, depending on whether the local tradition lends itself to it already or strongly resists it.

It is in and through the work milieu that the economic ideology of production is first acquired in the developing countries. In effect, the industrial working environment imposes on the workers a respect and value for technology, for productive work, and for the learning of universal and specific norms in the organization and operation of the firm. Any refusal to acquire these norms or difficulty in doing so constitutes an obstacle to progress in many developing countries, where adherence to the particularist norms of traditional society can slow down the rhythm of productivity increase.

Political ideologies

In many developing countries, industrialization was first imposed from the outside, generally by a foreign power. Such a situation did not favour the assimilation of the economic ideology of production by the local population; on the contrary, it was likely to engender opposition or resistance to the importation of a new spirit which threatened traditional values and established interests. Before they could be persuaded to participate actively in the movement towards industrialization and make it their goal, generally the people had to be motivated by a political ideology. In the developing countries, nationalism usually has fulfilled this function, sometimes coloured by a more or less radical socialism. Either by basing itself on certain traditional values or by transposing these values, nationalism has given economic development a meaning that is wider and more immediate; it has increased its relevance by providing a set of values and symbols capable of arousing collective and individual action. Thus, nationalism has served, in a way, to spiritualize economic development, to make it a second instrumental objective at the service of a higher goal. Political ideology therefore has been able to become a foundation and springboard for the economic ideology of production. Sometimes, of course, nationalism has impeded economic development when attempts have been made to effect certain objectives too hastily and when deception and illusion have been freely used to achieve its goals. The functional and complementary relationships between political and economic ideology are often complex and delicate.

Political ideologies and religion

Nationalism and socialism have often taken the form of a quasi-religious ideology, acting as a substitute for weakened religious feeling. In this regard, the secularization that follows industrialization has often been mentioned. It is true that the industrial world favours a clearer distinction between the sacred and the secular than was the case in many traditional societies. In particular, the prestige attached to religious professions has diminished and carried over into various other professions. But this secular phenomenon does not necessarily entail religious indifference. On the contrary, it may be accompanied by a renewed religious fervour, as has been observed in the developing countries and in the more industrialized countries. In fact, instead of serving as a substitute for religion, nationalism often becomes involved in or allied with religion, leading to the formation of national churches, tribal sects, secret societies and political and religious pressure groups. Moreover, the various gaps or discontinuities that economic development provokes between the life styles of traditional society and those of the industrial town engender states of insecurity and anxiety, and feelings of isolation and powerlessness, mainly in those sectors of the population which are least favoured by the change. This socio-psychological environment is highly conducive to the blossoming and expansion of religious movements, particularly those of the fundamentalist type.

Education

In the developing countries where the majority of the population are illiterate, education is a powerful agent of cultural and mental change. It opens up new ways of thinking, enlarges the perception of the world, demystifies the physical environment, develops rationality in knowledge and action, and effects socialization to specific universal norms of judgements and social relationships.

Mass media

Mass media, mainly the newspaper and the radio in the developing countries (television is not yet very widespread), also perform important socializing functions similar to those fulfilled by the school. But while they standardize information, they also serve to disseminate it. Daniel Lerner has emphasized that the techniques of mass communication contribute to the growth of what he has called psychic mobility or empathy, which he considers the psychological attitude essential to modernization. We have already seen that, for Lerner, empathy is the capacity to adapt oneself to various new or changing situations and to a constantly changing milieu. But the mass media teach one to perceive various situations and to imagine the position of those who act. Since in this way they sensitize and prepare for new and diverse experiences, Lerner calls them mobility multipliers.[16] The mass media thus break the ground for political participation, which Lerner considers to be an essential element in the modernization process.

Tradition and Development

Two criticisms

The model that we have just presented seeks to grasp the main traits which are generally observed in the progressive transformation from a traditional to an industrial society. It is really a transition from one type of social system to another.

Sociology is not yet in a position to elaborate a model which would present the logical or necessary stages of this transition. Thus, this is a dynamic model of a particular type, which seeks to define certain relationships between various points or elements of the changing system, and to pinpoint a few obstacles which are likely to block or slow down development.

But this model has been the object of two important criticisms. First, a model which presupposes an opposition and a total incompatibility between tradition and development is unilinear and too static. Second, the model neglects the great diversity of underdeveloped countries and, consequently, the multiplicity of roads to development. Let us consider these two criticisms in turn.

---

16. Lerner, *The Passing of Traditional Society*, pp. 52-54.

The linear model

Wilbert E. Moore, in particular, has shown the dangers of a linear model which describes development as a transition between two static states. According to a linear model, the original traditional society is in a sense frozen, as if it were in a state of lassitude. It is more or less abruptly awakened to economic progress, either by internal movement or, more generally, by the action of external influences. It then experiences a period of development and change, and finally attains the level of the developed society, where it becomes established and remains arrested for a second period.[17]

Such a grossly simplified model of development will probably never be proposed, in fact. But it is true that the radical opposition between the underdeveloped and developed countries has led many scholars to isolate the two types of society to the point where they appear as two fixed and practically static poles.

An incompatibility between tradition and modernity

The problem, however, is more subtle and complex than Moore's criticism reveals. Specifically, the question is whether there is a real and fundamental incompatibility between tradition and modernity, and between traditional society and developing society. If we return to the stages described by Rostow, we see that all the economic, political, social and mental structures of traditional society seem to be opposed to industrialization; it appears that economic progress can be effected only if there is a radical and total transformation of traditional society. Thus, to Rostow, tradition appears fundamentally incompatible with development; it is really its antithesis. This is why he says that the take-off phase is characterized mainly by the clear elimination of the traits of traditional society.

This position is not peculiar to Rostow; on the contrary, it is very widespread. For example, George M. Foster's analysis — which is very detailed — expresses the impact of technological change on traditional cultures.[18] More recently, Neil Smelser de-

---

17. Wilbert E. Moore, *Social Change* (Englewood Cliffs, N.J.: Prentice-Hall, Inc., 1963), p. 42.
18. George M. Foster, *Traditional Cultures: And the Impact of Technological Change* (New York: Harper and Row, 1962).

scribes the process of modernization as a series of discontinuities or breaks, which must be effected in the transition from pre-industrial to industrial society.[19]

Gusfield: the fallacies of the linear model

By basing his theory on the most recent ethnographic studies and by using, in particular, the case of India, Joseph Gusfield has denounced what he considers to be the fallacies of the linear model, which is too often employed to describe and analyze the transition from tradition to modernization.[20]

These fallacies are as follows:

1. It has been presumed that traditional societies have been stable for too long in their present or pre-development state. But it is clear that certain traditional societies, or those in the process of development whose history is known (such as India), are the product of an evolution which has often been complex and eventful.

2. Traditional culture has been described as a consistent body of norms and values, whereas it often manifests a diversity of values and choices.

3. A homogeneous social structure has been attributed to traditional society. But a great diversity of groups is found within it. In particular, some marginal foreign minorities — such as the Jews in Mediaeval Europe, the Mohammedans in Western Africa and the Chinese in Indonesia — have contributed to economic progress, innovation and the diffusion of productive economic attitudes.

4. *A priori*, it has been presupposed that tradition and development are in conflict, opposed to each other and mutually exclusive. But today, it is apparent that tradition and development not only can coexist, but even reinforce each other. For example, the extended family that was thought to be incompatible with industrialization seems, on the contrary, to adapt itself very well in some cases, and even to favour development, notably as a savings unit and as a basis for the creation of small firms, as has been observed in Madras, India. Similarly, to assert that the caste system is contrary to economic development, as is often done, is to see only

19. Neil J. Smelser, *Sociology: An Introduction* (New York: John Wiley and Sons, Inc., 1967), pp. 716-27.
20. Joseph Gusfield, "Tradition and Modernity." We should also mention Herbert Blumer, "Industrialization and the Traditional Order," *Sociology and Social Research* 48 (April 1964): 129-38.

one aspect of it and to neglect its contribution to the development of credit, to the division of labour, to the education of technical personnel, and to adaptation to the urban milieu. Again, India provides an example of this.

5. Finally, it has been presupposed that the process of modernization weakens traditions; however, tradition can itself become an ideology that is favourable to change. The nationalism of the new nations, which is the main support of development, is fed by tradition and seeks to synthesize it with modernization. And it is this neo-nationalism which serves to re-establish relationships and communication between the directing elites and the masses. Through this nationalism in which they find local values, the masses understand and accept the new objectives which are suggested to them.

The integration of tradition with modernization

Gusfield's criticisms express and synthesize the growing unease that a number of scholars have felt when they have tried to use the rigid model of the transition from tradition to modernization in order to understand and explain new phenomena in the developing countries. In contrast to the theory that a long and solidly established tradition has maintained from the time of Comte, Spencer, Tönnies and Durkheim, it is now accepted that there is neither firm opposition nor total incompatibility between traditional and industrial society. Undoubtedly the distinction between the two types of society remains valid when extreme cases or ideal types are compared. But in the analysis of development, a great number of observations today oblige us to recognize that modernization does not consist of a pure and simple destruction of traditional society, and a radical break with a social and mental structure which is irrevocably opposed to all innovation, or at least to the innovation required by industrialization. Can it be asserted that the modernization of the West has been the result of so total an upheaval? Wouldn't this overlook the fact that social change is never the complete negation of the past?

As we have noticed in the model of development elaborated earlier, the changes linked to modernization do not follow a single linear movement of rejection and adoption. On the contrary, it appears that the new is mixed with the old, and tradition is incorporated in and adapted to the new emerging society. Moreover, it can be expected that in Africa and Asia new variations of modern society will arise as a result of the union of the essential traits of modernity with those of societies which have a different tradition from Western society when it experienced industrialization and urbanization in the last century.

The Various Forms of Underdevelopment

The diversity of the underdeveloped countries

The second criticism that is directed at our model of development is that it presupposes that the underdeveloped or developing countries have sufficient traits in common that they can all be considered as a single class or in the same category. Specifically, it is assumed that all these countries face the same difficulties, suffer from the same handicaps, and proceed in roughly the same way in the development process. This criticism has been directed particularly at Rostow, whose five stages of growth are said to resemble railway stations through which all the countries on the route to development must necessarily pass.

To correct this fault, various writers have tried to construct classifications which take into account to a greater extent the diversity of the underdeveloped or developing countries. We will limit ourselves here to the relatively simple classification suggested by John Kenneth Galbraith.[21]

Galbraith: the criterion of obstacles to development

Galbraith starts with the following observation: all the underdeveloped or developing countries present two common traits — the poverty of the majority of their population, and obstacles which prevent them from surmounting the wall of poverty. In addition, they are distinguished by the fact that the same obstacles do not delay their development. Thus, according to Galbraith, *it*

---

21. John Kenneth Galbraith, *The Underdeveloped Country* (Toronto: CBC Publications, 1965). The interested reader will find a more elaborate analysis of another similar classification in Frederick Harbison and Charles A. Myers, *Education, Manpower, and Economic Growth, Strategies of Human Resource Development* (New York: McGraw-Hill Book Company, Inc., 1964).

is the type of obstacle to development which must serve as the criterion to differentiate the underdeveloped countries.

Classification of the Underdeveloped Countries

On the basis of this criterion, Galbraith distinguishes three classes or models of countries which experience difficulties in development.

The model of Africa south of the Sahara

In the first model, *the obstacle to development resides in the weakness of the cultural base of the society.* Specifically, by this Galbraith means that these countries suffer from a high illiteracy rate. There are a very limited number of individuals with higher education, and the educational system is clearly inadequate at all levels.

Galbraith calls this class the model of Africa south of the Sahara, because this is the situation which prevails, to varying degrees, in about a dozen African countries south of the Sahara Desert. Outside Africa, the same phenomenon is found in Haiti, Afghanistan and Saudi Arabia. In most cases these countries have been subjected to colonial regimes which have not helped to create the conditions favourable to take-off. When the colonizers withdrew, they left behind a country that was poorly equipped in human resources. The classic example is the Republic of the Congo, where only a very small number of university graduates existed at the time of independence.

The most serious consequence of this situation is the difficulty in establishing an efficient government, as a result of the lack of a competent and educated elite to occupy political and administrative positions. From this a vicious circle results: the weakness of the government delays the organization of the educational system, and the absence of a school system perpetuates the cultural weakness of the country.

These countries are constantly threatened with the resurgence of tribalism, anarchy and political disintegration, or the taking of power by men or groups who pursue only personal or particular interests.

The Latin American model

In the second model, the cultural basis is more extensive than in the first. The educational system, while imperfect, is sufficiently developed to produce an educated class from which is drawn a number of the necessary administrative and professional personnel.

Here, the obstacle to development resides in the social structure. The society is divided into two groups: a small minority of property owners, and a large mass of unskilled workers, mostly agricultural workers. But neither the owners nor the mass of workers have a sufficiently strong economic stimulant to raise the productivity of their work or capital. The workers, particularly those from the country, form a vast proletariat which can envisage no possibility of improving its lot. From the small holding that each family cultivates on the land of a large landowner, it can, at the most, derive a meager subsistence. In addition, it must avoid making profits, for these would be taken away in one way or another.

For the most part, the owners possess vast domains which are cultivated by a very cheap labour force with low output. Their holdings are so extensive that the owners derive a sufficiently satisfactory income that they need not be concerned with raising productivity. The non-owner members of the fortunate minority derive their income from government positions, army appointments, or professional occupations. Neither of these two groups — owners or non-owners — contributes positively to national production. Instead the rich minority lives on what Galbraith calls a non-functional income — that is, on an income which does not correspond to a service which is functionally useful in the national economy.

The vicious circle is completed by the fact that this non-functional income brings with it much more social recognition and prestige than does income stemming from industrial investments; for non-functional income indicates a share in power and authority.

In such a situation, the propertied classes are trapped in a social system which does not induce them to effect the transfers of capital required to activate the industrialization of the country and its economic development.

As its name indicates, examples of this model are particularly widespread in South and Central America; they can also be found in Iran, Iraq and Syria.

The model of Southeast Asia

The third model is particularly well represented by India and Pakistan; it applies also to the United Arab Republic, Indonesia and China.

Here the cultural base is extensive. Indeed, there is an abundance of educated people and a surplus of teachers, administrators and white-collar workers. The educational system, while unsatisfactory, is fairly widely established. Non-functional income is much less the general norm among the wealthy, and it is less valued socially than in the preceding model.

The obstacle to development stems from a lack of equilibrium between the productive factors. In these countries, the population increase has always been ahead of the increase in production. Thus the margin of capital available for industrialization always remains too small. These countries suffer from a chronic scarcity of capital and goods for consumption and from an irreducible surplus in the population. This results in economic stagnation, the permanent threat of scarcity and a great slowness in the modernization process.

Conclusion

These three models have the advantage of showing the diversity of conditions in the underdeveloped countries. In particular, they highlight the fact that the same factors do not have the same importance in the explanation of the economic backwardness of these countries. Thus, certain social values attached to property and power have a great weight in the second model, while the demographic factor strongly dominates the countries of the third model.

From this it follows that the same solutions are not applicable in all three cases, for the development process does not encounter the same obstacles and consequently cannot follow the same course. Each model requires a search for the appropriate circumstances for take-off, which cannot derive its impetus in the same way or under the impulse of the same forces.

Conclusion

Having laboriously constructed a general model of development, we have subjected it to the attack of two series of criticisms. What finally remains of the model?

In conclusion, it can be said that the criticisms of the general model of development do not invalidate it. Instead, they serve to make it less rigid; they guard against extreme simplifications and they emphasize the great diversity of real and concrete situations, and consequently the necessity for a certain relativism in their analysis.

Thus, these criticisms are valuable and useful. It is in this way, through successive slight alterations, that a valid model ultimately will be elaborated which will take into account reality as it is and in its entirety.

But one cannot have a true perception of the modernization process of the underdeveloped countries if one does not take a third element into account — the context of colonialism and decolonization in which the modernization process of most countries has taken place. The next chapter is devoted to the study of this problem.

Chapter 14
The Colonial System and Decolonization

In order to be complete, the model of development that we have presented and discussed in the preceding chapter must be placed within the context of colonialism and decolonization. In effect, almost all of the so-called developing countries are either colonies (or former colonies) or countries in the process of decolonization. And this fact profoundly affects their modernization process.

It can be said that there are two different forms of development: one results from *forces which are internal to the social system*, and the other is set in motion by *agents external to the system*. The Western industrial revolution of the eighteenth and nineteenth centuries is an example of the first type of development. The industrialization of Europe was produced by the Western bourgeoisie, who invested their own capital and used scientific and technical knowledge developed in the West. It is this type of development that sociology, from the time of Auguste Comte and Karl Marx up to the present, has analyzed most extensively. For a long time it was believed that it represented the universal and unique model through which every developing society must necessarily pass. This was the meaning of Comte's law of the three states; the same idea can perhaps be discerned in the five stages of development described by Rostow.

But the countries that are developing today are not in the same situation as the West was in the eighteenth century. They have been, and continue to be, subjected to the influence and competition of countries that are much further developed than they are. The first factors and agents of modernization came to them from these more advanced countries, or were even imposed on them; but at the same time, it is this dependence with regard to the more advanced countries that is the main obstacle to their development.

This phenomenon of dependence has been given the name of colonialism. As we will see later, it is a very profound dependence, which is not only economic and political, but also social and even psychological in nature.

In this chapter, we will present a brief analysis of the influence of colonization on the process of development. For greater clarity, we will consider *two successive periods* of the phenomenon: the colonial situation and decolonization. While it is not always easy to distinguish these two periods in reality, the distinction is analytically useful and valid.[1]

The Colonial System

The anthropology of colonized societies

It is only very recently that the underdeveloped or developing countries have been analyzed from the perspective of colonialism. Previously, anthropologists — to whom we owe most of the studies of archaic societies — sought mainly to understand and explain the internal functioning of these societies. They took into account the influence of external factors, but primarily from the perspective of *cultural diffusion*. By this they meant the way in which knowledge, technique, inventions and fashions are spread from one society to another following *contacts* established between two or several societies. The phenomenon of diffusion could already be observed between archaic societies, and it was the subject of a number of studies. Colonialism also seemed to be a phenomenon of diffusion, since the anthropologists were particularly sensitive to the breakdown of archaic societies which resulted from it. Because their attention was focused on the structure of the archaic society, they did not appreciate that relationships with the colonizing society took on the form of another more inclusive system — the colonial system.

---

1. For the research necessary for the writing of this chapter, we have benefited from the efficient assistance of M. Jacques Lamontagne, a graduate student in the Department of Sociology of the Université de Montréal.

With regard to anthropological studies of African peoples, Georges Balandier emphasizes:

> These were often conducted with reference to the "primitive" economy and social organization as affected by disturbances brought by the "modern" economy and the resulting problems. They neglected to refer to the colonial economy and the colonial situation, or to recognize the reciprocity of perspectives between the colonized and colonizing societies.[2]

Moreover, an important sector of the discipline of anthropology (notably American anthropology) studied archaic societies in exclusively cultural terms. Mainly under the influence of Malinowski, social reality was seen as a culture, rather than as a total social organization. Consequently, the colonial system as a form of social organization did not enter into the analytical framework. Again to quote Balandier:

> [These anthropological studies] mainly neglected this reference to the total society of the colony. What is really lacking is the very meaning of social reality, of the field of complex relationships formed by this reality, and of the antagonistic relationships expressed within it.[3]

Definition of the colonized society

The colony, or what Balandier calls the colonial situation, must thus be considered as a particular type of total society, or a type of social system with its own traits with regard to both its form of organization and cultural evolution, and the psychology of its actor-members.

For the purposes of our analysis, we will define the colonized society as follows: *it is a society which is economically not very advanced and whose economic, political, cultural and social development is subjected to all the relationships of dependence in which it finds itself necessarily involved with one or several societies which are economically more advanced.*

It may seem surprising, at first thought, that we define the colonized society mainly from the perspective of its development,

---

2. Georges Balandier, *Sociologie actuelle de l'Afrique noire*, 2nd edition (Paris: Presses universitaires de France, 1963), p. 10.
3. *Ibid.*, p. 24.

conditioned by its relationships of dependence. But in the very nature of colonized society, there is really *a dual problem of development*. First, a colonized society is a society that is *partially* developed by a colonizing society which seeks gain from it. The colonizing society introduces into traditional society some of the pre-con-
ditions for take-off described by Rostow. But at the same time, it
keeps a tight rein on development, either deliberately to protect
its interests or incidentally through the very colonial system it establishes.

Second, in the colonized society itself there is usually at least a
latent desire for autonomous development. It is precisely this desire which makes the colonial situation a problem for those who
are subjected to it, and which finally releases the mechanisms leading to full or relative independence.

But in order to grasp better the problems of development of the
colonized societies, we should analyze in greater detail the nature
of this type of society. In the next section we will outline the main
traits which are characteristic of the colonial system.

The Characteristic Traits
of the Colonial System

In particularly succinct terms, Georges Balandier characterizes the
colonial situation as follows:

> [It embodies] the domination imposed by a foreign
> minority that is "racially" and culturally different, in
> the name of a social (or ethnic) and cultural superior-
> ity, which is dogmatically asserted over an indigenous
> and materially inferior majority; the relating of hetero-
> geneous civilizations — a mechanical civilization with
> a powerful rapidly growing economy, of Christian ori-
> gin imposing itself on civilizations without complicat-
> ed techniques, with a backward and sluggish economy,
> and radically "non-Christian"; the antagonistic nature
> of the relationships between the two societies which is
> explained by the instrumental role to which the domi-
> nated society is condemned; the need to maintain dom-
> ination not only by the use of force but also through

the establishment of a set of pseudo-justifications and stereotyped behaviour.[4]

With this description as a starting point, we can elaborate in more detail a general model of the colonized society. For this purpose, we will use the elements provided by various writers, notably — in addition to Georges Balandier[5] — Raymond Kennedy,[6] Immanuel Wallerstein,[7] O. Mannoni,[8] Everett Hagen,[9] Albert Memmi[10] and Jacques Berque.[11]

Our model includes six traits which are found to some degree in every colonial situation. These are (1) foreign economic exploitation, (2) political dependence, (3) social and racial barriers, (4) social fragmentation, (5) the justificatory system and (6) psychological attitudes. We will describe each of these traits in detail and briefly analyze the consequences for development.

Foreign economic exploitation

Economic interest has been, and remains, the main motive for colonization. To the colonizer, the colony is a country whose re-

---

4. *Ibid.*, pp. 34-35.

5. In addition to Georges Balandier's *Sociologie actuelle de l'Afrique noire*, we should emphasize one of his articles in particular: "La situation coloniale: approche théorique," *Cahiers internationaux de sociologie* 11 (1951): 44-79.

6. Raymond Kennedy, "The Colonial Crisis and the Future" in Ralph Linton, ed., *The Science of Man in the World Crisis* (New York: Columbia University Press, 1945), pp. 306-46. Even though it was conducted over twenty years ago, this study by Kennedy still remains one of the best syntheses of the colonial situation. It will probably also interest the reader as an historical document. Writing in 1944, before the end of the war, surveying the different colonial countries Kennedy wrote: "Fortunately, two of the three most powerful states in the world, America and Russia, are themselves non-imperialist" (p. 341). It was at this period that the Americans said they were the holders of the most progressive attitude on the question of decolonization, while many Europeans criticized them for a dangerous liberalism and a lack of realism! If the predictions that Kennedy made on the stages of decolonization appeared advanced at that time, subsequent events have largely overtaken them!

7. Immanuel Wallerstein, *The Road to Independence* (Paris: Mouton, 1964) and by the same author, *Social Change: The Colonial Situation* (New York: John Wiley and Sons, Inc., 1966).

8. O. Mannoni, *Prospero and Caliban, The Psychology of Colonization*, trans. Pamela Powersland (London: Methuen & Co., 1956).

9. Hagen, *Theory of Social Change.*

10. Albert Memmi, *Portrait du colonisé, précédé du Portrait du colonisateur* (Korea: Buchef Chastel, 1957).

11. Jacques Berque, *Dépossession du monde* (Paris: Editions du Seuil, 1964).

sources he can exploit — resources which are useful and even necessary to the mother country for its enrichment or for the maintenance of its political power. Thus, depending on his needs and the resources of the colony, the colonizer may exploit the land, from which he derives certain products (sugar, coffee, bananas), the mines, the oil wells or the forests. To assist him in his enterprises, the colonizer must recruit part of the necessary labour force on the spot, and subsequently train and pay them. Through the new techniques that he imports, through the use of money and credit that he introduces or encourages, and through the values and patterns of behaviour that he brings with him, the colonizer is necessarily an innovator and an agent of social change. He disturbs an established order or an evolutionary process that was in motion before he arrived; he provokes the emergence of needs and desires which were hitherto unknown; he develops certain necessary services for his undertakings (railroads, a network of roads, a telecommunications system). In addition, the colonizer imports personnel (administrators and technicians) who will require various services from the local population.

In brief, in many traditional societies, colonization stimulates the first move towards economic development. But this move is slow to evolve into a force for autonomous development, because this type of economic exploitation slows down the development that it initiates. This is true for four main reasons. First, this type of development is voluntarily limited to certain resources and sectors. Thus we might call it sectional development; it is never total. In almost all cases, the colonizer takes care to preserve the subsistence economy parallel to the sector that he is developing according to his needs or interests, understanding the danger of competition that would arise if he destroyed it. Second, the products extracted from the colonized country are generally manufactured, not locally, but in the colonizing country, thus depriving the colony of an important factor in development. Third, since the salaries paid to the local labour force are always very low compared to those paid in the home country, a rather low standard of living and of aspiration is maintained. Finally, the local labour force can aspire only to subordinate posts since their mobility is restricted by the importation of technicians and administrators from abroad.

Political dependence

The second characteristic trait of the colonial situation is political dependence. All important political decisions concerning the colonized country are made by the government of the mother country; the latter maintains its own administrators in the colony, who are charged with carrying out decisions or having them carried out, and with transmitting essential information. If the colony has a local government (a council, a legislative assembly), it can make only limited decisions and, on other matters, may only submit recommendations or preferences to the home government.

The expression *political dependence* can be said to describe fully the colonial situation. The colonizer always discourages political participation by the local population, preferring to keep it in a state of complete dependence with regard to the decisions of the colonial authority (some authors use interchangeably the expressions *colonial situation* and *situation of dependence*). Historically, in all the colonies, the indigenous people who have sought to undertake political action which threatens this state of dependence, have been accused of being political agitators, and have been exiled or imprisoned. Most of the leaders of the new nations, from Gandhi to Nkrumah, have spent some time in colonial prisons. In the former Belgian Congo, no voluntary association of any kind could exist without the authorization of the administrators, who were ordered to supervise and control the creation of unauthorized associations.[12]

We should emphasize, however, that a colonial situation may exist without the political dependence that has just been described. This is the case in countries whose resources are exploited by foreign capital, but which keep at least a relative political independence. With this difference, the situation of these countries corresponds fairly closely to the general colonial model.

Social and racial barriers

The barriers which separate the colonizers from the colonized comprise the third trait of the colonial situation. The colonizing nation must establish a corps of civil servants, administrators,

---

12. Pierre Clément, "Formes et valeurs de la vie sociale urbaine" in Forde, ed., *L'industrialisation en Afrique*, pp. 500-505.

commissioners and military personnel in the colonized country; business agents, businessmen and settlers also come to settle there. Relationships between these foreigners and the indigenous population are limited to work or living requirements; otherwise, the colonizers live together. Since the foreigners are generally whites, the cleavage follows a racial demarcation, the famous colour line.

This cleavage is evident in the arrangement of colonial towns. Here one invariably finds the foreign quarter, which is different and separate from the rest of the town; domestics are the only members of the native population who may enter this quarter. Social or normal recreational relationships between natives and foreigners are practically impossible, for they are proscribed by an implicit code which is scrupulously obeyed by the two sides; violations are few, for fear of the sanctions they would entail. This is an excellent example of the efficiency of unofficial social control.

Social fragmentation

The cleavage between colonizer and colonized is only one aspect of the many divisions which make the colony a fragmented society. Within the indigenous population, new racial distinctions often emerge — among Indians, mulattos and non-Indians in South America; and between Asiatics and Africans in Africa. There are numerous divisions among ethnic groups, tribes, clans and castes. Among all these groups there sometimes exists a rigid and deep-seated hatred. These different groups are superimposed on each other, almost always according to an ancient hierarchy which has been transposed into the colonized society and is complicated by new hierarchies introduced by industrialization.

The colonial situation adds new divisions to these ethnic and racial divisions which predated colonization. In Africa, the degree of advancement — that is, of Westernization — was an important criterion for the grouping and classing of Africans among themselves;[13] P. Clément, for example, reports the existence in the Bel-

---

13. Readers of the *Asterix* series will remember that in *The Big Fight* the authors illustrate the alienation and confrontation between an "advanced" chief and a traditional chief in the colonial situation. As we know, the fantastic adventure of Asterix and his friend Obelix takes place in Gaul during the Roman occupation. Chief Cassius Ceramix, an "advanced" chief, no longer calls himself a Gaul but a Gallo-Roman; he makes a rule that his subjects must cut their hair in the Roman style and wear a toga; he calls his

gian Congo of voluntary associations which are open only to "advanced" blacks ("L'Association des evolués de Stanleyville" and "L'Association des evolueés femmes babua").[14] Similarly, missionary activities create a new opposition between the converted and the heathen; and the divisions between the Christian churches have been clearly re-established in the missionary countries.

This fragmentation of colonized society into groups that are often very small, rigidly differentiated, arranged in a hierarchy and hostile to each other is not likely to favour the collective action necessary for development. It tends to confirm the colonizer's opinion that the indigenous people are incapable of governing themselves without the risk of anarchy, despotism and civil war.

The justificatory system

Another trait of the colonial situation is that the colonizer constructs a justificatory system for himself which, for all practical purposes, forms what could be called the colonizing ideology. This is a set of rationalizations by which the colonizer explains his position in the colonized country, his superior status, and his behaviour towards the natives.

This ideology is based to a great extent on faith in the hereditary superiority of the white race. For example, one finds in it the following stereotypes and prejudices: coloured people lack the necessary moral and intellectual qualities to train themselves and exploit their country's resources; they do not know how to govern themselves without the risk of anarchy or despotism; colonization has greatly improved the living conditions of the natives, has provided a police force, various social services and a certain level of education, all of which gives the colonial undertaking a humanitarian character or makes it a civilizing mission; it would be futile to raise salaries, for the natives would only waste this money, and similarly there is no point in offering them too high a level of education, for they do not have the necessary intelligence to benefit

---

house his *domus* and, although a river flows through the village, he is going to build an aqueduct because, he says, "Aqueducts are more Roman". It is to him that the Roman centurion Nebulus Nimbus comes, to persuade him to fight Vitalstatistix, the chief of the unconquered village where Asterix and Obelix live. In this village besieged by Roman troops, the obstinate Gauls continue to defend their traditional way of life and independence.

14. Clément, "La vie sociale urbaine" in Forde, ed., *L'industrialisation en Afrique*, p. 504.

from it; in any case, since the natives do not demand anything better than what they now have, it would be useless to provoke aspirations which would only cause them dissatisfaction and frustration.

Even in the case of relationships between colonizers and colonized peoples of the same race, and sometimes of the same nationality, similar stereotypes are present. For example, a number of Britishers of the eighteenth century liked to describe their fellow-citizens who had emigrated to the American colonies as frustrated, ignorant trouble-makers who spoke bad English.[15]

When they form a minority (which is almost always the case), in imposing their authority and rule on the indigenous majority colonizers always need a reassuring ideology. The colonizer has a constant and more or less explicit fear of the masses that he dominates; and so the colonialist ideology explains to him why he can continue to dominate, and do so in peace. At the same time, this ideology authorizes him to discourage any form of autonomous development, since it presupposes the practical impossibility of this.

Psychological attitudes

Finally, between the colonizer and the colonized, a set of ambiguous relationships and attitudes develops. The colonizer, perceiving the colonized through a stereotyped image, treats them as minors who are only semi-responsible and always troublesome and worrying. His attitude will be comprised of a mixture of paternalism, contempt and fear. He will consider that the colonized need supervision, control and sanctions. Generally ignorant of their language, he will take cover behind this barrier in order to limit communication and maintain social distance. This will also enable him to entrust to loyal natives the responsibility of exerting controls and applying sanctions.

The colonized have an ambivalent attitude towards the colonizer. They endorse his image of them, recognizing themselves to be inferior to him; they admire and envy him, and seek to identify themselves with him. But the colonizer's world is always strange to them. It is inaccessible because of the social distance that he maintains; what Georg Simmel has called the visibility of the colonizer

---

15. André Maurois, *A New History of the United States*, trans. Denver and Jane Lindley (London: Bodley Head, 1948).

is too faint to enable them to imitate him perfectly and integrate themselves into his world. In addition, by the time the colonized have internalized and adopted the traits of the colonizer, he has already adopted others, so that they always lag behind.[16]

While they overvalue the image of the colonizer, who remains a distant and inaccessible reference point, the colonized must recognize themselves as different from him. They do not succeed in forming a valuable self-image, however, but remain dependent on his view of them. Finally, by rejecting the colonizer's image and by breaking it down (in a sort of murder of the father), the colonized seek to recognize and define themselves as different from him.[17] The admiration of the colonized for the colonizer ultimately leads to hostility and hate.

It is because of this psychological ambivalence of the colonized that one can speak of a fragmentation of their personalities, or a kind of depersonalization, as described by Jacques Berque in particular. This is the typical case of the *marginal* phenomenon — that is, of individuals and groups who succeed neither in identifying with the Other that they would like to be, nor in detaching themselves in order to be themselves and different from him.

The Points of Contact Between the Colonizers and the Colonized

The main traits of the colonial system that we have just described now enable us to distinguish what it is that makes it a completely special type of society: *it is a system composed of two sub-systems*

---

16. This is what David Riesman has called "the snake-like procession" when applying it to the university world in America. The body of the snake passes the same place as its head, but always later. David Riesman, "The Academic Procession," *Constraint and Variety in American Education* (New York: Anchor Books, 1958).

17. The description that Jean Ziégler gives of Patrice Lumumba's career corresponds to the sketch that we have just given. Coming from a poor environment, Lumumba entered the service of the colonial administration. This period marked his "will to integrate." Accused of stealing, he was imprisoned. His exit from prison in 1957 coincided with the beginning of his demands for the independence of the Congo. Jean Ziégler, *Sociologie de la Nouvelle Afrique* (Paris: Gallimard, 1964), pp. 189-214.

between which the points of contact are very limited. It is this fact that has long permitted the study of colonized societies without any reference to the context of the total colonial system. In addition, when we closely analyze the few points of contact between the two sub-systems, we realize that they have a remarkable particularity: *almost all of them serve to socialize the colonized sub-system (or certain groups of the colonized sub-system) in order to weld it into the colonizing sub-system.*

There are four main strategic points of contact between the two sub-systems: political power, the school, the working environment and the Church. Let us analyze them successively.

Political power

The political power of traditional society continues to exist in the colonial situation. Generally the same leaders and the same authority organizations are to be found. But the traditional political power is *redefined and reoriented*: there is no longer an autonomous, but rather a delegated authority, which serves as an intermediary between the population and colonial rule.

The traditional authority is entrusted with two particular functions by the colonizing authority. First, it is to act as a *sub-administrator*. The colonial authority will use local leaders to transmit and carry out directives, recruit personnel, organize public services, obtain information and so forth. Second, traditional authority is to perform a *policing* function. It will be counted on to keep order, maintain peace, and sometimes carry out punitive justice.

Through these two functions, the local authority becomes both a *socializing* agent and an agent of control. It is this authority which will teach the population to respect the new rules, and to accept new patterns of behaviour and values. For example, certain actions or activities which were previously accepted or tolerated in traditional society are now prohibited, and it is the local leaders who serve as socializing agents to help bring about the desired changes in attitudes and conduct.

The colonial administration also counts on the traditional leaders to serve as *symbols of integration* into the colonial regime in the eyes of the indigenous population. These leaders symbolize both the fact that traditional society has not been destroyed and the changes that must be accepted.

The school

In the colonial system, education can be organized and maintained by the colonial administration, by the Churches, or by philanthropic organizations. But as a general rule, there is a limited educational sector which offers schooling — particularly at the secondary and higher level — to only a limited portion of the population. The system of education serves to create an advanced elite, who will comprise the necessary administrative and technical personnel in government, business and the public services.

Drawn from traditional society but educated according to the programs, teaching methods and texts of the colonizing society, these personnel will serve as privileged intermediaries between the local administration and the population. They are depended on to understand both the natives and the colonizers; they are the main bridge between the two sub-systems.

This function, however, makes them the most marginal group in the colonized society. Also, as we will show later, it is among them that the most ardent champions of decolonization will be recruited.

The working environment

The colonizing society creates new working environments within the colony — administrative offices, public services, industry and commerce. In these working environments, the colonizer tries to reproduce the habits, climate, attitudes and behaviour which are familiar to him, and which he judges to be necessary and efficient.

The natives who are hired are trained to adopt behaviour and often values which to varying degrees are foreign to their original culture. They will be guided by both the respect that the colonizer imposes and the socializing pressure exerted through the working environment. In particular, the promotions given to the most advanced workers provide, at least for some workers, the motivation to identify with and conform to the culture recommended by the colonizing sub-system.

The Churches

In most colonial situations, a missionary activity can be observed which is parallel to colonization or complementary to it. The activity of the Churches is marked to some extent by religious evangelism; but it is almost always accompanied by various humanitarian works — the establishment of schools, hospitals, clinics, cooperatives and so forth.

Either through the religious conversions they effect or through the services they provide, the Churches also play the role of socializing agents. They contribute to the internalization of new norms of behaviour which apply not only to morality but also to sanitation, economic conditions and so forth. They transmit knowledge and values. They permit a certain form of identification with the colonial regime, but in a kind of tangential fashion — through the functions to which they permit access in the Church, and through the relationships that they establish between individuals belonging to the two sub-systems.

At the same time, the religious missions create marginal groups around them. The converted no longer belong completely to their traditional society, at least as long as they form only a small minority. This is true particularly when the traditional religion is strictly associated with collective life, as is true of most archaic societies. The colonizing society depends on these marginal groups to act as instigators of cultural change within their society, not only from the religious point of view but also in a more total way.

Socialization and dependence

We can enumerate other socializing factors in the colonized subsystem. There is the function that is fulfilled, for example, by a number of voluntary associations organized by the colonizer — old boys groups, religious societies, cooperatives and so forth. Based on the model of similar voluntary associations in the colonizing society, they take on a much more accentuated socializing function in the colonized society.

Finally, from this picture there emerges the fact that wherever the two sub-systems are in contact, the colonizing sub-system seeks to educate the members of the colonized sub-system. *But what is peculiar to this form of socialization is that it makes those who are socialized enter into a culture and a society which will always remain foreign to them. Also, it ultimately has the effect of socializing not for equality but for dependence.* This is a socialization which contributes to the recognition and acceptance of the other sub-system — that of the colonizer — as being not only different, but superior.

An important consequence follows. The points of contact eventually become *points which weld together* the two sub-systems.

Through the socializing relationships that the colonizer maintains with the colonized in the government, schools, work and the Churches, the colonizing sub-system attaches the colonized sub-system to it and partially transforms it without totally integrating it.

In this union, the colonized society comes to perceive and define itself only *in and through the relationships of dependence* that it maintains with the colonizing society.

Here microsociology and macrosociology meet in a reciprocity of perspectives. At the macrosociological level, the depersonalization of the collectivity corresponds to the depersonalization of individuals which we mentioned earlier. The collectivity is deprived of an identity. It no longer knows itself as it was previously, because it has experienced an abrupt break in its history. In addition, it cannot define its own historical action because it follows in the wake of a society whose history it does not recognize. The depersonalization of individuals and the loss of collective identity are thus the two trap-doors, at the psychological and sociological levels, of this same phenomenon of socialization to and within dependence.

The Introspective Phenomena of Colonized Society

The welding of the colonized society to the colonizing society never includes all of the former. The colonizing society attaches itself to the colonized society through certain ties: it creates advanced groups; it socializes some sectors of it; it transforms a part of its culture and social organization. But traditional society continues to exist, while experiencing changes of varying degrees of importance.

It is therefore not surprising that in the colonized society introspective as well as dependent phenomena are observed. By introspective phenomena, we mean various implicit forms of *refusal of the colonial system*, either through a return to traditional values or institutions, or through escape from immediate reality.

Refuge-values

Albert Memmi has talked of refuge-values to designate the process by which the colonized society takes up certain traditional values or creates new ones, suddenly attaching considerable importance to them. These values become life-buoys or symbols of something of oneself that one does not wish to lose. In this sense they can be said to present a sort of refuge in which the colonized society can still find itself, or in which it believes that it can recognize itself.

In this way, for example, kinship ties are seen to take on a new and tremendous value at the very moment when they are threatened by the geographical mobility of the population. Or common law may experience a new vitality and interest at the very time when the colonizers' law is being established. Some folk customs (songs, dances, costumes, crafts, cooking) and mythological beliefs can suddenly take on a symbolic aspect, recalling a past which increasingly appears as a long-lost paradise.

It is generally in its past, its history and its former social organization that colonized society will seek the values in which it takes refuge. When historical action no longer finds a future to construct, it will occupy itself with building an increasingly legendary past.

Messianism

Another introspective phenomenon which is fairly common in colonized society is the appearance of different forms of messianism or prophecy. Georges Balandier gives some striking African examples.

Generally, it is religious movements, sects and secret societies, inspired by some local prophet, which reconstruct a new and strongly syncretic mythology. In effect, elements of traditional religion are mixed with the colonizer's religion and remodelled in a new hybrid theology, in which — in a distorted but thinly disguised way — the frustrations and aspirations of the colonized society are expressed.

These forms of messianism, however, do not have the active strength of ideologies, and they do not suggest a specific historical action. Rather, they are derived from a sort of dream or from a utopia in its purest state.

The Colonial System and Development

From the preceding discussion, it can be seen that the colonial system stimulates the partial development of traditional society, but delays any process of total and autonomous development. From the perspective of development, one can say that the colonized society suffers from three weaknesses: *it is a peripheral, unbalanced and inhibited society*. Let us consider what this means in more detail.

A peripheral society

The colonized society can be considered to be located at the periphery of a circle of which the colonizing parent state would be the centre.[18]

The colony suffers from being both far from the centre and dependent on it. Being far from the centre, it does not benefit from the activity, energy and impetus harboured there; and it always lags behind the parent state. In addition, it is too exclusively and totally dependent on the metropolitan centre. It is from the centre that initiatives and impulses, and often also decisions, come. But it is mainly at the economic level that this dependence is apparent and serious. The colonial economy is constructed and directed solely according to the needs, interests and evolution of the parent state and for its benefit. This is what Albert Meister has called the "choker of the colonial pact."[19]

The colonized society is thus deprived of the internal elasticity and dynamism which are necessary for its autonomous development. It exists exclusively through and for the distant centre to which it is attached.

An unbalanced society

Second, and particularly from the economic point of view, the colonized society is profoundly unbalanced. Some sectors are exploited by the colonizer and are extensively developed; the rest of the society remains archaic and traditional, and is often at the lowest level of a subsistence economy. In addition, generally there is heavy exploitation of natural resources, while secondary industry remains almost non-existent.

The colonized society is unbalanced in many similar ways. A small educated group coexists with a population that is largely il-

---

18. This idea has been elaborated by Edward Shils, "Centre and Periphery," *The Logic of Personal Knowledge. Essays presented to Michael Polanyi* (London: Routledge and Kegan Paul, Ltd., 1961).
19. Albert Meister, *L'Afrique peut-elle partir? Changement social et développement en Afrique orientale* (Paris: Editions du Seuil, 1966), pp. 77-79.

literate; ultimately this leads the educated elite to uproot itself from the environment and go into exile. Modern towns grow up in a country that is still archaic. Unemployment is rife, while skilled labour is lacking.

The colonized society is unbalanced because, although the social system is maintained, it is partially disorganized. In addition, modern society, which is artificially superimposed on traditional society, does not really take root: it only accentuates further the disorganization of traditional society, to the point where ultimately the colonial system destroys itself.

An inhibited society

Finally, the colonized society's image of itself and the attitudes that it maintains make it a psychologically inhibited society. As it suffers from a deep feeling of inferiority and incapacity and takes refuge in the past, in legend or in utopic dreams, it is not provided with the individual and collective motivations which are essential for autonomous development.

Instead, in the colonized societies, a tendency can be observed to what the social psychologists have called withdrawal or immobility. What has often been called laziness among colonized peoples is only a form of this withdrawal, which results from the fragmentation of the personality that we mentioned earlier.

In addition to the economic handicaps (absence of capital and of a qualified labour force), these structural and psychological weaknesses of colonized societies make their development extremely difficult and problematical, and in some cases almost improbable.

Decolonization

Colonization is not a new or recent phenomenon; it goes back to the most ancient periods of known history. Great empires have dominated the history of humanity from the time of the Roman and Chinese Empires to that of the modern empires which have extended into Asia, Africa and the Americas. But there is an essential difference between the ancient and modern empires. Almost all the ancient empires were destroyed by external forces, whether these were the Barbarians or another competing empire, which were sufficiently powerful to shatter and divide them. *It is only in the modern empires that we have witnessed a general decolonization movement coming from within,* initiated and led to victory by the colonized countries themselves.

Of course, the ancient empires witnessed a number of revolts in the colonized countries; but most of these were repressed and stifled. In any case, they never entailed the move to liberation that we have seen recently. It is generally considered that the English colonies in America were the first to decolonize themselves in the eighteenth century in order to form a new independent nation — the United States.[20] In the nineteenth century, one by one the Spanish-American colonies obtained their political independence. In the twentieth century, it was the turn of the African and Asian countries to decolonize themselves.

Thus, while colonization is an old fact, decolonization is a new one which has recently appeared in human history and which is characteristic of the modern world. It can even be said that it is only in the last one or two decades that we have become conscious of the historical importance of decolonization, its complexity, and what it can represent for the future. This probably explains why it has not yet been the subject of many studies. We will attempt, however, to outline its main characteristics.

A process and a type of society

Decolonization can be considered in two ways. First, as its name indicates, it is an historical step or process; it is all the steps and actions by which a colonized society seeks its independence. But, at least in many cases, decolonization is also the fact that a new nation or a new total society of a rather particular kind is making its appearance. This type of society is designated by the name *post-colonial society.*

It is from these two perspectives that we will consider decolonization.

---

20. It is from this perspective that Seymour Lipset analyzed the American revolution and the society that emerged from it. Lipset, *The First New Nation.*

The Process of Decolonization

The vicious circle of the colonized society

The colonial system appears both as a closed and static system and as a potentially dynamic system. Its closed character results from the fact that a traditional or relatively undeveloped society is dominated by a foreign, more powerful and more advanced society. This domination destroys, blocks or inhibits the possibilities of change; it prevents the formation of local capital; it limits the skilled labour force to a certain sector or sectors of production, and holds them down to inferior levels of qualification and responsibility; it discourages initiative, the taste for risk, and self-confidence.

It is in this sense that we can speak of the vicious circle of colonized society. In fact, it has long seemed almost impossible for the colonized societies, or most of them, to break out of this vicious circle. In addition, one wonders whether, despite the appearance of political independence, the decolonized societies have succeeded in extricating themselves from the closed dependent system.

Factors in change

The colonial system, however, includes some potentially dynamic elements. The colonizing society sows seeds of change in the colonized society which mature more or less rapidly and can finally effect the breakdown of the colonial system. At least, such has been the case in contemporary colonized societies.

In particular, let us note three dynamic factors in the colonial system. First, the colonizing society introduces into traditional society a number of preconditions for take-off — modern means of transportation and communication, technological industries, patterns of economic behaviour, money and credit, and public services. While limited and even voluntarily restricted, these modern elements are henceforth present; the traditional society which has experienced them and their consequences can never turn back and return to its past circumstances.

Second, we have seen that colonialism rests essentially on an *imbalance* between, on the one hand, a society which is still traditional and which is maintained in a state of economic, political, cultural and even psychological dependence; and, on the other hand, an economic sector that is exploited by being developed within restricted and precise limits. But society is a total reality within which it is not easy to maintain indefinitely and artificially a tight compartmentalization and severe imbalance. It is the very principle of the social system that an artificially limited and un-balanced development ultimately stimulates a development process which is enlarged and extended to all of social reality — politics and culture, as well as the economy. And it is generally the colonial regime that these forces first attack as the major obstacle on the road to total development.

Finally, while it inhibits the dynamic motivations of personalities, the colonial system also produces frustrations, develops desires and aspirations, and provokes latent hostility. These psychological states can lead to the emergence of a will to individual and collective action which is directed both against the colonizer and towards the realization of more or less precise objectives.

The influence of these factors in modern colonized societies

Let us emphasize that here we perhaps have the explanation of the fact that it is only in modern times that we have witnessed a general move towards decolonization. The contemporary colonial system has produced disturbances, breaks and frustrations in traditional societies which are much more profound than was ever the case in the past. Never, in effect, has the contrast between traditional society and the innovations introduced by the colonizer been as great as it is in the modern world. Moreover, the rhythm of change has never been as rapid and abrupt as it is today.

It is natural that a greater and stronger imbalance should lead to individual and collective reactions which are more pronounced, more radical and more violent.

The action of elites

These factors provoke a move towards decolonization. But the decolonization process itself is unleashed and directed by the action of an elite, supported by a more or less important sector of the population. This elite is generally formed by a group that the colonizer defines as advanced. It is recruited among the intellectuals

— or at least among those who have undertaken advanced studies (sometimes even in the parent state) — among public administration personnel, students, members of the liberal professions, and sometimes certain traditional leaders.

Paradoxically, the groups and categories who comprise the main element of the elite which directs the movement towards colonization are those who have benefited from the colonial system and on whom the colonizer has counted for support.

The elite which suggests an action with a view to decolonization generally obtains the support of only a small minority of the population at the outset. It encounters the indifference, apathy and passivity of the rest of the people, and sometimes reactions of fear and open hostility. In addition, it conflicts with conservative elites, who fear losing acquired advantages in the change, or who consider that the venture entails more dangers than real promises.

The process of decolonization thus leads to a struggle between the indigenous elites, each of which presents a different definition of what ought to be the future of the collectivity.

Charismatic leaders

The decolonization elite very often crystallizes around one or a few strongly charismatic leaders. It is certainly a remarkable fact that decolonization has provoked the appearance of a number of charismatic figures. This was the case at the time of the American revolution — George Washington was invested with an almost legendary character, which has even continued to the present in the United States.[21] In the same way, Jean Ziégler notes that the revolutionary movement in Ghana was "completely dominated by the personality of Nkrumah,"[22] who was finally the subject of a "pseudo-religious consecration." Many other independence or decolonization movements also have had their charismatic leader: Bolivar in South America, Gandhi in India, Bourguiba in Tunisia, Sukarno in Indonesia, Fidel Castro and Che Guevara in Cuba and so forth.

The charismatic leaders provide inspiration at the same time as they serve as symbols for the independence movements. Through their writings, words and actions, they seek to express and represent what they perceive to be the aspirations of a dynamic sector of the colonized society, whose energies they try to channel towards a

---

21. *Ibid.*, chap. 1, for discussion of this aspect of the American revolution.
22. Ziégler, *Sociologie de la Nouvelle Afrique*, p. 83.

specific objective. In some cases, charismatic leaders have been able to perfect a strategy which has impressed the popular imagination by its originality and novelty, and sometimes also by the thought behind it. This was the case notably with Gandhi, who popularized various forms of non-violent revolutionary action — silent marches, peaceful obstruction, civil disobedience and hunger strikes.

Ideologies

One of the most important functions of elites and charismatic leaders is to create and spread the image of independence — that is, the ideology which rationalizes the motives for independence, specifies its means, and predicts its future. We have already seen the importance of ideology as a factor in social change and historical action. The process of decolonization cannot be undertaken without the production of what McClelland has called an ideological conversion, or without the existence of a guiding image, to use Chombart de Lauwe's expression. In effect, it is a revolutionary process (this will be analyzed in the next chapter); consequently, it requires a total reversal in perspective, and demands considerable individual and collective energies. Thus, it can be effected only if profound aspirations, desires and even dreams are given expression and validity in a formulation that is at least apparently coherent.

The ideology of decolonization is necessarily weighted with promises of a better tomorrow. It invokes the potential force of a collectivity which need only recognize itself; it includes both reactionary elements through its reference to the past, and progressive elements through its vision of the future. In its content, the ideology of decolonization is necessarily nationalistic. It encourages an ethnic, linguistic or national group to act unanimously, or it suggests the formation of a new national or federal collectivity. Sometimes, mingled with political concepts, there is also a strange combination of religious and mythical elements derived from traditional religion or from the religion of the colonizing society.

Mobilization

Through and by ideology, the process of decolonization requires *a capacity for mobilization*, particularly on the part of the elites and leaders. The concept of mobilization within the perspective of social change and historical action has recently been the subject of various theoretical and empirical studies.[23] By mobilization, we mean here the fact that *financial, technical, scientific, human or other resources are made available for collective action and are put under the control of an accepted authority.*

In the decolonization process, mobilization presupposes a *transfer of control* or a change in allegiance. The colonizing authority loses effective control of certain resources which pass into the hands of an unofficial authority composed of the elite and the leaders of the decolonization movement. But decolonization also requires the mobilization of non-mobilized resources — that is, those which have remained untapped.

In both cases, an elite's capacity for mobilization rests on its credibility, or on an act of confidence in itself and its promises for the future that it succeeds in inspiring. Decolonization is effected by means of a gamble on the future taken by a collectivity, or more often by a part of a collectivity. A decolonization movement is paradoxical — and consequently difficult to explain and interpret — because it is essentially an act of self-confidence undertaken by a collectivity that the colonial system has progressively robbed of self-confidence.

The chances of success of such an undertaking thus depend on the degree of mobilization of which an elite is capable in particularly unfavourable conditions. Clearly, then, for the purposes of studies of decolonization, it is important to develop precise techniques for measuring mobilization in a collectivity.[24]

The Post-Colonial Society

The society that emerges from the decolonization process is a complex reality which is generally very mobile, unstable and unbalanced, more divided than united, and often troubled by revolts and reversals of power. At least, this observation can be made in

---

23. Notably Karl W. Deutsch, "Social Mobilization and Political Development," *American Political Science Review* 55 (September 1961): 493-514; Gino Germani, "Démocratie représentative et classes populaires en Amérique latine," *Sociologie du travail* 3 (October–December 1961): 408-25; by the same author, "Social Change and Intergroup Conflicts" in Horowitz, *The New Sociology*, chap. 23; J. P. Nettl, *Political Mobilization* (London: Faber and Faber, 1967); Amitai Etzioni, "Mobilization as a Macrosociological Conception," *British Journal of Sociology* 19 (September 1968): 243-53.
24. This is what Karl Deutsch in particular has sought to do by measuring the degree of mobilization according to seven different dimensions in nineteen countries. But this is only a first approximation.

the cases of the United States after the American revolution, Bolivar's Colombia, and the new African nations.

Continued dependence

It is easier to effect political independence than to achieve economic independence. By definition, the economy of a colonized society is essentially dependent on more advanced economies. This situation is found both before and after political independence, but in the latter case it is complicated by the additional new problem of credibility — the new nation must gain the confidence of the foreign suppliers (states or private firms) that it must use in order to obtain capital, machines, credit and technicians. This problem arises at the very time when it is experiencing, or is in danger of, an exodus of capital, administrators and technicians, and when it must also mobilize those internal resources which have remained faithful to the colonial authority.

Political independence rarely entails an immediate rise in national production or in the standard of living. Rather, it provokes an economic crisis or a visible decline in the standard of living. The crisis can be all the more serious in that important resources must be devoted to social rather than economic investment — education, health and public administration.

The economic difficulties that the new nation experiences may in the end aggravate its economic dependence, instead of facilitating its liberation.

Deflected and frustrated aspirations

The temptation to maintain economic dependence is even stronger because it responds to the aspirations of important sectors of the population. Economic aspirations which are awakened and excited by the decolonization movement do not find their full satisfaction in the post-colonial society; instead, they are disappointed and betrayed. It may even be thought that political independence responds to these aspirations only if economic colonialism is perpetuated.

The aspirations aroused by the decolonization movement are those of a mass consumption society rather than a society of production. They are modelled on the circumstances and life styles of the colonizer, and there is a desire to reproduce them in the post-colonial society. This favours the continuation of a trade economy, rather than the take-off of an industrial economy.

Frustrated or deflected aspirations are not propitious to total and autonomous development. On the contrary, they form one of the most important obstacles to economic, and often to political, development in the post-colonial society.

South Americanization or control

The critical situation which follows decolonization can lead the post-colonial society in one of two very different directions: towards "South Americanization", or towards control.

South Americanization corresponds to an orientation of the liberal capitalist type. It consists of the reinforcement of a class, or certain propertied or privileged classes, who benefit from economic relationships with external markets either by direct association with them, or through the power and the indirect profit that they derive from economic colonialism. Between the privileged minority and the rest of the population, the economic and social gap remains very wide or continues to increase, since the channels of upward social mobility are practically blocked. This is the type of society that continues to prevail in South America after a century of political independence, and this is the origin of its name.

Control corresponds to a will and a plan for more collective total development. Concessions to certain privileged classes are almost non-existent, and control is thus based on an intense popular militant group. This is the Chinese or Cuban model. Alternatively, control may be authoritarian in nature, being accepted and maintained through certain agreements with some members of the propertied classes. This is the model of modified socialism. In the control model, in both its forms, political power is necessarily in the hands of a single party a dictatorial government or a military junta. But this can also be the case in the South Americanization model.

It should be recognized, however, that in the short term both models (control and South Americanization) create a considerable gap between a privileged ruling class and the majority of the population, which is mainly peasant. Given the limited resources available, and its low rate of productivity and growth, the post-colonial society is necessarily marked by a strong differentiation between the mass of the population and a privileged minority.

It is rather with regard to long-term perspectives of development that the two models differ. The South Americanization model appears doomed to stagnation, at least until its breakdown under the impact of a revolutionary movement. The control model offers more possibilities of development, as long as it does not crumble under idealism or corruption.[25]

Elites

The two types of models also differ in the kind of elite in power. In South Americanization, the power elite is really a class elite; this is perhaps the case that corresponds best to Mosca's description of the ruling class (see Chapter 12). Political, economic, cultural and religious power is concentrated in the hands of the same propertied and hereditary class whose wealth resides mainly in commerce and the ownership of land. But this wealth is marred by low productivity from the economic point of view, and it is constantly threatened by almost permanent inflation.

In the control model, the power elite is only relatively closed, for its members are recruited through educational channels and through alliance with the party in power. It is an elite whose common denominator is not social origin but the sharing of the same ideology, or at least of the same ideological basis, permitting a greater or lesser number of variations. In addition, given the clearly centralized nature of the government structure, this elite is more directly involved with political power, either through the numerous offshoots of the party or through those of public administration.

Struggles and conflicts

Too often, an important part of the energies of these elites is devoted to internal struggles. The life of post-colonial societies is troubled by many conflicts and disturbances. Whatever the regime, it must sometimes cope with popular revolts, mainly by peasants. The peasant masses, who generally form the majority of the population, have to suffer in particular from exploitation by the propertied classes in the South Americanization model, or from the policy of the rulers in the control model. Often savage and unorganized, these revolts are forcefully repressed, but their threat is ever-present.

---

25. On the subject of these two models, their sub-types and their evolution, see in particular, Meister, *L'Afrique peut-elle partir?*; also René Dumont, *L'Afrique noire est mal partie* (Paris: Editions du Seuil, 1962).

In the South Americanization model, the class elite is constantly threatened also by radical elites. The latter seek the support of the masses in order to develop a revolutionary movement capable of overthrowing the power elite and establishing a control regime. Variously tolerated, according to the more or less radical orientation of their ideology and according to the nature of political power, the opposition elite have great difficulty in fomenting anything more serious than local disturbances or revolts.

In the control society, the counter-revolutionary opposition is generally suppressed. This does not prevent it, however, from sometimes overthrowing the regime under certain favourable circumstances (through corruption of the rulers, for example). But the elite struggle is more often of an ideological kind; it opposes a more moderate to a more radical socialism, a more nationalist to a more internationalist socialism, and so forth.

Finally, let us emphasize that the national identity, under cover of which the decolonization process has been effected, can also be the subject of conflicts. In many cases, at the time of decolonization a fairly artificial national identity was propagated and adopted in which various racial, technical and linguistic groups were believed to be united. The difficulties and frustrations of the post-colonial situation cause this precarious union to disintegrate in favour of either renewed tribalism or regionalism based on various economic interests.

Post-colonial society, development and neo-colonialism

Effected in the name of autonomous development, political independence in itself cannot be said to entail either development or decolonization. In a great number of cases, the post-colonial society is a tortured, divided society which still suffers from extreme frustration. It is threatened by economic stagnation and a weakening of itself through its internal power struggles, and finally it may benefit only an already privileged minority. Both before and after independence, development remains problematical and subject to conditions which go beyond the general will alone.

Moreover, it has often been noted that a certain neo-colonialism burdens the post-colonial societies. This neo-colonialism can take on various forms: continued or even increased economic colonialism; ideological dependence on external imported models; imitation of former colonizers by elites in power; an educational system which closely copies that of an advanced nation, and so forth. Even though almost any social phenomenon can be criticized as being neo-colonial, it is a real fact whose influence on the development of a young nation is probably negative. But it should be recognized that it is a phenomenon that has not yet been analyzed in a rigorous fashion. It has been much more the subject of condemnation than of systematic studies.

Conclusion

In this chapter, we have attempted to add a dimension, which today is considered essential, to the analysis of the development of the underdeveloped countries, by placing this analysis within the total context of the colonial and post-colonial situation. While it has been necessary to treat this subject in a rapid — and often superficial — fashion, we hope that we have succeeded in showing that it is a complex phenomenon. It is largely because of the colonial and post-colonial context that the problem of underdevelopment remains so difficult to resolve in the contemporary world, and that one appears to move constantly further away from its resolution.

As to our analysis, let us add that the complexity of the subject stems not only from objective reality itself, but also from the fact that it is strongly charged with emotion. Decolonization is a *human problem* which sometimes seems to refuse to be enclosed in scientific language. We only hope to have treated it here in a way that is at the same time human and at least a little scientific.

Chapter 15
The Revolutionary Process

We have already noted the difficulty that there seems to be in carrying out an objective and scientific analysis of certain social realities. Ideologies, pressure groups, and perhaps to a greater extent colonialism and decolonization, all appear to slip away from the constraints of sociological analysis. But if a social phenomenon exists which even more often eludes sociological language, it is the revolutionary process. A complete contemporary literature has poeticized the revolution and revolutionaries, emphasizing the essentially tragic meaning of these moments of historical exaltation and almost total purity. Sociology seems to impose a triteness on revolution and revolutionaries, by reducing them to categories, types, factors and conditions, and by attempting to identify their mechanisms.

The revolutionary phenomenon leaves no one indifferent. Indeed, perhaps it is the most clearly discriminating of all social realities. If one's attitude towards the revolution is not favourable, it is because one is opposed to it; if one does not condemn it, then one accepts or desires it. The sociologist who tries to analyze revolution as a social phenomenon without condemning or condoning it in the end finds that he is suspected by everyone: the radicals criticize him for degrading the revolution with his false science; the conservatives accuse him of teaching revolution.

The sociology of revolution

The sociology of revolution does not intend to replace either the literature or the philosophy of revolutions; still less does it hope to serve as a substitute for, or to identify itself with, revolutionary or counter-revolutionary doctrines or ideologies. As we have already said, sociology is *one* of the perspectives from which man can view social reality. There are others, which are quite different from sociology and whose place it cannot take. The sociology of revolution must not be confused, then, with revolutionary or counter-revolutionary activity. Rather, it wishes to make this activity a subject of study, to attempt to understand it a little better by using the language and procedure characteristic of it.

In doing this, sociology certainly takes the poetry out of the event, at the same time that it makes it relative. But as a student of revolution, André Decouflé, says:

> If, as Fidel Castro was not afraid to recall in 1962 in the *Second Declaration of Havana*, "the duty of a revolutionary is to make revolution," that of the sociology of revolution is to escape from the normative danger. . . . The sociology of revolution must thus have as an equal basis the refusal to confuse itself with revolutionary doctrines, and care for a total analysis, both as rigorous and as neutral as possible, of revolutionary discourse from one end to another.[1]

Perhaps it is precisely because the revolutionary phenomenon risks leading sociology to the brink of the normative that, as Decouflé remarks again, "the sociology of revolution is still at the threshold of its existence."[2] Revolutions have been the subject of a great number of studies by historians or philosophers; but very few sociologists have yet dared to devote their research to them.

Revolution, social change and historical action

In the defence of sociologists, it should be emphasized that — contrary to what one is sometimes given to understand — revolution is not the sum total of either social change or historical action. It is

---

1. André Decouflé, *Sociologie des révolutions* (Paris: Presses universitaires de France, Collection "Que sais-je?," 1968), pp. 8-9.
2. *Ibid.*, p. 15.

only a moment, an event, and a rather rare one in the long history of human societies.

Nevertheless, sociology should take into account to a greater extent the fact that it is *a special and strategic moment*. Revolution is a sort of summit or ridge which clearly divides the history of a society into *before* and *after*, two phases which are profoundly different. As much by what precedes as by what results, it is an historical event whose relevance extends far beyond the immediate moment. The changes brought about by the revolution have repercussions far into the future, often in a manner that cannot be foreseen, and generally in a more profound way than one would have believed at the beginning. But revolution is often produced with an astonishing suddenness, first appearing as an accident, then revealing under analysis that it is the end of a long preparatory historical action.

Revolution has this strategic character in history (this explains why it has attracted the attention of historians to such an extent) because it presupposes and entails a considerable sum of social and mental changes. Revolution, in effect, is a break with a present that is judged unacceptable and intolerable; it is a radical refusal of the existing situation; it expresses a will to reconstruct a completely different social and human world. Thus, it can occur only following profound changes in the attitudes and consciousness of a collectivity, or a sector of a collectivity. And it brings in its wake still greater changes, both in mentality and in social organization.

The procedure of this chapter

Taking into account the position that the revolutionary phenomenon occupies in the history of societies, we have thought it necessary to treat it here as the final dimension of our analysis of social change and historical action. Given the scarcity of sociological studies on the subject, this chapter will serve both to show the limits of present sociological knowledge of revolution and to present what sociology can say about it.

We will approach the study of revolution from two perspectives. After defining what is meant by the revolutionary process, we will first see what is known of its antecedents — the factors and conditions that prepare for it. Then we will derive a number of characteristics which mark the revolutionary undertaking itself when it is considered as a special form of historical action.

Antecedents, Factors and Conditions of Revolution

What is revolution?

What do we mean by the revolutionary process? In the way in which we use this term, it serves to designate *a fierce and violent popular uprising whose aim is to overthrow an authority or a regime and to modify a situation*. Understood in this way, revolution is really a moment of history that is marked by a particular social effervescence as well as by a singular exaltation. It is an event that *one must be able to date* even though it is often difficult to do so in practice, particularly at the time that it takes place. Even historians sometimes do not agree on when a revolution has started and ended. It is nevertheless true that revolution is an *animated period* of history, and that this animated period is necessarily limited in time — that is, it has a beginning and an end.

Sometimes some phenomena are by extension called revolutionary. This is notably the case in expressions such as industrial revolution or technological revolution. Here one wishes to emphasize considerable and long-term changes entailed by certain technical or other transformations. It is clear that our definition does not include this type of revolution in what we call the revolutionary process.

Moreover, the revolutionary process implies *a plan to change the regime*. It is directed against an authority that it seeks to overthrow in favour of another. In this, revolution differs from a protest movement, which is designed to correct certain grievances. The revolutionary movement goes beyond this; it is the negation of an authority and a regime. A protest movement sometimes becomes a revolutionary process (as we will see later), but this is not necessarily the case.

Finally, we exclude from our definition the permanent state of revolution or the revolutionary society. We believe that these expressions stem from ideology rather than sociology. They refer to a certain conception of the post-revolutionary society. At the extreme, what is called revolutionary society seems instead to be guided by a counter-revolutionary ideology, in the sense that there is a wish to protect what the revolution has acquired against a new revolutionary process (leftist as well as rightist).

Marxist Sociology of the Revolutionary Process

Private property and the class struggle

Marxist sociology has analyzed the factors and conditions of the revolutionary process in greatest depth. We presented the main elements earlier — let us summarize them briefly.

From the Marxist point of view, the basic underlying cause of the revolutions that have marked human history is the private ownership of the means of production. Private ownership necessarily means the concentration of the means of production in the hands of a minority of property owners who exploit the productive work of a non-propertied labour force. The relations of production thus essentially become class relations — relations between the class who owns the resources, capital and instruments of production, and an alienated class who owns only its power to work, an asset that it must exchange in return for a salary.

The struggle of the exploited classes towards the overthrow of the propertied classes explains the revolutions which have appeared throughout history. But it is in industrial society that the contradictions between the forces of production and the relations of production have been most clearly evident. Industrial society has used considerable and extended means of production — capital, machines, labour force. From this there has resulted, on the one hand, an enormous concentration of wealth in the hands of the propertied class and, on the other hand, an unprecedented concentration of the labouring masses around the factories. The struggle between two basically unreconcilable classes is thus asserted most strongly in modern capitalist society. Indeed, it has become its dominant fact.

The historical role of the proletariat

The concentration of the labouring masses favours the formation of a revolutionary proletariat. In the capitalist regime, the workers are doomed to permanent, chronic and even increasing poverty. But, after they have formed a mass, they are in a better position than ever before to become aware of their situation, to develop a class consciousness and a politicized class consciousness. The alienated proletariat is thus destined to be an historical class. It is called on to rise against the dominant capitalist bourgeoisie and, by means of the revolution, to establish the dictatorship of the proletariat, which is preliminary to the classless communist society. The proletarian struggle and revolution are the beginning of, and the condition for, the coming of a new society and a new civilization that will mark the end of pre-history and the dawn of the liberation of man.

For this, the proletariat must become conscious of its political, social, cultural and ideological alienation. It is because the working class has always been deceived and bewildered by the culture and ideology of the propertied class that it has never been able to effect a complete revolution. In capitalist society, the role of the revolutionary working movement, of socialist inspiration, does not consist in creating class consciousness, but in making it crystallize and politicizing it by giving it precise objectives and a strategy for action.

Factors, conditions and agents of revolution

The Marxist sociology of revolution can be generally outlined in the following terms. The basic cause or root of the revolutionary process resides in the private ownership of the means of production. The *immediate cause* is the total alienation of the proletariat.

The main and essential *condition* of the revolutionary process is the crystallization and politicization of the class consciousness of the proletariat.

The *first agent* of revolution is the proletariat. The revolutionary socialist movement can be considered the *second agent*, which acts as the catalyst for the working class.

The revolutionary *process* is reduced to the class struggle and to the overthrow of the propertied class by the working class.

Finally, the *objective* is the disappearance of private property and the class society and their replacement by a communist and classless society.

A coherent, closed, and predictive or prophetic system

Marxist sociology provides the most complete, coherent and systematic explanation of the revolutionary process that can be found. In effect, it offers *a complete system for the interpretation of the revolutionary phenomenon in society*, notably in modern society.

All the elements of the process occur in a logical manner, and within a descriptive and totally explanatory structure.

This is what makes it *a closed system*. It is (or seems) necessary to accept or reject it as a whole, from the underlying basic cause through to the final objective that it accords the revolution. Precisely because the explanation of the revolutionary phenomenon is constructed as a system, it seems difficult to reject an element of it without destroying the whole.

The Marxist sociology of revolution is similarly systematic in that ultimately the explanation *predicts*. When the factors and conditions of the revolutionary process are known, one can deduce the consequences that must logically follow. The dictatorship of the proletariat and the classless communist society are the necessary outcome of the revolutionary process, as explained by Marxist sociology. This is why this sociology of revolution can be presented as both a scientific explanation and a program for action. But who can decide definitely — and on what basis — whether it is a scientifically based prediction, or a prophecy of ideological inspiration?

A few problems

The explanatory system of revolution provided by Marxist sociology poses still other specific problems. To what extent is the alienation of the proletariat an effective factor in the revolutionary process? Isn't there a level beyond which poverty engenders passivity and fatalism, rather than revolutionary action?

This brings us to ask under what circumstances the working class is the revolutionary agent described by Marx. Is class consciousness, even a politicized one, in itself a sufficient condition? Moreover, doesn't the Marxist explanation minimize the role of other groups or categories — notably intellectuals — in the revolutionary process?

The function of the revolutionary movement also appears fairly ambiguous. Isn't this often a less secondary agent than the Marxist interpretation would lead one to believe?

These questions, which are the subject of numerous discussions among Marxists as well as between Marxists and non-Marxists, have not been answered satisfactorily or with sufficient validity. Let us briefly indicate a few of the guideposts established by research to date.

The Revolutionary Antecedents

In a study undertaken a few years ago, Crane Brinton[3] attempted to carry out what he called the anatomy of revolution. He analyzed and compared the antecedents and development of four revolutions — the English Revolution (1640–1649), the French Revolution, the American Revolution and the Russian Revolution. These four revolutions have three features in common: they abolished an "old regime"; they profoundly altered not only the history of each of these countries, but also Western and even world history; and they were the source, at least at the beginning, of a modernization movement in these four countries.

Some tentative uniformities

From his comparative study, Brinton finally derives what he calls "some tentative uniformities" concerning the antecedents, factors, conditions and agents of the revolutionary process. There are seven of these, and they are worth summarizing.

1. The four revolutions were produced in societies which had experienced a certain degree of prosperity and economic development. Those who carried them out were not the poorest and most outlawed of men; their revolution was not a gesture of despair. Rather, it resulted from feelings of dissatisfaction, impatience and also hope, which arose from frustrated aspirations, unappeased desires, and limits or constraints which were judged unacceptable or intolerable.

2. The pre-revolutionary society was agitated by violent class hostilities. But it was not the most underprivileged classes who struggled against the propertied class — the untouchables rarely carry out a revolution against the aristocracy. The struggle took place and was the fiercest between classes close to each other. The bourgeoisie attacked and overthrew the aristocracy.

3. In all the pre-revolutionary societies, there was a change in allegiance on the part of the intellectuals, who became the most dangerous opponents of the ruling authority and of the dominant or propertied class. They fulfilled a dual function in the pre-revolu-

---

3. Crane Brinton, *The Anatomy of Revolution* (New York: Prentice-Hall, Inc., 1938 and 1952).

tionary period — to criticize the existing regime, and to define and propagate revolutionary ideology. This fact, which Brinton calls the desertion of the elites, according to him is one of the most general and surest indices of a pre-revolutionary state.

4. The governmental institution was paralyzed and suffered from inefficiency, either because it was negligent or incompetent or because it was overwhelmed by new situations and the problems with which it must cope.

5. The old ruling class, or at least a part of the ruling class, started to lose confidence in itself and in the virtues and qualities that traditionally gave it its strength and power. It lost confidence in its authority; above all, it no longer recognized the bases of its former authority. A part of the ruling class passed to the side of the revolutionary movement.

6. The government found itself at grips with serious financial difficulties which it appeared quite incapable of resolving. The State lacked funds; its credit was bad. One after the other, the expedients to which it resorted proved inefficient.

7. Faced with the first popular movements of discontent and agitation, the government resorted to force (police, army, militia) to keep control. But the government was clumsy in the use of force; it no longer controlled its troops. The intervention of the forces of order amplified the troubles. Policemen and military personnel deserted their units and went over to the side of the revolutionaries. Those who remained showed little heart for the protection and defence of the regime.

Discussion

Brinton is the first to recognize the tentative nature of these generalizations and to warn against abusing them. He admits that his conclusions are not equally applicable to the four revolutions studied. For example, his comment on the role of the bourgeoisie is certainly more valid for the English, French and American Revolutions than for the Soviet one. In addition, one should guard against claiming that each of Brinton's conclusions offers the same guarantees of validity in the case of any other revolution, particularly the most recent ones. This would be to exceed his intentions, and to ignore the warnings that he himself gives.

Nevertheless, one cannot help emphasizing that what is known of other revolutions seems to confirm completely some of Brinton's conclusions. In particular, in other revolutions one can perceive the

Figure 3

Aspirations which are satisfied and unsatisfied in
the revolutionary process

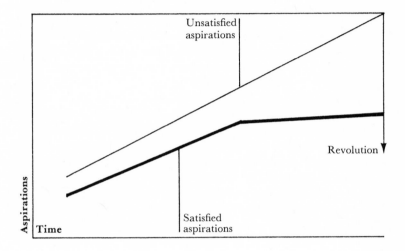

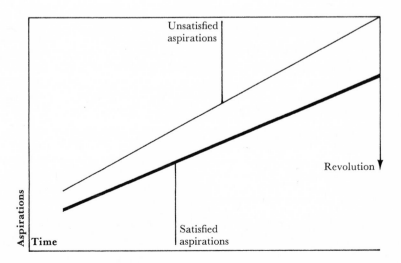

role that he accords to intellectuals, the disaffection of a part of the privileged class (notably youth) for its own ideology, the inefficiency of the State and the repressive use that it makes of the armed forces.

Economic frustrations

Let us add the conclusions of another study which confirm and develop Brinton's conclusions on the economic conditions favourable to the revolutionary process. When he too compared a number of revolutions, James C. Davies[4] came to the conclusion that revolution is linked to economic progress. Specifically, it seems that revolutions break out *when economic development is arrested* or broken, or in a more general fashion, *when economic development does not follow the rhythm of aspirations.*

Some aspirations are fulfilled as economic development progresses; but there are always some which are not, either because it is still not possible to satisfy them, or because they arise at a time when others are being satisfied. These unsatisfied needs comprise one of the motivations for continued economic expansion. But if economic development is stabilized or arrested, or if the unsatisfied aspirations grow too quickly to be satisfied by economic progress, there results a state of frustration, dissatisfaction and discontent which is propitious to the initiation of a revolutionary process.

These conclusions clearly support the observations made earlier on the turbulence of post-colonial societies, following the regime's failure to satisfy new aspirations and needs. Moreover, they emphasize the dynamic, complex relationships which link aspirations to economic development. In particular, they stress that these dynamic relationships can, under certain circumstances, produce the ferments for a revolutionary process.

Poverty and revolution

Finally, let us borrow a remark from Decouflé, who touches on a problem arising from the Marxist model:

> A correlation unequivocally established between misery and revolution has an implicit basis, a pseudo-deterministic conception of the "coming to consciousness" that

---

4. James C. Davies, "Toward a Theory of Revolution," *American Sociological Review* 27 (February 1962): 5-19.

more attentive observation must, it seems, avoid: the mass of the population would only become conscious of a state of misery if it decided, one day, through a secondary collective reflex, to lead to revolution. It knows misery, which is a familiar thing in its memory and its daily life.[5]

It is true that the Marxist sociology of revolution — or perhaps more specifically, a certain interpretation of it — can give rise to a sort of automatism; the alienated proletariat must necessarily develop a revolutionary class consciousness. This interpretation fails to recognize the role that the Marxist model also attributes to the socialist movement in the coming to consciousness and in the revolution.[6] It also does not take into account the fact that desperate misery has often led to savage revolts, and still more often to apathy, fatalism and to purely messianic movements rather than to authentic revolutions. We also know of revolutions "which are led by small groups of 'professional revolutionaries' without the participation of the populace which is still too miserable to accede to an awareness of a revolutionary scheme."[7]

The truth is very likely equidistant from the two extremes. There are enough examples to teach us that *poverty and misery are neither essential nor favourable conditions for the revolutionary process; on the other hand, the most underprivileged classes are not necessarily excluded from the revolutionary process.*

The absence of a general model

The preceding considerations finally lead to a modest (and perhaps disappointing) conclusion: sociology still does not possess a theory of the revolutionary process, or a proved and valid model for the interpretation and explanation of the phenomenon. The most coherent and complete model is undoubtedly the Marxist model; however, this must be considered with some reservations because of the trace of determinism (and perhaps of prophecy) included in it, and because it does not seem to respond to all situations and take all the facts into account.

---

5. André Decouflé, *Sociologie des révolutions*, p. 29.
6. It should be recognized that the role of the socialist movement in coming to consciousness and in the revolutionary process is a problem on which Marxists are far from agreed.
7. André Decouflé, *Sociologie des révolutions*, p. 23.

In order to explain the origins of the revolutionary phenomenon, sociology is reduced to a few general considerations of the kind that have just been presented, of which some are undoubtedly more banal than illuminating. The sociology of revolution remains an almost virgin territory for investigation.

The Revolutionary Venture

In this second part, we shall mention certain traits which are characteristic of what we are calling the revolutionary venture — that is, the actual revolutionary event, and the circumstances immediately surrounding it. First we will be concerned with revolutionary ideology, then with revolutionary development or the revolutionary cycle.

Revolutionary Ideology

A revolutionary tradition

There now exists a tradition of revolutionary thought which guides each new revolutionary ideology. This tradition has been formed over the last two or three centuries; it is inspired by the doctrine that has vitalized some of the great revolutions, those which form the main reference points in the history of revolutions. Thus, the English, French and Soviet Revolutions, which are very often taken as models, in particular have helped to establish and nourish the intellectual tradition of social revolutions. And the American Revolution has long been considered the prototype of the national revolution, even though it has recently lost its luster, at least outside the United States.

In the last decades, the Chinese and Cuban Revolutions have provided new patterns and elements for the revolutionary tradition, and more recently the Chinese Cultural Revolution has made a further contribution.

It can be said that today no revolution is completely innovative, for there is continuity from one revolution to another. The contemporary revolutions all draw on the same universal tradition; they all refer to the same great models.

But the tradition is developing. It is enriched and diversified by the contribution of new experiences and writings. It is not fixed and stable — indeed, it appears that by its very nature this tradition can never be definitive. It grows by drawing on a basic fund of experience, developing and expanding certain fundamental and major themes.

The rejection of the present

What makes each revolutionary ideology unique is that it radically criticizes a particular present situation which is finally judged unacceptable, intolerable and condemnable. Revolutionary ideology is essentially the total denial and rejection of the present in the name of a future which must be entirely different.

What is suggested for the future, however, can be explicit and precise, or not — and often it is not. But it is always guided by the same great generous and humanitarian principles which form the common basis of the revolutionary tradition: the freedom of man, total and real equality, collective well-being, a just society united in brotherhood. The terminology and language may vary; new sub-themes may emerge. But it is always in the light of the same major themes that the criticism, condemnation and rejection of the present are framed.

The principle of totality

The principle of totality of social movements — to use Alain Touraine's phrase (see Chapter 12) — is again found in revolutionary ideology. It appears in three distinct forms.

First, revolutionary ideology appeals to principles which have *a universal value*, which can be accepted by any man, in any society, and in any period. These principles are universally so valid that they almost seem to be axiomatic — the right of each person to happiness, freedom and so forth.

Second, the tradition of revolutionary ideology is formed largely on the basis of a representation of man as being overwhelmed or threatened *in his entire being* by present society. It is almost always the total man that revolutionary ideology proposes to save.

Finally, in order to save the whole man, revolutionary ideology proclaims *the reconstruction of the entire society* on new foundations. The revolution can never involve only a particular sector of society. If it seems to appeal to one social stratum, its intention is to use this group as a lever in order to transform the entire society.

Thus the proletariat is called upon to be the agent that will establish a new society which will be inhabited by a new man. Moreover, it is neither accident nor coincidence that the ideology of the student revolution leads to the reform of the total society; in this, it follows the revolutionary ideological tradition and the internal logic that drives it.

This triple principle of totality underlying the revolutionary tradition makes any criticism of the present necessarily radical and total. But it similarly confers on revolutionary ideology a certain *totalitarian character*; those who do not share it appear inevitably excluded from the new society that is proclaimed.

Reminder of the past

Many writers have noted the particular role of the past in revolutionary ideology. In effect, this ideology often suggests renewing a pure and legendary past, the past that existed before the corruption which leads to the condemnation of the present — the society that existed before private property, before the loss of freedom, before dependence, before the machine and technocracy, and so forth.

We must emphasize, however, that this does not mean taking a backward step. Revolutionary ideology wants to invent a new and original tomorrow. But the recollection of a lost past, where men seemed to be closer to an ideal state than they are today, serves as both a symbol and a promise.

Breaking with the present and the immediate past, revolutionary ideology thus suggests restoring an ancient past in an idealized future which will be closer to perfection than anything man has ever known.

Religious inspiration

This last remark finally leads us to emphasize the clearly religious but secularized inspiration underlying the revolutionary ideological tradition. Borrowing from the great religions — and particularly from Christianity — modern revolutionary ideology has translated and transposed into the everyday world those ideas that religion had applied exclusively to the mystical order: the freedom of the children of God, the equality of all before God, charity, union of the members of the mystical body and so on. These ideas, which were developed by religion with reference to what one can really call the supernatural society — that of the Kingdom of God and the saints — have been taken up by revolutionary ideologies and suggested as the ideal for temporal societies.

Thus, it is not surprising that the radical criticism of the present launched by revolutionary ideology sometimes recalls the condemnations of the great religious prophets with remarkable similarity.

The revolutionary vision of man and his destiny, of present society and its future is both *tragic and optimistic*, giving it an *apocalyptic* character. This vision is an attempt to express man's present drama, in which he is struggling with demons, and at the same time to promise him future salvation — but a salvation which he will have to earn. Finally, to complete the analogy with religious thought, it reminds man of a lost paradise and announces the coming of a better world.

We might suggest also that, because of these characteristics, ideology confers a certain *religiousness* on the revolutionary movement and the revolution itself. We can observe an almost mystical communion and exaltation; disinterested devotion and sacrifice at the service of collective salvation; essentially generous intentions; the pursuit of a high ideal of absolute purity; the exemplary and symbolic function of martyrs; evangelism and the struggle against hidden powers.

We will find these quasi-religious elements again in our analysis of the development of the revolutionary venture.

The Development of the Revolutionary Venture

A process of escalation

In many cases, the revolutionary plan does not appear immediately, at least for most of the actors. It emerges and unfolds progressively as a succession of responses or reactions to events. Except perhaps for a few leaders, *the revolutionary venture experiences an escalating development.*

Very often, the revolution has minor or even ordinary events as its immediate source. This was, for example, the case of the student revolution in Berkeley in 1964, which created the model and developed part of the ideology of subsequent student revolutions.

This revolution started with controversy concerning the availability of a small part of the sidewalk adjoining the campus for political propaganda.[8] Again, the revolutionary objective is not always apparent at first glance. For example, the war of American independence was first undertaken, not for the sake of independence, but to defend a certain concept of the British Empire held by those who had chosen to live in America.

In reality, every revolution is prepared long in advance, in both fact and spirit, but in a generally involuntary way. It results from a long succession of decisions and actions whose connection is not at first apparent, as well as from a progressive accumulation of hostility. The events that make the revolution explode — to adopt the usual terminology (which clearly describes the suddenness of most revolutions and the surprise with which they are met) — have little in common with the consequences they entail. What finally gives these events their density and impact is the explosive charge that has accumulated for some time.

Divisions and agreements

The escalation is mainly produced on the basis of a major acknowledgement, apparently confirmed by certain facts, of the immense and evidently irreducible gap which separates the conservatives from those who await, hope for and suggest changes. It thus becomes obvious that it is necessary to overthrow those in power and to destroy a regime of which nothing can be expected any longer.

Next, an image of the adversary to be overthrown is constructed, in which all the criticisms directed at the regime and all the hostility engendered by it are condensed. An appropriate terminology is created to designate the regime in a continually pejorative way; caricatures, slogans and songs make their contribution.

Inscribed in words as well as in facts is the total and irrevocable

---

8. On the development of this "revolution" and the evolution of its ideology, various documents and analyses will be found in Hal Draper, *Berkeley: The New Student Revolt*, with an Introduction by Mario Savio (the principal leader of the revolution (New York: Grove Press, Inc., 1965): Michael V. Miller and Susan Gilmore, eds., *Revolution at Berkeley* (New York: Dell Publishing Co., Inc., 1965); Seymour M. Lipset and Sheldon S. Wolin, eds., *The Berkeley Student Revolt: Facts and Interpretations* (Garden City, New York: Doubleday and Company Inc., 1965).

division between those in power and the revolutionary movement. This serves to create and maintain the unanimity of the revolutionary forces, and to enlist the considerable energy and resources required for any revolutionary undertaking.

Collective communion and exaltation

The revolutionary venture has certain heights or ultimate moments which are generally events experienced in a sort of collective exaltation and communion. Usually, these events are marked by acts or gestures which are particularly noble or courageous; or they announce or herald the victory and changes to come.

The event may be a battle, the capture of some locality or of a strategic or symbolic building, or the execution of a personality in power. The essential thing is that it should simultaneously symbolize the struggle against the regime, the unanimity and strength of the revolutionary movement, and the cause that it defends. It is what could be called *a special moment* in the revolutionary venture, in which the venture seems to reveal its total message and reunite all the energies that have been liberated.

Symbols

The preceding discussion indicates the central and dominant role of symbolism in the revolution, both in its development and in its ideological formulation. The revolution creates and maintains a great number of symbols. These serve to designate and distinguish the militants, overpower the adversaries, recall the past, mark changes and so on. People, places, dates and martyrs take on a symbolic value, through which they transmit a message, denounce the present, and announce the future.

One can even say that part of the revolution is effected through the intermediary of symbolic gestures — for example, capturing a place which, because of what it represents, will strike popular imagination and signify the beginning of the revolution or its victory; the trial and execution of adversaries or traitors, in order to clearly mark the end of a regime; the creation of institutions and organizations which anticipate the new order.

In addition, many revolutions have left behind them a great quantity of symbols which still bear witness to facts, ideas and people who have played a central role in the revolutionary venture.

Extremists and moderates

Behind the apparent unanimity of the revolutionary venture, however, great divisions are found. Up to now, we have spoken of the revolutionary movement in the singular; in reality, there are generally many revolutionary movements, which may oppose each other at the same time as they are all opposed to the regime in power. They may work together provisionally, form an alliance, or unite behind a common leader; their divisions persist and constantly threaten to reappear.

Perhaps the deepest division is the one which opposes those whom we will broadly call *the extremists* and *the moderates*. Every revolution has these two groups: the hardliners, who suggest the most radical objectives and the most violent means; and the moderates, who count on a more progressive evolution and want to resort to more peaceful methods.

The opposition between these two groups is even stronger in that they judge each other to be more dangerous than their common adversary. To them, the other group risks — through violence or moderation, according to the case — compromising the revolutionary venture and thus betraying the cause for which both are fighting.

The party and the masses

The complexity of the relationships between the revolutionary parties and the masses should be noted. The parties are supported, or say that they are supported, by the masses. They want to awaken them, educate them, and make them progress; at the same time they suggest giving them power.

The revolutionary movement is often confronted with the dilemma of whether to retain the control of the revolution or to give it over to popular power. This dilemma then causes supplementary divisions among those involved in the revolution. It was such a problem, for example, that opposed Rosa Luxembourg to Lenin; she favoured popular power and he, the action of the party. The same opposition is found in many other cases and in various forms.

The counter-revolution

A revolution cannot pursue its course without giving rise to a counter-revolution. Thus, the sociology of revolution should, as a necessary corollary, be called the sociology of counter-revolution.

The counter-revolution may arise at the beginning of the revolutionary process, or it may even precede it. It may take the form of repression, seeking to suffocate the budding revolution through force. Or instead, it can seek to suppress the revolution by offering compromises, by accepting a part of the revolutionary program, and by pledging itself to change. In this case, it will present progressive evolution, as opposed to revolution, as being ultimately more efficient.

The counter-revolution responds to the revolutionary images and symbols with counter-images and counter-symbols. It presents the imminent or actual revolution as threatening and bloody; it describes its nefarious consequences; it denounces the agitators, the instigators of troubles, the utopic revolutionaries, the professional revolutionaries and so on. The language and symbolism of the counter-revolution is no less colourful than that of the revolution.

It should not be believed, however, that the counter-revolution is reserved solely for those in power. *The counter-revolution sometimes arises among the very people who are carrying out the revolution,* on the basis of their internal divisions. Thus, the moderates, frightened by the course along which the extremists are driving their revolution, may construct either an open or underground counter-revolution.

The counter-revolution may arise again after a revolution. Then it suggests a return to the pre-revolutionary situation. But it can also draw together those who are discontented with the revolution and those who think that it has been cut short, with the hope, this time, of finishing the process that ended too soon.

Deceptions

In fact, it often happens that when the revolutionary process reaches the end of its cycle, it leaves deception and bitterness among a good number of those who have initiated and led it. In the last analysis, almost all revolutions appear to be betrayed, in one way or another, by a group or groups who have appropriated the profits. Those in power emerge strengthened and firmly established, indefinitely putting off the reforms for which the revolution was effected; or the moderates accept compromises which others judge to be unsatisfactory or even ridiculous; or the revolution, when accomplished, does not fulfill its promises.

In any case, it is a remarkable fact that almost all revolutions are finally the subject of disillusioned comments by those who carried them out as well as by those opposed to them. They have awakened and maintained very high aspirations and feelings; they have conscripted considerable energy; they have stimulated great currents of ideas and feelings. What results from them, finally, appears minute in proportion to the promises made and the effort involved.

Conclusions

We have tried to show that the revolution is a particularly intense moment of social life because of the conflicts that it arouses, the unanimities that it creates, the feelings that it awakens, and the symbolism that it develops. While historians study and evaluate revolutions in the light of their immediate consequences and long-term results, we believe that sociology should analyze the revolutionary phenomenon as *an animated social period*. Here some socio-psychological mechanisms appear to be enlarged under the microscope, while others are evident which are rarely observed and seldom found in everyday social life. Thus one can believe that the sociology of revolution highlights certain facets of social action, in which man reveals himself in his most generous and most brutal aspect.

Conclusion
What Is Sociology?

In the preceding fifteen chapters, we have not defined sociology; rather, we have attempted *to say what it is on the basis of what it does.* This, we believe, is a more realistic and valid procedure than the nominalist one, which would have consisted of starting with a formal definition or attempting to arrive at one. Sociology, like all other fields of scientific study, is difficult to encompass within the limits of a clear definition.

It may then seem paradoxical that, as a conclusion to this work, we should ask the question: what is sociology? Our intention is not to try to construct an arbitrary definition of sociology at this point. Instead, we want to suggest a few reflections on the nature of sociology — what it is and what it does. As a form of knowledge, sociology raises certain problems and creates certain ambiguities which are perhaps characteristic of all the social sciences, but which, in its case, seem to be more critical.

Sociology as a scientific field of study

Let us say at once that *to us sociology is a scientific undertaking.* It is as such that we have presented it in the preceding chapters. As a form of knowledge, it has the goal of scientifically understanding and explaining social reality.

As we have already said, this does not exclude or deny other forms of commentary on society — literary, poetical, critical, philosophical and so forth. Some literary or poetical works regard society more perceptively than can the sociologist. His procedure is necessarily more complex in that he is obliged to follow the long and often arid road which obeys the canons of the scientific method. This, however, is what makes sociology a scientific undertaking, and also gives it a unique and irreplaceable character.

The limits of our presentation

It is possible that our purpose has been slightly betrayed by the limits that we have tried to impose on our presentation. In effect, we have exposed only the outlines of *general sociology*, and this could ultimately create an exclusively theoretical, general, and perhaps even literary, image of sociology.

In fact, sociology includes a great quantity of empirical research. Some sociology, notably American, has been criticized for contenting itself with the accumulation of a mass of empirical observations, in a disorganized way and without reference to a theoretical model of research. We have reported or mentioned the conclusions of a number of empirical studies in the course of our presentation. But is within the framework of specialized sociology (which we have explicitly left aside) that most of the empirical studies are to be found.

Over the last few decades, research methods, and particularly the various different techniques for the analysis of data, have become more sophisticated. On occasion, we have thought it useful to mention some of these methods and techniques for research and analysis. But it was not part of our purpose to elaborate the subject further; on this question, a great number of works exist.

An impossible purpose?

Thus conceived as a whole, sociology clearly reveals its scientific purpose. Inevitably, not everything that claims to be sociological responds well to this purpose. It remains true, however, that we can perceive the scientific purpose of sociology when the discipline is considered as a whole.

This assertion, however, does not answer all questions. On the contrary, it gives rise to others. First, is this not an impossible purpose? Does social reality not escape from the form of knowledge that sociology claims to apply?

This problem has long stimulated many discussions, particularly in Germany where sociology has had to defend itself stoutly against historicism, which denied sociology in the name of the uniqueness of each historical event. Today these discussions have almost disappeared. Nevertheless, it is one of the peculiarities of sociology that one can still ask this very question while world sociological research occupies tens of thousands of researchers! If sociology is impossible, at least one can say that it exists!

Nevertheless, it should be recognized that the epistemological and methodological bases of sociology continue to be a problem. In effect, one can wonder what kind of knowledge man can succeed in having of a society in which he is immersed and by which he is formed. In what ways and by means of what fragments is this knowledge possible? Does the sociologist arrive at a special perception, or merely a distorted one, of *his society* and of *society*? Even if these questions are not widely discussed today, they have retained their validity.

The historic quality of sociology

A discussion of the epistemological and methodological bases of sociological knowledge would take us much too far. This is a question that stems from the philosophy and psychology of science and also, undoubtedly, from the sociology of science.

But we think that it is useful to conclude this work by calling attention to one aspect of this problem — that of *the historic quality of sociology*. Sociology is immersed in social history; it is part of it and is involved in it. It is difficult to ignore this and dangerous to deny it.

Here we will consider two consequences of this historic quality: history makes sociology a science in perspective, and it associates sociology with historical action.

Sociology in Perspective

A science immersed in its subject

In the Preface, we mentioned the tensions that characterize sociology: it wants to understand and explain historical societies and, through them, society; but at the same time, it is involved in the historical course of societies. Later we noted on several occasions that sociology is constructed, and continues to be constructed, as a science in perspective. Thus, by attempting to understand contemporary society (as well as other societies), sociologists have defined and elaborated their field of study. Their knowledge and interpretation of the social phenomenon thus depends on the societies that they observe and on the state of development of these societies.

But one can go further. Sociology is unconsciously marked by the perception that a society has of itself. The image that men have of their period and civilization is reflected in the theory that sociologists elaborate and in the studies they undertake. It can even be said that the sociologist does not escape from the images of his immediate environment — nation, social class, region, family and so forth. The ideologies surrounding him often provide him with the main elements of his sociological perception of the problems that interest him, and they influence the way in which he expresses and defines these problems. Sociology cannot exist completely outside the morality of the sociologist and his society; it inherits it and is strengthened by it.

An unfinished subject of study

Sociology is also a science in perspective in another sense: *it has inherited an unfinished subject of study*. By this we mean that the subject of its analysis is constantly changing. The physicist who studies the movements of the stars or atoms has the assurance that this matter is of a finished kind; its nature is given and constant. Newton was able to explain the universal law of gravity with the conviction that the planets do not invent new orbits or experience disturbances in their orbits. In the living order, the animal species are transformed, but according to a slow evolution which obeys precise laws or at least operates within given limits. Even the psychologist can have confidence in the constancy of the psychological structure of man.

This does not mean that these sciences have nothing more to discover. But we know that future discoveries are possible because of our present ignorance, rather than because of changes in the nature of reality.

In sociology, it is completely different. Society is an unfinished reality; it is always materializing by new routes and according to changing processes. It exists by being perpetually invented and redefined, by denying itself as such and making itself into something else. Thus, a sociology developed on the basis of the pre-industrial and feudal society of the Middle Ages would need to be revised today, not so much because of the errors of the mediaeval sociologists but because society has changed profoundly. And we must assume that the societies of the future will also develop in new, unforeseeable ways.

This is a very different situation from that of the sciences whose subject is complete. Einstein was able to correct and complete Newton's law of gravity on the basis of new hypotheses and mathematical formulations, not because the planet Mercury had changed its nature and orbit.

The challenge to be faced

Thus, sociology presents the unique feature of *being constructed while immersed in its forever unfinished subject of study*. The sociologist must know himself, and even wish himself, to be part of the subject, and simultaneously seek to detach himself sufficiently from it to see it from its various perspectives. In addition, the sociologist must recognize the limits imposed on his knowledge by the unforeseeable future course of societies.

In a somewhat exaggerated and simplified way, one could compare the sociologist's situation with that which the physicist and chemist would experience if our planet, instead of being attached to the solar system, followed a semi-free course in space, successively experiencing physical conditions (forces of attraction, atmospheric pressure) which were new and varied and likely to modify its trajectory as well as the phenomena being produced on its surface. In these conditions, one can imagine that physics and chemistry would still be possible. But their subject matter would never be finished; these sciences would become much more *difficult, mobile and hazardous*.

These three qualifications apply equally to sociology. Under a sometimes simplified exterior, it is an extremely difficult science because it is constantly influenced by the movement of the societies that it studies, in such a way that its observations, and even more its predictions, constantly remain hazardous.

This is the challenge to be faced — to elaborate in difficult conditions a form of knowledge that will be increasingly valid.

Sociology and Historical Action

There is something else — sociology modifies social reality while studying it. Society is not indifferent to the studies of it which are carried out; it responds, reacts and is guided by them to varying degrees.

This poses the very complex problem of the relationships between sociology and historical action — a problem which has been and continues to be widely discussed. Of course, we will not attempt to say anything definite on this subject. More modestly, we want to suggest some ideas for reflection.

Sociology and social criticism

Undoubtedly, sociology has arisen from the current of social criticism that is characteristic of modern society, and has been carried forward by this current. Social criticism has been fed from many sources, and has aroused various forms of knowledge and interpretation of society — theological, philosophical, moral, literary and poetical. Sociology is not all of social criticism, neither is it completely identified with it. But it has participated in social criticism and continues to do so.

It cannot be otherwise. Society is a moral reality. It appeals to norms and values; it constantly judges, evaluates and justifies itself in the light of new criteria; it invokes morality to enlist energies and mobilize resources.

The sociological undertaking is inscribed within this ethical context: first, the ethical context of the sociologist, whose values are seldom foreign to the work that he undertakes; and second, the ethical context of the entire society, which transposes and translates sociological studies, even the most neutral ones, to the level of value judgements and uses them for the various purposes of its historical action.

Thus, we should not be surprised that sociological research is subjected to moral judgements. It is criticized simultaneously (by sociologists as well as by non-sociologists) for being radical or conservative, bourgeois or revolutionary, linked or opposed to power, and so forth, depending on the point of view. Sociology belongs to the social facts that it studies; one can say that it is part of them in a unique way and more than any other scientific discipline, in that one cannot prevent it from becoming a subject of morality in the moral object that it studies.

The roots of sociology and its involvement in society's moral universe have taken on three forms, giving rise to what can be called three *traditions of intervention* in historical action.

The reforming theories

In the first tradition are ranged the great reforming theories. Here are found the interpretations of social organization and history that have been made with the explicit intention of denouncing the ills from which society suffers and proposing reforms for a superior human and social life. In this tradition thinkers and scholars coexist whose sources of inspiration and conclusions can be very different, if not opposed: Saint-Simon, Comte, Marx and Engels, de Tocqueville, Spencer, Tönnies, Sorokin.

In works of this kind, the scientific project has been pursued together with the reforming purpose, the latter serving as a motivation, inspiration and extension of the former. The scientific project and the plan for reform are often confused, to the point where sometimes it is difficult to dissociate them.

The critical analyses

The second tradition groups sociologists who have attempted to analyze certain aspects of contemporary society (or of certain societies) with the more or less explicit aim of emphasizing its weaknesses, lacks and dangers. This tradition is distinguished from the first in that these sociologists are less concerned with suggesting precise or original reforms than with pursuing critical analyses of contemporary society. In addition, the reforming purpose underlying their critical analyses is sometimes less explicit and evident than in the first case.

Generally, the works of C. Wright Mills are considered to be typical of this tradition, as are those of Thorstein Veblen and also, though to a lesser extent, David Riesman. Many sociologists have contributed to this tradition, even some of those who are habitually judged to be rather neutral. In the case of Mills and Veblen, almost their entire work is concerned with critical analysis; but a number of other sociologists have, on occasion, carried out analyses that can be grouped in the same category.

Strategic studies

The third tradition is composed of a set of empirical studies which sociologists have deliberately focused on what they considered to be social problems. This is a long and varied tradition which has produced studies of all kinds. It includes the large surveys carried out in England by Booth, Rowntree and the Webbs on the living conditions of the lower classes, and also the studies of Le Play and Halbwachs of the French workers. In the United States, among many others one can mention Bakke's studies of the unemployed, Wirth's study of the ghetto, Thrasher's of gangs, and Thomas and Znaniecki's study of immigrants.

Most of these studies are characterized by, and derive merit from, the great effort for objectivity made by their authors. These scholars wished to carry out a scientific work which would not be hampered by partiality, so that the fruit of their studies could serve to illuminate the mind, stimulate the conscience, and guide constructive action. In general, these authors did not question the total system; it can even be said that most of them accepted it. They were reformers rather than radicals.

Sociology at the service of all causes

When we consider these three traditions in sociology, we notice the plurality of tendencies and the diversity of ideologies which have guided sociological theory and empirical research. In sociology, we can find the trace of any ideology, and we can say that it serves all masters — those in power, reactionaries, moderate reformers and radicals.

A particular sociology which aims to be the least involved and the most strictly scientific is sometimes accused of supporting conservatism and those in power. This, in our opinion, simplifies things enormously. It would be easy to demonstrate that non-involved sociology has also had other ideological functions. Thus, Mills' work would not have been possible without the earlier more conservative studies of elites. And even Marcuse, who criticizes empirical sociology — in a way that is not always fortunate — resorts to what he calls non-ideological analyses of the facts in order to support his criticisms of the ideology of advanced industrial society.

There are sociologists of the left, of the right, and of the centre. Theoretical and empirical research is inspired by values, ideologies and moral norms which present the same range as exists in society. It would therefore be false to claim that sociology as a whole and in all of its work is either conservative or radical. It should even be hoped that this could never be said; for otherwise, sociology would be the reflection of a monolithic and enslaved society.

The amorality of sociology

If this is the case, the reason for it, in our opinion, is the fact that *sociology as such, as a scientific undertaking, only knows morality as a subject of study. It is he who practises it and those who use it — in fact, it is society — which gives sociology a moral orientation and purpose.*

We would go further. In our opinion, *sociology does not provide the criteria for a social ethic and critique of society.* It can effectively contribute factual and theoretical elements to guide the critique and ethic; but these proceed necessarily from criteria or principles which are beyond real sociological analysis — the philosophy of man, moral axioms and so forth. To our knowledge, sociology has never provided a single necessary reason for believing in freedom and the equality of man, any more than it has advocated the goodness or evil of human nature.

If we can hope that sociology will continue to favour the highest goals of humanity, that it will contribute to the full realization of man and to general well-being, it is because a sufficient number of minds will believe in these values to make them serve sociology. Otherwise, sociology could as easily benefit all forms of dictatorship, whatever the inspiration or justification.

An ethical problem

These remarks bring us to emphasize, in conclusion, that sociology poses ethical problems for the sociologist which are posed by few other scientific fields of study. At the same time, it raises problems of scientific and social ethics which are closely linked. He who practises sociology must, on the one hand, make it his rule to be guided by the strictest scientific norms; it is only on this condition that his science can make an original and valid contribution. On the other hand, he must question himself constantly about his personal values and choices and about those of his environment, knowing that his scientific work is never immune to their influence, for it can be exerted in a subtle way and often without the knowledge of the researcher.

At the same time, the sociologist is at least partially responsible for the use that is made of his science; he is responsible together with all the society to which he belongs. Sometimes he will find it necessary to detach himself from the aims that it is made to serve. But perhaps he should distrust even more the causes and ideologies with which he is in sympathy; they are likely to be the main threat to his intellectual and moral freedom. A sociology to which one adheres is not betrayed any less than a sociology to which one is enlisted.

The sociologist knows himself to be inevitably involved by his science in the current of the social and historical action that he studies. Perhaps more than others, he is responsible for an alert, clear and acute conscience, constantly renewed by the impetus which carries along every society and by the goals that the society pursues.

Further Reading

Part One: Social Action

For the reader who would like to go beyond the discussion of social action presented in the first part of this book there are a number of basic books.

Among what might be called the "great classics" of sociology, the following should be mentioned:

EMILE DURKHEIM, *Suicide*. Glencoe, Ill.: The Free Press, 1951.
This study, now three-quarters of a century old, has had great impact on modern sociology. Easy to read, it introduces the beginner in sociology to what might be called the "spirit" of sociological analysis. It is also an excellent example of a study where empirical research and theorizing are brought together.

JEAN PIAGET, *The Moral Judgment of the Child*. New York: The Free Press of Glencoe, 1948.
An internationally known psychologist, Piaget has published a great many books on child development. This one, which was influenced by Durkheim, illustrates well the complementarity of the processes of socialization and institutionalization. It shows especially how the child comes to take into account the norms and values of his surroundings, and how he finally internalizes them. One could also read with great profit two other books by Jean Piaget: *The Growth of Logical Thinking from Childhood to Adolescence* (New York: Basic Books, 1938), and *The Language and Thought of the Child* (New York: Harcourt and Brace, 1926).

GEORGE H. MEAD, *Mind, Self and Society*. Chicago: University of Chicago Press, 1934.

The influence of Mead on the development of sociology and social psychology has been very great, especially in the areas of the process of socialization, and the internalization of the social rules. This book also emphasizes the role of others in the development of self.

Besides these classics, many books published recently have dealt more fully with the topics that have been presented in Part One. The following are among those that may be regarded as the most important, for various reasons:

TAMOTSU SHIBUTANI, *Society and Personality; An Interactionist Approach to Social Psychology*. Englewood Cliffs, N.J.: Prentice-Hall, 1961.

Bringing together sociological and psychological studies, this book presents with great clarity the main results of recent research on motivation, interpersonal relationships, socialization and social control.

HANS GERTH and C. WRIGHT MILLS, *Character and Social Structure*. New York: Harcourt, Brace and Company, 1963.

This book is a little more difficult to read than the preceding one, but it goes more deeply into the sociological dimensions of human behaviour and social institutions. It especially emphasizes the symbolic aspects of behaviour and social structure.

A. KARDINER (in collaboration with R. LINTON, C. DUBOIS and J. WEST), *The Psychological Frontiers of Society*. New York: Columbia University Press, 1939.

This book was the outcome of an inter-disciplinary program involving psychiatrists and anthropologists. It has had a considerable impact on the school of thought called "culture and personality," which emphasizes the interrelationships and complementarity between these two basic elements of social action.

NEIL J. SMELSER and WILLIAM T. SMELSER, *Personality and Social Systems*. New York: John Wiley and Sons, Inc., 1963.

This is a reader which contains some sixty articles, most of which deal in some way with the various topics presented in the first five chapters of our book.

ERVING GOFFMAN, *The Presentation of Self in Everyday Life*. New York: Doubleday Anchor Books, 1959.
In this book, as well as in several others, Goffman has analyzed clearly the richness and intricacies of interpersonal relationships.

Many books and articles are available on the concepts that have been defined in Part One: culture, role, social control, values, symbols and ideologies. The following are worth mentioning:

RALPH LINTON, *The Cultural Background of Personality*. New York: Appleton-Century, 1945.
A classic presentation and discussion of the concepts of culture, role, and status and of the relationship between culture and personality.

HUGH DANIEL DUNCAN, *Symbols in Society*. New York: Oxford University Press, 1968.

W. LLOYD WARNER, *The Living and The Dead: A Study of the Symbolic Life of Americans*. New Haven: Yale University Press, 1959.
This book, as well as the previous one, deals with the place and role of symbols in social life, more specifically in political life.

CHAIM I. WAXMAN, ed., *The End of Ideology Debate*. New York: Clarion Books, 1969.
A collection of essays on the role of ideologies in social and political life. It presents a good overview of the debate over Daniel Bell's hypothesis on "the end of ideology" in the industrial society.

Some readers may wish to explore more deeply how sociologists have treated social action as an action system. Although they may be somewhat difficult reading for beginners in sociology, the following authors are the main representatives of this school of thought:

GEORGE C. HOMANS, *The Human Group*. New York: Harcourt, Brace and Company, 1950.
———, *Social Behavior: Its Elementary Forms*. New York: Harcourt, Brace and World, Company, 1961.
These two books are companion volumes and should be read together.

PETER M. BLAU, *Exchange and Power in Social Life.* New York: John Wiley and Sons, Inc., 1964.

TALCOTT PARSONS and EDWARD A. SHILS, eds., *Toward a General Theory of Action.* Cambridge, Mass.: Harvard University Press, 1951.

Although it is somewhat old now, since Parsons has published other more recent material, this book is probably Parsons' most readable work. Moreover, this is still the most succinct statement of Parsons' notion of social action, as well as his general system of action and its main sub-systems.

Part Two: Social Organization

The distinction between traditional society and technological society has been the subject of many studies and discussions. The number of relevant studies, both empirical and theoretical, increases still more if we include those dealing with the transition from one type of society to the other. The following works can be recommended:

ROBERT REDFIELD, *The Little Community* and *Peasant Society and Culture.* Chicago: The University of Chicago Press, Phoenix Books, 1960.

These two books, first published separately, have been reissued in one volume, which is very useful because they should be read together. In these books Redfield has developed his notion of "folk society," followed soon after by the concept of "peasant society." It is difficult to discuss these concepts without going back to Redfield.

EVERETT C. HUGHES, *French Canada in Transition.* Chicago: University of Chicago Press, 1943.

A lively monograph of a small town in Quebec, where traditional society and technological society meet and co-exist.

DANIEL LERNER, *The Passing of Traditional Society: Modernizing the Middle East.* New York: The Free Press, 1958.

Using data from different countries in the Middle East, Lerner sheds new light on the difference between traditional and technological society, and on the obstacles to the transition from one type to the other.

FLORENCE R. KLUCKHOHN and FRED L. STRODTBECK, *Variations in Value Orientation*. Evanston, Ill.: Row, Peterson and Company, 1961.
Besides being methodologically interesting for the research techniques used, this study focuses on the differences in value orientations to be found between traditional and technological societies.

DAVID RIESMAN (with NATHAN GLAZER and R. DENNEY), *The Lonely Crowd: A Study of the Changing American Character*. New Haven: Yale University Press, 1961.
In this book Riesman presented the three types of characters and social structures, which have since become so well-known. Riesman's book is one of the few bestsellers in the literature of sociology.

Much has been said and written on the new industrial society, or what is sometimes called the post-industrial age. Although not "sociological" in a strict sense, the following books are representative of different and even opposing schools of thought.

JACQUES ELLUL, *The Technological Society*. New York: Random House, Inc., 1967.

JOHN KENNETH GALBRAITH, *The New Industrial State*. New York: Signet Books, 1968.

THEODORE ROSZAK, *The Making of a Counter-Culture: Reflections on the Technocratic Society and Its Youthful Opposition*. New York: Doubleday and Company, Inc., 1969.

ALVIN TOFFLER, *Future Shock*. New York: Random House, Inc., 1969.

HERBERT MARCUSE, *One-Dimensional Man. Studies in the Ideology of Advanced Industrial Society*. Boston: Beacon Press, 1964.

WILLIAM H. WHYTE, Jr., *The Organization Man*. New York: Doubleday and Company, Inc., 1956.

The literature dealing with the analytical tradition in sociology is equally rich. These works are generally, by their very nature, at a higher level of abstraction than those already cited, and therefore more difficult to read. For this reason it is not easy to make a list of readings for beginners in sociology. We would suggest the following:

B. MALINOWSKI, "Culture," in *Encyclopedia of the Social Sciences.* New York: Macmillan Co., 1931.
This article is often referred to as the "manifesto" of the most orthodox form of functionalism. Malinowski has been very influential in both anthropology and sociology, and his article is therefore worth reading. Since a good part of it is purely descriptive, it is also pleasant reading.

ROBERT K. MERTON, *Social Theory and Social Structure,* revised edition. Glencoe, Ill.: The Free Press, 1957.
It is essential to supplement the reading of Malinowski by Merton, especially the first three chapters of this book, where Merton criticizes Malinowski's functionalism and explains his own conception of functional analysis. Several other chapters in this book are good illustrations of Merton's methodology and of his ability to relate empirical research and theory.

N. J. DEMERATH, and R. A. PETERSON, eds., *System, Change and Conflict: A Reader on Contemporary Sociological Theory and the Debate over Functionalism.* New York: The Free Press, 1967.
This books brings together the most important writing that has appeared over the last ten years dealing with functionalism, both pro and con. It is a very useful reader for anyone interested in the debate over functionalism and general theory in sociology.

TALCOTT PARSONS is generally regarded as the main representative of functionalism and systemic theory in sociology, although he has progressively developed a kind of structural-functionalism of his own. All Parsons' writings are difficult, both on account of his language and of the high level of generality of his theory. The best overall presentation of his thought is probably his own "An Outline of the Social System" in *Theories of Society,* eds. Talcott Parsons, Edward Shils, Kaspar D. Naegele and Jesse R. Pitts (New York: The Free Press of Glencoe, Inc., 1961), Volume I, 30-79. But perhaps the best summary of Parsons' general theory is in William C. Mitchell, *Sociological Analysis and Politics: The Theories of Talcott Parsons* (Englewood Cliffs, N.J.: Prentice-Hall, 1967).

MARION J. LEVY, Jr., *The Structure of Society.* Princeton: Princeton University Press, 1952.
Although similar in many respects to Parsons' general theory,

Levy's represents another approach to a structural-functional model of the social system. It is less sophisticated and less ambitious than Parsons', and also much easier to read.

WALTER BUCKLEY, *Sociology and Modern Systems Theory*. Englewood Cliffs, N.J.: Prentice-Hall, 1967.
This book is a fairly good representative of a new trend of thought, which emphasizes the use of general systems analysis in sociology. Buckley's criticism of Blau, Homans and Parsons is rather unfair, but he effectively demonstrates the pitfalls of mechanistic system models in the social sciences and the need for new models adapted to the systems of human action.

Part Three: Social Change and Historical Action

Social change has been approached in various ways and from different angles. But it can be said that the Marxist, or perhaps the Marxian tradition, provides the most coherent and global framework that has been evolved to explain historical change. If nothing else, it provides an explanation of change that is taking place in modern industrial societies as well as in the new emerging nations. Sociologists must therefore get acquainted with the Marxian sociology of change.

From this point of view, one should especially read, among Marx's works, The German Ideology *and* A Contribution to the Critique of Political Economy. *The following books will also be found helpful:*

T. B. BOTTOMORE and MAXIMILIEN RUBEL, *Karl Marx, Selected Writings in Sociology and Social Philosophy*. London: Penguin Books, 1956.

GEORGE LICHTHEIM, *Marxism, an Historical and Critical Study*. London: Routledge and Kegan Paul, 1964.

C. WRIGHT MILLS, *The Marxists*. New York: Dell Publishing Co., Inc., 1962.

ERNST FISCHER, *Marx in His Own Words*. London: Penguin Books, 1970.

IRVIN M. ZEITLIN, *Marxism: A Re-Examination*. Princeton, N.J.: Van Nostrand Company, Inc., 1967.

Some acquaintance with Marx's sociology is necessary to understand at least the first three books of the following list. The reader will find in these three books different judgements on Marx's theory of change and different ways of using Marxian sociology to explore the subject further. The last three books of the list are less directly influenced by Marxian sociology: they provide a good introduction to non-Marxian theories of change.

MAX WEBER, *The Protestant Ethic and the Spirit of Capitalism.* New York: Charles Scribner's Sons, 1958.

The reader will find in this book Max Weber's famous thesis on the historical links between Protestantism and capitalism in the Western world. It has often been regarded as an answer to Marx's dialectical materialism, although Weber himself has made clear that he did not want to propose a cultural determinism to oppose Marx's economic determinism.

RALF DAHRENDORF, *Class and Class Conflict in Industrial Society.* Stanford: Stanford University Press, 1959.

This book starts with an interesting summary and discussion of Marx's theory of class and class struggle. The author then presents his own model of social classes, power structure, and change in society, especially in modern society. The reader who has no great interest in theoretical discussions will find in the last chapters an illuminating analysis of the role of conflict in industrial societies.

T. B. BOTTOMORE, *Elites and Society.* London: Penguin Books, 1966.

In this little book, Bottomore gives a most interesting review and critical analysis of the theories of the role of elites in history and social change. From Pareto and Mosca down to Mills and the more modern studies, Bottomore shows clearly the evolution of the concept of elite. This book might be read in conjunction with Seymour M. Lipset and Aldo Solari, *Elites in Latin America* (New York: Oxford University Press, 1967).

DAVID C. MCCLELLAND, *The Achieving Society.* New York: The Free Press, 1961.

This piece of research has been inspired by Max Weber's thesis on the development of capitalism. It is also clearly related to the school of thought analyzed by Bottomore. McClelland maintains that he successfully isolated and measured what he calls the need for achievement in the personality. In this book he relates economic development at different historical periods and in different civilizations to the rate of the need for achievement. McClelland's studies have had a great impact on social psychology and should therefore be familiar to sociologists.

NEIL J. SMELSER, *Theory of Collective Behavior.* New York: The Free Press, 1962.

Smelser has developed an original conceptual model of social change, which is quite sophisticated, but at the same time clear and easy to grasp. The book contains a useful bibliography.

ROBERT A. NISBET, *Social Change and History: Aspects of the Western Theory of Development.* New York: Oxford University Press, 1969.

This is a fascinating critical analysis and discussion of the various theories of change and development in the social thought of the Western world, from classical Greek times to our own day.

In the last decade the process of modernization and the problems of the emerging nations have been analyzed in increasing depth by sociologists, as well as by economists, political scientists and social psychologists. The following list of books may serve as an introduction to the literature:

BERT F. HOSELITZ and WILBERT E. MOORE, eds., *Industrialization and Society.* Paris and The Hague: UNESCO and Mouton, 1963.

Most of the articles in this book, although a little dated now, are still worth reading. They provide a good introduction to the various problems of the developing nations.

CLARK KERR, JOHN T. DUNLOP, FREDERICK H. HARBISON AND CHARLES A. MYERS, *Industrialism and Industrial Man,* revised edition. New York: Oxford University Press, 1963.

This book summarizes the research on some factors and agents of development. The typology of elites in the developing countries is especially interesting, and may be valuable in research on social change.

FREDERICK H. HARBISON and CHARLES A. MYERS, *Education, Manpower and Economic Growth.* New York: McGraw-Hill, 1964.

This book is still one of the best analyses of the economic, social, cultural and political characteristics of the different states of development, from the least to the most highly developed countries. The authors have distinguished four stages of development, which they describe with a wealth of data. They finally present some "strategies" for the development of human resources.

EVERETT E. HAGEN, *On the Theory of Social Change*. Homewood, Ill.: The Dorsey Press, 1962.
In McClelland's line of thought, but using mainly Freudian psychoanalysis, Hagen explains both retreatism and revolt in the personalities of the underprivileged and the colonized.

CHARLES C. MOSKOS, *The Sociology of Political Independence*. Cambridge, Mass.: Schenkman Publishing Company, 1967.
This case study of the West Indies provides a good description of the process of creating a new nation, and illustrates how colonialism still prevails in various ways after political independence.

GUNNAR MYRDAL, *Asian Drama: Inquiry into the Poverty of Nations*, 3 volumes. New York: Random House, 1968.
These three massive books present a thorough picture of all aspects of poverty and development in modern Asia. It is probably the best piece of research on the subject, by a great mind, the author of *American Dilemma*.

Finally, sociology itself has increasingly become the concern of a number of sociologists. Its uses, its role, its epistemological foundations, as well as its relationship with economic and political power, have been scrutinized, especially in the last few years. Among the many works that have been published, one might pick out the following:

PAUL F. LAZARSFELD, WILLIAM H. SEWELL, HAROLD L. WILENSKY, eds., *The Uses of Sociology*. New York: Basic Books, 1967.
This book contains the most detailed description of the various fields of research and social policies where sociologists have been and still are active, with much practical information as well as discussions on theoretical and ethical problems.

P. A. SOROKIN, *Fads and Foibles in Modern Sociology, and Related Sciences*. Chicago: Henry Regnery Company, 1956.
This is a lively attack on sociology, mostly the American variety, by a leading modern sociologist. Although unfair in his generalizations, Sorokin's criticism is a healthy and useful exercise.

EDWARD SHILS, "The Calling of Sociology," in Talcott Parsons, Edward Shils, Kaspar D. Naegele and Jesse R. Pitts, eds., *Theories of Society*. New York: The Free Press, 1961, Volume II, 1405-1448.
In this long article Shils presents a broad overview of the development of sociology, the factors that favoured or inhibited its devel-

opment in the United States and in other countries, and its relationships with social criticism. He finally offers some personal reflections on the role of sociology in modern society.

C. WRIGHT MILLS, *The Sociological Imagination*. New York: Grove Press, 1961.

Mills delivers one of the hardest blows to both theoretical and empirical sociological research. This book is generally regarded as the main inspiration of critical or radical sociology which has developed in the last decade.

IRVING L. HOROWITZ, ed., *The New Sociology. Essays in Social Science and Social Theory in Honor of C. Wright Mills*. New York: Oxford University Press, 1965.

The first ten chapters deal with one aspect or the other of Mills' works. The others are pieces of research or theoretical discussions using more or less explicitly Mills' approach.

MAURICE STEIN and ARTHUR VIDICH, eds., *Sociology on Trial*. Englewood Cliffs, N.J.: Prentice-Hall, 1963.

The editors have gathered together some of the best critical appraisals of sociology that had been published in the 1950s.

ALVIN W. GOULDNER, *The Coming Crisis of Western Sociology*. New York: Basic Books, 1970.

One of the leading spokesmen of critical sociology makes an assessment of what he calls "academic" sociology, and shows how it is entirely dominated by the conservative ideology. Gouldner points out that the same may also apply to Marxist sociology in socialist countries.

Name Index

Subject Index

128; as membership milieu, *132-34, 135, 140*; in pre-industrial society, *248, 249*; in post-industrial society, *251, 253, 254*; and religion, *388, 391*; and revolutionary process, *533-34, 537*; and social change, *375-76, 409*; and social movements, *254, 442*; and social organization, *162, 181, 201, 202*; and social problems, *554*; and sociological perspective, *336, 550*; symbols of, 76; in technological society, *230, 232, 236-37, 363, 364, 366, 369*; in traditional society, *217*
Social control, definition of, *39*
Social evolution, *329, 337-38, 345, 348, 365-66, 367, 393, 407, 411, 416, 421, 426, 467-68, 490, 499, 502*; Comte's theory of, *157-60, 203, 329, 338, 345, 497*; Durkheim's theory of, *193-94, 330, 338, 352-54, 355, 356, 357*; Engels' theory of, *167-71, 329-30, 345, 370, 408, 476*; Marxist theory of, *167-71, 329-30, 338, 345, 408, 409-10, 476, 497*; Parsons' theory of, *197-99, 203-4, 205, 208, 318-19*; Spencer's theory of, *287-88, 330, 331, 338, 345, 353*
Social integration: and conflict theory, *419-20*; symbols of, *508*; theory of, *243-44, 407-8, 419-20, 425*
Socialization, *40-43, 95, 108-41, 273, 281, 315, 319, 320, 339-40, 359, 364-65, 408, 446, 483, 487, 488*; and colonialism, *508, 509, 510-11*; definition of, *108*
Social movements, *403, 406, 427, 441-47, 448, 452-55, 456, 487, 539*; definition of, *441*. *See also* Revolutionary process
Social organization, definition of, *149-50, 151-52*
Social organization, types of: Becker, *186*; Comte, *160-65, 171, 177-78, 191*; Cooley, *186*; Durkheim, *186, 192-97, 207*; Engels, *168-69, 171-78*; Janne, *362-65,*

366; MacIver, *186*; Marx, *168-69, 171-78*; Mumford, *361-65, 366*; Parsons, *199-203, 208*; Popper, *186*; Redfield, *186, 208*; Riesman, *357-60*; Spencer, *186, 188-91, 192-93, 194, 195, 207*; Tönnies, *181-86, 207*; Weber, *185-86*
Social process, definition of, *342-43*
Social reality, definition of, *21*
Social system: and cultural system, *309-10, 311, 312, 313*; function of, *313-14*; functional analysis of, *313-17*; Parsons' definition of, *309-10*; properties of, *267-68, 282-83*; structural components of, *312-13*; structure of, *311-13*
Societies, classification of, *144-255*; by Comte, *160-63*; by Durkheim, *195-96*; by Engels, *171-77*; by Janne, *362-65*; by Marx, *171-77*; by Mumford, *362-65*; by Parsons, *199-203*; by Riesman, *359*; by Spencer, *188-91*; by Tönnies, *182-84*. *See also* Technological society; Traditional society
Society, definition of, *12*
Status: achieved, *232*; ascribed, *231-32*; and authority, *418*; bureaucratic, *484*; and colonialism, *504-5*; and culture, *94*; and function, *270, 271, 272*; and law, *185*; and modernization, *481, 482, 483*; occupational, *233, 402*; of pressure groups, *450*; scale of, *261*; symbols of, *76-78, 145, 236*; in traditional society; *220*
Structural analysis, *287, 295, 296-98, 444*
Structural-functional analysis, *297, 299, 300, 311*
Structuralism. *See* Structure
Structural linguistics, *289, 291-92*
Structure: concept of, *151, 283-303, 306, 310, 311-24*; definition of, by Gurvitch, Lalane, Piaget, *295*; Parsons' definition of, *311, 312*
Sub-culture, *90, 241*
Symbolism. *See* Symbols
Symbols, *67-81*; of authority, *145*;